ACT

FOR

DUMMIES®

5TH EDITION

ACT FOR DUMMIES®
5TH EDITION

by Lisa Zimmer Hatch, MA, and
Scott A. Hatch, JD

WILEY

John Wiley & Sons, Inc.

ACT For Dummies®, 5th Edition

Published by
John Wiley & Sons, Inc.
111 River St.
Hoboken, NJ 07030-5774
www.wiley.com

Copyright © 2011 by John Wiley & Sons, Inc.

Published by John Wiley & Sons, Inc., Hoboken, NJ

Published simultaneously in Canada

For general information on our other products and services, please contact our Customer Care Department within the U.S. at 877-762-2974, outside the U.S. at 317-572-3993, or fax 317-572-4002.

For technical support, please visit www.wiley.com/techsupport.

Wiley also publishes its books in a variety of electronic formats. Some content that appears in print may not be available in electronic books.

Library of Congress Control Number: 2011930288

ISBN: 978-1-118-01259-8

Manufactured in the United States of America

10 9 8 7 6 5 4 3 2 1

WILEY

About the Authors

Lisa Zimmer Hatch, MA, and **Scott A. Hatch, JD,** have been preparing teens and adults to excel on standardized tests, gain admission to colleges of their choice, and secure challenging and lucrative professional careers since 1987. For virtually 30 years, they have administered their award-winning standardized test-preparation and professional career courses for live college lectures, online forums, and other formats through more than 300 universities worldwide.

Lisa and Scott have taught students internationally through live lectures, online forums, DVDs, and independent study opportunities. They have written the curriculum for all formats, and their books have been translated for international markets. Additionally, they wrote, produced, and appeared in the landmark PBS *Law for Life* series. Lisa and Scott continue to develop new courses for a variety of careers and extend their college admissions expertise to assist those seeking advanced degrees in law, business, and other professions. On behalf of Southwestern University School of Law, they recently taught an international comparative law seminar at the Universidad del Salvador in Buenos Aires, and they have established international student abroad classes at Cambridge University in England. Together they have authored numerous law and standardized test-prep texts, including *SAT II U.S. History For Dummies, SAT II Biology For Dummies, Catholic High School Entrance Exams For Dummies,* and *Paralegal Career For Dummies* (John Wiley & Sons, Inc.).

Lisa is currently an independent educational consultant and the president of College Primers, where she applies her expertise to guiding high school and college students through the admissions and financial aid processes. She dedicates herself to helping students gain admission to the colleges or programs that best fit their goals, personalities, and finances. She graduated with honors in English from the University of Puget Sound and received a master's degree in humanities with a literature emphasis from California State University. She is currently completing the UCLA College Counseling Certificate Program. She is the editor of the newsletter for the Higher Education Consultants Association (HECA) and the Rocky Mountain Association for College Admission Counseling (RMACAC).

Scott received his undergraduate degree from the University of Colorado and his Juris Doctor from Southwestern University School of Law. He is listed in *Who's Who in California* and *Who's Who Among Students in American Colleges and Universities* and was named one of the Outstanding Young Men of America by the United States Junior Chamber (Jaycees). He was also a contributing editor to the *Judicial Profiler* and *Colorado Law Annotated* and has served as editor of several national award-winning publications. His current books include *A Legal Guide to Probate and Estate Planning* and *A Legal Guide to Family Law,* which are the inaugural texts in B & B Publication's Learn the Law series.

Dedication

We dedicate *ACT For Dummies,* 5th Edition, to Alison, Andrew, Zachary, Zoe, Dan, Paige, and Ryan. Our family demonstrated patience, understanding, and assistance while we wrote this book, and we're very blessed to have them in our lives.

Authors' Acknowledgments

This book wouldn't be possible without the contributions of Henry Swider, Julia Diament, Zachary Hatch, and Zoe Hatch, who provided practice test material and helpful input. We also acknowledge the input of the thousands of students who've completed our test-preparation courses over the last 30 years. The classroom and online contributions offered by these eager learners have provided us with lots of information about what areas require the greatest amount of preparation.

Our project organization and attempts at wit were greatly facilitated by the editing professionals at Wiley Publishing. Our thanks go out to Tim Gallan and Chad Sievers for their patience and guidance throughout the process and to Amanda Langferman and Jessica Smith for their attention to detail and helpful suggestions during the editing process.

Finally, we wish to thank our literary agent, Margo Maley Hutchinson, at Waterside Productions in Cardiff for her support and assistance and for introducing us to the innovative *For Dummies* series.

We thrive on feedback from our students and encourage our readers to e-mail their comments and critiques to info@hatchedu.com.

Publisher's Acknowledgments

We're proud of this book; please send us your comments through our Dummies online registration form located at http://dummies.custhelp.com. For other comments, please contact our Customer Care Department within the U.S. at 877-762-2974, outside the U.S. at 317-572-3993, or fax 317-572-4002.

Some of the people who helped bring this book to market include the following:

Acquisitions, Editorial, and Media Development

Senior Project Editor: Tim Gallan

Executive Editor: Lindsay Sandman Lefevere

Copy Editors: Amanda M. Langferman, Jessica Smith

Technical Editors: Don & Diana Garner, Amy Nicklin

Assistant Editor: David Lutton

Editorial Manager: Michelle Hacker

Editorial Assistants: Rachelle S. Amick, Alexa Koschier

Art Coordinator: Alicia B. South

Cover Photo: © iStockphoto.com/Steve Shepard

Cartoons: Rich Tennant (www.the5thwave.com)

Composition Services

Project Coordinator: Bill Ramsey

Layout and Graphics: Carl Byers, Carrie A. Cesavice, Nikki Gately

Proofreaders: Lindsay Amones, Susan Moritz, Shannon Ramsey

Indexer: Infodex Indexing Services, Inc.

Publishing and Editorial for Consumer Dummies

Diane Graves Steele, Vice President and Publisher, Consumer Dummies

Kristin Ferguson-Wagstaffe, Product Development Director, Consumer Dummies

Ensley Eikenburg, Associate Publisher, Travel

Kelly Regan, Editorial Director, Travel

Publishing for Technology Dummies

Andy Cummings, Vice President and Publisher, Dummies Technology/General User

Composition Services

Debbie Stailey, Director of Composition Services

Contents at a Glance

Introduction 1

Part I: Coming to Terms with Reality: An Overview of the ACT 9
Chapter 1: Getting Your ACT Together: ACT 101 11
Chapter 2: Succeeding on the ACT 17
Chapter 3: Surviving the College Admissions Process 21

Part II: Serving Your "Sentence": The English Test 27
Chapter 4: Getting a Grip on Grammar 29
Chapter 5: Mastering the English Test 43
Chapter 6: It's Not What You Say but How You Say It: English Practice Questions 49

Part III: Don't Count Yourself Out: The Math Test 55
Chapter 7: Number Nuts and Bolts.. 57
Chapter 8: More Figures than a Beauty Pageant: Geometry Review............................ 71
Chapter 9: Algebra and Other Sleeping Aids 97
Chapter 10: Making Sense of Math Word Problems 117
Chapter 11: Numb and Number: Acing the Mathematics Test 129
Chapter 12: More Fun than a Root Canal: Mathematics Practice Questions 135

Part IV: Time to Read the Riot ACT: The Reading Test 143
Chapter 13: This, Too, Shall Pass(age): Sailing through the Reading Test 145
Chapter 14: Where Are CliffsNotes When You Need Them? Reading Practice Questions.... 153

Part V: Studying Brain Defects in Laboratory Rats: The Science Test 159
Chapter 15: From Frankenstein to Einstein: Excelling on the Science Test 161
Chapter 16: Faking Atomic Ache Won't Get You Out of This: Science Practice Questions 171

Part VI: Writing Rightly: The Optional Writing Test 181
Chapter 17: What to Expect from the ACT Writing Test... 183
Chapter 18: Excelling on Your Essay: The Writing Test Review...................................... 193
Chapter 19: Practicing Promptly with Practice Prompts: Essay Practice Questions 203

Part VII: Putting It All Together with Three Full-Length Practice ACTs 207
Chapter 20: Practice Exam 1... 209
Chapter 21: Practice Exam 1: Answers and Explanations 257
Chapter 22: Practice Exam 2... 299
Chapter 23: Practice Exam 2: Answers and Explanations 345
Chapter 24: Practice Exam 3... 387
Chapter 25: Practice Exam 3: Answers and Explanations 437

Part VIII: The Part of Tens 479

Chapter 26: Ten Wrong Rumors about the ACT 481
Chapter 27: Attention, Parents! Ten Ways You Can Help Your Student Succeed on the ACT 485

Index 487

Table of Contents

Introduction 1

   About This Book 1

   Conventions Used in This Book 2

   Foolish Assumptions 2

   How This Book Is Organized 3

      Part I: Coming to Terms with Reality: An Overview of the ACT 4

      Part II: Serving Your "Sentence": The English Test 4

      Part III: Don't Count Yourself Out: The Math Test 4

      Part IV: Time to Read the Riot ACT: The Reading Test 4

      Part V: Studying Brain Defects in Laboratory Rats: The Science Test 4

      Part VI: Writing Rightly: The Optional Writing Test 4

      Part VII: Putting It All Together with Three Full-Length Practice ACTs 5

      Part VIII: The Part of Tens 5

   Icons Used in This Book 5

   Where to Go from Here 5

   Figuring Out How Long All This Studying Will Take 6

Part 1: Coming to Terms with Reality: An Overview of the ACT 9

Chapter 1: Getting Your ACT Together: ACT 101 11

   What to Take to the ACT 11

   What Not to Take to the ACT 12

   What to Do If You Have Special Circumstances 13

   Guessing for Points to Maximize Your Score 13

   Your Number's Up: Scoring on the ACT 14

   What the ACT Expects You to Know 14

   Repeating the Test for a Better Score 15

Chapter 2: Succeeding on the ACT 17

   Surviving the ACT with Four Stress-Busters 17

      Inhaling deeply 17

      Stretching a little 17

      Thinking positive thoughts 18

      Practicing visualization 18

   Avoiding a Few Dumb Mistakes That Can Mess Up Your ACT 18

      Losing concentration 18

      Panicking over time 19

      Messing up numbering on the answer grid 19

      Rubbernecking 19

      Cheating 19

      Worrying about previous sections 20

      Worrying about the hard problems 20

      Forgetting to double-check 20

Chapter 3: Surviving the College Admissions Process 21

What's the Main Thing Colleges Look For? 21
How Do Higher ACT Scores Increase My Scholarship Chances? 22
Do Schools Care Whether I Repeat the ACT? 22
What Classes Should I Take in High School? 22
How Helpful Are Sports and Charity? 23
What Should I Say on the College Essay? 23
What Will They Ask Me in the Interview and What Should I Say? 23
How Do I Decide Which School Is Best for Me? 24
What's the Biggest Mistake Most Students Make in College Planning? ...24
How Do I Make My Final Decision? 25

Part II: Serving Your "Sentence": The English Test 27

Chapter 4: Getting a Grip on Grammar 29

Building a Solid Foundation: Grammar Basics 29
Reviewing the parts of speech 30
Verbs 30
Nouns 31
Pronouns 31
Adjectives 31
Adverbs 31
Conjunctions and prepositions 31
Piecing together the parts of a sentence 32
Subjects and predicates 32
Complements 32
Phrases and clauses 33
Punctuation rules for every occasion 33
Periods and question marks 33
Commas 33
Semicolons 35
Colons 35
Dashes 35
Apostrophes 35
Spotting Mistakes: Commonly Tested Errors 36
Picking up on pronoun errors 36
Unclear pronoun references 36
Faulty pronoun references 36
Improper pronoun forms 36
Getting subjects and verbs to agree 37
Calling out sentence fragments 38
Dealing with verb tense issues 38
Identifying problems with parallelism 39
Eliminating redundancy and wordiness 39
Sticking to standard expressions 39
Recognizing misplaced modifiers 41
Correcting miscellaneous mistakes 42

Chapter 5: Mastering the English Test 43

Figuring Out What the English Questions Want to Know 43
Seeing Is Believing: The Format of the Test 44
The passages 44

The question types 44
   Analyzing underlined words 44
   Dealing with writing questions 45
Their Pain, Your Gain: Looking Out for Traps That Others Fall into 47

Chapter 6: It's Not What You Say but How You Say It: English Practice Questions **49**

Part III: Don't Count Yourself Out: The Math Test 55

Chapter 7: Number Nuts and Bolts **57**
The Wonderful World of Numbers 57
   Keeping it real: Types of numbers 57
   Lining things up along the number line 58
   Understanding absolute value 58
   Getting familiar with prime and composite numbers 58
Minor Surgery: Basic Math Operations 59
   Adding and subtracting 59
   Multiplying and dividing 59
   Doing basic operations with odds and evens 60
   Doing basic operations with positives and negatives 60
Fractions, Decimals, and Percentages 61
   Converting fractions, decimals, and percentages 61
   Working with fractions 61
      Simplifying fractions 61
      Multiplying and dividing fractions 62
      Adding and subtracting fractions 62
      Mixing things up with mixed numbers 63
   Pondering percentages 63
Ratios and Proportions 64
   Ratios 64
   Proportions 65
Covering Your Bases: Exponents 66
Smooth Operator: Order of Operations 67
Average, Median, Mode, and More 67
   Doing better than average on averages 67
   Weighing in on weighted averages 68
   Mastering medians 69
   Managing modes 69
   Getting ready for range 69
Measuring Up: Units of Measurement 69
   Time 70
   Quantities 70
   Length 70

Chapter 8: More Figures than a Beauty Pageant: Geometry Review **71**
Toeing the Line 71
Analyzing Angles 72
Triangle Trauma 74
   Classifying triangles 75
   Sizing up triangles 75
   Zeroing in on similar triangles 76

Figuring out area and perimeter 78
Going Greek: The Pythagorean theorem...78
Taking the shortcut: Pythagorean triples..79
Thanks 4 Nothing: A Quick Look at Quadrilaterals 80
Missing Parrots and Other Polly-Gones (Or Should We Say "Polygons"?) 83
Measuring up polygons...83
Solving for volume..84
Adding to find total surface area 85
Running Around in Circles 86
Taking a Flight on the Coordinate Plane 91
Defining the coordinate plane..91
Knowing which formulas you need to guide your flight 92
Considering some advanced concepts 94

Chapter 9: Algebra and Other Sleeping Aids **97**
Variables 101 97
Abracadabra: Algebra 98
Solving for *x* in an equation...98
Adding and subtracting expressions...............................99
Multiplying and dividing expressions 100
Curses! FOILed again...100
Extracting by factoring..101
Substituting...104
Suffering Inequalities...104
Things Aren't Always What They Seem: Symbolism................105
Substituting for the variable in the explanation 106
Talking through the explanation and doing the operations........106
Too Hip to Be Square: Roots and Radicals..............................107
Adding and subtracting radicals...108
Multiplying and dividing radicals...108
Working from the inside out..109
Thinking Exponentially: Logarithms......................................109
Barely Functioning with Functions...110
Functions as symbols...110
Functions and the coordinate plane.................................110
Trying Your Hand at Trigonometry 111

Chapter 10: Making Sense of Math Word Problems **117**
Translating English into Math...117
Punching the Clock: Work Problems 118
Going the Distance: Rate Problems....................................120
Mixing Things Up: Mixture Problems....................................121
Getting Greedy: Interest Problems.....................................122
Figuring out simple interest...122
Finding percent growth...123
Picking Your Way through Percent Increase and Decrease 124
Practicing Probability..126
Rule 1: Create a fraction...126
Rule 2: Multiply consecutive probabilities 127

Chapter 11: Numb and Number: Acing the Mathematics Test **129**
What You See Is What You Get: The Format and Breakdown of the Math Test............129
Absence Makes the Heart Grow Fonder: What Isn't on the Math Test.......130
Getting into the Grind: The Approach 131

Time Flies When You're Having Fun: Timing Tips 132
  Skim for your favorite questions 132
  Start in the middle when plugging in the answer choices...................................132
  Kindly refrain from showing off everything you know..133
  Put aside two minutes to fill in the remaining ovals 133
Do's, Don'ts, and Darns: What to Do and Not Do on the Math Test 133
  Do get the lead out..134
  Don't start working until you've read the entire problem..................................134
  Do reread the problem with your answer inserted..134
  Don't strike out over a difficult question early on.......................................134

Chapter 12: More Fun than a Root Canal: Mathematics Practice Questions 135

Part IV: Time to Read the Riot ACT: The Reading Test 143

Chapter 13: This, Too, Shall Pass(age): Sailing through the Reading Test..............145
Facing Forty Questions: The Reading Test..145
  Timing...146
  Scoring..146
  Reading strategies 146
Identifying the Different Types of Reading Questions 148
  Main-idea questions..148
  Detail questions 149
  Tone, attitude, and inference questions...149
  Vocabulary-in-context questions...150
  Exception questions 150
Tips and Traps 150

**Chapter 14: Where Are CliffsNotes When You Need Them?
Reading Practice Questions..153**

**Part V: Studying Brain Defects in Laboratory Rats:
The Science Test.. 159**

Chapter 15: From Frankenstein to Einstein: Excelling on the Science Test............161
Too Graphic for Words: The Science Test's Format...161
The Android's Favorite: Data Representation 162
  Approaching data-representation passages with as little pain as possible.........163
  Reading tables, graphs, and diagrams: The data-analysis question 164
Experiments Galore: Research Summaries 165
  Identifying the study's purpose 165
  Following the experimental design and making valid conclusions 166
  Knowing what research-summary questions want to know 166
Warring Factions: Conflicting Viewpoints 167
  Devising your plan of attack..168
  Working through the conflict to find the right answer: Question styles............169

**Chapter 16: Faking Atomic Ache Won't Get You Out of This:
Science Practice Questions..171**
Passage 171
Initial Analysis..173
Questions...174

Part VI: Writing Rightly: The Optional Writing Test 181

Chapter 17: What to Expect from the ACT Writing Test 183

Rattling Your Writing with Some Loose Screws 183
  Writing before you think..184
  Panicking about time...184
  Not noticing your time limit 184
  Using creativity as a crutch 184
  Using words you don't know 185
  Being overly critical of yourself 185
  Writing like you speak...185
  Not taking a solid stand 185
  Pouring on too much controversy...................................185
  Repeating yourself over and over again 186
  Failing to edit your essay..186
Making the Grade: How the ACT Folks Score Your Essay 186
Reviewing Some Example Essays and Their Scores................186
  1 — 1 is the loneliest number: How not to be a 1 187
  2 — 2 little 2 late: Steering clear of coming in second 187
  3 — Still finding yourself on the wrong side of the tracks....188
  4 — Reaching 4 a better score 188
  5 — Shining brightly: A 5-star winner............................189
  6 — Unlocking the code to a perfect score 190

Chapter 18: Excelling on Your Essay: The Writing Test Review 193

Keeping It Simple: Making a Judgment 194
Fightin' with the Test's Words: Incorporating the Question 194
Putting Up Your Dukes: Deciding Your Position and Writing about It 195
Throwing a Good First Punch: The Hook..................................196
The Proof Is in the Pudding: Proving Yourself 197
  Using specific examples..197
  Mixing things up with a variety of examples....................197
Hamburger Writing: Organizing Your Essay 198
  The top bun: Introduction 198
  The three meats: Example paragraphs 198
  The lettuce, tomato, and special sauce: Transitions 199
  The bottom bun: Conclusion..200
Wielding the Red Pen: Editing and Proofing 200
  Staying alert with the touch method: Look for
    spelling mistakes and ghost words...............................200
  Getting a little R and R: Review for repetition 201
  Calling all action verbs: Be descriptive.........................201
  Avoiding problems with punk-tu-a-tion: Punctuate properly 201
  Handwriting check: Write legibly.....................................201

Chapter 19: Practicing Promptly with Practice Prompts: Essay Practice Questions 203

Writing Prompt 1 203
Writing Prompt 2 204

Part VII: Putting It All Together with Three Full-Length Practice ACTs 207

Chapter 20: Practice Exam 1 209

Chapter 21: Practice Exam 1: Answers and Explanations 257

English Test 257
Mathematics Test 265
Reading Test 276
Science Test 282
    Passage 1 282
    Passage 2 284
    Passage 3 286
    Passage 4 287
    Passage 5 288
    Passage 6 289
    Passage 7 291
Writing Test 293
Score One for Your Side: The Scoring Guide 294
Answer Key for Practice Exam 1 296

Chapter 22: Practice Exam 2 299

Chapter 23: Practice Exam 2: Answers and Explanations 345

English Test 345
Mathematics Test 354
Reading Test 365
Science Test 372
    Passage 1 372
    Passage 2 373
    Passage 3 375
    Passage 4 376
    Passage 5 379
    Passage 6 380
    Passage 7 381
Writing Test 384
Answer Key for Practice Exam 2 385

Chapter 24: Practice Exam 3 387

Chapter 25: Practice Exam 3: Answers and Explanations 437

English Test 437
Mathematics Test 446
Reading Test 461
Science Test 467
    Passage 1 467
    Passage 2 468
    Passage 3 470
    Passage 4 471
    Passage 5 472
    Passage 6 474
    Passage 7 475
Writing Test 476
Answer Key for Practice Exam 3 477

Part VIII: The Part of Tens 479

Chapter 26: Ten Wrong Rumors about the ACT 481

You Can't Study for the ACT 481
Different States Have Different ACTs 481
The ACT Has a Passing Score 481
The ACT Tests IQ 482
You Can't Use a Calculator on the ACT 482
You Should Never Guess on the ACT 482
The ACT Is Easier Than the SAT 482
The ACT Is the Same as the Achievement Test 483
You Have to Write an Essay 483
You Shouldn't Take Both the SAT and the ACT 483

Chapter 27: Attention, Parents! Ten Ways You Can Help Your Student Succeed on the ACT 485

Give Him Awesome Test-Prep Materials 485
Encourage Her to Study 485
Supply Him with a Good Study Environment 485
Take Practice Tests with Her 485
Model Good Grammar for Him 486
Help Her Memorize Math Formulas 486
Encourage Him to Read 486
Explore Colleges with Her 486
Get Him to the Test Site on Time 486
Help Her Keep a Proper Perspective 486

Index 487

Introduction

Welcome to *ACT For Dummies,* 5th Edition. This is a nondiscriminatory, equal-opportunity book. You're welcome to participate whether you're a genius or (like us) you need a recipe to make ice. Besides, the book's title is not a slam at you. You're not the dummy; the test is (and we've heard it called worse, believe us — especially the Friday night before the exam).

The goal of this book is to show you exactly how to survive the ridiculous situation called the ACT. No matter how excellent your high school teachers are (or were), they've prepared you for the real world, a world that, alas, has very little connection to the ACT. High school teachers can give you a good foundation in grammar, reading, science, and math skills (the areas tested on the ACT), but you may want to think of them as the friendly old GPs, the general practitioners whose job it is to keep you well and handle the little day-to-day problems. What do you do when you have a crisis, like the ACT, that's making you really sick? We like to think of *ACT For Dummies,* 5th Edition, as a loony but gifted specialist you can call when your situation becomes desperate.

No one wants to deal with the eccentric specialist for too terribly long. The goal of this book, just like the goal of the expert, is to come in with the Code Blue crash cart, deal with the situation, and then leave rapidly with as few lives destroyed as possible. This book has one goal: to prepare you for the ACT — period. We're not here to teach you every grammar rule ever created or every math formula that Einstein knew. We don't include any extra "filler" material to make this book look fat and impressive on bookstore shelves. If you want a thick book to use as a booster seat for the vertically challenged, go find *War and Peace.* If you're looking for something that you can use to prepare you for the ACT as quickly and painlessly as possible, again we say to you, welcome to *ACT For Dummies,* 5th Edition.

About This Book

You can't escape the ACT. Many colleges require you to take this entrance exam before they'll even look at your application. Virtually every college accepts scores from either the ACT or the SAT. (Wiley just so happens to publish *SAT For Dummies,* 8th Edition, by Geraldine Woods as well, should you choose to take that exam.) Many students decide to take both tests to see which one they do better on. Is that a good idea? Absolutely. If you have the option of taking either the ACT or the SAT, take both.

Many colleges emphasize ACT scores to compensate for grade inflation. That is, some high schools may give you an A for doing the same level of work that would gain you a C at other high schools. Because the ACT is the same for everyone (students nationwide take the exact same exam), colleges can use the scores to get inside your head and see what's really there. Think of this test as an opportunity, not a crisis: A good ACT score can overcome a low GPA. In just a few hours one fine Saturday morning, you can make up a little for years of messing up in school.

In *ACT For Dummies*, 5th Edition, you find out what types of questions are on the exam, which questions you should work on carefully, and which ones you're better off guessing at quickly. (Good news: The ACT has no penalty for wrong answers, so guess at absolutely every question you don't know.) We also help you figure out which approach to use for each type of question, and, perhaps most importantly, we show you some traps that are built into each question style. We've been test-prep tutors for many years and have developed a list of the "gotchas" that have trapped thousands of students over the years. We show you how to avoid being trapped, too.

This book is also full of the substantive information that you need to know, including grammar rules and geometry, algebra, and arithmetic formulas. Occasionally, we include some truly sick humor on the principle that, as you're groaning at our jokes, you won't notice that you're suffering from the questions. (Hey, as the mushroom said to his friends, "Of course, everyone likes me. I'm a fun-gi!")

Note to nontraditional students: The days of high school may be just a fading memory for you (along with your thin waistline and full head of hair). We recognize that not everyone taking the ACT is a high school junior or senior. Maybe you took a few years off to build your career or to nurture a family (or to pay your debt to society) and are now having to go back and review what you thought you had left behind years ago. As the Walrus said, "I weep with you; I deeply sympathize." It can be totally frustrating to have to deal with the subjunctive or pluperfect or quadratic equations all over again. Postpone your nervous breakdown. Things aren't as dismal as they look. You'll probably be surprised how quickly material comes back to you as you go through this book.

Conventions Used in This Book

To help you navigate the text, we use the following conventions:

- ✔ *Italics* point out new terms, add emphasis to a particular word or point, and denote variables in math problems.
- ✔ **Boldface** indicates the action part of numbered steps and the main items in bulleted lists.
- ✔ `Monofont` denotes website addresses. When this book was printed, some website addresses may have needed to break across two lines of text. Rest assured that we haven't put in any extra characters (such as hyphens) to indicate the break. So just type in exactly what you see in this book.

Foolish Assumptions

Although you could've picked up this book just because you have an insatiable love for English, math, reading, and science, we're betting you picked it up because you have to take the ACT. (Isn't it good to know at the outset that your authors have a remarkable grasp of the obvious?) And because we weren't born yesterday, we figure that you're taking the ACT in anticipation of applying to college. How exciting for you!

Because we've rarely met a person who actually looks forward to taking standardized entrance exams, we're lumping you into the category of "readers who are going into the ACT kicking and screaming." Okay, maybe we're being overly dramatic, but we've got a hunch that you're not especially excited about the prospect of spending four hours of precious sleeping-in time sitting in a stark classroom, darkening endless ovals on a bubble sheet under the watchful eye of a heartless proctor who continues to yell "Time!" before you've finished the section. Call us crazy!

Nevertheless, you picked up this book, so we assume that getting the best ACT score you can is important to you and that you care enough to sacrifice some of your free time to achieve that goal. Good for you!

Here are the other assumptions we've made about you while writing this book:

- ✔ You're a high school student, and, like most high school students, you carry a full course load, participate in a number of extracurricular activities, may even have a job, and prefer to carry on a social life. Or you may have already graduated from high school and may hold down a career and tend to a family. Either way, you don't want us to waste your time with a bunch of stuff that isn't on the ACT. For instance, as much as we enjoy creating vocabulary flashcards, we don't share those with you in this book because you don't need to memorize word meanings to ace the ACT.

- ✔ You're not all work and no play. We want to make studying for the ACT as painless as possible, so we've tried to lighten things up a bit with a few jokes. Forgive us, please. Some are really lame.

- ✔ Because you're college bound, you've spent some years engaged in a college-prep curriculum that includes algebra, geometry, and maybe a little algebra II and trigonometry. We're pretty sure you've had your fair share of English, social studies, and science classes and you've written an essay or two. Therefore, we don't bore you too much with the elementary stuff. (We do, however, cover the basic math and grammar concepts that you may have forgotten.)

After you've covered the information in this book, you may discover that you need more in-depth English or math review. Or maybe you just can't get enough of this stuff! Several Wiley publications are available to accommodate you. Dig more deeply into the rules of Standard English in *English Grammar For Dummies*, 2nd Edition, and find tons of grammar practice in the *English Grammar Workbook For Dummies*, 2nd Edition, both by Geraldine Woods. Those of you who are math challenged will find these books helpful: *ACT Math For Dummies* and *SAT Math For Dummies* by Mark Zegarelli; *Algebra I For Dummies*, 2nd Edition, and *Algebra II For Dummies* by Mary Jane Sterling; and *Geometry For Dummies*, 2nd Edition, by Mark Ryan.

How This Book Is Organized

We've broken this book into eight parts to help you quickly get to the chapters you need. The parts cover the following topics.

Part I: Coming to Terms with Reality: An Overview of the ACT

Part I is an overview of the exam, explaining what it tests, how the scoring works, and so on. You also get some tips on how to do well on the test, plus an overview of what colleges want from you.

Part II: Serving Your "Sentence": The English Test

Part II introduces the English portion of the ACT, explaining the format of the questions, suggesting how best to prepare for the test, and presenting a grammar review that refreshes your memory on all the piddly little points you once knew but have long forgotten.

Part III: Don't Count Yourself Out: The Math Test

The math part shows you strategies for doing well on this portion of the exam. As a sort of "gift with purchase," you also get four math reviews: basic math, geometry, algebra, and word problems.

Part IV: Time to Read the Riot ACT: The Reading Test

Sure you can read, but can you read fast enough to get through all the reading passages and answer all the questions on the ACT Reading Test? This part gives you strategies for doing so, saving you time and brain cells.

Part V: Studying Brain Defects in Laboratory Rats: The Science Test

This part introduces you to the Science Test, a test unique to the ACT. Here, you find out how to analyze various types of science passages and graphs, plus get techniques for doing your best on each type. You also find tips to help you recognize your own strengths and weaknesses and make the best use of your time.

Part VI: Writing Rightly: The Optional Writing Test

Okay, so you really don't have to take the ACT Writing Test. However, considering that many colleges and universities require the written essay, we recommend that you study the chapters in this section very carefully and plan to do some writing on test day.

Part VII: Putting It All Together with Three Full-Length Practice ACTs

This is the part you've either been waiting for or dreading. Here, you find three full-length ACTs that look similar to the real deal. And because reviewing your answers is often the best way to improve your test performance, we guide you through each practice test, explaining why right answers are right and wrong answers are wrong.

Part VIII: The Part of Tens

Assuming you've survived all the excitement, the book finishes up with the good stuff, The Part of Tens. Here, we dispel some myths about the ACT and list some ways your parents can help you succeed on test day.

Icons Used in This Book

Some information in this book is really, really important. We flag it by using an icon. Here's a list of the icons we use and details about what they mean:

Follow the arrow to score a bull's-eye by using the tips we highlight with this icon.

Burn this stuff into your brain or carve it into your heart; it's the really important material. If you skip or ignore the Remember icons, you won't get your money's worth out of this book.

This icon points out the "gotchas" that can kill you before you even know you're being hunted. Pay special attention to the cheesy notes marked with this mousetrap.

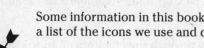

This icon marks sample problems.

This little page curl shows up on the corners of pages in chapters that contain only practice questions. Keep an eye out for it if you want to find these practice sessions quickly!

Where to Go from Here

You've probably heard the joke about the student who was debating over whether to buy a book at the bookstore. The sales clerk, eager to make his commission, proclaims, "Buy this book — it'll do half the work for you!" The student brightens up and exclaims, "Great! I'll take two!"

As much as we wish we could simply transfer test-taking material into your brain in one dump, we realize that learning it takes effort on your part. Meet us halfway. We've done our job by showing you what to study and how to go about it; now it's your turn. We suggest two ways to use this book:

- ✔ **Fine-tune your skills.** Maybe you're already a math whiz and just need help with the English grammar. Go right to the English review we provide in Part II. If, on the other hand, you're a grammar guru who wouldn't know a nonagon if you met one in a dark alley, turn to the math review we offer in Part III.

- ✔ **Start from scratch.** Grab a sack of food and some sharpened pencils, lock yourself in your room, and go through this book word for word. Don't worry; it's not as bad as it seems. Actually, starting from scratch is the preferred method. Many students make what we call the "mediocre mistake": They're good at one section, mediocre at a second, and dismal at the third. They spend all their time in their worst section and barely look at the sections that they're mediocre or good in. Big mistake! If you spend two hours studying something that's totally incomprehensible to you, you may improve your score a few points. If you spend two hours studying your mediocre material, you may improve your score by one or two points. A couple of points that you gain in your mediocre section are just as valuable as — and a heck of a lot easier to gain than — the same number of points you gain in your weakest section. Humor us and read the book from cover to cover. You'll pick up some great material . . . and a few new jokes along the way.

Regardless of whether you hunt and peck your way through the chapters or approach the first six parts consecutively, absolutely take the three practice tests in Part VII. How you choose to use the full-length practice tests is entirely up to you. However, may we suggest two tried-and-true methods?

- ✔ **Diagnostic:** Take the first practice exam to see how you score. Then devour the subject reviews and advice we provide in the first six parts of the book. Finish by taking the other two practice tests to see how much your score has improved.

- ✔ **Pure practice:** Devour the reviews and advice first and use the three full-length exams to practice and reinforce what you've learned in the rest of the book.

Either way, you may choose to save one of the exams to practice on during the days right before you take the ACT. That way, you can walk into the test site with the test questions fresh in your brain.

Figuring Out How Long All This Studying Will Take

In the real world, you have classes, family obligations, sports practices, and, if you're lucky, a social life. How on earth are you going to fit reviewing this book and studying for the ACT into your schedule? The answer is that you have to commit to this project and make it a priority. How many hours should you carve out of your schedule? Here's what we suggest.

Reading the ACT overview in the first three chapters shouldn't cut out too much of your free time, no more than 30 minutes. Other parts require more of an investment.

The five parts of the book that review English, math, writing, reading, and science contain one or two chapters that explain how to approach the subject at hand and one short chapter full of practice questions. Soaking up the information in the explanations and taking the short practice tests should take you about an hour or two per test subject.

Additionally, the English Test part features a very important grammar review that we strongly suggest you spend at least 2 hours working on. Even if you're good at grammar, this section features all sorts of persnickety grammar rules, just the type that (with your luck) you'd get caught on during the ACT. Finally, the Math Test part features four math reviews — number basics, geometry, algebra, and word problems — each of which should take you about an hour to fully absorb.

And don't forget the three full-length practice tests, of course. Each of the tests takes 2 hours and 55 minutes to complete, not including breaks. Give yourself about an hour to review the answer explanations for each exam. That should be enough time for you to review the answer explanations to every question and to take advantage of the opportunity to see shortcuts you may not have noticed or traps you luckily avoided. So taking and reviewing each exam should take you about 4 hours, for a total of approximately 12 hours. Here's the final timetable:

Activity	Time
Reading the ACT overview	30 minutes
Reviewing the approaches to the five test topics and working through the practice questions at 1.5 hours per topic	7.5 hours
Absorbing the four math review chapters at 1 hour per chapter	4 hours
Engrossing yourself in the grammar review chapter at 2 hours	2 hours
Enjoying the three full-length practice exams at 4 hours per exam	12 hours
Groaning in pain at the authors' lame jokes	15 minutes
Firing off letter complaining about authors' lame jokes (or sending along better ones!)	-15 minutes
TOTAL TIME	26 hours

Fear not: You don't have to do it all in a day. The last thing we're advocating is sleep deprivation! This book is designed so that you can start any part at any time. You don't have to have finished the general math chapter, for example, before you go through the general reading chapter.

Okay, are you ready? Are you quivering with anticipation, living for the moment when you can pick up your yellow No. 2 pencil and hold on for the thrill of a lifetime? (Or are you thinking, "These authors need to get a life!"?) Listen, you're going to take the ACT anyway, so you may as well have a good time learning how to do so. Laughing while learning is the whole purpose of this book. Take a deep breath, rev up the brain cells, and go for it! Good luck. Just remember that for you, ACT can come to stand for Ace Conquers Test!

Part I

Coming to Terms with Reality: An Overview of the ACT

In this part . . .

The reality is that you have to take the ACT. Reality bites. But by knowing what the ACT looks like and what you can expect, you may be able to bite back. Although you're undoubtedly eager to get right to studying for the ACT (Hello, what planet are *we* from?), please take a few minutes to go through this introductory material. Think of the ACT as a blind date: Knowing a little bit about what you'll encounter can lower your anxiety level at least a smidgen.

In addition, this part features a chapter that gives you vital info about how to beat stress, avoid careless mistakes, and recognize common ways you could mess up your score. Saving the best for last, this part also has advice from independent college counselors who present answers to the question, "What do colleges want from me?"

Chapter 1

Getting Your ACT Together: ACT 101

Are you the type of person who jumps into the cold water all at once instead of dipping your toe in a little at a time? If so, do we have a table for you! Table 1-1 gives you an overview of the ACT and shocks you with the entire kit and caboodle all at once.

Table 1-1	ACT Breakdown by Section	
Test	*Number of Questions*	*Time Allotted*
English	75	45 minutes
Mathematics	60	60 minutes
Reading	40	35 minutes
Science	40	35 minutes
Writing (optional)	1	30 minutes

If you add up the numbers, you find that you have 216 questions to answer in 205 minutes; 205 minutes is 3 hours and 25 minutes, or nearly 3½ hours. You get one 10-minute break between the second and third tests (the Mathematics and Reading Tests). If you opt not to take the optional Writing Test, you get to walk out right after the Science Test. If you include the time in the classroom spent giving out the tests, explaining the directions, checking your ID, answering the Interest Inventory questions, and so on, your whole morning is shot. You may as well figure on giving up 4 to 4½ hours for this test.

What to Take to the ACT

If you can't borrow the brain of that whiz kid in your calculus class for the day, you're stuck using your own. To compensate, be sure that you have the following with you before you leave for the ACT test center:

✔ **Admission ticket:** You should receive your ticket in the mail by about two weeks before the exam. If you don't have the ticket by then or if you got it but lost it, call the ACT Test Administration at 319-337-1270.

✔ **Pencils:** Take a bunch of sharpened No. 2 pencils with you. You may also want to take a big eraser (nothing personal — everyone makes mistakes) and a small pencil sharpener.

✔ **Map or directions:** Go to the test center a few days before the actual exam, and scope out your driving route and parking area. Often, the ACT is given at colleges that have parking lots far, far away from the test rooms. Drive to the college a few days in advance, park your car, and see just how long it takes you to get to the room. You don't need the stress of having to run to the test room at the last minute on test day.

✔ **Clothing:** Rumor has it some weird kids are lobbying for a special Nude ACT. Until it becomes available, though, you need to have some sort of external covering. Take a few extra layers. Schools that host the ACT often turn off the heat for the weekend (the ACT is usually offered on a Saturday), and the test room can be freezing cold. Alternately, in the summer, schools turn off the air conditioning, making the room boiling hot. Dress in layers and be prepared for anything.

✔ **Photo ID:** Showing the birthmark your boyfriend or girlfriend thinks is so cute isn't going to cut it with the test proctor. You need to bring a photo ID (student ID, driver's license, passport, military ID, FBI Most Wanted mug shot, whatever). If you don't have a photo ID, you can bring a letter of identification from your school. (The ACT website, www.actstudent.org, goes into detail about what this letter entails; we don't want to bore you with that information here.)

✔ **Eyeglasses:** Students taking the ACT frequently forget their reading glasses at home and then squint for the four long hours of the test. The ACT is enough of a headache on its own; you don't need eyestrain, as well. If you wear contacts, be sure to bring cleaning/wetting solution in case you have to take the lenses out and reinsert them. (Hey, all those tears can really mess up your lenses!)

✔ **Snack:** True, you get only one ten-minute break between the Math and Reading Tests, but that's enough time to gobble down something to jump-start your brain. We often suggest taking an energy bar or some peanuts, something with protein and carbohydrates. Scarfing down a candy bar is actually counterproductive; your sugar levels rise only momentarily and then drop down below where they were before you had your chocolate fix.

✔ **Watch:** Keeping track of time on your own timepiece is more efficient than wasting precious seconds seeking out the clock on the testing site wall. Place your watch on the desk where you can refer to it easily throughout the exam. If your watch has an alarm, turn it off so that you don't disturb the other students. If you don't know how to do so, borrow another watch. The proctor will take a beeping watch away from you.

✔ **Calculator:** The ACT gurus allow you to use a calculator only on the Mathematics Test. Although the ACT information bulletin has an entire quarter page detailing which calculators you can and cannot use, for all practical purposes, you can use any calculator (yes, even a graphing calculator) as long as it doesn't make a noise or have a computer algebra system. Make sure the one you bring has at least a square root function and, ideally, basic trigonometry functions. You may not use a laptop computer (don't laugh; you'd be surprised by how many students want to bring one to the test!) or a pocket organizer.

What Not to Take to the ACT

Do not, we repeat *do not,* take the following items with you to the ACT test room:

✔ **Cellphones and other electronic devices:** Leave your cellphone in the car. You aren't allowed to bring it into the test room. One student we know was dismissed from the test because he accidentally left his cellphone in his pocket, and it rang during the exam. The same goes for other electronics, such as iPads, PC tablets, or anything else that can access the Internet.

- ✔ **Books and notes:** Take it from us: Last-minute studying doesn't do much good. So leave all your books at home; you aren't allowed to take them into the test room with you. (Just be sure to fill your parents in on this rule. We once had a student whose mother drove all the way to the test center with her daughter's ACT prep book, thinking the girl needed it for the test. The mom actually pulled the girl out of the test to give her the book, resulting in the girl's nearly being disqualified from the test.)

- ✔ **Scratch paper:** You may not bring your own scratch paper to the test, and you don't receive any scratch paper during the exam. Fortunately, the exam booklet has plenty of blank space on which you can do your calculations.

What to Do If You Have Special Circumstances

Not everyone takes the ACT under the same conditions. You may have a special circumstance that can allow you to change the date of the ACT or the way you take your exam. Here are a few of the special circumstances that may affect how you take the ACT:

- ✔ **Learning disabilities:** If you have a diagnosed learning disability (LD), you may be able to get special accommodations, such as more time to take the test. However, you must specifically request such accommodations on your application form. Please note that in order to be eligible for special testing on the ACT, your LD must have been diagnosed by a professional and you should have a current individualized education plan at school that includes extended test time. Talk to your counselor for more information.

- ✔ **Physical disabilities:** If you have a physical disability, you may be able to take a test in a special format — in Braille, large print, or on audio. Go to the official ACT website (www.actstudent.org) for complete information about special testing.

- ✔ **Religious obligations:** If your religion prohibits you from taking a test on a Saturday, you may test on an alternate date. The ACT registration website specifies dates and locations in each state.

- ✔ **Military duty:** If you're an active military person, you don't complete the normal ACT registration form. Instead, ask your Educational Services Officer about testing through DANTES (Defense Activity for Nontraditional Educational Support).

Guessing for Points to Maximize Your Score

Scoring on the ACT is very straightforward:

- ✔ You get one point for every answer you get right.
- ✔ You get zero points for every answer you omit.
- ✔ You get zero points for every answer you get wrong.

The ACT is absolutely wonderful in that it doesn't penalize you for wrong answers. (In contrast, the SAT subtracts a fraction of a point for every question you miss.) Therefore, guessing on the ACT obviously works to your advantage. Never leave any question blank. We suggest that you save a couple of minutes at the end of each section just to go through the test and make sure that you've filled in an answer for every single question.

Your Number's Up: Scoring on the ACT

We once had a frustrated student tell us that the scores on the ACT looked a lot like measurements to him: 34, 29, 36. However, the ACT has four scores, which makes for a very strange set of measurements! The ACT scores are nothing like high school scores based on percentages. They're not even like the more familiar SAT scores that range from 200 to 800. Instead, they range from 1 to 36. Scoring on the ACT works like this:

✔ Each required test (English, Mathematics, Reading, and Science) receives a *scale score* between 1 (low) and 36 (high).

✔ The *composite score* is the average of the four required test scale scores.

✔ The English, Mathematics, and Reading Tests each receive a *subscore* between 1 and 18.

Don't assume that the subscores determine the total score. That would be too easy and too logical. The subscores are determined independently and don't necessarily add up to the total score in a section. Subscores show your performance on specific groups of questions within each of the tests that have subscores. For example, if you get Reading subscores of 11 in Social Sciences/Science and 16 in Arts/Literature, you know that you did better on the prose fiction and humanities passages than you did on the social science and science passages. Most colleges don't pay much attention to subscores when they make admissions decisions.

✔ If you take the ACT Plus Writing (which is the official title for the ACT with the optional Writing Test), you receive a Writing subscore that ranges from 2 (low) to 12 (high). The subscore is the sum of the scores you receive from each of the two people who grade your essay. You also get an additional Combined English/Writing score that ranges from 1 to 36. The ACT weighs this score based on two-thirds English and one-third Writing. The Combined English/Writing score doesn't get averaged into your composite ACT score.

✔ A *percentile score* tells you where you rank in your state and nationwide.

Look at the percentiles. Just knowing that you got a 26 doesn't tell you much. You need to know whether a 26 is in the 50th percentile, the 75th percentile, or the 99th percentile. If you get a 36, you have documented lifetime bragging rights because that's a perfect score!

The ACT website, www.actstudent.org/scores/understand/studentreport.html, provides a sample score report that shows you what all these scores look like when you and your colleges of choice receive them.

What the ACT Expects You to Know

The ACT tests the following subjects:

✔ **English:** The ACT expects you to know the fundamentals of grammar, usage, punctuation, diction, and rhetorical skills. For example, you must understand sentence construction — what makes a run-on and what makes a fragment. You need to know how to distinguish between commonly confused words, like *affect* and *effect* or *principal* and *principle.* You must be able to use the proper forms of words, distinguishing between an adjective and an adverb, and you must know the difference between a comma and a semicolon.

✔ **Mathematics:** The ACT requires basic skills in arithmetic, geometry, and algebra. If you've had two semesters of algebra, two semesters of geometry, and a general math background, you have all the math you need to answer about 90 percent of the questions. Unfortunately, the ACT also tests a little bit of trigonometry. If you haven't had trigonometry, don't worry. This book gives you the few things you need to know. The test has only a few trig questions (usually just four), and they're often so close to the end that you may not even get to them anyway (although you should definitely guess on them before time is called). Trig should be the least of your worries. Oh, and you don't have to know calculus. The ACT has no calculus questions. Happy day!

✔ **Reading:** The ACT expects you to be able to read a passage in a relatively short amount of time and answer questions based on it. Your reading skills are probably pretty set by now. If you're 17, you're not going to change the way you've been reading for the past 12 years. However, this fact doesn't mean you can't improve your ACT Reading score. Chapter 13 shows you a few tricks you can use to improve your speed and tells you how to recognize and avoid traps built into the questions.

✔ **Science:** You don't have to have any specific science background to ace the Science Test. The passages may test chemistry, biology, botany, physics, or any other science, but you don't have to have had those courses. The test gives you all the information you need to answer the science questions in the passages, diagrams, charts, and tables.

✔ **Writing (optional):** The ACT folks added this optional section to test your writing ability (an extremely important component for college success). Don't worry! You've been writing for years, and the ACT people know that you can't possibly write a perfect essay in a measly 30 minutes. They're not focusing on perfection; instead, they're looking at your thesis, your organization, and your ability to support your thoughts. The ACT doesn't require you to write the essay, but we suggest that you do. Quite a few colleges require the essay, and taking the ACT Plus Writing will assure that you meet their requirements. (If you're also submitting SAT scores, however, you don't need to take the ACT Writing Test because the required essay on the SAT meets the college requirement.)

Repeating the Test for a Better Score

Are you allowed to repeat the ACT? Yes. Should you repeat the ACT? Probably. Decide whether to repeat the ACT based on your answers to the following questions:

✔ **What errors did I make the first time around?** If your mistakes were from a lack of knowledge, that is, you just plain didn't know a grammar rule or a math formula, you can easily correct those mistakes with studying. However, if you made mistakes because you were careless or you daydreamed during the exam, you may have a personality quirk that's not as easy to change.

✔ **Why do I want to repeat the test?** Is your ego destroyed because your best friend got a better score than you did? That's probably not a good enough reason to retake the ACT. Do retake the exam if you're trying to get a minimum qualifying score to enable you to get into a college or into a scholarship program.

✔ **Can I go through this all over again?** How seriously did you take studying the first time around? If you gave it all you had, you may be too burned out to go through the whole process again. On the other hand, if you just zoomed through the test booklet and didn't spend much time preparing for the test, you may want a second chance to show your stuff.

✔ **Were my mistakes caused by factors that were not my fault?** Maybe you were in a fender-bender on your way to the exam, or perhaps you stayed up late the night before in an argument with your parents or your boyfriend or girlfriend. If you just weren't up to par when you took the exam, definitely take it again, and this time be sure to get a good night's sleep the night before.

The ACT doesn't automatically send colleges the scores for every time you take the test. It gives you the option of deciding which set of scores you want colleges to see. If you don't want to report the results of all your tests, keep these issues in mind:

✔ **The ACT automatically sends scores to the colleges you list on your test registration form.** If you want to wait until after you see your report to decide whether certain colleges can see your scores for a particular test administration, don't list those colleges with your ACT registration.

✔ **Many colleges figure your ACT composite score by averaging the highest scores you get in each section across all administrations of the test.** They refer to this practice as *superscoring* the ACT. If you get a 24 in English, a 21 in Math, a 23 in Reading, and a 25 in Science the first time you take the ACT and a 25, 20, 24, and 24, respectively, the second time, these colleges will figure your composite score by averaging your higher 25 English score, 21 Math score, 24 Reading score, and 25 Science score. Your composite score for each administration would be 23, but the composite score the colleges calculate would be 24. Therefore, you may want the colleges to get reports from all the times you take the ACT so that they can superscore your highest section scores.

✔ **Some colleges require you to report your scores from every test date.** Check with the admissions committee at the colleges to which you're applying to make sure they allow you to withhold score reports from particular test dates.

Chapter 2

Succeeding on the ACT

In This Chapter

▶ Mellowing, chilling, and relaxing before and during the ACT

▶ Identifying and sidestepping some easy ways to mess up your score

O n the wall of our office, we have a padded cushion that's imprinted with the words, "BANG HEAD HERE!" We've found that most of our students use it either to reduce stress (we guess one headache can replace another!) or — much more commonly — to express their exasperation over unnecessary, careless (we're trying not to say it, but okay — dumb!) mistakes. Going through the material in this chapter about how to relax before and during the ACT and how to recognize and avoid common mistakes can prevent you from becoming a head-banger later.

Surviving the ACT with Four Stress-Busters

Most people are tense before a test and often feel butterflies dancing in their stomachs. The key is to use relaxation techniques that keep your mind on your test and not on your tummy. To avoid becoming paralyzed by a frustrating question during the test, we suggest that you develop and practice a relaxation plan (perhaps one that includes the techniques we describe in the following sections). At the first sign of panic, take a quick timeout. You'll either calm down enough to handle the question, or you'll get enough perspective to realize that it's just one little test question and not worth your anguish. Mark your best guess and move on. If you have time, you can revisit the question later.

Practice a quick relaxation routine in the days before you take the exam so that you know just what to do when you feel panicky on test day.

Inhaling deeply

Stressing out causes you to tighten up and take quick breaths, which doesn't do much for your oxygen intake. Restore the steady flow of oxygen to your brain by inhaling deeply. Feel the air go all the way down to your toes. Hold it and then let it all out slowly. Repeat this process again several times.

Stretching a little

Anxiety causes your muscles to get all tied up in knots. Combat its evil effects by focusing on reducing your muscle tension while breathing deeply. If you feel stress in your neck and shoulders, also do a few stretches in these areas to get the blood flowing. You can shrug your shoulders toward your ears, roll your head slowly in a circle, stretch your arms over your head, or even open your mouth wide as if to say "Ahhh." (But don't actually say it out loud.)

Thinking positive thoughts

Any time you feel yourself starting to panic or thinking negative thoughts, make a conscious effort to say to yourself, "Stop! Don't dwell on anything negative." Then switch over to a positive track. For example, suppose you catch yourself thinking, "Why didn't I study this math more? I saw that formula a hundred times but can't remember it now!" Change the script to, "I got most of this math right; if I leave my subconscious to work on that formula, maybe I'll get it, too. No sense worrying now. Overall, I think I'm doing great!"

The ACT isn't the end-all, be-all of your life. Cut yourself some slack on test day. You probably won't feel comfortable about every question, so don't beat yourself up when you feel confused. If you've tried other relaxation efforts and you still feel frustrated about a particular question, fill in your best guess and mark it in your test booklet in case you have time to review it at the end, but don't think about it until then. Put your full effort into answering the remaining questions. Focus on the positive, congratulate yourself for the answers you feel confident about, and force yourself to leave the others behind.

Practicing visualization

Before the exam or during the break, practice visualization. Close your eyes and imagine yourself in the test room cheerfully looking at questions that you know the answers to, filling in the bubble grids to the right answers, finishing early, and double-checking your work. Picture yourself leaving the exam room all uplifted and then getting your scores and rejoicing five weeks later. Think of how proud of you your parents are. Imagine getting an acceptance letter from the college of your dreams. Picture yourself driving a fire-engine-red Ferrari ten years from now, telling the *Time* magazine reporter in the passenger seat that your success started with your excellent ACT scores. The goal here is to associate the ACT with good feelings.

Don't practice visualization during the test; you just waste time and lose concentration.

Avoiding a Few Dumb Mistakes That Can Mess Up Your ACT

Throughout this book, you discover techniques for doing your best on the ACT. We're sorry to say, however, that there are just as many techniques for messing up big-time on this test. Take a few minutes to read through these techniques in the following sections to see what dumb things people do to blow the exam totally. By being aware of these catastrophes, you may prevent them from happening to you. And no — the student who makes the greatest number of these mistakes doesn't receive any booby prize.

Losing concentration

When you're in the middle of an excruciatingly boring reading passage, the worst thing you can do is let your mind drift off to a more pleasant time (last night's date, last weekend's soccer game, the time that you stole your rival school's mascot and set it on the john in the principal's private bathroom — you get the point). Although visualization (picturing yourself doing something relaxing or fun) is a good stress-reduction technique to practice *before* the exam, it stinks when it comes to helping your ACT score during the test. Even if you have to pinch yourself to keep from falling asleep or flaking out, stay focused. The ACT is less than five hours of your life. You've probably had horrible blind dates that lasted longer than that, and you managed to survive them. This, too, shall pass.

Panicking over time

Every section on the ACT begins with directions and a line that tells you exactly how many questions are in the section and, therefore, how many minutes you have per question. The ACT is no big mystery. You can waste a lot of time and drive yourself crazy if you keep flipping pages and counting up how many more questions you have to do. You can do what you can do; that's all. Looking ahead and panicking are counterproductive and waste time.

Messing up numbering on the answer grid

Suppose that you decide to postpone doing Question 11, hoping that inspiration will strike later. But now you accidentally put the answer to Question 12 in the blank for Question 11 . . . and mess up all the numbers from that point on. After you answer Question 40, you suddenly realize that you just filled in Bubble Number 39 and have one bubble left — *aaargh!* Stroke City! It's easy to say, "Don't panic," but chances are that your blood pressure will go sky-high, especially when you eyeball the clock and see that only one minute remains.

If you have a good eraser with you (and you should), the wrong answers on the answer grid should take only a few seconds to erase. But how on earth are you going to re-solve all those problems and reread and reanswer all the questions? You're not; you're going to thank your lucky stars that you bought this book and took the following advice: When you choose an answer, *circle that answer in your test booklet first* and *then* fill in the answer on the answer grid. Doing so takes you a mere nanosecond and helps you not only in this panic situation but also as you go back and double-check your work.

Rubbernecking

Rubbernecking is craning your neck around to see how everyone else is doing. Forget those bozos. You have too much to do on your own to waste precious seconds checking out anyone else. You don't want to psych yourself out by noticing that the guy in front of you is done with his section and is leaning back whistling while you're still sweating away. Maybe the guy in front of you is a complete moron and didn't notice that the booklet has yet another page of problems — so he did only half the section. After you have the exam booklet in front of you, don't look at anything but it and your watch until time is called.

Cheating

Dumb, dumb, *dumb!* Cheating on the ACT is a loser's game — it's just plain stupid. Apart from the legal, moral, and ethical questions, let's talk practicality: You can't predict what types of grammatical mistakes will show up in the questions; what are you going to do, copy a textbook on the palm of your hand? All the math formulas that you need can't fit onto the bottom of your shoe.

Worrying about previous sections

Think of the ACT as five separate lifetimes. You're reborn four times, so you get four more chances to "do it right." Every time the proctor says, "Your time is up. Please turn to the next test and begin," you get a fresh start. The ACT rules are very strict: You can't go back to a previous section and finish work there or change some of your answers. If you try to do so, the proctor will catch you and you'll be in a world of hurt.

Worrying about the hard problems

The ACT contains some incredibly hard problems and questions. Forget about 'em. Almost no one gets them right, anyway. A ridiculously few students receive 36s every year, and if you get into the 30s, you're in a superelite club of only a few percent of the thousands and thousands of students who take the ACT annually. Just accept the fact that you either won't get to or can't answer a few of the hard questions and learn to live with your imperfection. If you do go quickly enough to get to the hard questions, don't waste too much time on them. See if you can use common sense to eliminate any answers. Then mark your best guess from the remaining choices. Keep reminding yourself that every question counts the same in a section, whether that question is a simple $1 + 1 = 2$ or some deadly word problem that may as well be written in Lithuanian.

Forgetting to double-check

If you finish a test early, go back and double-check the *easy* and *medium* questions. Don't spend more time trying to do the hard questions. If a question was too hard for you five minutes ago, it's probably still too hard for you. Your brain capacity likely hasn't doubled in the last few minutes. If you made a totally careless or dumb mistake on an easy question, however, going back over the problem gives you a chance to catch and correct your error. You're more likely to gain points by double-checking easy questions than by staring open-mouthed at the hard ones.

Every question counts the same. A point you save by catching a careless mistake is just as valuable as a point you earn, grunting and sweating, by solving a mondo-hard problem.

Chapter 3

Surviving the College Admissions Process

In This Chapter

▶ Pinpointing what the colleges really want from you

▶ Masterminding the right mix of academics, sports, and extracurricular activities

▶ Preparing for the all-important essay and interview

▶ Eliminating the biggest mistake most anxious applicants make

At this point in your life, you may be asking yourself, "What do I need to know about the college admissions process?" To help you out, we took this issue to a group of experts — members of the Higher Education Consultants Association (HECA; www.heca online.org). HECA members are experienced independent college consultants from all over the world who have helped thousands of students get into the schools that best meet their needs and fulfill their dreams. They visit dozens of colleges every year, talk with the admissions officers, and know what's important to them. This chapter offers you the responses we got from a handful of HECA members when we asked them about the issues that concern you most.

What's the Main Thing Colleges Look For?

"Colleges look for genuine applicants who submit genuine responses to the questions they ask. You wouldn't believe how far honesty goes in this process. Yes, curriculum, grades, and scores are important — this is an academic competition, after all. That said, you'd be surprised at how quickly a canned or generic essay response will move your application directly to the wait-list pile (even when all else is right on-target).

"It's hard to put yourself in the admissions officer's shoes, but imagine reading a lot of the same exact stuff — things spit right back at you from the college's website — to the point that you are literally reading the same phrases and responses over and over again. That's not compelling! What *is* compelling is seeing an essay that reflects the kind of student who fits well at your college and shows a genuine interest in, and knowledge about, your school. It's that kid colleges want to admit and who colleges think will come to their campus and contribute in a meaningful way. So think carefully about your response to those 'Why here?' supplemental essays and avoid a canned response." — Bari Norman, PhD, www.expert admissions.com

How Do Higher ACT Scores Increase My Scholarship Chances?

"In addition to increasing your chances of admission, higher ACT scores have another meaningful impact: larger scholarships. Most colleges engage in a strategy called *enrollment management,* which, in simple terms, means that colleges use 'academic,' 'merit,' or 'leadership' scholarships to attract students that they deem desirable. Many schools try to elevate the average test scores of their incoming freshman class, so they use these scholarships to attract students with higher test scores. This, in turn, will help the school increase its ranking. With a little research ahead of time, you can determine if a small investment of time in improving your score will provide you with a four-year financial reward. For instance, the Academic Achievement Award at the University of New Haven carries a renewable award of $7,000 to $11,000 a year and requires a minimum GPA of a 3.0 and a minimum ACT score of 21. However, the Distinguished Scholar Awards have a range of $12,000 to $15,000 and require the same minimum GPA of 3.0 but a minimum ACT score of 23. So, in this case, raising your ACT composite score by 2 points equates to more than $4,000 a year for four years. Enough to make the hours spent preparing for the test seem more than worth it." — James Maroney, www.collegetreasure.com

"Higher ACT scores may well result in a preferred financial aid package (more grants than loans) and/or a very attractive merit scholarship offer. Keep in mind that several hundred colleges now use enrollment management and financial aid leveraging techniques to attract the students they want. Typically, those who have achieved high grades and high test scores are more attractive and, thus, will receive preferential treatment when it comes time for grants and scholarships. Despite what you may have heard, families with no financial need are able to get scholarship aid at many fine colleges and universities if the student's grades and ACT scores are high enough." — Todd Fothergill, www.strategiesforcollege.com

Do Schools Care Whether I Repeat the ACT?

"Most schools are happy to have you repeat the ACT. It allows them to consider the results of your best work. A growing list of schools *superscore* results across multiple test dates. This means that they cherry-pick your highest subtest scores from different ACT sittings and use these to compute a new composite score." — Helane Linzer, PhD, www.ivymaven.com

What Classes Should I Take in High School?

"There are no specific courses that all students should take. Instead, you should take the most challenging college preparatory curriculum that you can succeed in. For graduation, most high schools require four years of English, three or four years of math, including geometry and two years of algebra, two or three years of science that includes at least one lab-based course, and two or three years of history or social science. Some colleges and universities expect to see additional coursework — four years of math or courses in fine or performing arts.

"Some students strive to boost their GPA by taking easier courses hoping for higher grades, but that strategy can sometimes backfire if the colleges they're applying to look closely at the difficulty level of their chosen curriculum. You need to consider the selectivity of the colleges you're applying to and plan accordingly. The most selective colleges want to see that you've taken the highest level of each subject offered at your school and then look at how well you've performed in those courses. Again, it's important to balance challenge with the ability to succeed. Not all students can be successful at the highest levels of all subjects, so you should consult with your teachers and school counselors to make the best course decisions for your situation." — Kimberly Davis, CEP, www.daviscollegeconsulting.com

How Helpful Are Sports and Charity?

"Colleges like to admit smart, interesting students. How do you show that you're interesting? By the activities you're involved with. Colleges don't generally care what activities you participate in, so you should choose those that you find most enjoyable. Contrary to popular belief, you don't need to be involved in a sport unless that is something that interests you. Volunteering, however, is always good to be involved with because it shows that you have an interest in others.

"The longer you do a particular activity, the better a college likes it. You should focus more on being really involved with a small number of activities than dabbling in a bunch of activities. If you can get a leadership position in an activity, that really helps you stand out when you apply to college." — Todd Johnson, www.collegeadmissionspartners.com

What Should I Say on the College Essay?

"When deciding on what you should write about for your college essay, be sure you're passionate about the topic. Don't worry about pleasing other people. Your topic needs to come from your heart, and if it does, it will read as an authentic and unique essay. If you try to write about something you're not passionate about or something you think will sound good, it will come across as cold and disconnected. The essay needs to reveal something about you and your character. Topics can range from an incident you witness — such as a bag boy at the supermarket being humiliated by a supervisor — to the plight of the homeless. Be sure to demonstrate the ability to think critically.

"Whatever your topic, approach the essay within the limits of your writing capabilities. There's nothing wrong with writing an expository essay where the thesis is clearly stated; just be sure to demonstrate your writing skills by focusing on a single topic and supporting your topic with clear and relevant details. Admissions people want to see that you can communicate your thoughts through writing and, at the same time, reveal something unique about yourself." — James E. Long, www.longrangesuccess.com

What Will They Ask Me in the Interview and What Should I Say?

"An admissions officer, a campus-trained student, or alumni of the school can do college interviews. They can be either informational or evaluative, but either way, interviews count in your favor. By making the effort to arrange an interview, you're showing serious interest in the school and helping them get to know you as a person rather than a list of grades, scores, and activities. This is your chance to shine! Don't wear jeans, sneakers, or a hat. Don't chew gum, and do put your phone away. Remember to smile, shake hands with confidence, make eye contact, speak clearly, and sit up straight. Come prepared to ask a few specific questions that are not easily answered by looking at the college website. Always send a thank-you note or e-mail within 24 hours.

"Interview questions generally fall into three categories, so if you can answer these questions, you'll be prepared:

✔ What do you have to offer the school academically, artistically, socially, athletically?

✔ What does the college have to offer you? How will it meet your needs?

✔ Open-ended questions where you have to answer WHY?

This is where they find out what kind of person you are. Practice coming up with three reasons for these types of questions. Why do your friends like you? Why do you like playing a particular sport? What has been your biggest disappointment? What's your favorite book?" — Colleen Reed, www.americancollegeconsulting.ca

How Do I Decide Which School Is Best for Me?

"Choosing the college that is best for you is the most important decision you've faced yet. With so many options and so many factors to consider, the college decision can cause more stress than all your previous choices combined! Luckily for you, you already have the skills you need to make this important decision.

"Consider this. How have you chosen your friends throughout the years? While choosing a friend is often a subconscious decision, you nonetheless start with a personal expectation for what a friend should be. Maybe the most important aspect of friendship is the ability to have fun together. Or maybe the most important aspect is loyalty. Whatever you prioritize in friendship, you have chosen your own friends accordingly.

"The college choice employs the same strategy. The most important question to start with is, 'What do you expect out of college?' After you have listed between ten and fifteen personal expectations for college, rank them according to how important they are to you. If you listed *fun,* you must ask yourself what will make college fun for you. If you listed *challenging,* think about what type of courses will offer the challenge you seek. Information about colleges is easy to find through school websites, campus tours, e-mail correspondence with the school, guidebooks, and word of mouth. If you take some time first to define what will make a college compatible to you, you will be able to search for the exact information you need from the schools you are considering." — Erin McKenzie, www.enroutecollege consulting.com

What's the Biggest Mistake Most Students Make in College Planning?

"As students approach the planning process for college, there are two broad areas that often trip them up. One has to do with academics while the other has to do with putting together a college list. A key to academic opportunity rests with the high school core curriculum. The more years you stick with English, science, math, history, and a foreign language, the greater your access will be to more colleges. (Some college systems recognize visual and performing arts as part of the core, and others don't.) Ditching core classes too soon or opting for a less rigorous senior year places you at risk, especially when vying for competitive colleges.

"The second big mistake that students make is how they put together a college list. Most focus on the *reach schools,* those easy-to-love colleges always on the radar of their friends and family. I believe it's important to build a college list from the bottom up, to create a solid foundation that supports the weight of the others. I call these *anchor schools.* Look first for the colleges that would love to have you apply, the ones that readily recognize your ability and talents. It's easy to fall in love with a number of colleges if you're willing to focus on the unique opportunities and passionate and knowledgeable teachers found on most campuses. A balanced college list is a key ingredient to successful college planning." — Gael M. Casner, www.collegefindedu.com

"The biggest mistake students make in their college planning is to presume that high school settings and resources are equal to collegiate ones. They are literally two different worlds. Consider this:

✔ High schools provide very structured experiences where most students attend a day that has been compartmentalized for them into class periods and activities, and they are grouped with the same students year after year. Imagine high school as a buffet table that has only one or two types of offerings on it, and in order to serve yourself, you need to ask permission. Now imagine a room full of multiple buffet tables, each with diverse and unlimited offerings with so many new people to meet, all in one spot. This is college life, where feeding your interests and intellect has unlimited possibilities, all of which you choose for yourself. This is how the two institutions differ from one another.

✔ The resources available to students in high school are more limited than those connected to the college experience, so the assumption by many when looking at the college picture is that they'll need the same, expanded setting (such as a large city) to broaden their experience. The limitations of high school can sometimes lead you to believe that a college must be located in a thriving metropolis or be large. However, *all* schools, large and small, urban or rural, have a thriving life to them, teeming with opportunities to choose.

"Don't rule out the possibility of attending a smaller college in a smaller city based only on your high school experiences. Find out all that a smaller institution has to offer. You may be surprised!" — Diane Schaefer, LCP, CEP, www.schaefereducationalplanning.com

How Do I Make My Final Decision?

For some students, making the final decision of where to attend college is the toughest part of the admissions process. If you find yourself struggling with your choice, stay as calm as possible. Take a step back and spend some time thinking about your individual goals, needs, personality, and what truly matters most to you in a college experience. Then evaluate each college individually based on those criteria. Keep in mind that there really is no perfect college; every school has pluses and minuses. Yet, there are happy, successful students at every college. After you've evaluated the colleges separately, compare them with each other, narrowing down the list to the one that seems to be the best match. Unfortunately, sometimes you'll have to make some tough choices, and we all have a tendency to mourn the 'one that got away.' Be careful not to let that cloud your vision about the great options you do have! Finally, remember that while deciding where to go is the last step in the long and tiring college application process, it's actually the first step in the next exciting phase of your life: attending college! Go forth confident that your choice is a good one." — Carolyn Z. Lawrence, AdmissionsAdvice.com

Part II

Serving Your "Sentence": The English Test

The 5th Wave   By Rich Tennant

PRONOUNS   AMATEURNOUNS

YOU   YOUS
THEY   YAWL
HE   WHOZITS
SHE
IT

In this part . . .

Lurking in the dark alleyways of the ACT is your first opponent, the English Test, one of four separate tests that you have to battle. The information in this part can help you win the fight (or at least lessen the slaughter!).

Remember those persnickety grammar rules you thought you'd left behind forever? Surprise! They're baaaaaack. This part refreshes your memory of those rules with a grammar review — one that uses enough stupid examples and silly jokes to keep you from dozing off. Following the grammar review is a chapter that tells you what the exam actually looks like, which questions are worth doing, and which questions you may as well just guess at wildly. Finally, the last chapter in this part is an abbreviated English Test: a dozen questions to make sure that what you've learned and reviewed is forever imprinted in your brain. Life just couldn't get any better.

Chapter 4

Getting a Grip on Grammar

- -

In This Chapter

▶ Solidifying your grasp on grammar basics

▶ Reviewing the parts of speech, sentence structure, and punctuation

▶ Identifying some commonly tested grammar errors

- -

The ACT English Test tests Standard written English. In the real world, you can use slang and casual English and still communicate perfectly well with your buddies, but on the ACT, you have to use the formal English that you learned in school. When you knock on a friend's door, for example, you call out, "It's me!" Right? Well, on the ACT, you have to say, "It is I."

About half of the ACT English Test questions test rhetorical skills, which cover general writing style and organization — in other words, the stuff you use every time you pick up a pen or turn on your word-processing program. The other half of the questions test what most people lump together in the general category they call English: punctuation, sentence structure, and basic grammar, including diction, subject/verb agreement, modifiers (adjectives and adverbs), and so on. That's the stuff you probably forget (or intentionally purge from your brain) ten minutes after being tested on it.

This chapter gives you a basic grammar review that brings back those thrilling days of yesteryear when you knew how to use the subjunctive and actually cared about the differences between adjectives and adverbs. The review starts off with the really easy stuff, but don't get too bored and drop out. The harder, picky stuff comes later, and chances are that's the stuff you really need to review.

You do not — we repeat, *do not* — have to fear defining something like the pluperfect. We're very careful to use technical terms sparingly throughout this material. Only teachers care about the technical names for all this grammar stuff. All you need to know is how to use the right rules, so don't worry about what to call things.

Building a Solid Foundation: Grammar Basics

The rules of grammar are really pretty logical. After you understand the basic rules regarding the parts of speech and the elements of a sentence, you have the hang of it. The following sections cover what you need to know to do well on grammar and usage questions. Bear with us as we run through the grammar basics. We promise to get through them as quickly as possible.

If you're a grammar guru, you may be able to skim or skip this section and focus on the later section "Spotting Mistakes: Commonly Tested Errors." If you encounter any confusing concepts or terms when you get there, come back to this section for some explanation.

Reviewing the parts of speech

Most of the English Test questions ask you to evaluate sentences. Every word in a sentence has a purpose, known as its *part of speech*. The parts of speech you should know for the ACT are verbs, nouns, pronouns, adjectives, adverbs, conjunctions, and prepositions.

Verbs

A sentence must have a *verb* to be complete. The three types of verbs are action verbs, the verb *to be,* and linking verbs.

- ✔ *Action verbs* state what's going on in a sentence.

- ✔ The verb *to be* links one part of a sentence to another, sort of like an equal sign in an equation.

- ✔ *Linking verbs* join the parts of a sentence together like the verb *to be,* but they give a little more information than the verb *to be* does. Common linking verbs are *feel, seem, appear, look, sound, taste,* and *smell.*

The ACT often tests you on using the right verb tense. The verb tenses you need to know for the test are present, past, future, present perfect, and past perfect. Table 4-1 gives you a quick summary of these tenses and shows you how to use them.

Table 4-1		Verb Tenses
Verb Tense	**Purpose**	**Examples**
Present	Shows an action or a condition that happens right now	Steve studies grammar every day. The dog is asleep.
Past	Shows an action or a condition that was completed in the past	Steve studied grammar in high school. The dog was asleep when I came in.
Future	Shows an action or a condition that hasn't happened yet but will happen	Steve will study grammar in college, too. The dog will be asleep when the guests arrive.
Present perfect	Shows an action or a condition that's already started and may continue or that happened at an undefined time	Steve has studied grammar for the exam. The dog has been sleeping for several hours.
Past perfect	Shows an action or a condition that happened before another one did	Steve had studied grammar for many weeks before he took the exam. The dog had been sleeping for several hours when the cat awakened him.

Nouns

You've undoubtedly heard *nouns* defined as persons, places, or things. They provide information about what's going on in a sentence and who or what is performing or receiving the action, such as the italicized nouns in this sentence: The social studies *teacher* gave the *students* five *pages* of *homework* regarding *countries* in *Europe*.

Pronouns

Pronouns rename nouns and provide a way to avoid too much repetition of nouns in a sentence or paragraph. You must be familiar with the three types of pronouns and their grammatical duties:

✔ **Personal pronouns rename specific nouns.** They take several forms: subjective, objective, possessive, and reflexive.

- The *subjective pronouns* are *I, you, he, she, it, we, you* (plural), and *they*, and (surprise, surprise) you use them as subjects in the sentence.

- The *objective personal pronouns* are *me, you, him, her, it, us,* and *them*. You use them as objects in a sentence.

- The *possessive pronouns* are *my, mine, your, yours, his, her, hers, its, our, ours, their,* and *theirs*.

- The *reflexive pronouns* are *myself, yourself, himself, herself, itself, ourselves, yourselves,* and *themselves*.

✔ **Indefinite pronouns refer to general nouns rather than specific ones.** Some common examples are *everyone, somebody,* and *anything*.

✔ **Relative pronouns connect descriptions to nouns.** Relative pronouns include *that, which,* and *who* (the subjective form), *whom* (the objective form), and *whose* (the possessive form).

Adjectives

Adjectives describe and clarify nouns. In the sentence "The putrid odor in the lab resulted in a bunch of sick students," *putrid* defines the kind of odor and *sick* describes the condition of the students. Without the adjectives, the sentence takes on a different and ridiculous meaning: The odor in the lab resulted in a bunch of students.

When you check a sentence on the exam for errors, make sure the adjectives are in the correct places so that each adjective describes the word it's supposed to.

Adverbs

Adverbs give extra information about verbs, adjectives, and other adverbs. They include all words and groups of words (called *adverb phrases*) that answer the questions where, when, how, how much, and why. In the sentence "The chemistry students gradually recovered from smelling the very putrid odor," *gradually* explains how the students recovered.

Many adverbs end in *ly,* but not all of them do. You know a word is an adverb if it answers the question where, why, when, how, how much, or why in the sentence.

Conjunctions and prepositions

Conjunctions and *prepositions* link the main elements of a sentence.

✔ **Conjunctions join words, phrases, and clauses.** The three types of conjunctions are *coordinating, correlative,* and *subordinating.* Don't worry about memorizing these terms; just know that they exist.

- The seven coordinating conjunctions — *and, but, for, nor, or, so,* and *yet* — are the ones you probably think of when you think of conjunctions.

- Correlative conjunctions always appear in pairs: *either/or, neither/nor,* and *not only/but also.*

- Subordinating conjunctions introduce dependent clauses and connect them to independent clauses. *Although, because, if, when,* and *while* are common examples of subordinating conjunctions. (For more on clauses, see the later section "Phrases and clauses.")

✔ **Prepositions join nouns to the rest of the sentence.** We'd need several pages to list all the prepositions, but common examples are *about, above, for, over,* and *with.* Prepositions always appear in prepositional phrases, which also include a noun. Prepositional phrases usually modify a noun (the students *in the band*) or a verb (the football player ran *down the field*).

Piecing together the parts of a sentence

The parts of speech we describe in the preceding section work together to form sentences. Every sentence has at least a subject and a verb, but most add a little bit (or a lot) more information.

Subjects and predicates

Every sentence has two parts: the subject and the predicate. The *subject* is the main actor in the sentence; it's the noun that's doing the action in the sentence or whose condition the sentence describes. The *predicate* is the verb and pretty much everything else in the sentence that isn't part of the subject.

Complements

Complements are parts of the predicate that add to the meaning of the sentence. In terms of the ACT, you need to be able to recognize the following complements in a sentence:

✔ **Predicate adjectives:** Adjectives that follow linking verbs and describe something about the subject. In the sentence "The dog is *brown* and looks *furry,*" *brown* and *furry* are predicate adjectives.

✔ **Predicate nouns and pronouns:** Nouns and pronouns that follow the verb *to be* and name the subject in a new way. In the sentence "The dog is a *collie,*" *collie* is a predicate noun. In "It was *she* who arrived late," *she* is a predicate pronoun.

✔ **Direct objects:** Nouns and pronouns that receive the action of action verbs. In the sentence "Dogs eat *meat,*" *meat* is a direct object; in "The dog licked *her* and *me,*" *her* and *me* are both direct objects.

✔ **Indirect objects:** Nouns and pronouns that receive the action of the verb when the sentence also contains a direct object. For example, in the sentence "The dog gave *Julia* the stick," *Julia* is an indirect object, and in "The dog gave *her* the stick," *her* is an indirect object.

The ACT doesn't ask you to locate complements in sentences, but if you know what they are, you'll be able to spot them and the errors that accompany them come test day.

Phrases and clauses

A sentence usually contains single words, phrases, or clauses that convey more information about the sentence's main message. *Phrases* and *clauses* are groups of words that work together to form a single part of speech, like an adverb or adjective. The difference between phrases and clauses is that clauses contain their own subjects and verbs; phrases don't.

The two types of clauses are independent and dependent:

✔ **Independent clauses express complete thoughts and can stand as sentences by themselves.** The sentence "Jeff opened the door, and the cat slipped out" contains two independent clauses.

✔ **Dependent clauses express incomplete thoughts and are, therefore, sentence fragments if left by themselves.** "Although the cat slipped out" is an example of a dependent clause. To convert any dependent clause into a complete sentence, you must add an independent clause, as in "Although the cat slipped out, Jeff caught it before it could run away."

Understanding the difference between independent and dependent clauses helps you recognize a bunch of errors, such as sentence fragments, reference problems, and punctuation errors.

Punctuation rules for every occasion

You use periods, commas, semicolons, and other forms of punctuation all the time when you write. But are you using them correctly? Punctuation rules are pretty straightforward. After you have them down, you can be sure you're practicing proper punctuation.

Periods and question marks

The two simplest types of punctuation to use properly are periods and question marks. Periods end sentences that aren't questions (like this one). Periods also follow initials, as in *J. K. Rowling,* and abbreviations, such as *etc.* But you don't use periods for initials in agency names, such as *ROTC* and *YMCA,* or for commonly used shortened forms, such as *ad* or *memo.*

Question marks end direct questions, like "When will dinner be ready?" However, you never put a question mark at the end of indirect questions, such as "Pam asked me when dinner would be ready."

Commas

The comma is perhaps the most misused punctuation mark in the English language. Whenever you see an underlined comma in the English Test, always know its purpose. Don't put a comma in a sentence just because you think it needs a pause.

Commas never separate a subject from its verb or a verb from its complement. Remember that simple fact and the following comma uses to take the guesswork out of placing commas:

✔ **Series:** In a series of three or more expressions joined by one conjunction, put a comma after each expression except the last one, as in the sentence "Rachel, Bryan, and Tyler bought sandwiches, fruit, and doughnuts for the picnic." Notice that no comma comes after *Tyler* and no comma comes before *doughnuts.*

✔ **Omitted words:** Use a comma to replace words omitted from a sentence. The comma replaces *and* in the second part of this sentence: I studied with Jerry yesterday, with Pam today.

✔ **Separation of clauses:** Put a comma before the conjunction when you join two independent clauses with a conjunction. Here's an example of what we mean: The polka-dot suit was Sammie's favorite, but she didn't wear it when she was feeling shy.

Also use a comma to set apart a beginning dependent clause from the rest of a sentence, as in "When Sammie feels shy, she doesn't wear her polka-dot suit." But don't put in a comma when the dependent clause comes after the independent clause. So the revised, no-comma-needed sentence looks like this: Sammie doesn't wear her polka-dot suit when she feels shy.

A run-on sentence happens when a sentence with two or more independent clauses has improper punctuation. Here's an example: I had a college interview yesterday morning and I'm pretty sure I knocked the interviewer's socks off. "I had a college interview yesterday morning" and "I'm pretty sure I knocked the interviewer's socks off" are independent clauses. You can't stick a conjunction between them to make a sentence. However, you have three other options:

- Put a comma before the *and:* I had a college interview yesterday morning, and I'm pretty sure I knocked the interviewer's socks off.

- Replace *and* with a semicolon: I had a college interview yesterday morning; I'm pretty sure I knocked the interviewer's socks off.

- Create two separate sentences by putting a period after *morning* and taking out the *and:* I had a college interview yesterday morning. I'm pretty sure I knocked the interviewer's socks off.

✔ **Nonessentials:** When a sentence includes information that's important but not crucial to the meaning of the sentence, you set off that information with commas on both sides (unless the nonessential info begins or ends a sentence — then you just use one comma). Sometimes determining whether an expression is essential is difficult, but following these guidelines can help:

- *Asides* consist of words such as *however, in my opinion,* and *for example* and are set apart from the rest of the sentence. Here's an example: In my opinion, Sammie looks smashing in her polka-dot suit.

- *Appositives* provide additional information about a noun that isn't critical to understanding the main idea of the sentence. In the sentence "The science teacher, Ms. Paul, scheduled a meeting with her top students," *Ms. Paul* lets you know the science teacher's name. Yet without that information, the sentence still retains its meaning. When a name is part of a title, as in the sentence "Professor Paul requested a meeting," don't use commas.

- *Titles and distinctions* that follow a name are enclosed in commas. Case in point: Georgia White, RN, is the first speaker for career day.

- *Abbreviations,* such as *etc., e.g.,* and *i.e.,* are enclosed in commas. Here's an example: Tyler pulled out the sandwiches, drinks, doughnuts, etc., from the picnic basket.

- *Dates and place names* contain what can be considered nonessential information and are, therefore, punctuated with commas. For example, "Mike attended school in Boulder, Colorado, from September 1, 2008, to May 23, 2011." Notice that commas appear on both sides of the state name and on both sides of the year in the date.

- *Nonrestrictive clauses* are by definition nonessential. Because nonrestrictive clauses always provide information that doesn't affect the meaning of a sentence, commas always set them apart from the rest of the sentence. The second clause in the sentence "The meeting took place in Ms. Paul's classroom, which is just down the hall from the library" provides important information, but the meaning of the sentence wouldn't change if that information were left out. You introduce nonrestrictive clauses with *which* rather than *that*.

Semicolons

The break a semicolon provides is more definite than the one a comma provides but less final than the break a period provides. Using semicolons is appropriate in the following instances:

- **To join two independent yet closely related clauses without a conjunction:** For example, the sentence "It's almost the weekend; I can finally relax" has two independent clauses that are closely related, so they appear together in the same sentence separated by a semicolon.

- **To begin a second clause with a conjunctive adverb:** Clauses that begin with conjunctive adverbs (such as *accordingly, also, besides, consequently, furthermore, hence, however, indeed, likewise, moreover, nevertheless, otherwise, similarly, so, still, therefore,* and *thus*) use a semicolon to separate them from another clause. Here's an example: I should relax this weekend; otherwise, I'll be tired all week. Note that a comma comes after the conjunctive adverb.

- **To provide clarity in complex sentences:** Semicolons appear in sentences that have a numbered series or when using commas would be confusing. See what we mean in this sentence: The secretary's duties include (1) creating, sending, and filing documents; (2) making and organizing appointments; and (3) scheduling and planning meetings.

Colons

Colons have several functions. You can use them in place of periods to separate two independent clauses (although semicolons usually fill this role). You can also use them to relate the introductory clause in a sentence to a relevant list of specifics, long appositive or explanation, or quotation. For instance, "Megan will be finished with her homework when she completes these three tasks: a rough outline for an essay, a worksheet of math problems, and the final draft of her chemistry report."

If the words before the colon don't form a complete sentence, then you've used the colon incorrectly, like this wrong construction: "Megan will be finished with her homework when she completes: a rough outline for an essay, a worksheet of math problems, and the final draft of her chemistry report." Deleting the colon fixes the problem.

Dashes

Dashes work like colons to introduce long appositives. They also separate a beginning series from the rest of a sentence and signal abrupt breaks in the continuity of a sentence. Here's an example: "A state championship, a college scholarship, and a Super Bowl ring — such were the dreams of the high school quarterback."

Apostrophes

Apostrophes have two purposes — creating contractions and forming possessives. The apostrophe takes the place of the missing letter or letters in a contraction. Think *they're* (they are), *can't* (cannot), *here's* (here is), and so on.

To show ownership of one noun by another, use an apostrophe. For example, a dog owned by a girl is "the girl's dog" and an opinion of a judge is "a judge's opinion." Here are some rules for forming possessives:

- ✔ **Most possessives are formed by adding *'s* to the end of a singular noun.** This statement is true even if the noun ends in *s*. Here are three examples: "Mrs. Roger's car," "the committee's decision," and "Charles's surgery."

- ✔ **If the possessive noun is plural and ends in *s*, only add the apostrophe.** Some examples include "the four boys' bikes" and "the Smiths' front porch."

None of the possessive pronouns contains an apostrophe. (*It's* is a contraction of *it is,* not the possessive form of it.) But indefinite pronouns *do* contain apostrophes, as in the sentence "Somebody's dog chewed my carpet."

Spotting Mistakes: Commonly Tested Errors

The ACT tests a bunch of English usage rules. The next sections highlight some of the errors that appear most frequently so that you're prepared to spot 'em without breaking a sweat.

Picking up on pronoun errors

If you see a pronoun in the underlined part of a sentence, check to make sure its reference is clear and it's in the proper form. That is, if it's used as an object, it needs to be in the objective form; if it's used as a subject, it needs to be in the subjective form.

Unclear pronoun references

If you can't tell which noun a pronoun refers to, something's wrong with the sentence. *It, that, this, these,* and *which* are some of the more common pronouns involved in this type of error, but no pronoun is immune to the issue. For example, the pronoun reference in the sentence "Bob and Tom went to the store, and he purchased a candy bar" is unclear. Because the subject of the first clause is plural, the pronoun *he* could refer to either Bob or Tom. You can correct this sentence by changing *he* to *Bob* (or *Tom*).

Faulty pronoun references

Plural nouns take plural pronouns, and singular nouns take singular pronouns. So the sentence "You can determine the ripeness of citrus by handling them and noting their color" has improper noun/pronoun agreement. *Citrus* is a singular noun, so using plural pronouns to refer to it is wrong. To correct this sentence, change it to "You can determine the ripeness of citrus by handling it and noting its color."

Improper pronoun forms

A pronoun needs to be in the same form (objective or subjective) as the noun it's substituting for. (See the section "Pronouns" for a list of pronoun forms.) This rule makes sense, doesn't it? The problem is that some of the rules about pronoun form have been violated so often in everyday speech that errors may not seem wrong to you when you see them.

Make sure you know these pronoun rules:

✔ **Use the subjective form when a pronoun is the subject of a clause.** The following construction is incorrect: Amy is taller than me. Why? Because *me* is the subject of an understood clause, and you can't use an objective pronoun as a subject. The correct construction is "Amy is taller than I (am)."

✔ **Use the subjective form of pronouns in compound subjects.** The construction "Him and me saw a movie last night" is wrong. *Him and me* is the compound subject of the sentence, so you have to use subjective forms. The correctly written version of this sentence is "He and I saw a movie last night."

✔ **Use the objective form for pronouns that serve as objects.** Writing "Jessie eats lunch with Dave and I every day" is inaccurate. *I* is the object of the preposition *with*, so it has to be in the objective form, as in "Jessie eats lunch with Dave and me every day."

If you have trouble figuring out what form a pronoun in a compound subject or object should be in, just take away the other noun or pronoun. For instance, you'd take Dave out of the sentence and say "Jessie eats lunch with me." Saying "Jessie eats lunch with I" sounds weird.

✔ **Use reflexive pronouns only when the receiver and the doer of an action are the same.** The sentence "Please return the forms to the secretary and myself" is wrong because you aren't the doer of the action of returning the forms; you're telling someone else to give the forms to you and your secretary. The correct version of this sentence is "Please return the forms to the secretary and me." Note that a sentence such as "He came up with the idea all by himself" is accurate because the doer and the receiver of the action are the same person.

✔ **Use *who* to refer to people, *which* to refer to animals and things, and *that* to refer to both.** You can't say, "There's the police officer which pulled me over yesterday." But you can say, "There's the police officer who pulled me over yesterday."

The next time your grammar teacher asks you to name two pronouns, you can be a smart aleck and shout out, "Who, me?"

Getting subjects and verbs to agree

Okay, so subjects and verbs don't actually fight, but they do sometimes disagree. To bring peace to the situation, you must pair plural subjects with plural verbs and singular subjects with singular verbs. If you see a verb in the underlined portion of the English Test, find the subject it goes with and make sure they agree.

When the subject isn't simple or obvious, finding it may be difficult. Just take a look at this sentence: Terry's continual quest to embellish his truck with a ton of amenities make it hard for him to stick to a budget. The subject is *quest* (a singular noun), but the interjection of "to embellish his truck with a ton of amenities" between the subject and verb may confuse you into thinking that *amenities* (a plural noun) is the subject. However, *amenities* can't be the subject of the sentence because it's the object of a preposition, and a noun can't be an object and a subject at the same time.

To spot subject/verb agreement errors in a complex sentence, focus on the main elements of the sentence by crossing out words and phrases that aren't essential to the point. Then check the subjects and verbs to make sure they agree. When you remove all the fluff from the sentence "Terry's continual quest to embellish his truck with a ton of amenities make it hard for him to stick to a budget," you get "Terry's quest make it hard." Now the problem is obvious! The singular noun *quest* requires the singular verb *makes*.

After you find the subject, you may not be able to tell whether it's plural or singular right away. Use these rules to help you decide:

- ✔ **A compound subject — two or more subjects connected by the word *and* — takes a plural verb.** A symphony and a fugue *are* (not *is*) beautiful.

- ✔ **The following words are always plural and, therefore, require plural verbs: *few*, *both*, *several*, and *many*.** Few students *enjoy* taking the ACT.

- ✔ ***Each*** **and *every* are always singular and require singular verbs.** The boys rarely agree. Each *has* his own opinion.

- ✔ **Indefinite pronouns are singular.** Everyone *eats* coconuts.

- ✔ **Five nouns (*some*, *any*, *most*, *all*, and *none*) may be singular or plural, depending on the noun in the phrase that follows them.** Most of the graduates *plan* to attend college. Some of the group *plans* to go out-of-state.

You can remember these words with the acronym S.A.M.A.N., the first letters of the words. Think of the sentence, "S.A.M.A.N. (Say, man), can you tell me which words are sometimes singular and sometimes plural?"

Calling out sentence fragments

Sentence fragments are incomplete sentences. They usually show up on the ACT either as dependent clauses that pretend to convey complete thoughts or as a bunch of words with something that looks like a verb but doesn't act like one.

Always keep the following in mind:

- ✔ **Dependent clauses by themselves are fragments because they don't provide complete thoughts.** "Although the stairs are steep . . ." is far from a complete thought.

- ✔ **Phrases that contain words that look like verbs but don't function as verbs can appear to be complete if you don't read them carefully.** In the sentence "The peacefulness of a morning warmed by the summer sun," *warmed* looks like a verb but doesn't act like one. Without a verb, the sentence leaves you hanging. You're not told what you're supposed to know about "the peacefulness of a morning warmed by the summer sun."

Having trouble spotting sentence fragments? Try reading the words under your breath. That way, you should be able to tell whether they express a complete thought.

Dealing with verb tense issues

Check the tenses of underlined verbs. Verb forms must be in the proper tense for a sentence to make sense. Review the purpose for each verb tense in Table 4-1 to help you spot incorrect tenses. For example, you know that using future perfect tense in "Yesterday, I will have read 300 pages" is incorrect because *yesterday* is in the past, and you don't use future tense to refer to past events.

The other verbs in a sentence give you clues to what tense a particular verb should be in. Generally, all verbs in a sentence should be in the same tense. For example, the sentence "I had read 300 pages in the book when my friends invite me to see a movie" must be incorrect because *had read* is past perfect tense and *invite* is present tense. You can correct the sentence by changing *invite* from present tense to past tense *(invited)*.

Whenever you see a verb in a usage question, check to make sure it agrees with its subject and that it's in the proper tense.

Identifying problems with parallelism

All phrases joined by conjunctions should be constructed in the same way. For example, the following sentence has a problem with parallelism: Ann spent the morning taking practice tests, studying word lists, and she read a chapter in a novel. Not all the elements joined by the *and* in this sentence are constructed in the same way. The first two elements are phrases that begin with a gerund (or *ing* form); the last element is a clause. Changing *read* to a gerund and dropping *she* solves the problem: Ann spent the morning taking practice tests, studying word lists, and reading a chapter in a novel.

When you see a sentence with a list of any sort, check for a lack of parallelism. Items in a series may be nouns, verbs, adjectives, or entire clauses. However, nonparallel verbs are the items that most commonly have errors. When a clause contains more than one verb, watch out for this particular error.

Eliminating redundancy and wordiness

Sentences that have awkward, wordy, redundant, or unclear constructions can be grammatically correct but still need fixing. The good news is that the right answer often just sounds better.

- ✔ **Using passive rather than active voice makes a sentence seem weak and wordy.** Passive voice beats around the bush to make a point. The passive voice in the following sentence hides who's doing the action: The speech was heard by most of the students. The sentence isn't technically incorrect, but it's better said this way: Most of the students heard the speech. Notice also that the sentence in active voice uses fewer words. When given the option, choose active voice over passive voice.

- ✔ **Repetitive language adds unnecessary words.** A sentence shouldn't use more words than it needs to. Saying "The custodian added an additional row of desks to accommodate the large class" is silly. The construction of "added an additional" is needlessly repetitive. The sentence reads better as "The custodian added a row of desks to accommodate the large class."

Sticking to standard expressions

English speakers use certain words in certain ways for no particular reason other than because that's the way it is. But sometimes even native English speakers fail to use idiomatic expressions correctly. It's common to hear people use *further* instead of *farther* when they mean distance or *less* instead of *fewer* when they refer to the number of countable items.

The only way to know proper idiomatic constructions is to study them, but you probably know many of them already. To help you out, Table 4-2 lists some commonly tested expressions and shows you how to use them correctly.

Table 4-2	**Commonly Tested Words and Expressions**	
Word or Expression	**Rule**	**Correct Use**
among/ between	Use *among* for comparing three or more things or persons and *between* for comparing two things or persons.	*Between* the two of us there are few problems, but *among* the four of us there is much discord.
amount/ number	Use *amount* to describe singular nouns and *number* to describe plural nouns.	I can't count the *number* of times I've miscalculated the *amount* of money I've spent on groceries.
as . . . as	When you use *as* in a comparison, use the construction *as . . . as*.	The dog is *as* wide *as* he is tall.
better/best worse/worst	Use *better* and *worse* to compare two things; use *best* and *worst* to compare more than two things.	Of the two products, the first is *better* known, but this product is the *best* known of all 20 on the market.
different from	Use *different from* rather than *different than*.	This plan is *different from* the one we implemented last year. (Not: This plan is *different than* last year's.)
effect/affect	Generally, use *effect* as a noun and *affect* as a verb.	No one could know how the *effect* of the presentation would *affect* the client's choice.
either/or neither/nor	Use *or* with *either* and *nor* with *neither*.	*Neither* Nellie *nor* Isaac wanted to go to *either* the party *or* the concert.
er/est	Use the *er* form (called the comparative form) to compare exactly two items; use the *est* form (called the superlative form) to compare more than two items.	I am *taller* than my brother Beau, but Darren is the *tallest* member of our family.
farther/further	Use *farther* to refer to distance and *further* to refer to time or quantity.	Carol walked *farther* today than she did yesterday, and she vows to *further* study the benefits of walking.
good/well	*Good* is an adjective that modifies a noun. *Well* is an adverb that usually answers the question how.	It's a *good* thing that you're feeling so *well* after your bout of the flu.
if/whether	*If* introduces a condition. *Whether* compares alternatives.	*If* I crack a book this summer, it will be to determine *whether* I need to study more math for the ACT.
imply/infer	To *imply* means to suggest indirectly. To *infer* means to conclude or deduce.	I didn't mean to *imply* that your dress is ugly. You merely *inferred* that's what I meant when I asked you whether you bought it at an upholstery store.

Word or Expression	Rule	Correct Use
lay/lie	Use *lay* and its irregular verb tense constructions (*laid, has laid, is laying*) to mean the act of putting or placing and to refer to what hens do. Use *lie* and its irregular verb tense constructions (*lay, has lain, is lying*) to mean the act of reclining or the state of resting or reclining. *Note:* To further confuse matters, the present tense of *lay* and past tense of *lie* are both *lay*.	I always *lay* a plastic cloth over the table to protect it. Grandma *is laying* out the silverware on the counter to see what requires polishing. The hen *laid* a dozen eggs last week, which is more eggs than it *has laid* in any other one-week period this year. My uncle *lies* down on the couch every afternoon for a nap. Yesterday, he *lay* there for three hours. I couldn't find my hat in the closet because it *was lying* on the floor. I think it *has lain* there for several weeks and would be *lying* there still if I hadn't seen it when I dropped my gloves.
less/fewer	Use *less* to refer to quantity (things that can be counted) and *fewer* to refer to number (things that can't be counted).	That office building is *less* noticeable because it has *fewer* floors. That glass has *less* water and *fewer* ice cubes.
less/least	Use *less* to compare two things and *least* to compare more than two things.	He is *less* educated than his brother is, but he isn't the *least* educated of his entire family.
like/as	Use *like* before nouns and pronouns; use *as* before phrases and clauses.	*Like* Ruth, Steve wanted the school's uniform policy to be just *as* it had always been.
many/much	Use *many* to refer to number and *much* to refer to quantity.	*Many* days I woke up feeling *much* anxiety, but I'm better now that I'm reading *Catholic High School Entrance Exams For Dummies*.
more/most	Use *more* to compare two things and *most* to compare more than two things.	Of the two girls, the older is *more* generous, and she is the *most* generous person in her family.

Recognizing misplaced modifiers

The ACT will surely test how well you can spot errors in modification. *Modifier* is a fancy term for words or phrases, such as adjectives and adverbs, that give more information about other words, usually nouns. Errors occur when modifiers are too far away from the words they modify and when what they're modifying is unclear.

Keep the following guidelines in mind whenever you're dealing with modifiers:

- ✔ **Modifiers must be as close to the words they modify as possible.** The sentence "Sam set down the speech he wrote on the desk" is incorrect because of a misplaced modifier. It sounds like Sam wrote the speech on the desk! The sentence "Sam set down his speech on the desk" is much better.

- ✔ **Beginning phrases must have a clear reference.** A beginning phrase in a sentence always modifies the subject of the sentence, so the sentence has to be constructed in a way that relates the phrase to the subject. Consider this sentence: Driving down the road, a deer darted in front of me. If you read this sentence literally, you may believe the *deer* drove down the road because the beginning phrase "driving down the road" refers to the subject of the sentence, which is *deer*. To make it clear that the driver — not the deer — drove down the road, you need to rewrite this sentence as follows: As I was driving down the road, a deer darted in front of me.

Because the test makers tend to focus on modification errors involving beginning phrases, be sure to check for this error every time you see a sentence with a beginning phrase.

- ✔ **Place *not only* and *but also* in parallel positions within a sentence.** People often place *not only* and *but also* incorrectly. Here's an example of a wrong way to use these expressions: Angelique *not only* was exasperated *but also* frightened when she locked herself out of the house.

See the problem? The phrase *not only* comes before the verb was, but the phrase *but also* comes before the adjective frightened. Correct it so that both elements come before adjectives: Angelique was *not only* exasperated *but also* frightened when she locked herself out of the house.

Correcting miscellaneous mistakes

The following list reveals some of the miscellaneous grammar mistakes that many people make every day. In the real world, you can live with these mistakes; on the ACT, they're deadly.

- ✔ **Hardly:** The word *hardly* is negative and often shows up in a trap double-negative question. Don't say, "Abe has *hardly nothing* to do this weekend after he finishes the ACT and is looking forward to vegging out in front of the TV." The correct version is, "Abe has *hardly anything* to do this weekend after he finishes the ACT and is looking forward to vegging out in front of the TV."

- ✔ **Hopefully:** Use *hopefully* only where you can plug in the words *full of hope.* "Hearing the telephone ring, Alice looked up *hopefully*, thinking that Steve might be calling her to apologize for sending her flowers on his ex-girlfriend's birthday."

Many people use the word *hopefully* incorrectly as a substitute for "I hope." The sentence "*Hopefully,* my ACT score will improve" is wrong. Your score won't improve unless you learn to say, "I hope that my ACT score will improve."

- ✔ **If/would:** Don't place *if* and *would* in the same clause. A common error is to say, "*If* I *would* have studied more, I would have done better." The correct version is, "*If* I *had* studied more, I would have done better" or "*Had* I studied more, I would have done better."

- ✔ **In regard to/in regards to:** The English language has no such expression as *in regards to.* Dump the *s;* the proper expression is *in regard to.* We need to have a heart-to-heart talk *in regard to* your making this mistake.

Chapter 5

Mastering the English Test

In This Chapter
▶ Knowing what skills the English Test tests
▶ Understanding the way the ACT presents English questions
▶ Avoiding falling for the ACT traps . . . or creating your own

When you open your ACT booklet, the first thing you see is the English Test. Your still-half-asleep brain and bleary eyes encounter 5 passages and 75 questions. Somehow, you're to read all the passages and answer all the questions within 45 minutes. That may seem like a lot of questions in a little bit of time, but the English questions really aren't super time-consuming. You'll be fine. Just take a deep breath, and read on to discover everything you need to know to succeed on the English Test.

Figuring Out What the English Questions Want to Know

The questions on the English Test fall into the following two categories:

- **Usage and mechanics:** A little more than half of the questions cover the ever-popular English topics of usage and mechanics. These questions include sentence structure (whether a sentence is a fragment or a run-on), grammar and usage (just about everything most people think of as English, such as adverbs, adjectives, and so on), and punctuation (don't worry — this isn't super hard; it's mostly just commas and semicolons).

- **Rhetorical skills:** Just less than half of the questions test rhetorical skills, such as organization (reordering the sentences in the passage), style (which expression, slang or formal, is appropriate within the passage), and strategy ("This passage would be most appropriate in which of the following types of books . . . ?").

Some questions are much more doable than others. For example, most students would agree that a simple grammar question asking about a pronoun reference or subject/verb agreement is easier to answer than an organization question expecting you to reposition a paragraph within the entire passage.

Seeing Is Believing: The Format of the Test

The ACT English Test passages look like standard reading comprehension passages — you know, the kind you've seen on tests for years. The difference is that these passages have many underlined portions. An underlined portion can be an entire sentence, a phrase, a word, or even just a punctuation mark. (You may want to take a quick look right now at the practice passage and questions in Chapter 6 to see what an English Test passage looks like. We'll wait.)

Okay, you're back. Here are the details about what information you get on the English Test and what you're expected to do with it.

The passages

The five passages cover a variety of topics. You may get a fun story that's a personal anecdote — someone talking about getting a car for his 16th birthday, for example. Or you may encounter a somewhat formal scientific passage about the way items are carbon-dated. Some passages discuss history; some, philosophy; others, cultural differences among nations. Some passages are fiction, such as excerpts from novels, both old and new. One type of passage is not necessarily more difficult than another. You don't need to use specific reading techniques for these passages (as you do with standard reading comprehension passages). Just read and enjoy — and be prepared to answer the questions that accompany the passages (see the next section for details).

Although these English passages aren't reading comprehension passages per se, you do need to pay at least a little attention to content instead of just focusing on the underlined portions. Why bother? Because a few of the questions at the end of the passages are reading comprehension–type questions that ask you about the purpose of the passage or what a possible conclusion might be. More about those in the later section "Dealing with writing questions."

The question types

The English Test has few questions in the standard interrogatory form. You won't see anything like "Which of the following is an adjective?" or "The purpose of the subjunctive is to do which of these?" Instead, you analyze underlined portions of passages and choose the answer that presents the underlined words in the best way possible. Thrown into the mix are several standard questions that ask you for the best writing strategy or the best way to organize sentences or paragraphs.

Analyzing underlined words

The majority of the test is about examining underlined words in a sentence. Your job is to determine whether the underlined portion is correct as is or whether one of the three alternate answer choices is preferable. The answer choices are (A), (B), (C), and (D) for the odd-numbered questions and (F), (G), (H), and (J) for the even-numbered questions. Choices (A) and (F) are always *NO CHANGE*. You select that choice if the original is the best of the versions offered. Occasionally, Choice (D) or (J) says, *OMIT the underlined portion*. Choose that answer when you want to dump the whole underlined portion and forget that you ever saw it. (And no, you can't do that with the entire test!)

Approach these types of questions methodically:

1. **Look for the obvious error or errors in the underlined words.** Chapter 4 summarizes the kinds of errors to look for, such as pronoun or punctuation problems, word choice issues, redundancy, and subject/verb agreement mistakes.

2. **Eliminate answer choices that don't correct the error.** If more than one choice corrects the error, choose the one that doesn't create a new error.

3. **If you don't see an error, examine the answer choices to make sure you haven't missed something.** If none of the alternatives are better than the original, choose NO CHANGE.

4. **Reread the sentence with the answer you've chosen inserted.** Don't skip this step. You may overlook a problem with your answer until you see how it works in the complete sentence.

Here's an example to demonstrate how to use this approach.

A full case of sodas, when opened by a horde of thirsty athletes who have been running laps, <u>don't go</u> very far.

(A) NO CHANGE

(B) do not go

(C) doesn't go

(D) doesn't get to go

The underlined part of the sentence contains a verb. Problems with verbs usually involve tense or subject/verb agreement. All the answers are in present tense, so the issue is probably subject/verb agreement. Find the subject that goes with "don't go." When you sift through the clauses and prepositional phrases, you see that the subject is *case*. Because *case* is singular, it requires the singular verb *doesn't*. Eliminate Choices (A) and (B) immediately because they don't correct the error. Choices (C) and (D) correct the verb problem, but Choice (D) adds unnecessary words and makes the sentence seem silly. So Choice (C) is correct.

Did you see the trap in this sentence? Some students think that *sodas, athletes,* or *laps* — each of which is plural — is the subject of the sentence. (*Laps* is especially tricky because it's right next to the verb.) In that case, they think the verb has to be plural, too, and choose Choice (A). You didn't fall for that cheap trick, did you?

If English isn't your first language, the diction and grammar questions are the key to your getting a good score on this test. When you studied English, you probably memorized rule after rule after rule, just the kinds of things that these questions test. In this situation, you actually have an advantage over American kids who haven't been tested on this stuff since the seventh grade. (In many American high schools, students start learning literature in the eighth or ninth grades and no longer focus on pure grammar.) Spend some time studying the grammar and usage rules in Chapter 4 and then head to Chapter 6 for practice on these types of questions.

Dealing with writing questions

A few of the questions in the English Test ask you to strategize about content, style, and organization. These questions usually come right out and ask you a question about the passage. The best way to approach these questions is by eliminating answer choices that can't be right.

Sometimes the answer to a question is a simple yes or no. Two of the answer choices provide the yes option; the other two give you the no option. First, you decide whether the answer to the question is yes or no. Then you choose the answer that provides the best reason for the yes or no answer.

Here's an example. Say that this question appears in an excerpt from a stuffy scientific journal article. Most of the passage is written in third person, but one paragraph suddenly switches to first person.

Given the topic and the tone of the passage, was the author's use of the pronoun *I* in this paragraph proper?

(F) Yes, because the only way to express an opinion is by using first person.

(G) Yes, because he was projecting his personal feelings onto the topic.

(H) No, because the use of *I* is inconsistent with the rest of the passage.

(J) No, because using *I* prevents the readers from becoming involved with the topic.

In this case, you're expected to get a feel for the tone of the passage as a whole. As soon as you read the question, decide whether using *I* is appropriate — *before* you even look at the answer choices. (If you don't have at least some idea in your brain *before* you look at the answer choices, they'll all look good.) Determine whether the answer is yes or no. Then focus on the two no choices or the two yes choices. Because most of the passage is in third person, the one paragraph in first person probably isn't right. So the answer to the question is most likely no. That narrows your focus to Choices (H) and (J). Choice (J) doesn't make sense. Using first person promotes rather than prevents reader involvement. Thus, the correct answer is (H).

Other writing questions may ask you about the structure or organization of sentences or paragraphs. If a passage has an organization question, it often warns you at the beginning by telling you that the paragraphs may or may not be in the right order. As you read, notice any inconsistencies in organization and put a mark in the margin whenever something doesn't seem to flow right. That way, you know where to look when you're asked an organization question like the following one.

To make the passage a coherent whole, Paragraph 4 should be placed:

(A) where it is now.

(B) at the beginning of the passage.

(C) after Paragraph 2.

(D) at the end of the passage.

First, look at the answer choices. If the paragraph seems out of place, the answer choices narrow down the places you can move Paragraph 4 to three. If Paragraph 4 provides introductory information that's discussed in later paragraphs, Choice (B) is probably right. If it builds on other paragraphs and concludes the ideas of the passage, Choice (D) is probably the one. If the paragraph contains information that links it directly to Paragraph 2, Choice (C) is probably the right answer.

Organization questions are often more time-consuming than others. Sometimes the best way to handle a question that asks you to move a paragraph or sentence is to make a quick guess and come back to the question later if you have the time. (Never leave any question blank; remember that the ACT doesn't penalize you for guessing.)

Their Pain, Your Gain: Looking Out for Traps That Others Fall into

We've taught the ACT for a couple of decades now. By this point, we've seen students fall for every trap the test makers have thought of — and some they probably never considered! Watch out for these most commonly tumbled-into traps:

- **Forgetting the NO CHANGE option:** Because the first answer choice — Choice (A) for odd-numbered questions, Choice (F) for even-numbered questions — is always NO CHANGE, students tend to gloss over it. Don't forget that you always have the option to keep things exactly the way they are.

- **Automatically choosing OMIT each time it shows up:** Although you may be tempted to shorten this section by screaming, "Dump it! Just dump the whole stupid thing!" every chance you get, don't fall into that habit. When you see the OMIT answer — either Choice (D) or Choice (J) — realize that it has the same one-in-four chance of being right as the other answers have. Consider it, but don't make it a no-brainer choice.

- **Automatically selecting the "other" word or grammar choice:** When you see *who* in a sentence, you're often tempted to change it immediately to *whom*. Yet if that same sentence said *whom* to begin with, you'd immediately change it to *who*. The temptation to *do* something, anything, is very strong. Don't change just for the sake of change.

- **Wasting time on the writing questions:** Some of the writing questions, like the attitude ones ("Would this essay be appropriate for a group of university professors?"), can be quite simple. But others, such as the ones that ask you to reposition sentences or complete paragraphs, can be incredibly time-wasting and frustrating. You may have to read and reread a paragraph, changing and rearranging the sentences again and again. You may be able to get the question right, but at what price? How much time do you chew up? How many more of the easy questions could you have gotten right in that time?

- **Ignoring the big picture:** Some questions are style questions. A style question expects you to sense the overall picture, to know whether the tone of the passage is friendly so that you can appropriately use a slang expression (for example, *totally lame*) or whether you need to be a bit more formal (*useless* rather than *totally lame*). If you focus on only the underlined portions and don't read the passage as a whole, you can easily miss this type of question.

Even if a question doesn't seem to expect you to understand the entire passage, you should still read a few sentences ahead of the question. How you correct a run-on or a fragment, for example, may depend on how the next few sentences are structured.

Chapter 6

It's Not What You Say but How You Say It: English Practice Questions

....

In This Chapter

▶ Putting your grammar skills to the test with a practice English passage
▶ Seeing the English Test questions in context

....

Y ou didn't think that we crammed those grammar and punctuation rules into your head just so you could lord your perfect speech over your friends, did you? Here we show you just how knowing the stimulating rules we cover in Chapter 4 comes in handy for the ACT. This practice chapter has one passage and 15 questions. Multiply that by 5 for the real ACT English Test. After you complete each question, you can review your answer by reading the explanation that follows.

Directions: Following are four paragraphs containing underlined portions. Alternate ways of stating the underlined portions follow the paragraphs. Choose the best alternative. If the original is the best way of stating the underlined portion, choose NO CHANGE. You also see questions that refer to the passage or ask you to reorder the sentences within a passage. These questions are identified by a number in a box. Choose the best answer.

Passage

[1] Marian Anderson possibly <u>will have</u> <u>the greatest</u> influence opening doors and
             1   2

gaining well-deserved opportunities for other African American singers than anyone else to

date <u>so far</u>. [2] Anderson, born in Philadelphia, Pennsylvania, had an early interest in music.
      3

[3] She <u>learns</u> to play the piano and was singing in the church at the age of six. [4] She gave
        4

her first concert at age eight<u>, when she was still a young child</u>.
                            5

[5] In 1925, Anderson won a concert hosted by the New York Philharmonic, beating out

<u>no less than</u> 300 singers. [6] <u>It launched her career but,</u> America was not quite ready for her
  6   7

fantastic voice, personality, or racial heritage.

In 1936, the White House <u>asking her</u> to give a performance. She confessed that this occa-
                      8

sion was <u>different than</u> other concerts because she was very nervous. She and Eleanor
       9

Roosevelt became <u>close friends, but</u> this friendship <u>between she and the First Lady became</u>
           10   11

evident when Anderson was snubbed by the Daughters of the American Revolution (DAR).

The DAR refused to let Anderson perform in Constitution Hall <u>in 1939, the White House</u> made
₁₂

arrangements for Ms. Anderson to sing on the steps of the Lincoln Memorial instead. [13]

In 1977, First Lady Rosalynn Carter presented Marian Anderson with a Congressional

Gold <u>Medal, making Ms. Anderson the first African American</u> to receive such an honor. Later
₁₄

she was inducted into the Women's Hall of Fame in Seneca Falls, New York. [15]

1. (A) NO CHANGE

   (B) has had

   (C) has

   (D) is having

Because Marian Anderson's influence has already been felt, future tense isn't appropriate.
Ms. Anderson has influenced and continues to influence. The verb tense that shows past
action that continues or may continue into the present and beyond is present perfect, so
the correct answer is (B). (See Chapter 4 for more information on verb tenses.)

2. (F) NO CHANGE

   (G) a greater

   (H) one of the greatest

   (J) a great

You need to read the entire sentence before deciding on an answer. If you read "the greatest
influence" all by itself, it sounds correct. However, if you continue to read the sentence, you
find the comparative *than*. You cannot say "the greatest influence than" but rather "a
greater influence than." The correct answer is (G).

Be very careful to read the entire sentence. You may save a few seconds by reading only the
underlined portion, but you'll sacrifice a lot of points.

3. (A) NO CHANGE

   (B) dating so far

   (C) so far dated

   (D) OMIT the underlined portion.

To date and *so far* are redundant; they mean the same thing. You can use one or the other
but not both. (Quick! Notify the Department of Redundancy Department!) The correct
answer is (D).

4. (F) NO CHANGE

   (G) has been learning

   (H) learned

   (J) is learning

Because Marian Anderson is no longer six years old, the sentence requires the past tense,
learned. **Hint:** If you aren't sure of the tense, check out the rest of the sentence. You're told
that Ms. Anderson "was singing," meaning the situation occurred in the past. So the correct
answer is (H).

5. (A) NO CHANGE

   (B) still a young child

   (C) still young

   (D) OMIT the underlined portion and end the sentence with a period.

   A person who is eight is still a young child — duh! The underlined portion is superfluous, unnecessary. Eliminate it. The period is necessary to finish the sentence. The correct answer is (D).

6. (F) NO CHANGE

   (G) less than

   (H) fewer than

   (J) no fewer than

   Use *fewer* to describe plural nouns, as in fewer brain cells, for example. Use *less* to describe singular nouns, like less intelligence. Because *singers* is a plural noun, use *fewer* rather than *less*. The correct answer is (J).

   If you picked Choice (H), you fell for the trap. You forgot to reread the sentence with your answer inserted. The meaning of the whole sentence changes with the phrase "fewer than 300 singers." In that case, you're diminishing the winner's accomplishment. The tone of the passage is one of respect. The author is impressed that Ms. Anderson beat out "no fewer than 300 singers." Keep in mind that you must make your answers fit the overall tone or attitude of the passage. If a passage is complimentary, be sure that your answers are, too.

7. (A) NO CHANGE

   (B) Launching her career,

   (C) Her career was launched, but

   (D) Upon launching it (her career),

   Be very suspicious of that two-letter rascal *it*. Always double-check *it* out because *it* is so often misused and abused. It must refer to one specific thing: "Where is the book? Here it is." In Question 7, it doesn't have a clear reference. It could mean that winning the concert launched her career, or it may seem that the New York Philharmonic launched her career. Another problem with Choice (A) is that pesky comma. It belongs before *but*, not after *it*. Choices (B) and (D) sound as if America launched Ms. Anderson's career: "Upon launching it . . . America was not quite ready . . . ." Be sure to go back and reread the entire sentence with your answer inserted. The correct answer is (C).

   Although the presence of passive voice in an answer is often an indication that the choice is wrong, that's not always the case. Passive voice may be okay if knowing who completed the action isn't important and when the choice that uses it is better than other choices with glaring grammar or punctuation problems.

8. (F) NO CHANGE

   (G) asked her

   (H) was asking her

   (J) asking

   The original is a fragment, an incomplete sentence. It tries to fool you into thinking that asking is the verb, but *ing* words all by themselves with no helping verbs to assist them can't work as verbs. The remedy is to change *asking* to the simple past verb *asked*. Because the sentence gives you a specific date, you know that the event happened at one point in the past. Therefore, Choice (H) is wrong. The White House wasn't in a continuous state of asking Ms. Anderson. So the correct answer is (G).

9. (A) NO CHANGE

 (B) different from

 (C) differed from

 (D) more different than

Standard English says *different from* rather than *different than*. Choice (D) adds more to the sentence to try to make *than* sound like a proper comparison term, but its addition also changes the meaning of the sentence. The White House concert wasn't more different than other concerts. It was simply different from other concerts that weren't as anxiety-provoking. The correct answer is (B).

Choice (C) changes *than* to *from,* but it introduces another verb into a sentence that already has a verb. You may not notice the problem if you don't reread the sentence with Choice (C) inserted. Always reread the sentence with your answer choice inserted before you mark the answer on your sheet to make sure you haven't missed something important.

10. (F) NO CHANGE

 (G) close friends, and

 (H) close friends — which

 (J) close and friendly,

The clause "but this friendship . . . became evident . . ." makes no sense in the context. Use *but* only to indicate opposition or change; use a comma and the word *and* to add to and continue a thought. The correct answer is (G).

11. (A) NO CHANGE

 (B) between the First Lady and she became

 (C) between her and the First Lady became

 (D) OMIT the underlined portion.

The pronoun is the problem in this question. *Between* is a preposition, which means that the pronoun and noun that come after it are objects of the preposition. Therefore, the pronoun has to be in objective form. The objective form of *she* is *her.* You can't omit the underlined words because the resulting clause has no verb. The correct answer is (C).

Many students tend to choose "OMIT the underlined portion" every time they see it, reasoning that it would not be a choice unless it were correct. Not so. If you decide to omit the underlined portion, be especially careful to reread the entire sentence. Often, omitting the underlined portion makes nonsense out of the sentence.

12. (F) NO CHANGE

 (G) in 1939; however, the White House

 (H) in 1939 but the White House

 (J) in 1939. Although the White House

To answer this question, you must correct the comma splice in the original sentence. You can't use a comma all by itself to join two independent clauses (complete sentences) in one sentence. You could separate them by putting a period after 1939 and capitalizing *the*. The answers don't give you that option, though. Choice (J) separates the clauses with a period, but adding *although* makes the second sentence a fragment. Another way to join two independent clauses together is with a semicolon. Choice (G) changes the comma to a semicolon and adds *however* for a smooth transition to the next thought. It properly places a comma after *however*, too. Choice (H) lacks a necessary comma before *but*. The correct answer is (G).

13. The author is considering inserting a sentence that presents a short list of other venues where Marian Anderson performed during her career. Would that insertion be appropriate here?

   (A) Yes, because the primary purpose of this paragraph is to emphasize the great number of places where Marian Anderson performed.

   (B) Yes, because it's always better to include many specific examples to advance an idea.

   (C) No, because the paragraph is about the obstacles that Marian Anderson had to overcome rather than the number of concert halls she performed in.

   (D) No, because providing a list of examples is never appropriate in an essay about a person's life.

When you see one of these "yes, yes, no, no" questions on the English Test, figure out the short answer to the question. Would a list of venues be appropriate? Probably not. (Please. The test is boring enough without having to read through a list of concert venues.) Ignore the yes answers for now and focus on the no choices. The paragraph seems to focus on the racial prejudice Anderson experienced rather than the number of places she performed in. So the correct answer is (C).

You can be pretty certain that Choices (B) and (D) are wrong. Both of them contain debatable words, such as *always* and *never*, that should raise a red flag for you. If you're thinking of choosing an answer that contains one of these all-encompassing words that leaves no room for exception, first make sure that something in the passage justifies the strong position.

14. (F) NO CHANGE

   (G) Medal, being the first African American

   (H) Medal; the first African American

   (J) Medal, the first African American

The original is okay the way it's written. The other choices make it sound like the medal was the first African American to receive such an honor. Choice (H) adds insult to injury by using a semicolon to do a comma's job. Note that the job of the semicolon is to separate two independent sentences; each sentence could stand alone. The correct answer is (F).

Don't forget that the sentence doesn't have to have an error. About 20 percent of the time the underlined portion requires NO CHANGE.

15. If the author of this passage were to add the following lines to the article, where would they be most logically placed?

    It was an era of racial prejudice, a time when people were still legally excluded from jobs, housing, and even entertainment merely because of their race. Thus, the early promise of success seemed impossible until something amazing for the times happened.

    (A) After Sentence 2

    (B) After Sentence 6

    (C) After Sentence 3

    (D) After Sentence 5

    You know from the answer options to look only in the first two paragraphs. Because the first sentence of the addition talks about racial prejudice, look in the beginning of the passage for something that mentions Marian Anderson's race. That topic is specifically discussed only in Sentence 6. So the correct answer is (B).

    Be sure to go back to the passage and reread the entire paragraph with the new lines inserted to make sure that they make sense.

    If you find yourself wasting too much time on a question like this one, your best bet is to eliminate answers if you can, guess, and move on. ***Remember:*** The ACT doesn't penalize you for wrong answers. Marking a guess for any question that has you stumped is to your advantage.

Part III
Don't Count Yourself Out: The Math Test

The 5th Wave   By Rich Tennant

"He ran some linear equations, threw in a few theorems, and before I knew it I was buying rust proofing."

In this part . . .

You knew it was coming, didn't you? You can't possibly get through a test-prep book without having a math review. Lucky for you, this part gives you three for the price of one: basic math, geometry, and algebra/trigonometry. Plus, we throw in a chapter that shows you how to answer those dreaded word problems. We've worked hard to make this stuff as painless as possible by throwing in the odd joke here and there and by using some examples that are a lot more fun than any you'd actually see on the ACT. After all, you're bound to experience a little bit of sensory overload as you cover three years of math in just three chapters.

But we don't waste your time. We don't insult you by starting too far back ("here are the multiplication tables you must know . . ."), and we don't give you material that's not tested (like calculus) just to impress you with *our* abilities. Instead, we emphasize what you're most likely to see on the test, reviewing all the formulas and even some of the math vocabulary, like prime and composite numbers.

This part also features a chapter on how to approach the math questions on the ACT, including what to do when you don't have a clue. You can discover how to recognize and avoid built-in traps, how to use the answer choices to save yourself time and headaches in solving the problems, and which questions are time wasters that are best to guess at quickly and leave behind in your dust.

To round out the part, we include a practice chapter with 12 questions that allows you to download some of the things you've been learning . . . and see whether you really can recognize those traps.

Chapter 7

Number Nuts and Bolts

In This Chapter

▶ Reviewing numbers and basic math operations

▶ Figuring out fractions, decimals, and percentages

▶ Reasoning through ratios, proportions, and exponents

▶ Finding order in operations and calculating the mean, median, mode, and range

▶ Considering units and measurements

You've seen them before. They crop up everywhere: your high school math tests, those dreaded achievement tests, and now your college entrance exam. Yes, we're talking about multiple-choice math questions. Take heart! Many of the math questions on the ACT cover the basics.

Even though you may already know most of the math that we discuss in this chapter, it never hurts to refresh your memory. After all, the questions on the ACT that ask about the basic math topics we cover here tend to be the easiest, so they offer you the best chance for getting correct answers. Brush up on your elementary school math, and you're sure to improve your score on the ACT Math Test.

The Wonderful World of Numbers

You're probably not surprised to find out that the math problems on the ACT involve numbers, but you also probably haven't thought about the properties of numbers in a long time. That's why we offer you a fairly complete number review here. (You can thank us later.)

Keeping it real: Types of numbers

Real numbers include integers, rational numbers, and those completely unreasonable irrational numbers.

✔ **Integers:** All the positive and negative whole numbers, plus zero. Integers aren't fractions or decimals or portions of a number, so they include –5, –4, –3, –2, –1, 0, 1, 2, 3, 4, 5, and continue infinitely on either side of zero. Integers greater than zero are called *natural numbers* or *positive integers;* integers less than zero are called *negative integers.*

Tread carefully when working with zero. It's neither positive nor negative.

✔ **Rational numbers:** All the positive and negative integers, plus fractions and decimal numbers that either end or repeat. For example, the fraction $\frac{1}{6}$ is a rational number. It can also be expressed as $0.1\overline{6}$.

✔ **Irrational numbers:** Numbers that can't be written as fractions, such as π and $\sqrt{2}$.

So when a question tells you to "express your answer in real numbers," don't sweat it. That's almost no constraint at all, because nearly every number you see is a real number.

Lining things up along the number line

You may have an easier time visualizing numbers if you see them on a number line. The *number line* shows all real numbers. Zero holds a place in the middle of the line. All positive numbers carry on infinitely to the right of zero, and all negative numbers extend infinitely to the left of zero, like this:

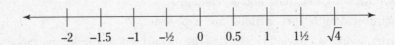

Understanding absolute value

The concept of absolute value crops up quite a bit on the ACT. The *absolute value* of any real number is that same number without a negative sign. It's the value of the distance a particular number is from zero on a number line (see the preceding section). For example, the absolute value of 1 is written mathematically as $|1|$. Because 1 sits one space from zero on the number line, $|1| = 1$. But because –1 also sits one space away from zero on the number line, $|-1| = 1$.

Absolute value relates only to the value that's inside those absolute value bars. If you see a negative sign outside the bars, the value of the result is negative. For example, $-|-1| = -1$.

Getting familiar with prime and composite numbers

The ACT expects you to know about *prime numbers,* which are all the positive integers that can be divided only by themselves and 1. A number that can be divided by more numbers than 1 and itself is called a *composite number*. Here are some other facts you should know about prime and composite numbers:

- ✔ 1 is neither prime nor composite.

- ✔ 2 is the smallest of the prime numbers, and it's also the only number that's both even and prime. (See the section "Doing basic operations with odds and evens" for more on even numbers.)

- ✔ 0 can never be a prime number because you can divide zero by every number in existence, but it's not considered to be a composite number either.

You don't need to memorize all the prime numbers before you take the ACT (yikes!), but do keep in mind that the lowest prime numbers are 2, 3, 5, 7, 11, 13, 17, 19, 23, and 29.

When you know how to recognize prime numbers, you can engage in *prime factorization,* which is just a fancy way of saying that you can break down a number into all the prime numbers (or *factors*) that go into it. For instance, 50 factors into 2 and 25, which factors into 5 and 5, giving you 2, 5, and 5 for the prime factors of 50.

Minor Surgery: Basic Math Operations

You don't have to be a brain surgeon to perform the basic mathematical operations of addition, subtraction, multiplication, and division, but you do have to train your brain to do these simple calculations without error. The following sections go over these basic operations so you don't miss questions because of silly calculation mistakes.

Adding and subtracting

Addition is when you combine two or more numbers to get an end result called the *sum*.

No matter what order you add a bunch of numbers in, you always end up with the same sum: $(2 + 3) + 4 = 9$ and $2 + (3 + 4) = 9$; $2 + 3 = 5$ and $3 + 2 = 5$.

When you *subtract* one number from another, you take one value away from another value and end up with the *difference* (the answer to a subtraction problem). So if $4 + 5 = 9$, then $9 - 5 = 4$.

Unlike addition, order *does* matter in subtraction. You get completely different answers for $20 - 7 - 4$ based on what order you subtract them: $(20 - 7) - 4 = 9$, but $20 - (7 - 4) = 17$. For another example, $2 - 3 = -1$ doesn't give you the same answer as $3 - 2 = 1$.

Multiplying and dividing

Think of *multiplication* as repeated addition with an end result called the *product*. The multiplication problem 3×6 is the same as the addition problem $6 + 6 + 6$. Both problems equal 18.

Multiplication is like addition in that the order in which you multiply the values doesn't matter: $2 \times 3 = 3 \times 2$ and $(2 \times 3) \times 4 = 2 \times (3 \times 4)$.

Another property of multiplication you need to know is the *distributive property*. You can multiply a number by a set of added or subtracted values by distributing that number through the other two values, like so:

$$2(3+4)=(2\times3)+(2\times4)=6+8=14$$

Of course, you can solve this problem by adding the numbers in parentheses $(3 + 4 = 7)$ and multiplying the sum by 2 $(7 \times 2 = 14)$. But when you start to add variables to the mix (see Chapter 9), you'll be glad you know about distribution.

Division is all about dividing one value into smaller values; those smaller values, or end results, are called *quotients*. Consider division to be the reverse of multiplication:

$$2\times3=6$$
$$6\div3=2$$
$$6\div2=3$$

In case the test throws some math terminology at you, know that the number at the beginning of any division problem is called the *dividend* and the number that goes into the dividend is called the *divisor*. So in the equation $6 \div 2 = 3$, 6 is the dividend and 2 is the divisor.

Doing basic operations with odds and evens

Even numbers are numbers that are divisible by 2 (2, 4, 6, 8, 10, and so on), and *odd numbers* are numbers that aren't divisible by 2 (1, 3, 5, 7, 9, 11, and so on). What's important to remember for the math questions is what happens to even and odd numbers when you add, subtract, multiply, or divide them by one another.

Here's what you need to know:

- ✔ When you add or subtract two even numbers, you get an even number.
- ✔ When you add or subtract two odd numbers, you get an even number.
- ✔ When you add or subtract an even number and an odd number, you get an odd number.
- ✔ When you multiply two or more even numbers, you get an even number.
- ✔ When you multiply an odd number by an even number, you get an even number.
- ✔ The only time you get an odd product is when you multiply two or more odd numbers.
- ✔ When you divide an even number by an odd number, you get an even number.
- ✔ The only time you get an odd quotient is when you divide an odd number by another odd number.

Knowing the rules for performing operations with odds and evens can be a big timesaver when you're trying to eliminate answer choices. For instance, if you have a problem that multiplies only even numbers, you can eliminate any odd-number answer choices without even doing the math!

Doing basic operations with positives and negatives

Know these important rules about performing the basic math operations with positive and negative numbers:

- ✔ When you multiply or divide two positive numbers, the answer is positive.
- ✔ When you multiply or divide two negative numbers, the answer is also positive.
- ✔ When you multiply or divide a negative number by a positive number, you get a negative answer.

You also have to know a thing or two (or four, actually) about adding and subtracting positive and negative numbers:

- ✔ When you add two positive numbers, your answer is positive: 3 + 5 = 8.
- ✔ When you add two negative numbers, your answer is negative: –3 + (–5) = –8.
- ✔ When you add a negative number to a positive number, your answer can be positive or negative: –3 + 5 = 2 and 3 + (–5) = –2.

If adding positive and negative numbers is confusing for you, check out the figure in the earlier section "Lining things up along the number line." Start at a number and move right for positive numbers and left for negative numbers. To solve the equation –3 + 5 = 2, find –3 on the number line and move right 5 spaces to 2. To solve the equation 3 + (–5) = –2, find 3 on the number line and move left 5 spaces to –2.

✔ If you subtract a negative number from another number, you end up adding the second number (the number you're subtracting) to the first, and your answer can be either positive or negative: 3 −(−5) is the same as 3 + 5, so the answer is 8; −5 −(−3) is the same as −5 + 3, so the answer is −2.

Fractions, Decimals, and Percentages

Fractions, decimals, and percentages all represent parts of a whole. The ACT asks you to manipulate these figures in all sorts of ways.

Converting fractions, decimals, and percentages

Because fractions, decimals, and percentages are different ways of showing similar values, you can change pretty easily from one form to another. Here's what you need to know:

✔ To convert a fraction to a decimal, just divide: $\frac{3}{4} = 3 \div 4 = 0.75$.

✔ To convert a decimal back to a fraction, first count the number of digits to the right of the decimal point. Then divide the number in the decimal over a 1 followed by as many zeros as there were digits to the right of the decimal. Finally, simplify the fraction (see the section "Simplifying fractions" for details): $0.75 = \frac{75}{100} = \frac{3}{4}$.

✔ To change a decimal to a percent, just move the decimal two places to the right and add a percent sign: 0.75 = 75%.

✔ To turn a percent into a decimal move the decimal point two places to the left and get rid of the percent sign: 75% = 0.75.

Working with fractions

Fractions tell you what part a piece is of a whole. The *numerator* is the top number in the fraction, and it represents the piece. The *denominator* is the bottom number of the fraction, and it indicates the value of the whole. If you were to cut a whole apple pie into 8 pieces and eat 5 slices, you could show the amount of pie you eat as a fraction, like so: $\frac{5}{8}$.

In the following sections, we show you how to do basic math operations with fractions. As a bonus, we also explain how to simplify fractions and work with mixed numbers.

Simplifying fractions

The ACT expects all fraction answers to be in their simplest forms. To simplify a fraction, first find the largest number you can think of that goes into both the numerator and denominator (called the *greatest common factor*). Then just divide the numerator and denominator by that number. For example, if you end up with $\frac{5}{10}$, you must simplify it further by dividing the numerator and denominator by 5: $\frac{5}{10} = \frac{1}{2}$.

Multiplying and dividing fractions

Multiplying fractions is easy. Just multiply the numerators by each other and then do the same with the denominators. Then simplify if you have to. For example:

$$\frac{3}{4} \times \frac{2}{5} = \frac{3 \times 2}{4 \times 5} = \frac{6}{20} = \frac{3}{10}$$

Always check whether you can cancel out any numbers before you begin working to avoid having to deal with big, awkward numbers and having to simplify at the end. In the preceding example, you can cancel the 4 and the 2, leaving you with

$$\frac{3}{{}_2 \cancel{4}} \times \frac{\cancel{2}^1}{5} = \frac{3 \times 1}{2 \times 5} = \frac{3}{10}$$

You get to the right solution either way; canceling in advance just makes the numbers smaller and easier to work with.

Dividing fractions is pretty much the same as multiplying them except for one very important additional step. First, find the *reciprocal* of the second fraction in the equation (that is, turn the second fraction upside down). Then multiply (yes, you have to multiply when dividing fractions) the numerators and denominators of the resulting fractions. For example:

$$\frac{1}{3} \div \frac{2}{5} = \frac{1}{3} \times \frac{5}{2} = \frac{5}{6}$$

Adding and subtracting fractions

Adding and subtracting fractions can be a little tricky, but you'll be fine if you follow these guidelines:

- **You can add or subtract fractions only if they have the same denominator.** Add or subtract just the numerators, like so:

$$\frac{1}{3} + \frac{4}{3} = \frac{5}{3}$$

$$\frac{3}{8} - \frac{2}{8} = \frac{1}{8}$$

- **When fractions don't have the same denominator, you have to find a common denominator.** To find a common denominator, you can multiply all the denominators, but doing so often doesn't give you the lowest common denominator. As a result, you end up with some humongous, overwhelming number that you'd rather not work with.

To find the lowest (or least) common denominator, think of multiples of the highest denominator until you find the one that all denominators go into evenly. For instance, to solve $\frac{4}{15} + \frac{1}{6}$, you have to find the lowest common denominator of 15 and 6. Sure, you can multiply 15 and 6 to get 90, but that's not the lowest common denominator. Instead, count by fifteens — because 15 is the larger of the two denominators — $15 \times 1 = 15$. But 6 doesn't go into 15. Moving on, $15 \times 2 = 30$. Hey! Both 15 and 6 go into 30, so 30 is the lowest common denominator.

Here's another example. To find the lowest common denominator for 2, 4, and 5, count by fives. What about 5? No, 2 and 4 don't go into it. How about 10? No, 4 doesn't go into it. Okay, 15? No, 2 and 4 don't go into it. What about 20? Yes, all the numbers divide evenly into 20.

Here's a trick for working with fractions with variables (see Chapter 9 for more about variables). Multiply the denominators to find the lowest common denominator. Then cross-multiply to find the numerators (see the later section "Proportions" for details on cross-multiplying).

Say you're asked to solve this problem:

$$\frac{a}{b} - \frac{c}{d} = ?$$

Find the common denominator by multiplying the two denominators: $b \times d = bd$. Then cross-multiply:

$$a \times d = ad$$
$$c \times b = cb$$

Put the difference of the results over the common denominator:

$$\frac{ad - cb}{bd}$$

Mixing things up with mixed numbers

A *mixed number* is a whole number with a fraction tagging along behind it, such as $2\frac{1}{3}$.

To add, subtract, multiply, or divide with mixed numbers, you first have to convert them into *improper fractions* (fractions in which the numerator is larger than the denominator). To do so, multiply the whole number by the denominator and add that to the numerator. Put the sum over the denominator. For example:

$$2\frac{1}{3} = \frac{(2 \times 3) + 1}{3} = \frac{7}{3}$$

Pondering percentages

In terms of percentages, the ACT usually asks you to find a percentage of another number. When you get a question like "What is 30% of 60?" evaluate the language like so:

- *What* means *?* or *x* (the unknown), or what you're trying to find out.

- *Is* means = (equals).

- *Of* means × (multiply).

Your job is to convert the words into math, like so: $? = 30\% \times 60$.

To solve this problem, convert 30% to a decimal (0.30) and multiply by 60. Tada! The answer is 18. Or, if you prefer, you could convert 30% to a fraction and multiply, like so:
$? = \frac{30}{100} \times \frac{60}{1} = \frac{1,800}{100} = 18$.

Sometimes a problem asks you to figure out what percent one number is of another. For example: The number 20 is what percent of 80? To solve this type of problem, just apply a little translation to the question to get a math equation you can work with.

The *number 20* is, of course, 20. You know that *is* means =. *What* gives you the unknown, or *x*, and *of* means multiply. Put it all together and you get this expression: $20 = x\% \times 80$. Now all you have to do is solve for *x*. Divide both sides by 80, and you get $\frac{20}{80} = x\%$, or $\frac{20}{80} = 0.25$.

Convert 0.25 to a percent by multiplying by 100 (or moving the decimal point two places to the right), and you have your answer: 0.25 = 25%. (See Chapter 9 for more details on how to solve for *x* and other variables.)

Here's a sample question to test what you know about parts of a whole.

What is 25% of $5\frac{3}{4}$?

(A) $\frac{37}{130}$

(B) $5\frac{3}{4}$

(C) $1\frac{7}{16}$

(D) $2\frac{3}{16}$

(E) 12

First, you don't need to do any calculations to eliminate Choices (B) and (E). 25% of $5\frac{3}{4}$ can't be $5\frac{3}{4}$ or 12. Then notice that the answer choices are in fraction rather than decimal form, so work the problem with fractions. When you convert 25% to a fraction, you get $\frac{1}{4}$. *Of* means multiply. So your equation is $\frac{1}{4} \times 5\frac{3}{4} = ?$. Convert the second fraction and multiply: $\frac{1}{4} \times \frac{23}{4} = \frac{23}{16} = 1\frac{7}{16}$. The correct answer is (C).

Ratios and Proportions

When you know the tricks we show you in this section, ratios and proportions are some of the easiest problems to answer quickly. We call them *heartbeat problems* because you can solve them in a heartbeat. Of course, if someone drop-dead gorgeous sits next to you and makes your heart beat faster, you may need two heartbeats to solve them.

Ratios

Here's what you need to know to answer ratio problems:

- **A *ratio* is written as $\frac{of}{to}$ or of:to.** The ratio *of* sunflowers *to* roses = $\frac{sunflowers}{roses}$. The ratio *of* umbrellas *to* heads = umbrellas:heads.

- **A *possible total* is a multiple of the sum of the numbers in the ratio.** For example, you may be given a problem like this: At a party, the ratio of blondes to redheads is 4:5. Which of the following could be the total number of blondes and redheads at the party? Megaeasy. Add the numbers in the ratio: 4 + 5 = 9. The total number of blondes must be a multiple of 9, such as 9, 18, 27, 36, and so on.

- **When a question gives you a ratio and a total and asks you to find a specific term, do the following:**

    1. **Add the numbers in the ratio.**

    2. **Divide that sum into the total.**

    3. **Multiply that quotient by each term in the ratio.**

    4. **Add the answers to double-check that their sum equals the total.**

Confused? Consider this example: Yelling at the members of his team, who had just lost 21–0, the irate coach pointed his finger at each member of the squad and called every player either a wimp or a slacker. If there were 3 wimps for every 4 slackers and every member of the 28-person squad was either a wimp or a slacker, how many wimps were there?

First, add the ratio: 3 + 4 = 7. Divide 7 into the total number of team members: $\frac{28}{7} = 4$. Multiply 4 by each term in the ratio: $4 \times 3 = 12; 4 \times 4 = 16$. Make sure those numbers add up to the total number of team members: 12 + 16 = 28.

Now you have all the information you need to answer a variety of questions. There are 12 wimps and 16 slackers. There are 4 more slackers than wimps. The number of slackers that would have to be kicked off the team for the number of wimps and slackers to be equal is 4. The ACT's math moguls can ask all sorts of things about ratios, but if you have this information, you're ready for anything they throw at you.

Be sure that you actually do Step 4 — adding the terms to double-check that they add up to the total. Doing so catches any careless mistakes that you may have made.

Proportions

The ACT may toss in a few proportion problems, too. A *proportion* is a relationship between two ratios where the ratios are equal. Just like with fractions, multiplying or dividing both numbers in the ratio by the same number doesn't change the value of the ratio. So, for example, these two ratios make up a proportion: 2:8 and 4:16, which you may also see written as $\frac{2}{8} = \frac{4}{16}$.

Often, you see a couple of equal ratios with a missing term that you have to find. To solve these problems, you *cross-multiply*. In other words, you multiply the terms that are diagonal from each other and solve for x. For example, to solve this equation $\frac{3}{8} = \frac{6}{x}$, follow these steps:

1. **Identify the diagonal terms: 3 and x; 6 and 8.**

2. **Multiply each set of diagonal terms and set the products equal to each other.**

   $$3 \times x = 3x$$
   $$6 \times 8 = 48$$
   $$3x = 48$$

3. **Solve for x.**

   $$x = 16$$

   For more on how to solve for x, go to Chapter 9.

Here's a sample ratio problem for you to try.

Trying to get Willie to turn down his stereo, his mother pounds on the ceiling and shouts up to his bedroom. If she pounds seven times for every five times she shouts, which of the following could be the total number of poundings and shouts?

(F) 75

(G) 57

(H) 48

(J) 35

(K) 30

Add the numbers in the ratio: 7 + 5 = 12. The total must be a multiple of 12 (which means it must be evenly divisible by 12). Here, only 48 is evenly divisible by 12, so the correct answer is (H).

Covering Your Bases: Exponents

Many ACT questions require you to know how to work with bases and exponents. Exponents represent repeated multiplication. For example, 5^3 is the same as $5 \times 5 \times 5 = 125$. When you work with exponents, make sure you know these important concepts:

- The *base* is the big value on the bottom. The *exponent* is the little value in the upper-right corner.

  In 5^3, 5 is the base and 3 is the exponent.

- The exponent tells you how many times to multiply the base times itself.

- A base to the zero power equals one. For example, $5^0 = 1$ and $x^0 = 1$.

- A base to a negative exponent is the reciprocal of itself.

  This concept is a little more confusing. When you have a negative exponent, just put the base and exponent under a 1 and make the exponent positive again. For example, $5^{-3} = \frac{1}{5^3}$. Keep in mind that the resulting number is not negative. When you flip it, you get the reciprocal, and the negative just sort of fades away.

- **To multiply like bases, add the exponents.** For example, $5^4 \times 5^9 = 5^{4+9} = 5^{13}$.

  You cannot multiply *unlike* bases. Think of it as trying to multiply dogs and cats — it doesn't work. All you end up with is a miffed meower and a damaged dog. You actually have to work out the problem: $5^2 \times 6^3 \neq 30^5 ; 5^2 \times 6^3 = 25 \times 216$.

- **To divide like bases, subtract the exponents.** For example, $5^9 \div 5^3 = 5^{9-3} = 5^6$.

  Did you think that the answer was 5^3? It's easy to fall into the trap of dividing rather than subtracting, especially when you see numbers that just beg to be divided, like 9 and 3. Keep your guard up.

- **Multiply the exponents of a base inside and outside the parentheses.** That's quite a mouthful. Here's what it means: $\left(5^3\right)^2 = 5^{3 \times 2} = 5^6$.

- **To add or subtract like bases that are variables that have like exponents, add or subtract the numerical coefficient of the bases.**

  The *numerical coefficient* (a great name for a rock band, don't you think?) is simply the number in front of the base. So the numerical coefficient in $5x^2$ is 5. Notice that it is *not* the little exponent in the right-hand corner but the full-sized number to the left of the base. Here are two examples of adding and subtracting bases that are variables that have like exponents:

  $$37x^3 + 10x^3 = 47x^3$$
  $$15y^2 - 5y^2 = 10y^2$$

  The numerical coefficient of any variable on its own is 1: $x = 1x$.

  You cannot add or subtract like bases with different exponents: $13x^3 - 9x^2 \neq 4x^3, 4x^2,$ or $4x$. The bases and exponents must be the same for you to add or subtract the terms. For more about working with variables, go to Chapter 9.

Smooth Operator: Order of Operations

When you have several operations (addition, subtraction, multiplication, division, squaring, and so on) in one problem, you must perform the operations in the following order:

1. **Parentheses.**

   Do what's inside the parentheses first.

2. **Power.**

   Do the squaring or the cubing (whatever the exponent is).

3. **Multiply or divide.**

   Do multiplication and division left to right. If multiplication is to the left of division, multiply first. If division is to the left of multiplication, divide first.

4. **Add or subtract.**

   Do addition and subtraction left to right. If addition is to the left of subtraction, add first. If subtraction is to the left of addition, subtract first.

An easy *mnemonic* (memory device) for remembering the order of operations is *Please Praise My Daughter And Son (PPMDAS):* Parentheses, Power, Multiply, Divide, Add, Subtract.

Here's a sample problem:

$$10(3-5)^2 + \left(\frac{30}{5}\right)^0 =$$

First, do what's inside the parentheses: $3 - 5 = -2$ and $\frac{30}{5} = 6$. Next, do the power: $-2^2 = 4$ and $6^0 = 1$. (Did you remember that any number to the 0 power equals 1?) Next, multiply: $10 \times 4 = 40$. Finally, add: $40 + 1 = 41$.

Average, Median, Mode, and More

Don't be surprised if the ACT asks you a few basic statistic questions. Most of these questions ask about average (also known as *average mean* or just *mean*), but you may see a few that deal with other related concepts, which is where the following sections come in.

Doing better than average on averages

To perform above average on questions about averages, you need to know how to apply the following formula for finding the average value of a set of numbers:

$$\text{Average} = \frac{\text{Sum of the numbers in the set}}{\text{Number of numbers in the set}}$$

For example, to find the average of 23, 25, 26, and 30, apply the formula and solve, like so:

$$\text{Average} = \frac{23 + 25 + 26 + 30}{4} = \frac{104}{4} = 26$$

You can use given values in the average formula to solve for the other values. In other words, if the exam gives you the average and the sum of a group of numbers, you can figure out how many numbers are in the set by using the average formula.

For example, Jeanette takes seven exams. Her scores on the first six are 91, 89, 85, 92, 90, and 88. If her average on all seven exams is 90, what did she get on the seventh exam? To solve this problem, apply the formula:

$$90 = \frac{Sum}{7}$$

Because you don't know the seventh term, call it x. Add the first six terms (which total 535) and x:

$$90 = \frac{535 + x}{7}$$

Multiply both sides by 7:

$$90 \times 7 = 535 + x$$
$$630 = 535 + x$$
$$95 = x$$

The seventh exam score was 95.

Weighing in on weighted averages

In a *weighted average,* some scores count more than others. Here's an example to help you see what we mean:

Number of Students	Score
12	80
13	75
10	70

If you're asked to find the average score for the students in the class shown in the preceding table, you know that you can't simply add 80, 75, and 70 and divide by 3, because the scores weren't evenly distributed among the students. Because 12 students got an 80, multiply 12 and 80 to get 960. Do the same with the other scores and add the products:

$$13 \times 75 = 975$$
$$10 \times 70 = 700$$
$$960 + 975 + 700 = 2,635$$

Divide not by 3 but by the total number of students, which is 35 (12 + 13 + 10 = 35):
$$\frac{2,635}{35} = 75.29.$$

Mastering medians

The *median* is the middle value in a list of several values or numbers. To find out the median, list the values or numbers in order, usually from low to high, and choose the value that falls exactly in the middle of the other values. If you have an odd number of values, just select the middle value. If you have an even number of values, find the two middle values and average them (see the previous section on averages). The outcome is the median.

Managing modes

The *mode* is the value that occurs most often in a set of values. For example, you may be asked what income occurs most frequently in a particular sample population. If more people in the population have an income of $45,000 than any other income amount, the mode is $45,000.

Getting ready for range

The *range* is the distance from the greatest to the smallest. In other words, just subtract the smallest term from the largest term to find the range.

The only trap you're likely to see in these basic statistics questions is in the answer choices. The questions themselves are quite straightforward, but the answer choices may assume that some people don't know one term from another. For example, one answer choice to a median question may be the mean (the average). One answer choice to a range question may be the mode. In each question, circle the word that tells you what you're looking for to keep from falling for this trap.

Try a sample statistics problem for yourself.

Find the range of the numbers 11, 18, 29, 17, 18, –4, 0, 11, 18.

(A) 33

(B) 29

(C) 19

(D) 0

(E) –4

Ah, did this one fool you? True, 33 is not one of the numbers in the set. But to find the range, subtract the smallest from the largest number: 29 – (–4) = 29 + 4 = 33. So the correct answer is (A).

Measuring Up: Units of Measurement

Occasionally, you may be expected to know a unit of measurement that the test makers deem obvious but that you've forgotten. Take a few minutes to review the following brief sections so you don't get stumped come test time.

Time

Make sure you know these time equivalents:

- 60 seconds = 1 minute
- 60 minutes = 1 hour
- 24 hours = 1 day
- 7 days = 1 week
- 52 weeks = 1 year
- 365 days = 1 year

Quantities

These quantity equivalents are handy for the ACT and baking:

- 16 ounces = 1 pound
- 2,000 pounds = 1 standard ton
- 2 cups = 1 pint
- 2 pints = 1 quart
- 4 quarts = 1 gallon = 16 cups = 8 pints

Length

Be sure to commit the following length measurements to memory:

- 12 inches = 1 foot
- 3 feet (36 inches) = 1 yard
- 5,280 feet (1,760 yards) = 1 mile

Everyone knows that 12 inches = 1 foot. But how many square inches are in a square foot? If you say 12, you've fallen for the trap. Actually, there are $12 \times 12 = 144$ square inches in a square foot.

Bonus: How many cubic inches are in a cubic foot? Not 12 and not even 144. A cubic foot is $12 \times 12 \times 12 = 1,728$ cubic inches.

Chapter 8

More Figures than a Beauty Pageant: Geometry Review

. . . .

In This Chapter

▶ Getting to the point with lines and angles

▶ Identifying the ins and outs of triangles and similar figures

▶ Centering in on polygons and circles

▶ Understanding the point of the coordinate plane

. . . .

Geometry is one of the areas that can mess you up on the ACT. But it's easy when you take the time to memorize some rules. This chapter provides a lightning-fast review of the major points of geometry so that you can go into the test equipped to tackle the geometry questions with ease.

Toeing the Line

You don't need to memorize the following definitions for the ACT, but you do need to be familiar with them. Here are the common terms about lines that may pop up on your test:

✔ **Line:** A straight path of points that extends forever in two directions. A line doesn't have any width or thickness. Arrows sometimes show that the line goes on forever in either direction. See line *AB* in Figure 8-1.

✔ **Line segment:** The set of points on a line between any two points on that line. Basically, a line segment is just a piece of a line from one point to another that contains those two points and all the points in between. See line segment *CD* in Figure 8-1.

Figure 8-1:
Line and line
segment.

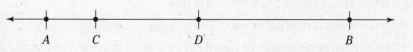

✔ **Midpoint:** The point halfway (an equal distance) between two endpoints on a line segment. In Figure 8-1, point *D* is the midpoint between points *A* and *B*.

✔ **Intersect:** To cross. Two lines can intersect each other much like two streets cross each other at an intersection.

✔ **Vertical line:** A line that runs straight up and down. Figure 8-2 shows you an example of a vertical line as well as the following three kinds of lines.

✔ **Horizontal line:** A line that runs straight across from left to right (refer to Figure 8-2).

✔ **Parallel lines:** Lines that run in the same direction and keep the same distance apart. Parallel lines never intersect one another (refer to Figure 8-2).

✔ **Perpendicular lines:** Two lines that intersect to form a square corner. The intersection of two perpendicular lines forms a right, or 90-degree, angle (refer to Figure 8-2).

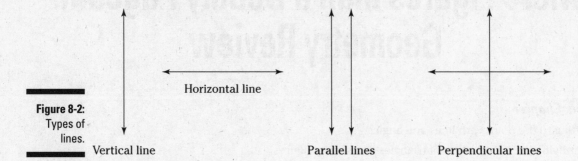

Figure 8-2:
Types of lines.

Horizontal line

Vertical line   Parallel lines   Perpendicular lines

Analyzing Angles

Angles are a big part of the ACT geometry problems. Fortunately, understanding angles is easy when you memorize a few basic concepts. After all, you don't have to do any proofs on the test. Finding an angle is usually a matter of simple addition or subtraction.

In terms of angles, these three rules generally apply to the ACT:

✔ No negative angles exist.

✔ No zero angles exist.

✔ You're extremely unlikely to see any fractional angles. (For example, an angle won't measure 45.50 degrees or $32\frac{3}{4}$ degrees.)

Here are a few other things you need to know about angles to succeed on the ACT:

✔ **Angles that are greater than 0 but less than 90 degrees are called *acute angles*.** Think of an acute angle as being a *cute* little angle (see Figure 8-3).

✔ **Angles that are equal to 90 degrees are called *right angles*.** They're formed by perpendicular lines and indicated by a box in the corner of the two intersecting lines (refer to Figure 8-3).

Don't automatically assume that angles that look like right angles are right angles. Without calculating the degree of the angle, you can't know for certain that an angle is a right angle unless one of the following is true:

• The problem directly tells you, "This is a right angle."

• You see the perpendicular symbol (⊥) indicating that the lines form a 90-degree angle.

• You see a box in the angle, like the one in Figure 8-3.

So the following angles aren't necessarily right angles:

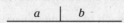

a $\quad$ b

✔ Angles that are greater than 90 degrees but less than 180 degrees are called *obtuse angles.* Think of obtuse as obese; an obese (or fat) angle is an obtuse angle (refer to Figure 8-3).

✔ Angles that measure exactly 180 degrees are called *straight angles.* (Refer to Figure 8-3.)

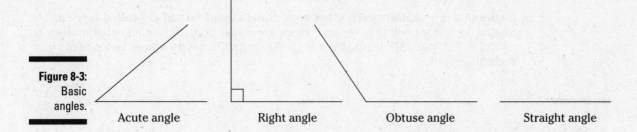

Figure 8-3:
Basic
angles.

Acute angle   Right angle   Obtuse angle   Straight angle

✔ Angles that total 90 degrees are called *complementary angles.* Think of *C* for corner (the lines form a 90-degree corner angle) and *C* for complementary (see Figure 8-4).

✔ Angles that total 180 degrees are called *supplementary angles.* Think of *S* for supplementary (or straight) angles. Be careful not to confuse complementary angles with supplementary angles. If you're likely to get these confused, just think alphabetically: *C* comes before *S* in the alphabet; 90 comes before 180 when you count (refer to Figure 8-4).

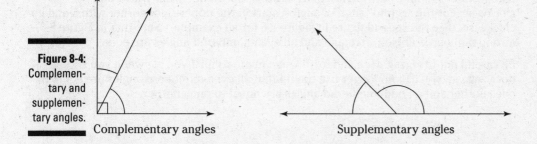

Figure 8-4:
Complemen-
tary and
supplemen-
tary angles.

Complementary angles   Supplementary angles

✔ Angles that are greater than 180 degrees but less than 360 degrees are called *reflex angles.* (See Figure 8-5 for an example.)

Note: Reflex angles rarely appear on the ACT.

Figure 8-5:
Reflex
angle.

320°

✔ Angles around a point total 360 degrees. (See Figure 8-6.)

✔ The exterior angles of any figure are supplementary to the interior angles and always total 360 degrees. (Refer to Figure 8-6.)

Figure 8-6:
Angles that
measure 360
degrees.

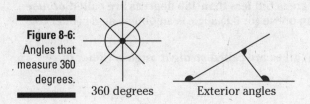

360 degrees   Exterior angles

✔ **Angles that are opposite each other have equal measures and are called *vertical angles.*** Just remember that vertical angles are *across* from each other, whether they're up and down (vertical) or side by side (horizontal). (Figure 8-7 shows two sets of vertical angles.)

Figure 8-7:
Vertical
angles have
equal
measures.

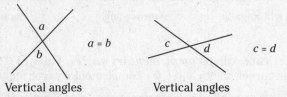

a = b   *c = d*

Vertical angles   Vertical angles

✔ **Angles in the same position around two parallel lines and a transversal are called *corresponding angles* and have equal measures.** (Figure 8-8 shows two sets of corresponding angles.)

When you see two parallel lines and a *transversal* (that's the line going across the parallel lines), number the angles. Start in the upper-right corner with 1 and go clockwise. For the second batch of angles, start in the upper-right corner with 5 and go clockwise. (See the second figure in Figure 8-8 for an example.) Note that in Figure 8-8, all odd-numbered angles are equal and all even-numbered angles are equal.

Be careful not to zigzag back and forth when numbering. If you zig when you should have zagged, you can no longer use the tip that all even-numbered angles are equal to one another and all odd-numbered angles are equal to one another.

Figure 8-8:
Correspond-
ing angles
have equal
measures.

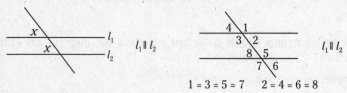

$l_1 \| l_2$

$l_1 \| l_2$

$1 = 3 = 5 = 7$ $2 = 4 = 6 = 8$

Triangle Trauma

Many of the geometry problems on the ACT require you to know a lot about triangles. Remember the facts and rules about triangles in this section, and you're on your way to acing geometry questions.

Classifying triangles

Triangles are classified based on the measurements of their sides and angles. Here are the types of triangles you need to know for the ACT:

- **Equilateral:** A triangle with three equal sides and three equal angles (see Figure 8-9).

- **Isosceles:** A triangle with two equal sides and two equal angles. The angles opposite equal sides in an isosceles triangle are also equal (refer to Figure 8-9).

- **Scalene:** A triangle with no equal sides and no equal angles (refer to Figure 8-9).

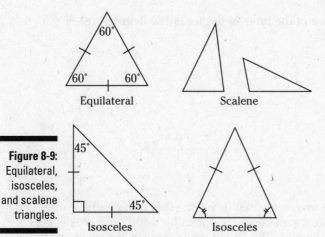

Figure 8-9:
Equilateral,
isosceles,
and scalene
triangles.

Sizing up triangles

When you're figuring out ACT questions that deal with triangles, you need to know these rules about the measurements of their sides and angles:

- **In any triangle, the largest angle is opposite the longest side.** (See Figure 8-10.)

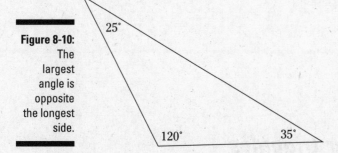

Figure 8-10:
The
largest
angle is
opposite
the longest
side.

- **In any triangle, the sum of the lengths of two sides must be greater than the length of the third side.**

  In other words, $a + b > c$, where a, b, and c are the sides of the triangle (see Figure 8-11).

Figure 8-11:
The sum of the lengths of two sides of a triangle are greater than the length of the third side.

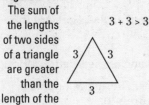

3 + 3 > 3

3 + 4 > 4
4 + 4 > 3

3 + 4 > 5
4 + 5 > 3
5 + 3 > 4

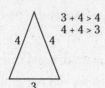

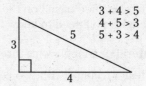

✔ **In any type of triangle, the sum of the interior angles is 180 degrees.** (See Figure 8-12.)

Figure 8-12:
The sum of the interior angles of a triangle is 180 degrees.

  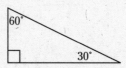

A trap question may want you to assume that different-sized triangles have different angle measures. Wrong! A triangle can be seven stories high and have 180 degrees or be microscopic and have 180 degrees. The size of the triangle is irrelevant; every triangle's internal angles add up to 180 degrees.

✔ **The measure of an exterior angle of a triangle is equal to the sum of the two remote interior angles.** (See Figure 8-13.)

Figure 8-13:
The measure of an exterior angle is equal to the sum of the two remote interior angles.

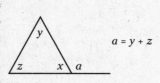

$a = y + z$

Zeroing in on similar triangles

Several ACT math questions require you to compare similar triangles. *Similar triangles* look alike but are different sizes. Here's what you need to know about similar triangles:

✔ **The sides of similar triangles are in proportion.** For example, if the heights of two similar triangles are in a ratio of 2:3, then the bases of those triangles are also in a ratio of 2:3 (see Figure 8-14).

Figure 8-14:
Similar triangles have proportionate sides.

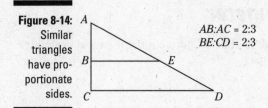

$AB:AC = 2:3$
$BE:CD = 2:3$

✔ **The ratio of the areas of similar triangles is equal to the square of the ratio of their sides.** For example, if each side of Figure A is $\frac{1}{3}$ the length of each side of similar Figure B, then the area of Figure A is $\frac{1}{9}$ or $\left(\frac{1}{3}\right)^2$ the area of Figure B. Figure 8-15 shows you what we mean. (See the next section for details on the area of triangles.)

Figure 8-15:
The relationship between the areas and sides of similar triangles.

 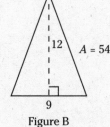

Figure A   Figure B

EXAMPLE

Two similar triangles have bases of 5 and 25. Which of the following expresses the ratio of the areas of the two triangles?

(A) 1:5

(B) 1:15

(C) 1:25

(D) 1:30

(E) 1:50

The ratio of the sides is 1:5 or $\frac{1}{5}$. The ratio of the areas is the square of the ratio of the sides: $\frac{1}{5} \times \frac{1}{5} = \frac{1}{25}$, which is the same as 1:25. So the correct answer is (C).

Bonus: What do you suppose the ratio of the *volumes* of two similar figures is? Because you find volume in cubic units, the ratio of the volumes of two similar figures is the *cube* of the ratio of their sides. If Figure A has a base of 5 and similar Figure B has a base of 10, then the ratio of their volumes is $1:2^3$, which is $\frac{1}{2} \times \frac{1}{2} \times \frac{1}{2} = \frac{1}{8}$.

REMEMBER

Don't assume that triangles are similar on the ACT just because they look similar to you. The only way you know two triangles are similar is if the test tells you they are.

Figuring out area and perimeter

To succeed on the Mathematics Test, you should be able to figure out the area and perimeter of triangles in your sleep. Memorize these formulas:

✔ **The area of a triangle is $\frac{1}{2}$ base × height.**

The height is always a line perpendicular to the base. The height may be a side of the triangle, as in a right triangle (see Figure 8-16a). But the height may also be inside the triangle. In that case, it's often represented by a dashed line and a small 90-degree box (see Figure 8-16b). The height may also be outside the triangle. You can always drop an altitude. That is, put your pencil on the tallest point of the triangle and draw a line straight from that point to where the base would be if it were extended (see Figure 8-16c).

✔ **The perimeter of a triangle is the sum of the lengths of its sides.** (See Figure 8-17.)

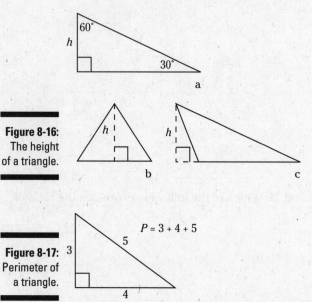

Figure 8-16:
The height of a triangle.

Figure 8-17:
Perimeter of a triangle.

$P = 3 + 4 + 5$

Going Greek: The Pythagorean theorem

The Pythagorean theorem plays a big role in the Math Test questions. Who knew an old Greek guy would have so much influence on your college education?

In any right triangle, you can find the lengths of the sides by using the *Pythagorean theorem,* which looks like this:

$$a^2 + b^2 = c^2$$

In this formula, *a* and *b* are the sides of the triangle and *c* is the hypotenuse. The *hypotenuse* is always opposite the 90-degree angle and is always the longest side of the triangle.

Keep in mind that the Pythagorean theorem works only on right triangles. If a triangle doesn't have a right — or 90-degree–angle you can't use any of the information in this section or the one that follows.

Taking the shortcut: Pythagorean triples

Having to work through the whole Pythagorean theorem formula every time you want to find the length of a right triangle's side is a pain in the posterior. To make your life a little easier, memorize these four common ratios, also called *Pythagorean triples,* in right triangles:

✔ **Ratio 3:4:5.** If one side of the triangle is 3 in this ratio, the other side is 4 and the hypotenuse is 5 (see Figure 8-18).

  Because this is a ratio, the sides can be in any multiple of these numbers, such as 6:8:10 (two times 3:4:5), 9:12:15 (three times 3:4:5), or 27:36:45 (nine times 3:4:5).

Figure 8-18: A 3:4:5 triangle.

✔ **Ratio 5:12:13.** If one side of the right triangle is 5 in this ratio, the other side is 12 and the hypotenuse is 13 (see Figure 8-19).

  Because this is a ratio, the sides can be in any multiple of these numbers, such as 10:24:26 (two times 5:12:13), 15:36:39 (three times 5:12:13), or 50:120:130 (ten times 5:12:13).

Figure 8-19: A 5:12:13 triangle.

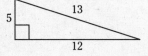

✔ **Ratio $s : s : s\sqrt{2}$, where s stands for the side of the figure.** Because two sides are equal, this formula applies to an isosceles right triangle, also known as a 45:45:90 triangle. If one side is 2, then the other side is also 2 and the hypotenuse is $2\sqrt{2}$ (see Figure 8-20).

Figure 8-20: Ratio for a 45:45:90 triangle.

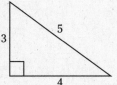

 This formula is great to know for squares. If a question tells you that the side of a square is 5 and wants to know the diagonal of the square, you know immediately that it is $5\sqrt{2}$. Why? A square's diagonal cuts the square into two isosceles right triangles (*isosceles* because all sides of the square are equal; *right* because all angles in a square are right angles). What is the diagonal of a square of side 64? $64\sqrt{2}$. What is the diagonal of a square of side 12,984? $12,984\sqrt{2}$.

You can write this ratio another way. Instead of writing $s : s : s\sqrt{2}$, write $\frac{s}{\sqrt{2}} : \frac{s}{\sqrt{2}} : s$, where s still stands for the side of the triangle, but now you've divided everything in the ratio by $2\sqrt{2}$. Why do you need this complicated formula? Suppose you're told that the diagonal of a square is 5. What is the area of the square? What is the perimeter of the square?

If you know the ratio $\frac{s}{\sqrt{2}} : \frac{s}{\sqrt{2}} : s$, you know that s stands for the hypotenuse of the triangle, which is also the diagonal of the square. If $s = 5$, then the side of the square is $\frac{5}{\sqrt{2}}$ and you can figure out the area or the perimeter. After you know the side of a square, you can figure out just about anything.

✔ **Ratio $s : s\sqrt{3} : 2s$.** This special formula is for the sides of a 30:60:90 triangle (see Figure 8-21).

Figure 8-21: Ratio for a 30:60:90 triangle.

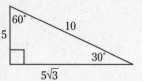

This type of triangle is a favorite of test makers. The important thing to keep in mind here is that the hypotenuse is twice the length of the side opposite the 30-degree angle. If you get a word problem that says, "Given a 30:60:90 triangle of hypotenuse 20, find the area" or "Given a 30:60:90 triangle of hypotenuse 100, find the perimeter," you can do so because you can find the lengths of the other sides (see Figure 8-22 for details).

Figure 8-22: Using the ratio for a 30:60:90 triangle to find the lengths of the triangle's sides.

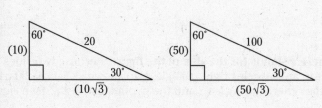

Thanks 4 Nothing: A Quick Look at Quadrilaterals

Another favorite figure of the ACT test-making folks is the *quadrilateral,* which is the fancy label mathematicians give shapes with four sides. Here's a summary of the four-sided figures you may see on the ACT:

✔ **A *quadrilateral* is any four-sided figure.**

The interior angles of any quadrilateral total 360 degrees. You can cut any quadrilateral into two 180-degree triangles (see Figure 8-23).

Figure 8-23:
A quad-
rilateral.

✔ **A *square* is a quadrilateral with four equal sides and four right angles.**

The area of a square is s^2 (or base $\times$ height) or $\frac{1}{2}d^2$, where d stands for the *diagonal* (see Figure 8-24).

Figure 8-24:
A square.

$A = s^2$

$A = \frac{1}{2}d^2$

✔ **A *rhombus* is a quadrilateral with four equal sides and four angles that are not necessarily right angles.** A rhombus often looks like a drunken square, tipsy on its side and wobbly.

The area of a rhombus is $\frac{1}{2}d_1d_2$ or $\frac{1}{2}$ diagonal$_1 \times$ diagonal$_2$ (see Figure 8-25).

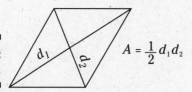

Figure 8-25:
A rhombus.

$A = \frac{1}{2}d_1d_2$

All squares are rhombuses, but not all rhombuses are squares.

✔ **A *rectangle* is a quadrilateral with four right angles and two opposite and equal pairs of sides.** That is, the top and bottom sides are equal, and the right and left sides are equal.

The area of a rectangle is length $\times$ width, which is the same as base $\times$ height (see Figure 8-26).

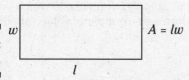

Figure 8-26:
A rectangle.

$A = lw$

✔ **A *parallelogram* is a quadrilateral with two opposite and equal pairs of sides.** The top and bottom sides are equal, and the right and left sides are equal. Opposite angles are equal but not necessarily right (or 90 degrees).

The area of a parallelogram is base $\times$ height. Remember that the height is always a perpendicular line from the tallest point of the figure down to the base (see Figure 8-27). Diagonals of a parallelogram bisect each other.

Figure 8-27:
A parallelo-
gram.

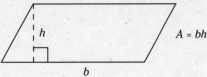

All rectangles are parallelograms, but not all parallelograms are rectangles.

✔ A *trapezoid* **is a quadrilateral with two parallel sides and two nonparallel sides.**

The area of a trapezoid is $\frac{1}{2}(\text{base}_1 \times \text{base}_2) \times \text{height}$. It makes no difference which base you label base_1 and which you label base_2, because you're adding them together. Just be sure to add them *before* you multiply by $\frac{1}{2}$ (see Figure 8-28).

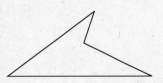

Figure 8-28:
A trapezoid.

Keep in mind that some quadrilaterals, like the one in Figure 8-29, don't have nice, neat shapes or special names.

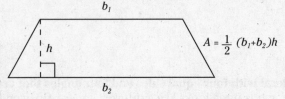

Figure 8-29:
Not all
quadrilater-
als have
special
names.

If you see a strange shape, don't immediately say that you have no way of finding its area. You may be able to divide the quadrilateral into two triangles, find the area of each triangle, and then add them together.

Knowing how to find the area of quadrilaterals (those with both neat and strange shapes) and other figures can help you solve *shaded-area* or *leftover* problems, in which you have to subtract the unshaded area from the total area. Here's an example of what a shaded-area figure may look like on the ACT:

Shaded areas can often be unusual shapes. Your first reaction may be that you can't possibly find the area of that shape. Generally, you're right, but you don't have to find the area directly. Instead, be sly, devious, and sneaky; in other words, think the ACT way! Find the area of the total figure, find the area of the unshaded portion, and subtract.

What is the area of the shaded portion of the circle inscribed in a square that follows?

(F) 64

(G) 16π

(H) $64 - 16\pi$

(J) $48 - 16\pi$

(K) 48

First, you have to find the area of the square. You know that the radius of the circle is 4, so the diameter of the circle, as well as the side of the square, is 8. Therefore, the area of the square is 64 ($A = s^2 = 8^2 = 64$). Next, find the area of the circle: $A = \pi r^2 = \pi(4^2) = 16\pi$. Then just subtract to find the shaded area: $64 - 16\pi$. The answer is Choice (H).

Missing Parrots and Other Polly-Gones (Or Should We Say "Polygons"?)

Triangles and quadrilaterals are probably the most commonly tested polygons on the ACT. What's a polygon? A *polygon* is a closed-plane figure bounded by straight sides.

Measuring up polygons

Here's what you need to know about the side and angle measurements of polygons:

- ✔ **A polygon with all equal sides and all equal angles is called *regular*.** For example, an equilateral triangle is a regular triangle, and a square is a regular quadrilateral.

  The ACT rarely asks you to find the areas of any polygons with more than four sides.

- ✔ **The *perimeter* of a polygon is the sum of the lengths of all the sides.**

- ✔ **The *exterior angle measure* of any polygon, also known as the sum of its exterior angles, is 360 degrees.** (An *exterior angle* is the angle formed by any side of the polygon and the line that's created when you extend the adjacent side.)

- ✔ **To find the *interior angle measure* of any regular polygon, also known as the sum of its interior angles, use the formula** $(n-2)180°$**, where *n* stands for the number of sides.** For example, to find the interior angle measure for a pentagon (a five-sided figure), just substitute 5 for *n* in the formula and solve:

  $$(5-2)180° = 3 \times 180° = 540°$$

  So the sum of the interior angles of a pentagon is 540°.

- ✔ **To find the average measure of one angle in a regular polygon, use the formula for the interior angle measure and divide by the number of sides (*n*) in the polygon:**

  $$\frac{(n-2)180}{n}$$

For example, to find the average measure of one angle in a pentagon, set up and solve this equation:

$$\frac{(5-2)\times 180}{5}=\frac{3\times 180}{5}=\frac{540}{5}=108$$

Because all angles are equal in a regular polygon, the same formula applies to finding an exact measurement of one angle in a regular polygon.

Note: If the test gives you a polygon, like the one in Figure 8-30, and does *not* tell you that it's regular, you can't solve for just one angle.

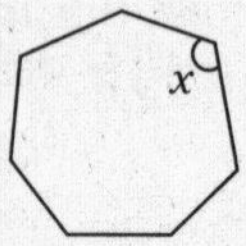

Figure 8-30:
You can't find the measure of just one angle in a polygon unless the ACT tells you the polygon is regular.

Solving for volume

The volume of any polygon is (area of the base) × height. If you remember this formula, you don't have to memorize any of the following specific volume formulas. If you take the time to memorize specific formulas, though, you'll use fewer steps to work out volume problems and you'll save some precious time.

✔ **Volume of a cube = e^3**

A *cube* is a three-dimensional square. Think of a die (one of a pair of dice). All of a cube's dimensions are the same; that is, length = width = height. In a cube, these dimensions are called *edges*. The volume of a cube is edge × edge × edge = edge^3 = e^3 (see Figure 8-31).

Figure 8-31:
Volume of a cube.

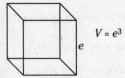

$$V = e^3$$

✔ **Volume of a rectangular solid = lwh**

A *rectangular solid* is a box. The base of a box is a rectangle, which has an area of length × width. Multiply that by the height to fit the original volume formula: Volume = (area of base) × height, or $V = lwh$ (see Figure 8-32).

Figure 8-32:
Volume of a rectangular solid.

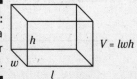

$$V = lwh$$

✔ **Volume of a cylinder** $= \left(\pi r^2\right)h$

Think of a *cylinder* as a can of soup. The base of a cylinder is a circle. The area of a circle is πr^2. Multiply that by the height of the cylinder to get the volume. Note that the top and bottom of a cylinder are identical circles. If you know the radius of either the top base or the bottom base, you can find the area of the circle (see Figure 8-33). (See the section "Running Around in Circles" for more on circles.)

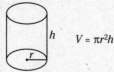

Figure 8-33:
Volume of a cylinder.

$V = \pi r^2 h$

Adding to find total surface area

The *total surface area* (TSA), logically enough, is the sum of the areas of all the surfaces of the figure. Here's what you need to know about TSA:

✔ **Total surface area of a cube** $= 6e^2$

A cube has six identical faces, and each face is a square. The area of a square is s^2; when working with cubes, we say edge^2 or e^2. If one face is e^2, then the total surface area is 6 times the area of one face or $6e^2$ (see Figure 8-34).

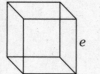

Figure 8-34:
Surface area of a cube.

$TSA = 6e^2$

✔ **Total surface area of a rectangular solid** $= 2(lw) + 2(wh) + 2(hl)$

You need to find the area of each of the six surfaces on the rectangular solid. The bottom and top have the area of length × width. The left side and right side have the area of width × height. The front side and the back side have the area of height × length. Together, they total $2(lw) + 2(wh) + 2(hl)$ or $2(lw + wh + hl)$. (See Figure 8-35.)

Figure 8-35:
Surface area of a rectangular solid.

$TSA = 2lw + 2wh + 2hl$

✔ **Total surface area of a cylinder** $= (\text{circumference} \times \text{height}) + 2\pi r^2$

The TSA of a cylinder is definitely the most difficult measure to figure out. Think of it as pulling the label off a can of soup, flattening it out, finding its area, and then adding that to the area of the top and bottom lids. The label is a rectangle. Its length is the length of the circumference of the circle. Its height is the height of the cylinder. Multiply length × height to find the area of the label.

You also need to find the area of the top and bottom of the cylinder. Because each is a circle, the TSA of the top and bottom is $2\pi r^2$. Then just add everything together (see Figure 8-36). (See the next section for everything you need to know about circles.)

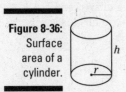
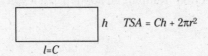

Figure 8-36:
Surface area of a cylinder.

$TSA = Ch + 2\pi r^2$

Running Around in Circles

Did you hear about the rube who pulled his son out of college, claiming that the school was filling his head with nonsense? As the rube said, "Joe Bob told me that he learned πr^2. But any fool knows that *pie* are round; *cornbread* are square!"

Circles are among the least complicated geometry concepts. To excel on circle questions, you must remember the vocabulary and be able to distinguish an arc from a sector and an inscribed angle from a central angle. Here's a quick review of the basics:

✔ A circle's *radius* goes from the center of the circle to its *circumference* (or perimeter). (See Figure 8-37.)

Figure 8-37:
The radius of a circle.

✔ A circle gets its name from its *midpoint* (or center).

For example, the circle in Figure 8-38 is called circle *M* because its midpoint is *M*.

Figure 8-38:
The midpoint of a circle.

Circle *M*

✔ A circle's *diameter* connects two points on the circumference of the circle, goes through the circle's center, and is equal to two radii (which is the plural of *radius*). (See Figure 8-39.)

Figure 8-39:
The diameter equals two radii.

✔ **A *chord* connects any two points on a circle.** (See Figure 8-40 for two examples.)

The longest chord in a circle is the diameter.

Figure 8-40:
Two
examples of
a chord.

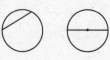

✔ **The area of a circle is πr^2.** (See Figure 8-41.)

Figure 8-41:
Area of a
circle.

$A = 16\pi$

✔ **The circumference of a circle is $2\pi r$ or πd because 2 radii equal one diameter.**

On the Math Test, you may encounter a wheel question in which you're asked how much distance a wheel covers or how many times a wheel revolves. The key to solving this type of question is knowing that one rotation of a wheel equals one circumference of that wheel.

✔ **A *central angle* has its endpoints on the circumference of the circle and its center at the center of the circle.**

The degree measure of a central angle is the same as the degree measure of its intercepted arc (see Figure 8-42). (Keep reading to find out what an arc is.)

Figure 8-42:
A central
angle.

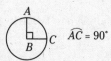

$\overset{\frown}{AC} = 90°$

✔ **An *inscribed angle* has both its endpoints and its center on the circumference of the circle.**

The degree measure of an inscribed angle is half the degree measure of its intercepted arc (see Figure 8-43).

Thales's theorem tells you that the endpoints of an inscribed angle in a semicircle create a right triangle. If *YZ* in the figure is the diameter of the circle, ∠*YXZ* is a right angle and △*YXZ* is a right triangle.

Figure 8-43:
An inscribed
angle.

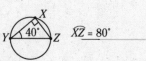

$\overset{\frown}{XZ} = 80°$

✔ **When a central angle and an inscribed angle have the same endpoints, the degree measure of the central angle is twice that of the inscribed angle.** (See Figure 8-44.)

Figure 8-44:
Central and
inscribed
angles with
the same
endpoints.

✔ **The degree measure of a circle is 360.**

✔ **An *arc* is a portion of the circumference of a circle.**

The degree measure of an arc is the same as its central angle and twice its inscribed angle (see Figure 8-45).

Figure 8-45:
An arc on a
circle.

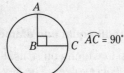 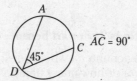

To find the *length* of an arc, follow these steps:

1. **Find the circumference of the entire circle.**

2. **Put the degree measure of the arc over 360 and then reduce the fraction.**

3. **Multiply the circumference by the fraction.**

✔ **A *sector* is a portion of the area of a circle.**

The degree measure of a sector is the same as its central angle and twice its inscribed angle.

To find the *area* of a sector, follow these steps:

1. **Find the area of the entire circle.**

2. **Put the degree measure of the sector over 360 and then reduce the fraction.**

3. **Multiply the area by the fraction.**

Finding the area of a sector is very similar to finding the length of an arc. The only difference is in the first step. Whereas an arc is a part of the circumference of a circle, a sector is a part of the area of a circle.

Here are a few examples of how the ACT may test you about circles.

What is the area of a circle whose longest chord is 12?

(A) 144π

(B) 72π

(C) 36π

(D) 12π

(E) Cannot be determined from the information given

The diameter of this circle is 12, which means its radius is 6 because a diameter is twice the radius. The area of a circle is πr^2, so $\pi 6^2 = 36\pi$. The correct answer is (C).

Choice (E) is the trap answer. If you know only that a chord of the circle is 12, you can't solve the problem. A circle has many different chords. You need to know the length of the longest chord, or the diameter.

A child's wagon has a wheel with a radius of 6 inches. If the wagon wheel travels 100 revolutions, approximately how many feet has the wagon rolled?

(F) 325

(G) 314

(H) 255

(J) 201

(K) 200

One revolution is equal to one circumference: $C = 2\pi r = 2\pi 6 = 12\pi$, which is approximately 12(3.14) or 37.68 inches. Multiply that by 100 to get 3,768 inches. Then divide by 12 to get 314 feet. The correct answer is (G).

Find the sum of $a + b + c + d + e$.

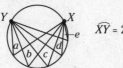

$\widehat{XY} = 20°$

Note: Figure not drawn to scale.

(A) 65 degrees

(B) 60 degrees

(C) 55 degrees

(D) 50 degrees

(E) 45 degrees

Although this figure looks a lot like a string picture you made at summer camp, with all sorts of lines running every which way, answering the question that goes along with it isn't as complicated as you may think. To get started, take the time to identify the endpoints of the angles and the center point. Each angle is an inscribed angle; it has half the degree measure of the central angle, or half the degree measure of its intercepted arc. If you look carefully at the endpoints of these angles, you see that they're all the same. They're all along arc *XY,* which has a measure of 20 degrees. Therefore, each angle is 10 degrees, for a total of 50. The correct answer is (D).

Find the length of arc *AC* in circle B below.

(F) 36π

(G) 27π

(H) 18π

(J) 12π

(K) 6π

Take the steps one at a time. First, find the circumference of the entire circle: $C = 2\pi r = 36\pi$. Don't multiply π out; problems usually leave it in that form. Next, put the degree measure of the arc over 360 and simplify. The degree measure of the arc is the same as its central angle, which is 60 degrees.

$$\frac{60}{360} = \frac{1}{6}$$

The arc is $\frac{1}{6}$ of the circumference of the circle. Multiply the circumference by the fraction:

$$36\pi \times \frac{1}{6} = 6\pi$$

The correct answer is (K).

After you get the hang of these, they're kinda fun. Right?

Find the area of sector *ABC* in circle B below.

Angle *ABC* = 90°

(A) 64π

(B) 36π

(C) 16π

(D) 12π

(E) 6π

First, find the area of the entire circle: $A = \pi r^2 = 64\pi$. Second, put the degree measure of the sector over 360. The sector is 90 degrees, the same as its central angle.

$$\frac{90}{360} = \frac{1}{4}$$

Third, multiply the area by the fraction:

$$64\pi \times \frac{1}{4} = 16\pi$$

The correct answer is (C).

Taking a Flight on the Coordinate Plane

The ACT likes to test you on coordinate geometry almost as much as shape geometry, so make sure you know a few basics about the coordinate plane. Coordinate geometry involves working with points on a graph that's officially known as the *Cartesian coordinate plane*. This perfectly flat surface has a system that allows you to identify the position of points by using a pair of numbers. The following sections take a closer look at the coordinate plane.

Defining the coordinate plane

Here are some terms you need to know to answer the ACT's coordinate geometry questions. Figure 8-46 shows you these terms on a coordinate plane.

- ✔ **x-axis:** The *x*-axis is the horizontal axis on a coordinate plane, where values or numbers start at the intersect point that has a value of 0. Numbers increase in value to the right of this point and decrease in value to the left of it. All points along the *x*-axis have a *y* value of 0.

- ✔ **y-axis:** The *y*-axis is the vertical axis on a coordinate plane, where values or numbers start at the intersect point that has a value of 0. Numbers increase in value going up from this point and decrease in value going down from it. All points along the *y*-axis have an *x* value of 0.

- ✔ **Origin:** The origin is the point (0, 0) on the coordinate plane; it's where the *x*- and *y*-axes intersect.

- ✔ **Quadrant:** The intersection of the *x*- and *y*-axes forms four quadrants on the coordinate plane, which just so happen to be named Quadrants I, II, III, and IV, as shown in Figure 8-46.

- ✔ **Ordered pair:** An ordered pair is made up of two coordinates, which describe the location of a point in relation to the origin. The horizontal (*x*) coordinate is always listed first, and the vertical (*y*) coordinate is always listed second. Point *A* in Figure 8-46 designates (2, 3).

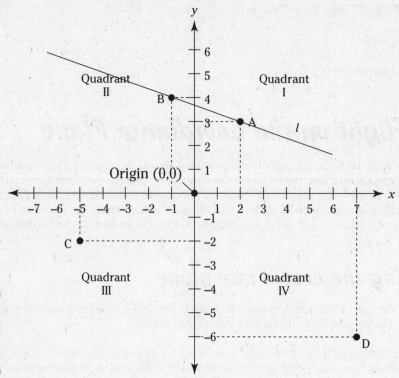

Figure 8-46:
The
coordinate
plane.

Knowing which formulas you need to guide your flight

When working with elements on the coordinate plane, keep these rules in mind:

✔ **A line connecting points with the same *x*- and *y*-coordinates — (1, 1), (2, 2), and (3, 3), for example — forms a 45-degree angle (see Figure 8-47).**

Figure 8-47:
A line
connecting
points with
the same
x- and *y*-
coordinates.

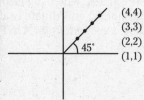

✔ **To locate the middle point of a line, use the *midpoint formula*: $M = \left(\dfrac{x_1 + x_2}{2}, \dfrac{y_1 + y_2}{2} \right)$.**

For example, to figure out the midpoint of a line that ends at points *A* (2, 3) and *B* (–1, 4) in Figure 8-46, use this formula:

$$\left(\frac{2+3}{2}, \frac{-1+4}{2} \right) = \left(\frac{5}{2}, \frac{3}{2} \right) = \left(2\frac{1}{2}, \frac{3}{2} \right)$$

✔ **To find the distance between two points, use the *distance formula*:**

$$\sqrt{(x_2 - x_1)^2 + (y_2 - y_1)^2}.$$

For example, you can figure the distance between points A (2, 3) and B (–1, 4) in Figure 8-46 by using this formula:

$$\sqrt{(-1-2)^2 + (4-3)^2}$$
$$\sqrt{(-3)^2 + (1)^2}$$
$$\sqrt{9+1}$$
$$\sqrt{10}$$

✔ *Slope* **measures how steep a line is.** It's commonly referred to as *rise over run*. Think of slope as a fraction. A slope of 4 is really a slope of $\frac{4}{1}$.

- A line with a negative slope goes from left to right (its left side is higher than its right side).

- A line with a positive slope goes from right to left (its right side is higher than its left side).

- A horizontal line has a slope of 0.

- A vertical line has an undefined slope.

- Parallel lines have the same slope.

One way to find the slope of a line is to locate two of its points and apply the formula for slope:

$$\text{Slope} = \frac{y_2 - y_1}{x_2 - x_1}$$

You can calculate the slope of line l in Figure 8-46 using Points A and B, like so:

$$\frac{4-3}{-1-2} = \frac{1}{-3} = -\frac{1}{3}$$

✔ **The *equation of a line* (or slope-intercept form) is *y = mx + b*.** The m is the slope of the line, and the b is where the line crosses the y-axis (called the y-intercept). So a line with an equation of $y = 4x + 1$ has a slope of $\frac{4}{1}$ and a y-intercept of 1.

You can draw a line on the plane if you know its equation. Find the y-intercept on the y-axis. Then use the slope to create the line. Go up by the slope's numerator and across by the slope's denominator.

Whenever you get an equation for a line that doesn't fit neatly into the slope-intercept form, go ahead and play with the equation a little bit (sounds fun, doesn't it?) to get it into the $y = mx + b$ format. That way, you can either solve the problem or get a visual idea of the graph of the line. For instance, if you see the equation $\frac{1}{3}y - 3 = x$, all you have to do is manipulate both sides of the equation until it looks like the slope-intercept form that you know and love:

$$\frac{1}{3}y = x + 3$$
$$y = 3x + 9$$

Voilà! You now know the slope of the line (3) as well as the y-intercept (9) by using some basic algebra. Pretty tricky!

Here's a sample question that tests your knowledge of the equation of a line.

What is the equation of a line with a slope $-\dfrac{2}{3}$ and a y-intercept of 7?

(F) $3x + 2y = 21$

(G) $-2x + 3y = 14$

(H) $2x - 3y = 21$

(J) $2x + 3y = 14$

(K) $2x + 3y = 21$

When you look at the answer choices, you see that they all have the same format: $ax + by = c$

You need to convert the equation to that format as well. Since the equation of a line is $y = mx + b$, you know that m is the slope and b is the y-intercept. So what are you waiting for? Plug in the values:

$$y = \left(-\frac{2}{3}\right)x + 7$$
$$3y = -2x + 21$$
$$2x + 3y = 21$$

The correct answer is (K).

Considering some advanced concepts

Occasionally, the ACT may ask you more complex questions about the coordinate plane. These questions are among the harder ones, and many students choose to hazard a guess for them and move on. That's perfectly fine, but if you want to give these questions an honest try, keep the following points in mind:

- ✔ **Use the *point-slope formula* if you have to find the graph of a line from its slope and one of its points.** The formula is $y - b = m(x - a)$, where m is the slope and (a, b) are the coordinates of the known point on the line.

- ✔ **Graphing a linear inequality is almost exactly the same as graphing the equation for a line, except a linear inequality covers a lot more ground on the coordinate plane.** While the graph of an equation for a line simply shows the actual line on the coordinate plane, the graph of a linear inequality shows everything either above or below the line on the plane. The graph appears as a shaded area to one side of the line. Figure 8-48 shows the graphs of several inequalities.

- ✔ **When you graph a quadratic equation (which you can find out more about in Chapter 9), it appears as a *parabola*, a curve shape that opens either upward or downward.** Two important properties of parabolas are

  - **The axis of symmetry:** This is the vertical line that bisects the parabola so that each side is a mirror image of the other.

  - **The vertex:** This is the rounded end of the parabola, which is the lowest point on a curve that opens upward and the highest point on a curve that opens downward. It's where the parabola crosses the axis of symmetry.

  The equation for a parabola is $y = a(x - h)^2 + k$, where the coordinate point (h, k) is the vertex. The vertical line $x = h$ is the axis of symmetry. If a is a positive number, the parabola opens upward. If a is negative, it opens downward. Figure 8-49 shows the graph of $y = x^2$. The values for h and k are 0, so the vertex is at the origin. The parabola opens upward because a is 1, a positive number.

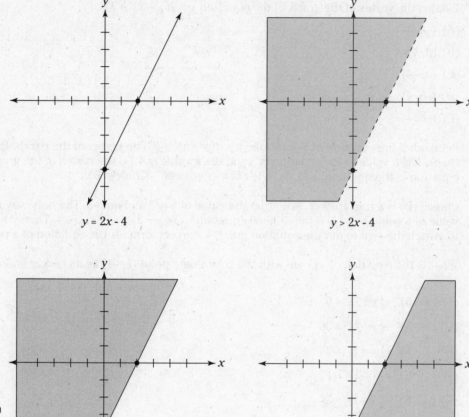

$y = 2x - 4$

$y > 2x - 4$

Figure 8-48:
Graphing
lines and
inequalities.

$y \geq 2x - 4$

$y \leq 2x - 4$

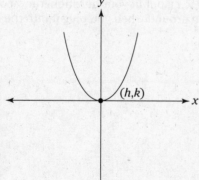

Figure 8-49:
A parabola
with its
vertex on
the origin.

(h,k)

✔ **The equation of a circle is $(x - h)^2 + (y - k)^2 = r^2$, where the center of the circle is point (h, k).** If the origin is the center of the circle, the equation would be $x^2 + y^2 = r^2$.

You can try a couple of practice questions to see how these advanced concepts may appear on the ACT.

What is the vertex of the graph of the equation $y = 2(x-3)^2 + 4$?

(A) $(-3, -4)$

(B) $(3, 4)$

(C) $(3, -4)$

(D) $(-3, 4)$

(E) $(-6, -4)$

Remember the equation of a parabola: $y = a(x-h)^2 + k$. The vertex of the parabola is (h, k). The h value in the equation is 3 and the k value is 4. So the vertex of the graph of the equation in the question is $(3, 4)$. The correct answer is Choice (B).

Choice (D) is a trap answer. Note that the value of h is 3 and not –3. The only way that the value of h could be –3 is if the original equation were $y = 2[x-(-3)]^2 + 4$. Then you'd have to switch the sign to put the equation into the correct form for the equation of a parabola.

What is the equation of a circle with the coordinate point (5, –1) as its center and a radius of 6?

(F) $(x-5)^2 + (y+1)^2 = 6$

(G) $(x-5)^2 + (y-1)^2 = 36$

(H) $(x-5)^2 + (y+1)^2 = 36$

(J) $(x+5)^2 + (y-1)^2 = 12$

(K) $(x-5)^2 - (y+1)^2 = 36$

The answer choices look so similar that you definitely need to know the details of the formula for a circle if you have any hope of getting this one right: $(x-h)^2 + (y-k)^2 = r^2$

Because you know the radius is 6, you also know the radius squared is 36, which means you can easily eliminate Choices (F) and (J). Choice (K) is obviously incorrect because you know that you have to add the two terms together in the formula for the circle; Choice (K) subtracts the two terms. That leaves you with Choices (G) and (H). Choice (G) would be okay if the center had the coordinate point of (5, 1), but in your question, the y-coordinate of the center is negative. So you switch the sign around when you plug it into the equation. The correct answer is (H).

Chapter 9

Algebra and Other Sleeping Aids

. . . .

In This Chapter

▶ Exploring variables and attacking algebra

▶ Setting inequalities straight

▶ Getting familiar with symbols, roots, and radicals

▶ Filling your time with logarithms and functions

▶ Triggering a response: SOH CAH TOA and other trigonometry

. . . .

Algebra is the study of properties of operations carried out on sets of numbers. That definition may sound like mumbo-jumbo, but, bottom line, algebra is just arithmetic in which symbols — usually letters — stand in for numbers. You study algebra to solve equations and to find the values of variables. The ACT gives you all sorts of opportunities to "solve the equation for x," so this chapter's here to review the basics of problem solving and to cover the essentials of more advanced topics, such as logarithms, functions, and trigonometry.

Variables 101

As you probably already know, you encounter a lot of variables in algebra problems. *Variables* are merely symbols that stand in for numbers. Usually the symbols take the form of the letters x, y, and z and represent specific numeric values. True to their name, variables' values can change depending on the equation they're in.

Constants, on the other hand, are numbers that don't change their values in a specific problem. In algebra, letters can refer to constants, but they don't change their values in an equation like variables do. To distinguish constants from variables, the ACT generally designates constants with the letters a, b, or c.

Think of variables as stand-ins for concrete things. For example, if a store charges a certain price for apples and a different price for oranges and you buy two apples and four oranges, the clerk can't just ring up your purchase by adding $2 + 4$ to get 6 and then applying one price. If he did, he'd be incorrectly comparing apples and oranges! In algebra, you use variables to stand in for the price of apples and oranges, something, for instance, like a for apple and o for orange. When you include variables, the equation to figure out the total price of your order looks something like this: $2a + 4o = $ total cost.

The combination of a number and a variable multiplied together is called a *term*. In the case of your fruit shopping spree, $2a$ and $4o$ are both terms. The number part of the term is called the *coefficient*. When you have a collection of these terms joined by addition and/or subtraction, you've got yourself an *algebraic expression*.

Terms that have the same variable (and the same exponents on those variables), even if they have different coefficients, are called *like terms*. For example, you may see an expression that looks something like this:

$$5x + 3y - 2x + y = ?$$

$5x$ and $-2x$ are like terms because they both contain an x variable; $3y$ and y are also like terms because they both contain the y variable.

If a variable doesn't have a coefficient next to it, its coefficient is 1; so y really means $1y$. To combine the like terms, add or subtract their coefficients. In this example, you combine the x terms by adding 5 and -2. To combine the y variable terms, you add the coefficients of 3 and 1. Your original expression with four terms simplifies to two: $3x + 4y$.

Abracadabra: Algebra

On the ACT, you work with variables to perform some basic algebraic procedures. We walk you through these procedures in the following sections.

Trivia Question: Where was algebra supposedly invented? ***Answer:*** Muslim scholars invented Algebra in Zabid, Yemen. See? You can't blame the Greeks for everything!

Solving for x in an equation

One of the first algebraic procedures you need to know is how to solve for x in an equation. To solve for x, follow these steps:

1. **Isolate the variable.**

   In other words, get all the x's on one side and all the non-x's on the other side.

2. **Add or subtract all the x's on one side; add or subtract all the non-x's on the other side.**

3. **Divide both sides of the equation by the number in front of the x.**

Try out this procedure by solving for x in this equation: $3x + 7 = 9x - 5$.

1. **Isolate the variable.**

   Move the $3x$ to the right by subtracting it from both sides. In other words, *change the sign* to make it $-3x$.

   Forgetting to change the sign is one of the most common careless mistakes that students make. To catch this mistake on the ACT, test makers often include trap answer choices that you'd get if you forgot to change the sign.

   Move the -5 to the left, changing the sign to make it $+5$. You now have $7 + 5 = 9x - 3x$.

2. **Add the x's on one side; subtract the non-x's on the other side.**

   $$12 = 6x$$

3. **Divide both sides by the 6 that's next to the x.**

   $$2 = x$$

If you're weak in algebra or know that you often make careless mistakes, plug the 2 back into the equation to make sure it works:

$$3(2) + 7 = 9(2) - 5$$
$$6 + 7 = 18 - 5$$
$$13 = 13$$

If you absolutely hate algebra, see whether you can simply plug in the answer choices. If this were a problem-solving question with multiple-choice answers, you could plug 'n' chug to get the answer.

$3x + 7 = 9x - 5$. Solve for x.

(A) 7

(B) $5\frac{1}{2}$

(C) 5

(D) $3\frac{1}{2}$

(E) 2

Don't ask for trouble. Keep life simple by starting with the simple answers first, and begin in the middle with Choice (C). That is, try plugging in 5. When it doesn't work, don't bother plugging in $3\frac{1}{2}$. That's too much work. Go right down to 2. The correct answer is (E).

If all the easy answers don't work, go back to the hard answer of $3\frac{1}{2}$, but why fuss with it unless you absolutely have to? Test makers often put mind-boggling choices at the beginning of the answers (or at the bottom, if you like to work upside down); skip them.

Adding and subtracting expressions

If a question asks you to add together two or more expressions, you can set them up vertically like you would for an addition problem in arithmetic. Just remember that you can combine only like terms this way. Here's an example:

$$3x + 4y - 7z$$
$$2x - 2y + 8z$$
$$\underline{-x + 3y + 6z}$$
$$4x + 5y + 7z$$

To subtract expressions, distribute the minus sign throughout the second expression and then combine the like terms. (To review the distributive property of multiplication, go to Chapter 7.) Here's an example of how to subtract two expressions:

$$\left(2x^2 - 3xy - 6y^2\right) - \left(4x^2 - 6xy + 2y^2\right) = 2x^2 - 3xy - 6y^2 - 4x^2 + 6xy - 2y^2 = -2x^2 + 3xy - 8y^2$$

Notice that distributing the minus sign changes the signs of all the terms in the second expression. Make sure you keep the signs straight when you subtract expressions.

Multiplying and dividing expressions

When you multiply a term by a *binomial* (an expression with two terms), you have to multiply the number by each term in the binomial, like so:

$$4x(x-3) = 4x(x) - 12x = 4x^2 - 12x$$

To divide a binomial, just divide each term in the binomial by the term, like so:

$$\frac{16x^2 + 4x}{4x} = 4x + 1$$

An easy way to multiply *polynomials* (expressions with many terms) is by stacking the two numbers to be multiplied on top of each other. Say you're asked to multiply these expressions: $(x^2 + 2xy + y^2)(x - y)$. Don't pass out! You can calculate this expression just like an old-fashioned arithmetic problem. Just remember to multiply each term in the second line by each term in the first line, like so:

$$
\begin{array}{r}
x^2 + 2xy + y^2 \\
\underline{x - y} \\
x^3 + 2x^2y + xy^2 \\
\underline{-x^2y - 2xy^2 - y^3} \\
x^3 + x^2y - xy^2 - y^3
\end{array}
$$

Line up your numbers during the first round of multiplication so that like terms match up before you add your first two products together.

Curses! FOILed again

When you have to multiply two binomials, use the FOIL method. *FOIL* stands for *First, Outer, Inner, Last* and refers to the order in which you multiply the variables in parentheses when you multiply two expressions. The result is a quadratic expression. You can practice FOILing by using the equation $(a + b)(a - b) = ?$ and following these steps:

1. **Multiply the *First* variables:** $a(a) = a^2$

2. **Multiply the *Outer* variables:** $a(-b) = -ab$

3. **Multiply the *Inner* variables:** $b(a) = ba$ (which is the same as ab)

   Remember that you can multiply numbers forward or backward, such that $ab = ba$.

4. **Multiply the *Last* variables:** $b(-b) = -b^2$

5. **Combine like terms:** $-ab + ab = 0ab$

   The positive and negative ab cancel each other out. So you're left with only $a^2 - b^2$.

Try another one: $(3a + b)(a - 2b) = ?$

1. **Multiply the *First* terms:** $3a(a) = 3a^2$.

2. **Multiply the *Outer* terms:** $3a(-2b) = -6ab$.

3. **Multiply the *Inner* terms:** $b(a) = ba$ (which is the same as ab).

4. **Multiply the *Last* terms:** $b(-2b) = -2b^2$.

5. **Combine like terms:** $-6ab + ab = -5ab$.

   The final answer is $3a^2 - 5ab - 2b^2$.

You need to out-and-out *memorize* the following three FOIL problems. Don't bother to work them out every time; know them by heart. Doing so saves you time, careless mistakes, and acute misery on the actual exam.

✔ $(a+b)^2 = a^2 + 2ab + b^2$

You can prove this equation by using FOIL to multiply $(a + b)(a + b)$.

1. **Multiply the *First* terms:** $a(a) = a^2$

2. **Multiply the *Outer* terms:** $a(b) = ab$

3. **Multiply the *Inner* terms:** $b(a) = ba$

4. **Multiply the *Last* terms:** $b(b) = b^2$

5. **Combine like terms:** $ab + ab = 2ab$

The final solution is $a^2 + 2ab + b^2$.

✔ $(a-b)^2 = a^2 - 2ab + b^2$

You can prove this equation by using FOIL to multiply $(a - b)(a - b)$.

Notice that the b^2 at the end is positive, not negative, because multiplying a negative times a negative gives you a positive.

✔ $(a-b)(a+b) = a^2 - b^2$

You can prove this equation by using FOIL to multiply $(a - b)(a + b)$.

Note that the middle term drops out because $+ab$ cancels out $-ab$.

Extracting by factoring

Now that you know how to do algebra forward (by distributing and FOILing), are you ready to do it backward? In this section, we show you how to switch to reverse gear and do some factoring.

Factors are the terms that make up a product. Extracting common factors can make expressions much easier to deal with. See how many common factors you can find in this expression; then extract, or *factor,* them out:

$-14x^3 - 35x^6$

First, you can pull out –7 because it goes into both –14 and –35. Doing so gives you $-7(2x^3 + 5x^6)$.

Next, you can take out the common factor of x^3 because x^3 is part of both terms. The simplified result is $-7x^3(2 + 5x^3)$.

You also need to know how to factor quadratic equations, which you accomplish by using FOIL in reverse. Say that the test gives you $x^2 + 13x + 42 = 0$ and asks you to solve for x. Take this problem one step at a time:

1. **Draw two sets of parentheses.**

    $(\quad)(\quad) = 0$

2. **To get x^2, the *First* terms have to be x and x, so fill those in first.**

    $(x\quad)(x\quad) = 0$

3. **Look at the *Outer* terms.**

    You need two numbers that multiply together to get +42. Well, you have several possibilities: 42 and 1, 21 and 2, or 6 and 7. You can even have two negative numbers:

–42 and –1, –21 and –2, or –6 and –7. You can't be sure which numbers to choose yet, so go on to the next step.

4. **Look at the *Inner* terms.**

    You have to add two values to get +13. What's the first thing that springs to mind? Probably 6 + 7. Hey, that's one of the possible combinations of numbers you came up with in Step 3 for the *Outer* terms! Plug them in and multiply.

    $$(x+6)(x+7) = x^2 + 7x + 6x + 42 = x^2 + 13x + 42$$

5. **Solve for *x*.**

    If the whole equation equals 0, then either $(x + 6) = 0$ or $(x + 7) = 0$. After all, any number times 0 equals 0. Therefore, when you solve for *x* for either of these possibilities, *x* can equal –6 or –7.

Solving quadratic equations is easy enough when the solutions come out to be nice round numbers. But occasionally the ACT requires you to solve a quadratic equation that isn't so pretty. When you can't simply solve a quadratic equation by factoring, you may have to resort to the quadratic formula:

$$x = \frac{-b \pm \sqrt{b^2 - 4ac}}{2a}$$

The quadratic formula is a reordering of the quadratic equation: $ax^2 + bx + c = 0$.

You use the formula when the ACT asks you to find the solution for *x* in a complex quadratic equation such as $3x^2 + 7x - 6 = 0$. Finding the factors for this equation is complicated, and splitting the equation into $(x \pm a)(x \pm b)$ form based simply on what you know about the factors of the last term can take all day. Instead, substitute the values for *a*, *b*, and *c* from the quadratic equation into the quadratic formula and solve for *x*. Here's an example problem to show you how to do so.

If $3x^2 + 7x - 6 = 0$, which of the following is a possible solution for *x*?

(F) $-\frac{1}{3}$

(G) $\frac{1}{3}$

(H) $\frac{2}{3}$

(J) 3

(K) 6

The values for *a, b,* and *c* in this equation are 3, 7, and –6, respectively. Plug these values into the quadratic formula and solve.

$$x = \frac{-b \pm \sqrt{b^2 - 4ac}}{2a}$$

$$x = \frac{-7 \pm \sqrt{7^2 - 4(3)(-6)}}{2(3)}$$

$$x = \frac{-7 \pm \sqrt{49 + 72}}{6}$$

$$x = \frac{-7 \pm \sqrt{121}}{6}$$

$$x = \frac{-7 \pm 11}{6}$$

$$x = \frac{-18}{6} \text{ or } x = \frac{4}{6}$$

$$x = -3 \text{ or } \frac{2}{3}$$

Whew! The correct answer has to be Choice (H) because –3 isn't an option.

You may be able to answer this question more quickly by substituting each of the answer choices for *x* in the original quadratic equation to see which one makes the right side of the equation equal zero. For instance, when you substitute 3 for *x*, you get $3(3)^2 + 7(3) - 6 = ?$. You don't need to do additional calculating to see that substituting 3 for *x* won't equal zero. It's unlikely that 6 will work, because substituting 6 for *x* would result in an even larger value than substituting the 3. Here's what you get when you plug in $\frac{2}{3}$:

$$3\left(\frac{2}{3}\right)^2 + 7\left(\frac{2}{3}\right) - 6 = ?$$

$$\left(\frac{3}{1}\right)\left(\frac{2}{3}\right)\left(\frac{2}{3}\right) + \left(\frac{14}{3}\right) - 6 = ?$$

$$\frac{12}{9} + \frac{14}{3} - \frac{6}{1} = ?$$

$$\frac{12}{9} + \frac{14}{3} \times \frac{3}{3} - \frac{6}{1} \times \frac{9}{9} = ?$$

$$\frac{12}{9} + \frac{42}{9} - \frac{54}{9} = ?$$

$$0 = 0$$

Choice (H) works! If it didn't, though, you'd have to perform the same calculations for the other answers. It's up to you to decide whether using the quadratic formula or the substitution method is faster for you.

Substituting

Suppose you have two algebraic equations with two different variables. For example, an ACT question may ask you to solve for x when $4x + 5y = 30$ and $y = 2 - x$. This problem calls for substitution!

All you really have to do here is substitute $2 - x$ for the value of y in the first equation:

$$4x + 5y = 30$$
$$4x + 5(2 - x) = 30$$
$$4x + 10 - 5x = 30$$
$$10 - x = 30$$
$$-x = 20$$
$$x = -20$$

So don't get discouraged if you see two different equations that have two different variables. They're not as hard to work with as you think!

Suffering Inequalities

Mathematical expressions don't always involve equal sides. You may in fact see a few *symbols of inequality,* or signs that mean values aren't equal to each other or that one value is greater or less than another.

Mathematics applies standard symbols to show how the two sides of an equation are related. You're probably pretty familiar with these symbols, but a little review never hurts. Table 9-1 gives you a rundown of the more commonly used algebra symbols that signify inequality. Expect to see them crop up here and there on the ACT.

Table 9-1	Mathematical Symbols for Inequality
Symbol	*Meaning*
$\neq$	Not equal to
$>$	Greater than
$<$	Less than
$\geq$	Greater than or equal to
$\leq$	Less than or equal to

When you use the greater than or less than symbols, always position the wide side of the arrow toward the bigger value, like so: $5 > 2$ or $2 < 5$.

Think of the greater than or less than symbols as sharks and the numbers as fish. The shark's open mouth always heads for the bigger fish, which just so happens to be the bigger value.

You can solve for x in simple inequalities the same way you do in equations. Just add or subtract the same number to or from both sides of the inequality, and multiply or divide both sides by the same number. Here's an example:

$$x + 6 \leq 0$$
$$x \leq -6$$

When you multiply or divide both sides of an inequality by a negative number, you have to reverse the direction of the inequality symbol. For example, when you simplify $-2x < 6$ by dividing both sides by -2 to isolate x, you must switch the symbol so that the final answer is $x > -3$.

You can also use inequalities to show a range of numbers instead of just one single value. For example, the ACT may show the range of numbers between -3 and $+2$ as an inequality, like so: $-3 < x < 2$. This expression, called a *compound inequality*, means that x could be any of these numbers: $-2, -1, 0$, and 1.

To show the range of -3 to $+2$ including -3 and $+2$, use the $\leq$ sign: $-3 \leq x \leq 2$. Now numbers represented by x include all of these possibilities: $-3, -2, -1, 0, 1$, and 2.

The following example problem shows you how inequalities may appear on the ACT.

If $3 > x > -1$ and x is an odd integer, what does x equal?

(A) 2

(B) 0

(C) 1

(D) −1

(E) −2

Use the process of elimination to narrow down your choices. The problem says that x is odd, so you know that Choices (A), (B), and (E) are wrong; 2, −2, and 0 aren't odd. Because x is greater than −1, it can't equal −1. Consequently, Choice (D) is also out. The answer must be Choice (C) because you know that x is between 3 and −1. Therefore, the possible integers for x are 2, 1, and 0. The only odd integer in that list is 1.

Things Aren't Always What They Seem: Symbolism

You may encounter a few basic types of symbolism problems on the ACT. To solve them, use this basic approach:

- Substitute the number given for the variable in the explanation.

- Talk through the explanation to see which constraint fits and then do the indicated operations.

Substituting for the variable in the explanation

You see a problem with a strange symbol. It may be a variable inside a circle, a triangle, a star, a tic-tac-toe sign, or something else. Realize that the symbol you see has no connection to the real world at all. Don't panic, thinking that your math teachers forgot to teach you something. The ACT makes up the symbols for each problem.

The ACT includes a short explanation with the symbol. Here are a few examples:

$$a \mathbin{\#} b \mathbin{\#} c = \frac{(a+b)^c}{b+c}$$

$$x * y * z = \left(\frac{z}{x}\right) + \left(\frac{y}{z}\right)^x$$

$$m @ n @ o = mn + no - om$$

Again, the symbols don't have any meaning in the outside world; they mean only what the problem tells you they mean, and that meaning holds true only for this problem.

Below the ACT's explanation of the symbols is the question itself. For example:

$$3 \mathbin{\#} 2 \mathbin{\#} 1 =$$

$$4 * 6 * 8 =$$

$$2 @ 5 @ 10 =$$

To solve symbol questions like these, use substitution. Plug in a number for the variable in the equation. Which number do you plug in? The one that's in the same position as that variable. For example:

$$a \mathbin{\#} b \mathbin{\#} c = \frac{(a+b)^c}{b+c}$$

$$3 \mathbin{\#} 2 \mathbin{\#} 1 = \frac{(3+2)^1}{2+1} = \frac{5^1}{3} = \frac{5}{3}$$

Because a is in the first position and 3 is in the first position, substitute 3 for a throughout the equation. Because b is in the second position and 2 is in the second position, substitute 2 for b throughout the equation. Because c is in the third position and 1 is in the third position, substitute 1 for c throughout the equation.

Do the same for the other problems.

$$x * y * z = \left(\frac{z}{x}\right) + \left(\frac{y}{z}\right)^x$$

$$4 * 6 * 8 = \left(\frac{8}{4}\right) + \left(\frac{6}{8}\right)^4 = 2 + 0.0316 = 2.316$$

$$m @ n @ o = mn + no - om$$

$$2 @ 5 @ 10 = (2 \times 5) + (5 \times 10) - (10 \times 2) = 10 + 50 - 20 = 40$$

This is the simpler of the two types of symbolism problems. Just substitute the number for the variable and work through the equation.

Talking through the explanation and doing the operations

The other type of symbolism problem you're likely to see on the ACT may seem more confusing until you've done a few. But then they become so easy that you wonder why you didn't get them before. Here's an example:

$(\otimes) = 3x$ if x is odd

$(\otimes) = \frac{x}{2}$ if x is even

Solve for $(\circledS) + (\circledS)$

To solve problems like this one, first talk through the explanation. You have something in a circle. If that something in the circle is odd, you multiply it by 3. If that something in the circle is even, you divide it by 2.

In the first half of the question, you have a 5 in the circle. Because 5 is odd, you multiply it by 3 to get 5 times $3 = 15$. In the second half of the question, you have an 8 in a circle. Because 8 is even, you divide it by 2: $8 \div 2 = 4$. Now all you have to do is add: $15 + 4 = 19$.

You still may think of this type of symbolism problem as a plug-in or substitution problem because you're plugging the number into the equation for x and working through it. However, you first have to figure out which equation to plug the number into, and that requires talking things through. You have to understand what you're doing in this type of problem. Here's another example for you to try:

$(\triangle) = 3x + \frac{1}{3}x$ if x is prime

$(\triangle) = x^2 + \sqrt{x}$ if x is composite

$(\triangle) + (\triangle) = ?$

Aha! To solve this problem, you have to remember some math vocabulary. No, prime numbers aren't the phone numbers with stars next to them in your little black book. A *prime number* is a number that can't be divided by any number other than 1 and itself; examples include 2, 3, 5, 7, 11, and 13. A *composite number* is a number that can be divided by one or more numbers other than 1 and itself; examples include 4, 6, 8, 9, 10, and 12.

The first thing you must do to solve the preceding example is decide whether the term in the triangle is a composite number or a prime number. Because 16 is a composite number, use the second equation. Square 16: $16 \times 16 = 256$. Then take the square root of 16, which is 4. Add them together: $256 + 4 = 260$.

Because 3 is a prime number, use the first equation for the second number in the triangle $3(3) + \frac{1}{3}(3) = 9 + 1 = 10$. Add the two solutions: $260 + 10 = 270$.

Too Hip to Be Square: Roots and Radicals

ACT math questions require you to know how to work with roots and radicals. For the purposes of the ACT, the two terms mean the same thing. The *square root* of a value is the number you multiply by itself to get that value. In other words, the square root of 9 (or $\sqrt{9}$) is 3 because you multiply 3 by itself to get 9. A cube root of a value is the number you multiply by itself 3 times to get that value. So the cube root of 27 (or $\sqrt[3]{27}$) is 3 because $3 \times 3 \times 3$ or $3^3 = 27$. To simplify working with square roots or cube roots (or any other roots), think of them as variables. You work with them the same way you work with x, y, or z.

Adding and subtracting radicals

Adding and subtracting radicals is easy to do as long as you remember a couple of guidelines:

✔ **To add or subtract like radicals, add or subtract the number in front of the radical.**

$$2\sqrt{7} + 5\sqrt{7} = 7\sqrt{7}$$
$$9\sqrt{13} - 4\sqrt{13} = 5\sqrt{13}$$

✔ **You *cannot* add or subtract unlike radicals (just as you cannot add or subtract unlike variables).**

$$6\sqrt{5} + 4\sqrt{3} = 6\sqrt{5} + 4\sqrt{3}$$

You can't add the terms and get 10.

 Don't glance at a problem, see that the radicals aren't the same, and immediately assume that you can't add the two terms. You may be able to simplify one radical to make it match the radical in the other term. For example:

$$\sqrt{52} + \sqrt{13} = ?$$

Begin by simplifying. Take out a perfect square from the term:

$$\sqrt{52} = \sqrt{4} \times \sqrt{13}$$

Because $\sqrt{4} = 2$, then $\sqrt{52} = 2\sqrt{13}$.

So you can add the two original terms:

$$2\sqrt{13} + \sqrt{13} = 3\sqrt{13}$$

Here's another example:

$$\sqrt{20} + \sqrt{45} = \left(\sqrt{4} \times \sqrt{5}\right) + \left(\sqrt{9} \times \sqrt{5}\right) = 2\sqrt{5} + 3\sqrt{5} = 5\sqrt{5}$$

Multiplying and dividing radicals

When you multiply or divide radicals, the motto is "just do it." All you do is multiply or divide the numbers and then pop the radical sign back onto the finished product. For example:

$$\sqrt{5} \times \sqrt{6} = \sqrt{30}$$
$$\sqrt{15} \div \sqrt{5} = \sqrt{3}$$

If you have numbers in front of the radical, multiply them as well. Let everyone in on the fun. For example:

$$6\sqrt{3} \times 4\sqrt{2} = (6 \times 4)\left(\sqrt{3} \times \sqrt{2}\right) = 24\sqrt{6}$$

 When you express the division of a radical as a fraction, you have to be careful. A fraction with a radical in the denominator is an irrational number (for more on irrational numbers, review Chapter 7). The ACT won't credit any answer choice with a radical in the denominator. Whenever your calculations result in a fraction with a square root in the denominator, you have to rationalize your answer. (That doesn't mean you justify to the teacher how on earth you came up with that answer; it means you get rid of the root in the denominator.) Don't worry. Rationalizing is easy. Just multiply both the top and the bottom by the square root in the denominator, like so: $\frac{1}{\sqrt{2}} \times \frac{\sqrt{2}}{\sqrt{2}} = \frac{\sqrt{2}}{2}$.

Find the value of $37\sqrt{5} \times 3\sqrt{6}$.

(F) $40\sqrt{11}$

(G) $40\sqrt{30}$

(H) $111\sqrt{11}$

(J) $111\sqrt{30}$

(K) 1,221

This problem calls for straightforward multiplication: $37 \times 3 = 111$ and $\sqrt{5} \times \sqrt{6} = \sqrt{30}$. The correct answer is (J).

Working from the inside out

When you see an operation inside the radical, do it first and then take the square root. For the following example, first solve the equation inside the radical using the common denominator of 360:

$$\sqrt{\frac{x^2}{40} + \frac{x^2}{9}}$$

$$\frac{x^2}{40} + \frac{x^2}{9}$$

$$\frac{9x^2}{360} + \frac{40x^2}{360}$$

$$\frac{49x^2}{360}$$

Now take the square roots: $\sqrt{49x^2} = 7x$ (because $7x \times 7x = 49x^2$) and $\sqrt{360} \approx 18.97$. Did you say that $\sqrt{360} = 6$? Nope! $\sqrt{36} = 6$, but $\sqrt{360} \approx 18.97$. Beware of assuming too much; doing so may lead you down the path to temptation.

Your final answer is $\frac{7x}{18.97}$. Of course, you can bet that the answer choices will include $\frac{7x}{6}$.

Thinking Exponentially: Logarithms

The ACT may include one or two questions that present you with a *logarithm,* which is essentially the number of times you multiply the base times itself to get the big number. The definition of a logarithm can be boiled down to taking this equation, $x = a^y$, and rearranging it to become $y = \log_a x$. It's just another way of saying y is the log to the base a of x.

So $\log_4 256$ is the number of times you multiply 4 (the base) by itself to get 256 (the big number, to use the technical term). In this case, $\log_4 256 = 4$.

Logarithms with a base of 10 are called *common logarithms.* Common logarithms may be expressed without the base. For example, $\log_{10} 100$ can be expressed simply as $\log 100$, and $\log 100 = 2$ because 2 is the exponent you'd use to show how many times you multiply 10 by itself to get 100.

If the ACT asks you to find the value for x in $\log_x 25 = 2$, you know what to do. Ask yourself what you multiply by itself 2 times to get 25. The answer is 5 because $5^2 = 25$.

If logarithms make your head spin, don't worry. You won't get too dizzy on the ACT because you're not likely to see more than one logarithm question on the Mathematics Test.

Barely Functioning with Functions

If you've never studied functions, don't worry. The ACT doesn't ask you a lot of function questions. And the ones that do appear are relatively easy. The two most common types are the easy plug-in kind and the more complex graphing kind.

Functions as symbols

Most of the function questions on the ACT are really just symbolism problems (see the earlier section "Things Aren't Always What They Seem: Symbolism" for more details). For example, you may see a problem like this one:

$$f(x) = (2x)^3. \text{ Solve for } f(2).$$

The *f* stands for function. To solve this problem, you do the same thing you do for symbolism questions: Talk through the problem. You say, "I have something in parentheses. My job is to multiply that something by 2 and then cube the whole disgusting mess." In other words, just plug in the 2 where you see an *x* in the explanation:

$$f(2) = (2 \times 2)^3 = 4^3 = 64$$

Here's another one to try out:

$$f(x) = x + x^2 + x^3. \text{ Solve for } f(10).$$

Just plug the 10 in for the *x:* $f(10) = 10 + 10^2 + 10^3 = 10 + 100 + 1{,}000 = 1{,}110$

Functions and the coordinate plane

The ACT may ask you to evaluate functions on the coordinate plane (see Chapter 8 for details on the coordinate plane). These problems can be a little more complex, but, lucky for you, the ACT doesn't include very many of them. So if this information flows right over your head, just let it go.

Say a test question tells you to find the following function on the coordinate plane: $f(x) = 2x^2 + 7, f(3)$. In other words, you're looking for the *f* of (*x*), and you're told that the value of *x* = 3. So the value of *f* (the function of *x*) is

$$f(3) = 2(3)^2 + 7$$
$$f(3) = (2 \times 9) + 7$$
$$f(3) = 18 + 7$$
$$f(3) = 25$$

In graphing terms, you know the *x* value is 3 (because the question tells you so), and the *y* value — the $f(x)$ — is 25. If you were to graph this on a coordinate plane, the ordered pair would be (3, 25). It's that simple.

Occasionally, the test makers may ask you to find a *piecewise function,* which is a function that's broken into pieces, or different segments. It's not much different from a "normal" function. You determine the function depending on how you define the possible values of the domain. Here's an example:

$$f(x) = \begin{cases} 2x-1, \ x \leq 1 \\ x+4, \ x > 1 \end{cases}$$

Notice that the function is split into pieces. The value of x determines the value of y just as it does in normal functions, but the y value of a piecewise function follows a different pattern depending on which of the two rules x falls under.

So, if $x = 0$ in the preceding function, it's less than 1, which means the first rule applies: $f(0) = 2(0) - 1$, and $f(0) = -1$. The point on the coordinate plane would be $(0, -1)$. If $x = 1$, $f(1) = 2(1) - 1$, and $f(1) = 1$. This point would be $(1, 1)$. You can graph these points and draw the line between. Just remember that the line is limited to x values that are equal to or less than 1.

If $x = 2$, then the second rule governs, and $f(2) = 2 + 4$, so $f(2) = 6$. When $x = 3$, $f(3) = 3 + 4$, so $f(3) = 7$. The points are $(2, 6)$ and $(3, 7)$. You can draw this line on the plane, too. A picture of these two functions on the coordinate plane would look something like this:

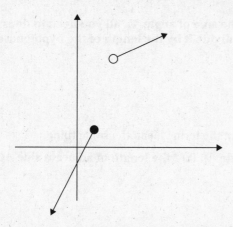

Trying Your Hand at Trigonometry

Many of our students cringe when they hear that the ACT has trigonometry questions. If you're cringing right now, too, relax and stand tall. The ACT has only a few trig questions, and this section covers what you need to know to answer those few even if you've never stepped foot in a trigonometry classroom.

ACT trigonometry questions concern trigonometric ratios. *Trigonometric ratios* express the relationships between the angles and sides of a right triangle in terms of one of its angles. You can answer almost every ACT trig question if you remember the mnemonic for the three basic trigonometric ratios, SOH CAH TOA.

SOH CAH TOA stands for

$$\text{Sine} = \frac{\text{Opposite}}{\text{Hypotenuse}}$$

$$\text{Cosine} = \frac{\text{Adjacent}}{\text{Hypotenuse}}$$

$$\text{Tangent} = \frac{\text{Opposite}}{\text{Adjacent}}$$

Are you scratching your head now and asking, "Opposite? Opposite *what?*" Take a look at this right triangle and consider the guidelines that follow it.

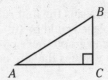

Side *AB* is the *hypotenuse* of the triangle. In relation to the angle at point *A*, side *BC* is the *opposite* side. The other side, the one that's not the hypotenuse or opposite angle *A*, is the *adjacent* side.

- ✔ **To find sin *A* (in other words, the sine of angle *A*), all you need to do is find the length of opposite side *BC* and divide it by the length of the hypotenuse (or *AB*).**

  $$\sin A = \frac{\text{opposite } A}{\text{hypotenuse}}$$

  $$\sin A = \frac{\overline{BC}}{\overline{AB}}$$

  Sine is usually abbreviated as *sin*; the terms mean the same thing.

- ✔ **To find cos *A* (the cosine of angle *A*), find the length of adjacent side *AC* and use the CAH part of SOH CAH TOA.**

  $$\cos A = \frac{\text{adjacent } A}{\text{hypotenuse}}$$

  $$\cos A = \frac{\overline{AC}}{\overline{AB}}$$

  Cosine is usually abbreviated as *cos*; they mean the same thing.

- ✔ **To find tan *A* (the tangent of angle *A*), use the TOA part of SOH CAH TOA.**

  $$\tan A = \frac{\text{opposite } A}{\text{adjacent } A}$$

  $$\tan A = \frac{\overline{BC}}{\overline{AC}}$$

  Yes, *tangent* is usually abbreviated as *tan*; they mean the same thing.

When you work with cosine and sine, keep these two very simple but very important points in mind:

- ✔ **No side in a triangle can be greater than the hypotenuse, so you can never have a sin greater than 1:** $\sin = \frac{\text{opposite}}{\text{hypotenuse}}$.
- ✔ **Because the side adjacent can't be greater than the hypotenuse, you can never have a cos greater than 1:** $\cos = \frac{\text{adjacent}}{\text{hypotenuse}}$.

These two bullets are so important that we're repeating them here. Burn this fact into your brain: Neither a sin nor a cos can be greater than 1.

Three additional trig ratios aren't covered by SOH CAH TOA. They appear less frequently on the ACT, so if you've had about all you can stand of trig, you can ignore them and still be okay on exam day. For those of you who can't get enough, they are secant (sec), cosecant (csc), and cotangent (cot). A standard angle designation in trig ratios is the theta symbol, θ. Here are the ratios for sec, csc, and cot:

$$\sec\theta = \frac{1}{\cos\theta}$$
$$\csc\theta = \frac{1}{\sin\theta}$$
$$\cot\theta = \frac{1}{\tan\theta}$$

Here's an example of just how far you can go when you SOH CAH TOA.

What is $\sin A$ if $\tan A = \frac{9}{40}$?

(A) $\frac{9}{41}$

(B) $\frac{40}{41}$

(C) $\frac{41}{40}$

(D) $\frac{40}{9}$

(E) $\frac{41}{9}$

Notice that you can eliminate Choices (C), (D), and (E) immediately if you realize that the sin can't be greater than 1. Because $\tan A = \frac{9}{40}$, you can draw a picture with opposite $A = 9$ and adjacent $A = 40$.

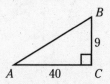

Use the Pythagorean theorem to determine the length of hypotenuse AB:

$$9^2 + 40^2 = (AB)^2$$
$$1{,}681 = (AB)^2$$
$$41 = AB$$

$$\sin A = \frac{\text{opposite } A}{\text{hypotenuse}}, \text{ so } A = \frac{9}{41}.$$

The correct answer is Choice (A).

In case you're interested (or just want to act interested to humor us), you can also find the sec and csc ratios for angle A. Because $\cos A = \frac{40}{41}$, $\sec A = \frac{41}{40}$. Because $\sin A = \frac{9}{41}$, $\csc A = \frac{41}{9}$.

The ACT may ask you to use basic geometric concepts to find the trig ratios of right triangles. Here's an example to show you how to master one of these slightly more complex ACT trig questions.

A right triangle has an angle with a degree measure of 30. Find cos 30°.

(F) $\frac{\sqrt{3}}{2}$

(G) $\frac{1}{2}$

(H) $\sqrt{3}$

(J) 1

(K) 2

Eliminate Choice (K). You know by now that no cos is greater than 1. And a right triangle with a 30-degree angle is a 30:60:90 triangle. So first draw a 30:60:90 triangle. (Remember that the ratio for this special triangle is $s : s\sqrt{3} : 2s$, where s stands for the length of the side. We discuss this ratio in detail in Chapter 8.)

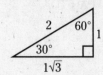

Then figure out the cos by using the CAH part of SOH CAH TOA.

$$\cos 30° = \frac{\text{adjacent } 30°}{\text{hypotenuse}} = \frac{\sqrt{3}}{2}$$

The correct answer is Choice (F). Choice (G) is the ratio for sine and Choice (H) is the ratio for tangent.

Why stop the fun? Try another.

A right triangle has an angle with a degree measure of 45. Find tan 45°.

(A) $\sqrt{2}$

(B) $\frac{\sqrt{2}}{2}$

(C) $\frac{1}{\sqrt{2}}$

(D) 0

(E) 1

Follow the same steps as you did for the previous example. First draw a 45:45:90 triangle. Remember that the ratio of the sides of this triangle is $s : s : s\sqrt{2}$, where s stands for the length of the side. (We discuss this ratio in Chapter 8.)

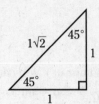

No nervous breakdowns, please

Try not to worry too much about the trigonometry questions that you'll face on the ACT. With a little practice, you should be able to handle just about anything the test makers throw at you regarding the material in this chapter. (And remember, the answer explanation chapters that follow each of the practice test chapters in this book take you through everything step by step.) If you're still confused after you take those exams or you're concerned about some of the more advanced trigonometry that has only a very slight chance of appearing on the test, don't worry. Keep chanting to yourself, "Only four, no more; only four, no more." The entire ACT has only four trig problems. So you can rest easy knowing that trigonometry won't make or break your ACT score.

Then figure out the tan by using the TOA part of SOH CAH TOA.

$$\tan 45° = \frac{\text{opposite } 45°}{\text{adjacent } 45°} = \frac{1}{1} = 1$$

The answer is Choice (E). If you picked Choice (A), you tried to find the ratio of the hypotenuse to one of the other sides, which isn't one of the three main trig ratios. Choice (B) is what you'd get if you were asked to find the sine or cosine of the 45-degree angle.

You know that Choice (C) can't be correct, because you can't have a radical in the denominator. If you were asked to find the sine or cosine of the 45-degree angle, you would have to rationalize the final answer: $\frac{1}{\sqrt{2}} \times \frac{\sqrt{2}}{\sqrt{2}} = \frac{\sqrt{2}}{2}$.

Chapter 10

Making Sense of Math Word Problems

In This Chapter

▶ Deciphering word problems by converting English to math

▶ Working through work problems and rate problems

▶ Thinking things out in mixture problems

▶ Dealing with interest problems and increased and decreased percents

▶ Sorting through probability problems

Not all the math questions on the ACT contain only one sentence or request that you simply "solve for *x*." In fact, many math questions require you to sift through a bunch of information to figure out what the real question is. These *word problems,* as they're called, require you to translate words into numbers and then arrange them in a way that makes mathematical sense. You know what we're talking about — those problems that tell you how fast Train A travels and what speed Train B moves at and then expect you to figure out exactly what hour the two trains will collide. Watch out!

Don't worry; we're here to help you make sense of all these words. Several words translate nicely into mathematical expressions, and many types of word problems lend themselves perfectly to specific formulas or strategies — all of which you discover in this chapter.

Translating English into Math

When you see a word problem on the Math Test, you may feel a little lost at first. Straightforward math equations seem so much more, well, straightforward. Even though word problems are written in English, they may seem like they're written in a foreign language. To help you with the translation, Table 10-1 provides you with some of the more common words you encounter in word problems and tells you what they mean (and look like!) in math terms.

Table 10-1	Common Words and Their Math Counterparts
Plain English	*Math Equivalent*
More than, increased by, added to, combined with, total of, sum of	Add (+)
Decreased by, diminished by, reduced by, difference between, taken away from, subtracted from, less than, fewer than	Subtract (−)
Of, times, product of	Multiply (×)
Ratio of, per, out of, quotient	Divide (÷ or /)
Percent	÷ 100
Is, are, was, were, becomes, results in	Equals (=)
How much, how many, what, what number	Variable (*x, y*)

Subtraction phrases such as "taken away from," "subtracted from," "less than," and "fewer than" require you to switch the order of the quantities you're subtracting. For example, "Ten decreased by six" means 10 – 6 (which equals 4), but "Ten subtracted from six" means 6 – 10, or –4.

As you read through a word problem, analyze its language to determine what math operations it involves. Keep this general process in mind:

1. **Determine what you're supposed to solve for, specifically what the x is in the equation.**

2. **Analyze the rest of the information to figure out how to arrange the equation to solve for x.**

Many of the word problems on the ACT like the following example, concern percentages.

To pay for college expenses, Ms. Bond takes out a loan in the amount of $650 with a simple interest rate of 8%. What is the total amount of the loan with interest?

(A) $658

(B) $52

(C) $702

(D) $1,170

(E) $1,300

The problem asks for the total amount (that's the x) of Ms. Bond's loan with (which means +) interest, so you have to add what she owes in interest to the original amount of the loan. Before you add the interest amount, you must find out what the amount of interest is. The language of the problem tells you that Ms. Bond has to pay an interest rate *of* (meaning ×) 8% (which means you divide 8 by 100). Written with numbers rather than words, the problem looks something like this:

$$x = (8 \div 100) \times 650 + 650$$

Perform the operation in parentheses first (as we explain in Chapter 7) to get 0.08. Next, multiply $650 by 0.08 to get $52. Ms. Bond pays $52 in interest. Add the interest amount to the loan amount to get your final answer: $650 + $52 = $702. The correct answer is Choice (C).

If you picked Choice (A), you added 8 to $650, which isn't the proper way to determine interest. Choice (B) is the correct interest amount but not the total amount of the loan plus the interest. If you opted for Choice (D), you incorrectly divided 8 by 10 rather than by 100 to come up with the interest amount. And Choice (E) is just $650 doubled.

Punching the Clock: Work Problems

Work problems ask you to find out either how much work two or more workers get done in a certain amount of time or how long it takes two or more workers to complete a task together or individually. Following is the standard formula for algebra work problems:

$$\text{Total production} = (\text{Rate of work} \times \text{Time})\text{Worker}_1 + (\text{Rate of work} \times \text{Time})\text{Worker}_2$$

Total production refers to the amount of work that gets done. When you encounter work problems, find the information in the story that fills in the formula. Then solve. Here's an example of how you can apply this formula to an ACT work problem.

Andy and Barbara are furniture movers. Andy can move 16 pieces of furniture per day, and Barbara can move 24 pieces per day. If they each work 8-hour days, how many pieces of furniture can the two of them move in 1 hour, assuming they maintain a steady rate?

(F) 2

(G) 5

(H) 40

(J) 160

(K) 320

This question asks you to find the amount of production and gives you the rate and the time. But to calculate the rate properly, you must state the hours in terms of days. Because a day is eight hours, one hour is $\frac{1}{8}$ of a day. Figure out how much Andy loads in one hour (or $\frac{1}{8}$ of a day) and add that to what Barbara loads in one hour:

$$\text{Total production} = \text{Andy's (Rate of work} \times \text{Time)} + \text{Barbara's (Rate of work} \times \text{Time)}$$
$$\text{Total production} = \left(16 \times \frac{1}{8}\right) + \left(24 \times \frac{1}{8}\right)$$
$$\text{Total production} = 2 + 3$$
$$\text{Total production} = 5$$

You now know that Andy and Barbara can load 5 pieces of furniture in one hour. So the correct answer is Choice (G).

If you picked Choice (H), you figured out the total production for one day rather than one hour. If you selected one of the other two choices, well, you were just guessing.

Another type of work problem gives you the amount of time two workers take to complete a job alone and then asks you to find the amount of time they need to complete the job when they work together. For these types of questions, time is the unknown. Let the job (or total production) = 1 because there's just one job to complete. Here's the formula for this type of work problem:

$$1 = \frac{\text{Time spent on job working together}}{\text{Time spent on job working along}} + \frac{\text{Time spent on job working together}}{\text{Time spent on job working along}}$$

The first fraction represents the effort of the first worker, and the second fraction represents (not surprisingly) the effort of the second worker. An ACT question that uses this equation may look like the following example.

Sally can finish sewing a quilt in 3 days; Meg completes a quilt in 9 days. How many days does it take for the two women to sew a quilt if they work together?

(A) 6

(B) 4.5

(C) 1

(D) 2.25

(E) 12

Apply the formula. The unknown for both women is how much time each spends when they work together, so make that the x for both of them. You know the amount of time each woman spends alone, so enter those figures into the formula:

$$1 = \frac{x}{3} + \frac{x}{9}$$

To add the fractions, make the denominators the same (flip to Chapter 9 if you need a refresher on how to do so) and solve:

$$1 = \frac{3x}{9} + \frac{x}{9}$$
$$1 = \frac{3x + x}{9}$$
$$9 = 3x + x$$
$$9 = 4x$$
$$2.25 = x$$

It takes the women 2.25 days to sew one quilt when they work together. So the correct answer is Choice (D).

You can eliminate Choices (A), (B), and (E) right away because the two women wouldn't take longer to sew the quilt together than Sally takes to sew it alone.

If you picked Choice (C), you either chose how many quilts they were making, or you guessed.

Going the Distance: Rate Problems

You can use the basic distance formula (Distance = Rate × Time) to solve any problem that involves distance, rate (a fancy name for speed), or time spent traveling. Sure, the formula looks easy on paper, but you can mess up quickly if you don't plug in your variables and numbers properly. With that in mind, check out this sample rate problem.

Paige can run a mile in eight minutes. How long does it take her to run $\frac{1}{10}$ of a mile at the same rate?

(F) 30 seconds

(G) 48 seconds

(H) 60 seconds

(J) 480 seconds

(K) 600 seconds

The problem tells you that Paige's distance is $\frac{1}{10}$ of a mile. You can figure her rate to be $\frac{1}{8}$ because she runs 1 mile in 8 minutes. And because the problem is asking how long she runs, you need to solve for time. Plug the numbers into the distance formula:

Distance = Rate × Time

$$\frac{1}{10} = \frac{1}{8} \times t$$

To find time, isolate *t* on one side of the equation by multiplying both sides by 8:

$$\frac{1}{10} \times 8 = t$$

$$\frac{8}{10} = t$$

So Paige runs $\frac{1}{10}$ of a mile in $\frac{8}{10}$ of a minute. Because $\frac{8}{10}$ isn't an answer choice, you must convert minutes to seconds. One minute equals 60 seconds, and $\frac{8}{10} \times 60 = 48$ seconds. The correct answer is Choice (G).

Choices (J) and (K) are obviously wrong because 480 seconds is 8 minutes and 600 seconds is 10 minutes, and you know that it takes Paige less time to run $\frac{1}{10}$ of a mile than it does for her to run a whole mile. Guessing is the only way you can come up with one of the other two answers.

TIP

Always check the possible answer choices for options that don't make any sense in the problem. You can toss those out right away and save your time for doing the math.

Mixing Things Up: Mixture Problems

A *mixture problem* is a word problem that looks much more confusing than it actually is. The hardest part for most students is knowing where to begin because most mixture problems involve a lot of different information. The best way to approach this type of problem is to make a chart; doing so helps you keep everything straight.

Say you're given this problem.

EXAMPLE

Marshall wants to mix 40 pounds of beads selling for 30 cents a pound with a quantity of sequins selling for 80 cents a pound. He wants to pay 40 cents per pound for the final mix. How many pounds of sequins should he use?

(A) 5

(B) 10

(C) 18

(D) 20

(E) 22

Before you start doing any math, make a chart to organize the different info the problem provides. Table 10-2 shows you what your chart should look like.

Table 10-2	Charting the Info Given in a Mixture Problem		
	Pounds	*Price per Pound*	*Total Price*
Beads	40	$0.30	$12.00
Sequins	*x*	$0.80	$0.80*x*
Mixture	40 + *x*	$0.40	$0.40 (40 + *x*)

Now you can reason it out. First, dump the decimal point because it makes the numbers easier to work with. (Officially, you multiply by 100 to get rid of the decimal point, but really you dump it.) The cost of the beads (1,200) plus the cost of the sequins (80x) must equal the cost of the mixture (1,600 + 40x). Now you have a workable equation:

$$1,200 + 80x = 1,600 + 40x$$
$$80x - 40x = 1,600 - 1,200$$
$$40x = 400$$
$$x = 10$$

Careful! Keep in mind what x stands for. It represents the number of pounds of sequins, which is what the question asks for, so in this case you don't have to do any more calculating. The correct answer is Choice (B).

Getting Greedy: Interest Problems

Problems often ask you how much interest someone earned on an investment. The ACT usually asks for simple interest, but it may also throw in a question or two that asks for percent growth. This section shows you how to succeed on both types.

Figuring out simple interest

Finding simple interest is pretty — PRTI, to be exact.

- ✔ P = Principal, which is the amount of money you begin with or the amount you invest
- ✔ R = Rate, which is the interest rate you're earning on the money (stated as a decimal)
- ✔ T = Time, which is the amount of time you leave the money in the interest-bearing account
- ✔ I = Interest, which is the amount of interest you earn on the investment

The formula is *PRT = I,* or Principal × Rate × Time = Interest.

Janet invested $1,000 at 5 percent annual interest for one year. How much interest did she earn?

(F) $5.00

(G) $50.00

(H) $70.25

(J) $75.00

(K) $500.00

This is the simplest type of problem. Plug the numbers into the formula, like so:

$$PRT = I$$
$$1,000 \times 0.05 \times 1 = 50$$

She earned $50 in interest. So Choice (G) is your winner.

Choices (F) and (K) try to trap you with variations on the decimal placement. You know that $5\% = \frac{5}{100} = 0.05$; be careful how you multiply.

Finding percent growth

One or two ACT questions may ask you for percent growth. Often it's in the context of how much an investment grows over time with a compounded interest rate. But the concept also applies to other values, such as population growth. Percent growth applies to any percent change repeated over a period of time.

For example, the ACT may ask you to figure out how much interest accrues on a bank account over several years. Don't panic! The good news is that a formula can help you. The bad news is that you have to memorize this formula for the test. That's not so bad, though, because the formula is really just *PRTI* for one year multiplied exponentially.

$$NV = IV \times (1+P)^Y$$

The *NV* stands for "new value," or the amount you end up with. *IV* is the initial value or the amount you started with. *P* is the percentage by which the value grows, and *Y* is the number of years or times the value changes. When you see a percentage growth question like this one on the ACT, you just plug the numbers into the formula and solve for the unknown.

Joe received $100.00 from his grandma for Christmas and deposited the full amount in a certificate of deposit on January 31st. The certificate of deposit earned a yearly interest rate of 5 percent. Joe made no withdrawals from or other deposits to the account. The certificate of deposit matured 10 years later on January 31st. How much money rounded to the whole dollar was in Joe's certificate of deposit account when it matured?

(A) $100.00

(B) $105.00

(C) $150.00

(D) $163.00

(E) $169.00

Because Joe's account earns interest every year, you use the formula for percent growth. The *IV* was $100.00. The percent change (*P*) was 5 percent or 0.05, and the number of years, or times, that interest was applied was 10. Plug these figures into the formula and solve for *NV*.

$$NV = 100 \times (1+.05)^{10}$$
$$NV = 100 \times (1.05)^{10}$$
$$NV = 100 \times 1.63$$
$$NV = 163$$

So the final answer is Choice (D).

If you used the formula for simple interest, you'd think that Joe earned $5.00 in interest and add that to his initial investment of $100.00 to mistakenly get Choice (B). Choice (C) is there to trap anyone who figured out simple interest and then just multiplied it by 10. You can't do that either. Whenever you're asked to find a repeated percentage of growth, you have to use the formula for percent growth. The ACT's interest problems aren't intentionally vicious. So you won't see anything really crazy, like "5 percent annual interest compounded quarterly for 3 months and 6 percent quarterly interest compounded daily," blah, blah, blah.

Useless but fascinating trivia: In Bulgarian, the word for *thank you* is pronounced *blah-go-dah-ree-uh*. But a shortened form, like *thanks,* is simply *blah*. If your mother takes you to task for being a smart aleck and going "blah, blah, blah" when she talks, you can innocently claim that you're practicing your Bulgarian and you're just thanking her for her wisdom.

Picking Your Way through Percent Increase and Decrease

You may see a problem that asks you what percent increase or decrease occurred in the number of games a team won or the amount of commission a person earned.

To find a percent increase or decrease, use this formula:

$$\% \text{ increase or decrease} = \frac{\text{Number increase or decrease}}{\text{Original whole}}$$

In basic English, to find the percent by which something has increased or decreased, you take two simple steps:

1. **Find the number (amount) by which the thing has increased or decreased.**

   For example, if a team won 25 games last year and 30 games this year, the number increase was 5. If a salesperson earned $10,000 last year and $8,000 this year, the number decrease was $2,000. Make that number the numerator (the top part) of the fraction.

2. **Find the original whole.**

   This figure is what you started out with before you increased or decreased. If a team won 25 games last year and won 30 games this year, the original number was 25. If the salesperson earned $10,000 last year and $8,000 this year, the original number was $10,000. Make the number you started out with the denominator (the bottom part) of the fraction.

You now have a complete fraction. Divide the fraction to convert to a decimal and multiply by 100 to make it a percentage.

In 2010, Coach Denges won 30 prizes at the county fair by tossing a basketball into a bushel basket. In 2011, he won 35 prizes. What was his percent increase?

(F) 100

(G) 30

(H) $16\frac{2}{3}$

(J) 14.28

(K) 0.166

The number by which his prizes increased, from 30 to 35, is 5. That's the numerator. The original whole, or what he began with, is 30. That's the denominator. So your fraction looks like this: $\frac{5}{30} = \frac{1}{6} = 16\frac{2}{3}\%$. The correct answer is Choice (H).

If you chose Choice (K), the test makers fooled you. The question asks for Coach Denges's *percent* increase. Choice (K) says that the increase was 0.166%, which is incorrect. The increase as a percentage was $16\frac{2}{3}\%$. If you chose Choice (J), you fell for another trap. You put the 5 increase over the 35 rather than over the 30.

Try another example.

Two years ago, Haylie scored 22 goals at soccer. This year, she scored 16 goals. What was her approximate percentage decrease?

(A) 72

(B) 37.5

(C) 27

(D) 16

(E) 0.27

Find the number of the decrease: 22 – 16 = 6. That's the numerator. Find the original whole from which she is decreasing: 22. That's the denominator. So your fraction looks like this: $\frac{6}{22} \approx 0.27$, or approximately 27 percent. The correct answer is Choice (C).

If you picked Choice (A), you put 16 over 22 instead of putting the decrease over the original whole. If you chose Choice (E), you forgot the difference between 0.27 and 0.27 *percent*. If you marked Choice (B), you put the decrease of 6 over the new amount, 16, rather than over the original whole. Note how easy these traps are to fall into. Our suggestion: Write down the actual formula and then plug in the numbers. Writing down the formula may be boring, but it takes only a few seconds and may save you points.

Here's a tricky question that many people try to do in their heads (instead of writing down the formula and plugging in the numbers); unfortunately, many of these people blow it big-time.

Carissa has three quarters. Her father gives her three more. Carissa's wealth has increased by what percent?

(F) 50

(G) 100

(H) 200

(J) 300

(K) 500

Did you fall for the trap answer, (H)? Her wealth has doubled, to be sure, but the percent increase is only 100. You can prove it with the formula: $\frac{75}{75} = 1 = 100\%$. (The number increase is 75 because she has three more quarters, or 75 cents. Her original whole was 75 cents.) The correct answer is Choice (G).

Don't fall into the trap of assuming that a 200 percent increase means that something doubled. When you double something, you increase it by 100 percent because you have to subtract the original "one" you began with. When you triple something, you increase by 200 percent because you have to subtract the original you began with. If you had three dollars and you now have nine dollars, for example, you have tripled your money but increased it by only 200 percent. Do the formula:

number increase = 6 dollars

original whole = 3 dollars

$\frac{6}{3} = 2 = 200\%$

Take a wild guess at what percent you increase when you quadruple your money? That's right, 300 percent. Just subtract the original 100 percent.

Practicing Probability

Probability questions are usually word problems. They may look intimidating, with so many words that make you lose sight of where to begin, but they aren't impossible to solve. In fact, by using the two simple rules we explain in the following sections, you can solve nearly every probability problem that the ACT tosses at you.

No matter what kind of probability problems you face, remember that probability can only be 0, 1, or a number in between 0 and 1. You can't have a negative probability, and you can't have a probability greater than 1, or 100 percent.

Rule 1: Create a fraction

To find a probability, use this formula to set up a fraction:

$$P = \frac{\text{Number of possible desired outcomes}}{\text{Number of total possible outcomes}}$$

The denominator is the easier of the two parts to begin with because it's the total possible number of outcomes. For example, when you're flipping a coin, you have two possible outcomes, giving you a denominator of 2. When you're tossing a die (one of a pair of dice), you have six possible outcomes, giving you a denominator of 6. When you're pulling a card out of a deck of cards, you have 52 possible outcomes (a deck of cards contains 52 cards), giving you a denominator of 52. When 25 marbles are in a jar and you're going to pull out one of them, you have 25 possibilities, giving you a denominator of 25. Very simply, the denominator is the whole shebang — everything possible.

The numerator is the total number of the outcomes you want. If you want to see heads when you toss a coin, you have exactly one desired outcome because the coin has only one head side, giving you a numerator of 1. Your chance of tossing heads, therefore, is $\frac{1}{2}$ — one possible heads and two possible outcomes altogether. If you want to roll a 5 when you toss a die, the numerator is 1 because the die has exactly one 5 on it. The probability of tossing a 5 is $\frac{1}{6}$ — one possible 5 out of six possible outcomes altogether.

If you want to draw a jack from a deck of cards, you have four chances because the deck contains four jacks: hearts, diamonds, clubs, and spades. Therefore, the numerator is 4. The probability of drawing a jack out of a deck of cards is $\frac{4}{52}$ (which reduces to $\frac{1}{13}$). If you want to draw a jack of hearts, the probability is $\frac{1}{52}$ because the deck contains only one jack of hearts.

A jar of marbles has 8 yellow marbles, 6 black marbles, and 12 white marbles. What is the probability of drawing out a black marble?

(A) $\frac{1}{6}$

(B) $\frac{3}{13}$

(C) $\frac{4}{13}$

(D) $\frac{6}{13}$

(E) 1

Use the formula. Begin with the denominator, which is all the possible outcomes: $8 + 6 + 12 = 26$. The numerator is how many outcomes result in what you want: 6 black marbles. The probability is $\frac{6}{26}$, which you can reduce to $\frac{3}{13}$, which is Choice (B).

If you came up with Choice (C) or (D), you figured out the probability of choosing a yellow or white marble, respectively. You know that Choice (E) can't be right. A probability of 1 means that there's a 100 percent chance that you'll pick a black marble.

A drawer contains 5 pairs of white socks, 8 pairs of black socks, and 12 pairs of brown socks. In a hurry to get to school, Austin pulls out a pair at a time and tosses them on the floor if they are not the color he wants. Looking for a brown pair, Austin pulls out and discards a white pair, a black pair, a black pair, and a white pair. What is the probability that on his next reach into the drawer he will pull out a brown pair of socks?

(F) $\frac{12}{25}$

(G) $\frac{8}{21}$

(H) $\frac{4}{7}$

(J) $\frac{3}{4}$

(K) 0

You use the same formula for this problem, but it's slightly more complicated. Austin began with 25 pairs of socks. However, Austin, that slob, has thrown 4 pairs on the floor already, which means only 21 pairs are left. The probability of his pulling out a brown pair is $\frac{12}{21}$, or $\frac{4}{7}$. The correct answer is Choice (H).

You know Choice (K) can't be right. Austin will eventually pull out a brown sock, so there's not a 0 probability of his doing so. Choice (F) incorrectly uses the original sock total to figure out the probability. Choice (G) is wrong because it mistakenly subtracts the scattered socks from the number of brown socks. No brown socks landed on the floor, so Austin still has 12 in the drawer to pull from.

Rule 2: Multiply consecutive probabilities

Rule 1 works nicely for questions that ask you for the probability of one event. Rule 2 tells you what to do if a question asks you to find the probability of more than one event. You just find the probability of each separate event. Then you multiply those probabilities together.

For example, to find the probability that you'll get two heads when you toss a coin twice, you first find each probability separately and then multiply the two. The chance of tossing a coin the first time and landing on heads is $\frac{1}{2}$. The chance of tossing a coin the second time and landing on heads is $\frac{1}{2}$. Multiply those consecutive probabilities: $\frac{1}{2} \times \frac{1}{2} = \frac{1}{4}$. The chance of getting two heads is 1 out of 4.

Think you get it? Try another just to make sure.

What's the probability of tossing a die twice and getting a 5 on the first toss and a 6 on the second toss? Treat each toss separately. The probability of getting a 5 is $\frac{1}{6}$. The probability of getting a 6 is $\frac{1}{6}$. Multiply those consecutive probabilities: $\frac{1}{6} \times \frac{1}{6} = \frac{1}{36}$. The chance of tossing a die twice and getting a 5 and a 6 is 1 out of 36.

Chapter 11

Numb and Number: Acing the Mathematics Test

In This Chapter
▶ Getting familiar with the format of the Math Test
▶ Taking a common-sense approach to the Math Test
▶ Speeding things up with some timing tips
▶ Knowing what to do — and what not to do — on the Math Test

*O*kay, you math whiz, here's a question for you. Quick, without your calculator, answer this question: How many seconds are there in a year? ***Answer:*** Exactly 12: January 2nd, February 2nd, March 2nd . . .

Your number's up. You can't escape the ACT Mathematics Test, no matter how hard you try. One of the four tests of the ACT is the one-hour Mathematics Test, whose questions, alas, aren't quite as much fun as the one we ask here. But don't worry. This chapter tells you what you need to know to ace the test.

What You See Is What You Get: The Format and Breakdown of the Math Test

No, the "breakdown" in the preceding heading doesn't refer to *your* (nervous) breakdown, but rather to the breakdown of the number and types of problems in the Mathematics Test. This 60-minute test features 60 questions (which makes figuring out your time per problem convenient, no?). The questions fall into pretty standard categories.

In the ACT bulletin and in many ACT study books, you have to slog through incredibly detailed analyses of the exact number of each question type on the test: 14 plane geometry questions, 4 trigonometry questions, blah, blah, blah. We refuse to put you to sleep with that sort of detail. We mean, it's not as if you have any control over the distribution of questions, right? (We can just see the letter: "Dear ACT: Please be sure that I have more geometry and fewer algebra problems — thanks . . . .")

The following is the short 'n' sweet version of the kinds of math questions you encounter in the dark alleyways of the ACT:

✔ **Pre-algebra:** (Normal people refer to this as *arithmetic.*) About 20 percent, or one-fifth, of the questions cover basic arithmetic, including such concepts as fractions and decimals and the dreaded word problems.

See Chapter 7 for the skinny on arithmetic and Chapter 10 for everything you need to know about word problems.

✔ **Elementary algebra:** You learn this type of material in your first semester or two of algebra. These questions test your ability to work with positive and negative integers, set up algebraic formulas, solve linear equations, and do the occasional FOIL problem. About 20 percent, or one-fifth, of the questions cover elementary algebra.

If you don't know what a FOIL problem is, don't despair. We discuss FOIL in excruciating detail in Chapter 9.

✔ **Intermediate algebra/coordinate geometry:** About 30 percent of the questions cover more difficult quadratic problems, as well as inequalities, bases, exponents, radicals, and basic graphing (finding points on an x, y–coordinate graph).

Turn to Chapter 8 if you need help with coordinate geometry and Chapter 9 if you're struggling with algebra.

✔ **Plane geometry and trigonometry:** About 23 percent of the questions cover plane figures (what you think of as "just plain figures," like triangles, circles, quadrilaterals, and so on). The trig questions make up only 7 percent of the test, so if you haven't had trig yet, don't freak out. Trig questions are very basic, covering trig ratios and basic trigonometric identities.

Learn what you need to know about plane geometry in Chapter 8, and go to Chapter 9 for a review of trigonometry basics.

Confused? Don't worry about the exact number of questions. Just remember two important points:

✔ You have 60 minutes to do 60 questions.

✔ One-third of the questions are arithmetic, one-third are algebra, and one-third are geometry.

Absence Makes the Heart Grow Fonder: What Isn't on the Math Test

Instead of obsessing over how awful the ACT Mathematics Test is, focus on a few of its good points — namely, what isn't on the test:

✔ **Calculus:** The ACT does not — we repeat, *does not* — test calculus. You don't even have to know how to pronounce *calculus* to get a good ACT Mathematics Test score. You also don't have to know trigonometry. Yes, 7 percent of the test (approximately four questions) covers trig concepts, but if you miss only four questions, we're happy, you're ecstatic, and your math score is outta sight.

✔ **Quantitative Comparisons, grid-ins, and so on:** The bizarre math questions found in some other standardized exams are also missing from the ACT. If you've taken the SAT, for example, you may have seen the Quantitative Comparison (or QC) question, which makes you compare two values to see which is greater, and the grid-in question, which asks you to answer the question outright with no multiple-choice options. You don't have to worry about those weird formats here. All the math questions on the ACT are in straightforward multiple-choice format.

All the math questions have *five* answer choices. The rest of the questions on the ACT have only four answer choices. Be sure to look at all the possible choices in the Math Test. We're always amazed by how many students, who are used to looking at answers A, B, C, and D or F, G, H, and J in the other ACT sections, totally don't see the E and K answer choices in the math section.

↙ **Traps:** Most math exams are full of nasty old traps. The ACT is not. It's not out to getcha, like other tests. Here, the questions really test your math knowledge, not your patience. You don't have to be quite as paranoid on the ACT as you do on other exams.

Getting into the Grind: The Approach

You've done multiple-choice math problems all your life. In fact, you probably don't have much more to learn about doing multiple-choice math questions. However, the following common-sense steps can help you stay focused as you move quickly through the Math Test:

1. **Identify the point of the question.**

   Yes, even the stupid word problems have a point. Each question is trying to get you to supply one specific piece of information. Does the question ask you to solve for a circumference or for an area? Do you have to state the value of x or of $2x$? Circle precisely what the question asks for. After you finish the problem, go back and double-check that your answer provides the circled information.

   We just said that the ACT is not out to trap you — but that doesn't mean you can't trap yourself. Among the answer choices are answers that you get by making careless errors. Suppose, for example, that the problem asks for the *product* of numbers, and you find the *sum.* Your answer will undoubtedly be there with the other wrong answers (and the one right one, of course). If the question asks for one-half of a quantity and you solve for twice the quantity, that answer will also likely be there. Because these types of answer choices are available to you, it's especially important that you identify *exactly* what the problem asks for and supply only that information.

2. **Budget your time and brain strain: Decide whether the problem is worth your time and effort.**

   You don't have to do every math problem in order, you know. Read the question and then predict how time-consuming it will be to solve. If you know you have to take several steps to answer the question, you may want to skip the problem and go back to it later. If you're not even sure where to start the problem, don't sit there gnawing at your pencil as if it were an ear of corn (unless you're Pinocchio, wood really isn't brain food). Guess and go.

   Guess, guess, guess! The ACT has no penalty for wrong answers. You're going to (or already have) read that statement hundreds of times throughout this book. We say it every chance we get to remind you that you can guess without fear of reprisal. Whenever you skip a problem, choose an answer, any answer, mark it on your answer sheet, and hope that you get lucky. Put a big arrow in the margin of the test booklet next to the question (not on the answer sheet, because it may mess up the computer grading) to remind yourself that you made a wild guess. But if you run out of time and don't get back to the question, at least you have a chance of guessing the answer right.

3. **Look before you leap: Preview the answer choices.**

   Look at the answer choices before you begin doing any pencil-pushing. Often, the choices are variations on a theme, like 0.5, 5, 50, 500, and 5,000. If you see those answers, you know you don't have to worry about the digit, only the decimal. Maybe the answers are very far apart, like 1, 38, 99, 275, and 495. You probably can make a wild estimate and get that answer correct. But if you see that the answers are close together (like 8, 9, 10, 11, and 12), you know you have to invest a little more time and effort into being extra careful when solving the problem.

   We'd be wealthy if we had a nickel for every student who groaned and complained as he or she looked at the answer choices, "Man, I didn't really have to work that whole problem out. I could've just estimated from the answer choices." Absolutely true.

4. Give yourself a second chance: Use your answer to check the question.

Think of this step as working forward and backward. First, work forward to come up with the answer to the question. Then plug the answer into the question and work backward to check it. For example, if the question asks you to solve for *x*, work through the equation until you get the answer. Then plug that answer back into the equation, and make sure it works out. This last step takes less time than you may think and can save you a lot of points.

Time Flies When You're Having Fun: Timing Tips

The most common complaint we hear from students about the Mathematics Test is, "There's just not enough time. If I had more time, I could probably do every single question, but I always run out of time." True enough. Although having one minute per question (60 math questions, 60-minute section) sounds good, you'll be surprised how fast time goes by. We have a few suggestions to help you make the best use of your time.

Skim for your favorite questions

We think of this technique as eating dessert first (something we always do). Go for the chocolate cake first (the easy questions) to make sure time doesn't run out before you get to the good stuff. Leave the green beans (the harder problems) for the end. If you run out of time (which happens to most test takers), at least you'll have finished the questions that you had the best chance of answering correctly.

If you decide to skip a question in any section on the ACT, make sure you mark any old answer for it on your answer sheet before you move on. You won't receive a penalty for wrong answers, so make sure you've bubbled in an answer for every question in the section before the proctor calls time.

Start in the middle when plugging in the answer choices

On many problems, you can simply plug in the answer choices to see which one fits. For example, suppose that the question is something like this:

$x + \frac{1}{2}x + \frac{1}{3}x = 110$. What is the value of *x*?

(A) 95

(B) 90

(C) 72

(D) 60

(E) 30

Yes, you can use a common denominator and actually work through the problem to find x directly. But it may be quicker and easier to plug in the answer choices. Start with the middle choice, Choice (C). If $x = 72$, then $\frac{1}{2}x = 36$, and $\frac{1}{3}x = 24$. But $72 + 36 + 24 = 132$, not 110. Because the sum is too big, you know the number you plugged in is too big as well. Go down the list, plugging in the smaller numbers. Try Choice (D). Let $x = 60$: $60 + 30 + 20 = 110$. That works! (See Chapter 7 for more on common denominators and Chapter 9 for more on variables like x.)

Kindly refrain from showing off everything you know

Some of the ACT problems have extraneous information. For example, a geometry problem may list all sorts of numbers, including lengths of sides and measures of interior angles. If the question asks you to find the area of a trapezoid, you need just the numbers for base and height. (Remember the formula? The area of a trapezoid is $\frac{1}{2}(b_1 + b_2) \times h$.)

Extra red-herring info can make you waste a lot of time. We already know that you're brilliant (you bought this book, didn't you?); you don't need to prove it by doing more than you're asked during the test. If you convert every problem into two or three new problems, you'll never finish the Math Test on time.

Put aside two minutes to fill in the remaining ovals

The ACT assesses no penalty for guessing. We like to say that over and over and over again until you're so exasperated that you want to cut off our air supply. It's critical to remember that you don't lose points for wrong answers; always keep in mind that wild guesses are worth making. Nothing is worse than that sinking feeling you get when the proctor calls time and you still have ten problems you haven't even looked at. If you save a few minutes at the end, you can wildly fill in some answers for those last ten problems. You have a good chance of getting at least a few of them correct.

The proctor is *supposed* to tell you when you have only five minutes left in the test. Before the test actually begins, you may want to remind your proctor to do so.

Do's, Don'ts, and Darns: What to Do and Not Do on the Math Test

Although the math questions are pretty straightforward, a few basic do's and don'ts are worth noting here.

Do get the lead out

Give your pencil a workout. If you have to solve a geometry problem, jot down the formula first and then just fill in the numbers. If you have the formula staring at you, you're not as likely to make a careless mistake as you would be if you tried to keep everything in your head. If the geometry problem has words, words, words but no picture, draw the picture yourself. When you plug in the answer choices or make up your own numbers to substitute for variables, write down what you plugged in and tried. We see students redoing the same things over and over because they forgot what they'd already plugged in. Doodle away. You get no scratch paper for the ACT, but the test booklet has plenty of white space.

Don't start working until you've read the entire problem

So you read the first part of a problem and start trying to solve for the area of the triangle or the circumference of the circle. But if you read further, you may find that the question asks only for a *ratio* of the areas of two figures, which you can figure out without actually finding the precise areas. Or you may solve a whole algebraic equation, only to realize that the question didn't ask for the variable you found, but for something else entirely. As we say in the "Getting into the Grind: The Approach" section, earlier in this chapter, circle the part of the problem that specifies exactly what it asks for.

Do reread the problem with your answer inserted

Very few students take this last critical step. Most test takers are so concerned with finishing on time that they solve the problem and zoom on to the next question. Big tactical error. Rereading the question in light of your answer can show you some pretty dumb mistakes. For example, if the question asks you for the average of 5, 9, 12, 17, and 32 and your answer is 75, you can immediately realize that you found the sum but forgot to divide by the number of terms. (And of course, 75 is one of the answer choices.) Maybe the question asks you to find one interior angle of a figure, and your answer is 190. If you look at the angle and see that it is *acute* (less than 90 degrees), you've made a mistake somewhere.

Don't strike out over a difficult question early on

Most standardized exams put their questions in order of difficulty, presenting the easy ones first, then the medium ones, and finally the hard ones. Things aren't as cut and dried on the ACT Mathematics Test. You may find a question that you consider really tough very early in the exam. Although *easy* and *hard* are subjective, many of our students over the years have been furious with themselves because they never looked at the last several questions — reasoning that if they couldn't get the earlier ones right, they obviously couldn't get the later ones at all. Wrong. We've seen some relatively simple questions, especially basic geometry questions, close to the end of the exam.

Chapter 12

More Fun than a Root Canal: Mathematics Practice Questions

In This Chapter

▶ Making your brain earn its keep with a handful of practice questions

▶ Testing your patience with the dreaded word problem

You've had so much fun reviewing algebra, geometry, and trigonometry that you simply can't wait to jump right in and practice what you know, right? Well, we don't want you to have to wait any longer to strut your stuff. Here's a set of a dozen math practice questions — give 'em your best shot!

Directions: Each of the following questions has five answer choices. Choose the best answer for each question.

1. $\dfrac{\left(a^4 \times a^3\right)^2}{a^4} =$

    (A) a^{36}

    (B) a^{10}

    (C) a^9

    (D) a^6

    (E) a^4

First, do the operation inside the parentheses. When you multiply like bases, you add the exponents: $a^4 \times a^3 = a^7$. When you have a power outside the parentheses, you multiply the exponents: $\left(a^7\right)^2 = a^{14}$. Finally, when you divide by like bases, you subtract the exponents: $a^{14} \div a^4 = a^{14-4} = a^{10}$. The correct answer is Choice (B).

If you picked Choice (D), you fell for a trap answer. If you said $a^4 \times a^3 = a^{12}$ and $a^{12 \times 2} = a^{24}$, you may have divided a^{24} by a^4 and gotten a^6. If you chose Choice (A), you fell for another trap. You may have reasoned that $a^4 \times a^3 = a^{12}$. Because 12 squared is 144, you may have thought that $\left(a^{12}\right)^2 = a^{144}$ and that $a^{144} \div a^4 = a^{36}$.

All these trap answers are intentional, put there to test whether you know how to perform operations with exponents. If you're still confused about how to multiply and divide like bases, turn to Chapter 7.

2. The ratio of knives to forks to spoons in a silverware drawer is 3:4:5. Which of the following could be the total number of knives, forks, and spoons in the drawer?

   (F) 60

   (G) 62

   (H) 64

   (J) 65

   (K) 66

   The total number of utensils must be a multiple of the sum of the numbers of the ratios. In other words, add 3 + 4 + 5 = 12. The total must be a multiple of 12. Only one answer choice — 60 — divides evenly by 12, so you know the correct answer is Choice (F).

   If you're confused about ratios (supposedly one of the easiest portions of the exam), check out Chapter 7.

3. An usher passes out 60 percent of his programs before the intermission and 40 percent of the remainder after the intermission. At the end of the evening, what percent of the original number of programs does the usher have left?

   (A) 60

   (B) 40

   (C) 24

   (D) 16

   (E) 0

   Whenever you have a percentage problem, plug in 100 for the original total. Assume that the usher begins with 100 programs. If he passes out 60 percent of them, he has passed out 60, leaving him with 40. Now comes the tricky part. After the intermission, the usher passes out 40 percent of the remaining programs: 40 percent of 40 is 16 ($0.40 \times 40 = 16$) and $40 - 16 = 24$. So the correct answer is Choice (C).

   Did you fall for the trap answer in Choice (E)? If you thought the usher first passed out 60 programs and then passed out the remaining 40, you believed that he had no programs left at the end of the evening. The word *remainder* is the key to this problem. The usher didn't pass out 40 percent of his original total, but 40 percent of the remaining programs.

   If you chose Choice (D), you made a careless mistake. The number 16 represents the percentage of programs the usher passed out after the intermission. The question asks for the percent of programs the usher had left. We suggest that you circle the portion of the question that tells you what you're looking for. When you double-check your work, review this circled portion first.

4. A salesman makes a commission of $1.50 per shirt sold and $2.50 per pair of pants sold. In one pay period, he sold 10 more shirts than pairs of pants. If his total commission for the pay period was $215, what was the total number of shirts and pairs of pants he sold?

   (F) 40

   (G) 50

   (H) 60

   (J) 110

   (K) 150

Let x be the number of pairs of pants the salesman sold. The number of shirts is $x + 10$ (because the problem tells you that the salesman sold 10 more shirts than pairs of pants). Set up the following equation:

$$\$1.50(x + 10) + \$2.50(x) = \$215$$

Now just follow these steps to solve for x:

1. **Multiply:** $1.50x + 15 + 2.50x = 215$

2. **Combine like terms:** $4.00x + 15 = 215$

3. **Isolate the x on one side:** $4.00x = 215 - 15$

4. **Subtract:** $4.00x = 200$

5. **Divide:** $x = 200 \div 4$, or $x = 50$

If you answered with Choice (G), you fell for the trap answer (after all that hard work)! Remember to go back and reread what the question is asking for. In this case, it wants to know the total number of pants and shirts sold. So you're not done working yet. If x (which equals 50) is the number of pairs of pants, then $x + 10$ (which is 60) is the number of shirts sold. (Note that 60 is a trap answer as well.) Combine $50 + 60$ to get the right answer, 110. The correct answer is Choice (J).

5. Kim and Scott work together stuffing envelopes. Kim works twice as fast as Scott. Together they stuff 2,100 envelopes in four hours. How long would Kim working alone take to stuff 175 envelopes?

(A) 20 minutes

(B) 30 minutes

(C) 1 hour

(D) 3 hours

(E) 6 hours

The ratio of Kim's work to Scott's work is 2:1. In other words, she does two out of every three envelopes. Scott does one out of every three envelopes, or $2,100 \div 3 = 700$. Scott does 700 in four hours, and Kim does 1,400 ($2,100 - 700 = 1,400$) in four hours. Divide 1,400 by 4 to find that Kim does 350 per hour. 175 is one half of 350. Therefore, in one half-hour (or 30 minutes), Kim can stuff 175 envelopes. The correct answer is Choice (B).

When you encounter a word problem like this one, don't start thinking about equations immediately. Talking through the problem may help you more than creating a bunch of equations.

6. If *DC* = 6 and point *O* is the center of the circle, what is the shaded area in the figure?

   (F) $72 - 18\pi$

   (G) $72 - 36\pi$

   (H) 9π

   (J) $36 - 18\pi$

   (K) $36 - 36\pi$

A *shaded area* is the leftover portion of a figure. To find a shaded area, you usually find a total area, find a subtotal area, and then subtract. In this figure, the shaded area is the total area of rectangle *ABCD* less the area of half the circle. If the side *DC* is 6, the radius of the circle is also 6.

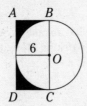

The area of a circle is πr^2; therefore, the area of this circle is $\pi 6^2 = 36\pi$. Be careful to remember that you're working only with a semicircle. The shaded area subtracts only half the area of the circle, so you know you have to subtract 18π. That immediately narrows the answers down to Choices (F) and (J).

Next, find the area of the rectangle. (The area of a rectangle equals length × width.) The width of *DC* is 6. Because the radius of the circle is 6, the diameter of the circle is 12. So *BC*, the diameter of the circle, is the same as the length of the rectangle. To find the area of the rectangle, simply multiply: $6 \times 12 = 72$. Finally, subtract: $72 - 18\pi$. The correct answer is Choice (F).

Shaded-area questions should be one of the easiest types of questions to get correct. If you got confused on this problem, flip to Chapter 8.

7. $5a^2 + (5a)^2 = 120$. Solve for *a*.

   (A) 2

   (B) 3

   (C) 4

   (D) 5

   (E) 6

First, deal with the parentheses: $(5a)^2 = 5a \times 5a$, which is $25a^2$. Then add like terms: $25a^2 + 5a^2 = 30a^2$. Finally, solve the equation for *a*:

$$25a^2 + 5a^2 = 30a^2$$
$$30a^2 = 120$$
$$a^2 = 120 \div 30$$
$$a^2 = 4$$
$$a = 2$$

The correct answer is Choice (A).

Choice (C) is the trap answer. If you divided 120 by 30 and got 4, you may have picked Choice (C), forgetting that 4 represented a^2, not a.

Of course, you also could simply plug in each answer choice and work backward to solve this problem. Here, if $a = 2$, then

$$5(2)^2 + (5 \times 2)^2 = 120$$
$$(5 \times 4) + 10^2 = 120$$
$$20 + 100 = 120$$
$$120 = 120$$

8. Three times as much as $\frac{1}{3}$ less than $3x$ is how much in terms of x?

(F) $9x$

(G) $8x$

(H) $6x$

(J) x

(K) $\frac{1}{3}x$

Working backward in this type of problem is usually the easiest way to solve it. One-third less than $3x$ is $2x$. You can calculate it this way: $3x - \frac{1}{3}(3x) = 3x - x = 2x$. Then just multiply by 3: $3 \times 2x = 6x$. The correct answer is Choice (H).

If English is your second (or third or fourth) language, a problem like this can be extremely difficult to understand. The math is easy to do, but the English is hard to translate. This type of problem is a good one for you to guess at quickly and just move on.

9. The following chart shows the weights of junior high school students. What is the sum of the mode and the median weights?

Weight in Pounds	Number of Students
110	4
120	2
130	3
140	2

(A) 230 pounds

(B) 235 pounds

(C) 250 pounds

(D) 255 pounds

(E) 258 pounds

This question tests vocabulary as much as it tests math. The *mode* is the most frequently repeated number. In this case, 110 is repeated more often than any other term. The *median* is the middle term when the numbers are arranged in order. Here you have 110, 110, 110, 110, 120, 120, 130, 130, 130, 140, 140. Of these 11 numbers, the sixth one, 120, is the median. And 110 + 120 = 230, so the correct answer is Choice (A).

Don't confuse *median* with *mean*. The *mean* is the average. You get the mean by adding all the terms and then dividing by the number of terms. If you confused median with mean, you'd really be in a quandary, because the sum of the mean and the mode is 232.73 and that answer isn't an option. If you picked Choice (B), you fell into a different trap. You thought that 125 was the *median,* because you added the first and last terms and divided by 2. Sorry. To find the median, you have to write out all the terms (all four 110s, both 120s, and so on) and then locate the middle term.

10. The ratio of the area of △*EBD* to △*ABD* is

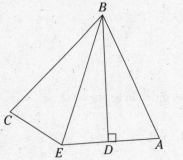

$CE = ED = DA$

(F) 3:2

(G) 3:1

(H) 2:1

(J) 1:1

(K) 1:2

The area of a triangle is $\frac{1}{2}bh$. The base of *EBD* is *ED*. *ED* is equal to *AD*, which is the base of △*ABD*. The bases of the two triangles are equal. The heights are equal, as well. By definition, the height of a triangle is a line from the tallest point perpendicular to the base. If the triangles have the same base and the same height, the ratio of their areas is 1:1. So the correct answer is Choice (J).

11.
$$\begin{array}{r} 95c5 \\ +3cbc \\ \hline ab3a2 \end{array}$$

Solve for the sum of $a + b + c$.

(A) 15

(B) 14

(C) 13

(D) 12

(E) 11

If you're rushed for time, this problem is a good one to guess at quickly. Remember that the ACT doesn't assess a penalty for wrong answers. Never leave an answer blank. Even a wild guess is worthwhile. However, if you do a few of these practice problems, you'll be surprised at how quickly you can get them right.

Don't panic. This problem is much easier than it appears. Start with the right-hand column, the ones or units column: $5 + c = 2$. You know that the 2 must be a 12 instead of just a 2 because you can't add a positive number to 5 and get 2, which means $c = 7$. Jot down $c = 7$.

When you carry the 1 to the tens column, you get $1 + 7$, which is 8, and $8 + b = a$. You don't know a yet . . . or do you? Go to the far-left column (the thousands column). If the answer is $ab3a2$, the variable a must equal 1. You can't add two four-digit numbers and get 20,000-something. The most you can get would be 10,000-something (for example, 9,999 + 9,999 = 19,998). Now you know that a is 1. Jot down $a = 1$.

Go back to the tens column: $1 + 7 = 8$ and $8 + b = 11$ (it can't be 1; it must be 11). Therefore, $b = 3$. Carry the 1 to the hundreds column: $1 + 5 = 6$ and $6 + c$ (which is 7) = 13. Yes, this is true — a good check. Carry the 1 to the next column: $1 + 9 = 10$ and $10 + 3$ is 13, which is what we said ab was in the first place. Therefore, $c = 7$, $b = 3$, $a = 1$, and $7 + 3 + 1 = 11$. The correct answer is Choice (E).

The most common mistake that students make on this type of problem is forgetting to carry the 1 to the next column. Double-check that you have done so.

12. $3\beta4 = \frac{1}{3} + \frac{1}{4}$. Solve for $\frac{2}{15}\beta\frac{2}{18}$.

   (F) 14

   (G) 14.5

   (H) 15

   (J) 16

   (K) 16.5

This problem is a symbolism problem, one that you should think through in words instead of heading for an equation. The symbol β indicates that you add the reciprocals of the two numbers. For example, the reciprocal of 3 is $\frac{1}{3}$, and the reciprocal of 4 is $\frac{1}{4}$. Therefore, add the reciprocals of $\frac{2}{15}$ and $\frac{2}{18}$: $\frac{15}{2} + \frac{18}{2} = \frac{33}{2} = 16.5$. The correct answer is Choice (K).

The β has this meaning for this problem only. The meanings of symbols vary from problem to problem; always read the problems carefully.

Part IV

Time to Read the Riot ACT: The Reading Test

The 5th Wave   By Rich Tennant

"Hey, Al! Do we hyphenate 'Doo Hickey?'"

In this part . . .

How long have you been reading now: 10 years? 12 years? The purpose of this part is not to teach you how to read. We assume that you can sound out the words and make at least a little sense of the passages. Instead, most of the material in this part discusses the types of questions you're going to encounter on the ACT Reading Test and the traps built into them. After you understand the techniques of handling each question type, you get to put the techniques into action with a full-out practice chapter with four abbreviated passages and eight questions.

Keep in mind that the reading passages in the ACT have little connection to the reading passages in the real world, so don't try to use the information we give you here on your reading assignments at school. Learn the techniques we describe here, use them on the ACT, and then file them away under "Been there, done that."

Chapter 13

This, Too, Shall Pass(age): Sailing through the Reading Test

. . . .

In This Chapter

▶ Getting to know the Reading Test passages

▶ Recognizing the different types of Reading Test questions

▶ Eliminating illusion, delusion, and confusion with some tips

. . . .

After working through an ACT Reading Test, a student said, "If I'd known it would end up like this, I never would have let my first-grade teacher show me how to read!" Now, that's just silly. If he hadn't learned to read, he'd be lost on the ACT and other sources of fine entertainment. The first day you spent with your ABCs prepared the way for this chapter, which explains the approach to the third section of the ACT — the Reading Test.

In this chapter, you find out what types of passages to expect and what the questions look like. After you know the ins and outs of excelling on the Reading Test, you'll be glad you learned to read.

Facing Forty Questions: The Reading Test

The Reading Test consists of four passages, each with 10 questions, for a total of 40 questions. Each passage is supposed to be similar in difficulty to materials you encounter during your freshman year of college. The test contains one passage on each of the following topics:

✔ **Prose fiction:** The first passage in the section is a fiction passage from a novel or a short story. Some of the fiction passages are very fun to read. But don't expect that you'll have read them before. In all the years we've been preparing students for the ACT, we've had only one student tell us she remembers having read the passage before in a novel. The ACT test makers obviously don't want to test you on what you're already familiar with (and maybe even have discussed in class); they want to test you on how well you evaluate a passage that's new to you.

✔ **Social studies:** The social studies passage comes after the prose fiction piece and covers sociology, anthropology, history, geography, psychology, political science, and economics. That's an incredibly wide range of topics when you think about it. The history passages are generally easier to understand; some of the psychology ones can be intense.

✔ **Humanities:** The third passage can be about music, dance, theater, art, architecture, language, ethics, literary criticism, and even philosophy. Most students tend to like the humanities passages because (believe it or not) they're actually interesting.

✔ **Natural sciences:** The last passage is what most people think about when they hear the word *science*. The natural sciences passage can cover chemistry, biology, physics, and other physical sciences.

Are you panicking right now, screaming, "I haven't taken physics! No fair!" Not to worry. The questions don't require you to know any particular subjects. Everything you need to answer the questions is right there in the passages, and you can go back to the passages as often as you like.

Timing

The Reading Test is 35 minutes long. Assuming you live to the average age of around 80, the Reading Test is only about 0.000000008 percent of your life. Now that doesn't seem so bad, does it? Because the test includes 40 questions, you need to spend just a little less than a minute per question. Remember that a little less than a minute includes reading the passage as well as working through the questions.

When you're finished with the prose fiction passage, glance at the clock. You should be no more than nine minutes into the section. If you've taken significantly more time than that to finish the first passage, you need to work more wisely (and quickly!) on the remaining passages.

Scoring

You get three reading scores. One is the total score, based on all four passages and 40 questions. Colleges pay the most attention to this score. Then you get two subscores: one in natural sciences/social studies (based, obviously, on the natural sciences and social studies passages) and one in arts/literature (based on the prose fiction and humanities passages). Though you may be interested to see which passages you did better on, colleges rarely put much emphasis on your reading subscores.

Reading strategies

You've probably been reading since you were about 5 years old. It's a little late for us to teach you the basics. But we can tell you how to make the best use of your time in this test. To do your best on this 35-minute test, follow these guidelines as you read through the passages and the questions that accompany them:

✔ **Preview the passages.**

You're naturally going to like one type of passage more than the others. Look for it and read it first, being extremely careful to shade in the correct bubbles on your answer grid as you answer the questions.

What happens if your brain takes a little vacation and you suddenly find you've filled in the bubbles all wrong? Maybe you started off by reading Passage 2, with Questions 11–20, but you filled in the bubbles for Questions 1–10? Hey, you laugh now, but mixing up the bubbles is easy to do, especially when you skip around. The first reaction usually is panic; first you erase all your answers, and then you try to remember what they were. Bad move. Here's how to handle this problem: As you answer a question, first circle the correct response in your booklet and then fill in the bubble for that response on the answer grid. That way, if you mess up and have to erase your answer grid, you can just glance at your answer booklet and find the right answers again.

✔ **Decide on a strategy.**

Some students do well under time pressures and can finish all four passages and the questions in the allotted 35 minutes. Those students often don't have to read slowly and carefully, getting every little morsel the passages have to offer; instead, they can read quickly to get the overall idea. Other students get so totally nervous if they have to rush, they mess up completely. If you're one of these students, a better strategy for you may be to concentrate on reading three of the passages carefully and answering all the questions correctly on them.

If you decide to focus on only three passages, be sure to fill in answers for the last passage. Remember, the ACT has no penalty for wrong answers, meaning that you should guess your brains out. Never ever leave an answer blank.

✔ **Pay special attention to the first and last paragraphs and to the first and last lines of each paragraph.**

Most writers (except writers of literature) pay attention to the maxim, "Tell 'em what you're gonna tell 'em; tell 'em; and tell 'em what you told 'em." In other words, the first sentence of a paragraph or the first paragraph of a passage usually gives the main idea and sets up the paragraph or the passage. The last sentence or paragraph summarizes what the previous sentences or paragraphs said. If you're absolutely short on time, you can often get away with focusing on these parts of the passage. Even if you're reading carefully and have plenty of time, think about these parts carefully.

This tip works best if the passage is a complete essay or short story. It doesn't work as well if the passage is an excerpt from a longer work. Occasionally, an excerpt seems to begin in the middle and end just as abruptly. However, most passages have some coherent format that you can use to your advantage.

✔ **Don't memorize!**

We see some students stop reading, gaze out into the distance, and mutter to themselves, counting off on their fingers. These students are obviously trying to memorize facts from the passage: "Let's see, the three basic elements that make up Kleinschwab's Elixir are . . . ." Stop! You don't have to memorize anything; in fact, doing so can be counterproductive. Although you naturally want to remember some of what you read, you can always go back to the passage as often as you'd like. When you go to the passage for information, you'll find it more quickly if you summarize (not memorize!) as you read.

✔ **Summarize.**

As you're reading, think about what you're reading and summarize it in your own words. Don't make things complicated. A simple "This passage is about the difference between the way the Greeks looked at nature and the way the Romans looked at nature" helps to focus your thoughts and answer those inevitable main-idea questions.

Question: Should you underline or outline as you go?

Answer: If doing so is your normal method of reading, yes. If you rarely outline or underline, doing so now may confuse you. Sometimes students who've been told to underline or outline spend more time worrying about what to underline than thinking about what's in the passage. Highlight key words (especially things like dates, proper names, unusual vocabulary, lists of examples, key transition words, and anything that really confuses you). Occasionally jotting a note in the margin to summarize a paragraph is particularly helpful. For example, next to Paragraph 1, you may write, "Need for elixir." Next to Paragraph 2, you may write, "Failed experiments." By Paragraph 3, you may write, "Success; uses of elixir." You get the idea. You're allowed to refer to the passages as often as you want; having an idea of what is where in the passage can save you precious seconds.

✔ **Look for relationships and connections.**

If the author contrasts two or more concepts, ask yourself what makes one idea different from the others. When a passage compares and contrasts theories, ideas, or techniques, keep track of which explanations apply to each and pay attention to which of the theories, ideas, or techniques the author seems to favor. Perhaps you're given thoughts in sequence. Try to keep track of what comes first, next, and last. For passages that talk about cause and effect, determine how one thing impacts another.

Question: Should you read the questions before you read the passages?

Answer: Skimming through the questions before you read the passage can help you. But you must practice this strategy a lot before you apply it during the test. The key word here is *skim*. Don't spend too much time on this step. Pick two or three questions to look at. Choose ones that are fairly short, don't have line references in them, and don't involve the main idea. (Questions with line references kindly point you to the passage, and the later section "Main-idea questions" tells you how to look for the main idea.) Your goal is to quickly pick up two or three things to mark as you read the passage. For instance, from a question that asks you to "describe the reason the author mentions the boycott of the corporation's products," you would hone in on the word *boycott*. Write *boycott* in the margins. When you read the paragraph about the boycott, star, circle, or draw a line from where you've written boycott to that area of the passage. Keep reading. That way, you'll know exactly where to go to answer the boycott question later.

Of course, you may be better off with the traditional method of jumping right into the passage without looking at the questions first. Try both techniques when you take the practice exams in this book to see which one works best for you (Chapters 20, 22, and 24 contain the practice exams).

Identifying the Different Types of Reading Questions

Although you may encounter many different types of reading questions on the ACT, the following types have shown up frequently in the past. Each of these question types requires a slightly different approach. Main-idea, tone, and some inference questions ask you about the passage as a whole, whereas detail, vocabulary-in-context, and other inference questions ask you about particular portions of a passage. The next sections break down each of these question types and explain how to answer them correctly.

Main-idea questions

A question may ask, "Which of the following is the main idea of the passage?" or "The primary purpose of Paragraph 3 is to do which of these?" You've likely tackled *main-idea questions* like these on other exams. As you answer them on the ACT, keep in mind these three characteristics of a main idea:

✔ **A main idea is broad and general.** It covers the entire passage (or the entire paragraph, if the question asks about a paragraph). Be sure not to choose a "little" answer. The mere fact that a statement is true doesn't mean it's the main idea. Suppose you have a question that asks you for the main idea of a passage about high school education. One answer choice says, "The ACT gives students the heebie-jeebies." No one can argue with that statement, but it isn't the main idea of the passage.

✔ **A main idea often repeats the topic sentence or key words.** If the passage is about Asian philosophy, the correct answer may have the words *Asian philosophy* in it. Don't immediately choose any answer just because it has those words, but if you're debating between two answers, the one with the key words may be the better choice.

✔ **A main idea is always consistent with the tone of the passage and the attitude of the author.** If the passage is positive and the author is impressed by the philosophy, the main idea will be positive, not negative or neutral. If the author is criticizing something, the main idea will be negative.

The best answer to a main-idea question is general rather than specific. If an answer choice for a main-idea question contains information that comes from just one part of the passage, it probably isn't the best answer. Here are some other ways to eliminate answer choices for main-idea questions:

✔ **Avoid answer choices that contain information that comes only from the middle paragraphs of the passage.** These paragraphs probably deal with specific points rather than the main theme.

✔ **Cross out any answer choices that contain information that the passage doesn't cover.** These choices are irrelevant.

✔ **See whether you can eliminate answer choices based on just the first words.** For example, if you're trying to find the author's main point in a natural science passage with an objective tone, you can eliminate answers that begin with more subjective words, like *argue* or *criticize*.

Detail questions

The *detail question* covers one particular point, not the passage as a whole. This question is one of the easiest to get correct, especially when the question gives you a line reference. You just go to the passage and find the specific answer. Some examples include "According to the passage, James confronted Gary about the business when which of the following occurred?" or "The results of the experiments were considered unacceptable because. . . ."

The key to answering detail questions is knowing where the information is in the passage so you can get to it quickly. (Here's where summarizing the main point of each paragraph as you read comes in handy; see the earlier section "Reading strategies" for more info.) Read the question carefully, and keep in mind that the right answer may paraphrase the passage instead of providing a word-for-word repeat.

If you're running short of time or your brain cells are about ready to surrender, look for this type of question and answer it first. You can often answer detail questions correctly even if you haven't read the entire passage. Find the key word in the question (such as *elixir*) and skim the passage for that word.

Tone, attitude, and inference questions

Tone, attitude, and *inference questions* ask you about information that a passage implies rather than states directly. Specifically, they test your ability to draw conclusions from the information that's actually in the passage. You have to read between the lines to find the answers to these questions. For instance, suppose you read a passage about hummingbirds. Information in one paragraph may state that hummingbirds fly south for the winter. Information in another paragraph may say that the Speckled Rufus is a kind of hummingbird. From this information, you can infer that the Speckled Rufus flies south in the winter.

You can usually spot inference questions because they often contain the words *infer* or *imply.*

When you face a tone, attitude, or inference question, look for the choice that extends the information in the passage just a little bit. Answer choices that make inferences that you can't support with what's stated in the passage are usually incorrect. Don't choose an answer that requires you to come up with information that isn't there. Sometimes knowing a lot about a passage's topic can throw you off because you may be tempted to answer questions based on your own knowledge rather than the passage.

Vocabulary-in-context questions

You may have to determine the meaning of a word by its use in context. These questions, creatively called *vocabulary-in-context questions,* are pretty easy to answer correctly because you can use the passage to figure out what the word in the question means.

The only potentially tricky part about these questions is that they may test you on unfamiliar definitions of words that you know the meanings of. Sometimes, ACT passages use common words in uncommon ways. For example, the author may mention that, "Lawrence was unable to cow Michael, despite his frequent threats." Although *cow* usually refers to a four-footed bovine, in this case, the word is used as a verb, meaning to intimidate or frighten. (Don't let the ACT cow you!)

The key to finding the best answer for a vocabulary-in-context question is to substitute the answer choices for the word in the passage. The answer choice that replaces the vocabulary word and makes sense is the right answer.

Exception questions

Most questions ask you to choose the one correct answer, but some questions are cleverly disguised to ask for the one answer that isn't true. We call these beauties *exception questions.* You can recognize them by the presence of a negative word (usually *except* or *not*) in the question: "The passage lists all of the following as reasons that Gary objected to the new model EXCEPT:" When you see questions worded this way, you know you're looking for the one answer choice that isn't true.

Exception questions aren't that difficult if you approach them systematically. Determining which answer choice doesn't appear in the passage takes time because you may think you have to look in the passage for the choice and not find it. But we have a better way to find the right (or should we say wrong?) answer. Instead of determining whether an answer *isn't* true, just eliminate the three true answers. Doing so leaves you with the one false (and therefore correct) answer. Identifying choices that are true according to the passage is much easier than determining the one choice that isn't. Take your time, and you'll do exceptionally well on exception questions.

Tips and Traps

The ACT isn't an especially tricky exam (unlike, say, the SAT, if you're taking it). However, some basic tips can prevent you from falling for the few traps that do exist . . . or from creating traps of your own.

✔ **Be willing to move around when time runs short.** Students often ask us, "Should I do the questions in order or skip around?" Our answer is that, for the most part, going in order is best. However, if you're running short of time, look for the "easier" types of questions. For most people, the easier questions are the detail questions, for which you may just go back and skim for a specific fact, or the vocabulary-in-context questions. A main-idea or primary-purpose question is also a pretty good candidate for doing quickly because you can answer it from your overall impression of the passage or by looking at just the first paragraph. Exception questions can often take a long time to answer because you have to find three statements that are true and then, by process of elimination, choose the one that isn't true.

✔ **Know how to eliminate wrong answers.** Using the process of elimination helps you weed out distracters and focus on the right answer. Sometimes you have to choose the best choice out of three pretty great choices. Other times you must choose from four really crummy options. Common wrong answers to reading comprehension questions include the following:

- **Choices that contain information that the passage doesn't cover:** Even if the information in these choices is true in real life, you can't pick them because the passage needs to be the source of the information. Eliminate these choices no matter how tempting they may be.

- **Choices that contradict the passage's main point, author's tone, or specific details:** After you've read the passage, you should be able to quickly eliminate most of the choices that contradict what you know about the passage.

- **Choices that don't answer the question:** Paying careful attention to the wording of each question can help you narrow down your answer options. For example, a question may ask about a disadvantage of something discussed in the passage. If one of the answer choices lists an advantage rather than a disadvantage, you can eliminate that choice without thinking twice.

- **Choices that contain debatable words.** *Debatable words* are words that leave no room for exception, such as *all, always, completely, never, every, none,* and so on. The rest of the answer may look pretty good except for that unrelenting word.

  Don't automatically throw out every answer that has one of these words. But if your answer contains a debatable word, make absolutely sure that information in the passage justifies the presence of that strong position.

✔ **Don't read more into the passage than what's there.** Many questions are based on information that the passage specifically states. Other questions are based on information that the passage implies. Don't take matters to extremes or bring in background information that you happen to have. Suppose that the passage talks about the fall of communism in the Soviet Union and its satellite countries. You can't automatically assume the author also believes that communism will fail in China. Don't choose the answer that takes the reasoning one step too far.

One final word: Try to enjoy the passages. We know; that's easy for us to say. But believe it or not, some of this reading material is very interesting. If you approach it with a negative attitude, your mind is already closed to it, making the material much more difficult to comprehend and remember. If you at least pretend that you're going to have a good time getting through it, you're much more likely to put things in perspective, get a better handle on the material, and maybe even learn something new.

Chapter 14

Where Are CliffsNotes When You Need Them? Reading Practice Questions

. . . .

In This Chapter

▶ Celebrating diversity: Practicing the various passage types

▶ Distinguishing the time-worthy questions from the time-waster ones

. . . .

On the actual ACT, the Reading Test consists of four full-length passages, each with about 750 words. Ten questions follow each passage. You have only 35 minutes to read the four passages and answer all 40 questions. This abbreviated practice exam (we want to ease you into this stuff slowly) has four shorter passages and a total of eight questions. Don't worry about timing now. Think about what type of passage you're dealing with (prose fiction, social science, humanities, or natural science) and identify each question type. See Chapters 20, 22, and 24 for the real tests, and check out Chapter 13 for everything you need to know about the Reading Test.

Directions: Answer each question based on what is stated or implied in the passage.

Passage 1 — Prose Fiction

This passage is adapted from the Robert Louis Stevenson novel *Kidnapped*.

Line Meanwhile such of the wounded as could move came clambering out of the fore-scuttle and began to help; while the rest that lay helpless in their bunks harrowed me with screaming and begging to be saved.

The captain took no part. It seemed he was struck stupid. He stood holding by the shrouds,
(05) talking to himself and groaning out aloud whenever the ship hammered on the rock. His brig was like wife and child to him; he had looked on, day by day, at the mishandling of poor Ransome; but when it came to the brig, he seemed to suffer along with her.

All the time of our working at the boat, I remember only one other thing; that I asked Alan, looking across at the shore, what country it was; and he answered, it was the worst possible
(10) for him, for it was a land of the Campbells.

We had one of the wounded men told off to keep a watch upon the seas and cry us warning. Well, we had the boat about ready to be launched, when this man sang out pretty shrill: "For God's sake, hold on!" We knew by his tone that it was something more than ordinary; and sure enough; there followed a sea so huge that it lifted the brig right up and canted her
(15) over on her beam. Whether the cry came too late or my hold was too weak, I know not; but at the sudden tilting of the ship I was cast clean over the bulwarks into the sea.

I went down, and drank my fill; and then came up, and got a blink of the moon; and then down again. They say a man sinks the third time for good. I cannot be made like other folk, then; for I would not like to write how often I went down or how often I came up again. All
(20) the while, I was being hurled along, and beaten upon and choked, and then swallowed whole, and the thing was so distracting to my wits, that I was neither sorry nor afraid.

Presently, I found I was holding to a spar, which helped me somewhat. And then all of a sudden I was in quiet water, and began to come to myself.

It was the spare yard I had got hold of, and I was amazed to see how far I had traveled from
(25) the brig. I hailed her indeed; but it was plain she was already out of cry. She was still holding together; but whether or not they had yet launched the boat, I was too far off and too low down to see.

While I was hailing the brig, I spied a tract of water lying between us, where no great waves came, but which yet boiled white all over, and bristled in the moon with rings and bubbles.
(30) Sometimes the whole tract swung to one side, like the tail of a live serpent; sometimes, for a glimpse, it all would disappear and then boil up again. What it was I had no guess, which for the time increased my fear of it; but I now know it must have been the roost or tide race, which carried me away so fast and tumbled me about so cruelly, and at last, as if tired of that play, had flung me and spare yard upon its landward margin.

1. The narrator compares the ship to the captain's wife and child to:

   (A) lament the captain's long separation from his family.

   (B) demonstrate the difficulty the captain has keeping focused on his job.

   (C) predict the captain's future madness.

   (D) show the depth of the connection the captain has to his ship.

   The focus of Lines 4–7 is on how the captain is upset by the condition of his ship. To compare his ship to his wife and child is to show how much he loves the ship and, thus, to emphasize the deep attachment he has to the vessel. So the correct answer is Choice (D).

2. By saying that he "got a blink of the moon" in Line 17, the narrator means that:

   (F) he foresaw his own demise.

   (G) he saw the sky as he came up out of the water to get air.

   (H) he was hallucinating as he was drowning.

   (J) he saw the captain with his pants down.

   Line 17 describes the narrator's dunking and near drowning. He was bobbing up and down in the water, going under the sea and then coming up for air, at which point he saw the moon. Make sure you answer the question in the context in which you find the statement; don't use your own common sense. And if you picked Choice (J) — which, of course, would never, ever appear on the actual exam — man, you're having altogether too much fun for the ACT! The correct answer is Choice (G).

Passage 2 — Social Science

Line Multinational corporations frequently have difficulty explaining to politicians, human rights groups, and (perhaps most important) their consumer base why they do business with, and even seek closer business ties to, countries whose human rights records are considered very bad by United States standards. The CEOs say that in the business trenches, the issue
(05) of human rights must effectively be detached from the wider spectrum of free trade.

Discussion of the uneasy alliance between trade and human rights has trickled down from the boardrooms of large multinational corporations to the consumer on the street who, given the wide variety of products available to him, is eager to show support for human rights by boycotting the products of a company he feels does not do enough to help its
(10) overseas workers.

International human rights organizations also are pressuring the multinationals to push for more humane working conditions in other countries and to, in effect, develop a code of business conduct that must be adhered to if the American company is to continue working with the overseas partner.

(15) The President, in drawing up a plan for what he calls the "economic architecture of our times," wants economists, business leaders, and human rights groups to work together to develop a set of principles that the foreign partners of United States corporations will voluntarily embrace. Human rights activists, angry at the unclear and indefinite plans for implementing such rules, charge that their agenda is being given low priority by the State
(20) Department. The President strongly denies their charges, arguing that each situation is approached on its merits without prejudice, and hopes that all the groups can work together to develop principles based on empirical research rather than political fiat, emphasizing that the businesses with experience in the field must initiate the process of developing such guidelines. Business leaders, while paying lip service to the concept of these
(25) principles, secretly fight against their formal endorsement as they fear such "voluntary" concepts may someday be given the force of law. Few business leaders have forgotten the Sullivan Principles, in which a set of voluntary rules regarding business conduct with South Africa (giving benefits to workers and banning apartheid in the companies that worked with U.S. partners) became legislation.

3. Which of the following best states the central idea of the passage?

   (A) Politicians are quixotic in their assessment of the priorities of the State Department.

   (B) Multinational corporations have little, if any, influence on the domestic policies of their overseas partners.

   (C) Disagreement exists between the desires of human rights activists to improve the working conditions of overseas workers and the practical approach taken by the corporations.

   (D) It is inappropriate to expect foreign corporations to adhere to American standards.

The main idea of the passage is usually stated in the first sentence or two. The first sentence of this passage discusses the difficulties that corporations have in explaining their business ties to certain countries to politicians, human rights groups, and consumers. From this statement, you may infer that those groups disagree with the policies of the corporations. So the correct answer is Choice (C).

Did you pick Choice (A) just because of the hard word, *quixotic?* It's human nature (we're all so insecure) to think that the hard word we don't know must be the right answer, but it isn't always so. Never choose an answer just because it has a word you can't define unless you're sure that all the answers with words you can define are wrong. *Quixotic* means idealistic, impractical (think of the fictional character Don Quixote tilting at windmills). The President's belief is not the main idea of the passage.

Just because a statement is (or may be) true doesn't necessarily mean that it's the correct answer to a question. Many of the answer choices to a main-idea question in particular often are true or at least look plausible. To answer a main-idea question, pretend that a friend of yours just came up behind you and said, "Hey, what'cha reading there?" Your first response is the main idea: "Oh, I read this passage about how corporations are getting grief from politicians and other groups because they do business with certain countries." Before you look at the answer choices, predict in your own words what the main idea is. You'll be pleasantly surprised how close your prediction is to the correct answer (and you won't be confused by all the other plausible-looking answer choices).

Choice (D) is a moral value, a judgment call. Who's to say what's appropriate and what's inappropriate? An answer that passes judgment, one that says something is morally right or morally wrong, is almost never the correct answer on the ACT.

4. Which of the following statements about the Sullivan Principles can best be inferred from the passage?

(F) They had a detrimental effect on the profits of those corporations doing business with South Africa.

(G) They represented an improper alliance between political and business groups.

(H) They placed the needs of the foreign workers over those of the domestic workers whose jobs would therefore be in jeopardy.

(J) They will have a chilling effect on future adoption of voluntary guidelines.

Choice (F) is the major trap here. Perhaps you assumed that because the companies seem to dislike the Sullivan Principles, they hurt company profits. However, the passage doesn't say anything about profits. Maybe the companies still made good profits but objected to the Sullivan Principles on principle. The companies just may not have wanted such governmental intervention even if profits didn't decrease. If you picked Choice (F), you read too much into the question and probably didn't read the rest of the answer choices.

In Choice (J), the phrase "chilling effect" means a negative or discouraging effect. Think of something with a chilling effect as leaving you cold. Because few corporations have forgotten the Sullivan Principles, you may infer that these principles will discourage the companies from agreeing to voluntary principles in the future. Thus, the correct answer is (J).

To get this question correct, you really need to understand the whole passage. If you didn't know what was going on here, you'd be better off just to guess and move on. An inference question usually means you have to read between the lines; you can't just go back to one specific portion of the passage and get the answer quickly.

Passage 3 — Humanities

Line Many people believe that the existence of lawyers and lawsuits represents a relatively recent phenomenon. The opinion that many hold regarding lawyers, also known as attorneys, is that they are insincere and greedy. Lawyers are often referred to as "ambulance chasers" or by other pejorative expressions.

(05) Despite this negativity, lawyers are also known for their fights for civil rights, due process of law, and equal protection. Lawyers were instrumental in desegregating the institutions in our society and in cleaning up the environment. Most legislators at the local, state, and federal level of government are lawyers because they generally have a firm understanding of justice and the proper application of statutory and case law.

(10) Lawyers are traditionally articulate public speakers, or orators, too. One of the finest legal orators was Marcus Tullius Cicero, who was an intellectually distinguished, politically savvy, and incredibly successful Roman lawyer. Cicero lived from 143–106 B.C. and was one of only a few Roman intellectuals credited with the flowering of Latin literature that largely occurred during the last decades of the Roman republic.

(15) Cicero's compositions have been compared to the works of Julius Caesar. Their writings have customarily been included in the curriculum wherever Latin is studied. Cicero was a lifelong student of government and philosophy and a practicing politician. He was a successful lawyer whose voluminous speeches, letters, and essays tend to have the same quality that people usually associate with pleading a case. His arguments are well structured,
(20) eloquent, and clear. Cicero perfected the complex, balanced, and majestic sentence structure called "periodic," which was imitated by later writers from Plutarch in the Renaissance to Churchill in the 20th century.

5. *Pejorative*, as it appears in Line 4, most nearly means:

   (A) comic.

   (B) dishonest.

   (C) self-serving.

   (D) uncomplimentary.

Get clues for answering this question from the information around the word. The passage classifies "ambulance chaser" as a pejorative expression. In the next sentence, the author uses the phrase "this negativity" to refer to the act of using pejorative statements for attorneys. Therefore, *pejorative* must have a negative connotation. You can eliminate Choice (A) — even though the thought of an overweight attorney running after a screaming ambulance may make you laugh. Plug the remaining choices into the sentence to see which one makes the best substitute for *pejorative*. The obvious answer is *uncomplimentary*. So the correct answer is Choice (D).

 If you picked Choice (B) or (C), you were probably thinking of words that describe the way that the author says many people think of attorneys. *Dishonest* is a synonym for *insincere*, and *self-serving* has a meaning that's similar to *greedy*. Trap answers like (B) and (C) are why you must read your answers in the context of the sentence. By doing so, you see that *pejorative* describes the expressions that others give to attorneys, not the attorneys themselves.

6. Which of these, according to the author, is a way that lawyers have positively contributed to society?

   (F) They have fought legislation designed to clean up the environment.

   (G) They have proposed laws to make "ambulance chasing" illegal.

   (H) They have taught public speaking skills to disadvantaged youth.

   (J) They have advocated for integration of public institutions.

The author covers the positive attributes of lawyers in the second paragraph, which mentions their contributions to cleaning up the environment and promoting integration. The passage doesn't say anything about the legalization of "ambulance chasing" or teaching public speaking, so you can eliminate Choices (G) and (H). Choice (F) is a little tricky if you don't read it carefully. Because Choice (F) says that attorneys have fought rather than promoted cleaning up the environment, it says just the opposite of what the passage states. So Choice (J) is the correct answer.

Passage 4 — Natural Science

Line Biomes are the major biological divisions of the earth. Biomes are characterized by an area's climate and the particular organisms that live there. The living organisms make up the "biotic" components of the biome, and everything else makes up the "abiotic" components. The density and diversity of a biome's biotic components is called its "carrying
(05) capacity." The most important abiotic aspects of a biome are the amount of rainfall it has and how much its temperatures vary. More rain and more stable temperatures mean more organisms can survive. Usually, the wetter a biome is, the less its temperature changes from day to night or from summer to winter. Biomes include deserts, rain forests, forests, savannas, tundras, freshwater environments, and oceans.

(10) Deserts are areas that get less than 10 inches of rain per year. Most deserts are hot (like the Sahara), but some are actually cold (like parts of Antarctica). Therefore, the thing that distinguishes deserts is their extreme dryness. The organisms that live in a desert need to be able to survive drastic temperature swings along with dry conditions, so the desert's carrying capacity is extremely low. Desert animals include reptiles like lizards and snakes and (15) some arachnids like spiders and scorpions.

Freshwater environments and oceans are also biomes. The freshwater biome includes elements like rivers, lakes, and ponds. These areas are affected by temperature swings, the amount of available oxygen, and the speed of water flowing through them. All of these are affected by the larger climate area the freshwater biome is in, which also affects the biotic (20) components. Algae, fish, amphibians, and insects are found in freshwater biomes. Oceans cover about 70 percent of the earth's surface, so they comprise the biggest biome. Temperature swings aren't nearly as wide in the oceans as they are on land, and there's plenty of water to go around. Therefore, the carrying capacity of the oceans is huge. The density and diversity of organisms isn't quite as high as in the tropical rain forest, but the (25) total number of organisms in the oceans is much bigger than all of the terrestrial biomes put together.

7. According to the passage, an accurate definition of "carrying capacity" of a biome would be:

   (A) the number and variety of living organisms it has.

   (B) the type of abiotic features it has.

   (C) its level of humidity.

   (D) how much its temperatures vary.

The first paragraph defines "carrying capacity" as the density and diversity of a biome's components. A good paraphrase for this definition is the number and variety of organisms, or Choice (A). The other answers refer to other characteristics of a biome that appear in the passage but don't define carrying capacity.

Don't immediately pick an answer choice just because you see it mentioned in the passage. The correct answer must apply specifically to the question being asked.

8. According to the passage, all of these elements affect the quality of a freshwater environment EXCEPT:

   (F) oxygen levels.

   (G) swings in temperature.

   (H) the larger climate in which it exists.

   (J) the policies of the country in which it exists.

The answer to this exception question comes straight from the passage. As you read the passage, mark the last paragraph to remind you later that it deals with freshwater biomes. That way, you know exactly where to go in the passage when the test asks you a question about freshwater environments (or biomes). Lines 17–18 say that freshwater biomes are affected by temperature swings, the amount of available oxygen, and the speed of water flowing through them, so you can eliminate Choices (F), (G), and (H). The passage doesn't cover issues that are unrelated to the natural environment, so the correct answer is Choice (J).

The best way to answer exception questions is to turn the wording around a bit. For example, you can approach this question by asking yourself to choose the answer that states something that *doesn't* affect the quality of a freshwater environment.

Part V
Studying Brain Defects in Laboratory Rats: The Science Test

The 5th Wave   By Rich Tennant

DOCTOR HORBUS OBSERVES THE CHEMICAL REACTION OF SULFURIC ACID TO PROF. DUNSON'S NEW LAB COAT USING A DRIBBLE BEACON.

©RICHTENNANT

In this part . . .

*W*e've had students complain that the ACT Science Test made them feel as confused as rats in a maze, but it's not quite that bad. This part introduces you to the three types of passages you'll see on the ACT Science Test. We explain what they look like, how to approach them, and when to run like heck and leave them alone. We also show you several of the most common questions that follow the passages and help you figure out what traps to look for. Then you get a chance to practice with a mini version of the test.

The material in this part does not — we repeat, *does not* — lecture on science per se. That is, we're not about to give you chemistry formulas or physics principles or biology maxims. That's not laziness or stupidity on our part (although you probably do know more about chemistry, physics, and biology than we do), but rather a matter of focus. The ACT Science Test doesn't expect you to know those sorts of things. The test makers give you all the information that you need to answer the questions right there in the passages themselves.

Chapter 15

From Frankenstein to Einstein: Excelling on the Science Test

• •

In This Chapter

▶ Eliminating brain strain by figuring out what you do and don't need to know

▶ Getting comfortable with data representation, research summaries, and conflicting viewpoints

▶ Identifying the different types of questions as well as the traps built into them

• •

Return your brain to the full upright and locked position. You don't have to use it as much as you may fear for the ACT Science Test.

So relax, unclench your hands, and take a few deep breaths. You are not, repeat *not*, expected to be able to remember the entire periodic table or to know the difference between the substantia nigra and a Lorentz transformation. After all, your grades in science classes appear on your transcript for the admissions officers to read if they really want to assess your science knowledge. The point of the Science Test (which aptly enough used to be called *Science Reasoning*) is to demonstrate that you have an important collegiate skill: the ability to approach novel information, sort it out, and draw conclusions from it. In other words, you don't have to know what a scientist knows, but you do need to be able to think as a scientist thinks.

Too Graphic for Words: The Science Test's Format

The Science Test consists of 40 questions that are based on seven passages (five to seven questions per passage). You have 35 minutes to answer these questions, which means you have about 5 minutes per passage.

Each passage should take you about 2 minutes to read and — at least partially — understand. As you go through the rest of this chapter, and especially as you're held spellbound by the excruciatingly detailed answer explanations to the practice exam questions in Part VII of this book, pay attention to which types of passages require a lot of upfront work and which ones you should straight-arm on your way to the questions.

Plan on allotting yourself approximately 30 seconds per question. You may not think 30 seconds is long enough, but some of the questions will be so easy that you'll answer them in a heartbeat and build up a reservoir of time, which you can then spend on the harder questions. But, of course, some of the questions will be so impossible that you'll want to sue your brain for nonsupport. If you can't answer a question within 30 seconds, take a guess and move on.

The ACT features three basic types of science passages: data representation, research summaries, and conflicting viewpoints. Each passage type requires a different approach to reading it and answering the questions that accompany it.

One of the best ways to prepare for the Science Test is to have a game plan for how you'll approach the passages come test day:

- Recognize which type of passage you're reading.
- Have a strategy for reading or evaluating it.
- Know which types of questions are likely to follow it.

The rest of the chapter provides a brief overview of what to expect and how to approach each type of passage.

The ACT has no penalty for wrong answers. Never leave any bubble blank even if you have no clue what that answer is. Fill in something and hope you get lucky.

The Android's Favorite: Data Representation

Of course, data-representation questions are Mr. Data's favorite, but they should be your favorite, too. Most students tell us that data representation is the easiest type of passage — not coincidentally because it usually has the least text to read. The ACT has three data-representation passages, each with five questions, for a total of 15 questions.

The data-representation questions are based on one or more tables, graphs, or diagrams, which are chock-full of information, and some brief text that precedes or follows them. Read the text so that you can get an idea about what point the tables, graphs, or diagrams are trying to make, but don't get hung up on any complicated terms or sentences. Here's an example of a data-representation passage.

Scientists studied the effect that variations in paraloxin had on the rate of samanity in the species *Braisia idioticus*. The results are summarized in Table 15-1.

Table 15-1	Example of a Data-Representation Table
Paraloxin (microshels)	*Samanity Rate (rics/sec)*
0	14
1	18
2	23
3	27
4	31
5	89
6	90
7	34
8	29
9	24

What? You don't know what paraloxin, samanity, rics, or microshels are? We're not surprised, considering that we just made them up. We're babbling here to make the point that you can get an idea of what the passage is discussing *without* having a clue about what all the terms mean. As you read the preceding passage, say to yourself, "When this thing called paraloxin is changed, samanity rate, whatever it is, may also change. I need to take a look at the table to see if this happens. The weird units simply measure paraloxin and samanity rate."

The actual ACT isn't as much fun as this book is. On the real test, all the science is dull and boring . . . we mean real. But our point is that if you don't know the big hairy terms, they may as well be made up as far as you're concerned. The ACT gives everyone, science geniuses and science morons alike, an equal chance by using unfamiliar science.

International students, this unfamiliar science is a boon for you. Yes, the passages can be difficult to read, but they're just as hard for a native English speaker as they are for you. The terminology is unfamiliar to everyone, giving you all an equal opportunity . . . and an equal headache.

The following sections show you how to approach a data-representation passage and how to answer the different types of questions that accompany it.

Approaching data-representation passages with as little pain as possible

When you encounter a data-representation passage on the test, we suggest that you use the following approach to get through it quickly and painlessly:

1. **Skim the introductory text.**

   Focus on getting an overview of what the passage is about. Don't get psyched out about unfamiliar terms, and don't try to understand every little thing.

2. **Look at the table, diagram, or graph that accompanies the text.**

   Identify what the graphic is displaying (for example, drug dosages, reaction times, kinetic energy, or astronomical distances).

3. **Look at what the columns, rows, axes, and so on represent and determine how they're related to one another.**

   An *independent variable,* or *controlled variable,* is the factor that the experimenter can change to a specific value, such as the amount of water added. The *dependent variable* is the factor that isn't under the experimenter's direct control, such as the amount of energy released. In other words, the dependent variable is dependent on the independent variable.

   The most typical relationship between columns, rows, axes, and so on is one in which one column, row, axis, and so on presents values for the independent, or controlled, variable and another shows what happens to the dependent variable. Figure 15-1 presents a classic relationship.

   Here, the amount of growth factor added is the independent variable, and the plant height is the dependent variable. The experimenter can't directly manipulate plant height. He or she can add a certain amount of growth factor but then has no choice but to wait and see what happens to the plant height.

   The ability to distinguish the independent from the dependent variable is essential for understanding many data-representation passages. You may even get a question directly asking about this distinction.

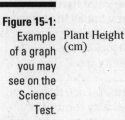

Figure 15-1:
Example
of a graph
you may
see on the
Science
Test.

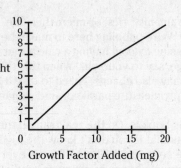

4. **Note the units of measurement.**

   Don't freak out if the units are unfamiliar to you. Data-representation passages always present units of measurement (even the bizarre ones) very clearly. The axes on graphs are usually labeled, legends typically accompany diagrams, and graphs and column and row headings usually include the units.

5. **Look for trends in the data, noting any significant shifts.**

   Take another look at Table 15-1. In the table, you see that samanity increases at regular intervals as paraloxin is gradually increased up through 4 microshels. Samanity rate hits a sharp peak when paraloxin rises to 5 and 6 microshels and then falls to levels comparable to those obtained when paraloxin was lower.

   In the plant growth graph in Figure 15-1, note that for the range of values shown on the graph, plant height steadily increases with increases in growth factor.

   When the value of one variable moves along a graph in the same direction as the value of another variable, those variables are said to have a *positive correlation,* or relationship. In the sample graph in Figure 15-1, plant height and the amount of growth factor added have a positive correlation; as one increases, the other increases also. A positive correlation can also apply to decreasing values; as one decreases, the other variable also decreases. Variables are said to have a *negative correlation,* or relationship, when one increases as the other decreases. The science questions test you on these two types of relationships. You've been forewarned. Now memorize them and conquer!

   Whatever you do, don't waste time trying to memorize the numbers! If a question requires specific details, you can always go back and look at the table for them. Why destroy any more brain cells than you absolutely have to?

Reading tables, graphs, and diagrams: The data-analysis question

The questions for data-representation passages ask you to perform some sort of data analysis. Don't panic; it sounds scarier than it is. The data-analysis question simply tests your ability to read the table, graph, or diagram and extract information from it.

Use the graph on plant growth shown in Figure 15-1 to answer the following question: What is the plant height when 5 mg of plant growth factor are used?

Find 5 mg along the horizontal axis, go up to the plotted line, and then go left to the vertical axis to read the value, which is 3 cm. Notice that you don't have to know anything about plants. You just have to look at what's in front of you.

What if a question asks you about a point or value that isn't actually plotted (or given) on the table? You can still answer the question. You *interpolate* by looking at the two closest values; in plain English, you just insert an intermediate term by estimating. For example, if you're given Table 15-1, you may be asked for the samanity rate when paraloxin is 1.5. Because the samanity rate is 18 when paraloxin is 1 and 23 when paraloxin is 2, the samanity rate when paraloxin is 1.5 is probably between 18 and 23. Given that the values go up in a regular fashion in this region of the table, you can reasonably say that the samanity rate is close to 20.5 when paraloxin is 1.5.

Along with interpolation, you have to worry about *extrapolation.* As the *extra* in its name implies, extrapolation asks you to come up with a value that's beyond the range depicted in the table or graph. In the plant growth graph shown in Figure 15-1, you probably safely predict that the straight upward line will continue for a while as growth factor moves past 20 mg, the last number presented in the horizontal axis. Therefore, you can make predictions about plant growth when growth factor is 21 mg by extending the line. However, you can't safely predict what will happen when growth factor is 50 mg. That number is far greater than what the graph shows. For all you know, the plants will die from an overdose of growth factor if they receive 50 mg.

Experiments Galore: Research Summaries

The ACT has three research-summary passages with six questions each. The research-summary questions make up 18 of the 40 questions on the Science Test. Like data-representation passages, research-summary passages usually include one or more tables or diagrams. But the research-summary passages are a little more sophisticated. Here, you must pay attention to what the researchers are testing in the experiments and how they perform the studies.

Fortunately, research-summary passages are predictable. You can expect each passage to tell you three important things:

- ✔ **Purpose of the study:** You may be very familiar with identifying the goal of the project or the purpose of the study, as you have probably done so on every lab write-up you've turned in since kindergarten. Sometimes the ACT is kind enough to do your work for you by stating or implying the purpose in the introductory paragraph.

- ✔ **Experimental design:** The passage tells you how the researchers have set up and controlled the experiment or study and provides information such as what apparatus they've used and which variables they've held constant.

- ✔ **Results:** The results are usually presented in the same table, chart, or graph format that we discuss in the section "The Android's Favorite: Data Representation."

The following sections discuss these three concepts in more detail and explain what you can expect from the science questions.

Identifying the study's purpose

The ACT expects you to understand some key principles of why the researchers created the experiment in the first place. But don't worry! Identifying the purpose of the experiment takes only a few seconds. Usually, the purpose is to examine what effect *x* has on *y*. After you pick up on the purpose, you must analyze how the researchers set up experiments to investigate these possible cause-and-effect relationships (see the next section for details).

Following the experimental design and making valid conclusions

A proper experiment systematically varies the factor that is the possible cause and holds all other factors constant. For example, if scientists want to investigate what effect having the flu has on one's ability to perform multiplication problems, a proper experiment would compare people who have the flu with those who do not, while keeping the groups equal in terms of such factors as age, mathematical ability, and the presence of psychological disorders. If the groups differ in one or more of these other factors, the researchers can't be certain that any observed difference in multiplication performance was a result of the flu. For instance, what would you think if the nonflu group, which consisted of 12-year-olds, did better on multiplication than the flu group, which consisted of 8-year-olds? You couldn't be certain whether age or the flu virus accounted for the difference.

Defective experimental designs, in which experimenters don't include proper controls, produce limited results. Some studies, by their very nature, can't adhere to an ideal experimental design. For example, if a scientist suspected that 2-year-olds who had been vaccinated for measles got more colds than 2-year-olds who hadn't been vaccinated, a proper design would be to give one group the vaccine and to withhold it from another group. However, the experimenters can't just keep one group of kids unvaccinated (mothers tend to get cranky when you make their kids sick "in the best interests of science"). Instead, the experimenters would have to try to collect data on how frequently the children came down with colds before they were immunized (children aren't immunized against measles until they're at least 1 year old) and perhaps collect data about children who haven't been vaccinated from kids whose parents have voluntarily kept them from vaccinations because of religious beliefs or allergies.

When an experiment lacks certain controls, take note of how the experiment's results are limited as you read the passage. A test question may ask you to come up with a good control. If you've already noted the limitation, you can quickly say what should've been done. If a question asks you what conclusions you can make, be very cautious. Coming up with definitive conclusions is hard to do when an experiment doesn't have proper controls.

The different studies presented in a research-summary passage may differ in terms of what factor the experimenters are manipulating. For example, one study may look at how flu affects multiplication ability or how multiplication ability varies according to the child's age. Another study may examine what dependent variable is being measured (multiplication drills in one study, word problems involving multiplication in the other). Identify the key way in which the studies differ. You may want to write some very brief notes in the margin to help you keep everything straight.

Although the studies you see on the ACT may differ somewhat, they're all designed to answer a key question stated in the purpose. Read each study with an eye toward how it addresses the big picture.

Knowing what research-summary questions want to know

Some of the research-summary questions are similar to the data-analysis questions we discuss in the section "Reading tables, graphs, and diagrams: The data-analysis question." The following question styles are also typical for research-summary passages:

  ✔ **Experiment-design questions:** These questions test your ability to follow the logic of the experimental design itself. Why or how was the experiment designed? What was the purpose of choosing one variable or one control?

✔ **Result/conclusion questions:** These questions ask you about the experiment's results; go figure! As you answer result/conclusion questions, be sure to pay attention to the question stem. If a question asks you about what you can conclude in Experiment 1 about the effects of one factor on the dependent variable, don't spend a lot of time searching through the information for Experiments 2 and 3.

When answering result/conclusion questions, be careful not to go overboard. Suppose that the study about the flu and multiplication (which we describe in the preceding section) showed that the flu group made substantially more errors on a multiplication drill than the nonflu group did. (For this example, assume that the study controlled for other factors.) Here's an example of a correct way of thinking about this experiment's results:

- *Question:* Which of the following statements is consistent with the study?

- *Answer:* The flu impaired the ability of the students studied to perform multiplication drills.

    Notice that this question asks for something probable, not a big, sweeping conclusion. You're not going out on a limb by saying that the flu seemed to have an effect. The study didn't prove that the flu was the definite cause of the multiplication difficulties, but the statement certainly follows from the data presented.

Now for an example of going too far (remember that this answer is *wrong!*):

- *Question:* What can be concluded about the effects of the flu?

- *Answer:* The flu impairs mathematical functioning by interfering with connections in the brain.

    Did the study investigate how the flu changed brain functioning? No! The study investigated multiplication drills. "Mathematical functioning" is much too broad a topic.

✔ **Additional-result questions:** The results of one study may have an effect on another study. When you come up against an additional-result question (one that presents you with a new set of results from a different but related experiment), your job is to determine how these new results fit into what you already know. Do the new results confirm what the initial studies showed, or are they in conflict? If they don't invalidate what you concluded earlier (from the initial experiments), do they limit what you can conclude? Perhaps the results of the flu and multiplication study investigated only children of elementary school age. If a question gives you the additional information that researchers observed no difference between the flu and nonflu groups when they studied high school students, you have to limit your conclusion about the flu's impairing-multiplication ability to a group of younger children. If the results with high school students were similar to the results with elementary school children, then you may generalize your conclusions to include a wider range of students.

Warring Factions: Conflicting Viewpoints

The ACT has one conflicting-viewpoints passage with seven questions. The conflicting-viewpoints passage is easy to recognize because it has two major portions of text with headings like "Scientist 1" and "Scientist 2" or "extinction by meteorites" and "extinction by natural selection." (Research-summary passages have headings, too, but their headings are almost always "Experiment 1, 2, 3" or "Study 1, 2, 3.")

The following sections show you how to tackle the conflicting-viewpoints passage and the questions that go with it.

Devising your plan of attack

The conflicting-viewpoints passage, as its title indicates, presents two different explanations about the same scientific situation. When you come up against such a passage on the Science Test, use the following approach to work through it:

1. **Read the introduction.**

   Find out what phenomenon the two viewpoints are debating. Maybe the scientists disagree on whether objects can travel faster than the speed of light or whether other planets in the solar system could support life.

2. **Read the first viewpoint and make some kind of brief notation (using your own words) about the author's main idea.**

   This main idea expresses the scientist's position on the situation discussed in the passage's introduction. Noting this main idea early on is important because you need to be able to identify, for example, that Scientist 1 says "pro" while Scientist 2 says "con." You don't want to become engrossed in a question that asks you to support Scientist 1 and forget that he or she took the "pro" side. (And yes, sometimes your notes to yourself *should* be as succinct as "pro" and "con" or "yes" and "no." The shorter the note, the less time you have to spend writing it.)

3. **Identify the evidence that the first scientist uses to support his or her main idea.**

   Does the evidence support the main idea, or is the scientist making a leap of faith? This "leap of faith" is called an *assumption*. Questionable assumptions open up the door for the other scientist to dispute the first scientist's argument and come up with an explanation of his or her own.

   Assumptions are usually pretty sneaky and can be well disguised. Suppose, for example, that the scientist claims that pandas are carnivores. He or she backs this up by showing that bears are carnivores. Do you see a gap between the main idea and the evidence? Evidence shows that *bears* are carnivores, but is that enough to say that *pandas* are carnivores? You can do so only if you assume that pandas are bears, which may or may not be true.

4. **Identify and analyze the second scientist's point of view.**

   After you finish with the first viewpoint, follow Steps 2 and 3 to identify and analyze the second viewpoint. Usually the second viewpoint is easier to follow because it's so predictable. The main idea of the second scientist is a statement that directly opposes the main idea of the first scientist.

   The evidence used in the second viewpoint may be different from the evidence used in the first viewpoint, but it may also be the same. The key difference lies in how the second scientist interprets the evidence. Don't look exclusively for differences between the two viewpoints. The ACT may throw in some similarities to see if you're paying attention.

When you're dealing with a conflicting-viewpoints passage, your job is to follow the logic of each viewpoint. Don't try to decide which viewpoint is correct. No one cares — not the ACT, not the college admissions office, and certainly not you. In fact, the ACT sometimes presents a viewpoint that's clearly false. For example, one scientist may claim that evolution takes place as a result of the inheritance of *acquired* characteristics. You know that this viewpoint is wrong. Think about it: If you gnaw your fingernails down to the bone worrying about the ACT, it doesn't follow that someday your children will be born with no fingernails! Again, worry only about the logic of the viewpoint, not whether it's right or wrong.

Bonus: Are you an onychophagist? Don't start fretting yet! It's not as serious as it sounds. *Onychophagia* is merely nail biting. The next time you want to get out of going to school, tell your mom that you're suffering from onychophagia. She may be too embarrassed to ask what it is and let you stay home.

Working through the conflict to find the right answer: Question styles

The questions in the conflicting-viewpoints passages are similar to the other two question types. If the scientific viewpoints relate to charts and graphs, the questions will ask you to analyze them. If the viewpoints regard interpretations of a particular experiment, you'll see questions about the way the experiment is designed and be asked to evaluate the results from the perspective of either scientist. Therefore, it's very important to keep track of each scientist's point of view. A couple of other question types that you don't see in the other two passage types appear for conflicting-viewpoints passages:

- ✔ **Comparing viewpoints:** These questions ask you to pick the answer that contains a statement on which both scientists would agree. The correct answers to these questions usually concern a fundamental concept of the scientific study or theory, something basic that each of the scientists can go along with. For instance, two scientists may present different viewpoints on whether Saturn can support life, but they may agree that it's possible in theory for some planet other than Earth to contain life.

- ✔ **Supporting or weakening conclusions:** Some questions ask you to support or weaken a scientist's viewpoint. The best way to strengthen a viewpoint is to come up with evidence that confirms that the scientist's assumptions are valid. The best way to weaken a viewpoint is to present evidence that casts doubt on the assumptions. For example, the assumption we discuss in the preceding section that pandas are carnivores because bears are carnivores is strengthened if pandas are bears. But it's weakened if pandas aren't bears.

Keep in mind exactly which of the two viewpoints you need to address for each question. Some of the wrong (trap!) answer choices deal with the other viewpoint and, as a consequence, don't answer the question.

The answer choices for a supporting or weakening question usually follow a predictable pattern. One choice, the correct answer, supports or weakens the correct viewpoint. One incorrect choice deals with the correct viewpoint but has the wrong effect on it (strengthens when you want to weaken, or vice versa). Another incorrect choice deals with the other viewpoint. Usually this choice strengthens the other viewpoint, so it's there to test your ability to keep the viewpoints straight. Occasionally, this incorrect choice weakens the other viewpoint. Such a choice is tough to eliminate, but remember that weakening (or strengthening) one viewpoint doesn't automatically strengthen (or weaken) the other. The third incorrect choice likely presents irrelevant evidence.

Because supporting/weakening the conclusion questions may be unfamiliar to you, here's an example of how to work through the answer choices for one. Suppose you have a passage about whether smoking cigarettes causes cancer. Scientist 1 says that it does, citing the fact that smokers have a higher incidence of cancer than nonsmokers do. Scientist 2 says that smoking cigarettes doesn't cause cancer, claiming that there's no proof that smoking causes the uncontrolled growth seen in cancer. Scientist 2 explains the association between smoking and cancer as a result of the fact that some people have a certain body chemistry that leads to both a smoking habit and cancer.

The first question asks you to identify evidence to support Scientist 1. Here are some very typical answer choices:

(A) Nicotine, a major cigarette ingredient, has been shown to cause cancer in laboratory rats. (This statement supports Scientist 1's theory and is the right answer.)

(B) Smokers invariably eat a lot of fatty foods, which have been shown to cause cancer. (This statement weakens Scientist 1's point of view by suggesting that another cause is at work.)

(C) Injecting rats with Chemical ABC caused them to seek out tobacco and also produced cancer cells. (This statement goes right along with Scientist 2's suggestion.)

(D) Lack of exercise causes heart disease. (This statement is irrelevant. It discusses neither cigarettes nor cancer.)

You don't care whether the answer choice's statement is actually true or false in the real world. For example, Choice (D), which claims that lack of exercise causes heart disease, may very well be true. So what? It has nothing to do with supporting Scientist 1's statement that smoking cigarettes causes cancer.

Chapter 16

Faking Atomic Ache Won't Get You Out of This: Science Practice Questions

In This Chapter

▶ Getting through the Science Test without blowing up your chemistry set

▶ Sorting through traps and tricks you may see on test day

*Q**uestion:* What happened to the band director when he stuck his finger into an electrical outlet? *Answer:* Nothing. He was a bad conductor!

If your store of science knowledge is so low that you don't even understand this joke, don't worry. You don't need any specific science knowledge to do well on the Science Test. Everything you need to answer the questions is stated or implied in the passages provided. (If you get the joke but don't laugh, maybe your standards are higher than our comedic ability!)

This chapter gives you a research-summary passage with twice the usual number of questions. On the actual ACT, a research summary has only 6 questions, not 12, as in this chapter. We give you double the usual number to give you an idea of the various ways in which the ACT can test the same basic points. For now, don't worry about the format or the timing. Review the material in Chapter 15; then apply that material to the questions in this chapter.

Directions: Read the science passage. Then complete the 12 questions that follow.

Note: To help you get a handle on the passage, we provide a quick analysis before we turn you loose on the questions. We suggest that you read through the whole passage followed by our brief analysis before moving on to the questions. Don't forget to read all the answer explanations after you're done!

Passage

By using electrical recording devices, scientists have shown that many cells in the part of the brain involved with processing visual information respond only to lines of a certain orientation. For example, some brain cells fire when vertical lines are present but do not respond to horizontal lines. Animals that rely on vision must have an entire set of cells so that at least some part of their brains responds when lines of a given orientation are present in their environment.

A major question is how much brain organization is affected by the animal's environment. The following series of studies investigates this possible environmental role in the development of rat vision.

Study 1

Scientists presented lines of various orientations to newborn rat pups while recording electrical activity from the visual part of the brain. No matter what the orientation, some cells fired while others did not.

These pups were able to walk around both vertical and horizontal obstacles without bumping into them.

Study 2

Scientists conducted the same test used in Study 1 on 6-week-old pups that were raised in a normal environment. Results matched those of Study 1.

Study 3

Scientists raised newborn rat pups for six weeks in a completely dark environment. The scientists recorded very little brain cell activity when the pups were presented with a wide variety of stimuli.

These pups had great difficulty navigating around various mazes. They bumped into both vertical and horizontal obstacles.

Study 4

Scientists placed newborn rat pups in an environment in which all they saw were vertical lines. At 6 weeks, none of their brain cells responded to horizontal lines, but their brain cells had more activity than what was found in Studies 1 and 2 when vertical lines were present.

These 6-week-old pups easily walked around a maze of vertical obstacles but bumped into and could not walk around horizontal obstacles placed in their paths.

Study 5

This study was identical to Study 4 except that the scientists exposed the rat pups to only horizontal lines. At 6 weeks, their brain cells showed no activity in response to vertical lines and, when presented with horizontal lines, showed increased activity as compared to the pups in Studies 1 and 2.

These pups negotiated a maze of horizontal obstacles but could not navigate around vertical obstacles.

Study 6

Scientists placed 6-month-old rats that were raised in a normal environment and had normal vision in a dark environment for six weeks. At the end of this time, these rats displayed a brain-cell firing pattern similar to that of the rats used in Studies 1 and 2.

Study 7

For six weeks, scientists exposed 6-month-old rats with normal vision and a prior normal environment to only vertical lines. Results were identical to those of Study 6.

Study 8

For six weeks, scientists exposed 6-month-old rats with normal vision and a prior normal environment to only horizontal lines. No difference was found between these rats and those of Study 7.

Initial Analysis

The passage isn't that bad. The language is a bit technical, but it's understandable. First, try to understand the introductory material, which tells you the point of the passage. Then determine what each study tells you. Don't spend much time trying to understand each study though. Get to the questions as quickly as you can.

The first paragraph basically says that brain cells controlling vision are specialized. Each cell does a particular job. To cover all possible jobs, a brain needs many different specialized cells.

You can grasp a concept more easily if you relate it to something in your own life. For example, think about how physicians specialize in their fields. An ophthalmologist treats your eyes. A dermatologist cures your zits. If you have a zit, the ophthalmologist doesn't treat you, just as a vertical-responding cell doesn't fire in response to a horizontal line.

The question in the second paragraph of the introduction is one you have probably heard applied to many aspects of development: How much of a characteristic is caused by your genes and how much by environment? For example, do you have a dazzling smile because you inherited good teeth from your parents or because you eat the right foods and brush after meals? Can you outrun the Road Runner because your parents are athletic or because you train very hard?

In Study 1, don't sweat the details regarding how the scientists measured the electrical activity. All you have to get from this study is that the scientists came up with a way to determine which cells respond to a certain type of line. The results of Study 1 make complete sense. Because the visual part of the brain has the whole spectrum of specialized cells, the fact that some, but not all, cells responded makes sense. If no cells responded, the animal would have a tough time seeing certain kinds of objects in the world. If all cells responded, the brain cells wouldn't be specialized.

The most significant result of Study 1 was that the cells responded the way they did soon after the pups were born. This result seems to indicate that the rat brain is wired the way it should be at birth and suggests that genes play a major, if not the only, role in determining how a rat brain handles vision.

On to Study 2. Its results make complete sense. If a newborn pup is well equipped to handle its visual world, six weeks of normal development wouldn't change that ability.

So far, no evidence implicates an environmental role in the development of rat vision. Ah, but so far, the experiments have been conducted in normal environments. What about abnormal environments?

Study 3 shows that after six weeks of no stimulation from the environment, the cells in the visual part of the brain didn't function properly. Do not, we repeat, *do not* immediately go overboard and say that a normal environment is necessary for normal responses. Remember that newborn pups had normal responses in Study 1. Instead, play it safe (think like a scientist and don't jump to conclusions too rapidly) and say that a normal environment seems to be necessary to maintain normal response from the visual part of the brain.

In Study 4, researchers denied the pups exposure to horizontal lines. You probably shouldn't be too surprised to find out that their brain cells didn't respond to horizontal lines or that the brain cells, at least functionally, didn't see the horizontal obstacles. After all, Study 3 shows that, when the cells in the visual part of the brain weren't given proper stimulation, they lost their ability to respond. The cells that normally responded to horizontal lines weren't stimulated, so they lost their ability to respond to horizontal lines.

Study 4 also indicates that at least some of these horizontal-responding cells converted to vertical-responding cells. This result provides strong support for the argument that favors environment over genetics. Under certain circumstances, the environment can change what the genes set up. (Using the analogy we used earlier in this section, you can inherit your parents' gorgeous teeth, but if you live on nothing but soda pop and candy bars, those gorgeous teeth are going to turn brown and fall out.)

You can breeze through Study 5. *Vertical* and *horizontal* switched roles and results perfectly. Everything is as expected; zoom on to the next study.

The results of Study 6 may surprise you. As in Study 3, the scientists deprived the rats of visual stimulation for six weeks. This time, however, everything was normal when they tested the rats. At the very least, you can deduce that being 6 months old makes a difference. A good scientist would reason that the visual part of the brain is flexible for at least some part of the first 6 months of a rat's life, but thereafter the wiring becomes somewhat permanent.

Study 7 follows from Study 6. The wiring of the visual part of a rat's brain becomes somewhat fixed at about 6 months old. You can't teach an old rat new tricks.

Finally, Study 8 also follows from Study 6. The environment loses much of its ability to influence the organization of the visual part of a rat's brain when the rat is about 6 months old.

In general, as you skim each research-summary passage on the Science Test, try to summarize briefly to yourself (and maybe even write a short note in the margin) what each study tested and what the conclusions were. Be sure to note the variables tested, such as the age of the rats and the horizontal or vertical lines.

Questions

1. On the basis of Study 1, can newborn rat pups see vertical lines?

   (A) No, because newborn rat pups have brain cells that respond to horizontal lines.

   (B) No, because newborn rat pups can move around horizontal obstacles.

   (C) Yes, because newborn rat pups have been exposed to many vertical lines in their environment.

   (D) Yes, because newborn rat pups have brain cells that respond to vertical lines.

The newborn pups' brains responded the way that you would expect if the rats were to get around in their environment, so the yes answers, Choices (C) and (D), are the most probable. Besides, Choices (A) and (B) give pretty weak reasons for the lack of responses. The ability to respond to horizontal lines doesn't make it impossible to respond to vertical lines.

Choice (C) is illogical; you can dump that choice by using your common sense alone. If the pups are newborns, how much exposure could they have had?

Choice (D) provides a good explanation, so it's the right answer. Because the pups had brain cells that responded to vertical lines, you can logically make the conclusion that the information from the vertical lines gets to the pups' brains, which, in turn, likely allows the pups to see the lines.

2. Scientists place a 3-week-old rat pup that was raised in a normal environment in a maze of vertical and horizontal obstacles. Which of the following is the most likely result?

    (F) The rat pup bumps into horizontal obstacles but gets around vertical obstacles.

    (G) The rat pup bumps into vertical obstacles but gets around horizontal obstacles.

    (H) The rat pup bumps into both vertical and horizontal obstacles.

    (J) The rat pup negotiates around both vertical and horizontal obstacles.

    If a newborn pup can get around the maze and a pup raised in a normal environment for six weeks can get around the maze, then you can logically conclude that a pup raised in a normal environment for three weeks would also be able to do so. Only Choice (J) has a pup that doesn't need a crash helmet, so it's your winner.

    Did you have Smart Students' Disease on this question and read more into the question? If you said, "Yeah, but what if . . ." and started imagining all sorts of horrible and unlikely possibilities ("Maybe the rat OD'd on cheese and staggered around . . ."), you made this problem much harder than it really was. Keep it simple, okay?

3. Scientists place a 6-month-old rat that was raised in a normal environment in a maze of vertical and horizontal obstacles. Which of the following is the most likely result?

    (A) The rat makes no attempt to get around the obstacles.

    (B) The rat negotiates around both vertical and horizontal obstacles.

    (C) The rat bumps into horizontal obstacles but gets around vertical obstacles.

    (D) The rat bumps into vertical obstacles but gets around horizontal obstacles.

    Did you try to answer this question based on Studies 1 and 2? Doing so worked for the previous question because it spoke of an age, 3 weeks, that was between newborn (Study 1) and 6 weeks (Study 2). In this question, the rat is older than the oldest pup in Studies 1 and 2, meaning that you can't be sure that the present trend continues. (Common sense tells you that the trend probably will continue, but you must be able to distinguish between what will probably happen and what will necessarily happen.)

    A more definitive answer comes from looking at Studies 6, 7, and 8. In these studies, scientists gave normal rats that had a normal environment for six months an abnormal environment for six weeks. The rat in this question didn't have to endure an abnormal experience. If the vision of the rats exposed to the abnormal environments turned out okay, then the rat that wasn't placed in such an environment should also be okay. So the correct answer is Choice (B).

    If you were really lost on this problem, you could eliminate Choice (A) right away because it's much too extreme. Answers with words like *rarely* and *infrequently* are right much more often than their dramatic counterparts like *no* and *never*. Because nothing indicates a favoring of vertical over horizontal lines or vice versa, you can eliminate Choices (C) and (D) as well.

4. Which of the following was not under the direct control of the experimenters?

    (F) the length of time that the rat spent in an abnormal environment

    (G) the number of brain cells that responded to horizontal lines

    (H) the age at which the rat was tested for visual response

    (J) the types of obstacles placed in a maze

When an experimental factor, or *variable,* is under the direct control of the experimenters, the experimenters can decide exactly how much (or what type) of that factor to use without having to depend on any intervening process. Choice (F) is clearly under the control of the experimenters. The experimenters can let the rat out of the maze (the environment) any time they want. Choice (J) is just as clear. The experimenters can throw in more vertical or horizontal obstacles at will.

Choice (H) is a little tougher to eliminate. You may think that the rat's age is up to the rat (or at least up to its parents), but the experimenters can decide exactly how old the rats have to be in order to be used in a certain part of the experiment.

By process of elimination, Choice (G) is correct. The experimenters can try to change this factor by changing the environment, but exactly how many cells respond depends on the way the rat's brain is set up and on how the rat's brain interacts with the environment.

The basic science info covered in Question 4 comes into play in many different passages. *Independent variables* — Choices (F), (H), and (J), in this case — are those that experimenters can manipulate independently of any other factor. For example, the experimenter can change the time spent in the dark environment from six weeks to five weeks without changing the type of obstacles in the maze. A *dependent variable* — Choice (G) in this case — depends on what else was done in the experiment.

5. What makes Study 6 important in relation to Study 3?

   (A) Study 6 shows that the effects of six weeks in darkness may depend on the rat's age when scientists place it in such an environment.

   (B) Older rats have more reliable brain-cell responses than younger rats.

   (C) Study 6 extends the findings of Study 3 by showing that longer periods of darkness also change brain-cell responses.

   (D) Study 6 contradicts the findings of Study 3 by showing that, when rats are placed in darkness for a longer period of time, the effect found in Study 3 disappears.

Dump Choices (C) and (D) immediately. Study 6 used older rats (ones that have been alive for a longer period of time), but these rats, as well as those of Study 3, were in darkness for only six weeks.

The ACT tests no expert knowledge. You can answer all questions based on what the passages state or imply. In other words, you aren't required to be an expert on rat brain physiology. Because only such experts know whether Choice (B) is true, you can reject it. Six weeks in darkness doesn't have such a devastating effect when the rats are older. The only answer left is Choice (A), which is correct.

6. Some humans who have suffered brain injuries have been able to recover a lost brain function by having the brain reorganize itself. On the basis of all the rat-vision studies, which of the following humans would be most likely to recover a lost function through brain reorganization?

   (F) a 50-year-old man who suffers a stroke (lack of oxygen to a certain region of the brain)

   (G) an 80-year-old woman who suffers a stroke

   (H) a 30-year-old combat soldier who suffers a bullet wound in the brain

   (J) a baby who has had part of the left side of his brain surgically removed along with a tumor

Calm down, calm down — no one expects you to know exactly how each of these brain traumas affects brain functioning. Everything you need to answer this question is there in the passage. The key is to pick up on the ages. Which rats showed a change from the ordinary response pattern when the environment changed? The young rats. Similarly, a young human's brain is likely to be more flexible than that of an older human. Haven't you always pointed out to your parents not to be so narrow-minded and set in their ways? Choice (J), which features the youngest human, is the correct answer.

If you're almost having a stroke right now arguing with me, us probably didn't notice how carefully the question was worded: "Which of the following humans would be *most likely* to . . . ?" True, you don't know for sure that the baby would have some lost brain function, but all you're asked is which of the answer choices is the most likely (and, no, "a student studying for the ACT" wasn't among them).

7. Scientists exposed a 1-year-old rat that was raised in a normal environment and had normal vision to only horizontal lines. Which of the following is the most reasonable prediction?

    (A) After three weeks, the cells in the visual part of the rat's brain fail to respond to vertical lines.

    (B) After six weeks, the cells in the visual part of the rat's brain fail to respond to vertical lines.

    (C) After six weeks, the cells in the visual part of the rat's brain respond to vertical lines.

    (D) After six months, the cells in the visual part of the rat's brain respond to vertical lines.

Study 8 shows that 6-month-old rats exposed to only horizontal lines for six months still have brain cells capable of responding to vertical lines. This info knocks out Choices (A) and (B). After six months, the wiring in the rat's visual part of the brain seems to be fixed, so you can assume that the 1-year-old rat's brain has fixed wiring.

Be careful of Choice (D). You can't say for sure what effects an exposure longer than six weeks will have. Choice (C) is a much safer (and correct!) choice.

Have you been noticing throughout these answer explanations how often you can narrow the answers down to two choices very quickly? If you're in a hurry or if you're confused, make a quick guess. Remember that the ACT doesn't penalize you for wrong answers.

8. In considering all the studies, which of the following is true regarding the brain-cell electrical measurements and the maze results?

    (F) The measurements and results are consistent with each other.

    (G) The measurements and results are consistent with each other only for newborn rat pups.

    (H) The measurements and results are consistent with each other only for rats more than 6 months old.

    (J) The measurements and results are inconsistent with each other.

When the electrical measurements showed reduced response to vertical lines, the rats couldn't negotiate around vertical obstacles. When the measurements showed reduced response to horizontal lines, the rats couldn't negotiate around horizontal obstacles. The electrical measurements and the maze results always provided the same information regarding what type of lines the rats could handle. So the correct answer is Choice (F).

9. Which of the following studies shows that environmental stimulation can lead to a change in the way the cells in the visual part of a rat's brain respond?

   (A) Study 4 only

   (B) Study 4 and Study 5 only

   (C) Study 5 and Study 8 only

   (D) Study 1, Study 5, and Study 8 only

   Study 1 was performed with newborn rat pups. With such minimal environmental stimulation, this study can't show that the environment has an effect. You can eliminate Choice (D).

   Study 4 looks good. Exposure to only vertical lines caused a loss of cells able to respond to horizontal lines and a gain of cells able to respond to vertical lines. Because the correct answer must have Study 4 in it, eliminate Choice (C).

   Study 5 is very similar to Study 4, except that the roles of the vertical and horizontal lines are reversed. Study 5 shows a loss of cells able to respond to vertical lines and a gain of cells able to respond to horizontal lines. So the correct answer is Choice (B).

   To check your work, verify that Study 8 doesn't work. Study 8 shows that the environment has no effect on 6-month-old rats. This study, taken by itself, lends no support to an environmental contribution.

10. If Study 4 is conducted but Studies 3 and 5 are not, can the scientists conclude that all cells in the visual part of a rat pup's brain require stimulation in order to function?

    (F) Yes, because some brain cells stop responding to horizontal lines.

    (G) Yes, because some brain cells respond to vertical lines.

    (H) No, because some brain cells respond to vertical lines.

    (J) No, because Study 4 does not test whether vertical-responding cells require stimulation.

    This question tests whether you understand that experimental results are limited when only certain conditions are tested. The results of Study 4 indicate only that horizontal-responding cells require stimulation early in a rat pup's life in order to function. Study 4 doesn't establish whether vertical-responding cells require such stimulation because the study doesn't examine what happens to the cells when they're deprived of vertical-line input. So without Studies 3 and 5, the scientists can't justify a conclusion regarding all cells. Eliminate Choices (F) and (G). For all you know, horizontal lines and the cells that respond to them can be special.

    Choice (H) is out because all this study establishes in regard to vertical lines is that the cells continue to respond when given vertical-line input. Perhaps the cells could have responded in the absence of such input.

    Choice (J) pinpoints the limitations of the study and is the correct answer. Studies 3 and 5 did test this factor and allow for a more general conclusion regarding brain cells and environmental input.

11. On the basis of all the studies, which of the following best summarizes the role of the environment in the development of a rat's visual brain-cell responses?

    (A) The environment has no effect.

    (B) Environmental input early in a rat's life contributes to the continuation of normal responding.

    (C) Environmental input can change the pattern of responses throughout a rat's life.

    (D) The environment is the only factor that influences the responses.

If Choice (A) were true, the pups in Studies 3, 4, and 5 would have normal visual responses. Eliminate Choice (A). If Choice (C) were true, the rats in Studies 6, 7, and 8 would show a change in response patterns. Choice (D) is at odds with Study 1. If the environment is the only factor, why do newborn rats show responses to all types of stimuli? This reasoning leaves only Choice (B), which is correct.

Are you noticing and using the wording in the questions and choices to help you choose and eliminate answers? The conservative language ("contributes to the continuation" rather than "directly determines") reinforces Choice (B) as the answer. Notice how easily you can contradict Choice (A), which contains the word *no*, Choice (C), which says *throughout,* and Choice (D), which includes *only*.

12. Which of the following studies would probably add the most new information to the work done in this set of experiments?

    (F) A study identical to Study 3, except that the pups are in the dark environment for seven weeks.

    (G) A study identical to Study 6, except that the rats are in the dark environment for five weeks.

    (H) A study identical to Study 6, except that the study uses 1-year-old rats.

    (J) A study identical to Studies 4 and 5, except that the rats are exposed only to diagonal lines.

Study 3 shows that six weeks of darkness almost entirely wipes out the cells' ability to respond. Perhaps seven weeks would cause a complete cessation of responding, but the point made from Study 3 (namely, that lack of visual stimulation leads to impaired brain-cell responding) has already been established. Therefore, the study mentioned in Choice (F) won't add much.

Study 6 strongly suggests that the response patterns in the visual part of a rat's brain are fixed enough at six months so that six weeks of an abnormal environment have no noticeable effect. If six weeks have no noticeable effect, why would five weeks be any different? Eliminate Choice (G). If the brain-cell responses are fixed by the time a rat is 6 months old, you can reasonably expect that a 1-year-old rat would show the same responses. Eliminate Choice (H).

The study mentioned in Choice (J) would help because it would show what happens to cells that respond to lines that are in between vertical and horizontal. This study would add some information regarding how precise the brain cells are in regard to lines in the environment. For example, is a diagonal line close enough to a vertical line that the exposure only to diagonal lines still allows the rat to respond to vertical lines? The answer to this question would increase understanding of how the environment interacts with the visual part of a rat's brain.

Part VI
Writing Rightly: The Optional Writing Test

The 5th Wave   By Rich Tennant

"C'mon Fogelman—talk! And I don't want to hear any of your nonparallel sentence structures, incomplete sentences, or dangling participles!"

In this part . . .

That's write — er — right! You *do* have a choice with
the ACT Writing Test. The test is optional, so you
can choose between spending an extra 30 minutes getting
writer's cramp or risking having your future college or
university become rather disappointed in you — because
there's a very real chance that they'll require this section
of the ACT. It's up to you, of course, but our advice is to
read the following chapters very carefully and opt to take
the Writing Test. Fear not! We give you the information
you need to put together an essay in record time that will
impress ACT readers. When it comes to choosing the
Writing Test, better safe than sorry!

Chapter 17

What to Expect from the ACT Writing Test

• •

In This Chapter

▶ Making your way to a high essay score by avoiding a few major writing errors

▶ Understanding the ACT scoring system as it relates to the Writing Test

▶ Viewing some sample essays and their scores

• •

The writing portion of the ACT is optional, meaning that you have the choice of spending an extra 30 minutes at the testing center. (How lucky for you!) Although it's optional, many colleges and universities require this section of the ACT, so taking this part of the test is in your best interest. After all, taking the Writing Test and assuming your college is going to require it is better than not having a score to submit. In other words, take the darn test. You have *nothing* to lose if your university doesn't want it and *everything* to lose if it does.

If you're already an excellent writer, which many of you probably are, this chapter gives you the added confidence you need to understand the ACT essay. If you're not the greatest writer, as many students aren't, don't despair. We're here to help. This chapter points out common pitfalls you need to avoid while writing your essay and explains the scoring system the ACT people use to grade your work. It then shows you how other people have tackled the ACT essay to make writing your own essay a little easier. We include sample essays with low scores for you to laugh at (don't worry, we don't include the writers' names) and essays with high scores for you to learn from. Generally, the test gives you a point-counterpoint topic and asks you to write about one side or the other. For information on the format of the Writing Test, see Chapter 18.

Rattling Your Writing with Some Loose Screws

Relax. You've been writing since the first grade, you have something to say, and this test is your way to prove it. All you need is a quick refresher on the basics of essay writing, which, lucky for you, we cover in the following sections. Avoid the pitfalls we describe here, and you'll be well on your way to a winning essay.

Although you may be scared to death of putting your ideas on paper with your name clearly indicated at the top of the page (who likes to be judged, anyway?), stop worrying. Your name is only on the first page, and the ACT scoring folks don't know what you look like.

Writing before you think

If you have no destination, you're bound to get lost. The most important part of your essay is having a strong structure and a clear idea of where you're going. If you put your pen to the paper without knowing what the heck you're going to say, you can bet your bottom dollar that the ACT folks won't know what you're saying either.

Make a quick plan before you start writing, and you'll avoid an essay that wanders aimlessly.

Panicking about time

Writer's block — when you simply can't think of anything to put down — often occurs in stressful situations and is frequently the result of a time crunch. You have 30 full minutes to complete the writing portion of the ACT. That's plenty of time to read the question, organize your thoughts, write your essay, and do a quick edit.

To get the most out of your 30 minutes, we suggest you break them down like this:

- ✔ 2 minutes to read the question
- ✔ 3 minutes to write your thesis and hook
- ✔ 5 minutes to organize your thoughts
- ✔ 17 minutes to write the bulk of your essay
- ✔ 3 minutes to edit and proofread

Notice that we don't include any time for panicking. Panicking takes 30 minutes just to get over, and, by then, your time's up!

Not noticing your time limit

Be aware of your time but don't panic. We know that's easier said than done. But remember that the ACT people know you don't have enough time to write the great American novel. However, they do expect you to produce a good, concise essay in the allotted time — which is why you absolutely must pick a position right away, use your time wisely, and stick to the time schedule. You don't have any time for deep, inner reflection, so don't engage in it.

Using creativity as a crutch

College admissions offices are looking for your creative individualism, but the folks at the ACT are looking for an essay. The ACT Writing Test gives you a *prompt,* or topic, to write about. The prompt is very specific, so now isn't the time to write a novel, a journal entry, or a poem. Although you may think you're being creative and impressive, the real creativity lies in impressing them with your writing skills. The Writing Test is the time to conform to the model of what the test makers want (which is an organized, well-thought-out essay that answers the question that they asked). But you can still throw a dose of *you* into the essay by using unique examples. Just make sure the structure and the language of the essay adhere to formal English standards. Provide what the test makers are looking for to get the score you want.

Using words you don't know

Nobody can be Shakespeare, especially in 30 minutes — not even Bill himself. When writing your essay for the ACT, you don't have the thesaurus button on your word processor in front of you — which actually may be a good thing. One of the worst mistakes you can make is using words that you think sound good but aren't absolutely sure how to use. Instead of trying to use words that you don't know, impress the ACT readers with your thoughts and your ability to communicate clearly. Using words you don't know or understand completely may give the ACT graders a laugh, but you won't be laughing when you see your score.

Being overly critical of yourself

Nobody writes the perfect essay in 30 minutes. Nobody! The graders know that, and you need to, too. Trying to be obsessively perfect does you more harm than good. If you spend too much time critiquing yourself, the ACT graders won't have anything to critique. And the good thing is that you don't have to be perfect to get a high score. You can get a good score in 30 minutes if you follow the suggestions and format in this book. Simply watch your time, stay organized, and express yourself clearly (and in your own words).

Writing like you speak

Everyone knows that speaking is much easier than writing. However, this test is neither the time nor the place to impress the test makers with your street vocabulary. Whatever you do, don't drop it like it's hot, don't think you're too cool for school, don't think you're kinda-like the, like, greatest, or like "ohmygod" this is so cool, or else it's your bad. In other words, you're not texting, you're not talking to your best friends, and you're not trying to communicate on the playground. You're writing for a bunch of old fogies who have no idea what the latest slang means. Stick to words that your grandparents understand.

Not taking a solid stand

Our definition of *wimp* is being indecisive. If you don't take a solid position with your writing, the graders are going to knock you down. You may read a question and think you can justify it in a few different ways, but nobody ever plays for two opposing teams. Don't be scared of picking a side even though you don't believe it. The ACT graders won't know that you don't actually believe what you've written. They only care that you sound confident and that you can support yourself.

Choose your thesis based on the number (and quality) of ideas you have to back it up, and your solid thesis and back-up punches will give you a winning score.

Pouring on too much controversy

The weekend before the ACT, you may be picketing your local politician, participating in a hunger strike for the dying kids in Africa, or living in the trees to save the forests from corporate logging. However, the ACT essay is not a forum for political activism. Remember, the people who score your essay come from all walks of life. You don't want to become too controversial and risk angering the reader so much that it affects your score. Remember that real people read your essay from their points of view and that your score may reflect their counterviews. Steer clear of controversy.

Repeating yourself over and over again

One of the biggest mistakes that you can make on the ACT Writing Test is saying the same thing again and again in different words. Don't try to lengthen your essay by repeating yourself. The test graders get it the first time. If you find yourself repeating sentences for lack of things to say, then you didn't spend enough time planning the essay.

The way to avoid too much repetition is by organizing your thoughts and coming up with specific and different examples to prove your thesis before you start writing.

Failing to edit your essay

One of the most embarrassing things that can happen to you on a perfect first date is having toilet paper stuck to your shoe and having your date tell you about it! Date over. To counteract potential faux pas like this one, make sure that you double-check your shoes before leaving the bathroom — a skill that you can also apply to finishing your ACT essay. (At last, a real-world skill you can finally use.)

Leave yourself time to proofread and check your essay for any obvious sentence structure errors, spelling mistakes, lack of clarity, missing or wrong punctuation, repetition, and illegible handwriting. By doing so, you eliminate any embarrassing toilet paper that's stuck to your writing before your date — or should we say your test grader — notices.

Making the Grade: How the ACT Folks Score Your Essay

You'll be happy to know that you personally get not one, but two, yes two, trained readers who score your essay. And if the first two don't agree, you get a third, yes third, reader all to yourself. Don't you feel special? The ACT guys sure think you are. Not only are you fortunate enough to receive a numerical score, but you even have the pleasure of reading the graders' individual comments on your writing. And yes, those comments appear on your high school and college reports, too. So we better get cracking. . . .

Here's the skinny on how you get your final Writing Test score: Two readers read your essay, and each one assigns it a numerical grade from 1 to 6. The sum of those ratings is your Writing Test subscore (2 to 12). When you choose to write the essay, the ACT people report the score as a combined English/Writing score. The English Test contributes two-thirds and the Writing Test contributes one-third toward that combined score. If you choose not to take the Writing Test, you get only the English Test score. The absence of the Writing Test score doesn't affect your ACT score in any other area.

Reviewing Some Example Essays and Their Scores

The ACT essay receives a score from 1 to 6. The lowest score you can achieve is — get this — a 1, and a 6 is the highest score. One of the best ways to avoid the common mistakes associated with receiving the lower scores is to read examples of all possible scores, which is where this section comes into play. Here we explain what you need to do to get the highest possible score on your essay by beginning with an example of an essay worthy of each score and then explaining why the sample deserves that particular score. Feel free to laugh at the ones with lower scores. We did. After reading these examples, you'll have a much better idea of what to avoid in your writing.

Here's the long-winded ACT prompt that all six of the sample essays were based on:

> In some high schools, many teachers and parents have encouraged the school to require school uniforms that students must wear to school. Some teachers and parents support school uniforms because they think their use will improve the school's learning environment. Other teachers and parents do not support requiring uniforms because they think it restricts individual freedom of expression. In your opinion, should high schools require uniforms for students?

> In your essay, take a position on the question. You may write about either one of the two points of view given, or you may present a different point of view on this question. Use specific reasons and examples to support your position.

 Remember that it doesn't matter which side you choose to write about. Picking one or the other won't matter in the ACT graders' eyes. All that matters is that you pick one side and support your opinion.

1 — 1 is the loneliest number: How not to be a 1

> I think students should have uniforms. There is a lot of gangsters at my school that where there pants to low and I don't really like it. If we had to where uniforms they wouldn't be allowed to do it. Girls should be able to wear shirts that show their stomach though since it looks good and everyone else likes it. There should also be a uniform against really stupid fashion. This should be imposed on teachers too. And principles. I think this is only fair. Why should we have to be the only ones who who have to have a uniform.

Being number 1 may be great for high school football, but it isn't great on your ACT test. This writer answers the question and chooses a side, but she doesn't support or back up her thesis. Not only does she fail to support her position, but she also goes off on a tangent and wanders throughout the essay. Her lack of focus, irreverent examples, and writing style merit a 1. Oh, and by the way, the number of spelling and word errors distracts the reader from her ideas and negatively influences the way the graders look at her essay.

2 — 2 little 2 late: Steering clear of coming in second

> I don't agree with the teachers and parents who think we should have uniforms. Our style of dress is what makes us individuals and sets us apart form each other.

> At my school students who dress in certain ways find others who are like them. You always know who is interested in the same stuff as you by what they wear. Imposing a uniform doesn't allow us to make friendships with people you are like ourselves.

> Uniforms would make people mad. Teachers would find it hard to control all their students because students would want to rebel. Kids wouldn't be able to find friends who are like them and this would cause them to rebel.

> These are just a few reasons why we should not have a uniform at school. There are many more reasons then just these but these are the most important.

To ACT graders, a 2 means you show weak skill in writing the essay. At least they think you have some sort of skill, but you can definitely improve it. This writer answers the question and shows that he can support his point of view, but his lack of organization leaves readers' heads spinning. The writer has paragraph structure in this essay, with an introductory paragraph and conclusion, but he's missing clear transitions between the two body paragraphs. His simple sentence structure lets everyone know that his writing skills may not be as high as they should be. A 2 may be better than a 1, but it isn't a score you should strive for.

3 — Still finding yourself on the wrong side of the tracks

In my opinion, kids should not have a uniform because it takes away freedoms that they should have. There are some clothing styles that teenagers wear that are not appropriate like tight revealing clothes. But to make students buy certain clothes like blue pants and white shirt infringes on their rights.

In America freedom of expression is very important and by forcing us to wear certain things schools are taking away one of our rights. If they start taking away this right, they might start taking away other ones too.

Uniforms are unfair because some families cannot afford them. Many kids would need a whole new wardrobe and their families would have a hard time buying this for them. Not only would they need clothes, but they also need clothes for outside of school. For poorer families this would be hard.

A uniform would take away some of our freedom of expression and it would be a financial strain for poorer families. I think that there should be no uniforms.

A 3 is almost a reason for celebration. Almost. This writer answers the question, gives reasons to support her ideas, and advances her argument. The essay maintains a semblance of structure. She presents a clear point of view with two supporting points that address the language presented in the prompt. Her sentences are more complex than the ones written by most eighth-graders, and she presents a clear conclusion that sums up her points.

However, she's still hanging around on the wrong side of the tracks. The ACT folks are starting to recognize her developing skill, but she still has room for improvement. Her essay would be better if she included a discussion of the counterargument and more fully developed her ideas. Her paragraphs aren't complete, and she doesn't include transitions to link her ideas and increase the essay's flow. Plus, she makes numerous punctuation mistakes. With a little work, this essay could make it to the right side of the tracks.

4 — Reaching 4 a better score

I believe that it would be a good idea for our schools to adopt uniforms. Some people argue that it would restrict student's freedom of expression, but I do not agree with this position. It is important that we have a right to express ourselves, but our society does not allow us to have unrestricted freedoms like this all the time. It is important to learn discipline, show respect for other's feelings and learn how to be successful operating in the real world. School uniforms create a better learning environment and also helps students prepare for their futures.

The most important benefit of imposing dress codes would be creating a better school environment. Students who are trying to concentrate and learn would be unfocused because of inappropriate clothing. Small clothing, tight tops, and sagging pants might be okay for after school but not appropriate for the classroom. Certain types of people might find profanity and obscene images offensive. Art and creative writing are better ways to express your creativity rather than on your clothing. Less distractions in the classroom would help a student to get a better education.

Another important benefit of having uniforms would teach students how to dress properly for different occasions. Clothes that you would wear to a party would not be appropriate for a dinner with your boyfriends parents. Likewise, you wouldn't wear your work clothes on a date. Some jobs in society require people to wear uniforms. Uniforms in schools help students to realize what the world is like and get ready to enter it.

Another important concern for students is trying to fit in. Uniforms take the emphasis off what you look like and put more emphasis on learning.

In conclusion, it is important for schools to require uniforms. Getting an education is the most important thing about school and uniforms take away distractions. Learning how to dress for the real world is also important. And it helps with the pressures of trying to fit in.

A score of 4 would make anyone want to run and frolic through green pastures because the ACT folks think you have adequate writing skills. You may not be the best, but at least you're average and your score is respectable. This writer takes a stance and acknowledges counterarguments. He maintains focus throughout the essay, and he supports each idea in the well-defined paragraphs with specific examples to make the graders happy. This writer demonstrates a simple organizational structure that works; it properly includes an introduction that sets up what the writer talks about in the body paragraphs and a conclusion that sums up his points without word-for-word repetition. This essay shows that the writer has learned adequate writing skills in school, even though he hasn't mastered perfect punctuation or impeccable word choice. (In the second paragraph, *less distractions* should be *fewer distractions,* and switching back and forth between third and second person isn't stylistically pleasing).

5 — Shining brightly: A 5-star winner

There is a debate now amongst parents and teachers about whether or not a uniform should be used in schools. I agree with the position that believes that uniforms will improve the learning environment in our schools. I think a dress code would significantly improve the excellence of our education. First, students would be able to focus on academics rather than the social facet of school. Second, the appearance of the school would improve and third, students would be better prepared for the working world.

The most crucial benefit of requiring uniforms would be to significantly reduce the distractions in the classroom. For students to be successful in the future it is important that we concentrate on the material being taught in the classroom. It is difficult to do this when you overhear students whispering about their newest Gucci purse or admiring their best friend's Prada shoes. Young people place such an emphasis on style and image rather than substance. In addition, students see school as a social venue rather than a learning environment.

Secondly, if the students and faculty are well groomed I believe that it improves the aesthetic appeal of the school. Formal attire is not necessary to achieve this. For example, requiring long pants and a collared shirt would be sufficient. Not only would the school look more professional, it would change the character of the school. Holding students to a higher standard would require them to do it for themselves. It would improve their maturity level as well.

Finally, sporting uniforms would prepare today's youth for the work of their future. A plethora of jobs require uniforms or a standard dress code. I think it is important for schools to not only prepare students academically for their future, but also in proper conduct and grooming. Just because someone has impressive qualifications doesn't mean they'll be hired if they look like they just rolled in from the beach. Allowing students to dress however they choose might eventually be harmful to their future success.

The opposing view feels that a dress code would hinder a student's freedom of expression, but I still think a dress code is a good idea. A dress code addresses the important issues at hand while at the same time allowing the student to find more appropriate ways of expression. It would be different if you could not paint or write creativity the way you chose in school because that would affect your freedom of expression.

In conclusion, I strongly support the idea of a dress code. Not only does it improve our learning environment but it also improves the character of the school and readies the student for a successful future.

A score of 5 gets you a gold star on the blackboard! It isn't ACT perfection, but it's pretty darn close. This writer is able to effectively address the issue by clearly answering the question and by addressing the counterargument. She presents a well-organized and fluid essay with a variety of specific examples. She develops the ideas in each paragraph and uses them to support her argument. This writer explores a cultural component that shows advanced critical-thinking skills and displays a mastery of vocabulary and precise word choice. Some problems with sentence structure and changing from third to second person within the same sentence keep it from receiving a perfect score, though.

6 — Unlocking the code to a perfect score

The trend of inappropriate dress in our schools is causing alarm in our parents and educators. This population argues that wearing inappropriate clothes is distracting in the classroom and interferes with the learning environment. They believe that requiring uniforms would provide a reasonable solution to the problem. Although those opposed to uniforms believe that a dress code would hinder the student's freedom of expression, I believe that the advantages far outweigh this potential disadvantage.

When freedom of expression begins to interfere with appropriate and clear education in the classroom, we have a serious dilemma and the issue needs to be addressed. The current lack of a dress code is not working. We are not breaking new ground when we suggest that the fashion that is spewed upon our youth in the mass media is riddled with sexual undertones. Examples can be seen in every teen magazine, youth-oriented television program, and in the most popular music videos. Further, clothing that advertisers would consider benign, stimulates and raises the hormone levels of every young male, which can be very distracting in the classroom. The only solution to help create an environment where learning takes precedence is to adopt school uniforms. Obviously, a uniform policy would be easier to enforce then a dress code and would bring many advantages to the entire academic population.

First and foremost, uniforms would help students to fight the materialistic world's values. Our society feels that designer labels, such as Gucci, Louis Vuitton, and Hilfinger, create self-worth and that without these, a person is open to cruel comments and non-acceptance. Many students cannot afford to "buy" their self-worth and are required to rise above the standards our society and media feeds them. As a teenager, acceptance is the most crucial aspect of their daily lives, and school uniforms take away the financial burden that our society imposes upon them. Although uniforms must be purchased, this is a minimal financial burden compared to overly high-priced current designer wear that students ask for.

Uniforms could also help curb gang related violence that occurs in many of our nation's schools. Specific colors, logos, and signs have been adopted into the lifestyle of gang members and each carries its own significance. What was once an ordinary red shirt could now be considered an intentional bullet fired in a gang battle. Uniforms decrease the division lines between gangs, as well as protect students who are ignorant to the unwritten laws that govern gangs.

For myself, uniforms would dramatically decrease the amount of time I spend preparing for my day. No longer would I need to delve into the bottom of my closet to find an outfit that I haven't worn this week. I do not need to worry that my best friends might come to school in the same outfit as I, because uniforms ensure that they will! Uniforms give me extra time to finish the homework I haven't done rather than spend time worrying about my wardrobe.

Those who argue that uniforms prevent creative expression are limiting their notion of creativity to fashion. There are many other ways to express creativity. In fact, requiring uniforms may actually encourage freedom of expression. Without the distraction created by questionable clothing, students may be better able to express themselves in art class, through scientific research, and with literary exploits. Uniforms help to ensure a learning environment that is free from distractions and fosters creative expression in areas that are important.

I highly value the worth of uniforms and feel they should be enforced throughout the entire school district. Solving problems in the entire district would help ensure a safer community, save money, encourage better learning, and give students a little extra time in the morning.

The secret to your success on the ACT is a 6, and with an essay like this, you can earn it. The ACT graders are practically drooling over this writer's style, because it recognizes the complexity of the issue, creates a clear thesis, and then supports it with well-thought-out and varied examples. The writer argues his side well and includes arguments from opposing points of view. His structure and organization is logical, and he includes transitions between his paragraphs. His writing displays his own unique wit and personality, and he concludes his essay with a reference to an anecdote in a prior paragraph. Given the time limits, this essay is nearly perfect. The occasional misplaced comma and misspelling of Hilfiger won't concern the graders.

Chapter 18

Excelling on Your Essay: The Writing Test Review

....

In This Chapter

▶ Figuring out what the ACT is looking for in your essay

▶ Breaking down the essay into manageable parts

▶ Exploring the top five editing techniques

....

Writing a great essay is totally different from writing a really great ACT essay. A great essay is one you plan and think about for days, write for days, and edit for even more days. The whole process usually takes a considerable amount of time. But on the ACT, you have to cram all that planning, thinking, writing, and editing into only 30 minutes, and, trust us, that's not enough time to write something worthy of a literary award. But don't fret! All you need to do is figure out what the test makers are looking for; then you can give them exactly that.

If you want to write an ACT essay that pleases your readers, make sure you do all of the following:

✔ **Make a judgment.** Doing so requires you to evaluate the question, decide your position, and clearly articulate it.

✔ **Develop a position.** Establishing a position requires you to explain your thoughts using examples, reasons, and details.

✔ **Maintain focus.** Staying focused requires you to stay on topic and make sure you don't add thoughts that aren't related to the prompt question.

✔ **Organize ideas.** Organizing your thoughts and ideas requires you to present your ideas in a logical way, using transitional words and sequencing your ideas so that they build on each other.

✔ **Communicate clearly.** Communicating clearly requires you to use a variety of sentence structures and vocabulary, and it requires you to spell correctly and make sure your grammar and punctuation are right.

To relieve your anxiety and help you manage the short amount of time you have to write the essay, we break down the essay into manageable chunks. If you follow the steps we outline in this chapter, writing the essay will be much easier than you think.

Keeping It Simple: Making a Judgment

Think of the ACT prompt as a courtroom. You're the judge, and two lawyers are presenting opposing sides to you. They give you their long, drawn-out narratives, practically putting you to sleep, before they finally present the question to you. Your job is to rule on the question, regardless of whether you know which lawyer is right. It's your courtroom. You must make a decision.

The writing prompt presents you with each opposing side in a long statement that addresses common high school ideas, such as curfews, dress codes, magazines in libraries, competition, or the act of compromising your beliefs.

The prompt may overwhelm you or bore you. It may include information that seems irrelevant. But no matter what, the end of the prompt gets to the point and asks you a question. Your first step is to decide which side to write about. You don't really have to believe it yourself; you just need to write about it with confidence. The ACT people don't know you, and they certainly won't go to your house to ask you to explain yourself further. The key to starting a strong essay is taking a strong position right away. Here's what you need to do first:

1. **Read the question.**

   Here's the sample prompt from Chapter 17 (we refer to it throughout the rest of this chapter):

   > In some high schools, many teachers and parents have encouraged the school to require school uniforms that students must wear to school. Some teachers and parents support school uniforms because they think their use will improve the school's learning environment. Other teachers and parents do not support requiring uniforms because they think it restricts individual freedom of expression. In your opinion, should high schools require uniforms for students?

   > In your essay, take a position on this question. You may write about either one of the two points of view given, or you may present a different point of view on this question. Use specific reasons and examples to support your position.

2. **Pay attention to the last two sentences of each paragraph.**

   Typically, the last two sentences in each paragraph of the prompt identify what you need to write about. Can you identify the exact question in the prompt in Step 1? The very last sentence in the first paragraph asks you a specific question, and the last sentence of the second paragraph tells you what to do:

   • In your opinion, should high schools require uniforms for students?

   • Use specific reasons and examples to support your position.

3. **Make a judgment regarding the question being posed by the prompt.**

   Do you think schools need to have uniforms? Or do you think students should come to school naked (just needed to wake you up here — did it work?). Don't just start writing before you decide what your position is.

Fightin' with the Test's Words: Incorporating the Question

Okay, so you've read the question and you've decided your position. Now it's time to write your first sentence. You can go the hard way and spend precious time trying to impress and sound really witty in the first sentence, or you can take our advice and *use the test's words*.

Using the test's words is the best route because it saves you time and guarantees that you've answered the question.

To use the test's words, all you have to do is rephrase the prompt and fill in your position. For example:

✔ **Prompt:** Should high schools require uniforms for students?

✔ **Your first sentence:** High schools should (or shouldn't) require uniforms for students.

Notice that we didn't come up with a single new word! We just moved the word *should* to become the third word in the sentence rather than the first. No brainpower needed here. No time wasted. Easy as pie. Keep in mind, however, that this is the most basic way of writing your first sentence. It may not get you a 6, but it definitely gets you started.

If you want to add a little more you into your first sentence, you can write something like this:

I believe that high schools should require uniforms for students.

Check that out! All we did was add to their sentence. We moved the *should* in their sentence and began our sentence with "I believe that . . ."

If you want to be a bit more dramatic, try something like the following (just make sure you answer the question clearly!):

A debate is being waged among teachers and parents regarding uniforms, and I believe that uniforms should be mandatory for all schools.

Taking the test makers' question and turning it around to use in your first sentence guarantees that you've answered the question. Now you can write more confidently because you know that you've already answered the question.

Putting Up Your Dukes: Deciding Your Position and Writing about It

Agree or disagree; it's that simple. Don't spend time debating with yourself and thinking, "Well, I kinda agree with the agree side but not really because . . ." You have no time for this silliness. Stop thinking so much! Don't you love teachers that tell you not to think? We know we do! Remember that the ACT folks don't care what you really feel; they just want an essay, and they want one in 30 minutes! After you've rephrased the question, just agree or disagree.

Here are two "nevers" to remember as you begin your essay:

✔ Never tell the ACT folks the reasons why you agree or disagree with the prompt in the first sentence.

✔ Never straddle both sides of an issue.

Throwing a Good First Punch: The Hook

Now that you've taken a stand and answered the question, you need to expand your first paragraph. Getting the reader's attention is key to keeping it throughout your essay. You must *hook* (grab the attention of) your reader right from the beginning. Think of the first paragraph as a funnel going from large thoughts to smaller ones.

✔ **The first sentence needs to capture the overall debate of the prompt.** For example, if your prompt is about school uniforms, you may want to write something like this:

> The appropriateness of uniforms is the subject of widespread debate.

Although you haven't yet stated your position, you've let the reader know that the essay is going to be about uniforms. You haven't given up your hand yet, which makes the reader want to continue reading your essay. Good job!

✔ **The second sentence needs to express both sides of the argument.** Representing both sides is easier than you think, because the original prompt gives you both sides of the debate. Reread the second and third sentences in the prompt. Reword them in your own voice and stick those thoughts right after your first sentence.

For example, you may write the following sentence about the uniform prompt:

> Although some people believe uniforms will improve the learning environment, others argue that uniforms may restrict individual freedom of expression.

Even though you're taking only one side, you need to include both in your introduction to show that you recognize both arguments. The ACT graders are sticklers for this point. Your score will be low if you fail to address the counterargument(s).

✔ **The third sentence establishes and expands on your position.** To establish your position, you merely have to state the three points that you'll cover in your essay to support your side and then state your side. These points eventually turn into your essay's three body paragraphs (see the section "The Proof Is in the Pudding: Proving Yourself" for details on writing the body paragraphs.)

For example, you may write the following sentence to take the position for uniforms in high schools:

> Because certain types of clothing can distract students, lead to school violence, and interfere with a student's ability to fit in, I believe that high schools should require uniforms for students.

Alternatively, you could vary your sentence structure by presenting your thesis separate from the sentence that presents your three points that will become your three body paragraphs:

> It's apparent to me that certain types of clothing can distract students, lead to school violence, and interfere with a student's ability to fit in. Therefore, I believe that high schools should require uniforms for students.

Your first paragraph is now complete:

> The appropriateness of dress codes is the subject of widespread debate. Although some people believe uniforms will improve the learning environment, others argue that uniforms may restrict individual freedom of expression. Because certain types of clothing can distract students, lead to school violence, and interfere with a student's ability to fit in, I believe that high schools should require uniforms for students.

The thesis should be the last sentence of your introduction paragraph. Don't give up your hand too early and don't neglect building the suspense.

The Proof Is in the Pudding: Proving Yourself

To create a great ACT essay, you must use specific examples, reasons, and details that prove your position on the prompt. The ACT folks are looking for two things here:

✔ Specific examples

✔ Variety of examples

Using specific examples

To get a handle on how specific your examples should be, consider the last time your parents questioned you about your Saturday night activities. We'll bet their questions included all the old stand-bys: Where did you go? Who was there? Why are you home so late? Who drove? How long has he had his license? You know that vague answers never cut it.

This skill that you've been practicing for years is going to come in handy when you take your ACT Writing Test, because you're already great at giving the specifics (or making them up). Really good examples discuss extremely specific details, events, dates, and occurrences. Your goal is to write in detail and to try not to be too broad and loose. For example, say that you're trying to find examples to support uniforms. You can conclude that allowing students to wear whatever they want leads to distraction among the students. Great, but you need to be more specific. You need to give an example from your life when you witnessed this distraction, or site a relevant article you've read. In other words, give dates, mention people, rat on your friends! Just choose examples that you know a lot about so that you can get down to the nitty-gritty and be extremely specific.

Mixing things up with a variety of examples

Over the past few years, you may have had to come up with a variety of excuses for breaking curfew — the car broke down, traffic was horrendous, the movie ran late, you forgot the time, you fell asleep . . . you know the routine. Again, thank your parents for helping you with yet another skill you can apply to the ACT Writing Test. Coming up with three specific examples about how you feel about uniforms just from your personal life is easy, but it's also boring.

Use a broad range of examples from different areas, such as literature, cultural experiences, your personal life, current events, business, or history. If you spend just a few moments thinking about the topic, you can come up with three great examples from varied areas.

So, to answer the question, "Should schools require students to wear uniforms?" you may come up with three examples like these:

✔ **Personal life:** A scenario where you saw a girl wearing a short skirt and teeny top and noticed how it interfered with other students' ability to concentrate

✔ **Literature:** An example from a magazine article you read about a high school shooting that explains how the boys who fired guns in their school were trying to hurt the kids who looked and dressed like jocks

✔ **Cultural experience:** The concern regarding wearing gang-related colors and logos and the potential implications doing so may have regarding violence in the schools

A nice variety of examples like these definitely gets the attention of the ACT folks and helps you sound like the smart writer that you are.

Hamburger Writing: Organizing Your Essay

Ever taken a bite of a big, juicy hamburger from a fast-food restaurant? Well, okay, we don't blame you for not wanting to see what's really lurking between the buns (even though it tastes darn good). But if you're feeling adventurous (and want to ace the essay part of the ACT), you may want to follow along as we dissect the classic fast-food burger and match each ingredient with a specific part of your essay. Yes, you heard right. Every great essay is organized like a big, juicy hamburger.

No matter what your prompt is, the ACT graders want to see a specific format to your writing. In other words, they don't want all the ingredients thrown in any old way. By following the organization we outline in the following sections, you can give the test graders a super-sized essay worthy of a supersized score.

The top bun: Introduction

The top bun includes the funnel of information that leads to your thesis. We show you how to write it in the previous sections. Now you can move on to the essay's body paragraphs.

The three meats: Example paragraphs

Think of your supporting arguments in terms of three different kinds of meat — perhaps two beef patties and some bacon or a chicken club with turkey and bacon. Each meat represents a separate paragraph in your essay, the purpose of which is to add specific examples that help prove the position that you state in your top bun. (Are you getting hungry yet?)

Each meaty paragraph needs to include the following elements:

✔ Three to five sentences

✔ A solid topic sentence that relates directly to your position (remember, you already wrote your three ideas in the top bun — your thesis)

✔ Variety of reasons, details, and examples that illustrate that specific topic

In the thesis we wrote about the uniform prompt, we said that clothing can be distracting (see the section "Throwing a Good First Punch: The Hook" for more on this sample thesis). You can use that thought as the topic sentence for your first meat paragraph. For example, you may open your first body paragraph with something like this:

Uniforms should be required because a variety of clothing choices can be very distracting in the learning environment.

Now you have to write a few sentences that prove that clothing can be distracting. Make sure that you use specific and clear examples from a variety of sources, including personal experience, history, culture, and literature. Don't stray off topic, or in this case, begin writing about anything other than the fact that clothing can be distracting. In other words, don't get distracted when writing about distraction!

Here's a sample meat paragraph that you (and the graders) can really sink your teeth into:

> Uniforms should be required because a variety of clothing choices can be very distracting in the learning environment. MTV and pop stars flash images of young girls wearing practically nothing, for example, a fashion that most teenagers try to emulate *(culture reference)*. However, wearing skimpy clothes and showing body parts can make some people look and react, which may interrupt an important part of class. That can be quite distracting when you're trying to learn the Pythagorean theorem *(personal experience reference)*. Furthermore, paying attention to the teacher is difficult when you hear people discussing another student's $150 Dolce and Gabbana jeans *(cultural reference)*. A uniform does away with these distractions by enforcing a more conservative style of clothing, allowing the focus in the classroom to remain on education rather than fashion.

Sounds good, right? Well, your essay isn't full, yet, even after a meaty paragraph like the last one. You still have two more meats to gobble down! Lucky for you, you've already decided which topics you're going to discuss in the next two meaty paragraphs: You mentioned distractions, school violence, and fitting in as part of your essay's introduction (see the section "Throwing a Good First Punch: The Hook" for details). You just wrote about distractions in the first meat paragraph, so your second meat is about school violence and your third is about fitting in.

To make things easier, structure the second and third examples exactly like you did the first one by including the following elements:

- A solid topic sentence that defends your position
- A few sentences in which you give reasons, details, and examples that support the topic of this paragraph
- A variety of examples taken from different areas, such as literature, culture, personal experience, and history

Your middle meats also need to address the opposition. In the case of the uniform debate, the prompt tells you that some say uniforms restrict personal freedom. Acknowledge this argument and then show why it's not strong enough to change your position. For example, you could point out that the clothes you wear aren't the only form of personal expression and that the lack of distractions created by uniforms may actually make it easier to express yourself in other areas, such as art, music, and writing.

The lettuce, tomato, and special sauce: Transitions

Like the sandwich, your essay needs to taste good (that is, read well) as a whole. Transitions serve as the special sauce and other burger fixins that help smooth out the differences between your paragraphs. You must include transitions between your first and second and second and third meat paragraphs. The best way to do so is by using transitional words, such as *secondly, finally, another idea, another example, furthermore,* and *in addition,* just to name a few.

The bottom bun: Conclusion

No matter how full of this essay you are by the time you add your three meaty paragraphs and all the saucy transitions, you need to consume the bottom bun before you're done. The bottom bun or conclusion of your essay needs to include the following two elements:

- A restatement of your position
- An expansion of your position that looks to the future

You can address both elements in three to four sentences. Just make sure you include your position, references to your meat topics, and one sentence that pulls everything together. Here's an example:

> Implementing a uniform policy would be beneficial *(restatement of your position)*. Requiring uniforms has the potential to limit distractions in the classroom, reduce school-related violence, and help students find more creative ways to fit in *(references to your meat topics)*. School uniforms would direct the appropriate focus back on education rather than on a fashion show *(looking toward the future)*.

Wielding the Red Pen: Editing and Proofing

With the finish line directly in front of you, all you have left to do is make a quick sprint (or should we say edit?) to the end of your essay. You absolutely must make time to proof your masterpiece. If you don't, your essay score will reflect your hasty goodbye. You're not finished until you've double-checked (and corrected) your writing. This section gives you five quick editing and proofreading techniques that can keep you from tripping before you cross the finish line.

Chapter 4 reviews the basic rules of grammar and sentence structure and reminds you of simple things to watch for when you check your sentences. Being the wonderful student that you are, you've probably already studied that chapter and are now ready to launch straight into editing. If you're a wonderful student who's been a little too busy lately, take some time to go over the grammar basics we cover in Chapter 4.

Staying alert with the touch method: Look for spelling mistakes and ghost words

Your brain is smarter than you think it is. When you proofread, your brain may see your writing the way you intended it to be rather than the way it really is. Your sentences may be missing just a few little words here and there, but, without them, your paragraphs and essay fail.

Use your pencil to physically touch every single word that you wrote. Doing so helps you find words that you omitted, catch simple spelling errors, and locate places where you've repeated words or thoughts. The smallest errors are often the most costly. The three easiest mistakes to catch are misusing *there, their,* and *they're; your* and *you're;* and *it's* and *its*. Touching the words as you proofread helps you outsmart your brain and catch these simplest of mistakes.

Getting a little R and R: Review for repetition

Rest and relaxation come after you've checked for repetition. Before you turn in your essay, be sure to read through it to see whether you've repeated yourself. Sometimes when examples are lacking, writers have a tendency to say the same things again and again, using different words. If you find that your essay reads like one long sentence, you need to spice it up and add some different thoughts.

Calling all action verbs: Be descriptive

You can't score a 6 if readers fall asleep in the middle of your essay. Wake them up by forcing them to read caffeine-filled words. In other words, use bold action verbs rather than mild-mannered, wimpy verbs. For example, instead of writing, "He ran to the store quickly," replace *ran* with *bolted, sprinted,* or *flew.* These words express more action and give the sentence movement. *Ran* is boring. Replacing boring verbs with verbs that create vivid pictures definitely improves your essay.

Avoiding problems with punk-tu-a-tion: Punctuate properly

Rebellion against authority may be your motto on most days, but you can't rebel against grammar and punctuation rules on the ACT essay. They always win. Here are the questions you need to ask yourself when you edit your essay for punctuation and other common grammar mistakes:

- ✔ Did I use the correct periods, exclamation points, and question marks?
- ✔ Did I capitalize the first words of my sentences and proper nouns?
- ✔ Do my subjects agree with my verbs?
- ✔ Did I use commas correctly?
- ✔ Are any of my sentences run-ons or fragments?
- ✔ Are my words spelled correctly?

Handwriting check: Write legibly

You need to get into med school before you can start writing like a doctor. If the ACT graders can't read your essay, how will they know how brilliant it is? Illegible writing is an easy error to catch as you proofread your essay. If *you* can't read your writing, erase what you can't read and rewrite it. Pencils with good erasers — what a useful invention!

Chapter 19

Practicing Promptly with Practice Prompts: Essay Practice Questions

. . . .

In This Chapter

▶ Using prompts to write practice essays

▶ Getting feedback from your parents and teachers

. . . .

In Chapters 17 and 18, you do a lot of reading about writing. But you'll never get better at writing without actually writing — which is why you've turned to this chapter. Here, we give you two sample prompts to practice with, and we suggest that you time yourself so that you get a sense of what 30 minutes of writing feels like. Practicing like this helps you avoid panicking when you take the real test.

Directions: Follow the guidelines in Chapters 17 and 18 and create an essay on each of the following two prompts. You don't have enough space to write your essay in this chapter, so grab some extra pieces of paper. One to one and a half pages for each essay should do the trick. (Just make sure you don't peek at our writing tips that follow each prompt until after you're done writing!)

Be sure to give yourself a good, long break in between essays. When you're done with each one, read through the tips we give you for writing each essay topic and assess your effort. Or, better yet, have your parents or English teacher read your essays for feedback.

Writing Prompt 1

Many successful people believe that a competitive environment fosters high achievement. In high schools, some parents and teachers think that competition between students encourages them to strive toward higher academic potential. Others think that academic competition negatively affects students' performance by causing undue stress and feelings of failure. In your opinion, should high schools encourage a competitive academic atmosphere?

In your essay, take a position on this question. You may write about either one of the two points of view given, or you may present a different point of view on this question. Use specific reasons and examples to support your position.

In this prompt, you have the option of either supporting or opposing a competitive high school environment. The question doesn't have a right answer; what's important is that you clearly and succinctly state and support the position you take.

Say, for example, that you support the concept of competition. In that case, you may begin your essay with a thesis statement about how fostering a competitive learning environment at the high school level is necessary to provide students with a taste of what's to come when they enter the real world. Your introduction may point out that the real world is very competitive and that the purpose of high school is to provide students with a foundation for success. Subsequent paragraphs may argue that many students thrive in a competitive environment and that measures like grading on a curve may encourage students to study more thoroughly and learn more in an effort not to fall behind. You must support your argument with examples, such as a quick summary of Darwin's Survival of the Fittest theory or the fact that the entire college admissions process is one big competition.

Be sure to include a nod to the opposing side. For example, you may explain how some people believe that an increasingly competitive environment in schools creates unnecessary stress at a time when students are still learning and becoming familiar with their own strengths and abilities and that high school is a time in students' lives when they should be able to hone their skills at their own pace, in whatever manner they learn most efficiently. To address this opposing side, point out that students who require extra time and attention may work with a tutor or log additional study hours in order not to be left behind . . . a luxury they're unlikely to see once they enter the far more cutthroat post-school job market.

Your closing paragraph is your last opportunity to make an impression on the reader. Use this paragraph to tie together the key points you made earlier in the essay. Present a succinct conclusion that brings the discussion full circle, perhaps by mentioning that more competitive high school students may become the leaders that help America compete with other nations worldwide.

Alternatively, you may choose to write against fostering a competitive environment at the high school level, choosing to write about how the high school years are the last chance students have to focus on learning by whatever methods are most effective for them as individuals. The rest of life can be likened to a competition, and, as most high school students have yet to reach adulthood, many of them simply are not ready to excel in a highly competitive environment. You may argue that the adolescent and teen years are stressful and emotionally taxing enough without the added stress of competition in the classroom, something most people become more equipped to handle as they enter adulthood.

When you address the opposing argument, you can say that while it's true that the future holds much competition, students will develop an ability to deal with that competition in college. You may note that students aren't required to apply for an education (although they may be in the case of private schools) until they reach the college level, and with good reason: They're simply not mentally and emotionally prepared for that level of competition in early adolescence.

Which side of the argument you choose to support isn't important; what's critical is that, regardless of your stance, you use solid examples and concise arguments to argue and support your case.

Writing Prompt 2

The prevailing attitude in many countries is that leaders must maintain the highest ethical and moral standards. Some people think that this attitude sets a good example for a country and its citizens. Others argue that leaders who show normal, human flaws connect them with their people and thereby enable progress and growth. In your opinion, should leaders always be accountable for high moral and ethical standards?

In your essay, take a position on this question. You may write about either one of the two points of view given, or you may present a different point of view on this question. Use specific reasons and examples to support your position.

In this prompt, you may argue for or against holding leaders to a higher moral and ethical standard than the common citizen. Say that you agree that leaders should be more accountable for their actions than the average person. Your thesis paragraph may state that leaders are leaders for a reason — because they embody the ideals of a given population and because anyone could be a leader if leaders shared the same flaws as everyone else.

Your subsequent arguments may cite examples of elected officials whose poor or lack of judgment resulted in problems for those they governed. For example, you may mention a politician who misused his power or access to government funds to help further his own agenda. You may note that a leader is inherently in a position to serve as a role model and should, therefore, be expected to act accordingly at all times while in the public eye.

You may choose to address the opposing side by stating that, while it's true that all humans are flawed by nature, leaders become leaders because of something exemplary about them. People elect and choose them because they aren't just like everyone else. Therefore, it's acceptable to hold them to a higher standard.

To wrap things up, your closing paragraph needs to echo, not directly repeat, the key points you make in the essay to support your initial argument.

Should you choose to support the opposing side, you may formulate your thesis around the idea that great leaders are a representation of the population they rule, flaws and all. They were chosen for a leadership role based on their ability to relate and identify with the people they govern, and this ability enables them to effectively make decisions in the best interests of their people. Strengthen your argument with real-life examples, such as citing a politician whose moral character is undeniably questionable and yet who is still revered as one of the best and most effective leaders of our time. Or offer a similar example of a leader whose questionable ethics didn't interfere with his or her ability to effectively rule a given population.

Providing inspirational examples of leaders who have been effective despite their character flaws has the added benefit of addressing the concerns of the opposition. You may point out that character flaws don't necessarily weaken a leader's accomplishments and may actually enhance the effectiveness of leaders who acknowledge their weaknesses. Perhaps leaders who are more representative of the common man may inspire others who work to overcome character flaws that they, too, may one day land a position of power and decision making. Plus, people are more likely to see flawed leaders as relatable, approachable figures who are more likely to have the general public's best interests at heart.

Conclude with a few lines that summarize the key arguments you make in your essay and draw a final conclusion as to why moral and ethical equals are the best choice for leadership roles.

Part VII

Putting It All Together with Three Full-Length Practice ACTs

The 5th Wave   By Rich Tennant

EDWARD SCISSORHANDS TAKES UP A HOBBY

"Have you ever tried speed reading without running your finger along the text?"

In this part . . .

It's the moment you've been waiting for: a chance to download all that stuff you've been cramming into your brain.

This part contains three full-length practice exams. We take these tests seriously, and you should, too. Take each test under actual test conditions, sitting in a quiet room and timing yourself. That way, you can get the full mind-numbing effect of plugging through the ACT. Open books are definitely out. (Sorry!) We have spies everywhere. We'll know if you cheat on these tests — you'll hear a knocking at your door one foggy night . . . .

Unlike the questions, however, the answer explanations don't have to be serious; in fact, they're a lot of fun. The chapter immediately following each of the tests provides explanations of the answer choices for each of the questions. You find out why the right answers are right and the wrong answers are wrong. We provide a lot of valuable information in each of the explanations, so we suggest that you read through all of them, even the ones for questions you answered correctly.

Ready? Show us what you can do.

Chapter 20

Practice Exam 1

● ●

You're now ready to take a sample ACT. The following exam consists of five tests: a 45-minute English Test, a 60-minute Mathematics Test, a 35-minute Reading Test, a 35-minute Science Test, and a 30-minute Writing Test.

For maximum benefit, take this test under the following normal exam conditions:

- ✔ Sit where you won't be interrupted (even though you'd probably welcome any distractions).
- ✔ Use the answer sheet provided to mark your answers.
- ✔ Set your timer for the time limits indicated at the beginning of each test in this exam.
- ✔ Do not go on to the next test until the time allotted for the test you're taking is up.
- ✔ Check your work for that test only; don't look at more than one test at a time.
- ✔ Do not take a break in the middle of any test.
- ✔ Give yourself one ten-minute break between the Math Test and the Reading Test.

When you've completed the entire practice exam, turn to Chapter 21, where you find detailed explanations of the answers as well as an abbreviated answer key. Go through the answer explanations to *all* the questions, not just the ones you missed. We include a plethora of worthwhile information, material that provides a good review of everything we cover in the other chapters of this book. We even make a few attempts at lame humor to keep you somewhat sane.

Note: The ACT Writing Test is optional. If you register to take the Writing Test, you'll take it after you've completed the other four tests. For information about the optional Writing Test, see Part VI.

Answer Sheet

Begin with Number 1 for each new test.

English Test

1. Ⓐ Ⓑ Ⓒ Ⓓ
2. Ⓕ Ⓖ Ⓗ Ⓙ
3. Ⓐ Ⓑ Ⓒ Ⓓ
4. Ⓕ Ⓖ Ⓗ Ⓙ
5. Ⓐ Ⓑ Ⓒ Ⓓ
6. Ⓕ Ⓖ Ⓗ Ⓙ
7. Ⓐ Ⓑ Ⓒ Ⓓ
8. Ⓕ Ⓖ Ⓗ Ⓙ
9. Ⓐ Ⓑ Ⓒ Ⓓ
10. Ⓕ Ⓖ Ⓗ Ⓙ
11. Ⓐ Ⓑ Ⓒ Ⓓ
12. Ⓕ Ⓖ Ⓗ Ⓙ
13. Ⓐ Ⓑ Ⓒ Ⓓ
14. Ⓕ Ⓖ Ⓗ Ⓙ
15. Ⓐ Ⓑ Ⓒ Ⓓ
16. Ⓕ Ⓖ Ⓗ Ⓙ
17. Ⓐ Ⓑ Ⓒ Ⓓ
18. Ⓕ Ⓖ Ⓗ Ⓙ
19. Ⓐ Ⓑ Ⓒ Ⓓ
20. Ⓕ Ⓖ Ⓗ Ⓙ
21. Ⓐ Ⓑ Ⓒ Ⓓ
22. Ⓕ Ⓖ Ⓗ Ⓙ
23. Ⓐ Ⓑ Ⓒ Ⓓ
24. Ⓕ Ⓖ Ⓗ Ⓙ
25. Ⓐ Ⓑ Ⓒ Ⓓ
26. Ⓕ Ⓖ Ⓗ Ⓙ
27. Ⓐ Ⓑ Ⓒ Ⓓ
28. Ⓕ Ⓖ Ⓗ Ⓙ
29. Ⓐ Ⓑ Ⓒ Ⓓ
30. Ⓕ Ⓖ Ⓗ Ⓙ
31. Ⓐ Ⓑ Ⓒ Ⓓ
32. Ⓕ Ⓖ Ⓗ Ⓙ
33. Ⓐ Ⓑ Ⓒ Ⓓ
34. Ⓕ Ⓖ Ⓗ Ⓙ
35. Ⓐ Ⓑ Ⓒ Ⓓ
36. Ⓕ Ⓖ Ⓗ Ⓙ
37. Ⓐ Ⓑ Ⓒ Ⓓ
38. Ⓕ Ⓖ Ⓗ Ⓙ
39. Ⓐ Ⓑ Ⓒ Ⓓ
40. Ⓕ Ⓖ Ⓗ Ⓙ
41. Ⓐ Ⓑ Ⓒ Ⓓ
42. Ⓕ Ⓖ Ⓗ Ⓙ
43. Ⓐ Ⓑ Ⓒ Ⓓ
44. Ⓕ Ⓖ Ⓗ Ⓙ
45. Ⓐ Ⓑ Ⓒ Ⓓ
46. Ⓕ Ⓖ Ⓗ Ⓙ
47. Ⓐ Ⓑ Ⓒ Ⓓ
48. Ⓕ Ⓖ Ⓗ Ⓙ
49. Ⓐ Ⓑ Ⓒ Ⓓ
50. Ⓕ Ⓖ Ⓗ Ⓙ

51. Ⓐ Ⓑ Ⓒ Ⓓ
52. Ⓕ Ⓖ Ⓗ Ⓙ
53. Ⓐ Ⓑ Ⓒ Ⓓ
54. Ⓕ Ⓖ Ⓗ Ⓙ
55. Ⓐ Ⓑ Ⓒ Ⓓ
56. Ⓕ Ⓖ Ⓗ Ⓙ
57. Ⓐ Ⓑ Ⓒ Ⓓ
58. Ⓕ Ⓖ Ⓗ Ⓙ
59. Ⓐ Ⓑ Ⓒ Ⓓ
60. Ⓕ Ⓖ Ⓗ Ⓙ
61. Ⓐ Ⓑ Ⓒ Ⓓ
62. Ⓕ Ⓖ Ⓗ Ⓙ
63. Ⓐ Ⓑ Ⓒ Ⓓ
64. Ⓕ Ⓖ Ⓗ Ⓙ
65. Ⓐ Ⓑ Ⓒ Ⓓ
66. Ⓕ Ⓖ Ⓗ Ⓙ
67. Ⓐ Ⓑ Ⓒ Ⓓ
68. Ⓕ Ⓖ Ⓗ Ⓙ
69. Ⓐ Ⓑ Ⓒ Ⓓ
70. Ⓕ Ⓖ Ⓗ Ⓙ
71. Ⓐ Ⓑ Ⓒ Ⓓ
72. Ⓕ Ⓖ Ⓗ Ⓙ
73. Ⓐ Ⓑ Ⓒ Ⓓ
74. Ⓕ Ⓖ Ⓗ Ⓙ
75. Ⓐ Ⓑ Ⓒ Ⓓ

Mathematics Test

1. Ⓐ Ⓑ Ⓒ Ⓓ Ⓔ
2. Ⓕ Ⓖ Ⓗ Ⓙ Ⓚ
3. Ⓐ Ⓑ Ⓒ Ⓓ Ⓔ
4. Ⓕ Ⓖ Ⓗ Ⓙ Ⓚ
5. Ⓐ Ⓑ Ⓒ Ⓓ Ⓔ
6. Ⓕ Ⓖ Ⓗ Ⓙ Ⓚ
7. Ⓐ Ⓑ Ⓒ Ⓓ Ⓔ
8. Ⓕ Ⓖ Ⓗ Ⓙ Ⓚ
9. Ⓐ Ⓑ Ⓒ Ⓓ Ⓔ
10. Ⓕ Ⓖ Ⓗ Ⓙ Ⓚ
11. Ⓐ Ⓑ Ⓒ Ⓓ Ⓔ
12. Ⓕ Ⓖ Ⓗ Ⓙ Ⓚ
13. Ⓐ Ⓑ Ⓒ Ⓓ Ⓔ
14. Ⓕ Ⓖ Ⓗ Ⓙ Ⓚ
15. Ⓐ Ⓑ Ⓒ Ⓓ Ⓔ
16. Ⓕ Ⓖ Ⓗ Ⓙ Ⓚ
17. Ⓐ Ⓑ Ⓒ Ⓓ Ⓔ
18. Ⓕ Ⓖ Ⓗ Ⓙ Ⓚ
19. Ⓐ Ⓑ Ⓒ Ⓓ Ⓔ
20. Ⓕ Ⓖ Ⓗ Ⓙ Ⓚ
21. Ⓐ Ⓑ Ⓒ Ⓓ Ⓔ
22. Ⓕ Ⓖ Ⓗ Ⓙ Ⓚ
23. Ⓐ Ⓑ Ⓒ Ⓓ Ⓔ
24. Ⓕ Ⓖ Ⓗ Ⓙ Ⓚ
25. Ⓐ Ⓑ Ⓒ Ⓓ Ⓔ
26. Ⓕ Ⓖ Ⓗ Ⓙ Ⓚ
27. Ⓐ Ⓑ Ⓒ Ⓓ Ⓔ
28. Ⓕ Ⓖ Ⓗ Ⓙ Ⓚ
29. Ⓐ Ⓑ Ⓒ Ⓓ Ⓔ
30. Ⓕ Ⓖ Ⓗ Ⓙ Ⓚ

31. Ⓐ Ⓑ Ⓒ Ⓓ Ⓔ
32. Ⓕ Ⓖ Ⓗ Ⓙ Ⓚ
33. Ⓐ Ⓑ Ⓒ Ⓓ Ⓔ
34. Ⓕ Ⓖ Ⓗ Ⓙ Ⓚ
35. Ⓐ Ⓑ Ⓒ Ⓓ Ⓔ
36. Ⓕ Ⓖ Ⓗ Ⓙ Ⓚ
37. Ⓐ Ⓑ Ⓒ Ⓓ Ⓔ
38. Ⓕ Ⓖ Ⓗ Ⓙ Ⓚ
39. Ⓐ Ⓑ Ⓒ Ⓓ Ⓔ
40. Ⓕ Ⓖ Ⓗ Ⓙ Ⓚ
41. Ⓐ Ⓑ Ⓒ Ⓓ Ⓔ
42. Ⓕ Ⓖ Ⓗ Ⓙ Ⓚ
43. Ⓐ Ⓑ Ⓒ Ⓓ Ⓔ
44. Ⓕ Ⓖ Ⓗ Ⓙ Ⓚ
45. Ⓐ Ⓑ Ⓒ Ⓓ Ⓔ
46. Ⓕ Ⓖ Ⓗ Ⓙ Ⓚ
47. Ⓐ Ⓑ Ⓒ Ⓓ Ⓔ
48. Ⓕ Ⓖ Ⓗ Ⓙ Ⓚ
49. Ⓐ Ⓑ Ⓒ Ⓓ Ⓔ
50. Ⓕ Ⓖ Ⓗ Ⓙ Ⓚ
51. Ⓐ Ⓑ Ⓒ Ⓓ Ⓔ
52. Ⓕ Ⓖ Ⓗ Ⓙ Ⓚ
53. Ⓐ Ⓑ Ⓒ Ⓓ Ⓔ
54. Ⓕ Ⓖ Ⓗ Ⓙ Ⓚ
55. Ⓐ Ⓑ Ⓒ Ⓓ Ⓔ
56. Ⓕ Ⓖ Ⓗ Ⓙ Ⓚ
57. Ⓐ Ⓑ Ⓒ Ⓓ Ⓔ
58. Ⓕ Ⓖ Ⓗ Ⓙ Ⓚ
59. Ⓐ Ⓑ Ⓒ Ⓓ Ⓔ
60. Ⓕ Ⓖ Ⓗ Ⓙ Ⓚ

Reading Test	Science Test
1. Ⓐ Ⓑ Ⓒ Ⓓ	1. Ⓐ Ⓑ Ⓒ Ⓓ
2. Ⓕ Ⓖ Ⓗ Ⓙ	2. Ⓕ Ⓖ Ⓗ Ⓙ
3. Ⓐ Ⓑ Ⓒ Ⓓ	3. Ⓐ Ⓑ Ⓒ Ⓓ
4. Ⓕ Ⓖ Ⓗ Ⓙ	4. Ⓕ Ⓖ Ⓗ Ⓙ
5. Ⓐ Ⓑ Ⓒ Ⓓ	5. Ⓐ Ⓑ Ⓒ Ⓓ
6. Ⓕ Ⓖ Ⓗ Ⓙ	6. Ⓕ Ⓖ Ⓗ Ⓙ
7. Ⓐ Ⓑ Ⓒ Ⓓ	7. Ⓐ Ⓑ Ⓒ Ⓓ
8. Ⓕ Ⓖ Ⓗ Ⓙ	8. Ⓕ Ⓖ Ⓗ Ⓙ
9. Ⓐ Ⓑ Ⓒ Ⓓ	9. Ⓐ Ⓑ Ⓒ Ⓓ
10. Ⓕ Ⓖ Ⓗ Ⓙ	10. Ⓕ Ⓖ Ⓗ Ⓙ
11. Ⓐ Ⓑ Ⓒ Ⓓ	11. Ⓐ Ⓑ Ⓒ Ⓓ
12. Ⓕ Ⓖ Ⓗ Ⓙ	12. Ⓕ Ⓖ Ⓗ Ⓙ
13. Ⓐ Ⓑ Ⓒ Ⓓ	13. Ⓐ Ⓑ Ⓒ Ⓓ
14. Ⓕ Ⓖ Ⓗ Ⓙ	14. Ⓕ Ⓖ Ⓗ Ⓙ
15. Ⓐ Ⓑ Ⓒ Ⓓ	15. Ⓐ Ⓑ Ⓒ Ⓓ
16. Ⓕ Ⓖ Ⓗ Ⓙ	16. Ⓕ Ⓖ Ⓗ Ⓙ
17. Ⓐ Ⓑ Ⓒ Ⓓ	17. Ⓐ Ⓑ Ⓒ Ⓓ
18. Ⓕ Ⓖ Ⓗ Ⓙ	18. Ⓕ Ⓖ Ⓗ Ⓙ
19. Ⓐ Ⓑ Ⓒ Ⓓ	19. Ⓐ Ⓑ Ⓒ Ⓓ
20. Ⓕ Ⓖ Ⓗ Ⓙ	20. Ⓕ Ⓖ Ⓗ Ⓙ
21. Ⓐ Ⓑ Ⓒ Ⓓ	21. Ⓐ Ⓑ Ⓒ Ⓓ
22. Ⓕ Ⓖ Ⓗ Ⓙ	22. Ⓕ Ⓖ Ⓗ Ⓙ
23. Ⓐ Ⓑ Ⓒ Ⓓ	23. Ⓐ Ⓑ Ⓒ Ⓓ
24. Ⓕ Ⓖ Ⓗ Ⓙ	24. Ⓕ Ⓖ Ⓗ Ⓙ
25. Ⓐ Ⓑ Ⓒ Ⓓ	25. Ⓐ Ⓑ Ⓒ Ⓓ
26. Ⓕ Ⓖ Ⓗ Ⓙ	26. Ⓕ Ⓖ Ⓗ Ⓙ
27. Ⓐ Ⓑ Ⓒ Ⓓ	27. Ⓐ Ⓑ Ⓒ Ⓓ
28. Ⓕ Ⓖ Ⓗ Ⓙ	28. Ⓕ Ⓖ Ⓗ Ⓙ
29. Ⓐ Ⓑ Ⓒ Ⓓ	29. Ⓐ Ⓑ Ⓒ Ⓓ
30. Ⓕ Ⓖ Ⓗ Ⓙ	30. Ⓕ Ⓖ Ⓗ Ⓙ
31. Ⓐ Ⓑ Ⓒ Ⓓ	31. Ⓐ Ⓑ Ⓒ Ⓓ
32. Ⓕ Ⓖ Ⓗ Ⓙ	32. Ⓕ Ⓖ Ⓗ Ⓙ
33. Ⓐ Ⓑ Ⓒ Ⓓ	33. Ⓐ Ⓑ Ⓒ Ⓓ
34. Ⓕ Ⓖ Ⓗ Ⓙ	34. Ⓕ Ⓖ Ⓗ Ⓙ
35. Ⓐ Ⓑ Ⓒ Ⓓ	35. Ⓐ Ⓑ Ⓒ Ⓓ
36. Ⓕ Ⓖ Ⓗ Ⓙ	36. Ⓕ Ⓖ Ⓗ Ⓙ
37. Ⓐ Ⓑ Ⓒ Ⓓ	37. Ⓐ Ⓑ Ⓒ Ⓓ
38. Ⓕ Ⓖ Ⓗ Ⓙ	38. Ⓕ Ⓖ Ⓗ Ⓙ
39. Ⓐ Ⓑ Ⓒ Ⓓ	39. Ⓐ Ⓑ Ⓒ Ⓓ
40. Ⓕ Ⓖ Ⓗ Ⓙ	40. Ⓕ Ⓖ Ⓗ Ⓙ

English Test

Time: 45 minutes for 75 questions

Directions: Following are five passages with underlined portions. Alternate ways of stating the underlined portions come after the passages. Choose the best alternative; if the original is the best way of stating the underlined portion, choose NO CHANGE.

The test also has questions that refer to the passage or ask you to reorder the sentences within the passages. These questions are identified by a number in a box. Choose the best answer and shade in the corresponding oval on your answer sheet.

Passage 1

About Giraffes

[1]

Last weekend my mother took <u>my younger</u>₁ <u>brother and I</u> to the zoo. <u>The zoo, it is not far</u>₂ <u>from our house,</u> is my favorite place to visit. <u>Along with enjoying being with</u>₃ my brother, too. My brother asked me which animal I liked best. I told him I had <u>trouble choosing between the</u>₄ <u>giraffe, the hippopotamus, and the zebra,</u> but I finally decided on the <u>last.</u>₅ We stood and watched the giraffe for an hour. The <u>keeper, noticing our</u>₆ <u>interest, and coming over to us to tell us about</u> <u>the animal.</u> I learned a lot I didn't know before.

[2]

For example, I learned that the word giraffe is thought to be derived from the Arabic word zirafah, which means "tallest of all." The name is <u>not inappropriate.</u>₇ Giraffes are the tallest animals on earth, and may reach a height of more than 15 feet. They have a more detailed scientific <u>name also interesting.</u>₈ Scientists officially call this animal *Giraffa camelopardalis* because <u>it considers them</u>₉ to look like a camel with the markings of a leopard.

[3]

It appears that no two sets of giraffe markings are alike. While most visitors to the zoo consider all giraffes to have the same markings, a trained eye can distinguish subtle differences. The patterns vary <u>from subspecies to subspecies,</u>₁₀ as does the location of the patterns. Some giraffes, for example, have spots running down their legs, and others do not. The colors can also vary, from a blackish hue to a light yellow. The colors serve the purpose of camouflaging the giraffe, <u>being that it</u>₁₁ blends in <u>well</u>₁₂ with the leaves of the trees in which it hides. The long neck of the giraffe is mistaken for a tree branch. The theory that the markings on a giraffe are comparable to the fingerprints of a human <u>has</u>₁₃ gained ground. [14] [15]

Go on to next page ⟶

1. (A) NO CHANGE
    (B) my younger brother and me
    (C) I and my younger brother
    (D) me and my younger brother

2. (F) NO CHANGE
    (G) The zoo is not far from our house, it
    (H) It is not far from our house (the zoo) and it
    (J) The zoo, which is not far from our house,

3. (A) NO CHANGE
    (B) I enjoy being with
    (C) I enjoy to be along with
    (D) Enjoying being along with

4. (F) NO CHANGE
    (G) trouble to choose between the giraffe, the hippopotamus, and the zebra,
    (H) trouble choosing among the giraffe, the hippopotamus, and the zebra,
    (J) trouble, to choose between the giraffe, the hippopotamus, and the zebra,

5. (A) NO CHANGE
    (B) latter
    (C) better
    (D) best

6. (F) NO CHANGE
    (G) keeper, noticed our interest, and coming over to tell us about the animal.
    (H) keeper noticing our interest by coming over to tell us about the animal.
    (J) keeper noticed our interest and came over to tell us about the animal.

7. (A) NO CHANGE
    (B) not appropriate
    (C) not appropriately
    (D) not inappropriately

8. (F) NO CHANGE
    (G) name, which is also interesting
    (H) name also interested
    (J) name, also interesting

9. (A) NO CHANGE
    (B) they consider it
    (C) they are considering them
    (D) it is considered

10. (F) NO CHANGE
    (G) from subspecies and subspecies
    (H) between subspecies
    (J) subspecies and subspecies

11. (A) NO CHANGE
    (B) which
    (C) to
    (D) OMIT the underlined portion.

12. (F) NO CHANGE
    (G) good
    (H) best
    (J) and does well

13. (A) NO CHANGE
    (B) have
    (C) have been
    (D) are starting to

14. The most logical and coherent placement of the last sentence of the passage is:
    (F) where it is now.
    (G) at the beginning of Paragraph 2.
    (H) at the end of Paragraph 2.
    (J) in the middle of Paragraph 3.

15. Which of the following sentences would be the best to conclude Paragraph 3?
    (A) Giraffes may be just as unique as human beings.
    (B) Giraffes are evolving and changing their color patterns to meet their environments.
    (C) Giraffes are the most colorful creatures in the animal kingdom.
    (D) Giraffes are my favorite animal.

Go on to next page

Passage 2

Alex Haley, *Roots* Author

[1]

Roots author Alex Haley turned <u>his African</u>
<u>ancestors</u> into a book <u>who's</u> emotional impact
                16   17
on African Americans cannot be overestimated.
Born in 1921 in Ithaca, New York, <u>his early years</u>
<u>were spent</u> with his grandmother in <u>Henning</u>
                                          18
<u>Tennessee</u>. Stories she told made Alex curious
      19
about his family history. 20

[2]

<u>As a child, writing was not one of Alex's</u>
<u>desired careers.</u> As an adult, Haley took a variety
        21
of jobs, eventually joining the Coast Guard and
becoming a cook. Unchallenged by his daily
routine in the U.S. Coast Guard, <u>Haley wrote</u>
<u>magazine articles, which</u> he sent to many
        22
different publishers, hoping to catch an editor's
attention. <u>Eventually,</u> his submissions were
        23
accepted, and occasionally he received payment
for his work. Haley's literary abilities <u>afforded</u>
<u>him an opportunity</u> to change his career. It is not
        24
every cook who can become a military journalist.
By 1959 when Haley retired from military service, he held the title of Chief Journalist.

[3]

Alex Haley wrote many articles on a variety
of topics, both domestic and international.
Eventually, he did family history research in the
National Archives in Washington, D.C. Haley took
more than a dozen years to do <u>the research and</u>
                                        25
<u>he traveled</u> more than half a million miles and
throughout more than three continents to work
in huge archives and small libraries. Researching
his ancestors <u>has taken them</u> to Juffure, a small
                    26
village in The Gambia. The Gambia's historian
spoke about Kunta Kinte, who was sent to the
United States on a British slave ship. <u>After Haley</u>
<u>completed his research, then he knew</u> he had
                    27
to tell everyone the story of Kunta Kinte. The
author emphasized that this <u>was the saga of not</u>
                                        28
<u>only</u> the Haley family but also the story of
African Americans. <u>That</u> African Americans
                          29
agreed was amply demonstrated by the fascina-
tion surrounding the mini-series developed from
the book. *Roots* continues to earn high ratings
every time it shows on television. 30

16. (F) NO CHANGE
    (G) stories about his African ancestors
    (H) his ancestors African stories
    (J) his African ancestors stories

17. (A) NO CHANGE
    (B) whos
    (C) thats
    (D) whose

Go on to next page

18. (F) NO CHANGE
    (G) Haley's early years were spent
    (H) Haley spent his early years
    (J) the years that Haley was early, he was spending

19. (A) NO CHANGE
    (B) Henning — Tennessee
    (C) Henning; Tennessee
    (D) Henning, Tennessee

20. The author is considering adding this sentence to the end of Paragraph 1:

    Haley was the oldest of three sons in his family.

    Given that the statement is true, would it provide information relevant to the paragraph?

    (F) Yes, because the first paragraph is about Alex Haley's family, and the sentence conveys important information about Haley's siblings.
    (G) Yes, because it explains why Haley was interested in his ancestors.
    (H) No, because it contradicts information presented earlier in the paragraph.
    (J) No, because it doesn't provide information that introduces Haley as an author.

21. (A) NO CHANGE
    (B) Alex's desires to become a writer were unstated when he was a child.
    (C) As a child, becoming a writer did not appeal to Alex.
    (D) OMIT the underlined portion.

22. (F) NO CHANGE
    (G) Haley wrote magazine articles which,
    (H) Haley, wrote articles for magazines that
    (J) Haley wrote magazine articles, that,

23. (A) NO CHANGE
    (B) Although
    (C) Because
    (D) Nonetheless,

24. (F) NO CHANGE
    (G) allow him to have an opportunity
    (H) enabled him an opportunity
    (J) have given him an opportunity

25. (A) NO CHANGE
    (B) research; therefore he traveled
    (C) research, he traveled
    (D) the research and traveled

26. (F) NO CHANGE
    (G) take him
    (H) took him
    (J) had brought him

27. (A) NO CHANGE
    (B) After Haley completed his research, he knew
    (C) When Haley, after completing his research, knew
    (D) Then, after he had completed his research, knew

28. (F) NO CHANGE
    (G) was not only the saga of
    (H) was of not only his saga but
    (J) saga was not only of

29. (A) NO CHANGE
    (B) Which
    (C) However,
    (D) OMIT the underlined portion.

30. This passage was written in response to a homework assignment to "Discuss the literary abilities of Alex Haley." Did the passage fulfill the assignment?

    (F) Yes, because the essay discussed the derivation of *Roots*.
    (G) Yes, because it informs the reader about the sources of Haley's ideas.
    (H) No, because the essay emphasizes Haley's life instead of his skill as a writer.
    (J) No, because the essay focuses more on Haley's family than on Haley.

Go on to next page

Passage 3

One Man's Opinion about Time Travel
by Carl Mack

Want to go back in time and <u>discussing</u>
₃₁
philosophy with Aristotle, rule with Nero, dine

with Lincoln? If you want to travel in time,

<u>a space ship is needed</u>. Why a space ship, you
₃₂

ask? The answer can be explained with a little

science (or at least in a way that a non-scientist,

like I, <u>think</u> is logical). The earth is rotating
₃₃
<u>on its axis, it is also</u> orbiting the sun. The sun
₃₄

travels along the outer arm of the Milky Way

galaxy, which meanders through space <u>on it's</u>
₃₅
<u>endless</u> journey through the infinite. As the earth

moves <u>from where it was to where it was now,</u>
₃₆
<u>moving you with it so you do not notice any</u>
₃₇
<u>change</u>. <u>This is why you think you are not</u>
₃₈
<u>moving even though you were.</u> In other words,

the earth is like a car in which you are a passen-

ger. If the car travels along a road at a rate of one

mile an hour and you move back in time one

hour (discounting all the movement of the earth

<u>itself)</u>; you will find yourself sitting on the road
₃₉

with the car heading toward you from one mile

away. When you went back in time in this exam-

ple, you did not take the car with <u>you; therefore,</u>
₄₀
it moved back in time and space to when and

where it was one hour earlier. Accounting for the

earth's movement, <u>the same is if you moved</u> in
₄₁

time. You would end up somewhere in space

waiting for the earth to catch up to you!

<u>And this is the reason because you</u> need a
₄₂
space ship; you have to travel to the point where

the earth was at the time you return. You have to

jump back to an earlier time than the time you

want so you can travel to the earth and arrive

"on time."

<u>Its said</u> that because no time travelers exist
₄₃
right now, time travel is impossible. It could be

that time travel is possible, but space travel

technology has not advanced enough to

<u>get them here yet</u>. [45]
₄₄

31. (A) NO CHANGE
     (B) be discussing
     (C) discuss
     (D) have discussed

32. (F) NO CHANGE
     (G) one needs a space ship
     (H) you can use a space ship
     (J) using a space ship is needed

33. (A) NO CHANGE
     (B) was thinking
     (C) had been thinking
     (D) thinks

34. (F) NO CHANGE
     (G) on it's axis, and it is
     (H) on its axis and also it is
     (J) on its axis and

35. (A) NO CHANGE
     (B) on its endless
     (C) on it's never-ending
     (D) not ending its'

Go on to next page

36. (F) NO CHANGE
    (G) from over there to here
    (H) from where it was before to where it was now
    (J) OMIT the underlined portion.

37. (A) NO CHANGE
    (B) and, you moving with it, then you do not notice any change
    (C) moved you with it so you do not notice any change
    (D) you move with it so you do not notice any change

38. (F) NO CHANGE
    (G) Because of this, you think you're not moving, but you are moving.
    (H) You're moving when you think you're not moving, and this is why.
    (J) OMIT the underlined portion.

39. (A) NO CHANGE
    (B) itself),
    (C) itself):
    (D) itself).

40. (F) NO CHANGE
    (G) you, therefore;
    (H) you; therefore
    (J) you, therefore,

41. (A) NO CHANGE
    (B) being the same if you moved
    (C) the same being true if you moved
    (D) the same would be true if you moved

42. (F) NO CHANGE
    (G) And this being the reason why you
    (H) Because of this is the reason you
    (J) Therefore, you

43. (A) NO CHANGE
    (B) People say
    (C) They are saying
    (D) OMIT the underlined portion.

44. (F) NO CHANGE
    (G) transport yet
    (H) take them here yet
    (J) get it here

45. Given that each of the following statements is true, which provides the best conclusion for this paragraph?
    (A) Therefore, time travel may be impossible.
    (B) They don't have the means to go backward to return to a future time.
    (C) Time travel may require more technology than is currently available.
    (D) So, time travel would allow people from different eras to converse.

Passage 4

The Findings of the Paleontologists

Paleontologists <u>have called</u> the preserved
                        46
fossilized burrows "Devil's Corkscrews" (or

Daemonelix) <u>from when</u> the time they were first
              47
found. <u>At that time then</u>, scientists thought the
       48
corkscrews might be <u>holes</u> left by the giant
                     49
tap roots of some unknown plant. But when

<u>however,</u> *Palaeocastor* skeletons were found
  50
in the bottoms of the spirals, almost everyone

had to concede that <u>they</u> were actually ancient
                     51
beaver burrows. Admittedly, the skeleton of

a Nothocyon <u>was being</u> found in one <u>burrow;</u>
             52
<u>but this</u> predator probably followed a beaver
  53
home for supper and just stayed. Three other

kinds of beavers lived around Agate (in what is

now Northwestern Nebraska in the United

States) in the early Miocene epoch, but their

bones have never been found in the <u>burrows,</u>

<u>in fact, no one</u> knows what they did for homes.
  54

Go on to next page ⟶

Perhaps <u>there burrows</u> were much shallower or
₅₅
were in the river banks where running water
soon destroyed them.

[1] It also explains why the paleontologists'
findings in Agate seem incompatible with the
divisions of epochs, periods, and eras; the divisions were based on breaks in a European sedi-
mentary record that reflected local events that
did not necessarily show up in North America's
sediments. [56] [2] Paleontologists can tell that no
dramatic change <u>lied</u> in store for the fauna at the
beginning of the M|iocene epoch and that many
Oligocene genera carried over into the new
epoch. [3] Some of the primitive animals that
had survived <u>in the extensive forests become</u>
<u>extinct</u> when the forests bega|n to dry out and
lose trees. [4] For the most part, however, the
record continued undisturbed, which is to be
expected where the accumulation of sediments
continued without interruption. [59] [60]

46. (F) NO CHANGE
    (G) calling
    (H) have been called by
    (J) used to be called

47. (A) NO CHANGE
    (B) from then
    (C) since
    (D) during

48. (F) NO CHANGE
    (G) At that time long ago
    (H) Then at that time
    (J) At that time

49. (A) NO CHANGE
    (B) holes,
    (C) holes:
    (D) holes;

50. (F) NO CHANGE
    (G) , nonetheless,
    (H) however
    (J) OMIT the underlined portion.

51. (A) NO CHANGE
    (B) the holes
    (C) they,
    (D) the holes,

52. (F) NO CHANGE
    (G) was
    (H) has been
    (J) is being

53. (A) NO CHANGE
    (B) burrow, however, this
    (C) burrow: but this
    (D) burrow, but this

54. (F) NO CHANGE
    (G) burrows. In fact, no one
    (H) burrows, no one, in fact,
    (J) burrows, because in fact no one

55. (A) NO CHANGE
    (B) they're burrows
    (C) their burrow's
    (D) their burrows

Go on to next page

56. The author is considering adding a sentence that provides the definitions of epoch, period, and era after Sentence 1. Should the author make this addition?

   (F) Yes, because Sentence 1 is the first time the author mentions epochs, periods, and eras.

   (G) Yes, because the main purpose of this paragraph is to show the differences among these three divisions, and knowing their definitions is crucial to understanding these differences.

   (H) No, because the author has adequately defined the three terms in the previous paragraph.

   (J) No, because the main point of this paragraph is to explain that changes to flora and fauna over the epochs were relatively minor and providing definitions of categories of time would be irrelevant.

57. (A) NO CHANGE
   (B) lay
   (C) lies
   (D) was laying

58. (F) NO CHANGE
   (G) within the extensive forests, became extinct
   (H) in the extensive forests became extinct
   (J) OMIT the underlined portion.

59. For the sake of logic and coherence, Sentence 1 should be placed where?
   (A) where it is now
   (B) after Sentence 4
   (C) after Sentence 2
   (D) after Sentence 3

60. Suppose the author's goal was to provide examples of how paleontologists can gain information from examining fossils. Would this passage fulfill that goal?

   (F) Yes, because the passage describes the methods paleontologists use to discover fossilized skeletons.

   (G) Yes, because the passage shows how fossilized skeletons provide paleontologists with information about what kinds of animals lived in various times.

   (H) No, because the passage focuses mainly on the duties of a paleontologist.

   (J) No, because although the passage provides examples of the types of fossilized skeletons paleontologists have found, it does not describe how these skeletons provide paleontologists with new information.

Passage 5

Vietnam

In 111 B.C., ancestors of the present-day Vietnamese, inhabiting part of what is now southern China and northern Vietnam, were conquered, there being the warlike forces of China's Han dynasty. Chinese rule lasted more than 1,000 years, since A.D. 939, when the Vietnamese ousted their conquerors and began a southward expansion that, by the mid-eighteenth century, reached the Gulf of Siam.

The Vietnamese were rent by internal political divisions, however, and for nearly two centuries contending families in the north and south struggled to control the powerless kings of the Le dynasty. During this period, Vietnam affectively was divided near the 17th parallel, just a few kilometers above the demarcation line established at the 1954 Geneva Conference.

Go on to next page

Vietnam <u>having been</u> reunited following a
₆₆
devastating civil war in the eighteenth century
but soon fell prey to the expansion of European
colonialism. <u>While the</u> French conquest of
₆₇
Vietnam began in 1858 with an attack on what is
now the city of Da Nang. France imposed control
gradually, <u>to meet</u> heavy resistance, and only in
₆₈
1884 was Vietnam officially incorporated into the
French empire.

Vietnam's resistance was the precursor of
nationalist activity directed against foreign rule.
By 1930, the Vietnam Nationalist Party had
staged the first significant armed uprising against
the French, <u>but its</u> virtual destruction in the ensu-
₆₉
ing French repression left the leadership of the
anticolonial movement to <u>those more adept at</u>
<u>underground organization and survival —</u> the
Communists. ⬚70 In that same year, the recently
formed Indochinese Communist Party (ICP)
<u>lead the way in setting up</u> short-lived "soviets" in
₇₁
Nghe An and Ha Tinh provinces, an action that
identified the ICP with peasant unrest.

The Vietnamese communist movement
began in Paris in 1920 when Ho Chi Minh became
a charter member of the French Communist
Party. Two years later, Ho went to Moscow to
study Marxist <u>doctrine, then he went</u> to China.
₇₂
While in China, he formed the Vietnamese
Revolutionary Youth League, setting the stage
for the formation of the ICP in 1930. French
repression of Nationalists and Communists

forced some of the insurgents underground.
<u>Other dissidents were imprisoned,</u> emerging
₇₃
later to play an important role in the anticolonial
movement. ⬚74 ⬚75

61. (A) NO CHANGE
    (B) conquered, due to the warlike
    (C) conquered by the warlike
    (D) overcome, by the warlike

62. (F) NO CHANGE
    (G) when
    (H) from
    (J) until

63. (A) NO CHANGE
    (B) expansion, that, by the mid-eighteenth century, made it to
    (C) expansion that by the mid-eighteenth century, reached
    (D) expansion that by mid-eighteenth century, reaching

64. (F) NO CHANGE
    (G) divisions; however, and
    (H) divisions. And however,
    (J) divisions, although

65. (A) NO CHANGE
    (B) in affect
    (C) in effect
    (D) ineffective

66. (F) NO CHANGE
    (G) being
    (H) having had been
    (J) OMIT the underlined portion.

67. (A) NO CHANGE
    (B) When the
    (C) Whenever the
    (D) The

Go on to next page

68. (F) NO CHANGE
    (G) meeting
    (H) and meeting
    (J) about to have met

69. (A) NO CHANGE
    (B) but it's
    (C) but, it's
    (D) so its

70. The author is considering changing this sentence by deleting the underlined portion. If the author did this, the paragraph would primarily lose:
    (F) information that is essential to the logical construction of the sentence.
    (G) information about why the Communists were able to take over leadership from the Vietnam Nationalist Party.
    (H) details about how the Vietnam Nationalist Party was able to withstand repression by the French.
    (J) interesting but irrelevant information about the anticolonial movement.

71. (A) NO CHANGE
    (B) took the lead in setting up
    (C) taking the led in setting up
    (D) taking the lead in setting up

72. (F) NO CHANGE
    (G) doctrine; then went
    (H) doctrine, and then going
    (J) doctrine, then went

73. (A) NO CHANGE
    (B) Other dissidents was imprisoned,
    (C) Other dissidents imprisoned
    (D) Other dissidents, imprisoned,

74. The author wishes to conclude this paragraph with a sentence that provides a smooth transition to the next paragraph, which describes the Vietnamese war for independence. Which of the following sentences provides the best transition?
    (F) This movement was not met without opposition, however, and revolution ensued.
    (G) Dissidents often emerge from prison eager to continue working for their causes.
    (H) Communist dissidents reacted to their Nationalist oppressors with violence.
    (J) Later, the United States would play a role in developing a stronger human-rights program in Vietnam.

75. This passage may have been written for which of the following purposes?
    (A) to ridicule the futility of fighting communism
    (B) to provide an historical overview of the government of Vietnam
    (C) to criticize foreign powers that attempt to control Vietnam
    (D) to show Ho Chi Minh's role in the development of modern communism

STOP DO NOT TURN THE PAGE UNTIL TOLD TO DO SO.
DO NOT RETURN TO A PREVIOUS TEST.

Mathematics Test

Time: 60 minutes for 60 questions

Directions: Each question has five answer choices. Choose the best answer for each question and shade the corresponding oval on your answer sheet.

1. A sales department wants to make a 12% profit on its product. If the cost of the product is $87, what will the selling price of the product have to be to achieve the desired profit?

   (A) $98.44

   (B) $97.44

   (C) $95.04

   (D) $92.14

   (E) $90.00

2. A board that's exactly $1\frac{1}{3}$ yards long is cut into three pieces. The first piece is 25 inches. The second piece is 10 inches. How long is the third piece?

   (F) 15 inches

   (G) 14 inches

   (H) $13\frac{1}{3}$ inches

   (J) 13 inches

   (K) $10\frac{1}{3}$ inches

3. Three friends, Mike, Ken, and Debi, earned an average of $50,000 each on a project. Their total earnings were exactly 40% of the total earnings of everyone in their company. How much were the total earnings of the entire company?

   (A) $600,000

   (B) $450,000

   (C) $375,000

   (D) $340,000

   (E) $40,000

4. Given that $(a+5)(a-6)=0$, which of the following is a true statement?

   (F) a could be +5 or +6

   (G) a could be –5 or –6

   (H) a could be –5 or +6

   (J) a could be +5 or –6

   (K) a could be 0

5. An office receives 80 calls a day for 6 days. In order to average 100 calls per day for 12 days, how many calls must the company get in the next 6 days?

   (A) 1,200

   (B) 1,100

   (C) 1,020

   (D) 720

   (E) 120

6. If x is an integer between 6 and 10, which of the following could be a true statement?

   (F) $x^2 = 144$

   (G) $\sqrt{x} = 2$

   (H) $2x = 14.5$

   (J) $3x = 24$

   (K) $\frac{1}{3}x = 1.5$

7. If one of the angles in a triangle is obtuse, which of the following is a true statement regarding the other two angles in the triangle?

   (A) They are in a ratio of 2:1.

   (B) They total 90 degrees.

   (C) One must be a right angle.

   (D) Both angles must be acute.

   (E) Both angles must be obtuse.

Go on to next page

8. 5% of $(a + b)$ = 10% of b. Which of the following must be a true statement?

    (F) $a > b$

    (G) $a < b$

    (H) $a = b$

    (J) $a + b = 0$

    (K) $a < 0, b < 0$

9. The square and isosceles triangle below have equal areas. x =

         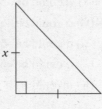

    Figure 1   Figure 2

    (A) $4\sqrt{2}$

    (B) $8\sqrt{2}$

    (C) $4\sqrt{3}$

    (D) $8\sqrt{3}$

    (E) $12\sqrt{3}$

10. The sides of a triangle are 6, 8, and 10. What is the degree measure of the angle between the sides measuring 6 and 8?

    (F) 15

    (G) 30

    (H) 45

    (J) 60

    (K) 90

11. The cost of a textbook increased by 25% from 2009 to 2010. In 2011, the cost of the textbook was $\frac{1}{4}$ below its 2009 cost. By what percentage did the cost of the textbook decrease from 2010 to 2011?

    (A) 0%

    (B) 20%

    (C) 25%

    (D) 40%

    (E) 75%

12. Which of the following is a factor of $a^2 - 8a + 15$?

    (F) $a + 5$

    (G) $a + 3$

    (H) $a - 1$

    (J) $a - 3$

    (K) $a - 15$

13. Jim was y years old m years ago. How many years old will he be in terms of y in 12 years?

    (A) $y + m + 12$

    (B) $ym + 12$

    (C) $y - m + 12$

    (D) $ym - 12$

    (E) $y - m - 12$

14. $\left(5x^2y^5\right)^2\left(3x^3y^4\right)^3 = ?$

    (F) $675x^{13}y^{22}$

    (G) $675^{36}y^{120}$

    (H) $15x^{36}y^{120}$

    (J) $15x^{13}y^{22}$

    (K) $15x^7y^{14}$

15. A circle with a radius of 4 inches has $\frac{1}{4}$ the area of a circle with a radius of how many inches?

    (A) 1

    (B) 2

    (C) 8

    (D) 16

    (E) 64

16. A hiker walks nonstop for 2 hours and 20 minutes and travels 7 miles. At what rate does he walk?

    (F) 2 mph

    (G) $2\frac{1}{10}$ mph

    (H) $2\frac{1}{2}$ mph

    (J) 3 mph

    (K) $3\frac{1}{2}$ mph

Go on to next page

17. A dollhouse is to be an exact replica of a collector's own home on a reduced scale. If the main bedroom of the dollhouse is 18 inches long by 24 inches wide, the real bedroom of 12 feet long is how many feet wide?

    (A) 24

    (B) 18

    (C) 16

    (D) 10

    (E) 8

18. Right triangles I and II (not shown) are similar figures. The angles of triangle I are in the ratio 1:2:3. If the perimeter of triangle I is $15+5\sqrt{3}$ and the shortest side of triangle II is 15, what is the perimeter of triangle II?

    (F) $150+20\sqrt{3}$

    (G) $60+15\sqrt{3}$

    (H) $60+5\sqrt{3}$

    (J) $45+15\sqrt{3}$

    (K) 45

19. When asked her age, Lael responded, "Take the square root of 625, add it to the square of 5, and take 40 percent of the resulting sum." Which of the following expresses Lael's age?

    (A) $L=\sqrt{(625+5)40}$

    (B) $L=0.40\cdot\sqrt{625+5^2}$

    (C) $L=0.40\cdot\sqrt{625}\cdot5^2$

    (D) $L=0.40+\sqrt{625}+5^2$

    (E) $L=0.40\left(\sqrt{625}+5^2\right)$

20. In a classroom of children, every child has either blond, brown, or red hair. The probability of randomly selecting a child with red hair is $\frac{1}{6}$. The probability of randomly selecting a child with brown hair is $\frac{1}{3}$. If 30 children have blond hair, how many children are in the classroom?

    (F) 30

    (G) 45

    (H) 60

    (J) 90

    (K) 120

21. If a is six greater than b, and the sum of a and b is –18, then $b^2 =$

    (A) 144

    (B) 36

    (C) 16

    (D) 4

    (E) 0

22. What is the interior degree measure of figure *ABCDE?*

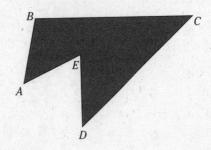

    (F) 900

    (G) 720

    (H) 540

    (J) 360

    (K) 300

23. A city is visited one month by 200 German, 320 American, 140 Moroccan, 180 French, and 240 Japanese tourists. If a circle graph were made representing the various categories, the angle made by the segment representing the French would be how many degrees?

    (A) 360

    (B) 270

    (C) 60

    (D) 1

    (E) $\frac{1}{6}$

Go on to next page

24. Nine friends intend to buy class rings at $85.00 each. The rings cost $864 per dozen if bought in a full dozen batch. If the friends can bring in three more students to purchase rings, how much would each friend save on the price of the ring?

    (F) $15.00

    (G) $14.33

    (H) $13.00

    (J) $12.75

    (K) $11.90

25. For all x and y, $\left(3x^2y + xy^2\right) - \left(2x^2y - 2xy^2\right) = ?$

    (A) $x^2 - x$

    (B) $x^2y - xy^2$

    (C) $x^2y + 3xy^2$

    (D) $5x^2 - xy^2$

    (E) $xy^2 + 3x^2y^2$

26. If line segment XY (not shown) goes from $(-2, 6)$ to $(4, 6)$, what are the coordinates of the midpoint of XY?

    (F) $(-1, 6)$

    (G) $(0, 0)$

    (H) $(1, 6)$

    (J) $(3, 0)$

    (K) $(3, 6)$

27. The ratio of olives to dates is 3:5, and the difference between the number of dates and the number of olives is 18. What is the total number of olives and dates?

    (A) 144

    (B) 72

    (C) 40

    (D) 27

    (E) 24

28. Given that x is an integer, for what value of x is $x + \frac{2}{3}x > 15$ and $x + 4 < 15$?

    (F) 8

    (G) 9

    (H) 10

    (J) 11

    (K) 12

29. A third of the product of 6 and 4 is the same as 3 less than $2x$. What is x?

    (A) 8

    (B) 7

    (C) 6

    (D) $\frac{11}{2}$

    (E) $\frac{5}{2}$

30. A gambler's lucky number is 12. On any roll of two dice, what is the probability that he will roll his lucky number?

    (F) $\frac{1}{2}$

    (G) $\frac{1}{3}$

    (H) $\frac{1}{6}$

    (J) $\frac{1}{12}$

    (K) $\frac{1}{36}$

31. Isosceles right triangle ABC has a perimeter of $20 + 10\sqrt{2}$. What is the area of the triangle?

    (A) $200\sqrt{2}$

    (B) 200

    (C) $100\sqrt{2}$

    (D) 100

    (E) 50

32. Paul wants to buy a new aquarium with the same volume as his old one. His old aquarium measures 6×4 units on the base and is 10 units tall. If his new aquarium has a base in which each side is 50 percent longer than the corresponding side in the old aquarium, approximately how many units tall will the new aquarium be?

    (F) 4.4

    (G) 4.5

    (H) 4.9

    (J) 5.0

    (K) 5.1

Go on to next page

33. Triangles *ABC* and *DEF* are similar figures. What is the perimeter of triangle *DEF*?

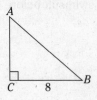

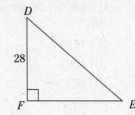

Area of *ABC* = 32

    (A) $56 + 28\sqrt{2}$

    (B) 84

    (C) $84\sqrt{2}$

    (D) $84 + 28\sqrt{2}$

    (E) $90\sqrt{2}$

34. Given that $-|3 - 3a| = -12$, which of the following could be *a?*

    (F) 5

    (G) 4

    (H) 3

    (J) 2

    (K) 1

35. Triangle *ABC* is an equilateral triangle with an area of 32. Triangle *DEF* is an isosceles right triangle with an area of 64. Which of the following represents the ratio of the sum of the interior angles in triangle *ABC* to the sum of the interior angles in *DEF*?

    (A) 4:1

    (B) 3:1

    (C) 2:1

    (D) 1:1

    (E) 1:2

36. Marcy bought eight items costing *x* cents each. She gave the clerk *y* dimes. In terms of *x* and *y*, how much change should Marcy get back?

    (F) $y - 8x$

    (G) $10y + 8x$

    (H) $10y - 8x$

    (J) $8x - y$

    (K) $8x - 10y$

37. Arc *AB* = 3 units. What is the circumference of Circle *O* in units?

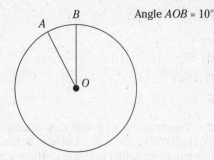

Angle *AOB* = 10°

    (A) $\dfrac{108}{\pi}$

    (B) 36

    (C) 36π

    (D) 108

    (E) 108π

38. Kim starts at point *X* and walks 50 yards straight north. Scott starts at the same point *X* and walks due east. The shortest distance between Kim and Scott is 120 yards. How many yards did Scott walk?

    (F) 130

    (G) 11,900

    (H) $\sqrt{13,000}$

    (J) $\sqrt{11,900}$

    (K) 50

39. What point on the graph of $x^2 - y = 4$ has an *x*-coordinate of 3?

    (A) $(3, -5)$

    (B) $\left(3, \sqrt{5}\right)$

    (C) $(3, 4)$

    (D) $(3, 5)$

    (E) $(3, 13)$

Go on to next page

40. An equilateral triangle has an altitude of $10\sqrt{3}$ units. What is the perimeter of the triangle?

    (F) 80

    (G) 60

    (H) 30

    (J) $20\sqrt{3}$

    (K) 20

41. An automatic water system fills an empty pool half full in one hour. Each hour thereafter the system fills one-half of the capacity that is still empty. After how many hours is the pool $\frac{1}{64}$ empty?

    (A) 12

    (B) 10

    (C) 7

    (D) 6

    (E) 5

42. If m pencils cost n cents, which of the following expresses the cost of p pencils?

    (F) mnp cents

    (G) $m + \frac{mp}{n}$ cents

    (H) $m + \frac{p}{n}$ cents

    (J) $n + \frac{p}{m}$ cents

    (K) $\frac{np}{m}$ cents

43. Hal can assemble 600 widgets in $2\frac{1}{2}$ hours. Faye can pack 200 widgets in 45 minutes. If Faye wants to work for exactly $4\frac{1}{2}$ hours and finish the same number of widgets as Hal, how many hours will Hal have to work?

    (A) 5

    (B) $4\frac{1}{2}$

    (C) $4\frac{1}{4}$

    (D) 4

    (E) $3\frac{3}{5}$

44. The cost of a swimsuit goes up 50% in June, down 20% in July, and down another 30% in August. The cost of the swimsuit in August is what % of the cost of the swimsuit before June?

    (F) 110%

    (G) 100%

    (H) 90%

    (J) 84%

    (K) 61%

45. A wheel covers a distance of 300π meters in 15 revolutions. What is the radius of the wheel?

    (A) 30π

    (B) 25

    (C) 20

    (D) 10π

    (E) 10

46. A prime number times a composite number must be

    (F) prime

    (G) composite

    (H) zero

    (J) a fraction

    (K) even

47. Sector AOC has an area of 120π square units. What is the circumference of the circle?

    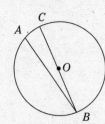

    Angle $ABC = 6°$
    O is the midpoint of the circle

    (A) $34,600\pi$

    (B) $1,200\pi$

    (C) 120π

    (D) $\frac{120}{\pi}$

    (E) $\sqrt{\frac{120}{\pi}}$

Go on to next page

48. On a circle with the equation $x^2 + y^2 = 25$, if the x-coordinate is -3, the y-coordinate could be:

    (F) -3

    (G) 0

    (H) 4

    (J) 9

    (K) 16

49. $(a+3)^2 + (a-4)^2 =$

    (A) $2a^2 - 2a + 25$

    (B) $2a^2 + 14a + 25$

    (C) $a^2 + 2a + 25$

    (D) $a^2 - 2a - 25$

    (E) $2a^2 - 2a - 4$

50. A jar that is now empty is going to be filled with red marbles and blue marbles. The person filling the jar wants the probability of drawing a red marble at random from the jar to be twice as great as the probability of drawing a blue marble at random. If the jar is going to contain 36 marbles, how many more must be red marbles than blue marbles?

    (F) 30

    (G) 24

    (H) 20

    (J) 18

    (K) 12

51. In the right triangle XYZ below, what is the value of tan Z?

    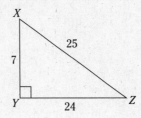

    (A) $\frac{7}{25}$

    (B) $\frac{7}{24}$

    (C) $\frac{24}{25}$

    (D) $\frac{25}{24}$

    (E) $\frac{24}{7}$

52. Which of the following is best expressed by the figure below?

    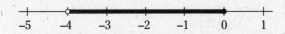

    (F) $x > -4$

    (G) $x < -4$

    (H) $-4 \leq x < 0$

    (J) $-4 < x \leq 0$

    (K) $-5 < x \leq 1$

53. If $4cx - \dfrac{3d}{e} = 4cy$, then $x - y = ?$

    (A) $-\dfrac{3d}{4ce}$

    (B) $-\dfrac{3d}{e} + \dfrac{1}{4c}$

    (C) $\dfrac{3d}{4e} - c$

    (D) $\dfrac{3d}{4ce}$

    (E) $\dfrac{3e}{e} + 4c$

Go on to next page

54. For all $a \neq 0$ and $b \neq 0$, what is the slope of the line passing through (a, b) and $(-a, -b)$?

(F) 0

(G) 1

(H) $\frac{a}{b}$

(J) $\frac{b}{a}$

(K) $-\frac{b}{a}$

55. From a lookout point on a cliff, the angle of depression to a boat on the water is 14 degrees, and the distance from the boat to the shore just below the cliff is 2 km. How far is the lookout from the water surface?

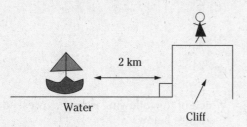

Water   Cliff

(A) $\frac{2}{\sin 14°}$

(B) $\frac{2}{\tan 14°}$

(C) $\frac{2}{\cos 14°}$

(D) $2 \sin 14°$

(E) $2 \tan 14°$

56. A laser printer is printing a novel. It prints 60 pages in the first hour, after which it breaks. Two hours later, the printer is fixed and resumes printing at the rate of 60 pages per hour. To finish the job on time, another laser printer that prints at the same rate is brought in and begins printing when the first printer is repaired. The two laser printers finish printing one hour later. The graphs of the number of pages printed (p) as a function of time (t) would most resemble which of the following?

(F)

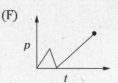

(G)

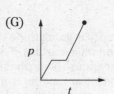

(H)

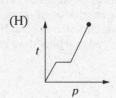

(J)

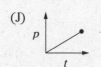

(K)

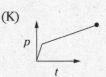

57. Which of the following is equivalent to $\frac{\sin^2 \theta + \cos^2 \theta}{\sec^2 \theta}$?

(A) $\cos^2 \theta$

(B) $\sin^2 \theta$

(C) $\tan^2 \theta$

(D) $\frac{1}{\cos^2 \theta}$

(E) $\sin^2 \theta + 1$

Go on to next page

58. On average, a cow and a half can give a pint and a half of milk in 36 hours. How many pints can three cows give on average in 72 hours? (All cows give milk at the same rate.)

    (F) 3

    (G) 4

    (H) 5

    (J) 6

    (K) 7

59. From an observer on the ground, the angle of elevation to a hot-air balloon is 21 degrees, and the distance from the observer to a point on the ground directly underneath the balloon is 1,500 meters. How many meters high is the balloon?

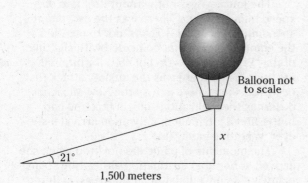

Balloon not to scale

x

21°

1,500 meters

    (A) $\dfrac{1,500}{\cos 21°}$

    (B) $\dfrac{1,500}{\tan 21°}$

    (C) $1,500 \sin 21°$

    (D) $1,500 \cos 21°$

    (E) $1,500 \tan 21°$

60. If A measures between 0° and 180° and $\tan A = \dfrac{4}{3}$, what are the possible values of $\cos A$?

    (F) $-\dfrac{3}{5}$ only

    (G) $-\dfrac{3}{5}$ and $\dfrac{3}{5}$

    (H) $-\dfrac{4}{5}$ and $\dfrac{4}{5}$

    (J) $\dfrac{3}{5}$ only

    (K) $\dfrac{4}{5}$ only

STOP DO NOT TURN THE PAGE UNTIL TOLD TO DO SO. DO NOT RETURN TO A PREVIOUS TEST.

Reading Test

Time: 35 minutes for 40 questions

Directions: Each of the four passages in this section is followed by ten questions. Answer each question based on what is stated or implied in the passage and shade the corresponding oval on your answer sheet.

Passage 1 — Prose Fiction

This passage is adapted from the short story "The Grass is Greener" by Julia Diament.

Line   She gave one last glance in the rearview mirror as the car rolled down the driveway. Seeing her mother blink back tears, she quickly looked away. It was hard enough leaving the
(05) small town that had served as her home, comfort zone, and safety net for the last 22 years — seeing her mother feign strength as the last of her little ones flew the coop only made the whole process that much harder.

(10)   Just like that, there she was, alone in the car with nothing but the open road in front of her. Only 2,500 miles to go until she reached her destination, a small, desert town in central Arizona she'd never seen before.

(15)   When she'd told her family, friends, and employer of her plans to venture into unchartered territory, she was met with mixed reactions. Particularly disappointing was the response of the manager of the restaurant where
(20) she worked.

"The grass is always greener," he said in response to her plan to start life anew in a drastically different environment.

Always a pessimist, she thought, and while
(25) she didn't exactly expect him to swing from the chandeliers upon hearing her news, a simple "good luck" would have sufficed.

"I give you two years," he snorted instead.

But she brushed off his comments, filled with
(30) excitement, anticipation, and determination to one day have the last laugh. She'd lived in the same small Northeastern town since she was born, and the time had finally come to spread her wings and explore potentially greener pastures,
(35) regardless of the careless comments made by those who had yet to venture more than 50 miles from everything they'd ever known.

The trip itself was eye opening. She'd never driven more than two hours at a time on her own, and here she was, embarking on a whole   (40) bunch of firsts: Her first solo cross-country drive, her first night alone in a hotel room, her first time putting down roots without the rest of her family, and the first time committing to a new home having not seen it first.   (45)

The journey was not without its share of speed bumps, either. There was the exorbitant speeding ticket in rural Texas, not to mention the empty gas tank that coincided with sighting of the "Prison area — Do not stop for hitchhik-   (50) ers" sign. Then there was the anxiety attack that occurred somewhere across the New Mexican desert as the realization sunk in that she had better find a job immediately upon arrival if she ever wanted to eat again.   (55)

The moments of panic did not stop when she arrived at her final destination either. She spent many nights on a deflated air mattress, endured the trials of living with a stranger with odd culinary and housekeeping habits, and made it   (60) through the general hiccups involved with any move: undelivered mail, poor cell phone reception, and the inability to find items she was *certain* she had packed. In time, these matters had a way of working themselves out, and before long,   (65) she was feeling genuinely happy, and, dare she say, at home in her new environment.

Years later, while visiting home one December on a holiday break, she stopped into the restaurant where she used to wait tables,   (70) hoping to show the manager who'd made the "grass is always greener" comment just how successful her big move had been, despite the negativity of so many naysayers. To her dismay, he had since been fired, and, last anyone had heard,   (75) was now mowing lawns and working odd jobs to make ends meet.

Go on to next page

I guess the grass is *always greener,* she thought to herself, feeling just a small amount of
(80) satisfaction at the misfortune of the man who had been so quick to rain on her parade several years back. As she returned to what had fast become her home away from home in the desert, and her lucrative job, growing group of friends,
(85) and satisfying romantic relationship, she couldn't help but remember her vow to have the last laugh. While she didn't take too kindly to the "grass is always greener" metaphor, she thought if the day ever came when she ran into her old
(90) manager, she knew exactly what to say: She who laughs last, laughs best.

1. The use of the word *exorbitant* in Line 47 most likely indicates that the traveler:

   (A) was traveling far above the posted speed limit.

   (B) considered the amount of the ticket unreasonable.

   (C) considered the ticket to be an unanticipated expense.

   (D) believed she was unfairly given the ticket.

2. When the author says she didn't expect her manager to "swing from the chandeliers" (Lines 25–26), she most likely means:

   (F) she did not expect him to become overwhelmed by excitement.

   (G) she did not expect him to offer her a raise to stay at the job.

   (H) she did not expect him to give her a going away party at a fancy restaurant.

   (J) she did not want him to have a breakdown upon hearing the news of her impending departure.

3. The traveler's attitude in the last paragraph can best be described as:

   (A) frustrated.

   (B) thoughtful.

   (C) bitter.

   (D) sarcastic.

4. Overall, the traveler is most likely to say that her move across the country was:

   (F) a complete failure because she experienced anxiety and loneliness.

   (G) a valuable learning experience that had both negative and positive aspects.

   (H) a primarily hazardous journey that made her wish she were back with her family and former employer.

   (J) completed solely because of boredom with her life in a small town in the Northeast.

5. That the restaurant manager who once made the "grass is always greener" comment eventually found himself mowing lawns is an example of:

   (A) resentment.

   (B) redundancy.

   (C) irony.

   (D) predestination.

6. All of the following were matters of concern for the traveler during her road trip EXCEPT:

   (F) hitchhiking prisoners.

   (G) staying alone in a hotel.

   (H) driving a manual transmission.

   (J) living apart from her family.

7. When the manager utters his "grass is always greener" comment, he is most likely implying that:

   (A) the traveler is likely to be pleased with the aesthetics of her new home.

   (B) his own life is superior to hers.

   (C) the traveler's new life in a new area of the country will not be as great as she thinks it will.

   (D) the traveler will never find a job like the one she is leaving.

Go on to next page

8. Which of the following was true for the traveler once she moved into her new home?

(F) She bought a new, more comfortable bed.

(G) She misplaced and was unable to locate many items that she had brought with her from home.

(H) She was afflicted by a particularly lengthy bout of hiccups.

(J) She had a roommate who prepared different foods from the ones she was used to.

9. Which of the following statements best describes the function of the tenth paragraph (Lines 56–67) in the passage as a whole?

(A) It indicates that, although the journey and transitional period were not without hardship, the traveler was able to overcome the obstacles that stood in her way and eventually feel comfortable with her move.

(B) It outlines many of the arguments that can be made against moving across the country.

(C) The paragraph provides insight into the neurotic and worrisome nature of the traveler.

(D) The paragraph provides evidence to support the passage's main theme that although travels are educational, in the end there's no place like home.

10. If the traveler was to describe her manager in one word, that word would most likely be:

(F) insecure.

(G) passive.

(H) optimistic.

(J) negative.

Passage 2 — Social Science

Symbolism in architecture is often overlooked by those who simply enjoy the aesthetic beauty of the buildings. The United States Capitol is one such example of a building that, while widely recognized, is rarely examined more than superficially and yet has a wealth of symbols that are relevant and of interest to the American people at large. Beginning as one small wing in 1800, the Capitol has been the site of the inauguration of most of the presidents since Thomas Jefferson took office in 1801. Abraham Lincoln's inaugural took place under scaffolding during increased construction in 1861. Throughout Lincoln's term, he responded to critics who complained about the cost of the construction by saying that the Capitol is a symbol of the unity of the nation, and that "if people see the Capitol going on, it is a sign we intend the Union shall go on." Lincoln is said to have begun and ended his presidency in the Capitol; his body was laid to rest in the Rotunda following his 1865 assassination.

Farmers and their place in U.S. history are symbolically represented by the products depicted on columns in the original Senate wing, including some of the period's most prevalent crops, corn and tobacco. (One ponders the fact that the sculptors hired to create such American symbols came from abroad.) Of course, some architectural items are more overt than symbolic, such as the Statue of Freedom that is atop the Capitol dome. On the base of the statue is incised *E Pluribus Unum,* which is Latin for "Out of many, one" and is also found on the Great Seal of the United States.

In 1814, the British, fighting the war of 1812, captured Washington and set out to destroy it, setting fire to most of its buildings, including the Capitol. While there was much damage inflicted upon the building, including the gutting of the interiors and the scarring of exteriors, there was not complete destruction during the conflagration because of a fortuitous rainstorm that hit Washington that evening. It was followed the next day by a windstorm that killed British officers, set off gunpowder explosions, and destroyed houses. The British officers decided to retreat, and the Capitol was spared.

One of the most striking features of the Capitol is its collection of artworks. While most tell stories about American history, some also present interesting facts about their artists. One such example is a piece by Samuel Morse. Perhaps best recognized in American history as

Line
(05)
(10)
(15)
(20)
(25)
(30)
(35)
(40)
(45)
(50)

Go on to next page

the inventor of the telegraph, Morse also worked
(55) as a painter. He painted a night session of the
House that featured each individual member,
having painstakingly convinced each member to
sit for him so that he could correctly portray
each likeness. A painting of the Marquis de
(60) Lafayette (who, incidentally, was the first foreign visitor to speak before a joint meeting of
Congress) still hangs in the House. Paintings that
adorn the Capitol walls trace the expansion of the
country as well. An Emanuel Leutze 1862 paint-
(65) ing, called *Westward the Course of Empire Takes
Its Way*, showed pioneers crossing a divide.

It is not just paintings that portray American
history — other forms of art found throughout
the Capitol do the same. For example, a Thomas
(70) Crawford bronze door shows Washington saying
goodbye in New York to his officers. The frieze
on the Rotunda depicts William Penn's treaty
with the Indians. Statues abound, including, perhaps surprisingly, one of a Confederate general,
(75) Floridian, Edmund Kirby Smith. Women and their
achievements are also recognized in Capitol art.
Amusingly nicknamed "Women in a Bathtub," an
eight-ton block of marble honors a trio of suffrag-
ettes: Elizabeth Cady Stanton, Susan B. Anthony,
(80) and Lucretia Mott. Also found are statues of
Ethan Allen, the Revolutionary War hero from
Vermont, Robert Fulton, the creator of the
steamboat, and John Gorrie, M.D., a physician
who patented the first ice-cream making machine
(85) in 1851 in an attempt to find something to cool
down his fevered patients.

The works of art featured throughout the
Capitol together help tell the stories of American
history, from relevant citizens to life-changing
(90) inventions and historical milestones. When one
looks beyond the obvious beauty of the Capitol,
the underlying rich history of its people becomes
visible.

11. The primary point of the first paragraph
(Lines 1–21) is that:

(A) presidents are usually sworn into office
on the steps of the Capitol.

(B) the Capitol is more than 200 years old.

(C) the Capitol holds much symbolism for
Americans.

(D) a beautiful building cannot truly be
appreciated unless one understands its
symbolism.

12. What did the author mean by saying that
Lincoln ended his presidency in the Capitol
(Lines 19–20)?

(F) Lincoln said goodbye to his party
members on the steps of the Capitol.

(G) Lincoln was involved in a scandal in
the Capitol that brought down his
presidency.

(H) Lincoln's body was returned to the
Capitol after he had been shot.

(J) Lincoln used the Capitol, not the
White House, as the official office of his
presidency.

13. Which of the following adjectives would the
author most probably use to describe the
fact that American symbols found in the
Capitol were sculpted by foreign artists?

(A) ironic

(B) ingenious

(C) perspicacious

(D) supercilious

14. As it is used in Line 29, the word *overt* most
nearly means:

(F) large.

(G) obvious.

(H) mysterious.

(J) artistic.

15. In Lines 41–42, *conflagration* most nearly
means:

(A) rainstorm.

(B) evening.

(C) bombing.

(D) inferno.

Go on to next page

16. Which of the following may best be inferred from the information in the third paragraph (Lines 35–47)?

    (F) American forces were superior to British forces of the time.

    (G) The British were so superstitious that they refused to fight after occurrences that seemed to favor the American cause.

    (H) The Capitol was completely destroyed by the British and had to be rebuilt.

    (J) If not for the intervention of natural forces, the Capitol most likely would have been completely destroyed.

17. According to the passage, one function of the art in the Capitol is to:

    (A) support and finance American art classes.

    (B) provide physical proof to Americans that their government uses their taxes in a judicious and egalitarian manner.

    (C) portray events in American history.

    (D) put on public display artworks by American artists presented to the president and Congress over the years.

18. The passage answers all of the following questions EXCEPT:

    (F) How did the sculpture "Women in a Bathtub" get its nickname?

    (G) What does *E Pluribus Unum* mean?

    (H) Who was the first foreign citizen to speak before a joint session of Congress?

    (J) What types of artwork other than paintings are found in the Capitol?

19. It is reasonable to infer that the author uses the phrase "perhaps surprisingly" (Lines 73–74) to imply that:

    (A) one would not expect a tribute to a former enemy of the Union in the Capitol.

    (B) one would not expect a Southerner to be honored in the North.

    (C) most statues are of civilians rather than military figures.

    (D) most statues are of people who are more famous than a relatively unknown general.

20. The author most likely listed the people portrayed in statues in the Capitol because the author wanted to:

    (F) prove that there is an equal representation of men and women statues.

    (G) show examples of the different types of artworks found in the building.

    (H) demonstrate the variety of people who have contributed to America.

    (J) provide a touch of comic relief.

Passage 3 — Humanities

The months are familiar to everyone. Nearly any small child can rattle off the twelve months of the year, and when students learn foreign languages, one of the first exercises they practice is saying the names of the months. Despite all that familiarity, however, one important piece of knowledge is still missing: an explanation of how and why the names of the months came into existence. Who decided on the names? Were the months named after people? Did the months always have the same names throughout history? The story of the months is a fascinating one and deserves more attention. (05) (10)

Every month's name tells a story. January is named after Janus, a Roman god who was depicted as having two faces, one looking forward and one looking back. *Janus* is the Latin term for an arch or gate (*janua* is door). The god Janus needed both of his faces. As the guardian of doors or gateways, he had to be vigilant for friends and foes coming from either direction. Of course, January is the first month of the year, but it wasn't always so. Until around 150 B.C., January was the eleventh month of the year. (15) (20)

February is one of the few months not named after a person. February is a form of *februare*, which was the Latin word for "to purify." This month's name came from the February 15 feast of purification. On that feast day, people attempted to atone for their sins and, as a result, hoped to appease the gods sufficiently to ensure healthy children and abundant crops in the next year. (25) (30)

March is named for Mars, whom many people have read about as the god of war. Few people realize that originally Mars was the god of springtime and new blossoms. Warriors would take the winter off from fighting and rest while the weather was too treacherous for battle. In the spring — around what we now think of as March — battles would resume. From this time line, Mars soon became better known as the god of war than of springtime. (35) (40)

Go on to next page

Not every month's name has a definitive provenance. Scholars debate the origins of the (45) name of April. Some writers and researchers claim that the word is from the Latin term *aperire,* meaning "to open," because the buds of new plants opened at this time of year. Other scholars believe the name April is perhaps the (50) namesake of the Greek goddess Aphrodite (abbreviated to Aphro). Aphrodite and Ares — whose Latin name was Mars — were a couple. Romantics prefer to think that as April follows March, Aphrodite followed Mars.

(55) May is also named after a goddess, Maika. She was the goddess of plants. Because flowers often blossom in May, naming the month after the goddess has an indisputable logic. Not much else is known about Maika.

(60) Not every month retained its original name over the years. For example, July and August weren't always known by those names. The original name for July was *Quintilis,* "fifth month." (Previously, the Latin calendar began with what (65) is now March. Therefore, the month of July was originally the fifth month.) August was previously called *Sextilis,* "sixth month." Likewise, September, October, November, and December were the seventh, eighth, ninth, and tenth (70) months. (The roots sept, oct, nov, and dec are common in many other words we use today. A septuagenarian is a person in his seventies; an octogenarian is a person in his eighties, and so on.) How did July and August get their new (75) names? When Julius Caesar was assassinated, Mark Anthony ordered the Roman senate to rename the fifth month (the month in which Caesar was born) after him. Quintilis became Julius, or July. Almost forty years later, Julius (80) Caesar's relative, Augustus Caesar, had August named after him. Augustus was born in September but chose to give August his name because that was the month in which he had made several of his most important conquests.

(85) The number of days in the months has changed throughout the years as well. It was a Roman superstition that even numbers were unlucky. Therefore, all months in the Roman calendar had an odd number of days, usually 31 or (90) 29. Even the number of days in the year has changed. In order to bring the Roman calendar back into sync with the solar year, one memorable year, 46 B.C., actually contained 445 days! The calendar of 365 days officially began on (95) January 1, in 45 B.C. Even that move, however, was not sufficient to balance the year with nature. To attempt to remedy the discrepancy, Pope Gregory XIII stated in 1582 that the day after October 4 should be October 15!

Of course, not every year has exactly 365 (100) days. Some years, known as leap years, have 366 days. A trivia question that many people believe they can answer is, "When do leap years occur?" Most people answer, "Every four years." They gloss over one very important fact, however. Not (105) every fourth year is a leap year. The century years — 1600, 1700, 1800, 1900, and 2000 — are not leap years unless they are evenly divisible by 400. For example, 1600 and 2000 are leap years, but 1700, 1800, and 1900 are not. (110)

21. As it is used in Line 2, "rattle off" most nearly means:

   (A) make a lot of noise.

   (B) recite quickly.

   (C) eliminate.

   (D) shake.

22. The main purpose of the passage is:

   (F) to explain how the months got their names.

   (G) to give reasons for the changes over time to the number of days in a year.

   (H) to explain the role of superstition in the naming of the months.

   (J) to suggest new, alternate names for the months in a year.

23. The passage states that Janus needed both of his faces for which of the following reasons?

   (A) He was the caretaker of warriors in battle.

   (B) He was the god of the beginning of the year.

   (C) As the god of doors and gateways, he had to look in two directions.

   (D) There were more days in the month named after him than there were in the other months.

24. According to the passage, which of the following months was named for a feast?

   (F) February

   (G) March

   (H) April

   (J) May

Go on to next page

25. With which of the following statements would the author most likely agree?

(A) Many people have misconceptions about the origin of the name of March.

(B) Many people believe that all the months are named after gods and goddesses.

(C) Scholars agree on the origins of the names of the months.

(D) The number of days in any month is determined by its lunar cycle.

26. As it is used in Line 92, the expression "into sync" most nearly means:

(F) on the same wavelength.

(G) in line.

(H) between.

(J) into the future.

27. The passage discusses all of the following EXCEPT:

(A) how July and August got their names.

(B) why the name of July was changed.

(C) how the calendar is balanced with the natural cycle.

(D) why Romans considered even numbers unlucky.

28. Which of the following is the main idea of the seventh paragraph (Lines 60–84)?

(F) Roman emperors had the power to change the calendar.

(G) The Roman calendar was different from the calendar we have today.

(H) Extra months were necessary to make the Roman calendar consistent with the calendars of the rest of the world.

(J) The names of the months of the Roman calendar have changed over time.

29. According to the author, which of the following is true about leap years?

(A) They have exactly 366 days.

(B) They occur in years that are equally divisible by 4.

(C) They do not occur in years that mark the beginning of a century.

(D) They occur every fourth year.

30. In Line 105, the author uses the phrase "gloss over" to mean:

(F) polish.

(G) finish.

(H) ignore.

(J) shine.

Passage 4 — Natural Science

Tales abound of the large snake of Trinidad, Surinam, and Bolivia known as the bushmaster. The bushmaster, found primarily in South and Central America, is the largest venomous (poisonous) snake in the New World. The names of (05) this snake tell much about it. The Latin name of the bushmaster is *Lachesis muta.* The *Lachesis* comes from Greek mythology, and refers to one of the three Fates. The Greeks believed that the Fates were women who determined how long (10) the "string" of a person's life would be. When the Fates cut the string, the person's life would cease. The bite of the *Lachesis muta,* the bushmaster snake, can indeed kill. It has been known to kill even humans (although the actual death (15) or injury may come from the bacteria on the snake's fangs, rather than from the venom itself). The *muta* part of the name is similar to our common word *mute,* and derives from the fact that although the snake shakes its tail — as does (20) the rattlesnake, to which it is related — when it senses danger, because there are no rattles on the bushmaster's tail, no noise is made.

A second name for the bushmaster is *concha pita,* meaning pineapple tail. This name reflects (25) the fact that the snake is covered in raised scales. The bushmaster can vary in color (most frequently in shades of brown), but is often tan with dark brown markings in the shape of diamonds. The snake's coloring serves as an excel- (30) lent camouflage in the forests where it lies. Bushmasters are usually solitary animals, coming together only during breeding. After breeding, the bushmaster female lays up to 12 eggs in a group called a clutch. While the eggs (35) are in the clutch, the bushmaster exhibits a strong maternal instinct, coiling around and protecting the eggs. This maternal instinct is quite rare among reptiles. When the eggs hatch — usually in two to three months — the young are (40) immediately capable of survival on their own.

The bushmaster is a type of pit viper. The *pit* in the snake's name comes from the fact that it has a hollow pit close to the eye. The pit is covered by skin to protect it. The purpose of the pit (45) is to sense heat. The heat is given off by the

Go on to next page

bushmaster's prey, which consists of warm-
blooded animals. The most common prey of the
pit viper is a rodent. Usually, a viper will bite its
(50) prey, then retreat, letting the venom do the
actual killing of the smaller animal. Should the
animal wander away during its death throes, the
bushmaster can follow the animal's scent to find
it later. Some bushmasters, however, bite their
(55) prey, then hold their fangs in the animal, often
lifting it off the ground. Bushmasters can
patiently stalk their prey, hiding under the leaves
or trees of the forest and waiting for the prey to
pass. For this reason, some scientists refer to
(60) bushmasters as ambush predators.

The bushmaster itself has few enemies.
Some larger species of snakes that are not susceptible to the pit viper's venom, such as certain
constrictors, can feed on the bushmaster. And
(65) like all snakes, the bushmaster may be attacked
by the large birds of prey. However, in the final
analysis, the greatest foe of the snake is
encroaching civilization. More and more of the
animal's habitat — forests that until recently
(70) were considered remote and uninhabitable by
humans — is being cleared. The bushmaster,
while not an endangered species, is undergoing
an alarming decline in numbers.

Some think that the bushmaster's reputation
(75) for ferocity is misplaced. True, the animal is
daunting by its sheer size. Some can reach
lengths of 12 feet. However, except when hunting
or attempting to breed, bushmasters are relatively placid, unaggressive creatures. Most of the
(80) injuries reported from bushmasters occurred
when hikers accidentally stepped on drowsing
snakes (whose coloration and silent warning
system rarely alert humans to the snakes' presence). They are nocturnal, and thus more aggres-
(85) sive at night than in the daytime.

31. The primary purpose of the passage is to:

(A) explain why bushmaster snakes are the
most poisonous snakes in the world.

(B) distinguish between truth and myth
regarding the bushmaster snake.

(C) suggest ways to use bushmaster snakes
to benefit mankind.

(D) explain the origins of the bushmaster's
name.

32. Which of the following is a question that
remains unanswered by the passage?

(F) Why is the snake colored the way it is?

(G) What is the purpose of the pits in the
viper's head?

(H) What does the bushmaster eat?

(J) How does a bushmaster attract its
mate?

33. According to the passage, which of the
following characteristics of a bushmaster
is rare among reptiles?

(A) the pits around its head

(B) the number of eggs it lays in one clutch

(C) its maternal instincts

(D) the lack of rattles on its tail

34. It can be inferred from the passage that:

(F) the bushmaster is not the world's largest venomous snake.

(G) bushmasters have more brightly
colored skins in the tropics.

(H) a bushmaster attacks only when
threatened.

(J) the bushmaster has become an
endangered species because the
Central American rainforests are being
threatened.

35. Which of the following is the reason the
bushmaster is called an ambush predator?

(A) It lives primarily in bushes in the
Amazon.

(B) It hides from its prey and then attacks
it secretly.

(C) It attacks only smaller animals.

(D) It feeds off only live flesh, not carrion.

36. Which of the following does the author mean
in Lines 74–75 by stating that "the bushmaster's reputation for ferocity is misplaced"?

(F) The bushmaster is fierce only at night.

(G) The bushmaster is becoming more
and more ferocious because it is
endangered.

(H) People are wrong in thinking that the
bushmaster is vicious.

(J) People fear the bushmaster.

Go on to next page

37. Which of the following information about bushmasters is most reasonable to infer from the second-to-last paragraph (Lines 61–73)?

    (A) They may become endangered soon.

    (B) Their venom is not deadly to birds of prey.

    (C) It is their presence in remote forests that makes those forests uninhabitable for humans.

    (D) They will be extinct within a decade.

38. The passage suggests that the reason hikers are frequently attacked by bushmasters is that the hikers:

    (F) disturb the snakes in their sleep.

    (G) enter the territories most fiercely defended by the snakes.

    (H) fail to pay attention to the snakes' audible warning system.

    (J) step on the snakes at night.

39. The main point of the last paragraph is that:

    (A) bushmasters sleep during the day.

    (B) bushmasters will attack to protect their young and their food.

    (C) bushmasters are quiet and hard to detect.

    (D) bushmasters are not as aggressive as some people believe.

40. Which of the following questions is NOT answered by the passage?

    (F) What are the primary enemies of the bushmaster?

    (G) How does a bushmaster locate its prey?

    (H) Why is the bushmaster considered to be aggressive?

    (J) Why does the bushmaster prefer to prey upon warm-blooded animals?

STOP DO NOT TURN THE PAGE UNTIL TOLD TO DO SO. DO NOT RETURN TO A PREVIOUS TEST.

Science Test

Time: 35 minutes for 40 questions

Directions: Following are seven passages and then questions that refer to each passage. Choose the best answer and shade in the corresponding oval on your answer sheet.

Passage 1

The amount of moisture in the air is designated as humidity. Weather reports typically present relative humidity, the percentage of the maximum amount of moisture the air can contain that is currently in the air. Air can contain more moisture at higher temperatures than at lower temperatures.

Relative humidity can be measured by comparing the temperature reading on a wet-bulb thermometer with the reading on a dry-bulb thermometer. Less humid air causes more moisture to evaporate from the wet bulb, thus lowering the temperature reading. Table 1 shows the relative humidity that is calculated at various air temperatures (dry-bulb) as a function of the difference between the wet-bulb and dry-bulb readings.

Table 1	Difference between Wet-Bulb and Dry-Bulb Readings									
	1	2	3	4	5	6	7	8	9	10
Dry-Bulb Reading (°C)	Relative Humidity (%)									
0	81	64	46	29	13					
2	84	68	52	37	22	7				
4	85	71	57	43	29	16				
6	86	73	60	48	35	24	11			
8	87	75	63	51	49	29	19	8		
10	88	77	66	55	44	34	24	15	6	
12	89	78	68	58	48	39	29	21	12	
14	90	79	70	60	51	42	34	26	18	10
16	90	81	71	63	54	46	38	30	23	15
18	91	82	73	65	57	49	41	34	27	20
20	91	83	74	66	59	51	44	37	31	24
22	92	83	76	68	61	54	47	40	34	28
24	92	84	77	69	62	56	49	43	37	31
26	92	85	78	71	64	58	51	46	40	34
28	93	85	78	72	65	59	53	48	42	37
30	93	86	79	73	67	61	55	50	44	39

Humid air feels warmer to a human than dry air does at the same temperature because the moisture in the air makes it harder for the human body to cool itself by evaporating water from its body. Table 2 shows what various temperatures feel like to a typical human at different relative percentages of humidity.

Go on to next page

Table 2 Relationship between Relative Humidity and Apparent Temperature (°C)

Relative Humidity	Air Temperature (°C)										
	21.1	23.9	26.7	29.4	32.2	35.0	37.8	40.6	43.3	46.1	48.9
	Apparent Temperature (°C)										
0%	17.8	20.6	22.8	25.6	28.3	30.6	32.8	35.0	37.2	39.4	41.7
10%	18.3	21.1	23.9	26.1	29.4	32.2	35.0	37.8	40.6	43.9	46.7
20%	18.9	22.2	25.0	27.8	30.6	33.9	37.2	40.6	44.4	48.9	54.4
30%	19.4	22.8	25.6	28.9	32.2	35.6	40.0	45.0	50.6	57.2	64.4
40%	20.0	23.3	26.1	30.0	33.9	38.3	43.3	50.6	58.3	66.1	
50%	20.6	23.9	27.2	31.1	35.6	41.7	48.9	57.2	65.6		
60%	21.1	24.4	27.8	32.2	37.8	45.6	55.6	65.0			
70%	21.1	25.0	29.4	33.9	41.1	51.1	62.2				
80%	21.7	25.6	30.0	36.1	45.0	57.8					
90%	21.7	26.1	31.1	38.9	50.0						
100%	22.2	26.7	32.8	42.2							

1. Which of the following is the best estimate of the apparent temperature when the air temperature is 35.0°C and the relative humidity is 75%?

(A) 51.6°C

(B) 54.0°C

(C) 56.9°C

(D) 57.3°C

2. Which of the following statements about the relationship between air temperature and apparent temperature is true?

(F) As air temperature increases, the relative humidity that produces an equivalent apparent temperature increases.

(G) As air temperature increases, the relative humidity that produces an equivalent apparent temperature remains constant.

(H) As air temperature increases, the relative humidity that produces an equivalent apparent temperature decreases.

(J) There is no relationship between air temperature and equivalent apparent temperature.

3. When the dry-bulb reading is 12.0°C, what is the wet-bulb reading, in °C, when the relative humidity is 78%?

(A) 2

(B) 10

(C) 12

(D) 14

4. The dry-bulb reading is the same as the air temperature. For a dry-bulb reading of 24.0°C and wet-bulb reading that is 4 degrees different, which of the following is the approximate apparent temperature in °C?

(F) 20

(G) 25

(H) 28

(J) 69

5. According to Table 1, under which of the following conditions is the amount of moisture in the area the least?

(A) dry-bulb reading of 0°C; wet-bulb reading 4.0°C different

(B) dry-bulb reading of 8.0°C; wet-bulb reading 6.0°C different

(C) dry-bulb reading of 16.0°C; wet-bulb reading 8.0°C different

(D) dry-bulb reading of 24.0°C; wet-bulb reading 10.0°C different

Go on to next page

Passage 2

A pharmaceutical company has developed a new drug for treating hay fever. It claims that the new drug causes less drowsiness than the current best-selling brand. To test this claim, the company ran the following three studies.

Study 1

Subjects were asked to perform a motor coordination task that required a high degree of alertness. Subjects who made fewer errors were judged to be less drowsy. Eight subjects were given a standard dosage of the new drug, and eight other subjects were given a standard dosage of the old drug. Four persons of each group of eight were tested one hour after ingesting the drug while the other four persons were tested eight hours after ingesting the drug.

Realizing that drug effects often depend on a subject's weight, the researchers weighed each subject who participated in the study. The number of errors and weights for each subject are presented in Table 1.

Study 2

After observing a wide range in the number of errors made by the subjects, the researchers repeated Study 1 but restricted the study to males who weighed 72 kilograms (kg). The results of this study appear in Table 2.

Study 3

This study was identical to Study 2 except that it tested only females who weighed 54 kg. The results of this study are shown in Table 3.

Table 1		Number of Errors on Coordination Task after Ingesting Drug			
Old Drug					
One hour after ingestion			*Eight hours after ingestion*		
Subject	Errors	Weight (kg)	Subject	Errors	Weight (kg)
1	38	75	5	37	71
2	52	55	6	33	73
3	44	70	7	52	53
4	57	54	8	45	55
Average # of Errors: 47.75			Average # of Errors: 41.75		
New Drug					
One hour after ingestion			*Eight hours after ingestion*		
Subject	Errors	Weight (kg)	Subject	Errors	Weight (kg)
9	30	73	13	32	70
10	49	53	14	52	50
11	42	55	15	46	51
12	34	70	16	35	71
Average # of Errors: 38.75			Average # of Errors: 41.25		

Go on to next page

Table 2   **Number of Errors on Coordination Task for 72-kg Males**

Old Drug			
One hour after ingestion		**Eight hours after ingestion**	
Subject	**Errors**	**Subject**	**Errors**
1	39	5	33
2	44	6	36
3	42	7	34
4	40	8	36
Average # of Errors: 41.25		**Average # of Errors: 34.75**	
New Drug			
One hour after ingestion		**Eight hours after ingestion**	
Subject	**Errors**	**Subject**	**Errors**
9	30	13	31
10	31	14	31
11	34	15	29
12	34	16	32
Average # of Errors: 32.25		**Average # of Errors: 30.75**	

Table 3   **Number of Errors on Coordination Task for 54-kg Females**

Old Drug			
One hour after ingestion		**Eight hours after ingestion**	
Subject	**Errors**	**Subject**	**Errors**
1	54	5	49
2	56	6	49
3	53	7	51
4	54	8	50
Average # of Errors: 54.25		**Average # of Errors: 49.75**	
New Drug			
One hour after ingestion		**Eight hours after ingestion**	
Subject	**Errors**	**Subject**	**Errors**
9	44	13	47
10	48	14	48
11	44	15	46
12	46	16	48
Average # of Errors: 45.5		**Average # of Errors: 47.25**	

Go on to next page

6. Which of the following is the most reason-able conclusion that can be made on the basis of Study 1?

    (F) The new drug is more effective than the old drug one hour after ingestion but not eight hours after ingestion.

    (G) Performance on the motor coordina-tion task deteriorates as time after ingestion of the old drug increases.

    (H) As compared to the old drug, the new drug improved the ability of experimen-tal subjects to perform the motor coor-dination task.

    (J) The new drug causes less drowsiness than the old drug one hour after inges-tion but not eight hours after ingestion.

7. Which of the following best summarizes why the researchers conducted Studies 2 and 3?

    (A) They wished to examine the effects of weight on drowsiness produced by the drug.

    (B) They were interested in whether the drug would affect men and women differently.

    (C) They wanted to eliminate a factor that caused variability in the results.

    (D) Most people who suffer from hay fever weigh approximately what the subjects in those studies weighed.

8. In comparison to Study 1, what is a primary limitation of Study 2?

    (F) Study 2 does not measure the effects of the drugs on females.

    (G) Study 1 suggests that the new drug may be more effective for a variety of subjects.

    (H) Study 1 shows that the new drug caused less drowsiness in a wider range of subjects.

    (J) Study 2 produced results that were more difficult to interpret.

9. If Study 3 included a group that was tested two hours after ingesting the old drug, which of the following would be the most reasonable prediction for the average number of errors made by this group?

    (A) 44

    (B) 49.5

    (C) 52

    (D) 56

10. Suppose that further study revealed that the group of subjects given the old drug and tested after eight hours in Study 1 was, under normal conditions, particularly profi-cient at performing the motor coordination task. How would this finding affect the overall results of the study?

    (F) It would add evidence that the new drug causes less drowsiness than the old drug at eight hours after ingestion.

    (G) It would suggest that side effects associ-ated with the old drug are more common eight hours after ingesting the drug than at only one hour after ingestion.

    (H) It would suggest that the new drug is more effective than the old drug at any time after ingestion.

    (J) It would require that the entire experi-ment be repeated with the same sub-jects being tested at both one hour and eight hours.

11. If later studies show that the new drug is at least as effective as the old drug in relieving hay fever and that the new drug produces no side effects other than drowsiness, would it be reasonable to recommend the new drug over the old drug to lightweight individuals suffering from hay fever?

    (A) Yes, but only if such individuals are given a lower dose than what was used in the current three studies.

    (B) Yes, because the evidence supports the claim that the new drug is at least as effective and produces less drowsiness.

    (C) No, because the individuals may oper-ate dangerous machinery within eight hours after ingesting the drug.

    (D) No, because the new drug differs from the old one with regard to how it affects the immune system, which is responsible for producing hay fever.

Go on to next page

Passage 3

A wide beach protects bluffs by spreading out the energy of waves and keeping them from eroding the soil and rocks that comprise the bluff (see Figure 1).

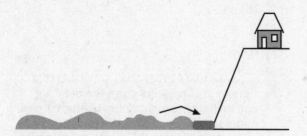

Figure 1: Simplified illustration of waves hitting a wide beach.

When water levels rise, bluffs become vulnerable to erosion because much of the beach is then underwater and the bluffs bear the brunt of the waves' force (see Figure 2).

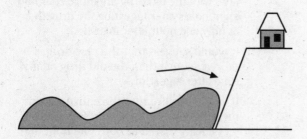

Figure 2: Simplified illustration of waves hitting a bluff when water level rises above beach.

To gain a better understanding of how natural forces can affect future water levels and bluff erosion, scientists studied the relationship between some key meteorological factors and water depth (deeper water means a higher water level) near the shore of an inland lake.

Study 1

Scientists measured precipitation and lake depth over a 30-year period and plotted the average depth against annual precipitation, as shown in Figure 3.

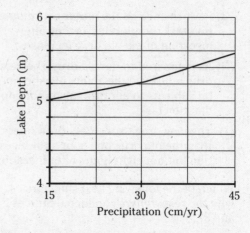

Figure 3: The average depth against annual precipitation.

Study 2

Because temperature affects water evaporation rate and a higher evaporation rate lowers water levels, scientists plotted the average depth against the mean annual temperature. This relationship is shown in Figure 4.

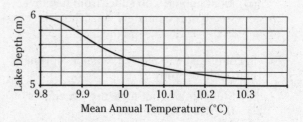

Figure 4: The average depth versus the mean annual temperature.

Go on to next page

Study 3

Wind is another factor that affects water evaporation rate, so scientists plotted the average depth against wind speed, as shown in Figure 5.

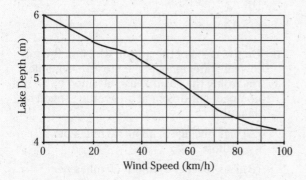

Figure 5: The average depth versus wind speed.

12. Suppose that only 10 cm of precipitation occurs in one year. Which of the following is the most reasonable lake depth estimate for that year?

   (F) 5.5 m

   (G) between 5.0 m and 5.5 m

   (H) between 4.0 and 5.0 m

   (J) 2.5 m

13. What is the most likely relationship between temperature and evaporation rate?

   (A) When temperature increases, evaporation rate increases.

   (B) When temperature increases, evaporation rate decreases.

   (C) When temperature increases, evaporation rate is unaffected.

   (D) When temperature decreases, evaporation rate increases.

14. After a year of low precipitation, high temperatures, and strong winds, the lake depth would probably be:

   (F) lower than average.

   (G) average.

   (H) a little higher than average.

   (J) much higher than average.

15. Are strong winds definitely good for the stability of the bluff?

   (A) Yes, because strong winds tend to lower water levels and help stimulate plant growth.

   (B) Yes, because strong winds deposit soil on the bluff and reduce soil fertility.

   (C) No, because strong winds raise temperatures.

   (D) No, because strong winds produce more powerful waves, which can crash into the bluff.

16. Which of the following is the dependent variable of the investigation?

   (F) precipitation

   (G) lake depth

   (H) mean annual temperature

   (J) wind speed

17. Without any additional information, which of the following would further knowledge of how weather affects the bluff?

   (A) measuring erosion as a result of precipitation, temperature, and wind speed

   (B) counting the number of homes built on the bluff

   (C) investigating the feasibility of constructing a protective seawall

   (D) measuring the tides over the course of several years

Go on to next page

Passage 4

The use of gasoline is directly related to the number of pollutants, such as hydrocarbons, nitrous oxide, and carbon monoxide, present in the air. As a result, drivers should take steps to minimize their gasoline consumption. One way to reduce this consumption is to drive at slower speeds. Figure 1 shows how gasoline mileage is affected by freeway driving speeds.

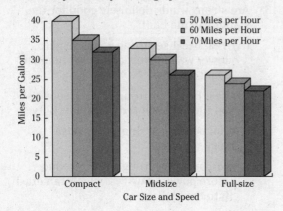

Figure 1: Effects of freeway driving speeds on gas mileage.

18. According to Figure 1, which of the following will produce the most pollutants on a 100-mile trip?

   (F) a compact car driven at 50 mph

   (G) a midsize car driven at 60 mph

   (H) a full-size car driven at 50 mph

   (J) a full-size car driven at 60 mph

19. You are in the desert with no gas in sight, and your gas gauge shows that you have very little gas left. According to the information in the chart, should you speed up to get to your destination?

   (A) No, because you use more gas at a higher speed.

   (B) No, because you need more time to find a gas station.

   (C) Yes, because the desert has very little pollution.

   (D) Yes, because your car operates for less time and, as a consequence, burns less gas.

20. Based on the chart in Figure 1, what is the best estimate of average miles per gallon for a full-size car driven at 55 mph?

   (F) 23

   (G) 25

   (H) 32

   (J) 37

21. On the basis of the graph, which of the following statements is the most reasonable regarding the gas mileage attained by a compact car driven at an average speed of 25 mph?

   (A) Gas mileage is about 40 miles per gallon.

   (B) Gas mileage is about 50 miles per gallon because gas mileage increases 8 miles per gallon for every 10 mph increase in speed.

   (C) Gas mileage is about 80 miles per gallon because gas mileage doubles when speed is cut in half.

   (D) Gas mileage can't be determined with any reasonable certainty because 25 mph is outside the range of numbers presented in the graph.

Go on to next page

22. Which of the following graphs best represents the relationship between freeway speed and pollutants emitted?

(F)

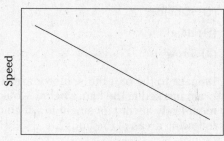

(G)

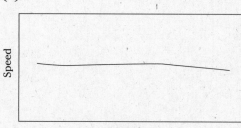

(H)

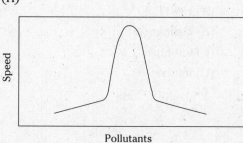

(J)

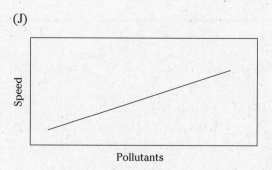

Passage 5

From stimulating the brains of patients undergoing neurosurgery, scientists have determined that a strip of the brain just in front of the central sulcus controls the motor neurons throughout the body. That is, this part of the brain controls the neurons that control the voluntary muscles. This motor area is illustrated in Figure 1.

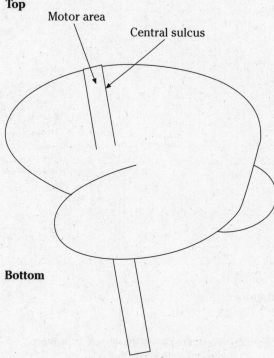

Figure 1: The part of the brain that controls the motor neurons in the body.

Go on to next page

Further work has mapped out the specific parts of this motor area that control certain parts of the body. The regions of the left half of the brain, which controls the right side of the body, are illustrated in Figure 2. There is a direct correlation between an area's size and the complexity of the coordination of the muscles it controls. The right side of the brain, which controls the left side of the body and is not illustrated, is a mirror image of the left side of the brain.

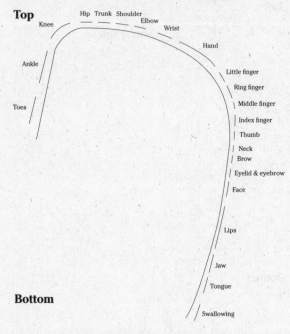

Figure 2: The motor regions of the left half of the brain control the right side of the body.

23. Which of the following is a true statement regarding the organization of the motor area shown in Figure 2?

   (A) No systematic relationship exists between how the motor area is organized and how the body is organized.

   (B) The region that controls the lips is larger than the area that controls all of the fingers.

   (C) The region that controls the hand is exactly equal in size to the region that controls the toes.

   (D) Some parts of the body are controlled by larger regions of the motor area than others.

24. From an inspection of Figure 2, which of the following areas involves the most complex coordination of muscles?

   (F) trunk

   (G) shoulder

   (H) hand

   (J) brow

25. Damage to the part of the motor area of the brain marked in the figure below would most likely affect movement in which of the following areas of the body?

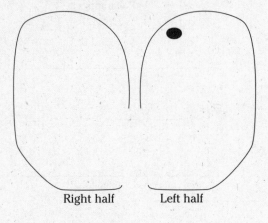

   (A) right lips

   (B) right knee

   (C) left hip

   (D) left jaw

Go on to next page

26. If it is true that the brain is organized so that related functions are under control of areas that are close to one another in the brain, which of the following is the most likely location for the part of the brain that controls speech production?

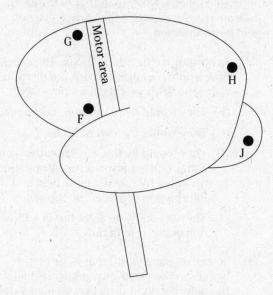

(F) location F

(G) location G

(H) location H

(J) location J

27. According to information in the passage, damage to the part of the motor area marked in the figure below will most likely affect:

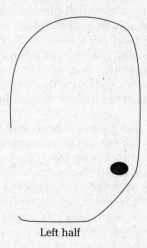

Left half

(A) vision.

(B) hearing.

(C) the ability to sense touch to the mouth.

(D) the ability to move facial muscles.

Go on to next page

Passage 6

Homing pigeons received their name because of their ability to find their way home even when they are hundreds of kilometers away. Scientists know that pigeons do not use visible landmarks to navigate because the birds can find their way home even after they have been transported in a covered box and released in an unfamiliar area. Scientists have offered several explanations for this acute navigational ability. Following are two of these hypotheses.

Sun Compass Hypothesis

Pigeons use the sun as a compass to orient themselves. Evidence for this theory comes from an experiment in which pigeons were placed in a circular cage with identical food cups evenly spaced just outside the cage. After being trained to go to the cup due east of the cage's center, pigeons were observed to go to the same cup even after the cage was rotated and the background scenery was changed. Pigeons failed to go to the east cup when the skies were overcast or when the experimenters used mirrors to alter the apparent position of the sun.

The pigeons use their internal clocks in conjunction with the sun to find their way home. For example, if the internal clock of a pigeon indicates noon while the bird observes the sun about to set, the pigeon knows that it is far to the east of its home and flies west to get there. A northern hemisphere bird that is due south of its home at noon sees that the sun is in the correct position as far as east and west are concerned but observes that the sun is higher in the sky than normal and therefore flies north to get home. Support for this mechanism comes from observing birds whose internal clocks have been experimentally shifted. Their orientation, with respect to the sun, is consistent with their internal clock, but because the clock is off, the pigeons fly in the wrong direction.

Magnetic Field Hypothesis

Holders of this hypothesis contend that pigeons do not rely on an internal sun-based clock calculation to orient themselves. They have observed that clock-shifted birds are just as accurate and fast as normal birds at finding their way home on overcast days.

Disruptions in the magnetic field surrounding the birds, on the other hand, affect the birds' orientation under such conditions. When bar magnets are placed on pigeons, they fly in random directions on overcast days. Similar results were obtained when scientists used electrical wires to induce an electrical field in a particular direction.

When the wires induced a magnetic field that pointed up through the birds' heads, the pigeons flew away from home. When the field pointed in the opposite direction, the birds flew toward home. These findings, along with the discovery that pigeons are capable of responding to a magnetic field much weaker than that of the earth, indicate that pigeons use the earth's magnetic field for orientation.

28. According to the Sun Compass Hypothesis, how would the pigeons with the disrupted magnetic fields orient on a sunny day?

   (F) They would fly in random directions.

   (G) They would fly toward home.

   (H) They would fly in a direction that is a compromise between the information provided by the magnetic field and the information provided by the sun.

   (J) They would fly straight but in a direction away from home.

29. Scientists have found that large disturbances in the earth's magnetic field affect the pigeons' flight direction on sunny days. Which of the following is the most reasonable statement that can be made on the basis of this finding?

   (A) The Sun Compass Hypothesis is completely false.

   (B) Pigeons do not use the sun for orientation.

   (C) The earth's magnetic field is the only factor that affects pigeon navigation.

   (D) The finding supports the Magnetic Field Hypothesis.

30. Which finding presented in the passage is consistent with the Sun Compass Hypothesis but inconsistent with the Magnetic Field Hypothesis?

   (F) The caged pigeons do not fly to the correct cup on overcast days.

   (G) Pigeons whose internal clocks have been experimentally shifted fly the wrong way on a sunny day.

   (H) Pigeons whose internal clocks have been experimentally shifted fly home on an overcast day.

   (J) Magnetic field disturbances affect pigeon navigation.

Go on to next page

31. The author of the Magnetic Field Hypothesis assumes that:

    (A) pigeons with magnets are not affected by the mere presence of metal.

    (B) magnets have absolutely no effect on pigeons on sunny days.

    (C) no birds use internal clocks to navigate.

    (D) pigeons do not use the sun to navigate.

32. According to the entire passage, what is a reasonable statement regarding what happens to pigeons whose internal clocks have been experimentally shifted when they are placed at their homes?

    I. They will fly away from home on a sunny day because the clock-sun calculation will indicate that they are away from home.

    II. They will stay home on a sunny day because they will recognize familiar landmarks.

    III. They will stay home on an overcast day because the magnetic field will indicate that they are home.

    (F) I and II only

    (G) I and III only

    (H) III only

    (J) I, II, and III

33. Some evidence indicates that homing pigeons can use barometric pressure to navigate. How does this evidence relate to the Sun Compass and Magnetic Field Hypotheses?

    (A) This evidence disproves both hypotheses.

    (B) This evidence is inconsistent with both hypotheses.

    (C) This evidence is consistent with the Sun Compass Hypothesis but inconsistent with the Magnetic Field Hypothesis.

    (D) This evidence may be consistent with both hypotheses.

34. Research shows that pigeons can orient to light that mimics conditions present on a partially overcast day in which blue sky is present but the sun's disk is blocked. If pigeons whose internal clocks have been experimentally shifted navigate home on such a day, which hypothesis is supported?

    (F) Sun Compass, because the pigeons responded correctly to the light.

    (G) Sun Compass, because the sun was blocked.

    (H) Magnetic Field, because the pigeons responded correctly to the light.

    (J) Magnetic Field, because the internal clock shift did not throw the birds off.

Passage 7

A typical chemical reaction can be represented as $A + B \rightarrow AB$. A and B are reactants that react to form product AB.

Chemists have measured the rate at which various products of reactions are formed and have found that the rate varies with the concentration of the reactants. For example, when the concentration of reactant A is doubled, the rate of formation of product AB may change, depending on the nature of the chemical reaction. The rate can remain the same, double, quadruple, or change in other ways. The concentration of reactant B affects the rate of product formation, but reactant B's effect can be different from that of reactant A. For example, you can have a reaction in which doubling the concentration of A doubles the rate of product formation, while doubling B's concentration quadruples the rate.

To learn more about the chemical reaction $H_3AsO_4 + 3I^- + 2H^+ \rightarrow H_3AsO_3 + I^{3-} + H_2O$, scientists ran a series of experiments to determine how the concentration of each reactant affects the rate of formation of the product H_3AsO_3.

Go on to next page

Experiment 1

Scientists combined 0.01 moles of H_3AsO_4, 0.20 moles of I^-, and 0.10 moles of H^+ in a liter of solution. H_3AsO_3 was formed at the rate of 2.8 units. Scientists repeated the reaction three times, using different amounts of H_3AsO_4 each time. The results are summarized in Table 1.

Table 1	Results of Varying H_3AsO_4 Concentration		
Concentration (moles/liter)			
H_3AsO_4	I^-	H^+	*Formation Rate (rate units)*
0.01	0.20	0.10	2.8
0.02	0.20	0.10	5.6
0.03	0.20	0.10	8.4
0.04	0.20	0.10	11.2

Experiment 2

This experiment was identical to Experiment 1 except that the scientists varied the concentration of I^- while holding the concentration of the other reactants constant. The results of these experimental trials are presented in Table 2.

Table 2	Results of Varying I^- Concentration		
Concentration (moles/liter)			
H_3AsO_4	I^-	H^+	*Formation Rate (rate units)*
0.01	0.20	0.10	2.8
0.01	0.40	0.10	5.6
0.01	0.60	0.10	8.4
0.01	0.80	0.10	11.2

Experiment 3

This experiment was identical to the other two, except that the concentration of H^+ was the one that varied. The results are presented in Table 3.

Table 3	Results of Varying H^+ Concentration		
Concentration (moles/liter)			
H_3AsO_4	I^-	H^+	*Formation Rate (rate units)*
0.01	0.20	0.10	2.8
0.01	0.20	0.20	11.2
0.01	0.20	0.30	25.2
0.01	0.20	0.40	44.8

Go on to next page

35. A chemist must make as much H_3AsO_4 as possible in a minute. If she can change the concentration of only one reactant, which reactant should she choose?

   (A) H_3AsO_4

   (B) I^-

   (C) H^+

   (D) any reactant

36. Why did the chemists vary the concentration of only one reactant at a time?

   (F) Varying the concentration of more than one reactant causes a violent explosion.

   (G) When the concentration of more than one reactant varies and the formation rate changes, how each reactant affects the formation rate is unclear.

   (H) Measuring the concentration of more than one reactant at the same time is difficult.

   (J) When the concentration of more than one reactant is varied, the amount of product formed is too great to make an accurate determination of the formation rate.

37. If the concentrations of H_3AsO_4, I^-, and H^+ are 0.02 moles/liter, 0.40 moles/liter, and 0.10 moles/liter, respectively, what is the formation rate?

   (A) 2.8 rate units

   (B) 5.6 rate units

   (C) 8.4 rate units

   (D) 11.2 rate units

38. If scientists combined 0.01 moles of H_3AsO_4, 0.20 moles of I^-, and 0.10 moles of H^+ in two liters of solution instead of the one liter that was used in the first trial of each experiment, what would happen to the formation rate?

   (F) The formation rate would decrease.

   (G) The formation rate would remain the same.

   (H) The formation rate would increase for a few seconds and then decrease.

   (J) The formation rate would increase.

39. If a fifth trial is performed in Experiment 3 in which 0.80 moles/liter of H^+ are used and all other concentrations remain unchanged, what would be the likely formation rate?

   (A) 22.4 rate units

   (B) 44.8 rate units

   (C) 89.6 rate units

   (D) 179.2 rate units

40. What happens to the formation rate of H_2O when the concentration of one or more reactants is increased?

   (F) The formation rate decreases.

   (G) The formation rate is zero.

   (H) The formation rate remains the same.

   (J) The formation rate increases.

STOP DO NOT TURN THE PAGE UNTIL TOLD TO DO SO.
DO NOT RETURN TO A PREVIOUS TEST.

Writing Test

Time: 30 minutes

Directions: Choose a position on the issue presented in the following writing prompt. Present your position in a logical, clear, and well-organized essay that follows the rules of Standard written English. Write your essay on a separate sheet of lined paper.

A recent report on the high school curriculum suggests that high schools should add five semesters of computer science courses to their graduation requirements. Researchers claim that computer science education is essential for graduates' success in the current technological environment and for the United States to continue to thrive in a global economy. School administrators oppose the addition, arguing that the new course requirements would impose an economic burden on high schools to hire new teachers and would deprive students of the opportunity to explore the arts and other elective courses. In your opinion, should high schools add a five-semester computer science requirement to their curricula?

Write an essay that takes a position on this issue. Your position can support either one side of the issue or the other, or you may introduce a different point of view on the question. Provide specific examples and reasons to support your opinion.

STOP DO NOT TURN THE PAGE UNTIL TOLD TO DO SO.
DO NOT RETURN TO A PREVIOUS TEST.

Chapter 21

Practice Exam 1: Answers and Explanations

• •

So you've completed Practice Exam 1 in Chapter 20 and now you want to check your answers and find out your score. Well, you've come to the right place!

In this chapter, we provide detailed answer explanations for each problem on the test to help you understand why one answer is correct and the others aren't. Along the way, you find zillions of tips, traps, and other valuable information you can use when you face the actual exam on test day. So be sure to read all the explanations carefully — yes, even the ones you got right!

After the explanations, you find the scoring guide that helps you determine what score you would've received if this practice test were real. If you're short on time, skip to the end of this chapter, where we provide an abbreviated answer key.

English Test

1. **B.** The easy way to choose between *me* and *I* in this situation is to ignore the other person. That is, read the sentence as, "My mother took I to the zoo." You would never say that; you would say, "My mother took me to the zoo." Choice (D) is incorrect because it's always better to put others before yourself!

2. **J.** Choice (F) is wrong. A sentence can't have two subjects, and this one has *zoo* and *it*. Changing *it* to *which* creates a *subordinate clause* (one that can't stand on its own) and eliminates the run-on sentence that Choice (G) creates.

3. **B.** The original sentence is a *fragment* because it has no verb. Choice (D) doesn't have a verb either, and Choice (C) includes the unnecessary word *along*. Choice (B) has a verb and expresses a complete thought.

4. **H.** *Among* compares more than two items; *between* compares exactly two. (As a way to remember this, note the *tw* in *between* and the *tw* in *two*.) Here, the sentence compares the giraffe, hippopotamus, and zebra, three animals, which means you use *among*.

   If you chose Choice (J), you got careless and didn't reread the sentence with your answer inserted. This final step can catch awkward sentences and save you a lot of points.

5. **A.** This question was pretty hard; pat yourself on the back if you got it right. *Latter*, an *er* form, compares two items. *Last*, an *est* form (without the *e*), is the right comparison term to use for the three animals. (If you missed this question, flip to Chapter 4.)

6. **J.** The original sentence is a fragment; it has no verb. It just hangs in the air, not expressing a complete thought. (You find yourself asking, "Well, what about the keeper?") Choice (J) completes the sentence with the verbs *noticed* and *came*, so it's the right answer.

Did you double-check the *ing* verbs, *coming* and *noticing,* in Choices (F), (G), and (H)? When *ing* verbs appear in sentences without the assistance of those trusty helping verbs, they can't function as verbs and complete the sentence. Always check sentences with *ing* verbs to make sure they include a helping verb to carry the load.

7. **A.** A double negative is a positive in English, just as it is in math. So "not inappropriate" means "appropriate." From the rest of the passage, you find out that a name meaning "tallest of all" is appropriate, given that the giraffe is the tallest animal. So this one's correct as is.

   Note: In some other languages, such as Spanish, a double negative does not make a positive and may not change the meaning of the sentence (as the double negative in Question 7 does). Those of you who speak languages other than English need to be especially careful not to make mistakes with double negatives.

8. **G.** If you chose (F), you probably have what we call Smart Students' Disease: You automatically, instinctively corrected the error in the sentence without even knowing it. Go back and look at the original and notice that what *interesting* refers to isn't clear. Adding *which* and a verb clarifies the situation, so Choice (G) is correct.

If you find that you have a lot of NO CHANGE answers, you're probably suffering from this insidious disease (too many brain cells can be as big of a problem as too few!). If you have a few minutes left at the end of the section, go back and check all your NO CHANGE answers to be sure that you didn't correct the errors in your head as you read.

9. **B.** Always, always, always check what the pronouns in a sentence refer to. In this case, *it* (singular) refers to *scientists* (plural), and *them* (plural) refers to *animal* (singular). Choice (B) fixes the problem. Choice (C) introduces the dreaded passive voice and provides no clear reference for *it*.

10. **F.** The correct formation is "from . . . to," not "from . . . and," and *subspecies* implies more than two members, which means you can't use *between* to show comparison. So this one's correct as is. Choice (J) changes the meaning of the sentence.

11. **B.** The word *being* is often wrong on the ACT, and, in this sentence, what *it* refers to is not at all clear. The expression "being that" is a sloppy construction. Use *which* in Choice (B) to express the same thought.

Choice (D) is the trap answer. Don't fall into the habit of choosing OMIT every time you see it. (Subconsciously, you may want to omit the whole darn exam, but that doesn't count!) Take a minute to reread how the sentence would work without the underlined portion, and you know something has to be there.

12. **F.** *Well* is an adverb and answers the question *how.* How does the giraffe blend in? It blends in well, so Choice (F) is right. If you chose Choice (G), see Chapter 4 for information on *good* versus *well.* If you chose (H) or (J), you changed the meaning of the sentence. A good general rule is to correct the error and then get outta there. In other words, don't do any more work or make any more changes than you absolutely have to.

13. **A.** The subject of the verb is *theory,* which is singular, so it requires the singular verb *has.* Hence, the sentence is correct as is. If you thought that *markings* or *fingerprints* was the subject of the sentence, you read too quickly.

14. **F.** To answer this question, take a quick glimpse at the answer choices. The options are in either Paragraph 2 or 3. The last sentence of the passage talks about how different the markings of giraffes are, which is the topic of Paragraph 3. Paragraph 2 discusses the giraffe's name, which means you can cross out Choices (G) and (H); the sentence has to be in Paragraph 3. The sentence is much more logical at the end of the paragraph where it is now than it would be in the middle, so Choice (F) is right.

Questions that ask you to order sentences or paragraphs can be pretty easy to answer if you concentrate on the options the answer choices give you.

15. **A.** The last paragraph talks about how unique the giraffes are, how their markings distinguish them from each other. Choices (B) and (C) are a little tricky. Yes, the last paragraph talks about how giraffes have different colors and blend in well with their surroundings. But it doesn't say anything about their evolving, nor does it indicate that other animals are less colorful. And Choice (D) contradicts what the author says in Paragraph 1 about his favorite animal. Choice (A) does the best job of picking up the theme of comparing giraffes to humans from the previous sentence and building on it.

16. **G.** The original sounds as if Mr. Haley were a magician who changed people into a book! The sentence means to say that *stories* about people were turned into a book. All the choices correct that problem, but Choices (H) and (J) include a new error because they don't make *ancestors* possessive. The stories belong to the ancestors, so they're the *ancestors'* stories. Choice (G) is correct.

17. **D.** This question was probably simple for you. *Who's* means "who is," as in, "Who's going to miss a question this easy?" The possessive of *who* (and *that* and *which,* too) is *whose,* Choice (D).

    Whos and *thats* aren't real words, unless you're talking about a bunch of thats or whos. And the only place we can imagine a bunch of whos is in Dr. Seuss's Whoville. But if you find yourself thinking of Dr. Seuss stories in the middle of the ACT, you may not have your priorities straight.

18. **H.** The original sentence sounds as though Haley's early years were born in New York, when obviously Haley was the one who was born there. So Choice (H) is the correct one here.

    When a sentence begins with a *verb phrase* (a phrase with some kind of verb in it but no subject), it relates to the first noun or pronoun after the comma. In this case, the noun that comes after the comma has to either be *Haley* or refer to Haley. You know Choice (J) doesn't correct the problem. But Choice (G) is tricky. It seems to start with Haley, or does it? It actually starts with "Haley's years," which still makes it sound like years were born in New York. Also, notice that Choices (F) and (G) contain passive voice, which is almost always wrong on the ACT.

19. **D.** You need a comma between *Henning* and *Tennessee* because you separate a state from a city with commas (not dashes or semicolons).

20. **J.** When you see these "yes, yes, no, no" questions, first answer the question with a yes or no answer. The proposed sentence probably isn't relevant because the rest of the paragraph shows how Haley's childhood led to his book. The information in the sentence doesn't relate back to that topic. Because the answer is probably no, check out Choices (H) and (J) first. Then cross out Choice (H); the sentence would be the first mention of Haley's siblings. Choice (J) sounds pretty good, and the first two choices don't include anything that persuades you to change your mind.

21. **D.** The underlined portion doesn't fit with the rest of the paragraph, which discusses Alex's military career. Likewise, Choices (A) and (B) don't fit, and Choice (A) contains passive voice. Another clue that you should nix the sentence is that it refers to Haley as *Alex* when the rest of the passage calls him *Haley.*

22. **F.** The sentence is correct as written. All the other choices use commas incorrectly. For instance, the comma goes before, not after, *which* in Choice (G); there's no reason for the comma after *Haley* in Choice (H); and surrounding *that* with commas in Choice (J) is doubly wrong.

23. **A.** *Eventually* shows that some time passed before Haley was published, which flows well from the previous sentence. Choices (B) and (C) make no sense, and Choice (D) indicates that his articles were accepted despite his submission of them. Hey, we'd like to get published without sending anything to publishers, but we're probably not so lucky!

24. **F.** "Afforded him an opportunity" is a correct expression. The verbs in Choices (G) and (J) are in the present tense, but the rest of the paragraph uses past tense verbs. Choice (H) is worded improperly; instead you could say "enabled him to gain an opportunity" or "gave him an opportunity."

Did you hesitate to choose Choice (F) because you'd already picked NO CHANGE in the two questions before this one? Don't let that pattern influence your answer. Base your choice on analyzing the question rather than the pattern of answer choice letters.

If you missed this one, you probably changed the wording unconsciously as you read. Always reread the answer you've picked in the full context of the sentence to make sure you haven't missed something.

25. **D.** The original version is a *run-on sentence:* two sentences incorrectly joined with *and* and no comma. Choice (C) creates another punctuation error, a comma splice; you can't join two independent clauses with just a comma. Haley traveled and researched at the same time (one didn't cause the other), so you can eliminate Choice (B). Plus, you need a comma after *therefore.* Choice (D) corrects the punctuation problem by eliminating *he.* Now the rest of the sentence isn't an independent clause, so the *and* works just great. If you're confused by commas, go to Chapter 4 to find out how to use them.

26. **H.** Whenever you see a pronoun in the underlined portion, make sure the pronoun is the right number (plural or singular) and has a clear reference. In this sentence, you don't know who *them* refers to. All the choices fix the problem by switching *them* to *him,* but Choice (G) incorrectly keeps the verb in present tense and Choice (J) improperly uses *brought,* which would only be okay if you were reading this book in The Gambia. If you live in Juffure and picked Choice (J), we'll let it slide.

In addition to pronoun errors, verb mistakes are among the most common errors on the English Test. Verbs may be in the wrong number (singular versus plural) or the wrong tense. Always double-check the verbs and pronouns.

27. **B.** If you picked Choice (A), you read too quickly. "After Haley . . . then he knew. . . ." You don't need both *after* and *then.* All the other choices eliminate the unnecessary *then,* but Choices (C) and (D) create incomplete sentences.

If two answer choices appear to be identical, one probably adds or deletes a critical word and is the correct answer choice. If you're confused, choose one of those two. (Always keep in mind that the ACT has no penalty for wrong answers. Always guess anytime you're not sure of the correct answer.)

28. **G.** Do you remember the rule about "not only . . . but also"? The rule (covered in Chapter 4, in case you've forgotten) is that "not only" and "but also" must come before like parts of speech. In other words, if "not only" is in front of a noun, "but also" must be in front of a noun, too. This question takes this rule one step further. "Not only" is in front of "the Haley family" which is a noun serving as an object, but "but also" is in front of "the story," which is *not* an object (it's a predicate noun, if you need specifics). Choice (G) puts "not only" in front of the other predicate noun in the sentence: "was not only the saga . . . but also the story."

You should have buzzers and alarms going off in your brain whenever you encounter one of the terrible twosomes. Diction questions, although not automatically wrong, require your careful attention. See Chapter 4 for more details.

29. **A.** *That* is actually the subject of this sentence, so you can't take it out as Choice (D) suggests. Choice (B) changes the sentence into a dependent clause, which makes it an incomplete sentence. Choice (C) simply makes no sense because it gives the sentence two verbs, *agreed* and *was.*

30. **H.** The passage gives an overview of Haley's history and explains how he came to write *Roots.* However, it doesn't analyze, or even mention, any other work. The reader gains no insight into Haley's ability, just into his background. So the answer has to be no, meaning your only two choices are (H) and (J). You can eliminate Choice (J) because it's not true.

Were you at all tempted to choose Choice (F) or (G) because they offer true statements? Remember that if the initial answer to a "yes, yes, no, no" question isn't right, the rest of the answer can't be right even if it's true.

31. **C.** Verbs in a series must be in parallel, or similar, form. You need to say the verbs this way: discuss . . . rule . . . dine.

32. **H.** The original version is in passive voice. In Standard English, the active voice is preferable. (Confused? Flip to Chapter 4, and enlarge your brilliance.) Choice (J) doesn't make the sentence any more active and is pretty darn wordy. Choices (G) and (H) are in active voice, but Choice (H) is better because it uses second person (you), which is consistent with the rest of the passage.

33. **D.** Don't let the "like I" fool you. The subject of the clause is *non-scientist,* not *I.* Just remember that the subject's not going to be in a part of the sentence that's enclosed in commas. The verb that goes with *non-scientist* is *thinks,* Choice (D). The verbs in the other choices are in past tense, which doesn't jive with the rest of the passage.

34. **J.** The original version is a pesky comma splice. Choice (G) corrects the comma error but incorrectly changes *its* (possessive) to the incorrect *it's* (the contraction of "it is"). Choice (H) creates a run-on sentence and adds a redundant *also.* You can correct the error with Choice (J), which takes away the second subject so that you're no longer joining two independent clauses.

35. **B.** The possessive form *its* is correct here; *it's* is the contraction of "it is." (We cover these and other commonly confused word duos in detail in Chapter 4.) Choice (C) keeps the wrong possessive form and introduces a synonym for *endless.* Choice (D) introduces yet another incorrect possessive form for *it.*

36. **J.** The pairing of the past-tense verb *was* with *now* makes no sense, which means you can cross out Choices (F) and (H). Referring to *there* and *here* in Choice (G) is ambiguous and means nothing. The best solution is to get rid of the underlined portion completely and just say "as the earth moves."

You're focusing only on correcting the underlined portion of the sentence. You'll have an opportunity to evaluate the rest of the sentence in the next question.

37. **D.** The underlined portion doesn't make clear what or who is doing the moving, and Choice (C) doesn't offer any solution. Choice (B) is confusing and wordy. With Choice (D), you know who's moving (you) and what happens as a result.

38. **J.** The underlined portion — and Choices (G) and (H) — states the same thought that was expressed in the preceding sentence and, thus, is unnecessary.

39. **B.** The stuff that comes before the semicolon is a dependent clause; the stuff after it is an independent clause. When a dependent clause begins a sentence, you separate it with a comma rather than a semicolon or a colon. (You can find more punctuation rules in Chapter 4.) The period in Choice (D) creates a sentence fragment, and you know how the ACT feels about fragments!

40. **F.** The original is correct. *Therefore* is a coordinating conjunction, and you have to put a semicolon between an independent clause and another independent clause that begins with a coordinating conjunction. You're not done, though, because you always need a comma after the coordinating conjunction.

If you're confused about coordinating conjunctions, go to Chapter 4. (Don't you wish you were like the ruler Sigismund who said the famous line that's quoted in all English classrooms: "I am the King of Rome and I am above grammar." We know a high school student who named her dog Sigismund in the man's honor.)

41. **D.** The original version uses an awkward construction, and Choices (B) and (C) create sentence fragments with no verbs.

The word *being* in an answer choice often signals a sentence fragment because it's a word that looks like a verb but doesn't really function as a verb without some assistance from a helping verb.

42. **J.** "The reason because" is an improper and redundant construction. A good writer is concise and succinct, so always look at the shortest answer first to see whether it works. In this case, Choices (F), (G), and (H) are redundant and unnecessarily wordy. Choice (J) is short and sweet — and right.

43. **B.** Don't rush to pick Choice (D) automatically. If you delete the underlined portion, the sentence begins, "That because." Yuck! The underlined pronoun has a big problem. The possessive form *its* isn't right; *said* doesn't belong to *it*. Choice (C) introduces a new pronoun, but you have absolutely no idea who *they* are. Choice (B) tells you that people are doing the saying.

44. **F.** You may have been suspicious of the underlined *them*. If you read the sentences that come before this one, though, you see that the only noun *them* could refer to is "time travelers." What *it* refers to in Choice (J) is a mystery, however, so you can cross that one out. You take things away from you and bring them to you, so changing *get* to *take* doesn't work, meaning that Choice (H) is out. In Choice (G), *transport* has no object, which means you don't know what's being transported. The best option is to leave the sentence the way it is.

45. **B.** The passage discusses how time travel would require one to go backward in a space ship to arrive at the same time, so Choice (B) concludes the paragraph in a way that's consistent with the main idea of the passage. The paragraph implies that time travel is possible, so if you chose Choice (A), you were expressing your own opinion. Choice (C) contradicts the point of the preceding sentence. Choice (D) may be true, but it's not the topic of the last paragraph.

Just because a statement is correct or is a fact doesn't mean it's the answer to the question. "Lincoln is the capital of Nebraska" is a fact, but it doesn't answer this question.

46. **F.** The present perfect tense, "have called," is correct in this sentence because paleontologists are still calling the burrows "Devil's Corkscrews." Choice (G) has an *ing* word posing as a verb, but you know it creates a sentence fragment. Choices (J) and (H) change the meaning of the sentence; they sound as if the scientists themselves were called "Devil's Corkscrews."

47. **C.** The correct expression is "since the time they were found," which means "from that time on." The other answers make no sense when you insert them into the sentence.

48. **J.** Choices (F) and (H) are redundant: The phrase "at that time" and the word *then* mean the same thing. Choice (G) replaces one redundancy with another. You don't need to say that a fossilized burrow was found long ago.

Have you noticed how often the shortest answer is the correct answer? Although you can't automatically assume that the shortest answer is always correct, consider it first.

49. **A.** The words after *holes* don't create a nonrestrictive clause or independent clause, so you don't need any punctuation mark after the underlined portion.

50. **J.** *But* and *however* mean the same thing, so you don't need both. Cross out Choices (F) and (H). *Nonetheless* makes no sense in the sentence; your best bet is to eliminate the underlined part altogether and choose Choice (J).

Are you remembering to double-check your answer choices by rereading the entire sentence with the choice inserted? If not, you're probably missing something.

51. **B.** In the original sentence, you can't tell whether *they* refers to the *skeletons* or the *spirals*. Choice (B) makes the reference crystal clear. You can't separate a subject from a verb with a comma, which means Choices (C) and (D) are wrong.

52. **G.** The verb tense in the underlined portion shows ongoing activity in the past, which is the wrong tense to show that the discovery happened once. The sentence calls for the simple past tense in Choice (G). Choices (H) and (J) also convey continuous activity and don't work in this sentence.

53. **D.** To separate two independent clauses joined by *but,* you need a comma rather than a semicolon or a colon. Semicolons connect two *independent clauses* (clauses that can stand on their own). You do use a semicolon before *however,* which makes the comma in Choice (B) wrong.

Are you about ready to enter a Clinic for the Terminally Confused? Don't worry about the terminology. Just review the basic punctuation tips we provide in Chapter 4.

54. **G.** You can't use a comma to connect two independent sentences. Choice (G) fixes the problem by inserting a period and a capital letter to make these separate sentences. Choice (J) is tempting, but it is unnecessarily verbose. Plus, "in fact" should be separated by surrounding commas.

55. **D.** *Their* is the possessive form of *they. There* is a place. (*Their* books are over *there.*) Because *their* is already possessive, you don't need the possessive *burrow's* in Choice (C). *They're* in Choice (B) is the contraction of "they are" and doesn't show possession.

56. **J.** Knowing the definitions of *epoch, period,* and *era* doesn't add anything to the paragraph. So the answer to the question is no. The author hasn't defined these terms anywhere else, so cross out Choice (H).

57. **B.** The correct conjugation of *lie* is lie, lay, and have lain. Well, isn't that just peachy? The past tense of lie is lay, and the ACT often tests the verbs to lie and to lay. So be absolutely certain that you know the distinction between them (*lie* has no object; *lay* requires an object) and their conjugations. We discuss these verbs in more detail in Chapter 4.

58. **H.** If the animals had survived in the past, they *became* extinct in the past. So you need the past tense in Choices (G) or (H). You can't separate a subject and verb with a comma, so Choice (G) is wrong. Omitting the underlined portion, which is Choice (J), makes nonsense of the sentence.

Don't fall into the habit of choosing the OMIT answer every time you see it. Be sure to reread the sentence that results when you omit the underlined words. Often, the resulting sentence makes no sense at all.

59. **B.** Look for clues in Sentence 1. It starts with *it,* and you don't know what *it* refers to. So it probably shouldn't be the first sentence of the paragraph; you can cross out Choice (A). If you put the sentence after Sentence 2, you still don't have a reference for *it.* Nothing in Sentence 3 provides a clue to what *it* is. But Sentence 4 ends with a mention of the accumulation of sediment. This accumulation also explains why the findings seemed incompatible. Bingo! Choice (B) is your winner.

Questions that ask you to reorder sentences or paragraphs can take longer than others to answer. If you're pressed for time and encounter one of these questions, eliminate obviously incorrect answers and guess from the rest.

60. **G.** The passage is all about what scientists can learn from fossils, so the answer is probably yes. The problem with Choice (F) is that the passage doesn't discuss methods of discovery (although that wouldn't answer the assignment even if it did). Choice (G) sounds right, but check the last two choices just in case. The passage isn't about paleontologists; it's about fossils. Choice (H) is out. Choice (J) isn't true; the passage give examples of fossils, like the "Devil's Corkscrews," that have provided scientists with information about the past.

61. **C.** The Han Dynasty conquered the Vietnamese. Find the most succinct, concise way to say this without creating additional errors. Choice (D) would be okay if it didn't have that unnecessary and downright wrong comma. The words that come after the comma contain essential information, so they shouldn't be separated from the rest of the sentence with a comma. Choice (B) has the same comma problem and awkward phrasing to boot.

62. **J.** Had you read the phrase "since A.D. 939" by itself, it would seem logical, but you know from the first sentence that the rule lasted since 111 B.C. rather than A.D. 939. Choices (F) and (H) can't be right. Choice (G) doesn't make sense; the answer has to be Choice (J) because 111 B.C. until A.D. 939 is "more than 1,000 years."

Sometimes you have to read the entire sentence and a few sentences before or after it to know which word fits best.

63. **A.** The commas are correctly placed in the original sentence. All the other options contain comma problems. Choice (B) sneaks in a comma after *expansion,* but the clause that follows is a restrictive clause that's essential to the meaning of the sentence and shouldn't be separated. Choices (C) and (D) punctuate the nonessential phrase "by the mid-eighteenth century" incorrectly with just one comma. A nonessential phrase has to have commas on either side of it unless it ends or begins a sentence. Lucky for you, though, you don't have to figure out whether the phrase is essential or not, because none of the answer choices gives you the option of eliminating the commas altogether.

64. **F.** If you got this question correct, kudos to you! Normally, the word *however* is used as a conjunctive adverb (no this isn't some sort of disease, though trying to remember its definition might make you kind of queasy; go to Chapter 4 for some relief) that initiates an independent clause and therefore requires a semicolon to separate it from the rest of the sentence. For example, "I was careful; however, I still missed the question." In this case, however, (just like in this sentence you're reading right now) the *however* is a mere aside, so the commas surrounding it are just fine. Choice (J) changes the meaning of the sentence, and Choice (H) neglects the comma that needs to come before *however* (to say nothing of the fact that it makes no sense).

65. **C.** *Affectively* with an *a* has to do with emotion and is hardly ever used. The same goes for "in affect." The intended wording for this sentence is Choice (C), the idiomatic expression "in effect," which means "to have the effect or purpose of." So the division "for all intents and purposes" existed near the 17th parallel. Choice (D) changes the meaning of the entire sentence. *Ineffective* means "not skillful," not "efficient."

66. **J.** If the word *but* weren't there, the original form would work: "Vietnam, having been reunited, soon fell prey. . . ." But the word *but* is right there in the sentence, and you can't change it, which means the verb has to be in simple past tense. Choices (G) and (H) aren't simple past tense; in fact, Choice (G) isn't a verb at all. All is not lost, though; Choice (J) allows you to delete the "to be" verb altogether and leaves *reunited* as the verb in simple past tense.

67. **D.** The word *while* turns the entire sentence into a *subordinate clause* (an incomplete sentence or fragment). And so do *when* and *whenever* in Choices (B) and (C). Eliminating *while* makes the sentence complete.

Double-check the word *while* each time you encounter it. Subordinate conjunctions, such as *while, when, although,* and *despite,* often (on the ACT) begin sentence fragments.

68. **G.** The original sentence sounds as if France's purpose in gradually imposing control was to meet heavy resistance. But the sentence really means that France met heavy resistance as it was gradually imposing control. Choice (G) properly shows the simultaneous relationship. Choice (H) has an unnecessary *and.* (We live by the motto, "When in doubt, leave it out." It's a good thing we're test-prep experts and not surgeons!) Choice (J) has an awkward construction and verb tense issues.

69. **A.** This question tests *its* (possessive form) versus *it's* (contraction of "it is"). Here, the uprising belongs to *it,* making the possessive correct and narrowing the answers down to (A) and (D). *So* indicates a corresponding thought; *but* correctly indicates a contrary thought.

70. **G.** Approach this question methodically. If you take out the underlined portion, the sentence still makes sense, which means you can cross out Choice (F). From the context of the sentence, you know that *those* in the underlined portion refers to the Communists and

Choice (G) is probably right. The Vietnam Nationalist Party was practically destroyed, so Choice (H) isn't a contender. Consider Choice (J): The information is about the anticolonial movement, but it's not irrelevant (it tells you specifically why the leadership was successful). So the best answer is Choice (G).

71. **B.** *Led* is the past tense of *lead.* As in, we led you right into a trap. The required word here is the noun, *lead,* meaning the front position. (Rudolph takes the *lead* when pulling Santa's sleigh.) Choice (D) takes away the verb in the sentence and turns it into a fragment, so you know (B) is your winner.

72. **J.** The original sentence is a comma splice. A comma isn't the right punctuation mark for joining independent clauses; leave that job for the semicolon, and cross out Choice (F). Choice (H) introduces a different verb form that isn't parallel with the rest of the sentence. Choice (J) eliminates *he,* which corrects the comma splice because the remaining part of the sentence is no longer an independent clause. The comma before *then* is there to replace the missing *and.*

If you chose (G), you fell for the trap. The original sentence could use a semicolon, but Choice (G) eliminates the subject *he* so that the last part of the sentence is no longer an independent clause and the semicolon is no longer correct.

73. **A.** Choice (B) has the singular verb *was* with the plural subject *dissidents.* Choice (C) sounds as if the dissidents were doing the imprisoning rather than being imprisoned. Choice (D) turns the sentence into a fragment.

74. **F.** The last sentence of the passage mentions that some dissidents emerged to participate in the anticolonial movement. The question tells you that the next topic is the war for independence. The only answer that touches on both of these subjects is Choice (F). It refers to the movement and points to revolution (which is another way of saying war for independence). Choice (J) is completely unrelated to either subject. Choice (G) relates to the last sentence of the passage but doesn't point to the war for independence. If you read too quickly, you might pick Choice (H). But the passage implies that Nationalists and Communists were allies rather than enemies, so that answer doesn't make sense.

When an ACT question asks you to provide the best transition, choose an answer that contains a little bit of the previous subject and a little bit of the next subject.

75. **B.** ACT passages are rarely negative; they don't ridicule or criticize. So you can eliminate Choices (A) and (C) right away. Choice (D) is too specific. Ho Chi Minh appears only in the last paragraph.

The purpose of a passage is usually very broad and general: to introduce a topic, to give an overview, or to discuss or explain an idea. When in doubt (remember that the ACT has no penalty for guessing), choose the most generic answer.

Mathematics Test

1. **B.** Multiply $87 by 0.12 (which is the same as 12 percent) to get $10.44. Add that to the original $87, for a total of $97.44.

   You can take a small shortcut for problems like this one. Multiply 87 by 1.12, because that's the same as 112 percent, to get $97.44 immediately. You cut out one additional step.

2. **J.** This problem requires just simple subtraction and knowing that there are 3 feet in a yard. That means that $1\frac{1}{3}$ yards is 3 feet + 1 foot, or 4 feet, for a total of 48 inches. Subtract: $48 - 25 = 23$; $23 - 10 = 13$.

You can eliminate Choices (H) and (K) immediately, because you're cutting off whole inches, not fractions. If you chose either Choice (H) or (K), you confused $\frac{1}{3}$ of a yard (which is a foot) with $\frac{1}{3}$ of an inch.

3. **C.** The three friends averaged $50,000 each, which means their total was $150,000 ($3 \times 50,000 = 150,000$). Create the equation where T stands for Total: $150,000 = 40$ percent T or $150,000 = 0.4T$. Divide both sides by the value next to the variable:

$$T = \frac{150,000}{0.4}$$
$$T = 375,000$$

Were you looking for an answer like "It cannot be determined"? If so, you were probably confused because you don't know exactly how much money each individual made. Maybe Debi made $100,000 and both Mike and Ken together made $50,000. But their individual amounts are irrelevant. The only important point is that three people together made $150,000.

4. **H.** One of the two parenthetical expressions must equal zero, because the product of zero and anything else is zero. That means that either $a = -5$ (because $-5 + 5 = 0$) or $a = 6$ (because $6 - 6 = 0$).

Although this is an easy problem to do, it's also an easy problem to miss with a careless mistake. As soon as you see that the answer choices are variations on a theme, with the positive and negative signs making all the difference, go back and double-check that you didn't make a silly mistake.

5. **D.** If the office wants 100 calls a day for 12 days, it wants 1,200 total calls ($100 \times 12 = 1,200$). It has 480 calls ($80 \times 6 = 480$). Subtract: $1,200 - 480 = 720$.

If you picked Choice (E), you fell for the trap! The question doesn't ask how many calls per day the office receives; it asks how many calls altogether the office receives. Sure, if the office needs to have 720 calls in 6 days, that's 120 calls per day ($720 \div 6 = 120$), but that's not what the question wants to know. ***Remember:*** The mere fact that the answer you got is staring you in the face doesn't mean it's the correct answer to the problem.

6. **J.** The key here is knowing that an integer is a whole number (for example, 1.5 is not an integer). For Choice (F) to be true, x would have to be 12, which is too large. For Choice (G) to be true, x would have to be 4, which is too small. For Choice (H) to be true, x would have to be 7.25, which is not an integer. For Choice (K) to be true, x would have to be 4.5, which is both too small and not an integer. Only Choice (J) works, because if $3x = 24$, $x = 8$. (If number definitions are fuzzy in your memory, turn to the thrilling pages of Chapter 7.)

7. **D.** Knowing geometry vocabulary (which we cover in Chapter 8) helps with this question. An *obtuse angle* is more than 90 degrees, and an *acute angle* is greater than 0 but less than 90 degrees. The interior angles of a triangle total 180 degrees. If one angle is greater than 90 degrees, the sum of the other two angles must be less than 90 degrees. Each of the remaining two angles, therefore, must be acute.

If you have trouble remembering the difference between obtuse and acute angles, think of this: An *obtuse* angle is an *obese* angle because it's fatter than a 90-degree angle; an *acute* angle is *a cute* little angle because it's smaller than a 90-degree angle.

8. **H.** An easy way to deal with percentages is to use the number 100. In this case, say that $(a + b) = 100$. Then 5 percent of $100 = 5$. That means that 10 percent of $b = 5$. Solve for b: $0.10b = 5$. Divide both sides by the value next to the variable: $b = 5 \div 0.10 = 50$. If $a + b = 100$, then $a = 50$ and $a = b$.

Are you saying, "Yeah, but what if I plug in something other than 100? How do I know it works with other numbers? Okay, we'll prove it to you. Try plugging in another number. (If you want to make life harder, go ahead!) Choose something truly bizarre, like -37. Let $(a + b) = -37$. Then 5 percent of $-37 = -1.85$. If $-1.85 = 10$ percent of b, solve for b:

−1.85 = 0.1b. Divide both sides by the value next to the variable: −1.85 ÷ 0.1 = −18.5. If $(a + b)$ = −37 and b = −18.5, then a = −18.5 as well. Son of a gun, it works! (But the moral of the story is: Plug in 100 when dealing with percentages. It makes life so much easier.)

9. **B.** The area of a square is side × side, or side^2. In this case, that's 8^2, or 64. That means the area of the triangle is also 64. The area of a triangle is $\frac{1}{2}b \times h$. In this case, that's $\frac{1}{2}x(x)$, or $\frac{1}{2}x^2$. Create the equation: $\frac{1}{2}x^2 = 64$. Multiply by 2 to get rid of the fraction: $x^2 = 128$. Take the square root by simplifying: $\sqrt{128} = \sqrt{64} \times \sqrt{2}$. The square root of 64 = 8, giving you a final answer of $8\sqrt{2}$.

10. **K.** You can solve this problem very quickly if you recognize that the triangle's ratio 6:8:10 is double the ratio of 3:4:5. A 3:4:5 ratio is a very common ratio for the sides of right triangles. (We cover this ratio in Chapter 8.). Bingo! A right triangle has one 90-degree angle; the answer has to be Choice (K).

11. **D.** An easy way to solve a problem like this is to plug in 100 for the original price of the book. In 2009, the book cost $100. If the price rose by 25 percent, it went up $25 to a total of $125. In 2011, the price was $\frac{1}{4}$, or 25 percent, below its 2009 cost. That means that it was $25 below the original $100, or $75.

If you picked Choice (A) or Choice (E), you fell for a trap. Choice (A) catches careless students who think, "The price rises 25 percent and then falls $\frac{1}{4}$, or 25 percent, for a 0 percent change." Wrong. Reading the question carefully tells you that you need to know the percent decrease from 2010 to 2011, which is from $125 to $75. The formula for percent increase or decrease is

$$\frac{\text{Number increase or decrease}}{\text{Starting (original) number}}$$

In other words, the denominator is the number you begin with, which, in this case, is 125 (because the question asks for the change from 2010, not from 2009). The number decrease is $50 (125 − 75 = 50). Finally, $\frac{50}{125} = \frac{4}{10} = 40\%$.

Choice (E) traps readers who forget that they're trying to find a percentage decrease and find just the year 2011 price.

12. **J.** The easiest way to do this problem is to look at the last term in the expression — the 15. What two numbers multiply to 15 and add to 8? You could choose 3 and 5 or −3 and −5. If you choose 3 and 5, you have $(a + 3)(a + 5)$, giving you $a^2 + 8a + 15$, thanks to the FOIL method we describe in Chapter 9 (*FOIL* stands for First, Outer, Inner, Last). You need $(a − 3)(a − 5)$, which multiplies to $a^2 − 8a + 15$.

13. **A.** A simple way to do this problem is to plug in numbers. Say that Jim is 20 years old now. Let m = 5. That means that 5 years ago, he was 15, such that y = 15. In 12 years, he will be 20 (his current age) + 12, which is 32. Look for an answer that works out to 32 when you plug in your numbers. Choice (A): $y(15) + m(5) + 12 = 32$.

14. **F.** First, square or cube each expression: $\left(5x^2y^5\right)\left(5x^2y^5\right) = 25x^4y^{10}$ and $\left(3x^3y^4\right)\left(3x^3y^4\right)\left(3x^3y^4\right) = 27x^9y^{12}$. Then multiply the products.

Before you go through all the button pushing to find the product of 25 and 27, check the exponents in the two terms: $x^4\left(x^9\right) = x^{13}$. You've narrowed the answers down to Choices (F) and (J). Next, you can eliminate Choice (J) because $25 \times 27 > 15$. What looked like a "pain in the posterior" problem is over with in a flash.

This question is relatively easy if you remember how to work with bases and exponents. To multiply like bases, add the exponents. To work with a "power to a power," that is, with one exponent inside parentheses and one outside, multiply the exponents. (If we've totally left you in the dust, go to Chapter 7. This stuff is easy once you get the hang of it.)

15. **C.** The area of a circle is πr^2, or 16π for the first circle. Because 16π is $\frac{1}{4}$ of 64π, you need a circle with an area of 64π, which means its radius must be 8: $\left(8^2\right)\pi = 64\pi$.

If you chose (A), you went backward and didn't think the problem through. If the second circle has a bigger area, it must have a bigger — not smaller — radius. The fact that 1 is $\frac{1}{4}$ of 4 is irrelevant. If you chose (D), you simply took 4 times the first circle's radius.

Remember that you get the ratio of the areas of similar figures by squaring the ratio of their sides (or radii). In other words, if the radii are in a ratio of 1:2, their areas are in a ratio of 1:4.

16. **J.** The formula for rate, time, and distance is $rt = d$: rate × time = distance. The rate is 2 hours and 20 minutes, which is $2\frac{1}{3}$ hours or $\frac{7}{3}$ hours, and the distance is 7 miles. Plug what you know into the formula: $r\left(\frac{7}{3}\right) = 7$. Multiply both sides by 3 and solve for r: $r = 3$.

17. **C.** To find the ratio of the dollhouse to the real house, set up a proportion. The ratio of the bedroom lengths is 18 inches to 12 feet. The answer has to be in feet, so change inches to feet. Because 18 inches is the same as 1.5 feet and 24 inches is the same as 2 feet, the ratio is $\frac{1.5}{12}$ and the proportion to find the width is

$$\frac{1.5}{12} = \frac{2}{x}$$

Cross-multiply and solve for x: $1.5x = 24$ and $x = 16$.

Did you notice that you can eliminate answers (A), (D), and (E) by using common sense? You can eliminate (A) because the length of the real bedroom is not 18 feet and the dollhouse is built to scale; the width cannot be 24 feet. Because the floor is wider than it is long (24 inches to 18 inches in the dollhouse), the answer must be more than 12 feet.

18. **J.** Two figures are similar if their sides (and angles) are in proportion. In this case, if the right triangles are similar, then the angles of triangle II are also in the ratio 1:2:3, which just happens to be a 30:60:90 triangle. (See Chapter 8 for a refresher on similar figures, the interior angles of a triangle, and the properties of special right triangles, like the 30:60:90 triangle.)

The ratio of sides in a 30:60:90 triangle is $s : s\sqrt{3} : 2s$, where s stands for the shortest side. So, if the shortest side of triangle II is 15, the other two sides measure $15\sqrt{3}$ and 30. Add the three sides together to get a perimeter of $45 + 15\sqrt{3}$.

19. **E.** Make sure you know what this word problem is asking for before you start doing any math. It doesn't want the solution to the equation but rather the equation itself. For these types of questions, going backward is often easier. "Forty percent of everything" means 0.40 times everything else, so you can eliminate Choices (A) and (D). Adding the square of 5 is simply $+5^2$. Choice (C) is wrong because it multiplies rather than adds 5^2. And 5^2 doesn't belong under the square root sign, which means you can cross out Choice (B). Only Choice (E) is left.

Read every choice. If you're rushed (and who isn't?), you may do too much work by anticipating what the question is asking for and actually solving the equation. No one really wants to know Lael's age, just the equation for finding it.

20. **H.** Find the percentage of redheaded and brown-haired children in the class by adding the probabilities of choosing either one: $\frac{1}{6} + \frac{1}{3} = \frac{1}{6} + \frac{2}{6} = \frac{3}{6} = \frac{1}{2}$. If half the children don't have blond hair, the other half of the children do have blond hair. That means the number of blondes, 30, is half the number of children, making the total 60.

21. **A.** Set up equations from the wording of the question: $a = 6 + b$ and $a + b = -18$. Substitute the value of a in the first equation for a in the second equation and solve for b: $(6 + b) + b = -18$; $6 + 2b = -18$; $2b = -24$; $b = -12$. So $b^2 = 144$.

22. **H.** You can find the interior angles of any polygon by using this formula: $(n-2) \times 180°$, where n stands for the number of sides. Here $n = 5$ and $(5-2)180 = 3(180) = 540$.

Notice that it makes no difference whether the figure is regular (all sides and angles are the same) or irregular. The exam may give you some truly bizarre-looking figures; don't let them intimidate you. The interior angle formula is the same no matter how grotesque the figure is.

23. **C.** The total number of tourists is the sum of $200 + 320 + 140 + 180 + 240 = 1,080$. The French are $\frac{180}{1,080}$ or $\frac{1}{6}$ of the total. A circle has 360 degrees, and $\frac{1}{6}$ of 360 is 60. If you chose Choice (E), you fell for the trap and didn't finish working the problem.

24. **H.** This problem is easier than it looks. If the rings cost $864 for 12, divide $864 by 12 to get $72. The price per ring drops from $85 to $72, a difference of $13.

25. **C.** Remove the parentheses and distribute the minus sign: $3x^2y + xy^2 - 2x^2y + 2xy^2$.

When you distribute the minus sign, it changes the sign of every element in the parentheses. Confusing signs is one of the most common careless errors in algebra problems.

Combine the like terms, $3x^2y - 2x^2y + xy^2 + 2xy^2 = x^2y + 3xy^2$, and mark Choice (C).

26. **H.** Line segment XY must be a horizontal line parallel to the x-axis, because the y-coordinate does not change. If the line segment goes from -2 to $+4$, it's 6 units long. The midway point would be 3 units along. Start at -2 and count: From -2 to -1 is 1 unit. From -1 to 0 is 2 units. From 0 to 1 is 3 units.

If you chose (K), you fell for the trap. Yes, you're moving 3 units to the right, but you're moving from -2. You go from -2 to 1, not to 3.

27. **B.** Add the numbers in the ratio: $3 + 5 = 8$. The total must be a multiple of 8, eliminating Choices (A) and (D). Try each of the remaining answers. If the total is 72, there are 9 groups (because 8 into 72 is 9). Multiply: $9 \times 3 = 27$ and $9 \times 5 = 45$. Subtract: $45 - 27 = 18$. You have a winner! (***Bonus trivia:*** Did you know that olive trees can live to be more than 2,000 years old? Just think, this question may be plaguing students two millennia from now!)

28. **H.** The easiest way to answer this question is as follows: Plug in the answer choices. We suggest you start with the middle term. That way, you can see whether the answer is too high or low and then choose your next plug-in accordingly.

If x is 10, then $10 + \frac{2}{3}(10) = 10 + 6.66 \approx 17$, which is certainly more than 15. The first equation is valid. Try the second: $10 + 4 < 15$. Is $10 + 4 < 15$? Yes. The answer is (H).

Just to convince those Doubting Thomases in the crowd, try another answer. Take Choice (G), for instance: $9 + \frac{2}{3}(9) = 9 + 6 = 15$. Because the first equation doesn't work, don't even bother with the second. If you take the time to check, you'll see that none of the other answers work.

When you make up your own numbers to plug in, you have to check every single answer, in case more than one works. (If more than one works, plug in new numbers and try again.) But when you plug in the answer choices, you can stop as soon as one works. On the ACT, only one answer can be correct.

29. **D.** This question tests your ability to translate English into that foreign language called algebra. If you've drawn a blank, use the handy translation guide we provide in Chapter 10. "A third" means $\frac{1}{3}$ and "of" means multiply. The product of 6 and 4 translates to 6×4. So far you've got $\frac{1}{3} \times (4 \times 6)$. "Is" means = and "three less than $2x$" means $2x - 3$. The final translated equation is $\frac{1}{3} \times (4 \times 6) = 2x - 3$. Now just solve for x: $8 = 2x - 3$; $11 = 2x$; $x = \frac{11}{2}$.

Did you think the answer was Choice (E)? If so, you subtracted 3 from 8 instead of adding and ended up with $8 - 3 = 5$ rather than $8 + 3 = 11$.

30. **K.** The only way to roll a 12 is to roll double sixes. The probability of rolling any number on a six-sided die (one of a pair of dice) is 1 out of 6, or $\frac{1}{6}$. Multiply consecutive probabilities: $\frac{1}{6}$ (for the first die) $\times \frac{1}{6}$ (for the second die) $= \frac{1}{36}$.

The probability rules you need to know for the ACT are pretty easy, and after you know them well, you'll ace all the probability questions. Take the time to review them in Chapter 7. In case you're wondering, the probability of your getting a probability question on the ACT is probably 100 percent.

31. **E.** The sides of an isosceles right triangle are in the ratio $s : s : s\sqrt{2}$, where s is one of the equal sides. The equation for the perimeter (p) of an isosceles right triangle, then, is $2s + s\sqrt{2} = p$. You know the perimeter of the triangle is $20 + 10\sqrt{2}$, which means that s must be 10. Use that information to find the area. The area of a triangle is $\frac{1}{2}bh$, and the sides of an isosceles right triangle are the base and height, such that $\frac{1}{2}(10)(10) = 50$.

32. **F.** The formula for the volume of a rectangular solid (a box or a fish tank, for instance) is lwh. The volume of the first tank is $6 \times 4 \times 10 = 240$. The sides of the base of the second tank are 50 percent longer than those of the first tank. If one side of the first tank is 6, the second tank has a side of $6 + \frac{1}{2}(6)$, or $6 + 3 = 9$. If the other side of the first tank is 4, the second tank has a side of length $4 + \frac{1}{2}(4)$, or $4 + 2 = 6$. Apply what you know to the volume formula: $9 \times 6 \times h = 240$. Solve for h to get $4.\overline{44}$, or approximately 4.4.

33. **A.** You can find the height of $\triangle ABC$ by applying the formula for the area of a triangle: $\frac{1}{2}bh$. The area is 32 and the base is 8, so $\frac{1}{2}8h = 32$. Solve for h to discover that the height is also 8. Therefore, the figure is an isosceles right triangle. Because similar figures have sides in proportion, $\triangle DEF$ is also an isosceles right triangle, making its base 28.

You could use the Pythagorean theorem to find the length of the hypotenuse, but you know from reading Chapter 8 that the ratio of the sides of the isosceles right triangle is $s : s : s\sqrt{2}$. That means the hypotenuse of $\triangle DEF$ is 28 and the perimeter is $28 + 28 + 28\sqrt{2}$, or $56 + 28\sqrt{2}$.

If you chose Choice (B), you just added all the numbers and said to heck with that pesky square root sign. No can do. You can't add roots and nonroots. If you picked Choice (C), you kept the square root sign but added everything together anyway. If adding roots and nonroots confuses you, go to Chapter 9 for a quick refresher.

34. **F.** The straight lines indicate absolute value, which is always positive. Therefore, $3 - 3a$ must equal 12 or –12. If $3 - 3a = 12$, $|3 - 3a| = 12$ and $-|3 - 3a| = -12$. If $3 - 3a = -12$, $|3 - 3a| = 12$ and once again $-|3 - 3a| = -12$. For $3 - 3a = 12$, $-3a = 9$ and $a = -3$, which is not one of the answer choices. For $3 - 3a = -12$, $-3a = -15$ and $a = 5$, which is Choice (F). If you chose Choice (H), you forgot to change the sign when you moved the 3 to the other side of the equal sign.

Why not take a simple shortcut? Plug in the answer choices. The ACT is nice enough to give you the answer for each problem; all you have to do is plug and chug through the answer choices until you find it. Only Choice (F) works for Question 34.

Note that the question carefully asks for which *could* be true. The answer choices never try to trap you by putting in two correct answers. If more than one value works in a problem, the ACT offers only one as an answer choice.

35. **D.** This problem is much easier than it looks. The sum of the interior angles of any triangle is 180° no matter what the size of the triangle is. Therefore, the interior angles of both triangles total 180°; 180:180 = 1:1.

If you chose Choices (A), (C), or (E), you let the areas of the triangles distract you.

36. **H.** The easy way to do this problem is to plug in numbers. Say the items cost 1 cent each for a total cost of 8 cents. Marcy forked over 2 dimes, for a total of 20 cents. Her change is the difference: 20 – 8 = 12. Go through each answer choice, plugging in 1 for x and 2 for y. The answer that comes out to be 12 is the winner. Choice (F) becomes 2 – 8 = –6. Nope. Choice (H) is 20 – 8 = 12. You have your answer.

37. **D.** The ratio of the arc length to the circumference is equal to the ratio of the arc measurement to 360°. $\overarc{AB} = \frac{10}{360}$ or $\frac{1}{36}$ of the circumference. Set up the proportion and cross-multiply: $\frac{3}{C} = \frac{1}{36}$; $1C = (3)(36)$; $C = 108$.

38. **J.** You can create a right triangle like this one from the paths of Kim and Scott:

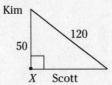

You may have looked at this triangle quickly, thought that it was one of those famous 5:12:13 PT (Pythagorean theorem) triples, and picked Choice (F). Sorry, it's not that easy this time (but we like the fact that you thought of the triples, which do show up often on this test).

Note that 120 is the hypotenuse, which in a 5:12:13 triangle is 13, not 12. So you have to solve this one the old-fashioned way by applying the Pythagorean theorem: $50^2 + b^2 = 120^2; 2,500 + b^2 = 14,400; b^2 = 11,900; b = \sqrt{11,900}$.

If you picked Choice (G), you avoided one trap but fell into a second. The 11,900 represents a side *squared*. To find the side, take the square root of 11,900.

39. **D.** Plug 3 in for x in the equation: $9 - y = 4$; $y = 5$ when $x = 3$. The coordinates are (3, 5).

40. **G.** The altitude (or height) divides the equilateral triangle into two 30:60:90 triangles, as shown here:

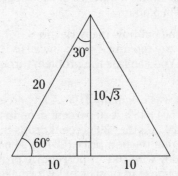

You know this because an altitude is always perpendicular (90 degrees) to the base and an equilateral triangle has three 60-degree angles. That means the bottom-left angle is 60 degrees, the angle in the middle is 90 degrees, and the angle at the top has been split into two, making it into two 30-degree angles.

The ratio of the sides of a 30:60:90 triangle is $s : s\sqrt{3} : 2s$, where s is the smallest side (the side opposite the 30-degree angle). The height of the triangle forms the side that measures $s\sqrt{3}$, which means $s = 10$. Therefore, each side of the original triangle is 2(10) or 20. 20 + 20 + 20 = 60, so Choice (G) is your answer.

41. **D.** The easy way to do this problem is to take it one step at a time. After one hour, the pool is half empty. After the next hour, it is one-fourth empty (because $\frac{1}{2} \times \frac{1}{2} = \frac{1}{4}$). You can make a little chart of the progression, like the one that follows:

Hour	Capacity Left
1	$\frac{1}{2}$
2	$\frac{1}{4}$
3	$\frac{1}{8}$
4	$\frac{1}{16}$
5	$\frac{1}{32}$
6	$\frac{1}{64}$

Scan the answer choices before you begin solving the problem. Doing so tells you how precise you need to be. Because three of the answers are so close — (C), (D), (E) — you have to solve the problem exactly. Had the answers been far apart, like 12, 6, and 0, you could have estimated.

42. **K.** The easy way to do this problem is to plug in numbers. Let $m = 5$ and $n = 10$. If five pencils cost 10 cents, each pencil costs $\frac{10}{5}$, or 2 cents. So you know the cost of one pencil is $\frac{n}{m}$. Because m is in the denominator, you can already narrow down your answers to Choices (H) and (K). Multiply the cost per pencil ($\frac{n}{m}$) by the number of pencils (p) to get $\frac{n}{m} \times p = \frac{np}{m}$.

43. **A.** First, find out how many 45-minute increments are in 4.5 hours, or 270 minutes: $\frac{270}{45} = 6$. Faye, therefore, assembles 6 batches of 200 widgets, or 1,200 widgets. Hal assembles 600 in 2.5 hours, or 1,200 in 5 hours.

Don't bother figuring out how many Hal does in 1 minute, or in 45 minutes, or in any other increment. That's way too much work. Because 1,200 is 2 times 600, Hal works for 2×2.5 hours, or 5 hours. You can talk the problem through instead of getting involved in lengthy calculations.

44. **J.** Say that the suit was originally $100. A 50 percent increase raises the price to $150: $100 + (100 \times 0.50) = 150$. A 20 percent drop in the price puts the cost at $120: $150 - (150 \times 0.2) = 120$. Another 30 percent drops the price to $84: $120 - (120 \times 0.3) = 84$. Now you can easily see that the new price ($84) is 84 percent of the original price ($100). That's the beauty of working with 100 for percentage problems. Yes, the answer is true no matter what number you choose to plug in, but why make life any harder than it already is?

Choice (G) is the trap answer. Did you simply write down +50 – 20 – 30 = 0, meaning there was no change? If so, the new cost would be 100 percent of the old cost, but, as we explain in the preceding paragraph, the decreases aren't all percentages of the same number.

45. **E.** A revolution of a wheel is the same as the circumference of a wheel. If the wheel goes 15 revolutions and 300π meters, you divide 300π by 15, and each revolution is 20π. Remember that $C = 2r\pi$. To find r, apply the formula: $20\pi = 2r\pi; 20 = 2r; 10 = r$.

46. **G.** A little vocabulary lesson here: *Prime numbers* are numbers that have no positive integer factors other than 1 and themselves. Examples are 2, 3, 5, and 7. *Composite numbers* do have positive integer factors other than 1 and themselves. Examples are 4, 6, and 9.

Because a composite number already has more factors than just 1 and itself, multiplying it by yet another number keeps it composite.

To tackle a problem of this sort, plug in both types of numbers. Try to plug in numbers that eliminate answer choices. For instance, 3 (prime) × 9 (composite) = 27. The answer isn't a prime number, zero, a fraction, or an even number, so eliminate Choices (F), (H), (J), and (K).

47. **C.** To visualize sector *AOC*, draw a straight line from point *A* to point *O* on the figure in the practice test in Chapter 20. An *inscribed angle* (one that has a vertex on the circle) has half the measure of its central angle so $\angle AOC = 12°$. (If you forgot this, turn to Chapter 8.) Because a circle has 360°, $\angle AOC = \frac{12}{360}$ or $\frac{1}{30}$ of the circle, so the area of sector *AOC* must be $\frac{1}{30}$ of the area of the circle. Multiply the area of sector *AOC* by 30 to find the area of the circle: $120\pi \times 30 = 3{,}600\pi$.

Because the area of a circle is πr^2, the radius of this circle must be 60: $\pi r^2 = 3{,}600\pi$; $r^2 = 3{,}600$; $r = 60$. When you know the circle's radius, you can apply the formula for circumference: $C = 2r\pi$; $C = 2(60)\pi$; $C = 120\pi$.

Did you automatically eliminate Choice (C) because it was the same value as the area of the sector? Don't make quick assumptions; complete the calculation.

48. **H.** Don't be intimidated if you don't remember anything about circles or their equations. Simply plug the –3 into the equation and solve for *y*: $-3^2 + y^2 = 25; 9 + y^2 = 25; y^2 = 16; y = \pm 4$.

If you insist on getting excessively paranoid, don't freak out and think that the right answer choice has to be both –4 and +4. The question asks you what *could* be an answer; either is possible.

49. **A.** You can, of course, apply FOIL (First, Outer, Inner, Last; see Chapter 9) to multiply each expression out and then add the products. But you don't have to do that much work or spend that much time if you remember that $(a + b)^2 = (a^2 + 2ab + b^2)$. Substitute 3 for *b* and you've got $a^2 + 6a + 9$. Next recall that $(a - b)^2 = (a^2 - 2ab + b^2)$. Substitute 4 for *b* to get $a^2 - 8a + 16$. Now add the two equations vertically, like so:

$$\begin{array}{r} a^2 + 6a + 9 \\ a^2 - 8a + 16 \\ \hline 2a^2 - 2a + 25 \end{array}$$

You can eliminate Choices (C) and (D) immediately because you know that $a^2 + a^2 \neq a^2$. Don't forget to narrow down the answers as you go to avoid making a careless mistake.

When the answers have variations on a theme, such as positive and negative versions of the same numerals, be sure to watch your signs carefully. Double-check this type of problem as soon as you finish it.

50. **K.** If there are going to be two colors of marbles and red has twice the chance of being drawn as blue, red marbles must be $\frac{2}{3}$ of the total and blue marbles must be $\frac{1}{3}$ of the total. That way, the probability of drawing a red marble is twice as great as the probability of drawing a blue marble. Now all you have to do is multiply: $\frac{2}{3} \times 36 = 24$ and $\frac{1}{3} \times 36 = 12$. The difference between 24 and 12 is 12.

51. **B.** Do you remember that great saying you learned in trig: SOH CAH TOA ("soak a toe, uh")? If not, you can review everything you need to know in Chapter 9. For this problem, you need to know that $\tan Z = $ opposite/adjacent. The length of the side opposite *Z* is 7, and the length of the side adjacent to *Z* is 24. Therefore, $\tan Z = \frac{7}{24}$.

52. **J.** The unshaded circle means that point is not included on the graph. Therefore, –4 is not part of the graph and you can eliminate Choice (H). The shaded circle means that point is included on the graph. Look for an answer that says the graph can be equal to 0. Choice (J) works well.

Choice (F) is far too broad. Numbers greater than –4 are infinite and would be off the graph. Choice (G) is too broad for the same reason: Numbers less than –4 are infinite. Choice (K) is the trap answer. The graph doesn't go all the way to –5.

53. **D.** Get the terms that have x and y in them on one side and all the terms that have nothing to do with x and y on the other side. Subtract $4cy$ from both sides: $4cx - 4cy - \frac{3d}{e} = 0$. Add $\frac{3d}{e}$ to both sides: $4cx - 4cy = \frac{3d}{e}$. Factor out $4c$: $4c(x - y) = \frac{3d}{e}$. Then divide by $4c$ to isolate $x - y$ on one side of the equation: $x - y = \frac{3d}{4ce}$.

54. **J.** You have to memorize the slope equation to solve this type of problem:

$$slope = \frac{y_2 - y_1}{x_2 - x_1}$$

Substitute the appropriate x- and y-coordinates into the equation:

$$\frac{b - (-b)}{a - (-a)} = \frac{2b}{2a} = \frac{b}{a}$$

Note: Which point you choose for y_2 doesn't matter, but after you choose y_2 (or b), you must choose the x-coordinate in the ordered pair for x_2 (or a).

55. **E.** To find the angle of depression, first draw a horizontal line from the lookout point. The line forms the 14-degree angle. The horizontal line is parallel to the water's surface. When parallel lines are cut by a transversal, the alternate interior angles are *congruent* (the same):

So you can draw a right triangle with a 14-degree angle:

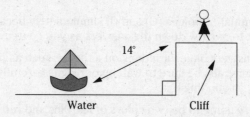

You know the side *adjacent to* (next to) the 14-degree angle measures 2 km, and you're trying to find the measure of the opposite side, so the trigonometric function you need is the tangent: $\frac{\text{opposite}}{\text{adjacent}}$. Apply the formula and solve for x: $\tan 14° = \frac{x}{2}$; $2 \tan 14° = x$ degrees.

56. **G.** Wait! You don't need to drag out your graphing calculator for this one. This problem requires more common sense than anything else. First, look for a graph that shows that nothing was printed for two hours. This narrows the field quickly to Choices (G) and (H), which look almost exactly alike. The difference, however, is that the horizontal portion on Choice (G) shows that the number of pages (p) remained steady for a period of time. If you look closely, you see that Choice (H) holds the time (t) rather than the pages (p) steady for a period of time, which is wrong.

57. **A.** The key to answering this question is to remember the equation $\cos^2\theta + \sin^2\theta = 1$. If you have trouble remembering this doozy of an equation, think of a right triangle with a hypotenuse of 1, as in $x^2 + y^2 = 1^2$ (think Pythagorean theorem).

Because $\cos\theta = \dfrac{\text{adjacent}}{\text{hypotenuse}} = \dfrac{x}{1} = x$ and $\sin\theta = \dfrac{\text{opposite}}{\text{hypotenuse}} = \dfrac{y}{1} = y$, then $x^2 + y^2 = 1^2$. You can rewrite this as $\cos^2\theta + \sin^2\theta = 1$.

To get back to the problem at hand, use this equation:

$$\frac{\sin^2\theta + \cos^2\theta}{\sec^2\theta} = \frac{1}{\sec^2\theta}$$

Because $\sec\theta = \dfrac{1}{\cos\theta}$, $\sec^2\theta = \dfrac{1}{\cos^2\theta}$. Make the final substitutions:

$$\sec^2\theta = \frac{1}{\cos^2\theta} = \frac{1}{\sec^2\theta} = \frac{1}{\frac{1}{\cos^2\theta}} = 1 \times \frac{\cos^2\theta}{1} = \cos^2\theta$$

Now take a deep breath!

Most students aren't comfortable with these complex trig questions. If you're one of them, take heart. Questions with this level of difficulty don't crop up too often, and they're usually at the end of the Mathematics Test. Don't spend too much time trying to figure them out. Mark any old answer on your answer sheet, and skip merrily along to the next question. You don't have to get all the problems right to get a very good score; you can afford to miss several of them.

58. **J.** This problem is one of the oldest tricks in the books; test makers include it to try to get students to waste time doing a lot of mathematical calculations, setting up algebraic equations full of p's and c's, and running through calculator batteries. Forget the frenzy; you can solve this problem simply by talking through it.

The first thing to realize is that you can't have a cow and a half, so double that to get three cows. Twice as many cows (three instead of $1\frac{1}{2}$) can give twice as much milk (three pints instead of $1\frac{1}{2}$) in the same number of hours.

Don't stop there and choose (F). The cows produce 3 pints of milk in 36 hours, but the question asks you for the amount of milk they produce in 72 hours.

You have the right number of cows. You double the number of hours: $36 \times 2 = 72$. The same number of cows in double the time can give double the milk: $3 \times 2 = 6$ pints. This problem is much easier than it looks . . . unless you make it hard.

59. **E.** The unknown height is opposite the 21-degree angle. Because 1,500 is the side adjacent to 21 degrees, you can use the tangent formula: $\dfrac{\text{opposite}}{\text{adjacent}}$. So $\tan 21° = \dfrac{x}{1,500}$. Solve for x: $1,500 \tan 21° = x$.

60. **J.** If, like most people, you don't remember anything about the unit circle, draw a right triangle:

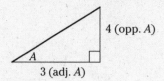

If one leg is 3 and the other is 4, the hypotenuse must be 5. The triangle is a 3:4:5 right triangle. Therefore, $\cos A = \dfrac{\text{adjacent}}{\text{hypotenuse}}$; $\cos A = \dfrac{3}{5}$.

If you have any extra time by the end of the test section (which we highly doubt), you can verify that the answer is Choice (J) by drawing a unit circle:

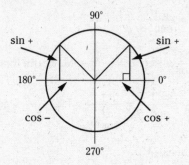

Because $\tan A = \dfrac{\text{opposite } A}{\text{adjacent } A}$, $\tan A = \dfrac{\sin A}{\cos A}$ in the unit circle.

Because $\tan A$ is positive, $\sin A$ and $\cos A$ must both be positive or both be negative. Between 0 degrees and 90 degrees, $\sin A$ and $\cos A$ are both positive. But between 90 degrees and 180 degrees, $\sin A$ is positive and $\cos A$ is negative, ruling out any possibility that A is between 90 degrees and 180 degrees and that $\cos A$ is negative.

Depending on what math level you're taking in school, you may not have even learned this stuff in class yet. Don't worry; the ACT has only a few questions like it. And look on the bright side: Quickly guessing on this question frees up more time for you to return to the other questions you can double-check now that you have the time.

Reading Test

1. **B.** *Exorbitant* means "overpriced" or "very expensive," so Choice (B) is the most obvious answer. Even if you didn't know the definition of *exorbitant,* you could eliminate Choices (A) and (D). The passage doesn't mention what the posted speed limit was, and the narrator never suggests that she didn't deserve the ticket. Choice (C) may have tempted you because speeding tickets are rarely anticipated, but *exorbitant* doesn't mean "unexpected."

You're supposed to choose the best answer out of the four options. To know which is the best, use that secret weapon known as *POE,* or the process of elimination. By eliminating answers you know can't be right, you help isolate the answer that fits the best.

2. **F.** The narrator's indication that her boss is always a pessimist leads you to believe that she doesn't expect him to provide an overly positive reaction to her news, but that's really all you know. You can't assume a lack of specific expectations like a raise offer or party, so

eliminate Choices (G) and (H). Just because someone's a pessimist doesn't mean he's prone to breakdowns; Choice (J) is a bit too extreme. The most general and least extreme option is Choice (F).

3. **B.** The question very kindly directs you specifically to the last paragraph, where the narrator reflects on her decision to move. Her thoughts about the success she has experienced because of her move indicate satisfaction that her boss's earlier prediction that she would fail hadn't come true. Therefore, the best answer of the four is Choice (B); she uses the paragraph to thoughtfully consider the effects of her move. Choices (A) and (C) are way too extreme for the tone and content of the last paragraph. She feels successful rather than frustrated or bitter. You may have had a little more difficulty eliminating Choice (D), though. There is a hint of sarcasm in the last paragraph when she feels "a small amount of satisfaction" that the boss who told her that the grass is always greener ended up mowing lawns, but this reference is just one part of the entire paragraph and suggests a little irony rather than full-blown sarcasm.

For questions that ask you for the purpose or tone of an entire paragraph or passage, choose answers that apply to the whole passage or paragraph, not just part of it.

4. **G.** You can probably cross out Choices (F) and (J) because they contain disputable words. A "complete failure" means that no part of her move was successful. Unless the passage comes right out and says that there was nothing good about the move, you know Choice (F) has to be wrong. The word that should warn you away from Choice (J) is *solely,* which is another way of saying *only.* Boredom may have been one reason that the narrator wanted to move, but it wasn't the sole reason. That leaves you with Choices (G) and (H). Although the narrator experienced a few setbacks in her travels, you can't say that the trip was mostly hazardous. She did make it to her destination, after all. POE leads you to Choice (G), the most generic, and therefore best, summary of the narrator's experience.

5. **C.** *Irony* means "using humor to suggest the opposite of something's literal meaning." It's ironic (and a little amusing) that the manager used the "grass is always greener" cliché to suggest that the narrator wouldn't make it away from home when the manager then ended up in the position of literally keeping the grass green. Although the manager may have had a feeling of resentment, which is Choice (A), that feeling doesn't relate the cliché to his new profession. If you picked Choice (B), redundancy, you'd have to think the manager had had a lawn-mowing career in the past, and Choice (D), predestination, implies that the boss was somehow able to foresee his future career, an idea that nothing in the passage supports.

6. **H.** If doing so helps you focus, you can rephrase this question to "Which of the following wasn't the narrator concerned about?" Now just eliminate her concerns. The first paragraph suggests that the narrator was worried about leaving her home and family for the first time, so you can cross out Choice (J). Although the narrator doesn't come right out and say that she was worried about staying by herself in a hotel room, she does list it as one of her "firsts" at Line 42, which tells you that it was an unfamiliar experience. You may not want to eliminate Choice (G) right away, but it's probably wrong. The next paragraph describes her uneasiness when she sees the sign about not stopping for hitchhikers in the prison area. That sounds like a concern! Nowhere in the passage is there any mention of whether she drives a manual or automatic transmission, so you can confidently pick Choice (H) as the best answer.

7. **C.** The common phrase "the grass is always greener" has nothing to do with the actual appearance (or aesthetic) of the landscape, so you can toss out Choice (A). Choice (B) is probably wrong, too; the manager utters the phrase in reference to the narrator's life, not his, and, while the manager may think that the narrator won't be as happy with her next job, that thought doesn't relate well to the common understanding of the phrase "the grass is always greener," and Choice (D) contains a red flag in the word *never.*

Answer choices in the Reading Test that have debatable words, such as *never, always,* and *completely,* are probably wrong. Consider them carefully before claiming them as right answers.

8. **J.** The information you need to answer this question comes from the tenth paragraph. Cross out Choice (F) because, although you may think it would be a good idea for the narrator to get a new bed to replace the faulty air mattress, the passage never says that she actually makes that wise purchase. Choice (H) confuses physical hiccups with the kind that mean "glitches." The narrator wasn't really afflicted with hiccups. You may be tempted to choose Choice (G). The passage does say that she can't find a few things, but the narrator refers to these items as things she was "certain she had packed," which implies that she had left them at home rather than misplaced them in the new abode. Choice (J) works best. Because she says that her roommate has "odd culinary" habits, you can assume that her roommate creates dishes that the narrator isn't very familiar with.

9. **A.** Although Choices (B) and (C) may have a little truth to them, the key is the phrasing of the question. The right answer has to reflect the purpose of the whole paragraph. Choice (D) misstates the real theme of the paragraph. The point isn't that there's no place like home. If that were true, the narrator would have ended up back in her small hometown. Choice (A) provides an excellent summary of the point of the paragraph and fits with the theme of the whole passage.

Just because something in an answer choice is true doesn't necessarily mean that it's the right answer to the question.

10. **J.** The narrator refers to her manager as a pessimist; that's all you need to choose Choice (J) because *negative* is a synonym for *pessimistic.* She certainly doesn't think he's an optimist; that's the opposite of a pessimist. You may get the impression that the manager becomes insecure because he was wrong about the narrator's success, but that assumption doesn't have enough support from the passage. The narrator definitely doesn't think the manager is passive. His rude comments wouldn't come from a passive person, so you can eliminate Choice (G), too.

11. **C.** Choices (A) and (B) are true statements but are much too specific to be main ideas. A main idea, whether of a paragraph or the whole passage, is broad and general. Choice (D) is tricky, but it goes too far. The passage neither states nor implies that a building cannot be appreciated without understanding symbolism; it simply informs the reader of the symbolism within the Capitol. Hence, (C) is the right answer.

12. **H.** In Lines 20–21, you're told that Lincoln's body was laid to rest under the Rotunda after he was assassinated. The other answers are neither given nor implied in the passage.

When you're asked what the author means, be sure to go back to the passage and find the answer in the context of the passage. Don't try to use your common sense or dredge up what little you remember from American history.

Bonus trivia: Speaking of Lincoln, did you know that one of his nicknames was the Perpendicular Pronoun? The 6'4" president was criticized for using the word "I" in his speeches, something considered improper at the time.

13. **A.** If something is *ironic,* it contradicts what you'd normally expect. For example, it would be ironic if the firehouse burned down. Here, it's ironic that the symbol of America, the Capitol, is filled with works by foreign artists. Choice (B), *ingenious,* means clever or resourceful. Choice (C), *perspicacious,* means shrewd or perceptive, and Choice (D), *supercilious,* means arrogant.

Did you pick Choice (C) or (D) because you thought, "Ooh, big word! I don't know what it means, so it must be the right answer!"? If so, you're not alone. Many students automatically choose the longest, hardest word. Usually, the totally bizarre word you've never seen before is there to distract you. Don't choose a word you don't know unless by process of elimination you're absolutely positive that the words you do know are wrong.

14. **G.** This type of question is merely plug 'n' chug; plug each answer choice into the context and see which one works best. The sentence says, ". . . more overt than symbolic," meaning less hidden symbolism and more open, obvious meaning.

15. **D.** The third paragraph talks about the buildings being on fire and then says that the rainstorm prevented the conflagration from destroying everything. From this, you can deduce that a conflagration is a fire and that the rainstorm doused the fire, making Choice (D) the right one. After all, *inferno* is a synonym for fire.

If you chose Choice (A), you fell for the trap. The conflagration itself isn't the rainstorm; it's just the opposite.

16. **J.** The paragraph talks about how a rainstorm put out the fire and how a windstorm killed British forces. From this, you can infer that Nature helped save the Capitol, making Choice (J) the right one. Choice (F) is a value judgment: Who's to say who's superior and who's inferior? (In case you're wondering, value judgments are rarely correct answers.) Choice (G) is a trap. It may be true that the British superstitiously thought that the world was conspiring against them and in favor of the Americans, but that implication is too much of a stretch for you to make. Choice (H) is just plain wrong. The paragraph tells you that the Capitol was damaged but not destroyed.

17. **C.** Sometimes the obvious answer is in fact the correct answer. The fourth paragraph specifically says that most artwork tells a story about American history, making Choice (C) the way to go. The other answers may be true, but they aren't mentioned in the passage. When a question begins with the words, "According to the passage," the answer usually comes straight from the passage. This type of question is a gift to you. The only way to get it wrong is to outsmart yourself by making the question harder than it really is.

18. **F.** If EXCEPT questions throw you, focus on what you're supposed to look for. This particular question asks for what's *not* stated in the passage, so begin by crossing out answer choices that you remember reading about. You read the definition of *E Pluribus Unum* ("Out of many, one,") in the second paragraph. The fourth paragraph tells you that Lafayette was the first foreigner to address a joint session of Congress. The second-to-last paragraph gives several examples of the subject matter of the Capital's artwork. That same paragraph mentions the nickname "Women in a Bathtub," but it doesn't include an explanation of the nickname's origin.

An EXCEPT question (or any negatively phrased question, such as, "The author would most likely DISAGREE with which of the following statements?" or "Which of the following is NOT true?") can be a time-wasting question, a good one to guess at quickly and go on if you're running out of time.

19. **A.** The passage talks about such patriots as Washington, Jefferson, Lafayette, and Penn. The author is probably surprised to find a statue of a former enemy among the others.

A little common sense goes a long way. Use POE (process of elimination) to get this question right. Nothing in the passage implies that the Capitol art honored only Northerners. You know the Capitol's art includes statues of women as well as statues of men. And some of the people honored, like Washington and Lafayette, are in fact military heroes, not civilians.

20. **H.** The author mentions men and women, confederates and foreigners, doctors and Indians. So you can reasonably assume that his purpose is to show the diversity of people who have helped make America the nation it is. If you chose Choice (J), you were indulging in a little wishful thinking! Yes, mentioning the man who invented ice cream may have been slightly funny, but it's unlikely the author was trying to provide any comedy in this passage.

21. **B.** The easy way to answer this question is to plug 'n' chug. Plug each answer choice into the sentence and chug, or read, through it. The sentence, "Nearly any small child can recite quickly the twelve months of the year," makes the most sense.

Choices (A) and (D) are traps. Yes, when you rattle something, you can shake it and it makes noise, but those particular uses aren't appropriate in this particular sentence. Words have more than one meaning. Your job is to identify which meaning works best in the context of the sentence.

22. **F.** The first paragraph specifically states that a piece of information is missing: how the names of the months came into existence. The majority of the rest of the passage explains the names, so Choice (F) is the winner here.

If you picked Choice (G) or (H), you fell for the "But I know I read that!" trap. Just because the passage mentions an answer choice doesn't mean that it's the main idea of the passage. A main idea is a general, underlying theme that runs through most of the passage. A good way to identify a main idea is to pretend that you're answering a buddy's question: "Hey, what did you just read?" In this case, you would respond with something like, "Oh, I read a passage about how the months got their names." Often, you can predict the correct answer to a main-idea question before you even read the answer choices.

23. **C.** Lines 19–21 state, "As the guardian of doors or gateways, he had to be vigilant for friends and foes coming from either direction." This specific-information question should have been very easy for you. It simply asks you to find one fact from the passage. You don't have to interpret anything or draw any conclusion.

Recognizing specific-information questions on the test is important. If you're running short on time, invest your time in these questions, because you can almost always get them right.

24. **F.** When a question begins with the words, "According to the passage," it's usually quite simple. The answer to this particular question is right there in the passage, almost word for word, in Lines 27–29, which state, "This month's name came from the February 15 feast of purification." If you missed this question, get in the habit of summarizing paragraph topics as you read each passage.

25. **A.** The fourth paragraph implies that because people know Mars was the god of war, they assume that the month of March got its name from warfare. But the author states that the origin of the name actually referred to the fact that war was postponed until the springtime and that Mars was also the god of springtime.

Choice (B) is close but not quite right. The author discusses that most of the months are named after gods and goddesses but never states or implies that most people believe that all months are named for gods and goddesses. (Be careful not to read too much into the answer.) Choice (C) is definitely wrong. The fifth paragraph talks about how not every month's name has a definite *provenance,* or known origin. And Choice (D) is off the wall: The passage mentions nothing about lunar cycles.

26. **G.** This question should have been relatively easy (unless you were too burned out to go back and look at how the expression is used in the passage). Plug the answer choices into the sentence and see which one works best. It's logical to say, "In order to bring the Roman calendar back in line with the solar year. . . ." Choice (F) would be a good second choice, but "on the same wavelength" isn't as precise as Choice (G). The passage is about time designations rather than radios.

27. **D.** The second-to-last paragraph states that Romans considered even numbers unlucky but never says why.

Often, when a question asks which of the following isn't discussed, the answer has a *why* in it. Passages often state facts but may not give the why and wherefore behind those facts.

28. **J.** Because the question asks for a main idea, look for the most general answer. The passage mentions Choices (F) and (G), but they aren't the main point. A main idea often is located in the topic, or opening, sentence of the paragraph. The topic sentence of this paragraph states, "Not every month has retained its original name over the years."

29. **A.** The author states that most people believe every fourth year is a leap year, but that's not the case, so Choice (D) is wrong. The passage says that century years aren't leap years unless they're evenly divisible by 400, but that doesn't necessarily mean that all leap years are divisible by 400. So Choice (B) is wrong, too. Nothing in the paragraph about leap years implies that leap years can't occur in years that begin a century, so you can eliminate Choice (C). The answer has to be Choice (A) because it's the only one left; plus, the passage tells you that leap years have 366 days.

30. **H.** The key to answering this one correctly is to insert every answer choice into the sentence to see which one makes the most sense. The author discusses how people don't realize something (that not every fourth year is a leap year), which means that they ignore a fact.

This question is very typical of vocabulary-in-context questions. Sure, you know what *gloss* normally means, but the ACT rarely uses a word in its normal sense. In fact, the normal sense of the word is usually the trap. Choices (F) and (J) here are the trap answers. By the way, did you notice that Choices (F) and (J) are basically the same? Because you can't have two right answers, both must be wrong.

31. **B.** A primary purpose is general and broad, not specific. The overall agenda of this passage is to differentiate between what's true and false about bushmasters. So Choice (B) is the best answer. Choice (D) gives information that's stated only briefly in the passage; it isn't the purpose of writing the passage. The passage doesn't mention Choice (C) at all. Choice (A) is the trap answer. The passage states that bushmasters are poisonous, but it doesn't explain why.

32. **J.** The best way to answer this question is with POE: Find three questions that appear in the passage and whatever is left is the correct answer. The second paragraph states that the bushmaster's coloring aids in its camouflage. The third paragraph tells why the bushmaster has the pits in its head. The third paragraph also tells you that the bushmaster eats rodents. Although the passage does talk about the maternal instincts of the bushmaster, it doesn't discuss mating habits or attracting a mate.

If you're rushed for time, this question is a good one to guess at quickly and come back to later if you can. (The ACT has no penalties for wrong answers, which means that you never want to leave an answer blank.)

33. **C.** The second paragraph states, "This maternal instinct is quite rare among reptiles." So Choice (C) is the right answer.

When a question begins with the words, "According to the passage," it's usually a freebie for you, a complete gift. If you know that you aren't going to be able to answer all the questions in time, or if your brain is mush and you're losing focus (we speak from experience!), look for an "According to the passage" question.

If you chose Choice (D), you fell for the trap. Yes, the first paragraph states that the bushmaster has no rattles on its tail, unlike the rattlesnake. But the passage doesn't say that this lack of rattles is rare among reptiles. The author differentiates two snakes; he doesn't make a generalization about all snakes.

34. **F.** The first paragraph states that the bushmaster is the largest venomous snake in "the New World." From this careful distinction (not "the largest snake in the world," but "the largest snake in the New World"), you can infer that larger snakes are found elsewhere in the world.

Choice (H) is tempting, but it's a trap. The bushmaster perhaps attacks humans only when threatened, but the passage implies that the bushmaster attacks its prey for food, even though the prey (like rodents) doesn't threaten the snake.

35. **B.** The third paragraph discusses how bushmasters hide from and then ambush their prey.

You didn't fall for that piece of lame humor in Choice (A), did you? "Ambush" has nothing to do with bushes in the Amazon!

36. **H.** Words have more than one meaning. Much of the ACT reading test asks you to interpret how the author uses certain words instead of just knowing their straightforward dictionary meanings. To *misplace* does mean to lose, but that's not how the author means the term in this instance. He is saying that people have the wrong idea — that bushmasters are not really fierce or vicious.

The key to answering this question is to continue reading. The real answer is in the text that follows the lines given in the question. Careless readers who go only where the question directs them miss this type of question every time.

37. **A.** The paragraph discusses how the bushmasters' numbers are declining, although the bushmaster is not yet an endangered species. The author implies, without coming right out and stating, that the bushmaster may become endangered as more and more of its habitat is removed. Choice (C) goes too far. The fact that hikers hike in the forest proves that the snakes don't make those areas uninhabitable. Choice (D) is far too specific. You can't know if — or when — the snakes will become extinct. A common trap on the ACT is offering a very strongly worded answer that is rarely correct.

38. **F.** The last paragraph states that the hikers step on sleeping snakes because of the snakes' coloration and their lack of rattles. So Choice (H) is wrong. Choice (J) is the trap answer. The passage says that hikers step on the snakes when they're asleep, but the snakes are nocturnal, so they probably aren't sleeping during the night.

39. **D.** This question is tricky. Choice (A) states a fact — that bushmasters do sleep during the day — but it isn't the main point of the paragraph. Choice (B) states a fact that seems logical, based on common knowledge about wildlife in general (that most animals — including humans — will attack to protect their young and their food). But it's not the main point of the paragraph either. The last paragraph mentions Choice (C) when it states that the bushmaster's coloration and silent warning system rarely alert humans to the snake's presence . . . ." But that's not the main point of the paragraph. The main point (as introduced by the topic sentence of the paragraph) is that the bushmaster is not as ferocious and aggressive as its reputation would make you believe.

When a question asks you for the main idea, whether of the entire passage or of just a paragraph, try to predict an answer before you look at the choices. Pretend that someone just asked you what you're reading. Your response, which in this case may be something like, "People think that this snake is more dangerous than it really is," is the main idea.

40. **J.** If you're rushed for time, a negatively phrased question ("Which was NOT . . .") is a good one to guess at quickly. Answering this question is really like answering three separate questions, because you have to find three questions the passage *does* answer and then identify which question it does *not* answer by process of elimination. The fourth paragraph talks about enemies of the bushmaster. The third paragraph discusses how a bushmaster locates its prey. The last paragraph explains why some people consider the bushmaster aggressive.

Choice (J) can be a little tricky. The author mentions that the bushmaster preys on warm-blooded animals, but he never tells *why* the bushmaster has that preference. (If you missed this question, don't feel too bad. Many people miss negatively phrased questions, which is why we suggest that you not waste too much time on them.)

Science Test

In each of the following sections, we explain how to interpret the tables and figures, as well as the introductory text, that accompany each passage in the Science Test. After all, it's important that you read all the introductory material before you try to answer any of the questions. Then we go into more detailed explanations of the specific questions and their answers.

Passage 1

Before going to the questions that relate to Passage 1, make sure you have some idea about how the two tables work. To figure the relative humidity in Table 1, find a dry-bulb reading in the left-hand column and move right to the appropriate difference between wet-bulb and dry-bulb readings. For example, for a dry-bulb reading of 20 degrees Celsius (C), the relative humidity is 59 percent when the wet-bulb reading is 5 degrees different from the dry-bulb reading. The major trend to note in Table 1 is that humidity increases with higher temperatures (as you move down the table) and decreases with increased differences between the two bulb readings (as you move to the right).

As you look at Table 2, note that the apparent temperature, as explained in the sentence immediately preceding the table, is what a given combination of humidity and air temperature would feel like to a typical human. The table shows, for example, that the apparent temperature at 70 percent relative humidity and an air temperature of 23.9 degrees C is 25.0 degrees C. The trends are that apparent temperature increases with increasing humidity, consistent with the common knowledge that high humidity is uncomfortable, and that apparent temperature increases with increasing air temperature, consistent with the common-sense notion that the hotter it gets, the hotter it feels.

1. **B.** All four of the choices are between 51.1 for 70 percent and 57.8 for 80 percent (see Table 2). Because 75 percent is halfway between 70 percent and 80 percent, the number you're looking for should be close to halfway between 51.1 and 57.8.

   Choice (B) is a little less than halfway, but that's okay because the number should actually be closer to 51.1 (the number for 70 percent). 51.1 is closer to 45.6 (the number for 60 percent) than it is to 57.8 (the number for 80 percent). In other words, as the relative humidity levels progress evenly, the apparent temperature intervals in this range get larger. The gap between the apparent temperatures for 75 percent and 80 percent should be larger than the gap between such temperatures for 70 percent and 75 percent. Choice (B) is 2.9 away from 51.1 and 3.8 away from 57.8.

2. **H.** The choices all have to do with the point at which air temperature and apparent temperature are equivalent. According to Table 2, at an air temperature of 21.1 degrees C, the apparent temperature is the same at 60 percent and 70 percent relative humidity. When the air temperature is 23.9 degrees C, this equivalence occurs at 50 percent humidity. At 26.7 degrees C, the humidity is between 40 percent and 50 percent. This trend of having lower humidity to make the two temperatures equal continues as air temperatures increase (as you move to the right on the table). Choice (H) is the only choice that expresses this relationship.

   One of the keys to success when you're approaching data-representation and research-summary passages is to pick up on trends.

3. **B.** Read the introductory material to see that the wet-bulb reading is lower than the dry-bulb reading because the evaporation of water from the wet bulb lowers the reading. So the wet-bulb reading in this case is 2 degrees C lower than 12 degrees C, or 10 degrees C, which is Choice (B). If you don't pick up on the idea that the wet-bulb reading is lower than the dry-bulb reading, you can at least figure that there's a difference of 2 from 12, making the answer Choice (B) or (D). Although even a wild guess is appropriate on the ACT (because you don't get a penalty for wrong answers), a 50-50 guess heightens your chances of getting a correct answer.

   Did you look at Table 1, find the dry-bulb reading of 12 degrees C, look across until you got to 78 percent relative humidity, look up the table until you saw the number 2, and then put down Choice (A)? The problem is that the 2 represents the *difference* between the dry-bulb reading and the wet-bulb reading. Be sure to read the introductory material for each passage on the Science Test!

4. **G.** To answer this question correctly, you must combine information from the two tables. Wrong answer (J) corresponds to the relative humidity that occurs in the situation described in this question. To answer the question, you must take this 69 percent relative humidity and go to Table 2. The 69 percent figure is close to 70 percent, so use the 70 percent row and move under the column marked 23.9 (23.9 is close to 24, the dry-bulb reading and, hence, the air temperature, in this question). The row and column match up at 25.0, making the answer Choice (G).

Notice that trap answer (F) comes from simply subtracting 4 from 24 and that trap answer (H) comes from adding 24 and 4. If you got either of these choices, you probably picked up on the word *different* in this question and didn't engage the brain cells sufficiently to think through how to get the apparent temperature.

5. **A.** Although you know that low moisture causes a greater difference between the two bulbs (thanks to the passage's introduction), don't go for Choice (D) so quickly. A look at Table 1 reveals that the relative humidities for Choices (A), (B), (C), and (D) are 29 percent, 29 percent, 30 percent, and 31 percent, respectively. To find the actual, as opposed to relative, amount of moisture in the air, one must multiply these percentages by the maximum amount of moisture that the air can hold at the various temperatures. Because this maximum amount increases with increasing temperature, Choice (A) must be the answer over Choice (B) because, in Choice (A), you multiply the 29 percent by a lower number. You can dismiss Choices (C) and (D) because both the percentages and the numbers the percentages are multiplied by (the maximum moistures) are higher.

Passage 2

The important point to take away from the introductory paragraph is that the purpose of the study is to test which drug makes subjects less drowsy. Although the pharmaceutical company is probably concerned with how effectively its drug alleviates hay fever, the study presented here doesn't measure this factor.

The description of Study 1 tells you that drowsiness was tested by counting the number of errors that subjects made on a task that requires alertness. Picture yourself as an experimental subject. If you're drowsy from a pill as you perform a motor task that requires alertness, how do you think you'll do? You'll probably make many mistakes. The statement that subjects who made fewer errors were judged to be less drowsy jives with your imagined scenario. The rest of the description of Study 1 tells you that the two drugs were compared at two different times, creating four groups of subjects. Each group had four subjects, making the study symmetrical and straightforward to follow.

Like you do with data-representation passages, be sure to examine the data closely in this research-summary passage and look for major trends. Table 1 reveals that the subjects taking the new drug made fewer errors on average than those taking the old drug. This difference was far more pronounced for the groups that were tested one hour after ingestion. The errors associated with the old drug were much lower at eight hours than at one hour. This finding makes sense when you realize that the effects of drugs tend to wear off with time. The new drug didn't show this decrease in the number of errors, perhaps because it wasn't making its subjects too drowsy to begin with.

How does weight figure in? A scan of Table 1 shows that the heavier subjects made fewer errors than the lighter subjects. The drowsiness caused by the drug seems to be greater in those who weigh less. Some reflection on outside knowledge can help you understand this finding: Who gets a higher dosage of a pain reliever, an adult or a baby? An adult who received a baby's dose wouldn't feel much lessening of the pain.

Now that you've gotten a handle on Study 1 and Table 1, notice what happened in the next two studies. Study 2 was basically a repeat of Study 1 except that the experimenters took out a factor that caused some variability. Table 2 shows much of what Table 1 shows but also indicates that the new drug caused fewer errors than the old drug even at eight hours. The difference in averages of the two eight-hour groups may not seem great (34.75 versus 30.75), but such a difference is probably significant when the table shows how little variability exists within each group of four.

Study 3 was identical to Study 2 except that the subjects weighed less and were female. The number of errors was higher (remember how the lighter subjects made more errors in Study 1), but the trend of the results was virtually identical to that of Study 2.

6. **J.** Note the purpose of the study mentioned in the introduction and the description of Study 1. This study was designed to test the extent to which the drugs make test subjects drowsy. It didn't examine how effective the drugs were in relieving hay fever, so eliminate Choice (F). Choice (J) follows nicely from our analysis of Study 1. Don't choose Choice (G) just because the numbers decrease. You must remember that lower numbers mean *fewer* errors, or a *better* performance. Choice (H) is wrong because no data show how well the subjects did on the task before taking the drug. You need that data before you can conclude anything about the drug's improving performance.

7. **C.** Once again, analyzing the results before you look at the questions makes answering the questions much easier. From the given information, you know that the researchers eliminated a source of variability by using subjects who were all the same weight. Choice (C) expresses this idea. With less variability, researchers can be more confident that any differences observed between drugs or between times is a consequence of the drug taken or the time since ingestion. Small differences between groups don't mean much if the results for both groups range widely. Such small differences may be significant if one group is consistently a little higher than the other group.

Choice (D) is the easiest choice to eliminate. Where in this study can anybody find the weight of typical hay fever sufferers? (The answer is nowhere!) A comparison of Studies 2 and 3 could provide some information regarding Choice (A), but Study 1 already provides such information. Remember that the question is basically asking why the researchers went on to conduct Studies 2 and 3. Choice (B) is tempting because the subjects in Study 2 were male and the subjects in Study 3 were female, but the description of the studies doesn't mention the sex of the subjects as something that was of major concern to the researchers. Besides, the way Studies 2 and 3 are designed, it's impossible to look at them and determine whether the greater number of errors in Study 3 came about because the subjects were lighter or because the subjects were female.

8. **H.** Here's your chance to use some common sense. Study 2 may have produced results with less variability, but all Study 2 shows when taken by itself is that the new drug is probably better with regard to producing drowsy side effects only for males of a certain weight. Hence, Choice (J) is wrong. Choice (H) is correct because it points out that Study 1 used a wider range of subjects. Choice (F) may look enticing, but you don't know the sex of the subjects used in Study 1. Perhaps the subjects in Study 1 were also all male. Eliminate Choice (G) because the studies were concerned with drowsiness, not the effectiveness of the drug.

9. **C.** Table 3 indicates that the average for the one-hour group was 54.25, while the average for the eight-hour group was 49.75. You can reasonably expect that the average for the two-hour group would be in between these two averages, which means you can cross out Choices (A), (B), and (D).

10. **F.** The question tells you that the average you see for the group that took the old drug and was tested eight hours after ingestion is probably a bit lower than the average would've been if subjects who were not particularly proficient at the motor task had been used. With regular, everyday, less-coordinated people, the average would probably be higher than the 41.75 shown. With this higher average, the gap between the new and old drugs would be higher than the current 0.5 and would strengthen the claim that the new drug produces less drowsiness at eight hours, which you can make with Studies 2 and 3. Thus, Choice (F) makes sense.

The next two choices have key flaws. To make a case for Choice (G), you'd have to know that the old drug at eight hours normally produces more errors than the old drug at one hour. You may not assume that less-coordinated subjects would make that many additional errors. Another problem with Choice (G) is that it mentions side effects in general when the study simply investigated drowsiness. The best way to eliminate Choice (H) is to realize that the choice mentions the drugs' effectiveness, which these studies didn't investigate.

Choice (J) makes some sense. Many studies do use the same subjects for different parts of the study. One advantage of such an experimental design is that different groups are equated for overall ability because the different groups have the same people. One problem with Choice (J), though, is that the subjects may do better at eight hours because the subjects already had a chance to practice at one hour — not because the drowsiness has worn off.

A more serious problem with Choice (J) is that it uses the extreme word *require*. Remember that absolute choices are rarely correct on the ACT.

11. **B.** Even if you wanted to be ultraconservative and not recommend the new drug, the reasons given in Choices (C) and (D) aren't logical. You have no way of knowing what the patients will do, and even if you did, such information doesn't have much to do with the new drug versus the old drug. In fact, the evidence points to the superiority of the new drug at both one and eight hours. If the individual is going to operate dangerous machinery, it's better that he or she do so with the new drug, which doesn't produce as much drowsiness. Choice (D) doesn't follow from the information in the question or in the studies, so get rid of it because the ACT doesn't expect you to use any specialized knowledge of the immune system that isn't covered in the passage. In addition, Choice (D) provides no indication as to which drug is superior regarding its effect on the immune system.

Choice (B) is consistent with the studies and the information in the question and doesn't make any outlandish statement such as, "The new drug is vastly superior to the old drug with respect to all short-term and long-term effects." Choice (A) is out primarily because the ACT doesn't want you to practice medicine without a license. You'd have to know a lot more about the new drug's pharmacological actions before making such a statement. Another point is that the new drug seemed better than the old drug when the dosages of the drugs were equated. Why would you say that the new drug is okay only if the dosage is reduced?

Passage 3

The first two paragraphs and figures provide background information, as is often done on the ACT. Don't worry about understanding all the details. The main point is that when water levels rise, the waves are more likely to hit the bluff. When this happens, the bluff erodes.

Don't waste time thoroughly analyzing each study or Figures 3 through 5. Often, you can use common sense on these science passages. Study 1 shouldn't shock you; you should expect that precipitation leads to greater lake depth.

Study 2 is somewhat more complex than Study 1. The key is to observe in Figure 4 that higher temperatures are associated with lower water levels (less depth). This relationship makes sense if you reason that high temperatures increase evaporation rate (think about how fast you dry off when you get out of a pool on a hot day) and that an increased evaporation rate lowers water levels.

The results of Study 3 are similar to those of Study 2. Like high temperatures, strong winds lead to high evaporation, which, as you see in Study 2, lowers water levels. You see this relationship in Figure 5. Link Studies 2 and 3 together in your mind to help you nail down the relationship among high temperature, strong wind, high evaporation, and less water association.

12. **H.** A quick look at Figure 3 reveals that lake depth goes down as precipitation goes down. Because lake depth is 5.0 m when precipitation is 15 cm/year, Choices (F) and (G) are unreasonable. Choice (J) is too precise and is also improbable. A doubling of precipitation

from 15 cm/year to 30 cm/year results in only a 0.5 m change in lake depth. The change from 10 cm/year to 15 cm/year is not as great as the 15-to-30-cm change, so the lake depth changing from 2.5 m to 5.0 m would not make sense. Choice (H), although not certain, is a safe thing to say and is the answer. Such safe answers are good bets on the ACT.

13. **A.** Experimenters conducted Study 2 under the premise that temperature affects evaporation rate. The researchers already know that high evaporation rates lower water levels. Figure 4 shows an association between high temperature and low water levels. If high temperatures result in low water levels and high evaporation rates result in low water levels, high temperatures probably lead to high evaporation.

Common sense counts when answering questions in this section. Choice (A) is logical and fits in with basic science. You have probably observed that liquids disappear faster when the temperature is hot. Also, when evaporating, water changes from a liquid to a gas. Which state is associated with a higher temperature? The gas, so high temperatures and high evaporation go together.

14. **F.** Although you can't determine what happens to lake depth with certainty (because several unmentioned factors are involved), the question asks what probably will happen. Therefore, the most obvious choice is safe. Low precipitation is associated with low water levels. High temperatures and strong winds increase evaporation rates, which lower water levels. When all three factors are connected to low water levels, you can safely say that the water level will be lower than average. So Choice (F) is the winner.

15. **D.** Study 3 provides some evidence that strong winds can be good for the bluff because such winds lower water levels. With low water levels, more waves will hit the beach rather than the bluff. However, the word *definitely* in the question makes Choice (A) incorrect. Other factors, one of which is mentioned in Choice (D), also exist. Does the fact that powerful waves can lead to erosion on the bluff make sense? Yes, it does, reinforcing Choice (D) as the right answer.

As with Choice (A), Choice (B) is wrong because you can't definitely say things are good. In addition, wind is more likely to erode the soil on the bluff than to deposit soil on it. Choice (C) is out because you can't say that wind raises temperatures (which may be good for the bluff).

16. **G.** The lake depth depends on the temperature and the amount of precipitation and wind. In a cause-and-effect relationship, the cause is the independent variable, and the effect or result is the dependent variable. So Choice (G) is right.

Another reason to pick Choice (G) is that the other three choices are all factors that the scientist examines for their effects on lake depth. If you want to select Choice (F), you'd also have to select Choices (H) and (J). Because all three answers can't be correct, all three choices must be wrong.

17. **A.** Because Choices (B) and (C) mention nothing about the weather, strike them out. Choice (A) provides helpful information because it's similar to the passage's investigation but more direct; it measures weather elements that affect the bluff through erosion rather than water level. Choice (D) is out because tides are the result of gravitational pull from the moon and the sun, which is not a weather factor.

Passage 4

At last, a graph you can actually relate to. You probably know that a compact car gets more miles per gallon than a full-size car does, as the graph in Figure 1 shows. The graph also shows that for each car size, gas mileage is better at slower speeds — which is why, logically enough, speed limits were lowered during the energy crisis of the 1970s.

The information presented before the graph is no big shock. When cars burn gas, they pollute the air. The more gas burned, the more pollution. To put this idea together with the graph, figure that the cars that get better gas mileage use less gas to travel a given distance; therefore, they do not pollute as much as large cars do.

18. **J.** Reasoning backward from the information given in the passage, the car that produces the most pollutants is the one that uses the most gas. Which car uses the most gas? The one that gets the worst gas mileage — Choice (J).

19. **A.** When you drive a car faster, you get fewer miles per gallon than when you drive that car slower. In other words, you have to use more gas to go a given distance. So Choice (A) is correct.

    Eliminate Choice (B) because time isn't the critical factor in your finding a gas station. The probability of your finding a gas station increases with the distance driven, not the time driven.

    You probably eliminated Choices (C) and (D) as soon as you saw that they began with "Yes." (Good for you!) Choice (C) looks tricky but it's wholly irrelevant. If you're facing being stranded in the middle of the desert, you probably don't care too terribly much whether your car is going to pollute. The key factor is whether you run out of gas. (Besides, just because an environment is relatively unpolluted doesn't give you license to pollute it.) Choice (D) is only half true. You will operate your car for less time; however, gas consumption is a function of distance, not time.

20. **G.** The logical solution is to figure that the answer is in between the miles per gallon for a full-size car driven at 50 mph and 60 mph. These figures are 26 and 24, respectively, making 25 the answer.

    Choice (F) is illogical because it's a worse gas mileage than what a full-size car driven at 60 mph gets. Remember, gas mileage should be higher when you reduce speed.

    If you chose Choice (H) or (J), you made the test maker's day. These answers are designed to trap careless readers who don't notice that the figures are the mileage that midsize and compact (not full-size) cars would get at 55 mph.

21. **D.** If you got this question right, congratulations — you're thinking like a scientist. Making projections beyond the range of numbers presented in a graph is risky. In the graph, statistics are given for speeds between 50 and 70 mph. The 25-mph figure cited is far outside of this range.

    Try hard not to outsmart yourself. You can't simply figure that if slowing down between 70 and 50 mph increases gas mileage, further decreases in speed will improve gas mileage even more. Too many factors that you don't know about are involved (for example, the engine may have to work harder when lower gears are used at lower speeds).

    Recognize when you may make a reasonable extrapolation and when you may be going too far, right into a trap. In Question 20, you can logically estimate a number (because 55 is between 50 and 60, both of which appear on the chart). In this question, you can't logically make an estimate because the chart doesn't cover the number in question.

22. **J.** Cars use more gas when speed increases, which means that cars also emit more pollutants when speed increases. Only Choice (J) shows that pollutants increase as speed increases for the entire range of speeds.

Passage 5

Did you take one look at this problem and tell a friend, "Pull the plug; I'm obviously brain dead!"? You don't need to be intimidated by the terms. No one expects you to be a neurosurgeon. All the ACT wants you to understand is that certain parts of the brain control certain muscles in the body. The figures simply indicate the locations of these controlling regions.

23. **D.** Scan the options. You can eliminate Choice (A) right away because there definitely seems to be a system in the organization of the motor area. The motor area moves from the lower body parts (toes and ankles) to the upper body parts (facial features) with the middle parts (hips and hands) in between. Be wary of Choice (C) because it contains the word *exactly*. The figure is a rough drawing that probably doesn't show any exact information, and the hand area actually looks a little larger than the toe area. The area of the region that controls the little, ring, middle, and index fingers and thumb appears to be larger than the area dedicated to just the lips, so Choice (B) isn't right. Choice (D) is the only one left.

Did Choice (D) fool you because it seemed too easy? Sometimes, especially for science questions that ask you to estimate information from charts and figures, the most general and obvious answer is the correct one. Don't make the questions more difficult than they are.

24. **H.** One simple way to reason through this question is to see that the hand area is much larger than the areas for trunk, shoulder, and brow. If Choice (F) is the answer, then why not Choices (G) and (J), too? They're all about the same size. And don't forget to use your common sense. You can logically think that the more complex areas of the body require more brain control.

25. **B.** Figure 2 shows that the dot is in the knee area, narrowing the options to Choices (B) and (C). Because the left half of the brain controls the right side of the body (see the text before Figure 2), the correct answer is Choice (B).

This question offers a classic example of when thinking about the diagram and the accompanying notes for a few moments before jumping right into the questions can help. The paragraph below the first figure states that one side of the brain controls the opposite side of the body (left brain, right body, and vice versa). Knowing that fact sends you quickly to the right answer.

26. **F.** To know what locations H and J control, you'd have to have specific science knowledge. Unless you're a brain surgeon, you probably don't have all this info right at your fingertips. Remember that the ACT doesn't expect you to have specific knowledge but only to deduce information from a chart, table, graph, or picture. The passage tells you nothing about locations H and J, so you know right away that they're wrong.

Location G is near the top of the brain, which, according to Figure 2, is involved with the lower part of the body. Location F is near the face, lips, and jaw area. These parts of the body have more to do with speech, making Choice (F) the more logical choice. (Although you've heard of body language, your knees don't really chatter up a storm!)

27. **D.** This question (the entire question set, actually) deals with the motor area of the brain, so focus on choices that mention muscle functions. Hey! You can quickly eliminate Choices (A), (B), and (C) because all three have to do with control of the senses. Choice (D) is the only answer that involves motor skills.

Don't spend too much time fretting about Choices (A), (B), and (C). Knowing how the brain controls sensory functions requires too much specialized knowledge for the ACT. The ACT wants to make sure that your brain functions but doesn't expect you to know a lot about how all brains function.

Passage 6

The introduction is certainly simple enough. Try to rephrase it in your own words: Pigeons are able to find their way home, but exactly how they do so is unknown.

Try to identify one key point in each paragraph. In the first paragraph of the Sun Compass Hypothesis, all you need to understand is that the birds seem to use the sun's position to locate the cup. Don't get hung up on trying to figure out more than that.

The main idea of the second paragraph is about internal clocks; when the internal clock provides incorrect information, errors result. This information suggests that the birds use the clock and compare the clock's info with the position of the sun.

This type of passage isn't called conflicting viewpoints for nothing. Just as you've grasped the main idea and logic of the first hypothesis, along comes a second hypothesis. The Magnetic Field Hypothesis states that pigeons don't always use their internal clocks with the sun. But be careful not to go too overboard with this conclusion. All the findings say is that when the sun isn't available, the birds don't compare their internal clocks with the sun to orient themselves. That's not to say that pigeons never use the sun, even though the author of the Magnetic Field Hypothesis chooses to ignore it. The findings simply suggest that the sun isn't essential for orientation. Because the pigeons found their way home, they seem capable of using other information.

Finally, rephrase the gist of the second paragraph. The paragraph presents some evidence that shows that magnetic fields influence pigeon orientation. This evidence suggests that pigeons may use the earth's magnetic field to find their home but doesn't mean that they must use the field.

28. **G.** The Sun Compass Hypothesis says that homing pigeons use the sun. Because the pigeons can see the sun, they'll use the sun and fly home. Choices (F) and (H) are more consistent with the other hypothesis, which suggests that the magnetic field is a major player in the birds' orientation. Choice (J) has real problems; it's inconsistent with both hypotheses. If the sun is key, the birds will fly in the correct direction unless their internal clock is altered. If the magnetic field is the most important element, the birds will continue to fly in random directions because the fields are distorted.

29. **D.** The Magnetic Field Hypothesis states that pigeons use the earth's magnetic field to orient themselves. A finding that shows that changes in this field change the way pigeons fly is certainly consistent with this hypothesis. The experiments with the magnets and electrical wires produced similar results, which were used to support the Magnetic Field Hypothesis.

Were you shrewd enough to notice that Choices (A) and (B) basically say the same thing? Because you can't have two correct answers, both answers must be wrong. Besides, Choices (A) and (B) are much too extreme. The sun may be overruled by a large disturbance in the magnetic field, but to say that the sun has no effect is going too far. Choice (C) has the same problem with extremism. The word *only* is too limiting (choices containing *only* are rarely correct). The pigeons still seem to use the sun under normal conditions.

30. **F.** If you chose Choice (J), you were 180 degrees wrong: Choice (J) is the major piece of support for the Magnetic Field Hypothesis. Choice (H) is almost as bad as Choice (J); the Magnetic Field author also used this info in his hypothesis. Choice (G) is consistent with the Sun Compass Hypothesis, but the Magnetic Field author can respond by saying that the magnetic field is a factor that's sometimes overruled on sunny days. By process of elimination, Choice (F) is correct. With no sun, the Sun Compass Hypothesis would predict that the pigeons would have trouble. On the other hand, the Magnetic Field Hypothesis would predict that the magnetic field should guide the pigeon, especially on a day when the sun is blocked.

31. **A.** Because a question like this one is hard to predict an answer for, go through the answer choices. Choice (A) appears good. The author has to assume that the pigeons aren't affected by metal, because, if pigeons were affected by the mere presence of metal, the author couldn't conclude that the magnets were responsible for throwing the pigeons off because metal material (not necessarily magnetic material) may have disoriented the pigeons.

Choice (B) is too extreme (remember, a hedging answer is almost always better than a definite answer, so go for the wimpy words) and seems to contradict the author's idea that magnets are important. No information regarding what happens when magnets are worn on sunny days is available.

The downfall of Choice (C) is also extremism. The author may accept that internal clocks may be used on sunny days. What makes this choice particularly bad is that it generalizes for all birds. You have no information regarding other bird species, so you have no way of knowing what the author assumes about this point.

Finally, Choice (D) is wrong because the author may accept that the pigeons may use the sun under certain conditions. The author's main point is that magnetic fields are used.

32. **G.** Here's a case where opposites don't attract. If two statements are contradictory, they can't both be right. Eliminate Choices (F) and (J) immediately because they include both I and II together. Doing so means that III has to be correct — because the remaining answer choices, (G) and (H), both contain III. Don't strain any brain cells trying to think about it. (Okay, if you insist: Option III is consistent with the Magnetic Field Hypothesis. When the sun is wiped out as a factor, the magnetic field plays an important role.)

Option I looks good because of its similarity to the Sun Compass evidence cited in the passage. Option II is out because the beginning of the passage rules out landmarks. With I in and II out, only Choice (G) can be the answer.

33. **D.** A major idea to get from this passage is that the two hypotheses present factors that homing pigeons may use to navigate. The evidence doesn't suggest that the sun or the earth's magnetic field is essential.

Both hedging and looking for exceptions are good ideas when you're dealing with science passages. Very rarely do you see an *absolute,* or something that must be true. Note the very safe, wimpy language in the correct answer, Choice (D).

Evidence that brings up another possible factor doesn't contradict either hypothesis. This reasoning eliminates Choices (A) and (B). You can easily dump Choice (C); if barometric pressure is consistent with one hypothesis, it has to be consistent with the other.

34. **J.** According to the Sun Compass Hypothesis, pigeons whose internal clocks have been experimentally shifted should make mistakes when light is present. The pigeons didn't make mistakes, so Choices (F) and (G) are out. The Magnetic Field Hypothesis, on the other hand, uses evidence that the clock-shifted pigeons didn't make errors to build up support for its claim. Choice (G) is wrong because pigeons didn't respond correctly to the light; a clock-light calculation should have pointed them in another direction. The pigeons did respond correctly, but they didn't use the light to do so. If they had, they would've gone another way. Choice (J), the correct answer, is similar to the info presented in the first paragraph of the Magnetic Field Hypothesis.

Passage 7

Start off by summarizing to yourself the passage's main idea, which tells you why the passage was written. Although the introduction may seem long and complicated, all it's saying is that the concentration of what you start with affects how fast you get a product as the chemical reaction takes place.

When you look at the experiments, don't get hung up on the chemical formulas. You can skim over them for the moment. (Remember: You're not required to have any scientific background to answer these questions. You don't need to memorize the Periodic Table or know anything about chemistry.) Just try to identify the information the tables give and the conclusions you can draw from the tables.

The key factor to note is that an increase of any reactant increases the formation rate. Increases in H^+ lead to larger increases in formation rate than do increases in the other two reactants.

35. **C.** H_3AsO_3 is the product, so the change that increases the formation rate the most is the change that produces more H_3AsO_3 in a given amount of time. From the passage's introduction, you know that increases in H^+ lead to the largest increases in formation rate.

36. **G.** The chemists varied only one concentration at a time so that you can easily observe how each reactant affects the formation rate. For example, Table 1 shows that doubling the concentration of H_3AsO_4 doubles the formation rate, while Table 3 shows that doubling the concentration of H^+ quadruples the formation rate. If both these reactants are doubled, the formation rate is eight times the original rate, but without knowing anything beforehand, scientists can't tell which reactant, if any, has a greater effect on the rate. So Choice (G) is the right answer here.

In general, you can interpret experiments more easily when the experimenters change only one factor at a time. This type of experimental methodology question is a frequent one on the ACT.

The other choices don't make sense. Why would an explosion occur? No explosion occurs even when the concentration of a given reactant is four times the original amount. You can reasonably think that changing the concentration of a couple of reactants by small amounts wouldn't lead to any calamities. So Choice (F) is out. This type of reasoning also rules out Choice (J). In Experiment 3, scientists measure a rate that's almost 20 times the original rate. Even if measuring greater rates is difficult, the scientists can take care not to change the concentrations of two or three reactants by too great an amount.

Choice (H) is not at all PC (politically correct). The ACT will not have you believe that scientists are not up to a task. Even if measuring two or more concentrations is difficult, you can rest assured that the scientists would find a way. Besides, who said that the concentrations had to be measured at the same time? Why not measure each concentration separately and then dump all the reactants in at once?

37. **D.** This question asks how the given concentrations compare with the original concentrations (the concentrations that appear in the top line of each table). The concentrations of the first reactants are doubled, while the concentration of H^+ is the same. Table 1 shows that when the concentration of H_3AsO_3 is doubled, the formation rate doubles from 2.8 to 5.6 rate units. Table 2 reveals that doubling the concentration of I^- also doubles the formation rate. When each concentration is doubled, as is the case in Table 2, the formation rate equals 2×2 or four times the rate obtained when the original concentrations are used $(4 \times 2.8 = 11.2)$.

38. **F.** With two liters of solution instead of one and the same amounts of reactants, the concentration of each reactant decreases. In each experiment, increasing concentration increases formation rate, so decreasing concentration decreases formation rate.

39. **D.** Get rid of Choices (A) and (B) immediately. There's no reason for the rate to go down when the concentration of H^+ goes up. Throughout Table 3, the rate increases. A sudden reversal makes no sense.

Don't fight the ACT. Rarely, very rarely, does the Science Test contain traps. The logical conclusion is usually correct; the reasonable interpretation of a table or chart or graph is usually the right one.

Did you pick Choice (C)? Don't feel bad. It's tempting to think that doubling the concentration of H^+ from 0.40 moles/liter to 0.80 moles/liter would double the formation rate, but look at Table 3. Did doubling the concentration from 0.10 to 0.20 merely double the rate? No, doubling the concentration quadrupled the rate, making Choice (C) too low. The answer is Choice (D), which is four times the rate when the concentration of H^+ is only 0.40 moles/liter.

40. **J.** Uh-oh: Where did H_2O come from? Don't panic. The equation written in the introduction indicates that H_2O is formed when H_3AsO_3 is formed. Well, what happens to the formation rate of H_3AsO_3 when reactant concentration increases? All the experiments show that this formation rate increases. Because H_2O is also formed when H_3AsO_3 is formed, the increase in the formation rate of H_2O makes sense.

Don't think that questions in this test necessarily follow the same order of the passage. That is, Question 1 doesn't have to come from the introduction and Question 6 from the last paragraph. As you can see in Question 40, the last question can be from the first part of the passage. To help you keep everything straight, we suggest that you jot down your thoughts — your summary of the passage — in the margin of the test booklet. You may need to go back and refer to your notes a few times.

Writing Test

If you wrote the optional essay for this test, check it over and make sure your essay contains these necessary features:

- ✓ **An obvious position:** Did you take a stand and stick to it? Remember that which side you take isn't a big deal. How well you support your position makes or breaks your essay. You should take only a few seconds to choose which side to argue before you start writing.

- ✓ **A strong thesis:** Did you create a thesis that answers the question posed by the prompt and sets up your essay? Try to slip in some of the wording from the prompt. Make sure your thesis introduces the two or three main points you use to back up your stand on the issue.

- ✓ **A steady focus:** Every element of your essay should be about your thesis. Make sure you didn't stray off topic.

- ✓ **Good organization:** We know it sounds boring, but your essay must have an introduction, body, and conclusion. Make sure you devote each paragraph in the body to a discussion of one of your two or three main supporting points. Check out the hamburger organization plan that we outline in Chapter 18 to help you evaluate the organization of your essay.

- ✓ **Excellent examples:** Professional essay readers really love to see creative, descriptive examples that strengthen your points. Vivid details draw readers in and endear them to your writing prowess.

- ✓ **Clear and interesting writing:** Check your essay for sentence structure variety, precise word choice, and impeccable spelling, grammar, and punctuation.

The prompt gives you the option of writing for or against adding five semesters of computer science to the graduation requirement. (It also says you can advocate for another option, but why would you put yourself through the extra work of coming up with something new?) The essay prompt itself has no right answer. You can be for the new requirement or against it. You just have to pick one and move on.

For example, if you decided that the new requirement is a good idea, you might set up your essay this way:

- ✓ **Thesis/Introduction:** Your thesis could be that, given the steady increase of technological advancement, the computer science requirement is necessary for high school students' future success in higher education and in their careers.

- ✓ **Body:** Your first body paragraph could be about how computer science classes would better prepare students for success in higher education, either in college or vocational school. You could state that even seemingly non-technological college courses, such as sociology or history, may require students to know enough about computers to prepare presentations using computerized software.

The next paragraph could cover how computer knowledge is essential in existing and future careers. Pepper your comments with an example of your Uncle Stu who was passed up for a promotion because he didn't know how to work the new computerized inventory system at his manufacturing job. Show that as the rest of the world becomes increasingly technological, high school students must either comply and accept new methods of business and communication or fall behind. Without technological advances, everyone would still be handwriting letters to be delivered by mule train.

You could address the opposition in the third paragraph. You may point out that high school students can study the arts in an extracurricular environment. Use your cousin Marissa, who performs in local theater productions, as an example.

✔ **Conclusion:** Conclude with a short summary paragraph that encapsulates the main point of your essay.

If you decided to take the opposing position, your essay could focus on the drawbacks of sacrificing the arts for new computer science requirements. The thesis could point out that with resources in schools already stretched so thin, the curriculum change comes at too high a cost. You could show the contribution that the arts make to producing caring people with an integral understanding of what it means to be human and that an ephemeral knowledge of the latest technology can't redeem the loss of this sense. You could point out the drawbacks of technological saturation with examples of how face-to-face communication has suffered as a result of the rise of alternative methods of communication, like texting and instant messaging. And perhaps add that high school students already have a better understanding of technology than their parents. An additional argument could be that technology changes too much to keep up with in a high school setting, but a core curriculum of classic subjects provides students with the thinking ability they need to learn new skills for college and beyond.

In a nutshell, which position you took isn't important. How you supported your stance and the quality of your supporting information is very important.

When you're finished reviewing your essay, ask your English teacher to look over your masterpiece for writing errors and to provide general comments about your essay's organization and strength in addressing the given prompt.

Score One for Your Side: The Scoring Guide

The ACT scoring may be weird (Why is 36 the high score? Why not a 21 or a 49 or a 73?), but it is very straightforward. Follow these simple directions to score your practice exam:

1. **Count the number of correct responses in each of the practice tests: English, Mathematics, Reading, and Science (see the answer key at the end of the chapter).**

   Do NOT subtract any points for questions you missed or questions you didn't answer. Your score is based only on the number of questions you answered correctly. That number is called your *raw score*.

2. **Locate your raw score in Table 21-1 and move to the left to find the *scale score* that corresponds to your raw score.**

   For example, a raw score of 50 on the English Test gives you a scale score of 21.

3. **Add your four scale scores and divide that sum by 4; the resulting average is your *composite score*.**

   For example, say that your scale scores were 23, 31, 12, and 19; your composite score would be 85 ÷ 4 = 21.25, or 21.

Table 21-1	Scoring Guide			
Scale Score	**Raw Scores**			
	English	**Mathematics**	**Reading**	**Science**
1	0–1	0	0	0
2	2	–	1	–
3	3	1	2	1
4	4–5	–	3	–
5	6–7	–	4	–
6	8–9	2	5	2
7	10–11	3	6	3
8	12–13	–	7	4
9	14–16	4	8	5
10	17–19	5	9	6
11	20–22	6–7	10	7
12	23–25	8	11–12	8–9
13	26–28	9–10	13	10
14	29–31	11–12	14	11–12
15	32–35	13–14	15	13–14
16	36–37	15–17	16	15
17	38–40	18–19	17	16–17
18	41–43	20–22	18–19	18–19
19	44–45	23–24	20	20–21
20	46–48	25–26	21	22
21	49–50	27–29	22	23–24
22	51–53	30–32	23	25
23	54–55	33–34	24	26–27
24	56–57	35–37	25	28
25	58–59	38–40	26–27	29
26	60–62	41–42	28	30
27	63–64	43–45	29	31
28	65–66	46–48	30	32
29	67	49–50	31	33
30	68–69	51–53	–	34
31	70	54–55	32	35
32	71–72	56	33	36
33	73	57	34	37
34	–	58	35	38
35	74	59	36	39
36	75	60	37–40	40

Answer Key for Practice Exam 1

English Test

1. B	14. F	27. B	40. F	53. D	66. J
2. J	15. A	28. G	41. D	54. G	67. D
3. B	16. G	29. A	42. J	55. D	68. G
4. H	17. D	30. H	43. B	56. J	69. A
5. A	18. H	31. C	44. F	57. B	70. G
6. J	19. D	32. H	45. B	58. H	71. B
7. A	20. J	33. D	46. F	59. B	72. J
8. G	21. D	34. J	47. C	60. G	73. A
9. B	22. F	35. B	48. J	61. C	74. F
10. F	23. A	36. J	49. A	62. J	75. B
11. B	24. F	37. D	50. J	63. A	
12. F	25. D	38. J	51. B	64. F	
13. A	26. H	39. B	52. G	65. C	

Mathematics Test

1. B	13. A	25. C	37. D	49. A
2. J	14. F	26. H	38. J	50. K
3. C	15. C	27. B	39. D	51. B
4. H	16. J	28. H	40. G	52. J
5. D	17. C	29. D	41. D	53. D
6. J	18. J	30. K	42. K	54. J
7. D	19. E	31. E	43. A	55. E
8. H	20. H	32. F	44. J	56. G
9. B	21. A	33. A	45. E	57. A
10. K	22. H	34. F	46. G	58. J
11. D	23. C	35. D	47. C	59. E
12. J	24. H	36. H	48. H	60. J

Reading Test

1. B	8. J	15. D	22. F	29. A	36. H
2. F	9. A	16. J	23. C	30. H	37. A
3. B	10. J	17. C	24. F	31. B	38. F
4. G	11. C	18. F	25. A	32. J	39. D
5. C	12. H	19. A	26. G	33. C	40. J
6. H	13. A	20. H	27. D	34. F	
7. C	14. G	21. B	28. J	35. B	

Science Test

1. B	8. H	15. D	22. J	29. D	36. G
2. H	9. C	16. G	23. D	30. F	37. D
3. B	10. F	17. A	24. H	31. A	38. F
4. G	11. B	18. J	25. B	32. G	39. D
5. A	12. H	19. A	26. F	33. D	40. J
6. J	13. A	20. G	27. D	34. J	
7. C	14. F	21. D	28. G	35. C	

Chapter 22

Practice Exam 2

• •

*R*eady to see how you do on a sample ACT? The following exam consists of five tests: a 45-minute English Test, a 60-minute Mathematics Test, a 35-minute Reading Test, a 35-minute Science Test, and a 30-minute Writing Test.

To get the most bang for your buck, take this test under the following normal exam conditions:

- ✔ Sit where you won't be interrupted or tempted to use your cellphone or play video games (even though it seems downright cruel).
- ✔ Use the answer sheet provided to give you practice filling in the dots.
- ✔ Set your timer for the time limits indicated at the beginning of each test in this exam.
- ✔ Do not go on to the next test until the time allotted for the test you're taking is up.
- ✔ Check your work for that test only; don't look at more than one test at a time.
- ✔ Don't take a break during any test.
- ✔ Give yourself one ten-minute break between the Math Test and the Reading Test.

When you finish this practice exam, turn to Chapter 23, where you find detailed explanations of the answers as well as an abbreviated answer key. Go through the answer explanations to all the questions, not just the ones that you missed. You'll find a cornucopia of valuable information that provides a good review of everything that we cover in the other chapters of this book. We've even thrown in a few cheesy jokes to help you get through it.

Note: The ACT Writing Test is optional. If you register to take the Writing Test, you'll take it after you've completed the other four tests. For details about the optional Writing Test, see Part VI.

Answer Sheet

Begin with Number 1 for each new test.

English Test

1. Ⓐ Ⓑ Ⓒ Ⓓ
2. Ⓕ Ⓖ Ⓗ Ⓙ
3. Ⓐ Ⓑ Ⓒ Ⓓ
4. Ⓕ Ⓖ Ⓗ Ⓙ
5. Ⓐ Ⓑ Ⓒ Ⓓ
6. Ⓕ Ⓖ Ⓗ Ⓙ
7. Ⓐ Ⓑ Ⓒ Ⓓ
8. Ⓕ Ⓖ Ⓗ Ⓙ
9. Ⓐ Ⓑ Ⓒ Ⓓ
10. Ⓕ Ⓖ Ⓗ Ⓙ
11. Ⓐ Ⓑ Ⓒ Ⓓ
12. Ⓕ Ⓖ Ⓗ Ⓙ
13. Ⓐ Ⓑ Ⓒ Ⓓ
14. Ⓕ Ⓖ Ⓗ Ⓙ
15. Ⓐ Ⓑ Ⓒ Ⓓ
16. Ⓕ Ⓖ Ⓗ Ⓙ
17. Ⓐ Ⓑ Ⓒ Ⓓ
18. Ⓕ Ⓖ Ⓗ Ⓙ
19. Ⓐ Ⓑ Ⓒ Ⓓ
20. Ⓕ Ⓖ Ⓗ Ⓙ
21. Ⓐ Ⓑ Ⓒ Ⓓ
22. Ⓕ Ⓖ Ⓗ Ⓙ
23. Ⓐ Ⓑ Ⓒ Ⓓ
24. Ⓕ Ⓖ Ⓗ Ⓙ
25. Ⓐ Ⓑ Ⓒ Ⓓ
26. Ⓕ Ⓖ Ⓗ Ⓙ
27. Ⓐ Ⓑ Ⓒ Ⓓ
28. Ⓕ Ⓖ Ⓗ Ⓙ
29. Ⓐ Ⓑ Ⓒ Ⓓ
30. Ⓕ Ⓖ Ⓗ Ⓙ
31. Ⓐ Ⓑ Ⓒ Ⓓ
32. Ⓕ Ⓖ Ⓗ Ⓙ
33. Ⓐ Ⓑ Ⓒ Ⓓ
34. Ⓕ Ⓖ Ⓗ Ⓙ
35. Ⓐ Ⓑ Ⓒ Ⓓ
36. Ⓕ Ⓖ Ⓗ Ⓙ
37. Ⓐ Ⓑ Ⓒ Ⓓ
38. Ⓕ Ⓖ Ⓗ Ⓙ
39. Ⓐ Ⓑ Ⓒ Ⓓ
40. Ⓕ Ⓖ Ⓗ Ⓙ
41. Ⓐ Ⓑ Ⓒ Ⓓ
42. Ⓕ Ⓖ Ⓗ Ⓙ
43. Ⓐ Ⓑ Ⓒ Ⓓ
44. Ⓕ Ⓖ Ⓗ Ⓙ
45. Ⓐ Ⓑ Ⓒ Ⓓ
46. Ⓕ Ⓖ Ⓗ Ⓙ
47. Ⓐ Ⓑ Ⓒ Ⓓ
48. Ⓕ Ⓖ Ⓗ Ⓙ
49. Ⓐ Ⓑ Ⓒ Ⓓ
50. Ⓕ Ⓖ Ⓗ Ⓙ

51. Ⓐ Ⓑ Ⓒ Ⓓ
52. Ⓕ Ⓖ Ⓗ Ⓙ
53. Ⓐ Ⓑ Ⓒ Ⓓ
54. Ⓕ Ⓖ Ⓗ Ⓙ
55. Ⓐ Ⓑ Ⓒ Ⓓ
56. Ⓕ Ⓖ Ⓗ Ⓙ
57. Ⓐ Ⓑ Ⓒ Ⓓ
58. Ⓕ Ⓖ Ⓗ Ⓙ
59. Ⓐ Ⓑ Ⓒ Ⓓ
60. Ⓕ Ⓖ Ⓗ Ⓙ
61. Ⓐ Ⓑ Ⓒ Ⓓ
62. Ⓕ Ⓖ Ⓗ Ⓙ
63. Ⓐ Ⓑ Ⓒ Ⓓ
64. Ⓕ Ⓖ Ⓗ Ⓙ
65. Ⓐ Ⓑ Ⓒ Ⓓ
66. Ⓕ Ⓖ Ⓗ Ⓙ
67. Ⓐ Ⓑ Ⓒ Ⓓ
68. Ⓕ Ⓖ Ⓗ Ⓙ
69. Ⓐ Ⓑ Ⓒ Ⓓ
70. Ⓕ Ⓖ Ⓗ Ⓙ
71. Ⓐ Ⓑ Ⓒ Ⓓ
72. Ⓕ Ⓖ Ⓗ Ⓙ
73. Ⓐ Ⓑ Ⓒ Ⓓ
74. Ⓕ Ⓖ Ⓗ Ⓙ
75. Ⓐ Ⓑ Ⓒ Ⓓ

Mathematics Test

1. Ⓐ Ⓑ Ⓒ Ⓓ Ⓔ
2. Ⓕ Ⓖ Ⓗ Ⓙ Ⓚ
3. Ⓐ Ⓑ Ⓒ Ⓓ Ⓔ
4. Ⓕ Ⓖ Ⓗ Ⓙ Ⓚ
5. Ⓐ Ⓑ Ⓒ Ⓓ Ⓔ
6. Ⓕ Ⓖ Ⓗ Ⓙ Ⓚ
7. Ⓐ Ⓑ Ⓒ Ⓓ Ⓔ
8. Ⓕ Ⓖ Ⓗ Ⓙ Ⓚ
9. Ⓐ Ⓑ Ⓒ Ⓓ Ⓔ
10. Ⓕ Ⓖ Ⓗ Ⓙ Ⓚ
11. Ⓐ Ⓑ Ⓒ Ⓓ Ⓔ
12. Ⓕ Ⓖ Ⓗ Ⓙ Ⓚ
13. Ⓐ Ⓑ Ⓒ Ⓓ Ⓔ
14. Ⓕ Ⓖ Ⓗ Ⓙ Ⓚ
15. Ⓐ Ⓑ Ⓒ Ⓓ Ⓔ
16. Ⓕ Ⓖ Ⓗ Ⓙ Ⓚ
17. Ⓐ Ⓑ Ⓒ Ⓓ Ⓔ
18. Ⓕ Ⓖ Ⓗ Ⓙ Ⓚ
19. Ⓐ Ⓑ Ⓒ Ⓓ Ⓔ
20. Ⓕ Ⓖ Ⓗ Ⓙ Ⓚ
21. Ⓐ Ⓑ Ⓒ Ⓓ Ⓔ
22. Ⓕ Ⓖ Ⓗ Ⓙ Ⓚ
23. Ⓐ Ⓑ Ⓒ Ⓓ Ⓔ
24. Ⓕ Ⓖ Ⓗ Ⓙ Ⓚ
25. Ⓐ Ⓑ Ⓒ Ⓓ Ⓔ
26. Ⓕ Ⓖ Ⓗ Ⓙ Ⓚ
27. Ⓐ Ⓑ Ⓒ Ⓓ Ⓔ
28. Ⓕ Ⓖ Ⓗ Ⓙ Ⓚ
29. Ⓐ Ⓑ Ⓒ Ⓓ Ⓔ
30. Ⓕ Ⓖ Ⓗ Ⓙ Ⓚ

31. Ⓐ Ⓑ Ⓒ Ⓓ Ⓔ
32. Ⓕ Ⓖ Ⓗ Ⓙ Ⓚ
33. Ⓐ Ⓑ Ⓒ Ⓓ Ⓔ
34. Ⓕ Ⓖ Ⓗ Ⓙ Ⓚ
35. Ⓐ Ⓑ Ⓒ Ⓓ Ⓔ
36. Ⓕ Ⓖ Ⓗ Ⓙ Ⓚ
37. Ⓐ Ⓑ Ⓒ Ⓓ Ⓔ
38. Ⓕ Ⓖ Ⓗ Ⓙ Ⓚ
39. Ⓐ Ⓑ Ⓒ Ⓓ Ⓔ
40. Ⓕ Ⓖ Ⓗ Ⓙ Ⓚ
41. Ⓐ Ⓑ Ⓒ Ⓓ Ⓔ
42. Ⓕ Ⓖ Ⓗ Ⓙ Ⓚ
43. Ⓐ Ⓑ Ⓒ Ⓓ Ⓔ
44. Ⓕ Ⓖ Ⓗ Ⓙ Ⓚ
45. Ⓐ Ⓑ Ⓒ Ⓓ Ⓔ
46. Ⓕ Ⓖ Ⓗ Ⓙ Ⓚ
47. Ⓐ Ⓑ Ⓒ Ⓓ Ⓔ
48. Ⓕ Ⓖ Ⓗ Ⓙ Ⓚ
49. Ⓐ Ⓑ Ⓒ Ⓓ Ⓔ
50. Ⓕ Ⓖ Ⓗ Ⓙ Ⓚ
51. Ⓐ Ⓑ Ⓒ Ⓓ Ⓔ
52. Ⓕ Ⓖ Ⓗ Ⓙ Ⓚ
53. Ⓐ Ⓑ Ⓒ Ⓓ Ⓔ
54. Ⓕ Ⓖ Ⓗ Ⓙ Ⓚ
55. Ⓐ Ⓑ Ⓒ Ⓓ Ⓔ
56. Ⓕ Ⓖ Ⓗ Ⓙ Ⓚ
57. Ⓐ Ⓑ Ⓒ Ⓓ Ⓔ
58. Ⓕ Ⓖ Ⓗ Ⓙ Ⓚ
59. Ⓐ Ⓑ Ⓒ Ⓓ Ⓔ
60. Ⓕ Ⓖ Ⓗ Ⓙ Ⓚ

Reading Test	Science Test
1. Ⓐ Ⓑ Ⓒ Ⓓ	1. Ⓐ Ⓑ Ⓒ Ⓓ
2. Ⓕ Ⓖ Ⓗ Ⓙ	2. Ⓕ Ⓖ Ⓗ Ⓙ
3. Ⓐ Ⓑ Ⓒ Ⓓ	3. Ⓐ Ⓑ Ⓒ Ⓓ
4. Ⓕ Ⓖ Ⓗ Ⓙ	4. Ⓕ Ⓖ Ⓗ Ⓙ
5. Ⓐ Ⓑ Ⓒ Ⓓ	5. Ⓐ Ⓑ Ⓒ Ⓓ
6. Ⓕ Ⓖ Ⓗ Ⓙ	6. Ⓕ Ⓖ Ⓗ Ⓙ
7. Ⓐ Ⓑ Ⓒ Ⓓ	7. Ⓐ Ⓑ Ⓒ Ⓓ
8. Ⓕ Ⓖ Ⓗ Ⓙ	8. Ⓕ Ⓖ Ⓗ Ⓙ
9. Ⓐ Ⓑ Ⓒ Ⓓ	9. Ⓐ Ⓑ Ⓒ Ⓓ
10. Ⓕ Ⓖ Ⓗ Ⓙ	10. Ⓕ Ⓖ Ⓗ Ⓙ
11. Ⓐ Ⓑ Ⓒ Ⓓ	11. Ⓐ Ⓑ Ⓒ Ⓓ
12. Ⓕ Ⓖ Ⓗ Ⓙ	12. Ⓕ Ⓖ Ⓗ Ⓙ
13. Ⓐ Ⓑ Ⓒ Ⓓ	13. Ⓐ Ⓑ Ⓒ Ⓓ
14. Ⓕ Ⓖ Ⓗ Ⓙ	14. Ⓕ Ⓖ Ⓗ Ⓙ
15. Ⓐ Ⓑ Ⓒ Ⓓ	15. Ⓐ Ⓑ Ⓒ Ⓓ
16. Ⓕ Ⓖ Ⓗ Ⓙ	16. Ⓕ Ⓖ Ⓗ Ⓙ
17. Ⓐ Ⓑ Ⓒ Ⓓ	17. Ⓐ Ⓑ Ⓒ Ⓓ
18. Ⓕ Ⓖ Ⓗ Ⓙ	18. Ⓕ Ⓖ Ⓗ Ⓙ
19. Ⓐ Ⓑ Ⓒ Ⓓ	19. Ⓐ Ⓑ Ⓒ Ⓓ
20. Ⓕ Ⓖ Ⓗ Ⓙ	20. Ⓕ Ⓖ Ⓗ Ⓙ
21. Ⓐ Ⓑ Ⓒ Ⓓ	21. Ⓐ Ⓑ Ⓒ Ⓓ
22. Ⓕ Ⓖ Ⓗ Ⓙ	22. Ⓕ Ⓖ Ⓗ Ⓙ
23. Ⓐ Ⓑ Ⓒ Ⓓ	23. Ⓐ Ⓑ Ⓒ Ⓓ
24. Ⓕ Ⓖ Ⓗ Ⓙ	24. Ⓕ Ⓖ Ⓗ Ⓙ
25. Ⓐ Ⓑ Ⓒ Ⓓ	25. Ⓐ Ⓑ Ⓒ Ⓓ
26. Ⓕ Ⓖ Ⓗ Ⓙ	26. Ⓕ Ⓖ Ⓗ Ⓙ
27. Ⓐ Ⓑ Ⓒ Ⓓ	27. Ⓐ Ⓑ Ⓒ Ⓓ
28. Ⓕ Ⓖ Ⓗ Ⓙ	28. Ⓕ Ⓖ Ⓗ Ⓙ
29. Ⓐ Ⓑ Ⓒ Ⓓ	29. Ⓐ Ⓑ Ⓒ Ⓓ
30. Ⓕ Ⓖ Ⓗ Ⓙ	30. Ⓕ Ⓖ Ⓗ Ⓙ
31. Ⓐ Ⓑ Ⓒ Ⓓ	31. Ⓐ Ⓑ Ⓒ Ⓓ
32. Ⓕ Ⓖ Ⓗ Ⓙ	32. Ⓕ Ⓖ Ⓗ Ⓙ
33. Ⓐ Ⓑ Ⓒ Ⓓ	33. Ⓐ Ⓑ Ⓒ Ⓓ
34. Ⓕ Ⓖ Ⓗ Ⓙ	34. Ⓕ Ⓖ Ⓗ Ⓙ
35. Ⓐ Ⓑ Ⓒ Ⓓ	35. Ⓐ Ⓑ Ⓒ Ⓓ
36. Ⓕ Ⓖ Ⓗ Ⓙ	36. Ⓕ Ⓖ Ⓗ Ⓙ
37. Ⓐ Ⓑ Ⓒ Ⓓ	37. Ⓐ Ⓑ Ⓒ Ⓓ
38. Ⓕ Ⓖ Ⓗ Ⓙ	38. Ⓕ Ⓖ Ⓗ Ⓙ
39. Ⓐ Ⓑ Ⓒ Ⓓ	39. Ⓐ Ⓑ Ⓒ Ⓓ
40. Ⓕ Ⓖ Ⓗ Ⓙ	40. Ⓕ Ⓖ Ⓗ Ⓙ

English Test

Time: 45 minutes for 75 questions

Directions: Following are five passages with underlined portions. Alternate ways of stating the underlined portions come after the passages. Choose the best alternative; if the original is the best way of stating the underlined portion, choose NO CHANGE.

The test also has questions that refer to the passages or ask you to reorder the sentences within the passages. These questions are identified by a number in a box. Choose the best answer and shade in the corresponding oval on your answer sheet.

Passage 1

Food Trends
by Joel Shapiro

Recently, it has been a current trend in the
                                        1
food service industry to decrease fat content and sodium. This trend, which was spearheaded by the medical community as a method of fighting heart disease, has had some unintended side effects obesity and heart disease — the very
    2
thing the medical community was trying to fight.

Fat and salt are very important parts of a diet. It is required to process the food that we
      3
eat, to recover from injury, to stay hydrated, and for several other bodily functions. Fat and salt are required parts of diet. When fat and salt are
         4
removed from food, the food tastes as if it is missing something. As a result, people will eat more food to try to make up for that missing element. Even worse, people tend to compensate by eating more junk food. Such as potato chips,
                              5
soda, candy, and doughnuts, my favorite. Junk food is full of fat and salt; by eating more junk food people will get more salt and fat than they need in their diet.

There is another interesting side effect of removing salt and fat from food — less flavor. It took me several years to figure out why the food that I was getting at restaurants had lesser flavor
                                        6
as time went by but the food that I prepare at home continued to have strong flavors. I discover
                                              7
the answer in a bowl of chili. I had been making chili (my family's favorite dish and one that I serve at least once a week) with low-fat meats, following the current trend toward low-fat food. One day at the grocery, the store had run out of the low-fat meat, so I bought some meat with much higher fat content than I normally purchase. The chili I made from this meat tasted much better than the previous chili.
                          8

From that point on, I experimented, with
                   9
ingredients that were not low in fat. The resulting dishes were much more satisfying than before. In addition, I found that people I served them to didn't eat as much. After talking at several,
                                  10
I discovered that they found the meals much more satisfying than they had in the past.

Go on to next page

Therefore, they ate less. And, as a result, ending up eating less calories than they had with the low-fat meals.
    [1] Salt is a more difficult ingredient to judge. [2] If there is too much, the meal doesn't taste good, and diners will push the food aside uneaten. [3] If there isn't enough, the dish tastes like something is missing and diners will eat more food to obtain enough salt. 12

    Salt also helps bring out the flavors of the dish. The trick is to find just the right amount. I generally do this by tasting. As I cook, I taste the sauce or food that I am preparing. If it tastes like "something is missing," then I add a little salt. I stir it in, give it a few minutes and then try it again. Eventually, it tastes perfectly.

    Fat and salt enhance the way foods taste and are important parts of any diet. Including an adequate amount of both of them in your meals will reduce your urge to snack between meals (often on unhealthy, empty-calorie treats) and will improve the flavor of your food. However, be careful not to go overboard. Moderation is key; it's possible to consume too much of both, being not good for the health. 15

1. (A) NO CHANGE
    (B) Recently, there has been a current trend in the food service industry
    (C) A recent trend in the food service industry has been
    (D) Recently, having trended toward in the food service industry

2. (F) NO CHANGE
    (G) effects, including obesity
    (H) affects, such as obesity
    (J) affects: obesity

3. (A) NO CHANGE
    (B) It's
    (C) They are
    (D) OMIT the underlined portion.

4. (F) NO CHANGE
    (G) Fat, and also salt, are required parts of diet.
    (H) When on a diet, fat and salt are required.
    (J) OMIT the underlined portion.

5. (A) NO CHANGE
    (B) food, including potato chips, soda, candy, and doughnuts, my favorite
    (C) food, such as potato chips, soda, candy, and, my favorite doughnuts
    (D) food, potato chips, soda, candy, and doughnuts are my favorites

6. (F) NO CHANGE
    (G) less and less
    (H) lesser and lesser
    (J) the least

7. (A) NO CHANGE
    (B) discovering
    (C) discovered
    (D) had discovered

Go on to next page

8. (F) NO CHANGE

(G) the previous chili's

(H) the flavor of the previous chili

(J) the first one's

9. (A) NO CHANGE

(B) on; I experimented,

(C) on, I experimented;

(D) on, I experimented

10. (F) NO CHANGE

(G) After talking with any number of them,

(H) After talking to several of them,

(J) After talking afterwards to several people,

11. (A) NO CHANGE

(B) As a result, they are eating less food and consuming less

(C) As a result, they consumed less

(D) And, as a result, they consumed fewer

12. The writer wants to add the following sentence to this paragraph:

Although it has no calories, salt can affect how much food people consume.

This sentence would most logically be placed:

(F) before Sentence 1.

(G) after Sentence 1.

(H) before Sentence 3.

(J) at the end of the paragraph.

13. (A) NO CHANGE

(B) tastes well

(C) tastes perfect

(D) perfectly tastes

14. (F) NO CHANGE

(G) which isn't healthy

(H) not being too healthy

(J) and that is for the health not good

15. The author wants to emphasize the importance of having the right amounts of fat and salt and discourage against eliminating them altogether by adding this sentence to the end of the last paragraph:

However, if you eat no salt or fat, you are likely to overeat and become obese.

Should the author include this addition?

(A) No, because the addition would be redundant.

(B) No, because the sentence contradicts information that the author states in the first paragraphs of the passage.

(C) Yes, because the sentence provides information that the reader needs to know and cannot find elsewhere in the passage.

(D) Yes, because the paragraph does not adequately conclude the passage without the inclusion of the sentence.

Passage 2

Native American Government

[1] The question has been asked how Native American tribes, whom govern themselves do so.
16
[2] Most tribal governments are organized democratic, that is, with an elected leadership.
17
[3] The governing body is referred to as a council, it is composed of persons elected by
18
vote of the eligible adult tribal members. [4] The presiding official is the chairman, although some tribes use other titles, such as principal chief,
19
president, or governor. [5] An elected tribal council, recognized as such by the Secretary of the Interior and the people working for him, have authority to speak and act for the tribe and
20
represent it in negotiations with federal, state,
21
and local governments. 22

Go on to next page ⟹

Just what do tribal governments do? They generally define conditions of tribal membership, regulate domestic relations of members, prescribe rules of inheritance for reservation property not in trust status, levy taxes, regulate property under tribal jurisdiction, control conduct of members by tribal ordinances, and they administer justice.

What role do Native Americans have in the American political system? They have the same obligations for military service as do other U.S. citizens. They have fought in all American wars since the Revolution, they served on both sides in the Civil War. Eli S. Parker, a Seneca from New York, was at Appomattox as an aide to General Ulysses S. Grant when Lee surrendered, and the unit of Confederate Brigadier General Stand Watie, a Cherokee, was the last to surrender. It was not until World War I that Native American's demonstrating patriotism (6,000 of the more than 8,000 Native Americans who served in the war were volunteers) moved Congress to pass the Indian Citizenship Act of 1924. One reads in your history books about using the Navajo Marines of their language as a battlefield code, the only such code that the enemy could not break. Today, one out of every four Native American men is a military veteran, and 45 to 47 percent of tribal leaders is a military veteran. [30]

16. (F) NO CHANGE
(G) tribes go about governing themselves
(H) tribes who go about governing them and do so
(J) tribes, who, governing themselves, do so

17. (A) NO CHANGE
(B) democratically
(C) in a way that is democratic
(D) OMIT the underlined portion.

18. (F) NO CHANGE
(G) council; however, it is
(H) council, but is
(J) council and is

19. (A) NO CHANGE
(B) such as, principal
(C) like principle
(D) like, principle

20. (F) NO CHANGE
(G) had
(H) has
(J) having

21. (A) NO CHANGE
(B) be representing it
(C) to represent them
(D) representing them

22. The most logical and coherent location for Sentence 4 would be:
(F) where it is now.
(G) before Sentence 1.
(H) after Sentence 1.
(J) after Sentence 5.

23. (A) NO CHANGE
(B) and administering
(C) and administer
(D) and to be administering

Go on to next page

24. (F) NO CHANGE
    (G) They did fight
    (H) It has fought (the tribal)
    (J) Fighting

25. (A) NO CHANGE
    (B) when the Native Americans, who demonstrated
    (C) that the Native Americans' demonstrated
    (D) when the Native Americans'

26. (F) NO CHANGE
    (G) in history books
    (H) in their history books
    (J) in one of their history books

27. (A) NO CHANGE
    (B) the use by Navajo Marines of their language
    (C) Navajos using their Marine language
    (D) the Navajo Marines language use

28. (F) NO CHANGE
    (G) only code such
    (H) only code, such
    (J) only such code,

29. (A) NO CHANGE
    (B) is military veterans
    (C) are military veterans
    (D) is a veteran of the military

30. Given that the author was supposed to write an essay that predicts the roles Native Americans will play in future wars, does this passage fulfill this goal?
    (F) No, because the primary purpose of the passage is to explain the responsibilities of tribal governments.
    (G) No, because the passage discusses only current and past events.
    (H) Yes, because the passage is mostly about the contributions of Native Americans to the military.
    (J) Yes, because the most logical topic for the next paragraph of the passage would be how Native Americans will contribute to future wars.

Passage 3

A Trip to Lassen

Every summer, my family takes a car trip to one of this countrys great national parks. Last summer we had the pleasure of spending several days in Lassen Volcanic National Park in Northern California. As we were there, the park ranger gave us a lot of interesting information about the park's geology, biology, and history.

[1] Apparently, the theory of plate tectonics claim that as the expanding oceanic crust, which is the thinnest of the two types, forces its way under the continental plate margins; it pierces deeply enough into the hot areas of the earth to liquefy again. [2] Compartments of molten rock (called magma) result. [3] About half a million years ago, Mount Tehama gradually building up here throughout countless eruptions. [4] These become the feeding chambers for volcanoes, like the one that created Mount Tehama. [5] Mount Tehama fell long before Lassen Peak came into existence, but it's caldera ruptured, which is why there's no big lake there now. 40

The park's flora is a mix of species that are native to the Sierra Nevadas from varieties that emanate from the Cascade Mountains. The result is that the park in all areas boast more than 700 plant species, which is amazing when you consider that nearby Mount Shasta has less than 500. 43 Around two thirds of the species are at the northern limit of their range in the park, which

Go on to next page

means that about one third of the species, those from the Cascades, are at their southern limit.

The park ranger told us that historians have a difficult time determining what life was like for those who occupied the Lassen area long ago. They do know, though, that it was a meeting point for four groups of Native Americans; Atsugewi, Yana, Yahi, and Maidu. Its harsh weather conditions, generally high elevation, and itinerate deer populations made the Lassen area pretty much uninhabitable in the winter months. Therefore, Native American groups probably just lived here during warmer months when they could better engage in hunting and gathering. 45

31. (A) NO CHANGE
    (B) one of these countrys' great national parks
    (C) one of this country's great national parks
    (D) one of this country's great national park's

32. (F) NO CHANGE
    (G) Whenever
    (H) While
    (J) During our time while

33. (A) NO CHANGE
    (B) claim when
    (C) claims that whichever
    (D) claims that as

34. (F) NO CHANGE
    (G) crust, the thinnest of the two types of crust
    (H) crust which is the thinner type
    (J) crust, which is the thinner of the two types of crust,

35. (A) NO CHANGE
    (B) margins, it pierces
    (C) margins; however, it pierces
    (D) margins and piercing

36. (F) NO CHANGE
    (G) resulting
    (H) results
    (J) resulted

37. (A) NO CHANGE
    (B) was built up here, going through countless
    (C) had builded up here through uncounted
    (D) built up here through countless

38. (F) NO CHANGE
    (G) as
    (H) as if
    (J) likely

39. (A) NO CHANGE
    (B) but its caldera
    (C) and Tehama's caldera
    (D) therefore, the caldera that it had

40. To make this paragraph more logical and coherent, Sentence 4 should be positioned:
    (F) where it is now.
    (G) after Sentence 2.
    (H) before Sentence 1.
    (J) after Sentence 5.

Go on to next page ⟶

41. (A) NO CHANGE
    (B) and
    (C) form
    (D) to

42. (F) NO CHANGE
    (G) boasts and has
    (H) boasts over
    (J) have more than

43. At this point in the essay, the author is considering adding a specific description of the kinds of plants that grow on Mount Shasta. Should the author make this addition?

    (A) No, because the essay is about Lassen Volcanic Park rather than Mount Shasta.

    (B) No, because Mount Shasta has fewer species of plant life than Mount Tehama.

    (C) Yes, because the main topic of the paragraph is a discussion of plant species.

    (D) Yes, because it is always a good idea for a writer to provide many specific details in an essay.

44. (F) NO CHANGE
    (G) of Native Americans: Atsugewi,
    (H) of Native Americans, these are Atsugewi,
    (J) that are comprised by Native Americans — Atsugewi,

45. Which of these best describes the function of the last paragraph?

    (A) It summarizes the information discussed in the previous paragraphs.

    (B) It presents a personal opinion that contradicts information that the author presents at the beginning of the passage.

    (C) It introduces a topic not previously discussed in prior paragraphs.

    (D) It supports the author's hypothesis that the Lassen area is only inhabitable during the winter months.

Passage 4

One Boy's Role Model

As a young boy, I having dreamed of
₄₆
following in the footsteps of explorer Richard Halliburton, who it is fair to say has been my
₄₇
hero since childhood. Let other boys dream
₄₈
of being Viking warriors or knights in shining armor. I have always wanted to be a world-famous explorer, going places no one has ever been or returning to places where civilization flourished long ago.

Richard Halliburton lived the life I always wanted to live, and he wrote about it in ways that motivated me as a youngster and still have the power to thrill me as a man. I am especially captivated by his stories of his trip to Pompeii,
₄₉
which he calls the city that rose from the dead. A few miles past Naples, Italy along the slopes of
₅₀
Vesuvius, this city is found. It is much the same as it was before the eruption in A.D. 79, with wine jars still lying on the ground and ruts in the streets from the passing chariots still visible.

[1] He calls these chilling effects the volcano's "tantrums" and mentions that, while the locals treat them casually, he himself cannot
₅₁
help that consider what future explorers would think if they found his body, complete with tourist guide, wristwatch, and toothbrush. 52
[2] Halliburton makes his writing accessible by including familiar references that everyone can relate to, such as graffiti on the walls.

Go on to next page

[3] <u>And describing the signboards</u> and posters
53

in perfect condition that display announcements

of gladiator contests and proclaim catchy quota-

tions. [4] (My favorite is, "Good health to any-

body <u>who invites me to dinner</u>.") [5] Neither too
54

wordy <u>or too concise</u>, the <u>explorer's writing</u>
55   56

<u>appeals</u> to the secret fears of all of us by men-

tioning that, as he sat in his hotel room that

<u>evening and looks out over</u> the landscape, he
57

could see flashes of red light shooting up from

<u>the summit of it</u>. 59 60
58

46. (F) NO CHANGE
     (G) As a young boy, I dreamed of
     (H) As a young boy, I am dreaming of
     (J) Dreaming, as a young boy, of

47. (A) NO CHANGE
     (B) whom, it is fair to say,
     (C) who, it's fair to say,
     (D) of whom it is fair to say,

48. (F) NO CHANGE
     (G) Let other boy's dream
     (H) Dreams that other boys have
     (J) Other boys dream,

49. (A) NO CHANGE
     (B) fascinated at
     (C) captivated about
     (D) apprehended with

50. (F) NO CHANGE
     (G) This city is found a few miles past
         Naples, Italy, along the slopes of
         Vesuvius.
     (H) Located a few miles past Naples, Italy,
         along the slopes of Vesuvius, you find
         this city.
     (J) Along the slopes of Vesuvius, a few
         miles past Naples Italy is where this
         city is located.

51. (A) NO CHANGE
     (B) he cannot help but
     (C) he himself cannot help it that
     (D) he himself cannot help but

52. The author most likely includes Halliburton's
     reference to "a tourist guide, wristwatch,
     and toothbrush" in Sentence 1 to:
     (F) show how far hygienic practices have
         come since A.D. 79.
     (G) add a touch of humor to the prospect
         of having Halliburton's body found in a
         lava flow.
     (H) let the reader know what kinds of items
         an explorer carries with him.
     (J) emphasize just how devastating the
         effects of Vesuvius were on Pompeii.

53. (A) NO CHANGE
     (B) And like — <u>the signboards</u>
     (C) Along with mentioning the signboards
     (D) He also mentions the signboards

54. (F) NO CHANGE
     (G) invite me to dinner
     (H) invite him to dinner
     (J) OMIT the underlined portion.

55. (A) NO CHANGE
     (B) or, too, concise
     (C) nor too concise
     (D) nor concise enough

56. (F) NO CHANGE
     (G) explorer, writing, appeals
     (H) explorer and his writing appeals
     (J) explorer's writing having appealed

57. (A) NO CHANGE
     (B) evening and is looking out over
     (C) evening, having looked over
     (D) evening and looked out over

Go on to next page

58. (F) NO CHANGE
    (G) its summit
    (H) their summit
    (J) the summit of Vesuvius

59. To make the last paragraph more logical and coherent, Sentence 1 should be:
    (A) positioned where it is now.
    (B) positioned before Sentence 4.
    (C) positioned after Sentence 5.
    (D) OMITTED, because there are no other references to volcanoes in the essay.

60. This essay on Richard Halliburton would most likely appear:
    (F) in an encyclopedia entry about famous Italian explorers.
    (G) on the editorial page of a small newspaper.
    (H) as part of a memoir written by an older gentleman.
    (J) in a geography textbook.

Passage 5

Bird Mating Habits

The courting ritual of many birds <u>that</u> 61 includes elaborate dances and posturing. Some birds have intricate <u>set routines that never vary,</u> 62 patterns that are repeated continuously in a dance as old as the species itself. Other birds appear to be improvising, making up steps as they go along and adapting their movements to fit the situation. Some of the dancers appear <u>more warlike than romantic</u> 63 with puffed-out chests and aggressive strutting. Some of the dancers even charge the objects of their affections. A type of pheasant, called the tragopan, pops out from behind a rock to show himself to the female. <u>While</u> 64 one would expect the female to be surprised or at least startled, more often than not she is what one zoo curator called "amazingly unimpressed."

Another part of the mating ritual is <u>to be</u> 65 <u>providing</u> an appropriately enticing home, <u>often called a bower,</u> 66 for the female. The nesting areas are decorated with everything and anything the bird can find, including twigs, feathers, small rocks, trash bag pieces, <u>and sometimes there are even broken glass shards</u>. 67 Some experts have noted that the birds with the less attractive plumage, dull light brown birds with no exceptionally attractive coloring, create the <u>more colorful and elaborate</u> 68 bowers, perhaps as compensation.

Not all birds are plain-colored. The male tragopan (found in southern Tibet) has a bright yellow face and a red head. The wattled pheasant has a dark body but a fan of snowy, almost painfully white tail feathers. He also has a blue wattle around the head and <u>red irises in the eye region</u>. 69 The bird of paradise can range from black to bright orange and blue. You may know that a peacock has "eyes" on its tail feathers, but did you know that a pheasant <u>is with them</u>, 70 too? The Argus pheasant can raise his wing feathers, which are decorated with a pattern that seems to resemble eyes. <u>This is why the Argus pheasant got its name,</u> 71 after Argus, the watchman in Greek

Go on to next page

mythology who had a hundred eyes. Some birds are so stunning that people who observed them in captivity theorized that the birds must have come from the Garden of Eden, the only place that could possibly support such beauty.

<u>The courtship dances of birds have been emulated by humans.</u> In New Guinea, <u>for example.</u> <u>Warriors</u> wear large headdresses made with bird of paradise feathers and dye their bodies to resemble those of their favorite birds. 74 75

61. (A) NO CHANGE
    (B) which
    (C) those
    (D) OMIT the underlined portion.

62. (F) NO CHANGE
    (G) sets of routines, and they never vary,
    (H) routines and sets, never varying,
    (J) routines,

63. (A) NO CHANGE
    (B) as warlike than romantic
    (C) more warlike as romantic
    (D) as warlike as romantic

64. Which of the following substitutes for the underlined word would be the LEAST appropriate?
    (F) Although
    (G) Whereas
    (H) Because
    (J) Even though

65. (A) NO CHANGE
    (B) to have provision for
    (C) to have provided
    (D) to provide

66. (F) NO CHANGE
    (G) often called a bower —
    (H) often called, a bower
    (J) often, called a bower

67. (A) NO CHANGE
    (B) and even sometimes there are broken shards of glass
    (C) and, sometimes, even broken glass shards
    (D) and, sometimes, even, you find broken glass shards

68. (F) NO CHANGE
    (G) most colorful and elaborate
    (H) mostly colorful and elaborate
    (J) more than colorful and elaborate

69. (A) NO CHANGE
    (B) red irises
    (C) red in the irises region
    (D) red irises in the regions of the eye

70. (F) NO CHANGE
    (G) with them
    (H) has them
    (J) also has them

71. (A) NO CHANGE
    (B) The Argus pheasant was named
    (C) This is the reason why they named the Argus pheasant
    (D) Therefore, the name is the Argus pheasant

72. (F) NO CHANGE
    (G) Humans have been emulating the courtship dances of birds.
    (H) The courtship dances of the bird has been emulated by humans.
    (J) Humans have emulated the courtship dances of birds.

Go on to next page

73. (A) NO CHANGE

    (B) for instance; warriors

    (C) for example: Warriors

    (D) for example, warriors

74. Which of these sentences is the best choice to come after the last sentence?

    (F) The costumes the men perform in are thought by some to resemble the appearance of those same birds.

    (G) Then they strut and posture in patterns that imitate the dance routines of the birds they look like.

    (H) Tragopans are commonly called horned pheasants because they have two horns that stand up during their courtship dance.

    (J) New Guinea is an island in the South Pacific and the most linguistically diverse area in the world.

75. Suppose the writer had been assigned to write an essay that includes a description of a courtship ritual of birds. Did the author complete the task successfully with this essay?

    (A) Yes, because the author describes how male pheasants attract female pheasants by building a bower.

    (B) Yes, because the author presents a theory and then provides examples of how that theory is manifested in real life.

    (C) No, because the author describes the coloring of only a few types of pheasants.

    (D) No, because the author includes a paragraph about how humans dance like birds.

STOP DO NOT TURN THE PAGE UNTIL TOLD TO DO SO.
DO NOT RETURN TO A PREVIOUS TEST.

Mathematics Test

Time: 60 minutes for 60 questions

Directions: Each question has five answer choices. Choose the best answer for each question and shade the corresponding oval on your answer sheet.

1. Five cheerleaders and ten football players contributed to a coach's retirement party. Each cheerleader gave the same amount of money, exactly twice as much as each football player gave. If together the 15 friends donated $480, how much money did each football player give?

   (A) $5

   (B) $15

   (C) $22

   (D) $24

   (E) $26

2. What is the fourth term in the arithmetic sequence 2, 5, 8 . . . ?

   (F) 9

   (G) 10

   (H) 11

   (J) 12

   (K) 13

3. Let $x = -3$. Which of the following is equal to $2x - (3y - 3x) + 4y$?

   (A) $y + 15$

   (B) $y + 12$

   (C) $y - 12$

   (D) $y - 15$

   (E) $7y - 15$

4. What is the measure of angle *LMX*?

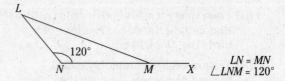

$LN = MN$
$\angle LNM = 120°$

   (F) 150°

   (G) 120°

   (H) 100°

   (J) 60°

   (K) 30°

5. Jarnelle can assemble 300 widgets in an hour. To be eligible for a raise, she must be able to raise her rate of assembly by 25 percent. At the new rate, how many widgets could Jarnelle assemble in 8 hours? (Assume a steady rate with no breaks.)

   (A) 6,125

   (B) 3,000

   (C) 375

   (D) 300

   (E) 75

6. To solve the following proportion, *a* must be which of the following?

$$\frac{3}{5} = \frac{a}{25}$$

   (F) 20

   (G) 18

   (H) 15

   (J) 12

   (K) 5

Go on to next page

7. What is the number of square units in the area of an isosceles right triangle with a hypotenuse of $5\sqrt{2}$?

   (A) $2\sqrt{2}$

   (B) 25

   (C) $12.5\sqrt{2}$

   (D) 12.5

   (E) $10+5\sqrt{2}$

8. Which of the following is another way of expressing $6a-\left[(a-3)-a\right]$?

   (F) $4a+3$

   (G) $5a-3$

   (H) $6a-3$

   (J) $5a+3$

   (K) $6a+3$

9. Veronica buys a car on sale for 25 percent off the original price but has to pay a 5 percent luxury tax on the sale price. If the before-sale price of the car is \$18,000, how much does Veronica pay for the car?

   (A) \$18,900

   (B) \$14,400

   (C) \$14,175

   (D) \$13,500

   (E) \$4,500

10. A floor with a length three times its width has a perimeter of 640 feet. What is its area in square feet?

    (F) 100,000

    (G) 19,200

    (H) 14,400

    (J) 8,800

    (K) 6,000

11. If $a=3$ and $b=10$, which of the following is the closest approximation to

    $$\frac{a+b(a-b)^2(a^2-b)}{b(a^2+b)}?$$

    (A) 10

    (B) 2.5

    (C) –1

    (D) –2.5

    (E) –8

12. Three angles, x, y, and z, share the same vertex and lie along a straight line. If $x=\frac{1}{2}y$ and $y=\frac{2}{3}z$, how much is $z-x$?

    (F) 90°

    (G) 85°

    (H) 80°

    (J) 70°

    (K) 60°

13. What is the answer when $5a^3b^4+3a^2b^3$ is subtracted from $a^3b^4-2a^2b^3$?

    (A) $-4a^3b^4-5a^2b^3$

    (B) $-4a^3b^4+a^2b^3$

    (C) $6a^3b^4+a^2b^3$

    (D) $4a^3b^4+a^2b^3$

    (E) $4a^3b^4+5a^2b^3$

14. If a 30:60:90 triangle has a perimeter of $30+10\sqrt{3}$, what is its area in square units?

    (F) $2,000\sqrt{3}$

    (G) 2,000

    (H) $100\sqrt{3}$

    (J) $50\sqrt{3}$

    (K) $10\sqrt{3}$

15. The average scores of students on a final exam are as shown on the chart below.

Dustin	Kristiana	Leoni	Tim	Deidre
75	82	79	91	93

    What is the positive difference between the mean and the median of their scores?

    (A) 84

    (B) 82

    (C) 12

    (D) 5

    (E) 2

16. Rectangle $ABCD$ has a diagonal of 6 units, and one side measures 3 units. What is the perimeter, in units, of the rectangle?

    (F) 24

    (G) $12+12\sqrt{3}$

    (H) $12+6\sqrt{3}$

    (J) $6+6\sqrt{3}$

    (K) 6

Go on to next page

17. Which of the following is true of the pair of numbers 4 and 6?

    (A) Their least common multiple is 24.

    (B) Their least common denominator is 4.

    (C) Neither number has any prime factors.

    (D) The least prime factor of both numbers is 3.

    (E) The least common multiple of both numbers is 12.

18. For all x and y, $\left(3x^2y + xy^2\right) - \left(2x^2y - 2xy^2\right) =$

    (F) $x^2 - x$

    (G) $x^2y - xy^2$

    (H) $x^2y + 3xy^2$

    (J) $5^2y - xy^2$

    (K) $x^4y^2 + 3x^2y^4$

19. What is the number of square units in the total surface area of this cylinder, including both ends?

    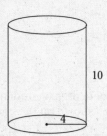

    (A) 16π

    (B) 40π

    (C) 100π

    (D) 104π

    (E) 112π

20. What is the slope of a line parallel to the line $2x + 3y = 6$?

    (F) $\dfrac{4}{3}$

    (G) 1

    (H) $\dfrac{3}{4}$

    (J) $-\dfrac{2}{3}$

    (K) 0

21. What is $\left(2a^2 + ab - 8\right) - \left(3a^2 - 2ab + 8\right)$?

    (A) $ab + a^2$

    (B) $3ab + a^2 - 16$

    (C) $3ab + a^2$

    (D) $3ab - a^2 - 16$

    (E) $ab - a^2 - 16$

22. Jessica and Josh want an average score of 95 for five exams. Jessica's scores are 93, 92, 90, and 100. Josh's scores are 95, 97, 89, and 94. For each student to average a 95 for the five exams, how many more points does Josh need to get than Jessica on the last test?

    (F) 5

    (G) 4

    (H) 2

    (J) 1

    (K) 0

23. Simplify $2y - \left(4 - 3y\right) + 3$.

    (A) $-y - 12$

    (B) $-y + 7$

    (C) $5y - 7$

    (D) $5y - 1$

    (E) $5y + 1$

24. If the shaded area in the square below is $144 - 36\pi$, what is the diagonal of the square?

    (F) $11\sqrt{2}$

    (G) $12\sqrt{3}$

    (H) $12\sqrt{2}$

    (J) $6\sqrt{2}$

    (K) 6

Go on to next page

25. What is the measurement in degrees of *x?*

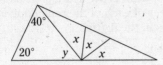

Note: Not drawn to scale

(A) 10

(B) 20

(C) 30

(D) 40

(E) 50

26. A machine sorts ball bearings. Due to a mechanical problem, the machine drops half the ball bearings per cycle. If the machine finishes its fifth cycle with 11 balls still remaining in the machine, how many balls were in the machine at the end of the first cycle?

(F) 704

(G) 352

(H) 176

(J) 88

(K) 44

27. Five friends are going to share computer time. Each of the five will pay $22.20 for his share. If the friends want to drop their individual price paid down to under $12.00 each, how many additional friends must join in sharing the price of the computer time? (Assume all friends pay equal shares.)

(A) 8

(B) 5

(C) 4

(D) 3

(E) 2

28. If $\frac{1}{a} = 4$ and $\frac{1}{b} = 5$, how much is $\frac{1}{ab}$?

(F) $\frac{1}{20}$

(G) $\frac{1}{9}$

(H) 9

(J) 20

(K) 200

29. The circumference of Circle *O* is 10π units. What is the area of triangle *ABC* in square units?

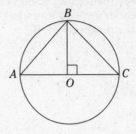

(A) 10

(B) $10 + 10\sqrt{2}$

(C) 20

(D) 25

(E) 50

30. If $4^{-x} = 64$, what is the value of *x?*

(F) –4

(G) –3

(H) 0

(J) 3

(K) 4

31. In the right triangle *XYZ* below, what is the value of tan *Z?*

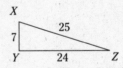

(A) $\frac{7}{25}$

(B) $\frac{7}{24}$

(C) $\frac{24}{25}$

(D) $\frac{25}{24}$

(E) $\frac{24}{7}$

Go on to next page

32. After a slower reader increased her reading speed by 25 percent, she was still 50 percent slower than a faster reader. Before the slower reader increased her speed, the faster reader's speed was what percent of the slower reader's speed?

    (F) 300%

    (G) 250%

    (H) 225%

    (J) 200%

    (K) 125%

33. The current pushes a swimmer back 2 feet for every 2 yards she swims. If she needs to cover 500 yards and each stroke takes her 5 yards, how many strokes must she take?

    (A) 1,000

    (B) 700

    (C) 500

    (D) 150

    (E) 100

34. A farmer can plow x rows in y minutes. Which of the following represents the number of rows the farmer can plow in w hours?

    (F) $60xyw$

    (G) $\frac{x+7}{60} \cdot w$

    (H) $\frac{w}{60} \cdot x$

    (J) $\frac{w+x+y}{60}$

    (K) $60\frac{x}{y} \cdot w$

35. If $f(x) = 1 + x^3$, what is $f(-5)$?

    (A) 126

    (B) 124

    (C) −124

    (D) −125

    (E) −126

36. Two interior angles of an octagon sum up to 480. What is the average measure in degrees of each of the remaining interior angles in the figure?

    (F) 180

    (G) 175

    (H) 150

    (J) 125

    (K) 100

37. Square $RSTU$ has a perimeter of 48. If A, B, C, and D are the midpoints of their respective sides, what is the perimeter of square $ABCD$?

    (A) 32

    (B) $24\sqrt{2}$

    (C) 24

    (D) $12\sqrt{3}$

    (E) $12\sqrt{2}$

38. What is the perimeter of the figure shown below?

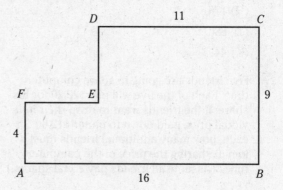

    (F) 75

    (G) 60

    (H) 59

    (J) 56

    (K) 50

Go on to next page

39. Given that a and b are integers and $a + b = 26$ and $a \neq b$, what is the largest possible value for ab?

    (A) 169

    (B) 168

    (C) 165

    (D) 26

    (E) 13

40. If $x \neq 4$, simplify for $\frac{\sqrt{x}+2}{\sqrt{x}-2}$.

    (F) -1

    (G) $\frac{x+4}{x-4}$

    (H) $-\sqrt{x}-1$

    (J) $\frac{x+4\sqrt{x}+4}{x-4}$

    (K) $-\sqrt{x}+4$

41. $64^{\frac{2}{3}} = ?$

    (A) 0

    (B) 4

    (C) 8

    (D) 16

    (E) 32

42. Set A = (2, 3, 4, 5, 6, 7, 8, 9)

    Set B = (3, 6, 9, 12, 15)

    Let a be a number from Set A and b be a number from Set B. Define $a @ b$ as the sum of all prime numbers from Set A and all nonprime numbers from Set B. What is the value of $a @ b$?

    (F) 61

    (G) 60

    (H) 59

    (J) 51

    (K) 50

43. A cookie jar contains nine chocolate chip cookies, six oatmeal cookies, and four sugar cookies, and there are no other cookies in the jar. Paul pulls out and eats a chocolate chip cookie, an oatmeal cookie, a chocolate chip cookie, a sugar cookie, and an oatmeal cookie. What percent probability is there that the next time he reaches into the jar, he'll pull out a chocolate chip cookie?

    (A) $66\frac{2}{3}$

    (B) 50

    (C) 40

    (D) $33\frac{1}{3}$

    (E) $\frac{1}{2}$

44. A street has a number of billboards. Starting at one end of the street, the billboard advertising milk is the 13th. From the other end of the street, the billboard is the 14th. How many billboards are there along the street?

    (F) 24

    (G) 25

    (H) 26

    (J) 27

    (K) 28

45. The trinomial $x^2 + 7x - 8$ can be factored as the product of two linear factors, in the form $(a \pm b)(x \pm b)$. What is the polynomial sum of these two factors?

    (A) $2x - 7$

    (B) $2x + 7$

    (C) $2x - 6$

    (D) $2x + 6$

    (E) $2x - 8$

Go on to next page

46. $3a + 5b = 10$. Solve for b in terms of a.

    (F) $5 - \dfrac{5}{2}a$

    (G) $2 - \dfrac{3}{2}a$

    (H) $2 - \dfrac{3}{5}a$

    (J) $2a - \dfrac{3}{2}$

    (K) $2a - \dfrac{3}{5}$

47. If $-4mx - \dfrac{3b}{c} = 4my$, then $x + y =$?

    (A) $\dfrac{-3b}{4mc}$

    (B) $\dfrac{-3b}{8mc}$

    (C) $\dfrac{-3b}{16m^2c}$

    (D) $\dfrac{-6b}{4m^2c}$

    (E) $\dfrac{-3b}{c} - 4m$

48. What is the solution set of $a(a + 4) = 12$?

    (F) {6, –2}

    (G) {–6, 6}

    (H) {–6, 2}

    (J) {12, 0}

    (K) {4}

49. What is the simplified form of
    $x\big[(3 + x)(4x) + 2\big]$?

    (A) $4x^3 + 12x^2 + 2x$

    (B) $2x^3 + 12x^2 + 2x$

    (C) $12x^3 + 4x^2 + 2x$

    (D) $4x^3 + 2x^2 + 4x$

    (E) $4x^3 + 4x^2 + 12$

50. A car passed a designated point on the freeway and traveled for 2 hours at 80 m/hr. Then, in an effort to save gas, the driver slowed to 70 m/hr for 1 hour. The driver stopped for gas and lunch for 1 hour and then traveled 80 m/hr for 1 hour. The graph of the driver's distance (d) from the designated point as a function of time (t) would most resemble which of the following?

    (F) d

    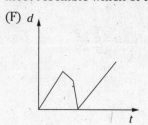

    (G) d

    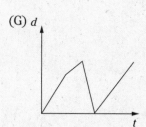

    (H) d

    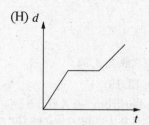

    (J) d

    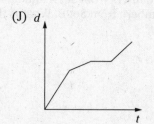

    (K) d

    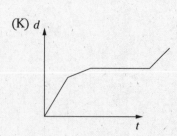

Go on to next page

51. What is the sum of the two solutions to the equation $x^2 - 5x + 6 = 0$?

    (A) –5

    (B) –1

    (C) 1

    (D) 5

    (E) 6

52. Which of the following represents the graph of the solution set of $x + 1 \le 8$?

    (F)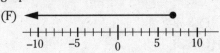

    (G)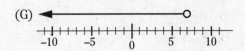

    (H)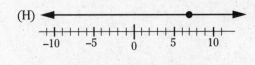

    (J)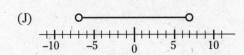

    (K)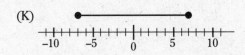

53. A line's equation is $x + 2y = 4 - (x + y)$. Its equation may also be expressed as $y = ?$

    (A) $\frac{3}{4} + \frac{2x}{3}$

    (B) $\frac{4}{3} + \frac{2x}{3}$

    (C) $\frac{4}{3} - \frac{2x}{3}$

    (D) $\frac{1}{4} - \frac{2x}{3}$

    (E) $\frac{2x}{3}$

54. Which of the following is equivalent to $\dfrac{\sin^2\theta + \cos^2\theta}{\sec^2\theta}$?

    (F) $\cos^2\theta$

    (G) $\sin^2\theta$

    (H) $\tan^2\theta$

    (J) $\dfrac{1}{\cos^2\theta}$

    (K) $\sin^2\theta + 1$

55. What is the simplified form of $\dfrac{7}{2 + \sqrt{3}}$?

    (A) 21

    (B) $7 + \sqrt{3}$

    (C) $7 - 7\sqrt{3}$

    (D) $14 + 7\sqrt{3}$

    (E) $14 - 7\sqrt{3}$

56. For all $a \ne 0$, what is the slope of the line passing through $(2a, -b)$ and $(-a, -b)$ in the usual (x, y) coordinate plane?

    (F) 0

    (G) $\dfrac{2b}{3a}$

    (H) $\dfrac{3a}{2b}$

    (J) $3a$

    (K) undefined

57. Three painters take ten hours to paint four rooms. How many hours will 9 painters take to paint 12 rooms?

    (A) $1\frac{1}{3}$

    (B) $3\frac{1}{3}$

    (C) 6

    (D) 10

    (E) 30

58. Which of the following is equal to $\dfrac{10.8(10^{-3})}{400(10^{-5})}$?

    (F) $0.027(10^2)$

    (G) $0.0027(10^{-2})$

    (H) $0.27(10^{-2})$

    (J) $0.0027(10^2)$

    (K) $27(10^{-2})$

Go on to next page

59. Georgia buys q quarts of milk at d dollars per quart and b boxes of cereal at $d + 1$ dollars per box. Which of the following expressions represents the total amount spent?

(A) $qd + bd + 1$

(B) $(q+b)(d+1)$

(C) $(q+b)(2d+1)$

(D) $d(q+b)+b$

(E) $bd(q+b)$

60. Find the area of rectangle $ACEG$.

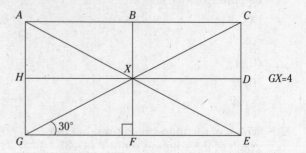

GX=4

(F) $8\sqrt{2}$

(G) $8\sqrt{3}$

(H) 16

(J) $16\sqrt{2}$

(K) $16\sqrt{3}$

STOP DO NOT TURN THE PAGE UNTIL TOLD TO DO SO.
DO NOT RETURN TO A PREVIOUS TEST.

Reading Test

Time: 35 minutes for 40 questions

Directions: Each of the four passages in this section is followed by ten questions. Answer each question based on what is stated or implied in the passage and shade the corresponding oval on your answer sheet.

Passage 1 — Prose Fiction

This passage is excerpted from the novel *The Twelve* by William Gladstone.

Line   Max knew from the beginning that there was a purpose to his life and an important destiny that he had been called upon to fulfill. This understanding wasn't something tangible, how-
(05) ever. There was a voice in his head that spoke of a reason for which he had been born, yet there were no words — just colors and powerful vibrations. His inner world, this secret playground, was filled with beauty and elegance, and it made
(10) Max very happy.

He seemed to be able to summon knowledge on any subject but had a particular attachment to the art of mathematics and exhibited an uncanny ability and proficiency with numbers,
(15) which constantly swirled around in his mind, vibrating in a multitude of colors. Even before he could walk, he was able to multiply triple-digit numbers in his head.

And this talent adopted a three-dimensional
(20) component. He imagined boxes placed vertically and horizontally and at tangents without end. He envisioned each box as the universe complete unto itself and would contemplate the shape, direction and lack of beginning or end within
(25) each box or collection of boxes.

Such exercises afforded him pleasure, as did most things in life. However, there remained one constant reminder that all was not perfect.

Louis.

(30) Despite the violence he experienced at the hands of his older brother, Max considered Louis his best friend. Their uncanny link caused Max to feel great empathy for his sibling, and it seemed as if they both remembered the blissful
(35) paradise that had been the womb.

From the moment of his birth, Max accepted that wherever he was, he was exactly where he was supposed to be in life and was completely at peace with the idea.

(40) Louis, on the other hand, was angry that he had been forced to leave that perfect state of being and that the world had greeted him with a stranglehold. Thus, he had come into this world kicking and screaming and remained in a constant state of revolt. (45)

That Max felt no such thing angered Louis even more, and he was determined to make his brother's life as miserable as his own by virtue of force and fear. Even as toddlers, Louis would attack Max, pinning him to the floor and choking (50) him, and then retreat as soon as Max started to cry. When the adults came running, he had achieved a safe distance, and they never realized the level of the violence. Since Max couldn't express himself, they remained utterly ignorant. (55)

Eventually Max learned to play dead. He found it otherwise impossible to resist, since Louis was filled with such superhuman strength when enraged that it would take more than one adult to subdue him, had they even been aware (60) of the need.

And despite his inherent inclination to be optimistic, Max found that the constant attacks began taking their toll. He never felt safe at home and knew that, whatever successes he achieved (65) at school, or in any aspect of life, he would suffer for it.

As the attacks increased, he seriously considered ending his life in order to escape his tormentor. (70)

At the age of seven, he contemplated stabbing himself in the stomach with a butter knife. While in his secret, inner world, he had seen the potential for his existence and was excited for the possibilities that lay ahead, the outer world (75) presented him with a very large, unavoidable obstacle.

His decision made, he picked up the knife.

Yet as he pushed the soft-edged blade into his tummy, he remembered the quiet, inner (80) voice from early infancy. So he put the knife aside, realizing in that moment that he had a purpose — a true mission — and even though there might be obstacles in his path, he would have the courage to face whatever came his way. (85)

Once he'd learned how to escape his brother's choke holds.

Go on to next page

(90) As a toddler, despite his lack of coherent speech, Max exhibited leadership qualities by taking charge of any group.

As he grew, he excelled in every subject at school and had real joy in learning. He was very good in sports and at twelve years old was Westchester County's fastest runner in the fifty-
(95) yard dash. Max joked that it was running away from Louis that had led him to become such a fast runner.

When he graduated from eighth grade, he was valedictorian, president of the student coun-
(100) cil and captain of the football, wrestling and baseball teams. He had an extraordinary sense of anticipating where the ball or opponents might be headed, he always seemed to be in the right place at the right time, and the idea of making an
(105) error never occurred to him.

He expected himself to be perfect in everything he did . . . and so, he was. Yet these expectations didn't yield the anxiety experienced by most children.

(110) There was no question that he was loved by his parents, and thanks to his father's success, he had material abundance. So, despite the torments leveled in his direction by his brother, Max managed to survive his early adolescence.

1. Which of the following best expresses the main point of the first paragraph (Lines 1–10)?

   (A) Max lived in a constant state of optimism and positive thinking.

   (B) Max thought in colors and vibrations rather than in prose.

   (C) Max recognized that his thought process was different from others.

   (D) Max knew he was put on this earth for a reason, and while he had yet to determine exactly what that reason was, he was comforted by it.

2. The word *tangible,* as it is used in Line 4, most likely means:

   (F) vague or elusive.

   (G) concrete.

   (H) affirmative.

   (J) changeable.

3. Throughout his early adolescence, Max exhibited natural talent in all of the following areas EXCEPT:

   (A) mathematics.

   (B) track.

   (C) gymnastics.

   (D) football.

4. The selection below that best summarizes the passage as a whole is:

   (F) Max was able to overcome the most troubling obstacle in his life, his brother Louis, and become an overachiever despite the hardships he'd suffered at his brother's hands.

   (G) Max lived a life plagued by feelings of inadequacy as a result of the cruelty he suffered growing up alongside Louis.

   (H) Max's ability to hide the traumas in his home life enabled him to excel academically and through sports.

   (J) Max was intellectually superior to his peers from a very early age and suffered socially as a result.

5. The author would most likely say that Max thought about ending his life because:

   (A) his failure to be able to communicate verbally with his parents left him feeling he needed to take drastic measures to call attention to Louis's abuse.

   (B) the hardships he suffered at the hands of his brother seemed impossible to overcome despite his belief that he held a special purpose in this world.

   (C) he knew almost from birth that he was drastically different from his peers, and the thought of spending his whole life feeling like an outsider was too much to bear.

   (D) he felt that if he didn't take his own life, Louis would do so for him and he no longer could stand living in fear.

Go on to next page

6. When the author refers to *exercises* in Line 26, he means:

   (F) using his mind to position imaginary shapes.

   (G) rudimentary calisthenics.

   (H) multiplying six-digit numbers in his head.

   (J) playing dead in front of Louis.

7. The author feels that Max exhibited leadership skills in his early years by:

   (A) exhibiting a penchant for empathizing with others.

   (B) showing an appreciation for those he didn't necessarily get along with, such as his unexplainable fondness for his brother Louis despite his cruel nature.

   (C) approaching obstacles in his life in a calm, organized manner.

   (D) demonstrating he could take charge of a group.

8. The author would most likely say that Max differed from most children his age in all but which of the following ways?

   (F) He desperately yearned for the approval of his parents and teachers.

   (G) He failed to speak throughout the majority of his childhood.

   (H) He was unaffected by the high expectations adults placed on him.

   (J) He felt from birth onward that he was exactly where he was supposed to be in life.

9. In Lines 75–77, when the author says, "the outer world presented him with a very large, unavoidable obstacle," he is most likely referring to:

   (A) Louis.

   (B) Max's unmatchable intellect.

   (C) Max's lack of communication skills.

   (D) society as a whole.

10. Which of the following best describes Max's progression throughout the passage?

    (F) He spent his early years living in near-constant fear but devoted his later youth to instilling fear in others.

    (G) He began life socially inept and was able to overcome struggles and excel in a variety of social situations.

    (H) He lacked self-esteem throughout his early childhood but then became downright narcissistic as the years progressed.

    (J) He spent his early years in fear of his cruel older brother but was later able to capitalize on the experience.

Passage 2 — Social Science

This passage is adapted from *How to Develop Self-Esteem in Your Child: 6 Vital Ingredients* by Dr. Bettie Youngs.

What is the work of childhood? Each stage of a child's development presents its own set of tasks and demands, all focused on gaining self-knowledge or selfhood. The work of each stage is pretty well-defined. (05)

Until the age of two, a child primarily views himself as part of his mother (or father, if he is the primary caretaker). Upon reaching two, he develops the ability to be aware that he is really separate from her. This situation presents him with the (10) task of establishing autonomy — separateness. The two words that best describe his new-found selfhood, that he is in fact a separate person, are "no" and "mine." Possession is the tool he uses to enforce that sense of separate self. (15)

Having realized his separateness, the three-year-old goes on to master his environment. Mastery plays an important role in his perception of self. It influences his feelings of being capable or not capable. His need for success in (20) his endeavors at this stage is crucial. He labors over each of his accomplishments. He is slow and methodical and takes forever to do each task. Needing feedback to know if he has been successful, he strives for recognition of these (25) achievements. ("Watch me, Mommy! Watch me, Mommy!") That he has something to offer nurtures his sense of competence and proves his value.

Go on to next page

(30)   Parents are the name of the game for the five-year-old. At this age, the mother is the center of the child's world. He not only wants to please her, but he also wants to be near her, wants to talk with her, wants to play with her, (35) and wants to help her around the house. The five-year-old's adoration of his parents is unquestionably heartwarming. The result is almost totally parent-pleasing behavior. In his determination to do everything just right, he'll ask per- (40) mission for the simplest thing, even when he needn't; and he will then beam with pleasure when the parent smiles and gives permission.

     Age six can be described as the stage of "me-ness." Self-centeredness comes before other- (45) centeredness. While children were in the preschool stage, they discovered that they were separate from their parents, although they still kept their parents as the center of their existence. At six, they must shift the focus from their parents to (50) themselves. They now place themselves at the center of their world instead of parents or others. Although they may appear to be excessively self-centered and unconcerned with the needs and feelings of others, this is an important (55) milestone in their development. They are now ready to undertake the task of being receptive to their own interests and attempting to understand them.

     At age 16, it is not uncommon for a child to (60) experience feelings of being confused, embarrassed, guilty, awkward, inferior, ugly, and scared, all in the same day. In fact, a teenager can swing from being childish and petulant to being sedate, or from acting rational to irratio- (65) nal, all in the same hour. It's a time of confusion and uncertainty. The goal is to experience intimacy; he needs to belong. This is a time of duality. The 16-year-old wants to be with others, yet he wants to be alone; he needs his friends, but (70) he will sabotage them if they appear to outdo him; he'll root for a friend out loud, but he'll secretly wish for his friend's failure. Age 16 is a time when he wants total independence, but he is not capable of it. He doesn't really want to live (75) without his parents, although he believes that they are roadblocks hindering his life.

     The final stage of development in childhood is establishing total independence. In changing from being dependent on others to being self- (80) dependent, children confront some pretty big (and frightening) issues. They have three tasks. Their first task is to determine vocation. A child needs to ask what he is going to do with his life. Underlying this task is the self-esteem need to be (85) somebody, to experience positive feelings of

strength, power, and competence. Second, he needs to establish values. The goal is to sort out his own values and to decide which ones to keep and which ones to discard. Following this step is the only way that he can develop integrity. (90) Perhaps most striking is his need to establish a workable and meaningful philosophy of life. Reevaluating his moral concepts will mean searching for his own personal beliefs, complete with facing religious, ethical, and value-laden ide- (95) ologies. Developing personal convictions will be influenced by his level of self-esteem, especially if a conflict exists among what he believes, what his family believes, and what his friends find acceptable. Third, he needs to establish self-reliance. (100)

11. The author's primary purpose in writing this passage is to:

   (A) show that early childhood learning is important because it provides the foundation for life.

   (B) analyze the causes behind low self-esteem in children.

   (C) denounce child psychologists.

   (D) discuss the various behaviors associated with the ages of children.

12. According to the author, the ultimate goal of children is to gain:

   (F) recognition.

   (G) selfhood.

   (H) praise.

   (J) competence.

13. The author uses the comment "Watch me, Mommy! Watch me, Mommy!" to make the point that three-year-olds:

   (A) recognize that they are individuals, separate from their parents.

   (B) do tasks in order to please their parents.

   (C) need outside acknowledgment of their accomplishments at a specific age of development.

   (D) are prone to repeating themselves.

Go on to next page ⇒

14. Which of the following is another way of stating "Parents are the name of the game" (Line 30)?

   (F) Parents design games and activities to entertain and stimulate their children.

   (G) The names parents give their children determine their sense of self-worth.

   (H) Parental gamesmanship influences children's development.

   (J) Parents are of prime importance to their children.

15. You may infer from the fifth paragraph (Lines 43–58) that the author considers a lack of sensitivity in six-year-olds:

   (A) abnormal and rare.

   (B) cute at that age but unacceptable in adults.

   (C) precocious because such egotism does not usually begin until the teenage years.

   (D) vital in order for children to recognize their separateness from their parents.

16. Which of the following phrases best expresses the idea of the sixth paragraph (Lines 59–76)?

   (F) The goal is to experience intimacy.

   (G) This is a time of duality.

   (H) Age 16 is a time when a child wants total independence.

   (J) A 16-year-old believes that parents are roadblocks hindering his life.

17. As used in Line 82, *vocation* means:

   (A) rest and relaxation.

   (B) geographical area.

   (C) romance.

   (D) career.

18. The author mentions all of the following as specific tasks in establishing self-dependence EXCEPT:

   (F) figuring out what to do in life.

   (G) determining moral concepts.

   (H) developing self-reliance.

   (J) avoiding conflicts between what he believes and what others believe.

19. Which of the following best describes the organization of the passage?

   (A) Concepts are discussed in order from most important to least important.

   (B) Discussions begin with a presentation of a theory followed by proven facts.

   (C) Discussions are ordered chronologically.

   (D) The author presents beliefs and then offers predictions.

20. It may be reasonably inferred from the passage that all stages of childhood have as their ultimate goal:

   (F) fiscal security.

   (G) recognition.

   (H) independence.

   (J) parental respect.

Passage 3 — Humanities

El Greco painted *The Burial of Conde Orgaz* in Toledo, Spain, during the years 1586–88. Almost 400 years later, Joseph Beuys, a post–World War II German artist, initiated his artistic career with mixed media drawings that com- (05) bined pencil with colored ink or watercolor on creased paper, one of which he entitled *Kadmon*. Although the two artists painted different sub- jects in different time periods, in different coun- tries, with different media and in different styles, (10) they convey a common meaning. Both works demonstrate the relationship between the spiri- tual and material world and explore the human position within these worlds.

El Greco received his formal art training in (15) Crete and Italy, but he created his master works in Spain, a country known both for a heightened sense of spirituality and a feeling for the real and tangible. His formal training was a blend of Byzantine mysticism and Italian Mannerism. (20) During his early years he learned from Cretan monks to make flat, mystical icons in the Byzantine tradition. He then studied under Jacopo Bassano and Titian in Venice, but was most influenced by his apprenticeship to (25) Tintoretto, who introduced him to the emotion, force, and strong movement characteristic of Mannerism. These early influences coupled with a short stay in Rome, where he was stimulated by the work of Michelangelo, supplied the back- (30) ground for the unique style El Greco achieved when he settled in Toledo to paint religious com- missions from churches and convents. Not only

Go on to next page

did El Greco receive diverse artistic training, but (35) he also received a well-rounded spiritual, histori- cal, literary and scientific education from his early humanistic schooling and his eclectic group of friends in cosmopolitan Toledo. His paintings combined his varied artistic and intel- (40) lectual influences to portray the interplay between the spiritual world and the material world. Considered by many to be his master- piece, *The Burial of Conde Orgaz* reflects his forceful ability to illustrate both worlds.

(45) Like El Greco, Joseph Beuys experienced a variety of personal and artistic influences that inspired him to portray spiritual and earthly themes in his works. Beuys grew up in the tiny German town of Kleve, and his youth was influ- (50) enced by the small community's predominant Catholicism and its bucolic natural setting. According to Christopher Lyon, Beuys's art grew out of Beuys's attempts to deal with the chaotic aftermath of World War II, and his early drawings (55) portray both the personal and political schisms created by the war's devastation. His early works reveal his vivid imagination and demonstrate what Lyon calls a "mythic approach to his life and art," a technique Beuys continued to explore (60) more fully in his studies at the Dusseldorf Academy of Art and in his unique performance art demonstrations in later years. *Kadmon*, one of Beuys's earliest works, portrays his fascina- tion with the relationship between the mystic (65) and the tangible.

El Greco and Beuys chose different subjects to portray the interplay between the heavens and the earth. Because his art was commis- sioned by churches and because art before the (70) advent of photography served not only aesthetic purposes but also as a record of history, El Greco most often re-created specific religious events. Unobstructed by the limitations of church spon- sorship and freed by modern artistic exploration, (75) Beuys chose more primordial subject matter for his interpretations.

The Burial of Conde Orgaz uses the burial of an esteemed and religious Spanish count, who had died over 250 years before its painting, as a (80) means of portraying the relationship between the heavens and the earth. The brilliantly colored oil on canvas painting, measuring 16 feet high and almost 12 feet wide, adorns one wall of the Church of San Tome in Toledo. The painting con- (85) tains two main settings. The lower scene depicts an ornately robed Saint Stephen and Saint Augustine gently lowering the armored body of Conde Orgaz into an unseen grave. Surrounding the saints is a group of clergy and noblemen in varying states of worship and mourning. Above (90) this scene hover the inhabitants of heaven.

In contrast to the generally well-defined fea- tures of the figures in the lower scene, the fig- ures in the heavens are blurred and ethereal. The dominant figure among the angels and saints (95) is the blue and red clothed Virgin Mary, who appears to be taking petitions from a seemingly endless string of souls. Mary's gaze is not directed at the petitioner's, however. She is gently reaching for the soul of Conde Orgaz that (100) floats toward her in the undefined form of a baby. Alongside Mary, Saint Peter watches hold- ing the keys to heaven. Above and somewhat at a distance, Christ sits as Lord over the scene. The only connections between the two scenes are (105) the flames that leap from the torches held by the noblemen to the heavenly realm, the cross held by one of the clergy, and the eyes of the priest as he gazes toward the soul of Conde Orgaz. These connections suggest that the division between (110) heaven and earth, spiritual and material, can only be transcended by the Spirit, symbolized by the flames, Christ, symbolized by the cross, and, perhaps, through the knowledge of the priest.

21. The author's primary purpose in writing this passage is most likely to:

(A) prove that El Greco produced works of art with spiritual themes while Beuys produced works that emphasized bucolic themes.

(B) show the similarities between two seemingly dissimilar artists.

(C) reveal the various influences on the work of El Greco and Beuys.

(D) demonstrate that great works of art have the power to transcend the tangi- ble world and unite the material world with the spiritual world.

22. It is reasonable to infer from the passage that El Greco's artistic education:

(F) resulted from an intricate combination of religious and nonreligious influences.

(G) was largely a product of his formal train- ing at the Dusseldorf Academy of Art.

(H) reached its height during his appren- ticeship to Michelangelo.

(J) was more diverse and richer than the artistic educations received by other artists of his day.

Go on to next page →

23. The author would say that El Greco and Beuys used different subjects to showcase the interplay between the heavens and the earth because:

    (A) El Greco's vocation was supported by the church, but Beuys was not obligated to create works for a particular sponsor.

    (B) Beuys's art was influenced by primeval subjects, whereas El Greco's art was inspired by his passion for history.

    (C) the two had differing religious views.

    (D) the two came from different socioeconomic backgrounds.

24. The word *schisms* in Line 55 refers to:

    (F) solutions.

    (G) religious beliefs.

    (H) fascinations.

    (J) divisions.

25. All of the following figures are depicted in El Greco's *The Burial of Conde Orgaz* EXCEPT:

    (A) Saint Augustine.

    (B) clergy and noblemen.

    (C) the Virgin Mary.

    (D) Tintoretto.

26. It is the author's belief that *The Burial of Conde Orgaz* suggests that the separation between the spiritual and material worlds can be overcome by:

    (F) Saint Peter because he holds the keys to heaven.

    (G) the flame, which to the author is a representation of the Holy Spirit.

    (H) wealth and power as symbolized by the torches held by the noblemen.

    (J) the petitions of an endless line of souls.

27. The passage states that El Greco painted his most accomplished works in:

    (A) Italy

    (B) Crete

    (C) Spain

    (D) Germany

28. The passage implies that a significant influence on Beuys's art was:

    (F) a blend of Byzantine mysticism and Italian Mannerism.

    (G) studying the works of El Greco.

    (H) growing up in a small, rural town in Germany.

    (J) his Catholic school upbringing.

29. The author would say that a possible similarity between the works of El Greco and Beuys is that both of them:

    (A) were created using watercolors.

    (B) explored the interplay between the spiritual and material worlds.

    (C) were influenced by earlier German artists.

    (D) portrayed the same subject matter.

30. As presented in Line 5, "mixed media drawings" most likely refers to drawings that:

    (F) have been reproduced in a variety of different formats.

    (G) have been created using more than one artistic technique.

    (H) have been displayed in public settings and then reproduced to appear in print publications.

    (J) have received mixed critical reviews in the media.

Go on to next page

Passage 4 — Natural Science

Line
Thrombosis refers to abnormal clotting that causes the blood flow in a blood vessel to become obstructed. Venous thrombosis refers to such an obstruction in a vein, often at some site

(05) of inflammation, disease, or injury to the blood vessel wall. The clot (thrombus) may remain fixed at the site of origin, adhering to the wall of the vein. Or the clot (or a fragment of it) may break loose to be carried elsewhere in the circu-

(10) latory system by the blood. The migratory clot or fragment is then called an embolus.

In pulmonary embolism, the clot or fragment breaks free from its site of origin, usually a deep vein of the leg or pelvis, and is carried by the

(15) blood through progressively larger veins into the inferior vena cava, a very large abdominal vein that empties into the right side of the heart. The embolus is pumped through the right side of the heart and into the pulmonary artery, whose

(20) branches supply blood to the lungs. Depending on its size, the embolus may pass through the larger pulmonary branches, but may eventually enter a branch too narrow to allow it to pass. Here it lodges, obstructing blood flow to the lung

(25) tissues supplied by that vessel and its finer divisions "downstream" from the embolus.

The clinical consequences of pulmonary embolism vary with the size of the embolus and the extent to which it reduces total blood flow to

(30) the lungs. Very small emboli cause so little circulatory impairment that they may produce no clinical signs or symptoms at all. In fact, among the estimated 300,000 patients who experience pulmonary embolism each year, the great majority

(35) suffers no serious symptoms or complications, and the disorder clears up without significant aftereffects.

However, in a significant percentage of patients, the pulmonary embolism is massive,

(40) sometimes reducing total pulmonary blood flow by 50 percent or more; and the consequences may be grave: seriously strained circulation, shock, or acute respiratory failure. Massive pulmonary embolism causes some 50,000 deaths

(45) each year in the U.S.

Certain classes of patients are more likely than others to develop venous thrombosis with its attendant risk of pulmonary embolism. Disorders that increase susceptibility include

(50) venous inflammation (phlebitis), congestive heart failure, and certain forms of cancer. Women are more susceptible during pregnancy and during recovery from childbirth than at

other times, and those taking birth control pills appear to be at slightly higher risk than are (55) women who do not. Postoperative patients constitute a high-risk group, particularly following pelvic surgery and orthopedic procedures involving the hip. Any operations requiring that the patient be immobilized for prolonged peri- (60) ods afterward exacerbate the risk of this problem. Among patients recovering from hip fractures, for example, the incidence of venous thrombosis may run as high as 50 percent.

Venous thrombosis can sometimes be diag- (65) nosed by the presence of a swollen extremity with some evidence of inflammation or a clot that can be felt when the affected vein is examined. But sometimes venous thrombosis produces no clear-cut clinical signs so that other (70) tests may be needed to confirm the diagnosis.

One such test entails injecting fibrinogen tagged with a radioactive isotope of iodine into the blood. Fibrinogen has a strong affinity for blood clots and is incorporated into them, carry- (75) ing its radioactive label with it. The clot can then be located with a radiation-sensing device.

Another diagnostic technique, called venography, involves injecting a dye (one that shows clearly on X-rays) into the vein where obstruc- (80) tion is suspected. The X-ray venogram provides very detailed information on the extent and location of the obstruction.

A third technique uses sensitive instruments that measure blood flow in vessels of the extrem- (85) ities to detect any circulatory impairment that may result from thrombosis.

Signs of nonfatal pulmonary embolism may include sudden shortness of breath, chest pain, increased heart rate, restlessness and anxiety, a (90) fall in blood pressure, and loss of consciousness. But clinical symptoms may vary by their presence or absence and in their intensity, and their similarity to symptoms that may result from other disorders can make the diagnosis of pul- (95) monary embolism difficult on this basis alone.

Pulmonary angiography (X-ray visualization of the pulmonary artery and its branches after injection of a radiopaque dye) is the most reliable diagnostic technique, but it is a complex test that (100) cannot be done routinely in all patients. A somewhat simpler test involves injecting extremely fine particles of a radioactively labeled material such as albumin into a vein and then scanning the lungs with a radiation detector while the par- (105) ticles traverse the pulmonary blood vessels.

Go on to next page ⟶

31. The purpose of the first paragraph (Lines 1–11) is to:

    (A) analyze the causes of blood clots.

    (B) describe types of blood clots.

    (C) predict who is most likely to get a blood clot.

    (D) inform the readers of steps to take for the prevention of blood clots.

32. Which of the following best describes the difference between a thrombus and an embolus?

    (F) A thrombus is in the lung; an embolus may be anywhere.

    (G) A thrombus is usually fatal; an embolus is rarely fatal.

    (H) A thrombus remains stationary; an embolus moves within the circulatory system.

    (J) A thrombus is larger than an embolus.

33. It is reasonable to conclude from the passage that pulmonary embolism:

    (A) may clear up on its own.

    (B) is invariably fatal.

    (C) is more severe in children than in adults.

    (D) may be prevented by following a specific diet.

34. According to the passage, a common origin for a pulmonary thrombosis is in the:

    (F) heart.

    (G) brain.

    (H) leg.

    (J) arm.

35. In Line 48, the phrase "attendant risk" refers to:

    (A) risks faced by those who aid others.

    (B) risks that accompany something else.

    (C) minimal, almost nonexistent, risks.

    (D) risks that are higher for women than men.

36. The word *exacerbate* in Line 61 means:

    (F) reduce.

    (G) cure.

    (H) exaggerate.

    (J) worsen.

37. The author suggests which of the following about pulmonary angiography (Line 97)?

    (A) It diagnoses a specific type of pulmonary embolism that is more complex than other types of embolisms.

    (B) Its use of radiopaque dye creates severe allergic reactions in some patients.

    (C) It involves the use of radioactive particles that are injected into a vein and then detected with a radiation detector.

    (D) The test has properties that prevent it from being used repeatedly on some patients.

38. Which of the following is the best title for the passage?

    (F) How to Cure Pulmonary Embolisms

    (G) How Blood Clots Develop

    (H) Means of Preventing Blood Clots and Embolisms

    (J) Description and Diagnosis of Blood Clots

39. The reason that the author introduces the three tests discussed in Lines 72–87 is to:

    (A) lament the high cost of diagnosis.

    (B) prove that any blood clot can eventually be diagnosed.

    (C) describe the means of confirming a suspected diagnosis.

    (D) reject the premise that all blood clots are fatal.

40. According to the author, using clinical symptoms to diagnose pulmonary embolisms:

    (F) is cheaper and more time-effective than using high-tech machinery.

    (G) should be done cautiously and in conjunction with other tests.

    (H) can be done only in the least acute cases.

    (J) cannot be done routinely on all patients.

STOP DO NOT TURN THE PAGE UNTIL TOLD TO DO SO. DO NOT RETURN TO A PREVIOUS TEST.

Science Test

Time: 35 minutes for 40 questions

Directions: Following are seven passages and then questions that refer to each passage. Choose the best answer to each question and shade in the corresponding oval on your answer sheet.

Passage 1

In the pole vault, the pole acts to convert the energy generated by an athlete running down a runway into a force that lifts the athlete over a crossbar. The most advanced vaulters use stiff poles that quickly convert the horizontal energy into the lifting force. Beginning vaulters are not strong, fast, or skillful enough to bend a stiff pole as needed to generate substantial vertical lift. Beginning vaulters must use more flexible poles.

To test the suitability of two materials for use in poles, scientists subjected three miniature poles to two laboratory tests. Pole No. 1, made of fiberglass, is 50 cm long, with a diameter of 1 cm and a mass of 1 kg. Pole No. 2, also made of fiberglass, is also 50 cm long but has a diameter of 1.5 cm and a mass of 2.25 kg. Pole No. 3, made of carbon fiber, is 50 cm long, 1.5 cm in diameter, and has a mass of 1 kg.

Study 1

Scientists tested the three poles to determine how much force is required to bend the poles to an 85-degree angle. Table 1 shows the results.

Table 1	Results of Bent-Pole Test
Pole	**Force in Newtons (N)**
1	4.9
2	5.8
3	6.3

Study 2

Scientists bent each pole to an 85-degree angle and then allowed the pole to snap back to a straight position. Table 2 shows the time required for each pole to snap back.

Table 2	Results of Snap-Back Test
Pole	**Time in Milliseconds (msec)**
1	733
2	626
3	591

1. According to the results of the two tests, the relationship between the force required to bend a pole and the time needed for the pole to snap back to its regular position is that:

(A) the greater the force required to bend the pole, the more time required for the pole to snap back.

(B) the greater the force required to bend the pole, the less time required for the pole to snap back.

(C) for only the fiberglass poles, the greater the force required to bend the pole, the more time required for the pole to snap back.

(D) for only the fiberglass poles, the greater the force required to bend the pole, the less time required for the pole to snap back.

Go on to next page

2. On the basis of Study 1, the relationship between pole mass and stiffness is that:

    (F) poles with greater masses are stiffer.

    (G) fiberglass poles with greater masses are stiffer.

    (H) poles with smaller masses are stiffer.

    (J) there is no relationship between pole mass and pole stiffness.

3. Which of the following is a controlled variable in this study?

    (A) pole diameter

    (B) force required to bend poles

    (C) time for poles to return to vertical

    (D) force generated when poles return to vertical

4. Kinetic energy results from the actual motion of an object, while potential energy is a measure of the energy that results if an object were to move from a certain location. During a pole vault, virtually all the energy is in the form of potential energy:

    (F) when the vaulter is running down the runway.

    (G) when the pole is bent.

    (H) as the pole unbends and sends the vaulter upward.

    (J) as the vaulter falls into the pit.

5. Ideally, vaulters like to use long poles because the poles reach closer to the crossbar. If a pole is too long, though, a vaulter has difficulty carrying it down the runway because of its mass. Given these considerations, the material that is best suited for a very long pole is:

    (A) fiberglass, because it snaps back relatively slowly.

    (B) fiberglass, because it has a relatively high mass-to-volume ratio.

    (C) carbon fiber, because it is relatively stiff.

    (D) carbon fiber, because it has a relatively low mass-to-volume ratio.

6. On the basis of the entire study, which of the following would be the most appropriate pole for the beginning pole vaulter?

    (F) Pole 2

    (G) Pole 1

    (H) Pole 3

    (J) either Pole 2 or Pole 3

Passage 2

Very few humans live to the age of 100. In other words, almost all members of the human population who were born in a given year will die within 100 years. Scientists, health professionals, and life insurance agents are interested in examining how many people in a population will live to be a certain age. One way to measure this information is to look at how much of the population has died after a certain number of years. A graph documenting the results of one such study is presented in Figure 1.

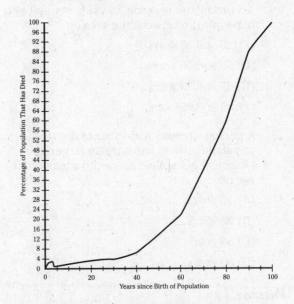

Figure 1: How much of the population has died after a certain number of years.

7. According to Figure 1, approximately what percentage of the human population lives to at least 80 years of age?

    (A) 10 percent

    (B) 40 percent

    (C) 60 percent

    (D) 80 percent

Go on to next page ⟶

8. The increase in percentage of deaths is highest for which of the following intervals?

(F) 0 to 20 years

(G) 20 to 40 years

(H) 40 to 60 years

(J) 60 to 80 years

9. Suppose a study eliminates infant mortality (children dying at birth or very shortly thereafter) from consideration. How will the graph change?

(A) The quick rise that is recorded on the graph just after 0 years will disappear.

(B) The graph will show a higher percentage of deaths at 20 years.

(C) The graph will become slightly flatter between 60 and 80 years.

(D) The horizontal range of the graph will extend past 110 years.

10. According to the graph, the largest number of people die between the ages of:

(F) 20 and 30 years.

(G) 50 and 60 years.

(H) 65 and 75 years.

(J) 85 and 95 years.

11. A person who was a member of the study population would still have an 80 percent chance of being alive at around a maximum age of:

(A) 15 years.

(B) 35 years.

(C) 55 years.

(D) 80 years.

Passage 3

A radioactive substance is one that contains atoms with nuclei that change into other types of atomic nuclei. For example, a uranium nucleus can lose two protons and two neutrons and become a thorium nucleus. Atoms of some radioactive substances change more frequently than others. Over time, the rate of change for any substance slows as a greater percentage of atomic nuclei change to a final, more stable state.

Devices can measure the number of atomic changes that take place at a given time. Each of these changes is commonly called a disintegration. Table 1 and Table 2 show the disintegration rates for two unknown substances.

Table 1 Substance A Disintegrations

Time (hours)	Disintegration Rate (millicuries)
0	200
5	100
10	50
15	25
20	12.5

Table 2 Substance B Disintegrations

Time (hours)	Disintegration Rate (millicuries)
0	2,000
4	1,000
8	500
12	250
16	125

12. It is reasonable to deduce that after 20 hours the disintegration rate for Substance B will be about:

(F) 0 millicuries.

(G) 12.5 millicuries.

(H) 62.5 millicuries.

(J) 200 millicuries.

13. If Substance A starts with 10,000,000 radioactive atoms, the number of atoms present at 15 hours will be:

(A) 666,667.

(B) 1,250,000.

(C) 3,333,333.

(D) 5,000,000.

Go on to next page

14. The disintegration rate of Substance B is 1,500 millicuries:

    (F) at about 2 hours.

    (G) at exactly 2 hours.

    (H) at about 3 hours.

    (J) at exactly 3 hours.

15. Given that the half-life of a radioactive substance is the time it takes for half of the radioactive atoms to disintegrate, the substance with the shorter half-life is:

    (A) Substance A, because it reaches its half-life after 5 hours.

    (B) Substance A, because it will be completely disintegrated after 25 hours.

    (C) Substance B, because the disintegration rate fell to half its original value in 4 hours.

    (D) Substance B, because it was measured for 16 hours instead of 20.

16. Radioactive substances are potential health hazards because the particles emitted from radioactive substances can damage parts of the human body. Therefore, humans should take great care to limit the amount of radioactivity they are exposed to. Which of the following is safest for a human to handle?

    (F) Substance A after 5 hours

    (G) Substance A after 20 hours

    (H) Substance B after 8 hours

    (J) Substance B after 16 hours

Passage 4

When sunlight heats the earth's surface, much of that energy is radiated back to the atmosphere. Although some of this re-radiated energy escapes to space, a significant amount of it is reflected back to the earth's surface by molecules in the atmosphere. These molecules — water, nitrous oxide, methane, and carbon dioxide — trap re-radiated energy in the same way that glass in a greenhouse does and warm the earth. Hence, the term "greenhouse effect" has been used to refer to the warming of the earth caused by the gases' keeping heat within the earth's atmosphere.

Scientists agree that the greenhouse effect results in higher temperatures on earth but disagree as to whether recent increases in atmospheric carbon dioxide will lead to undesirable global warming. Two scientists discuss this possibility.

Scientist 1

Ancient ice cores from Antarctica indicate that the concentration of carbon dioxide in the atmosphere and global mean temperatures have followed the same pattern of fluctuations in levels over the past 160,000 years. Therefore, the increase in atmospheric carbon dioxide concentration from 280 parts per million to 360 parts per million that has occurred over the past 150 years points to significant and detrimental climatic changes in the near future. The climate has already changed: The average surface temperature of the earth has increased 0.6°C in the past hundred years, with the ten hottest years of that time period all occurring since 1980. Although 0.6°C may not seem large, changes in the mean surface temperature as low as 0.5°C have dramatically affected crop growth in years past. Moreover, computer models project that surface temperatures will increase about 2.0°C by the year 2100 and will continue to increase in the years after even if concentration of greenhouse gases is stabilized by that time. If the present trend in carbon dioxide increase continues, though, carbon dioxide concentration will exceed 1,100 parts per million soon after 2100 and will be associated with a temperature increase of approximately 10.0°C over the present mean annual global surface temperature.

Scientist 2

The observed increases in minor greenhouse gases such as carbon dioxide and methane will not lead to sizeable global warming. Water vapor and clouds are responsible for more than 98% of the earth's greenhouse effect. Current models that project large temperature increases with a doubling of the present carbon dioxide concentration incorporate changes in water vapor, clouds, and other factors that would accompany a rise in carbon dioxide levels. The way these models handle such feedback factors is not supported by current scientific knowledge. In fact, there is convincing evidence that shows that increases in carbon dioxide concentration

Go on to next page ⟹

would lead to changes in feedback factors that would diminish any temperature increase associated with more carbon dioxide in the atmosphere. The climatic data for the past hundred years show an irregular pattern in which many of the greatest jumps in global mean temperature were too large to be associated with the observed increase in carbon dioxide. The overall increase of 0.45°C in the past century is well under what the models would have predicted given the changes in carbon dioxide concentration. As with the temperature models, recent increases in atmospheric carbon dioxide have not risen to the extent predicted by models dealing solely with carbon dioxide levels. The rate of carbon dioxide concentration increase has slowed since 1973. Improved energy technologies will further dampen the increase so that the carbon dioxide concentration will be under 700 parts per million in the year 2100.

17. Which of the following is an assumption made by Scientist 1?

(A) Feedback factors have little effect on the magnitude to which increased carbon dioxide will increase temperature.

(B) Humans will not be able to limit their activities that contribute to rising carbon dioxide levels.

(C) A rise in the global mean temperature of 1.0°C is not significant.

(D) Temperature fluctuations will match carbon dioxide changes when carbon dioxide changes are abrupt.

18. A scientific article states that "Scientists will soon develop computer models that accurately account for feedback factors." This statement is consistent with:

(F) only the viewpoint of Scientist 1.

(G) only the viewpoint of Scientist 2.

(H) the viewpoints of both Scientist 1 and Scientist 2.

(J) the viewpoint of neither Scientist 1 nor Scientist 2.

19. Which of the following is the most likely reason that the two scientists present different figures for the temperature rise that has occurred over the past hundred years?

(A) It has been difficult to determine the mean global temperature with complete accuracy.

(B) Scientist 2 uses figures that do not take account of the rise in atmospheric carbon dioxide.

(C) Scientist 1 notes that all ten of the hottest years in the last hundred years have come since 1980.

(D) It has not been established that global warming is a threat to the earth.

20. Indicative of rising temperatures, a large block of the Larson B Ice Sheet in Antarctica recently broke off, raising water levels around the world and increasing the vulnerability of coastal areas to flooding. In light of this information, which of the following predictions would be most consistent with Scientist 1's viewpoint?

(F) Feedback factors will retard the future rate of ice sheet disintegration.

(G) The amount of ice that will break off will double with a doubling of atmospheric carbon dioxide.

(H) The breakup of the ice sheet will minimize global warming.

(J) Coastal areas will be more prone to flooding in the next hundred years.

21. Scientists 1 and 2 would most likely agree with which of the following statements about atmospheric carbon dioxide levels?

(A) Increasing carbon dioxide levels affect other factors.

(B) Humans will never be able to stabilize atmospheric carbon dioxide levels.

(C) The rate of increase in carbon dioxide levels will rise throughout the next hundred years.

(D) Carbon dioxide levels are directly linked to temperature.

Go on to next page

22. Scientist 1's claim about the significance of increased global temperatures over the past hundred years is most vulnerable to the criticism that:

    (F) the carbon dioxide increases that she presents have taken place over the past 150 years.

    (G) she does not specify which years since 1980 have been hottest.

    (H) she does not specify whether the change in crop growth she cites was caused by an increase or decrease in temperature.

    (J) the figures she presents for temperature increases over the next hundred years are greater than the figure she provides for the past hundred years.

23. It is reasonable to infer from Scientist 2 that:

    (A) humans will be able to adapt to any problem produced by global warming.

    (B) a change in atmospheric water vapor could significantly affect global temperatures.

    (C) atmospheric carbon dioxide levels will never reach 1,100 parts per million.

    (D) atmospheric carbon dioxide levels will eventually stop increasing.

Passage 5

Angiosperms, or flowering plants, typically produce flowers seasonally. The various angiosperm species produce their flowers at different times of the year. For example, some flowers bloom in early spring, while others bloom in the summer. Research has shown that these flowering plants respond to changes in day length. A cocklebur, for example, does not produce flowers during the time of year that has days longer than 15.5 hours. When the length of day drops below this figure, flowering occurs. This type of flower is known as a short-day (SD) plant. Long-day (LD) plants do the opposite. These plants do not flower until the length of day exceeds a certain critical value. Plants that do not respond to changes in day length are called day-neutral (DN) plants. The following experiments investigate what aspect of changing day length is responsible for the plants' responses.

Experiment 1

Botanists raise both SD and LD plants in a greenhouse under long-day conditions. As expected, the SD plants do not flower, and the LD plants do flower. When a brief period of darkness interrupts a long day, the LD plants continue to flower.

Experiment 2

Scientists raise both SD and LD plants in a greenhouse under short-day conditions. The SD plants flower, and the LD plants do not flower. When a brief flash of light interrupts the long night, the SD plants stop flowering and the LD plants begin to flower.

Experiment 3

Experimenters perform a yearlong study in which they raise both SD and LD plants in several greenhouses. The light/dark cycle corresponds to the day-length changes that occur normally over the course of a year. Daytime temperatures differ in each greenhouse. All SD plants flower at the same time of year. As expected, all LD plants flower at a different time than the SD plants do, but the LD plants all flower at the same time when compared to one another.

Experiment 4

Conditions are identical to those of Experiment 3, except that while daytime temperatures are kept the same across all greenhouses, nighttime temperatures vary. SD and LD plants still flower at different times of the year, but the plants vary considerably as far as when each plant begins to flower. For example, SD plants in greenhouses with warmer nighttime temperatures flower at a different time than do SD plants in cooler greenhouses.

Go on to next page

24. On the basis of Experiments 1 and 2, the most critical factor in determining whether SD and LD plants will flower is the:

    (F) total number of daytime hours.

    (G) total number of nighttime hours.

    (H) number of uninterrupted daytime hours.

    (J) number of uninterrupted nighttime hours.

25. Cocklebur, an SD plant, and spinach, an LD plant, are both raised on an 8-hour day, 16-hour night cycle. If a brief flash of light is presented in the middle of the 16-hour night, the most likely result will be that:

    (A) neither plant will flower.

    (B) cocklebur will flower; spinach will not.

    (C) spinach will flower; cocklebur will not.

    (D) both plants will flower.

26. The variable that the experimenters do not directly control is:

    (F) type of plant.

    (G) flowering.

    (H) amount of light.

    (J) temperature.

27. Are the results of Experiments 3 and 4 consistent with the results of Experiments 1 and 2?

    (A) No, because Experiments 3 and 4 use a wider variety of plants.

    (B) No, because temperature does not change in Experiments 1 and 2.

    (C) Yes, because both sets of experiments suggest that the plants respond to a night factor rather than a day factor.

    (D) Yes, because both SD and LD plants are used in all the experiments.

28. Which of the following best represents the shape of a line graph that records flowering activity as a function of day length for an LD plant that starts to flower when day length exceeds 15 hours?

(F)

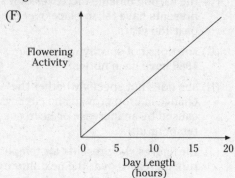

(G)

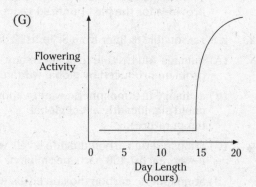

(H)

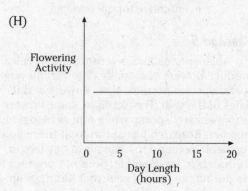

(J)

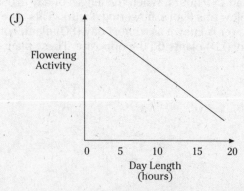

Go on to next page ➡

29. Near the equator, day length varies little throughout the year. That is, periods of day and night are virtually equal every 24 hours. Assuming proper soil, water, and other essential conditions, the plant that would most likely flower when grown near the equator would be:

    (A) an LD plant that flowers only when the daylight exceeds 14 hours.

    (B) an SD plant that flowers only when the day length falls between 6 and 11 hours.

    (C) a DN plant.

    (D) an SD plant that flowers only when daylight falls below 8 hours.

Passage 6

Matter exists in three phases: solid, liquid, and gas. In general, these phases are defined by how far apart the particles in the substance are. Particles are typically closest together in a solid and farthest away from one another in a gas.

Temperature is clearly related to phases. As temperature rises, particles move faster and farther away from one another and matter changes from a solid to a liquid to a gas. The temperature at which matter changes from liquid to gas is called its boiling point.

Pressure also affects phases of matter. A substance that is a gas at a certain temperature and low pressure may become a liquid at the same temperature if pressure is increased.

Figures 1 and 2 summarize the relationship among temperature, pressure, and phase for both bromine and water.

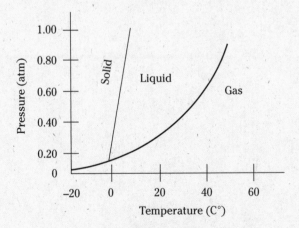

Figure 1: Bromine phases.

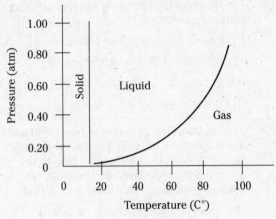

Figure 2: Water phases.

30. At 60°C and 1.00 atm, water is:

    (F) a solid.

    (G) a liquid.

    (H) a gas.

    (J) in the process of changing from a solid to a liquid.

31. Sublimation occurs when a solid changes to a gas without going through a liquid phase. A point at which sublimation can occur is when:

    (A) bromine is at –20°C and 0.05 atm.

    (B) bromine is at 0°C and 0.80 atm.

    (C) water is at 0°C and 0.80 atm.

    (D) water is at 80°C and 0.50 atm.

32. At 30°C, as pressure is decreased from 0.6 atm to 0.3 atm, it is true that:

    (F) bromine changes from a gas to a liquid.

    (G) bromine changes from a liquid to a gas.

    (H) water changes from a solid to a liquid.

    (J) water changes from a gas to a liquid.

Go on to next page

33. For which of the following are the particles farthest apart?

    (A) bromine at –10°C and 1.00 atm

    (B) bromine at 50°C and 0.80 atm

    (C) water at 0°C and 0.40 atm

    (D) water at 100°C and 0.60 atm

34. At high altitudes, pressure is lower and softening spaghetti in boiling water takes longer than it does at sea level. According to the information in the passage, the most reasonable explanation for this effect is that:

    (F) ice crystals form on the spaghetti.

    (G) air temperature is lower at high altitudes.

    (H) the boiling point is lower at lower pressure and lower temperatures are not as effective at softening spaghetti.

    (J) at lower pressure, water boils at a higher temperature and reaching this temperature takes longer.

Passage 7

Radon is a gas that is emitted from the earth's crust in small quantities. Radon can readily be detected in wells. An accidental discovery of excessive radon emission in an earthquake-prone area led seismologists to study the association between radon emission and earthquakes. Such an association could prove valuable in perfecting ways to predict earthquakes.

Study 1

Scientists selected four sites that had experienced recent earthquakes and measured radon emissions in several wells located near the epicenter (the point on the earth's surface above the focus of an earthquake). At each well, the scientists recorded the percentage by which that well's radon emission exceeded the average radon emission found in wells throughout the world. This percentage was called the differential. These measurements are depicted in Figures 1 through 4.

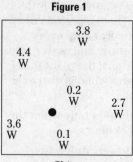

Figure 1

3.8 W
4.4 W
0.2 W
2.7 W
3.6 W
0.1 W

China
Magnitude - 7.9
Average differential - 2.5

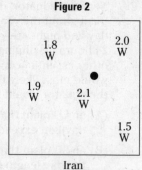

Figure 2

1.8 W
2.0 W
1.9 W
2.1 W
1.5 W

Iran
Magnitude - 6.9
Average differential - 1.9

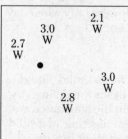

Figure 3

2.1 W
3.0 W
2.7 W
3.0 W
2.8 W

California, USA
Magnitude - 7.2
Average differential - 2.7

Figure 4

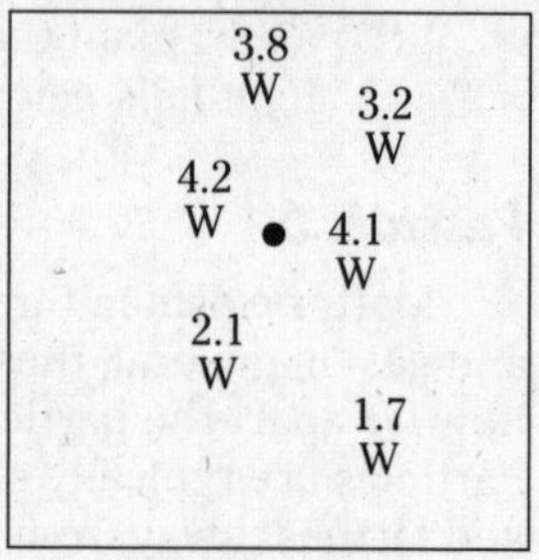

3.8 W
3.2 W
4.2 W
4.1 W
2.1 W
1.7 W

Chile
Magnitude - 7.5
Average differential - 3.2

Legend for all figures

● = Epicenter

Number = Percent that radon emission is greater than normal (differential)

W = Well

Scale: 1 cm = 100 km

Go on to next page

Study 2

To study whether the differential varied depending on the magnitude of an earthquake, seismologists made a scatter plot of the average differential against earthquake magnitude for each site. Figure 5 shows this scatter plot.

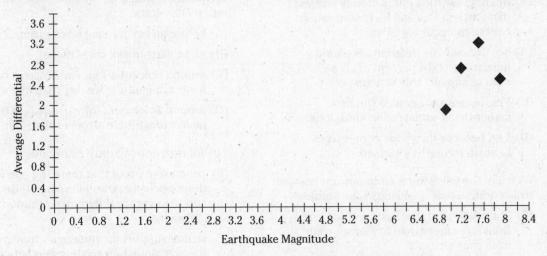

Figure 5: Scatter plot of average differential and earthquake magnitude.

35. It is reasonable to conclude from Study 1 that:

(A) there is no correlation between earthquakes and increased radon emissions.

(B) some evidence suggests a correlation between earthquakes and increased radon emissions.

(C) radon emissions of wells more than 1,000 km from the epicenter of an earthquake do not increase.

(D) radon emissions at an earthquake's epicenter are more than 5 percent greater than normal levels for the entire earth.

36. Which of the following would strengthen the claim that increased radon emissions are associated with earthquakes?

(F) Scientists measure radon emissions from wells near the epicenter of an earthquake in the Caribbean and record measurements that do not differ significantly from average radon emissions throughout the world.

(G) For each of the locations depicted in the figures for Study 1, scientists study wells that were 500 miles from the epicenters and find that these wells had similar emission differentials to those recorded at wells near the earthquakes' epicenters.

(H) Scientists find a location with a 7.9 magnitude earthquake and an average emission differential of 3.6.

(J) Scientists discover more earthquake activity at the epicenters depicted in the figures for Study 1.

Go on to next page

37. Do the findings in Study 1 support the conclusion that radon emissions cause earthquakes?

    (A) No, because the results merely suggest that earthquakes and increased radon emissions occur together.

    (B) No, because the differentials would have to exceed 4 percent at all well sites to support this conclusion.

    (C) Yes, because every well site had higher-than-normal radon emissions.

    (D) Yes, because the radon comes from beneath the earth's surface.

38. Which of the following is an important control condition that is lacking in the studies?

    (F) The studies fail to measure radon emissions from more than five or six wells from each site.

    (G) The studies do not measure radon emissions from sites that experienced earthquakes with magnitudes greater than 8.0.

    (H) The studies do not take into consideration radon emissions from sites that have not had an earthquake in more than 400 years.

    (J) The studies do not include radon emission measurements from the same sites before the earthquakes occurred.

39. A study that would provide useful information to make a determination of whether radon emissions can be used to predict earthquakes would be one that measures radon emissions:

    (A) before an earthquake takes place.

    (B) as an earthquake takes place.

    (C) around epicenters for earthquakes that have a magnitude weaker than 6.9.

    (D) around epicenters for earthquakes that have a magnitude stronger than 7.9.

40. The information in Study 2 provides:

    (F) conclusive proof that there is a correlation between earthquake magnitude and the average differential of radon emissions.

    (G) strong support for the theory that there is almost no relationship between the occurrence of earthquakes and higher radon emissions.

    (H) a visual depiction of the relationship between earthquake magnitude and the percentage that its radon emissions exceed average levels.

    (J) a visual record of the negative correlation between earthquake magnitude and average differential.

STOP DO NOT TURN THE PAGE UNTIL TOLD TO DO SO. DO NOT RETURN TO A PREVIOUS TEST.

Writing Test

Time: 30 minutes

Directions: Choose a position on the issue presented in the following writing prompt. Present your position in a logical, clear, and well-organized essay that follows the rules of Standard English. Write your essay on a separate sheet of lined paper.

As an alternative to traditional fundraising, the school board is proposing to fund school activities and athletic equipment by contracting with a large soft drink company to place advertisements on school buses and gymnasium walls. The contract with the soft drink company will generate about $200,000.00 per year for the district, much more than can be raised by traditional fundraising methods like magazine sales. A parents' organization opposes the contract, stating that soft drink advertisements on school buses and inside school buildings send the message that the school endorses student consumption of soft drinks despite research that shows that soft drink consumption may lead to obesity. In your opinion, should schools raise funds by contracting with soft drink companies to advertise on school buses and within school buildings?

Write an essay that takes a position on this issue. Your position can support either one side of the issue or the other, or you may introduce a different point of view on the question. Provide specific examples and reasons to support your opinion.

Chapter 23

Practice Exam 2: Answers and Explanations

● ●

You've completed the practice exam in Chapter 22, and now you can't wait to check your answers and discover your score. Well, this chapter is your key to doing just that.

Here, we go over the right and wrong answers to each question in the practice exam. As part of our explanations, we include tons of valuable information that you'll be able to use when you face the real ACT on exam day.

If you're short on time, skip to the end of this chapter, where we provide an abbreviated answer key. Be sure to check out Chapter 21 when you're done looking over this chapter; there, you find the scoring guide that helps you determine what score you would've received if this practice test were real.

English Test

1. **C.** You probably noticed a couple of problems with the underlined portion. Perhaps the most obvious is that *recently* and *current* have the same meaning, so having them both in the sentence is downright redundant. One of them has to go. They both still appear in Choice (B), which means you can ditch that answer. That leaves you with Choices (C) and (D). Choice (D) sounds awkward, and it makes the sentence a fragment with no verb. The answer has to be Choice (C) because it gets rid of the repetition and takes care of the *it* in the original sentence that doesn't clearly refer to any particular noun.

   Whenever you see an underlined pronoun, check to make sure that its reference is definite rather than vague.

2. **G.** Chapter 4 discusses the difference between *effect* and *affect*. An *effect* is a result, and you usually see it used as a noun. To *affect* is to concern or influence, and you usually see it used as a verb. The use of *effect* is correct here. Take note: Your not knowing the distinction between these two words can adversely affect your ACT score.

   Knowing *effect* is correct enables you to narrow the answers down to Choices (F) and (G). Choice (F) is wrong because the phrase "obesity and heart disease" gives more information about the types of side effects (it sort of renames *side effects*) and, therefore, needs to be set off with commas or, in this case, a comma and a period.

3. **C.** In the sentence, the pronoun *it* can refer to either of two things — fat or salt or both. Find the answer choice that clarifies the pronoun reference. Choice (B) doesn't eliminate *it*. It just changes "it is" to a contraction. With Choice (C), though, the plural pronoun *they* makes it clear that both fat and salt are required. Omitting the pronoun altogether takes away the subject of the sentence and makes it a fragment, so Choice (D) is definitely out.

   Some students get into the bad habit of choosing OMIT every time they see it. Although we understand your urge to toss out everything you can get your hands on (including those annoying proctors who call time before you're finished), doing so isn't always the best policy.

4. **J.** The sentence repeats the ideas conveyed in the first and second sentences of the paragraph without adding anything new, so it has no reason for being in the passage at all. Choice (J) allows you to put an end to the needless repetition. Besides, Choices (G) and (H) create new errors that you don't want to deal with. Choice (G) has a subject/verb agreement problem, and Choice (H) contains the dreaded passive voice.

5. **B.** Well, you can't stick with Choice (A) because it creates a sentence fragment; you need a subject and verb to go with the "such as" phrase. Check the answer choices to see what you can do about the problem. Cross out Choice (D). By now you know that you can't have two sentences combined as one without bringing in some form of punctuation. Choice (C) corrects the fragment, but it creates a new error with the comma before "my favorite." For the comma to work there, you'd have to see another comma after "my favorite" to show that the words are an aside. You have to go with Choice (B) because it fixes the fragment and properly punctuates the aside.

6. **G.** The author means to imply that restaurant food is getting progressively blander. Strangely, you don't use the word *lesser* to show a gradual lessening. (You usually use it to describe people: "a lesser man would have thrown his book out the window, but I held on to mine.") The phrase "less and less" shows a progressive reduction, so Choice (G) is right. Choice (J) is wrong because *least* implies a comparison of at least three items, not the two (flavor before and flavor now) referred to here.

7. **C.** From the context of the passage, you know that the verb needs to be in the past tense. Neither Choice (A) nor Choice (B) has a past tense verb. Choice (D) sets the action in the past but uses the past perfect tense, which indicates an action that was going on in the past while something else happened. The best verb for this simple sentence is the simple past tense, *discovered*.

Often, to determine the tense of a verb, you need to read a little before and after the sentence with the underlined portion. The sentence for this question introduces a story about something that happened in the past. You wouldn't know that unless you read ahead a little.

8. **F.** The original version is fine. It compares the current chili to the previous chili: "This chili is better than that chili." Choices (G), (H), and (J) compare two different (and therefore incomparable) things. They all compare chili to flavor. You have to compare chili to chili and flavor to flavor. It's a subtle difference, but get used to it because the ACT likes to test you on impeccably proper comparisons.

9. **D.** The first comma in the underlined portion is okay because it comes after an introductory phrase. The comma after *experimented,* though, isn't right. The information that comes after *experimented* is essential to the meaning of the sentence. For the sentence to be relevant, you need to know what kind of experimenting the author conducted. You use commas to separate nonessential elements from the rest of the sentence, but don't get commas involved with essential parts of a sentence. Semicolons join independent clauses, so you can cross out the answers that contain semicolons — Choices (B) and (C). Choice (D) is the only one left.

10. **H.** You don't talk *at*; you talk *to* or *with*. Cross out Choice (F) and look at the other options. All of them correct the preposition problem, but Choice (J) has needless repetition with its addition of *afterwards*. Choice (G) changes *several* to the wordier and more awkward "any number." The best answer is Choice (H).

Don't let *them* in Choice (H) scare you away. In this case, *them* clearly refers to the people because we're pretty sure the author didn't talk to the dishes, which is the only other possibility.

11. **D.** The underlined portion has two main problems. First, it has no verb, so the sentence is a fragment. Second, it uses *less* to describe the quantity of calories. Remember, you use *fewer* to describe plural nouns and *less* for singular concepts. All the choices fix the sentence fragment, but only Choice (D) changes *less* to *fewer*.

12. **G.** Before you try to place the sentence, notice that it talks only about salt and its effects on how people eat. Then use the answer choices to help you figure out the most logical position for it in the paragraph. Choice (F) suggests placement at the beginning of the paragraph. Sentence 1 already provides a nice transition from the previous paragraph, so you probably don't want to change it. Putting the sentence after Sentence 1, however, makes sense. Putting the new sentence, which makes the general statement that salt affects food intake, before Sentences 2 and 3 is logical because those sentences go on to give more detail about how salt actually affects food intake. You can eliminate Choice (H) pretty easily because you don't want to separate two sentences with specific information with a more general sentence. Putting the new sentence at the end of the paragraph seems redundant.

13. **C.** This question may have stumped you. You know that you use adverbs to describe how the action verb is carried out. At first glance, you may think the underlined portion uses the adverb *perfectly* correctly. However, *taste* isn't an action verb in this sentence. It's a linking verb. Therefore, you need to use the adjective *perfect* instead. "To taste perfectly" literally means to taste in a perfect way. Someone who tastes perfectly has perfect taste buds and an exquisite ability to taste. This sentence means to say that the food tastes perfect, and food doesn't have taste buds.

14. **G.** We're confident that you recognized that Choice (G) was the proper way to write the words in the underlined portion. The clause needs a subject and verb; "which is" satisfies this need. Choice (H) moves some words around and adds an ambiguous *too,* but it doesn't supply the clause with a subject and verb. Choice (J) comes through with a subject and verb — that is — but because it's worded so awkwardly, you can scratch it out.

15. **A.** The sentence just restates the information in the last two sentences of the passage. Because it doesn't add any relevant information, you should vote no on inserting it. Choices (A) and (B) give you that option. You can cross out Choice (B), though, because the problem isn't that the sentence is contradictory; the problem is that it's repetitive. Even if you weren't sure whether the sentence belonged, you could have eliminated Choice (C) because you know the information appears elsewhere in the passage. If the sentence says the same thing as the original ending sentence, it doesn't conclude the passage any better. So Choice (D) is also out.

16. **G.** The subject of the underlined clause is *who,* which means using the objective form *whom* is wrong and so is Choice (F). The other choices fix that problem, so the sentence must have other issues, too. Look carefully at Choice (J). The original sentence surrounds the phrase "who governing themselves" with commas, so it shouldn't be essential to the sentence. In other words, the sentence should still make sense if you take it out. When you take it out, the question being asked is "how Native American tribes do so." Well, that's certainly confusing! Choose the construction that best identifies the real question being asked. Choice (G) gets the job done with "[how] tribes go about governing themselves." Choice (H) doesn't finish the thought and leaves you hanging, which is downright uncomfortable.

If you get confused about when to use *who* and *whom,* substitute *him* with an *m* for *whom* with an *m*. If *him* works, *whom* is proper. If *him* doesn't work, use *who*.

17. **B.** An adverb, which usually ends in *ly,* answers the question *how*. How are most tribal governments organized? Democratically. Choice (C) is grammatically correct, but it's unnecessarily awkward and prolix. (No, prolix isn't an expensive brand of watch. *Prolix* just means wordy.) Why say that a government is organized "in a democratic way" when you can say *democratically* instead? If you delete the underlined portion with Choice (D), you know that the government is organized but not how. The sentence would read, "Most tribal governments are organized, that is, with an elected leadership." That choice seems to say that the definition of organized is having an elected leadership, which isn't true.

Many students fall into a bad habit on the ACT. They choose the OMIT answer every time they see it. But OMIT has no better or worse chance of being correct than any other answer choice.

18. **J.** The original is a comma splice, or two sentences (independent clauses) that are incorrectly joined. When you take out the subject of the second part of the sentence, that part of the sentence is no longer an independent clause; the simple conjunction *and* makes it part of the predicate of the main sentence. Choice (H) changes the meaning of the sentence and incorrectly puts a comma before the conjunction. The comma is only proper before the conjunction when an independent clause follows the conjunction. Choice (G) doesn't have any punctuation errors, but *however* indicates that the second sentence contradicts the first sentence, which isn't what the author is going for.

19. **A.** This question tests the distinction between *principal* and *principle*. *Principal* (with a *pal*) means main or primary. (You may have learned in about sixth grade that "The principal is your pal, your buddy.") *Principle* (with an *le*) is a rule. Knowing this distinction narrows your answers to Choices (A) and (B). You can cross out Choice (B) because you don't put a comma before the elements in a series.

20. **H.** If you missed this easy question, you probably read it too quickly. This sentence has a problem with subject/verb agreement. The subject of the sentence is *council*. *Council* is singular and requires the singular verb *has*. So Choice (H) is right.

Did you let yourself get bamboozled by the prepositional phrase? The phrase "by the Secretary of the Interior and the people working for him" can't be the subject of the sentence because the nouns in the phrase are *objects* of the preposition *by,* and nouns can't be subjects and objects at the same time (see Chapter 4 for more grammar details).

21. **A.** *Tribe* is singular. (*Tribe* is a collective noun. Collective nouns look plural, but they're usually singular.) Because *tribe* is singular, it requires the singular pronoun *it* rather than *them*. So Choices (C) and (D) can't be right. Choice (B) avoids the pronoun agreement problem, but it creates a new error with its lack of parallel structure. Verbs in a series must be in the same grammatical form: to speak, act, and represent.

22. **F.** Giving the names for the presiding official of the council before you even mention the council and the presiding official doesn't make sense, so you know that Sentence 4 has to come after Sentence 3. Go ahead and cross out Choices (G) and (H). Sentence 3 mentions the presiding official. Talking about the various names for the presiding official right after the paragraph mentions the council itself makes more sense than waiting to do so in a sentence or two later. Therefore, Choice (F) is the best option.

23. **C.** No need to break into a cerebral sweat for this pretty simple question. Verbs in a series must be in parallel form. This very long sentence has a number of verbs, and all are in the simple present: define, regulate, prescribe, levy, regulate, and control. The last verb must be in the same form as well — administer — so you can eliminate Choices (B) and (D) immediately. The original unnecessarily makes the last entry in the list a clause by adding the subject *they*.

24. **J.** The original sentence is a comma splice. You can't use a comma to join two sentences into one. You can't change the punctuation, so you have to do something to the underlined portion to change the first part of the sentence into an incomplete sentence (one that can't stand alone). Choices (G) and (H) don't cut it because both of them still contain a subject and a verb ("they did" and "it has"). The only choice that doesn't contain a verb and that, therefore, eliminates the independent clause is Choice (J).

25. **C.** You don't have to think too hard about Choice (A) because it doesn't form the possessive correctly. The sentence refers to more than one Native American, so you have to form a plural by putting the apostrophe after the *s*. Choice (B) sets up a nonrestrictive clause, "who demonstrated patriotism," but it doesn't have a comma after *patriotism,* so it doesn't work. The *when* in Choice (D) leaves you with an incomplete thought. You don't know what happened when the patriotism moved Congress. The correct answer needs to complete the proper construction of "it was not until . . . that . . . ." Choice (C) fits the bill and uses the proper possessive form.

26. **G.** The original sentence improperly contains both third and second person. One reads in one's history book or you read in your history book, but one doesn't read in your history book. Choices (C) and (D) change second person to third person but introduce a number problem in the process. *Their* is plural, and *one* is singular. So those answers don't work. Choice (G) has to be right.

27. **B.** Choice (A) makes no sense. It sounds like the Navajo Marines — rather than their language — were used as code. You have to find another option. Choice (C) is tempting, but it changes the meaning of the sentence. The Navajos didn't use the Marine language; they used the Navajo language. Choice (D) doesn't work either. The Navajo Marines' language didn't make up the code; the Navajo language did. Besides, *Marines* needs to be in possessive form. Even though it's in passive voice, Choice (B) is the best answer.

Sometimes the best answer of the four isn't the one you'd create if you had the chance. Sure, active voice is better than passive voice, but you don't have any other option in this case. You have to take what you can get.

28. **F.** In the original sentence, *such* is an adjective that correctly describes the noun *code.* Switching *code* and *such* in Choice (G) gives you "the only code such that the enemy could not break." In that construction, "such that" should describe how a verb acts. But the sentence doesn't have a verb for the phrase to describe. Cross out Choice (G) and the similar construction in Choice (H). As a general rule, eliminate any answer choices like Choice (J) that put a comma before *that. That* introduces a restrictive or essential clause that commas shouldn't set apart.

29. **C.** *Percent* is plural because it refers to *leaders,* which is a plural noun. So you need a plural verb, *are,* and a plural predicate noun, *veterans.*

This question is an example of one of the rare instances when a prepositional phrase *does* affect subject/verb agreement. With *percent,* you have to look at the object of the preposition. For example, 50 percent of the *house* is infested with termites, but 50 percent of the *houses* in the neighborhood *are* infested with termites.

And speaking of termites, here's a quick joke: What did the termite say when he walked into the saloon?

"Is the bar tender here?"

30. **G.** The passage talks about what tribal governments do and what role Native Americans play in the political system, including their contributions to past wars, but nowhere does it predict the future. So you need to choose a no answer, either Choice (F) or (G). Between the two, Choice (G) is a better answer. (Notice how we used *between* and *better* to compare two choices?) Choice (F) isn't true. The passage doesn't focus mainly on tribal government; it talks equally as much about Native American contributions to military service.

31. **C.** The underlined portion contains a possessive form error. The great national parks belong to the country, so it should be "country's great national parks." The sentence refers to only one country (ours), so you can't choose the plural possessive form in Choice (B). Although both Choices (C) and (D) correct the possessive form of *country,* Choice (D) creates another possessive error by adding an apostrophe to *parks.* Nothing belongs to the park. The word was fine in plural form just the way it was.

32. **H.** The *as* in the sentence probably sounded strange to you when you first read it. It should have because it's not idiomatically correct to say "as we were there." You use *as* to indicate two events that happen at exactly the same time. The park ranger didn't give them information at the precise moment they got to the park. It happened at an indeterminate time during their stay or *while* they were there. Saying *whenever* seems to imply that the family had visited the park several times and that the park ranger gave them information whenever they were there. Choice (J) is redundant; the phrase "during our time" and the word *while* mean the same thing. Choice (H) is best.

33. **D.** The subject of the sentence is *theory,* not "plate tectonics." *Theory* is singular and needs a singular verb, *claims.* So you can narrow down the answers to Choices (C) and (D). You can eliminate Choice (C), though, because *whichever* makes no sense in the context of the sentence.

An underlined portion that features a verb often tests subject/verb agreement. Go back and identify the specific subject, and, in most cases, ignore the prepositional phrase.

34. **J.** When you compare two things, you use the *er* form rather than the *est* form. Cross out Choices (F) and (G). Choice (H) can't be right because it doesn't have commas on either side of the nonrestrictive clause that begins with *which.*

Clauses that begin with *which* are nonrestrictive, or not essential, to the sentence. As nonrestrictive clauses, they should always have commas on both sides separating them from the rest of the sentence (or a comma and a period if they end the sentence).

35. **B.** You can't use a semicolon to join a dependent clause ("as the expanding oceanic crust . . . plate margins") and an independent clause ("it pierces deeply . . . to liquefy again"). So you know Choices (A) and (C) are out. Instead, you use a comma like the one in Choice (B) to separate a beginning dependent clause from the independent clause. Choice (D) takes away the independent clause at the end and creates an incomplete sentence that leaves you confused and frustrated. You don't need that kind of stress in the middle of a test! If you need to review dependent and independent clauses, look at Chapter 4.

36. **F.** The sentence is fine the way it is. The subject of the sentence is *components,* which is plural, so the sentence requires a plural verb, *result.* If you thought the subject was *rock,* you fell for the trap answer, Choice (H). If you picked Choice (G), your answer created a sentence fragment with no verb. Choice (J) unnecessarily changes the verb to past tense. Insert your answer into the original sentence to make sure it fits. *Result* fits because the rest of the paragraph is in the present tense.

37. **D.** The original is a fragment with no verb. Without the assistance of a helping verb, *building* isn't a verb. Alter the *ing* verb (which is often an indication of an error) to *built* to change the sentence to the simple past tense. Choice (B) is wordy and awkward and makes it sound like the mountain was built like you'd build a house.

We hope you didn't fall for Choice (C). The English language has no such word as *builded.* The past tense of *build* is *built.* (Come, come now, don't leave in a huff over that cheesy answer. As Groucho Marx would say, "Wait a minute and a huff!")

38. **F.** *Like* compares similar objects. That is, *like* usually connects two nouns. *As* compares situations or actions. So you can eliminate Choices (G) and (H). Choice (J) changes the meaning entirely. *Likely* means probably; *like* means similar to.

39. **B.** The possessive form of *it* is *its,* not *it's.* Choice (B) corrects the problem without changing the meaning of the sentence.

40. **G.** Sentence 4 begins with "These become feeding chambers . . . ." So the sentence that comes before it must deal with something that could become feeding chambers. Sentence 3 ends with *eruptions,* but eruptions most likely don't become feeding chambers; therefore, you can cross out Choice (F). Look for another location for Sentence 4. Most paragraphs don't begin with an ambiguous concept like *these,* so you can eliminate Choice (H). By process of elimination, you know Sentence 4 comes after either Sentence 2 or Sentence 5. Sentence 5 just refers to a lake. A singular lake wouldn't become plural feeding chambers. Cross out Choice (J) and pick Choice (G). You don't even have to examine Sentence 2, but if you did you'd see that it refers to compartments of molten rock, which could become chambers.

41. **B.** You probably got a sense that something was wrong with this sentence when you read it, but exactly what was wrong may not have been obvious. Instead of spending a bunch of time trying to figure it out, just plug in answer choices to see which one works best. Say that the flora is a mix of species from the Sierra Nevadas *and* varieties from the Cascades. The other answer choices don't fit. So Choice (B) is your winner.

42. **H.** The subject is *park,* which is singular and requires a singular verb, like *boasts.* Therefore, you can eliminate Choices (F) and (J). Choice (J) changes *boast* to *have,* but *have* isn't singular either. *Boast* must be the verb that belongs in the sentence. Choice (G) doesn't cut it because it sounds as though the park is doing some boasting and also has 715 plant species. "To boast" simply means "to be proud to have" — as in you and your friends can boast some of the highest ACT scores around if you learn the tricks and the traps of the exam. Choice (H) is the right answer.

43. **A.** What do you think? Is a description of the types of plants that grow on Mount Shasta appropriate? Probably not. Besides being a little boring, a description of Mount Shasta's flora isn't really relevant to a passage about Mount Tehama in Lassen Park. Cross out Choices (C) and (D). Although Mount Shasta does have fewer plant types than Lassen Park, the smaller number of plant types isn't the reason that a description of them is inappropriate. You wouldn't want to see that description even if Mount Shasta had more plants than Lassen Park. The best answer is Choice (A).

44. **G.** You don't use a semicolon to introduce a series; instead, you use the colon or perhaps the dash. The punctuation marks in both Choices (G) and (J) work in the sentence, but Choice (J) replaces *of* with the wordy and unnecessary phrase "that are comprised by." Choice (G) is better. If you selected Choice (H), you created a comma splice, which is the result of joining independent clauses with a comma and no conjunction.

45. **C.** This last paragraph presents an entirely new topic about Lassen Park. So cross out Choice (A) and pick Choice (C). Previously, the passage gave a physical description of the land and discussed its plant life. This paragraph introduces you to the humans who inhabited the area. The paragraph doesn't contradict anything in the rest of the passage, and thinking that the author would say that the park only sustains life in the snowy winter months is just plain silly.

46. **G.** You may be surprised to find out that "having dreamed" doesn't function as a verb. It actually functions as a noun but looks like a verb. Therefore, the original sentence is a fragment and needs a change. Choice (J) doesn't help because *dreaming* is a noun, too. Because the writer is no longer a young boy, you're looking for a past tense verb. You find it in Choice (G).

Remember that *ing* words often make complete sentences into incomplete sentences or fragments because they only look like verbs. Choose an *ing* word if you're looking for a noun, but don't expect it to work as a verb without a little help from a helping verb.

47. **A.** This question brings up the whole *who* versus *whom* dilemma. Use *who* for subjects and *whom* for objects. In this sentence, *who* is the subject of the clause "who has been my hero." So you know that *who* is the proper form. Cross out Choice (B). The objective form *whom* is okay in Choice (D) because it's the object of the preposition *of,* but if you change *who* to "of whom," the clause loses its subject and the sentence makes no sense. Choice (C) tries to separate "it's fair to say" as a nonessential clause, which would be fine except that the answer choice doesn't put a comma after *say.* You have to stick with Choice (A) here.

48. **F.** If you picked Choice (J), you answered too quickly. The simple subject and verb in Choice (J) may seem better than the original, but Choice (J) also puts a comma after *dream* and separates the verb from its object, which is a no-no in the grammar world. Choice (H) creates a sentence fragment, and Choice (G) incorrectly turns *boys* into a possessive.

49. **A.** This question tests the use of prepositions. You can't be fascinated at or captivated about something. "Apprehended with" in Choice (D) is an awkward word choice for the sentence. Going with Choice (A) is best here.

50. **G.** This question is an interesting one because all the answer choices are pretty bad. Your job is to choose the least awful among them. (Hmm, sounds rather like a mixer dance, doesn't it?) The original is in passive voice and is missing the comma after *Italy.* At first glance, Choice (H) may seem promising. It's in active voice and properly puts commas before and after *Italy.* Look at it carefully, though. A beginning phrase always describes the subject of the sentence. This answer literally states that *you* (not the city) are located a

few miles past Naples. You probably wish you were in Naples rather than taking practice ACT tests, but, unfortunately, that's not the point of this sentence. Choice (J) has a whole mess of comma problems. You have to separate the country name (Italy) from the city name (Naples) with commas on either side. Choice (G) is in the passive voice (is found) rather than the active voice, but it doesn't have the punctuation or modifier errors that the other choices have, and passive voice isn't that big a problem in this sentence. It's really not important who exactly finds the city. The point is that it's found or located near Naples. Choice (G)'s the best of four rather lackluster choices.

51. **B.** Be wary of reflexive pronouns, such as *itself, himself, themselves,* and so on. The test makers often use them incorrectly on the ACT to make sure you're paying attention. They can't act as subjects the way that *himself* does in the underlined portion. The only answer that corrects the problem is Choice (B). Saying "cannot help but" is idiomatically correct.

52. **G.** The author shows Halliburton's sense of humor with this addition. He records how Halliburton makes light of the idea of being overcome by a volcano by imagining what it would be like for future explorers to excavate him and his typical tourist items. The only answer that demonstrates this lighthearted spirit is Choice (G). The passage isn't about hygienic practices or even a list of what the well-equipped explorer wouldn't leave home without. Cross out Choices (F) and (H), and, while you're at it, mark out Choice (J). The author seems to be interested in the effects of the volcano on Pompeii, but the list doesn't emphasize Vesuvius's devastation.

53. **D.** The original sentence doesn't have a verb. It's a fragment. The only answer choice that supplies a verb is Choice (D). None of the others makes the sentence complete.

54. **F.** *Anybody* is singular and requires the singular verb *invites*. Eliminate Choices (G) and (H) immediately. Choice (J) may be tempting, but the sentence doesn't have a comma before the underlined portion, which means it's a restrictive, or necessary, clause. Omitting a necessary clause would deprive the sentence of something that is, well, necessary. Choice (F) is the only way to go.

55. **C.** *Neither* always goes with *nor* (and *either* always goes with *or*). Whenever you see the word *neither,* make sure that *nor* follows hard on its heels. Choices (A) and (B) pair *neither* with *or,* so you can scratch them out right away. You can cross out Choice (J), too. It changes *or* to *nor,* but it changes the meaning of the sentence by replacing *too* with *enough.*

When you find a simple grammar or diction error, change only that part and leave the rest of the sentence alone. In general, changing as little of the sentence as possible is the way to go.

56. **F.** The underlined portion is fine the way it is. Choice (J) makes the sentence a fragment. The plural subject in Choice (H) doesn't agree with the singular verb. Choice (G) is awkward and changes the thing that's doing the appealing from the writing to the explorer.

57. **D.** The underlined verb is in the wrong tense. It refers to a past event, but *looks* is present tense. The only answer that's in the simple past tense is Choice (D): ". . . he sat in his hotel room . . . and looked out."

58. **J.** Whenever you see a pronoun in the underlined part of a sentence, make sure it has a clear reference. The only noun that *it* could refer to here is *landscape,* and you don't often refer to the summit of a landscape. So you can cross out Choice (F). Choice (G) doesn't solve the problem of the unclear pronoun, and Choice (H) compounds the problem by introducing an unclear plural pronoun. Only Choice (J) defines which summit the light flashes shoot from.

59. **C.** First, eliminate Choice (D). Even if you thought you should omit the sentence, references to volcanoes occur throughout the passage, so Choice (D) is wrong. Sentence 1 refers to "these chilling effects," so you know that it needs to go after a sentence that mentions some sort of chilling effects. You also need to know who *he* refers to. Nothing in the last sentence of the preceding paragraph provides a reference for either. So cross out Choice (A) and note that the remaining choices give you the option of putting the sentence after Sentence 4 or Sentence 5. The best answer is Choice (C). The chilling effects can refer to the flashes of light from the volcano.

60. **H.** Given the tone of the passage, you can eliminate Choices (F) and (J). It's not objective and formal enough to be an encyclopedia or textbook entry. The passage doesn't express an editorial opinion, so by process of elimination, it must be the memoir of an older gentleman, which makes sense. The author reminisces about when he was young, which is perfectly appropriate for a memoir.

61. **D.** The sentence as it is doesn't express a complete thought; it's a fragment. Leaving out the word *that* makes the sentence complete.

62. **J.** A *routine* is something that's set and doesn't vary. Therefore, the original version is redundant and unnecessarily wordy. The author can make the point just as clearly with the one word *routines*.

63. **A.** The language used to compare warlike and romantic is fine the way it is. The proper construction is *more . . . than . . . .* Choices (B) and (C) improperly pair *as* with *than* and *more*. You can pair *as* with *as* to show similarity, but the original sentence doesn't show a similar relationship between warlike and romantic. So Choice (D) is out.

64. **H.** Because you're looking for the one word out of the four that doesn't work, find the answer choice that means something different from all the others. *Although, whereas,* and *even though* show contrast. *Because* shows cause and effect. Choice (H) is the one that doesn't belong with the others.

65. **D.** The underlined part needs to be a verb form that functions as a noun. One of the verb forms that can be a noun is the infinitive form, *to + verb*. You find the infinitive in Choice (D). Another form is the *ing* form of the verb without any helping words. In this case, the *ing* form would be *providing,* but it's not an option. The other choices are unnecessarily wordy and confusing.

66. **F.** The original version, with the aside set apart in commas, is correct. Choice (G) is inconsistent; to separate nonessentials in a sentence, you need two commas or two dashes but not one of each. Choices (H) and (J) don't include the whole aside within the commas.

67. **C.** Items in a series must be parallel in form. For example, you wouldn't say, "The ACT is thrilling, exciting, and a challenge." Instead, you'd say, "The ACT is thrilling, exciting, and challenging." Here, only Choice (C) eliminates the final clause and keeps the sequence of items in the same form — all nouns. (We cover parallelism in Chapter 4.)

68. **G.** You can safely assume that there are more than two types of birds and more than two types of bowers. Therefore, the correct superlative is *most,* which is used to compare three or more things, rather than the comparative form *more,* which is used to compare just two things.

69. **B.** The iris is the colored part of the eye. Saying "irises in the eye region" is redundant because you don't have irises in your ears or your tummy!

70. **H.** Saying that a pheasant "is with" eyes on its feathers doesn't make sense. Just as the peacock *has* eyes on its feathers, the pheasant *has* eyes as well. So Choice (H) is the winner here. Choice (J) is the trap. It creates unnecessary repetition. Inserted, it would make the sentence read, ". . . a pheasant also has them too."

Be sure to reread the sentence with the answer you've chosen inserted. Doing so may take a few seconds, but it helps you prevent mistakes in questions like this one.

71. **B.** The original version is wordy and awkward. Choose the simplest answer to make the point. Choices (C) and (D) are just as verbose as the original version. Also, in Choice (C), just who are *they?* Mysterious bird-naming people?

Although the shortest answer isn't always the best answer, it's always an answer worth checking out. We suggest plugging in the shortest answer first to see whether it works.

72. **G.** The original sentence uses passive voice, but it clearly states that the humans are the ones doing the action. Therefore, you need to find the option that changes the construction to active voice. Choice (H) makes things worse by keeping passive voice and creating a subject/verb agreement problem. Both Choice (G) and (J) make *humans* the subject of

the sentence, and deciding which one does it best may be a little tricky. Choice (G) is in the present perfect progressive tense, and Choice (J) is in the present perfect tense. The distinction between the two tenses is subtle, and you probably won't be tested on it too often. The progressive tense in Choice (G) tells you that the emulation has occurred in the past and is still happening today. Choice (J) implies that humans have emulated birds in the past, but there's no indication that they still are. The next sentence tells you that humans in New Guinea are currently emulating birds, so the best answer is Choice (G). It tells you that bird emulating is still alive and well in present society.

73. **D.** The original version is a fragment, an incomplete sentence with no verb. Connecting it to the next sentence takes care of the problem. Just make sure you use the proper punctuation. You can use a semicolon to connect two groups of words only if both are complete sentences. And the colon's only appropriate when everything that comes before it is a complete sentence. You already know that first part is a fragment. Separate the beginning phrase from the rest of the sentence with a comma, Choice (D).

> **Bonus trivia:** Speaking of New Guinea, birds aren't the only interesting creatures there. Did you know that Papua, New Guinea, has several types of kangaroos that live in the top layers of trees? Just imagine walking along through the trees and looking up to see a kangaroo! (You'd probably think you were hallucinating from studying too much for the ACT!)

74. **G.** The main idea of the paragraph is that humans try to dance like birds. The next sentence advances the idea by giving details about what humans in New Guinea wear to copy birds. To pick the best next sentence, cross out Choices (H) and (J). Both of them discuss topics that have nothing to do with the ways that humans emulate birds. Choosing between Choices (F) and (G) may be a little trickier. Both sentences provide more detail about how particular humans copy the birds. Choice (F), though, pretty much says the same thing as the sentence that comes right before it. To get more detail about how humans emulate birds in their dances, pick Choice (G). It stays on topic and adds new information.

75. **A.** The question just asks whether the essay contains a description of a bird courtship ritual. The first and second paragraphs contain several examples, so the answer has to be yes. You can cross out Choices (C) and (D). The author presents facts, not theories, so the best answer is Choice (A).

Read carefully so you know exactly what the question asks. Notice that this question didn't ask you whether the main theme was about bird courtship rituals. If you picked Choices (C) or (D), you probably assumed the question was asking for the overall purpose of the essay rather than only one aspect.

Mathematics Test

1. **D.** The official, algebraic way to do this problem is to let the amount each cheerleader gave be c and the amount each football player gave be f. Then $c = 2f$. Because there are five cheerleaders, their total amount equals $5c$ or $10f$. The ten football players also gave $10f$. The final equation is

$$10f + 10f = 480$$
$$20f = 480$$
$$f = 24$$

After you finish the problem, double-check your answer by plugging it in and talking through the problem. Doing so takes only a few seconds and can save you from making silly mistakes. If each football player gave $24, then the ten of them gave $240. Each cheerleader gave twice as much as each football player, or $48, so the five of them also gave $240 ($5 \times 48 = 240$) and $240 + $240 = $480.

The ACT was nice enough to give you answer choices; why not take advantage of them? You can do this whole problem without algebra by simply plugging in the answer choices. Start with the middle value. If the middle value doesn't work, you'll know whether the number must be greater or less than that choice. First, $22 \times 10 = 220$ and $44 \times 5 = 220$ and $220 + 220 = 440$. Because 440 isn't enough, go to the next higher number, Choice (D). Plug in the numbers: $10 \times 24 = 240$, $5 \times 48 = 240$, and finally $240 + 240 = 480$.

2. **H.** Find the relationship between the first three terms: $2 + 3 = 5$, $5 + 3 = 8$, and $8 + 3 = 11$.

If you thought this question was too easy, keep in mind it's only Question 2. Questions tend to get harder as you move through the Math Test.

3. **D.** First, plug in –3 for x. Then $2x = 2(-3) = -6$ and $-3x = -3(-3) = 9$.

The minus sign outside the parentheses in the given equation $2x - (3y - 3x) + 4y$ changes the +9 to –9. (Remember that you have to distribute the minus sign through the parentheses.) You now have $-6 + -9 = -15$. Narrow the answers down to Choice (D) or (E). Next, solve for y: $-3y + 4y = y$. So the answer is $y - 15$, or Choice (D).

Make a habit of crossing out answers as you go. This method can prevent you from working through an entire problem and then choosing the wrong answer because you forgot the first part of the problem by the time you did the second part.

4. **F.** If two sides of a triangle are equal, their angles also are equal. Because all three angles of a triangle total 180 degrees, the two unmarked angles must be 60 degrees total ($180 - 120 = 60$) or 30 degrees each ($60 \div 2 = 30$). Angles along a straight line are *supplementary,* or total 180 degrees. Therefore, $180 - 30 = 150$; the exterior angle measures 150 degrees.

The measure of an exterior angle is equal to the sum of the measures of its two remote interior angles. Here, the *remote* (in other words, "not next to") interior angles are *NLM*, which is 30, and *LNM*, which is 120, for a total of 150.

Did you notice that Choice (F) is the only possible answer? It's the only choice greater than 120. Because an exterior angle equals the sum of two remote interior angles, it must be $120 + x$; x isn't equal to 0. Therefore, the exterior angle is greater than 120.

5. **B.** First, use your common sense to eliminate Choices (C), (D), and (E). If Jarnelle can already assemble 300 widgets in one hour and is going to raise her rate and work eight hours, she certainly is going to assemble a lot more widgets than these answers show. That knowledge quickly narrows the answers down to Choices (A) and (B).

Next, find that 25 percent or one-fourth of 300 is 75, Choice (E), which you have already eliminated. (One good reason to eliminate choices as you go is to avoid falling for traps like this one.) If she increases her rate by 75, Jarnelle can now assemble 375 widgets in one hour — Choice (C). In eight hours, she can assemble $375 \times 8 = 3,000$ widgets.

Another way to estimate is to say that 375 is about 400 and $400 \times 8 = 3,200$. Only Choice (B) is remotely close.

6. **H.** To solve a proportion, first cross-multiply: $3 \times 25 = 75$ and $5 \times a = 5a$. Then make the products equal: $75 = 5a$. Finally, divide both sides through by 5: $a = 15$.

7. **D.** The sides of an isosceles right triangle are in the ratio $s : s : s\sqrt{2}$. The $s\sqrt{2}$ is the hypotenuse. (If you don't remember this formula, go to Chapter 8.) Each side or leg of the triangle, therefore, has to be 5. The area of a triangle is $\frac{1}{2}bh$. In an isosceles right triangle, the two legs are the base and the height, making the area of this triangle $\frac{1}{2}(5)(5) = \frac{1}{2}(25) = 12.5$.

Choice (B) traps students who forget to multiply the base and height by one-half. Choice (E) is the perimeter, not the area. Because answer choices often have such "variations" to trap a careless test taker, circle what the question is asking for. Before you fill in the oval on the answer sheet, refer to that circled info again to be sure that you're answering the right question.

Did the phrase "square units in the area" confuse you? Not to worry. Just think of it as area.

8. **K.** Start by distributing the negative to the bracketed part of the equation. (To help you remember this principle, write a negative 1 in front of the parentheses.) Negative 1 times *a* is –*a*. Negative 1 times –3 is +3, which immediately eliminates Choices (G) and (H). Negative 1 times –*a* is +*a*. Combine like terms: $6a - a + a = 6a$.

When the answers are all "variations on a theme" like Question 8's answers, double-check that you're keeping your positive and negative signs correct.

9. **C.** First, find 25 percent or $\frac{1}{4}$ of 18,000: $\frac{18,000}{4} = 4,500$. But don't pick Choice (E) because that's just the discount. Subtract it from \$18,000 to get \$13,500. Then take 5 percent of \$13,500, which is \$675. That's the luxury tax, so add it to \$13,500 to get \$14,175.

If you chose Choice (A), you added the sales tax to the original cost, not to the sales cost. If you picked Choice (B), you assumed that a discount of 25 percent and a tax of 5 percent is the same as a discount of 20 percent. That logic is wrong because the percentages are percentages of different *wholes* (in the first case, the percent is of the original price; in the second case, the percent is of the sale price). Whenever you're dealing with percentages, keep in mind that a percentage is part of a whole and double-check that you have started with the correct whole.

10. **G.** This problem is easier than it looks. Draw a rectangle of width *x* and length 3*x* (because the problem tells you that the length is 3 times the width). Add all the sides to find the perimeter: $x + 3x + x + 3x = 8x$. The perimeter is 640, so $8x = 640$ and $x = 80$. If *x*, the width, is 80, then 3*x*, the length, is 240. The area of a rectangle is length × width: $80 \times 240 = 19,200$.

11. **D.** Before you do any math, circle the words *closest approximation*. Those words are a clue that the problem is going to be a pain in the posterior — that you'll probably deal with some very weird numbers. More importantly, though, they're a clue that you don't have to work the problem through to the bitter end but that you can estimate a final answer.

Next, plug and chug. Put the numbers in and work the problem through, like so:

$$= \frac{3 + 10(3-10)^2(9-10)}{10(9-10)}$$

$$= \frac{3 + 10(49)(-1)}{190}$$

$$= \frac{3 - 490}{190}$$

$$= -\frac{487}{190}$$

Here's where you estimate: $\frac{487}{190} = 2.56315789$, which is closest to 2.5. Just don't forget the negative sign!

This type of problem is great to do if word problems are hard for you. This question consists of numbers, numbers, and more numbers. However, this problem can also catch those who are prone to making careless errors. The more calculations you do, the greater the chance of a careless error. Double-check your answers to questions like this.

12. **K.** Angles along a straight line total 180 degrees. Forget about all the fraction stuff, and start off by plugging in nice, simple numbers that meet the requirements. Say, for example, that $x = 1$. That means that $y = 2x$ and $z = 3x$. See how neatly things work out? You're often rewarded for plugging in simple numbers. Then you have $x + 2x + 3x = 180$, $6x = 180$, and $x = 30$. If $x = 30$, then $y = 60$ and $z = 90$. Yes, it works. Now just go back and answer the question: $z - x = 90 - 30 = 60$.

13. **A.** This problem looks a lot harder than it is; don't let yourself be intimidated. First, be sure that you get the wording straight. You're subtracting the first term from the second term. Think of this as "second term minus first term." If you overlooked this wording, you may have fallen for a trap and picked Choice (D) or (E).

Second, check that the variables are the same and are to the same power or you can't subtract them. For example, you can do $5a^3 - 3a^3$, but you can't do $5a^3 - 3a^2$ (unless, of course, you know the value of a). When the variables and *exponents* (or powers) are the same, you can ignore them and just subtract the *numerical coefficients* (the numbers in front of the variables): $1 - 5 = -4$. (Because no number is in front of the a^3b^4, you assume its coefficient is a 1.) Now your answer has to be Choice (A) or (B). Subtract the coefficients in front of the a^2b^3: $-2 - 3 = -5$.

14. **J.** The sides of a 30:60:90 triangle are in the ratio $s : s\sqrt{3} : 2s$, where s is the shortest side. (If this ratio doesn't sound familiar to you, flip to Chapter 8.) Draw the figure like this:

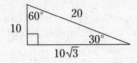

You know s is the height, opposite the 30-degree angle and $s\sqrt{3}$ is the base, opposite the 60-degree angle. The area of a triangle is $\frac{1}{2}bh$:

$$A = \frac{1}{2}(10)\left(10\sqrt{3}\right)$$
$$A = 5 \times 10\sqrt{3}$$
$$A = 50\sqrt{3}$$

15. **E.** This question is as much vocabulary as it is math. A *mean* is the average of numbers: Add the numbers together (420) and divide by the number of numbers ($420 \div 5 = 84$). A *median* is the middle number when you put the numbers in order.

If you picked Choice (D), you fell for the trap of thinking that 79 was the median because it was the "middle number." You have to put the numbers in sequential order first: 75, 79, 82, 91, 93. Now you can see that 82 is the median. Take the mean minus the median: $84 - 82 = 2$.

Bonus trivia: While we're talking vocabulary, do you know what the mode is? A *mode* is the most repeated term, the one that shows up the most. For example, if the numbers were 2, 3, 2, 4, 5, the mode would be 2.

16. **J.** Draw a rectangle with a diagonal with a length of 6 that splits it into two 30:60:90 triangles. The ratio of sides of a 30:60:90 triangle is $s : s\sqrt{3} : 2s$. If the $2s$ side is 6, then s is 3, and the $s\sqrt{3}$ is $3\sqrt{3}$.

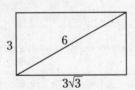

Add the sides to find the perimeter: $3 + 3 + 3\sqrt{3} + 3\sqrt{3}$.

17. **E.** If you missed this relatively simple question, you probably got careless. In Choice (A), although 24 is indeed a common multiple of 4 and 6 (meaning that both terms divide evenly into it), 24 is not the least common multiple. The least common multiple is 12, Choice (E).

To find a least common multiple quickly, list the multiples of the largest number: 6, 12, 18, 24 . . . . Then find the lowest number that both original numbers go into. In this case, both 6 and 4 go into 12.

Choice (B) can't be right because 4 doesn't go into 6. Choice (C) isn't even logical. All numbers, except 0 and 1, can be factored down into prime numbers; that's what prime numbers are, the least positive integer factors. Choice (D) is wrong because the least prime factor of 4 is 2. (If you thought it was 1, you need to flip to Chapter 7. By definition, 1 isn't a prime number.)

18. **H.** First, remove the parentheses: $3x^2y + xy^2 - 2x^2y + 2xy^2$.

    The last term becomes positive because of the negative sign in front of the second set of parentheses. Remember to distribute the negative sign throughout the parentheses: $-1(-2xy^2) = +2xy^2$. Confusing signs is one of the most common careless errors you can make when solving algebra problems.

    Then combine like terms: $3x^2y - 2x^2y + 2xy^2 + xy^2 = x^2y + 3xy^2$.

19. **E.** The key to this problem is knowing the formula for the TSA (total surface area) of a cylinder: $2\pi r^2 + 2\pi rh$. We explain this formula in Chapter 8.

    The $2\pi r^2$ represents the areas of the top and bottom circles: Here, $4^2\pi = 16\pi$. Add the top and bottom areas: $16\pi + 16\pi = 32\pi$. The $2\pi r$ represents the circumference of the cylinder, which, if cut, would be the length of the base of a rectangle:

    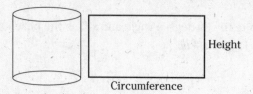

    Circumference

    The area of a rectangle is lw. Here, that's $2\pi r$ times height, which is $(2)4\pi \times 10 = 80\pi$. Then all you have to do is add: $32\pi + 80\pi = 112\pi$.

20. **J.** Parallel lines have the same slope, so you can use the same formula for the parallel line. Isolate the y value to get the slope-intercept form: $y = mx + b$ (where m is the slope of the line). Given that $2x + 3y = 6$, subtract $2x$ from both sides: $3y = 6 - 2x$. Then to get rid of the 3, divide everything by 3. You're left with $y = -\frac{2}{3}x + 2$. The slope is $-\frac{2}{3}$ because it's the value for m in the formula.

21. **D.** First, distribute the negative sign that's outside the parentheses, making the second expression $-3a^2 + 2ab - 8$. Then combine like terms: $2a^2 - 3a^2 = -a^2$. The answer has to be either Choice (D) or (E).

    Next, $ab + 2ab = 3ab$. Between Choices (D) and (E), only Choice (D) works.

22. **K.** To find Jessica's missing test score, use the mean formula to create an equation with x representing the fifth missing test score: $\frac{93 + 92 + 90 + 100 + x}{5} = 95$. Solve the equation for x to find that $x = 100$.

    Use the same method to find Josh's missing test score: $\frac{95 + 97 + 89 + 94 + y}{5} = 95$. Solve for y: $y = 100$. Subtract the two scores: 100 (Jessica's needed score) – 100 (Josh's needed score) = 0. The answer is Choice (K).

    If you picked Choice (F), you fell for the trap. The question doesn't ask for the difference between the score Josh needs and his current average score. Make sure you know exactly what information the question asks you for before you shade in your answer.

23. **D.** Remove the parentheses by distributing the negative sign; in other words, change the signs of the values in the parentheses: $2y - (4 - 3y) + 3$ becomes $2y - 4 + 3y + 3$. Combine the $2y$ and the $3y$ to get $5y$ and -4 and 3 to get -1. Put them together and you have $5y - 1$.

24. **H.** The value of the shaded area is what remains after you've subtracted the area of the unshaded portion (the circle) from the area of the entire figure (the square). The formula for the area of a square is s^2. The formula for the area of a circle is πr^2. Play Sherlock Holmes and do a little deducing. The radius of the circle is half the diameter, and the diameter is the same length as the sides of the square, which means the radius is half of s. Now you

    can set up an equation to find the length of each side of the square: $s^2 - \left(\frac{1}{2}s\right)^2 \pi = 144 - 36\pi$.

    You could go through the process of solving for s, but it's faster to continue your powers of deduction: s^2 must equal 144 and 144 is the perfect square of 12. The square's side lengths are 12.

Draw the diagonal of the square. It creates two isosceles right triangles. The ratio of sides in an isosceles right triangle is $s : s : s\sqrt{2}$. If the side of the square is 12, the diagonal (which is the same as the hypotenuse of the triangle) is $12\sqrt{2}$.

25. **B.** First, find out the value of angle y inside the triangle. Because the angles of a triangle total 180 degrees, $y = 180 - (20 + 40) = 120$. Next, the three x angles and the y angle total 180 degrees because they form a straight line. Therefore, $120 + 3x = 180$ and $3x = 60$, so $x = 20$.

26. **H.** Sometimes the hardest part of a math problem is figuring out where to start. Use the test answers to help you with this one and work backward. If the machine is losing half the ball bearings every cycle, double the answer five times to track it down: 11 (end of fifth cycle) $\times 2 = 22$ (end of fourth cycle); $22 \times 2 = 44$ (end of third cycle); $44 \times 2 = 88$ (end of second cycle), $88 \times 2 = 176$ (end of first cycle).

27. **B.** Note that the problem says each person wants to pay *under* $12, not exactly $12. This problem is relatively easy if you plug in the answer choices instead of trying to make equations. Start in the middle with Choice (C). Currently, if the 5 friends pay $22.20 each, the total cost of the time is $111.00. If 4 more friends join them, for a total of 9 people, divide $111 by 9 to get $12.33 — just *over* $12. You know you must have more people but probably just one more because you're so close. Plug in Choice (B). If you add 5 people, you have 10 people sharing the $111 cost. Divide 111 by 10 to get $11.10, which is under $12.

28. **J.** Cross-multiply to solve for a and b:

$$\frac{1}{a} = 4$$
$$4a = 1$$
$$a = \frac{1}{4}$$

$$\frac{1}{b} = 5$$
$$5b = 1$$
$$b = \frac{1}{5}$$

Therefore

$$\frac{1}{ab} = \frac{1}{\left(\frac{1}{4}\right)\left(\frac{1}{5}\right)} = \frac{1}{\frac{1}{20}} = 20$$

If you picked Choice (F), you forgot to divide by multiplying the reciprocal. If you answered with Choice (G) or (H), you added the 4 and 5 instead of multiplying them.

29. **D.** The circumference of a circle is $2\pi r$. If the circumference is 10π, then $r = 5$. The area of a triangle is $\frac{1}{2}bh$. The base, AC, is $2r$, or 10. The height, OB, is equal to r, or 5. So the area of the triangle is half of 5 times 10, which is 25.

30. **G.** You probably figured out that $4^3 = 64$, but don't get too excited and merrily pick Choice (J). If you substitute a positive 3 for x, you end up with $4^{-3} = -64$ because three negatives make a negative. That tells you that x has to be -3, such that $4^{-(-3)} = 4^3 = 64$ because two negatives result in a positive.

31. **B.** Do you remember that great saying you learned in right triangle trig: SOH CAH TOA ("soak a toe uh")? If not, review Chapter 9. To find tan Z, you need to use TOA or $\frac{\text{opposite}}{\text{adjacent}}$. The value of the side opposite of Z is 7; its adjacent side (the one that's not the hypotenuse) has a value of 24. The answer is $\frac{7}{24}$, Choice (B).

32. **G.** When you deal with percentages, start by plugging in 100. Say that the slow reader originally read at 100 words per minute. Then when she increased her speed by 25 percent, she read at 125 words per minute (because 25 is 25 percent of 100). If she reads at only

50 percent of, or half as fast as, the fast reader, the fast reader reads 250 words a minute. The fast reader's speed, 250, is what percent of the slow reader's original speed of 100? Create an equation (250 *is* what percent *of* 100):

$$250 = x\% \times 100$$

$$2.5 = x\%$$

$$x = 250\%$$

If you picked Choice (D), you got careless and found what percentage the fast reader's speed is of the slow reader's increased speed rather than of her original speed. Circle precisely what the question is asking you so that you don't fall for traps like this one.

33. **D.** For every 2 yards (6 feet) that she swims, the swimmer actually progresses only 4 feet (because she loses 2 feet for every 2 yards). That means 1 yard swum = 2 feet covered. If 1 stroke is 5 yards, she goes 10 feet in that one stroke. The swimmer needs to cover 500 yards, or 1,500 feet, meaning that she has to take 150 (that is $\frac{1,500}{10}$) strokes.

34. **K.** One easy way to do this problem is to plug in numbers. Let $x = 5$ and $y = 10$. The farmer can plow 5 rows in 10 minutes or 1 row every 2 minutes. Therefore, the farmer can plow 30 rows in 1 hour (because 1 hour = 60 minutes). Let $w = 2$, such that the farmer works for two hours. If he can plow 30 rows in 1 hour, he can plow 60 rows in 2 hours. The answer to the problem is 60. Go through all the answer choices, plugging in your values for x, y, and w, to find which one works out to 60. Choice (K) does the trick:

$$\frac{60(5)}{10} \times 2 = \frac{300}{10} \times 2 = 30 \times 2 = 60$$

35. **C.** The only way to miss this problem is to intimidate yourself, to make the problem seem harder than it really is. Even if you haven't studied functions in school (that little f stands for *function*), you can solve this problem by following directions. Talk your way through the problem. Say to yourself, "I have something in parentheses. That means I cube the something, then add one." In this case, the *something*, the x, is given as –5. So cube –5 to get –125. Then add 1 to get –124. That's all there is to it!

The answer choices are full of traps for the careless student. If you incorrectly cubed –5 and got positive 125 and then added 1, you picked Choice (A). If you correctly cubed –5 and got –125 and then incorrectly added 1 and got –126, Choice (E) was waiting for you. And if you chose Choice (B), you combined both mistakes, cubing –5 to get the wrong answer of +125 and then subtracting rather than adding 1.

Just because the answer you got is in front of you doesn't mean it's the right answer. The test makers are aware of commonly made mistakes and put them on the test to tempt you.

36. **K.** An octagon has 8 sides. The formula for the total interior angle measure of a figure is $(n - 2)\,180$, where n stands for the number of sides. (We go over this formula in Chapter 8.) Here, $8 - 2 = 6$ and $6 \times 180 = 1,080$. Subtract 480 to get 600. An octagon has 8 angles. The question accounts for two of them, leaving the remaining 6 angles to sum up to 600 degrees. Divide 600 by 6 to get 100.

37. **B.** The four sides of a square are equal. Because square *RSTU* has a perimeter of 48, its sides measure $48 \div 4 = 12$. If points *A*, *B*, *C*, and *D* are midpoints, then each one divides the sides of the larger square into lengths of 6 units:

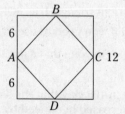

Each side of square *ABCD* is the hypotenuse of an isosceles right triangle. The ratio of the sides of an isosceles right triangle is $s : s : s\sqrt{2}$. That means the hypotenuse of each triangle is $6\sqrt{2}$. Multiply the side length by 4 to get a perimeter of $24\sqrt{2}$.

38. **K.** This problem is much easier than it looks. You don't have to find the lengths of each and every side. Just pretend you moved line *FE* to be at the same height as *DC*. That makes line *FC* the same length as *AB*. Then pretend you moved line *ED* to the left and put it on top of the short line *AF*. That makes line *AD* the same length as *BC*. Now take $16 \times 2 = 32$ and $9 \times 2 = 18$; then add them together for a total of 50.

39. **B.** You get the largest product by using the middle or median terms. Here, $13 + 13 = 26$ and $13 \times 13 = 169$, but 169 can't be the answer because *a* can't have the same value as *b*.

    Therefore, you have to choose the next two largest terms, $12 + 14$. Multiply 12 and 14 to get 168.

40. **J.** Does this problem make you think of Egyptian hieroglyphics? Join the crowd. Instead of just saying, "That's history, Babe!" and guessing at this problem, make it easier to solve by plugging in numbers. Choose to substitute a value for *x* that doesn't equal 4 and is a perfect square; 9 works. Now solve the equation with 9 sitting in for *x*:

$$\frac{\left(\sqrt{9}+2\right)}{\left(\sqrt{9}-2\right)} = \frac{3+2}{3-2} = \frac{5}{1} = 5$$

Keep in mind that 5 is the answer to the problem. It isn't the value of *x*. Jot down the 5 to the side, draw a circle around it, put arrows pointing to it — do whatever it takes to remind yourself that the answer you want is 5. Now go through each answer choice, seeing which one comes out to be 5. Only Choice (J) works:

$$\frac{\left(9+4\sqrt{9}+4\right)}{9-4} = \frac{9+12+4}{5} = \frac{25}{5} = 5$$

Be very careful not to substitute 3 for *x* because $x = 9$ and $\sqrt{x} = 3$. Keep track of the values by writing "$x = 9$" and "answer = 5" in the margins of your test booklet.

When you plug in numbers, go through every single answer choice, *soporific* (sleep inducing) as it may be. If you started with Choice (K), for example, and made a careless mistake, you would assume that Choices (J), (H), and (G) didn't work either . . . and probably select Choice (F) by process of elimination. If you take just a second to work out Choice (F), though, you see that it too is wrong, alerting you to the fact that you made a mistake somewhere.

Check out the CD if you purchased the Premier edition for another explanation.

41. **D.** The cubed root of 64 is 4, and 4 squared is 16: $64^{\frac{2}{3}} = \left(\sqrt[3]{64}\right)^2$.

    Questions with exponents and bases are among the easiest ones on the whole exam to answer correctly. If you're confused about how to work this problem, go to Chapter 9.

    This type of problem, because it involves only numbers and no words, is perfect for students who get headaches just looking at some of those lengthy word problems.

42. **H.** A *prime number* has no positive integral factors other than one and itself. (We discuss prime numbers in detail in Chapter 7.) The prime numbers in Set A are 2, 3, 5, and 7, which add up to 17. (Did you forget 2? 2 is the only even prime number.) Note that 9 isn't prime because it factors into 3×3. The nonprime (also called *composite*) numbers from Set B are 6, 9, 12, and 15, which add up to 42. The sum of 17 and 42 is 59.

Not all prime numbers are odd (2 is a prime number), and not all odd numbers are prime (9 is not prime).

43. **B.** To find probability, use this fraction:

$$\frac{\text{Number of possible desired outcomes}}{\text{Number of total possible outcomes}}$$

The cookie jar originally contained 19 cookies, but Paul ate 5 of them, leaving 14 total. That's the denominator. The jar originally contained 9 chocolate chip cookies, but Paul ate 2 of them, leaving only 7. That's the numerator. The fraction is $\frac{7}{14}$, which reduces to $\frac{1}{2}$ or 50%.

If you picked Choice (E), you fell for the trap. The question asks for the *percent* probability. Choice (E) would be saying one-half of one percent, not 50 percent.

44. **H.** You didn't need to make an equation to solve this problem. There's a much easier way. Draw a simple diagram that shows 13 marks so that the 13th dash has a *B* for billboard:

$$\underset{1\quad2\quad3\quad4\quad5\quad6\quad7\quad8\quad9\quad10\quad11\quad12\quad13}{—\;—\;—\;—\;—\;—\;—\;—\;—\;—\;—\;—\;—}\;\text{B}$$

Then count backward from 1 and place the *B* on the 14th mark in a diagram like this one:

$$\text{B}\;\underset{14\quad13\quad12\quad11\quad10\quad9\quad8\quad7\quad6\quad5\quad4\quad3\quad2\quad1}{—\;—\;—\;—\;—\;—\;—\;—\;—\;—\;—\;—\;—}$$

Put the two diagrams together and count the marks:

$$—\;—\;—\;—\;—\;—\;—\;—\;—\;—\;—\text{B}—\;—\;—\;—\;—\;—\;—\;—\;—\;—\;—\;—\;—$$

If you were careless and thought that you could just add, you probably marked Choice (J), 27. Drawing the diagram shows you that you have to account for the billboard's spot from both ends of the street, so you have to subtract 1 from the sum, making the total 26.

45. **B.** Take this problem step by step. First, factor the expression. The product of the last terms has to be –8 and their sum has to be 7. The two values that have a product of –8 and a sum of 7 are –1 and 8. That means that $x^2 + 7x - 8$ factors into $(x + 8)(x - 1)$. Add the two expressions: $(x + 8) + (x - 1) = x + 8 + x - 1 = 2x + 7$. If you need a refresher on how to factor trinomials, turn to Chapter 9.

46. **H.** The wording "in terms of" can be confusing, so ignore it. You're simply solving for *b*. Solve this problem the same way you solve other algebra problems. First, get all the *b*'s on one side and all the non-*b*'s on the other side. Subtract 3*a* from each side: $5b = 10 - 3a$. Next, divide both sides by what is next to the *b*:

$$\frac{5b}{5} = \frac{10 - 3a}{5}$$
$$b = 2 - \frac{3}{5}a$$

Notice that you must divide each term on the right side of the equation by 5.

47. **A.** Your goal is to get all the terms with *x* and *y* on one side of the equation and all the terms without *x* and *y* on the other side of the equation. To do so, first add 4*mx* to each side:

$$-4mx - \frac{3b}{c} = 4my$$
$$-4mx + 4mx - \frac{3b}{c} = 4mx + 4my$$
$$-\frac{3b}{c} = 4mx + 4my$$

To solve for *x* and *y*, factor out 4*m* and divide:

$$-\frac{3b}{c} = 4m(x + y)$$
$$\frac{-3b}{4mc} = x + y$$

The most common mistake students make on this type of problem is confusing their − and + signs. As soon as you get an answer, turn around and double-check it immediately. You can be pretty sure that the test makers will include in the answer choices whatever you get if you mess up the − and + signs.

48. **H.** First, distribute a through the parentheses: $a(a+4)=a^2+4a$. Form a quadratic equation by subtracting 12 from both sides of the resulting expression: $a^2+4a-12=0$. Next, factor the expression into $(a+6)(a-2)=0$. Finally, make the parenthetical expressions equal to 0 and solve for a: $a=-6$ or $a=2$.

49. **A.** Follow the order of operations. First, multiply the parenthetical expressions: $(3+x)(4x)=3(4x)+4x^2=12x+4x^2$. Add 2 to get $4x^2+12x+2$. Next, multiply everything by the x outside the brackets: $x(4x^2+12x+2)=4x^3+12x^2+2x$.

This problem is great to do if you're running out of time. Figuring out what you have to do doesn't take much effort, and actually doing the work doesn't take much time. The only mistake you're likely to make is a careless one, so be sure to double-check your work.

50. **J.** Get rid of Choices (F) and (G) right away. These choices show that the distance equals 0 at one time beyond the starting time. But the car never moves back to the initial designated point. Choice (H) doesn't feature an interval when the car slows to 70 m/hr; instead, it shows that the car moved forward at a constant speed, stopped, and then resumed the constant speed. So it's out, too. Choice (K) is close, but the gas/lunch interval (horizontal line) lasts too long. Choice (J) is correct.

51. **D.** The two solutions of the equation result from factoring in the form of $(x\pm\_)(x\pm\_)=0$. The values that fill in the blanks are the ones that have a product of 6 and a sum of −5. The values that multiply to 6 and add up to −5 are −2 and −3, so the factored equation looks like this: $(x-2)(x-3)=0$.

To solve for x, make either expression inside the parentheses equal to 0:

$x-2=0$ when $x=2$

$x-3=0$ when $x=3$

The solutions are $x=2$ and $x=3$. Double-check your work:

$(2-2)(2-3)=0$

$(3-2)(3-3)=0$

Everything checks out. The sum of the solution is $2+3=5$, or Choice (D).

52. **F.** If $x+1$ is less than or equal to 8, then x is less than or equal to 7 $(x+1\le8; x\le7)$. The graph that includes 7 and all numbers less than 7 is Choice (F).

If you chose Choice (G), you fell for the trap. You neglected to account for the "or equal to" portion of the inequality and left 7 out of the solution.

53. **C.** First, distribute the negative sign: $x+2y=4-x-y$. Add y to and subtract x from both sides: $3y=4-2x$. Then divide both sides by 3 to isolate the y: $y=\dfrac{4}{3}-\dfrac{2x}{3}$.

54. **F.** The key to answering this question is to remember the equation $\cos^2\theta+\sin^2\theta=1$. If you have trouble remembering this, think of a right triangle with a hypotenuse of 1, as in $x^2+y^2=1^2$ (think Pythagorean theorem).

Because $\cos\theta=\dfrac{\text{adjacent}}{\text{hypotenuse}}=\dfrac{x}{1}=x$ and $\sin\theta=\dfrac{\text{opposite}}{\text{hypotenuse}}=\dfrac{y}{1}=y$, then $x^2+y^2=1^2$.

You can just rewrite this as $\cos^2\theta+\sin^2\theta=1$.

Use this equation to solve the original problem: $\dfrac{\sin^2\theta + \cos^2\theta}{\sec^2\theta} = \dfrac{1}{\sec^2\theta}$.

And because $\sec\theta = \dfrac{1}{\cos\theta}$, $\sec^2\theta = \dfrac{1}{\cos^2\theta}$.

Make the final substitutions: $\sec^2\theta = \dfrac{1}{\cos^2\theta} = \dfrac{1}{\sec^2\theta} = \dfrac{1}{\dfrac{1}{\cos^2\theta}} = 1 \times \dfrac{\cos^2\theta}{1} = \cos^2\theta$.

These difficult trig problems aren't very common on the ACT; they usually appear only at the end of the math section. Don't spend too much time trying to figure them out. If you get to one of these problems and you're running out of time, mark your best guess and move along to the next question. As long as you do well on most of the other problems, you don't have to answer these difficult questions correctly to get a good score.

55. **E.** Multiply both the top and the bottom of the fraction by $2-\sqrt{3}$ (known as the *conjugate of the denominator,* just in case you care). Doing so makes the denominator equal to 1, so you can just ignore it from that point on: $\left(2+\sqrt{3}\right)\left(2-\sqrt{3}\right) = 2^2 + 2\sqrt{3} - 2\sqrt{3} - 3 = 4 - 3 = 1$. Multiply the numerator by $2-\sqrt{3}$ and you have your answer: $7\left(2-\sqrt{3}\right) = 14 - 7\sqrt{3}$.

This problem is great to do if you're short on time. It looks incredibly complicated, but all you have to do is multiply both the top and the bottom by the conjugate of the denominator.

56. **F.** The most straightforward way to approach this problem is to remember that slope is change in rise over change in run, or $\dfrac{y_2 - y_1}{x_2 - x_1}$. In this case, $y_2 - y_1 = -b - (-b)$, which comes out to be $-b + b$, and $x_2 - x_1 = a - 2a$, which comes out to be $-3a$. Substitute and you get slope $= \dfrac{0}{-3a} = 0$.

You may have recognized that $y = -b$ in both points, which means y is constant and the line is horizontal.

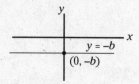

Horizontal lines have a slope of 0, reinforcing that Choice (F) is the answer.

If you did this problem upside down and got $\dfrac{-3a}{0}$, you thought it was undefined (because division by 0 is undefined) and chose Choice (K).

57. **D.** Choice (E) is a sucker bet. Just because the problem multiplied both the number of painters and the number of rooms by 3 doesn't mean that you multiply number of hours by 3.

If three times as many painters are working, they can do the job in one-third of the time one painter takes. If you're confused, reword the problem in your own terms. Suppose that you take three hours to mow a lawn. If your two friends chip in and help you, the three of you can work three times as fast and get the job done in just one hour. The same is true here. Three times the number of painters (from 3 to 9) means they can finish the job in one-third the time: $\dfrac{10}{3} = 3\dfrac{1}{3}$.

If you chose $3\dfrac{1}{2}$, you didn't finish the problem. Nine painters would do the same job — that is, paint four rooms — in $3\dfrac{1}{2}$ hours. But the number of rooms is three times what it was, so this factor triples the amount of time needed. Triple $3\dfrac{1}{2}$ to get ten hours. Yup, you're back to the original amount of time, which unfortunately was probably the first answer your "common sense" told you to eliminate.

Think about this problem logically. The painters take one-third the time, but they do three times the work. The one-third cancels out with the 3 to get you right back where you started.

58. **F.** First, write out each expression separately. $10.8\left(10^{-3}\right)$ means to move the decimal point three places to the left. (***Remember:*** A negative power means the number gets smaller, shifting the decimal point to the left, not to the right.) The result is 0.0108. Do the same for the denominator. $400\left(10^{-5}\right)$ means to move the decimal point 5 places to the left, giving you 0.004. Next, divide 0.0108 by 0.004 to get 2.7. Finally, figure out which of the expressions is equal to 2.7. The expression $0.027\left(10^{2}\right)$ means to move the decimal point two places to the right (a positive exponent makes the number larger, meaning the decimal point shifts to the right, not the left), giving you 2.7.

This question is probably the easiest one to make a careless mistake on in this whole exam. If you're going to do a problem of this sort, be sure that you can commit the time to the problem. Do the problem carefully, double-checking your decimal point as you go and then triple-checking it after you're finished.

59. **D.** You can make this question easy, or you can make it hard. You want to do it the easy way, you say? Great: Plug in numbers. You can choose any numbers that your heart desires, but we suggest that you keep them small. Why waste time on a lot of multiplication? Let $q = 1$; Georgia buys 1 quart of milk. Let $d = 2$; the milk costs 2 dollars a quart. (Your numbers don't have to make fiscal sense; maybe it's rare yak's milk. You have better things to worry about.) Let $b = 3$. She buys 3 boxes of cereal at 3 dollars a box ($d + 1 = 2 + 1 = 3$). Now you can easily figure the total. One quart of milk at 2 dollars a quart equals 2 dollars. Three boxes of cereal at 3 dollars a box equals 9 dollars. Add them up to get 11 dollars. Plug the values for q, d, and b into the answer choices and see which one equals 11. Choice (D) is your winner.

Keep two important concepts in mind when you plug in numbers: First, keep the numbers small and easy to work with. Second, jot down the numbers as you create them. That is, write to the side: $q = 1$, $d = 2$, and $b = 3$. Confusing the numbers (saying $d = 3$ or $b = 1$, for example) is super easy to do in the pressure of the exam. Take just a nanosecond to put down the assigned values and refer to them constantly.

Here's the algebraic way to solve this problem: The amount spent for milk is (q quarts) (d dollars/quart) = qd (when you cancel the quarts). Then the amount spent for cereal is (b boxes)($d + 1$ dollar/box) = $b(d + 1)$ = $bd + b$ (when you cancel the boxes). Add these two expressions together: $qd + bd + b$. Factor out the d: $d(q + b) + b$.

If you think the algebra is straightforward, you're right . . . as long as you set up the original equation correctly. Unfortunately, too many people have no idea how to set up the equation and end up doing it upside down, inside out, or whatever. If you plug in numbers, you can talk your way through this relatively difficult problem in just a few seconds.

60. **K.** The interior angles of any triangle add up to 180 degrees. You're given two of the three angles of triangle *GFX* — 30° and 90°. Solve for the other angle: $180 - (30 + 90) = 60$. A 30:60:90 triangle has a special ratio for its sides: $s : s\sqrt{3} : 2s$, where s is the shortest side and $2s$ is the hypotenuse (the side opposite the 90-degree angle). Side *GX* is $2s$, the hypotenuse, which means that $s = 2$ and the other sides are 2 and $2\sqrt{3}$. If *FXS* is 2, then *XB* is 2 and *FB* is 4. The height of the rectangle is 4. If side *GF* is $2\sqrt{3}$, then *FE* is also $2\sqrt{3}$ and the length of the rectangle is 2 $(2\sqrt{3})$ or $4\sqrt{3}$. The area of a rectangle is lw, so $4 \times 4\sqrt{3} = 16\sqrt{3}$.

Reading Test

1. **D.** To answer this question, focus on the first paragraph. The paragraph implies Choice (A) and comes right out and states Choice (B), but neither of these points is what the paragraph is all about. The answer that best summarizes the paragraph is Choice (D) because it includes all the paragraph's elements. The first paragraph doesn't compare Max's thought process with other people's thought processes, so you can eliminate Choice (C).

Cross out answers that mention only one part of the passage or paragraph in question. Remember that the best answer to a main-point question is the one that incorporates as much of the material as possible without making unreasonable assumptions.

2. **G.** You may know that *tangible* means capable of being perceived with the senses. If you don't, though, you can still answer this question correctly. Examine the sentence. *Tangible* describes something that Max's understanding is *not*. The next sentence elaborates. Max's understanding has come from "a voice in his head," but the voice seems to convey colors and vibrations rather than words. Sounds pretty fuzzy, doesn't it? Start plugging in the answer choices to see which one fits. Eliminate Choice (F) because it has an opposite meaning. It's not that his understanding *wasn't* vague. Choice (G) sounds good. Colors and vibrations don't provide something concrete. Check Choices (H) and (J) just to be sure. Neither works. The understanding did affirm Max's sense of purpose, and understanding that comes from something nebulous, such as inner voices without words, is probably able to change. Stick with Choice (G).

3. **C.** Cross out all the answers that appear in the passage. The second paragraph is all about Max's mathematical talent; Lines 93–95 tell you that he excelled in the 50-yard dash, which is a track event; and you read about his aptitude for football in Line 100. No part of the passage references gymnastics. Eliminate Choices (A), (B), and (D), and fill in the bubble for Choice (C).

4. **F.** Answers that aren't accurate or that cover only one part of the passage have to be wrong. The second-to-last paragraph says that Max expected to be perfect in everything and achieved perfection without being anxious about it. In other words, he didn't feel inadequate. Cross out Choice (G). Choice (H) implies a cause-and-effect relationship between Max's ability to hide his trauma and his academic and athletic successes. The passage doesn't say that Max tried to hide the trauma, so it definitely doesn't link his trauma to his successes. Nothing in the passage tells you that Max suffered socially. In fact, it tells you that he was student council president and captain of three athletic teams. Eliminate Choice (J). Choice (F) provides the best summary of the passage.

5. **B.** When you read the passage, you may have marked Lines 68–85 as Max's suicide thoughts. Go there to answer this question. The author clearly states that Max "seriously considered ending his life in order to escape his tormentor." Choice (C) contains no mention of Louis, Max's tormentor, so it has to be wrong. The paragraphs that discuss Max's suicide attempt don't mention his parents, so you'd have to assume too much to pick Choice (A). You're down to Choices (B) and (D). Both seem pretty good, but Choice (B) is better. It includes both his fear of his brother and his understanding of his purpose in life, the two elements the author gives in the 10th through 13th paragraphs. Choice (D) requires you to assume information that isn't stated in the passage about Max's reasons for considering suicide.

Eliminate answer choices that make assumptions that you can't justify with specific information in the passage.

6. **F.** The author's use of the word *such* before *exercises* means that he's referring to a previous thought. The prior paragraph talks about Max's ability to position imaginary shapes, not his ability to do physical exercises, so you can mark your pencil through Choice (G). Choice (J) is out because the author hasn't even mentioned Louis before this paragraph. The author mentions Max's ability to multiply large numbers when he was a baby, but he specifically states that the numbers were three-digit numbers rather than six-digit ones, so Choice (H) is out. Choice (F) correctly equates exercises with Max's mental movements of imaginary shapes.

7. **D.** Lines 88–90 tell you that Max displayed leadership skills even as a toddler by taking charge of any group. Choice (D) says exactly that. The other answer choices provide true statements about Max's attributes, but these characteristics aren't ones that the author specifically says provide proof of Max's early leadership tendencies.

8. **F.** Eliminate the answer choices that make true statements about Max and that describe qualities that aren't true of most other children. Choice (J) is an excellent paraphrase of Lines 36–39; Max did think he was exactly where he was supposed to be in life. Cross out (J). Most children don't go through the majority of their childhood without speaking, but Lines 54–55 and Lines 88–89 suggest that Max couldn't express himself verbally. Cross out Choice (G). Lines 107–109 say that, unlike other children, Max didn't get anxious about the expectations he had for himself. Choice (H) is out. By process of elimination, Choice (F) is the best answer. Nowhere in the passage does the author indicate that Max experienced a yearning for approval. On the contrary, it implies that Max wasn't worried about what other people thought of him.

Questions that require you to read through the whole passage to find out what's not in it can be very time-consuming. If you find that you're spending more than a minute to answer these types of questions, eliminate answers you know aren't right, guess from the remaining options, and move on.

9. **A.** This one should've been pretty easy. The question refers you directly to a line in the passage, so you know exactly where to go to find the answer. The paragraph before the one that mentions Max's obstacle says that Max considered ending his life to escape his tormenter. The tormenter is his obstacle. From the passage, you know that his tormenter is his brother, Louis. Fill in the bubble for Choice (A). If you want to be sure you're right, look at the other choices. Max recognizes that his intelligence is beneficial, and his lack of verbal communication doesn't seem to bother him. He seems to have no problem with general society, only his brother.

10. **J.** If you picked Choice (F), you probably did so because you didn't read the whole answer; the passage doesn't say that Max ever instilled fear in others. You can cross out Choice (H) because the author never suggests that Max lacked self-esteem or was self-absorbed. Choice (G) focuses just on social situations, and the passage covers more than Max's social development. The best answer is Choice (J) because it takes into consideration Max's overall life success and the cause of his early struggles.

11. **D.** You should have dumped Choice (C) right away. The ACT isn't going to write a passage whose primary purpose is to trash (*denounce* means to put down or to bad-mouth) someone, especially a professional such as a child psychologist. Main-idea, primary-purpose, or best-title answers are almost always positive or neutral, not negative.

Choice (B) is tempting. The passage does mention self-esteem (and if you're smart enough to look at the attribution, you'll see that the excerpt, in fact, comes from a book on self-esteem), but it never mentions anything about *low* self-esteem.

Choice (A) is also tricky. It just sounds so pompous and correct: "provides the foundation for life." La-di-da. However, the passage discusses children up to the age of 16, which is well beyond "early childhood." So by process of elimination, you know Choice (D) is the winner.

The primary purpose of many passages is to describe, discuss, or explain something. Those three words are so often the correct answer to a main-idea or primary-purpose question that you should immediately give them serious consideration. (They're not *always* right, of course — but almost always.)

12. **G.** This question is a gift to you. The answer is right there in the second sentence of the passage — selfhood.

If you chose Choice (J), you fell for the trap. Yes, children work to achieve competence at various tasks throughout the stages of childhood, but all the tasks lead to the ultimate goal of selfhood. Don't choose an answer simply because the passage mentions it. Be sure that the answer you choose refers to the specific question being asked.

13. **C.** The third paragraph mentions this cry of a child to make the point that he needs feedback and recognition of his achievements. So Choice (C) is right.

Choice (A) is a true statement that the passage discusses; however, it isn't the answer to this specific question. Be careful that you don't choose a statement merely because it's true and appears in the passage. Doing so is like saying, "There are 360 degrees in a circle," when the teacher asks you for the capital of Romania. Sure, the statement is true, but what does it have to do with the matter at hand?

Choice (B) is tempting, but the passage discusses parent-pleasing behavior later in the fourth paragraph, not in conjunction with the given quotation.

14. **J.** This question traps rushed students who don't go back to see how the passage uses the statement in context. Lines 31–32 say that "the mother is the center of the child's world." True, the other answers mention games, but the phrase "the name of the game" was used metaphorically in this instance. To say that something is the "name of the game" means that it's the main idea, the point of the whole activity. For example, getting into college is the name of the game when you're studying for the ACT. If you didn't need a good ACT score to get into school, would you really go through all this mind-numbing studying? (You would? Just for our jokes? We're flattered, but whoa — get a life!)

15. **D.** The author states that this separateness is an important milestone in children's development, indicating that this separateness is vital. (A *milestone* is an event marking a significant stage in life. For example, getting a driver's license is a milestone to teenagers.)

Did you notice that all the wrong answers are negative and only the correct answer is positive? If you're guessing (the ACT has no penalty for wrong answers, so a guess is always worthwhile), dump the negative answers and go for the positive one. The ACT rarely trashes anyone or anything and is all sweetness and light.

16. **G.** The theme of the passage is the confusion between wanting two opposite things, such as demanding to have freedom from parents but being afraid to let go of them.

Obviously, every answer comes right from the passage itself, so they all look familiar and "sound right." For a question like this one, ignore the answer choices at first. Reread the passage and identify its main idea in your own words. Then go back and find which answer best expresses that idea. If you look at the answer choices first, they'll all look good. Try to predict the answer first.

17. **D.** This question should have been a pretty easy one. But you do need to examine more than just the indicated sentence; read the few sentences surrounding it. The next sentence says, "A child needs to ask what he is going to do with his life." Choice (D) is your answer.

You didn't fall for the cheap trick in Choice (A), did you? A *vocation* is not the same thing as a *vacation*. If you fell for Choice (B), you confused a *vocation* with a *location*.

18. **J.** The author talks about self-dependence in the last paragraph, so focus your attention there. The paragraph mentions three tasks a child has to accomplish to achieve self-dependence. If you were paying attention as you read through the passage, you probably underlined these tasks with your pencil.

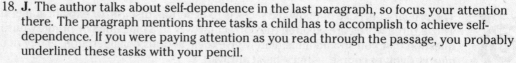

Whenever a passage introduces a series, underline or star that part of the passage. The ACT often tests you on lists of information.

As you read each task in the paragraph, cross out the corresponding answer choice because you're looking for the answer choice that doesn't show up in the passage. The first task is to determine vocation, which is the same as figuring out what to do. Eliminate Choice (F). Next, the author mentions establishing values. As you continue to read through the paragraph, you see that the author equates values with moral concepts. You can cross out Choice (G). Choice (H) is a word-for-word copy of the third task, so you can mark through that answer. The remaining option is Choice (J). The passage suggests that the child needs to work through conflicts with his beliefs rather than avoid conflicts.

19. **C.** The passage discusses the various stages of children by their ages. *Chronological* means in order of time. If you didn't get this question right, you outsmarted yourself and tried to make matters more difficult than they really were. Believe it or not, not every single question on the ACT is out to get you.

20. **H.** You could answer this question based on either the last paragraph or the first paragraph. The final paragraph discusses how the final stage of development is establishing total independence. If total independence is the final stage, then the ultimate goal is that independence. The first paragraph also discusses how the purpose of childhood development is to achieve selfhood or self-knowledge.

21. **B.** The last line in the first paragraph states that the works of both artists convey spiritual themes, so you can eliminate Choice (A). The passage does talk about what influenced the two artists, which is Choice (C), but because this topic appears only in the second and third paragraphs, it's probably not the main reason for the passage. The passage is specifically about the works of El Greco and Beuys; it doesn't make a statement about great works of art in general. You can cross out Choice (D). Choice (B) paraphrases the intent of the last two sentences of the first paragraph. The two artists are different, but they paint similar themes.

You often find the answer to a main-theme question in the first or last paragraph of the passage.

22. **F.** Get your pencil moving and mark straight through Choice (G). Beuys, not El Greco, studied at Dusseldorf Academy. The second paragraph says that El Greco received diverse artistic training, but it doesn't compare the level of diversity to other artists of his day. Choice (J) requires you to assume too much. You're down to Choices (F) and (H). Studying with Michelangelo gave El Greco the background for his unique style, but he continued to develop his style in Toledo. You don't have enough information to say that El Greco's training didn't go further after he apprenticed under Michelangelo. Process of elimination leaves you with Choice (F). The second paragraph says that El Greco's training resulted from a combination of formal art studies and a variety of intellectual influences.

This question was likely easier to answer if you kept track of and marked paragraph topics as you read the passage. If you marked that the second paragraph deals with El Greco's artistic training, you knew just where to go to answer this question.

23. **A.** Choice (A) is pretty much a paraphrase of information in the fourth paragraph. That paragraph tells you that El Greco painted mostly religious themes because churches commissioned his work. Beuys wasn't limited by church sponsorship. The first part of Choice (B) works, but the second part doesn't. The wishes of the churches he painted for — not his own passions — determined El Greco's subjects. The passage doesn't discuss the particular religious views of either painter, so you can cross out Choice (C). Likewise, the passage doesn't go into the socioeconomic backgrounds of the artists. Eliminate Choice (D).

24. **J.** The sentence states that the devastation of the war caused *schisms,* so it can't be a particularly positive word. So Choices (F) and (H) are out. When you replace the word with "religious beliefs," you say that the devastation of war created "political religious beliefs," which doesn't make sense. So Choice (G) doesn't work. The clear answer is Choice (J): Personal and political divisions are often a result of a devastating war.

25. **D.** Focus on the fifth and sixth paragraphs, which describe the Orgaz painting. All the choices are part of the picture except Choice (D). Tintoretto only appears in the second paragraph as one of the artists whom El Greco apprenticed under.

26. **G.** The answer to this question is in the final sentence of the passage, where the author states that the connections suggest that "the division between heaven and earth, spiritual and material, can only be transcended by the Spirit, symbolized by the flames." The paragraph mentions Saint Peter, the torches of the noblemen, and the petitions of the endless line of souls — Choices (F), (H). and (J) — but the author specifically designates Choice (G), the flame representing the Holy Spirit, as the thing that has the power to overcome the separation between the spiritual and material worlds.

27. **C.** The third paragraph states that El Greco painted his masterworks in Spain, which is Choice (C). Although he trained in Italy, Choice (A), and Crete, Choice (B), he didn't paint his masterworks there. The passage mentions that German artists influenced Beuys, but it never makes a connection between El Greco and Germany. So cross out Choice (D).

28. **H.** You know Choice (F) is wrong because Byzantine mysticism and Italian Mannerism were El Greco's influences. The third paragraph states that Beuys's art developed from his having to deal with the effects of World War II on the small German town where he grew up. That statement makes a good case for Choice (H). The passage touches on a number of similarities between El Greco and Beuys, but it never suggests that El Greco influenced Beuys, which is what Choice (G) says. The fourth paragraph refutes Choice (J). Religious factors heavily influenced El Greco, not Beuys. And just because Beuys came from a predominantly Catholic town doesn't mean he had a Catholic upbringing.

When a question asks you to find out what the passage implies or suggests, don't assume too much. You have to be able to support all your assumptions with specific information from the passage.

29. **B.** This question is an easy one. Without much thought, you can cross out Choice (C). The passage never says that El Greco had German influences. The first paragraph specifically states that the artists painted different subjects with different media, so Choices (A) and (D) are out. The last sentence of the first paragraph says that both works "demonstrate the relationship between the spiritual and material worlds," which Choice (B) paraphrases.

30. **G.** If you're an artist or know anything about art, this question probably wasn't too hard for you. "Mixed media" refers to artworks that artists create using a mixture of techniques. If you don't know much about art, though, don't worry. Just use the passage to answer the question. In the first paragraph, the author says that Beuys used pencil, colored ink, watercolor, and creased paper to create a work, which tells you that "mixed media" involves using more than one kind of artistic medium or technique. The paragraph describes original artwork rather than reproductions, so Choices (F) and (H) don't fit. Choice (J) is in there to catch test takers who associate *media* only with journalism. The passage doesn't ever mention the way critics viewed the artists' works, so Choice (J) is irrelevant.

Be sure to rely on information in the sentence to answer vocabulary-in-context questions. If you answer these questions based only on what you know about the word or phrases, you'll probably get them wrong. You have to do some detective work and look for clues in the passage.

31. **B.** The first paragraph simply introduces blood clots, mentioning fixed and migratory clots. So Choice (B) is your answer.

Did you remember that *describe* is one of the Big Three? By Big Three, we mean the three words that are often (not always, but frequently enough to merit your attention) the correct answers to a primary-purpose question: discuss, describe, and explain.

32. **H.** The first paragraph tells you that a *thrombus* is a clot; an *embolus* is simply a migratory clot. Choice (H) is the winner here. The other answers may or may not be true. The passage doesn't give you enough information to decide.

33. **A.** Lines 34–37 state that, among pulmonary embolism patients, "the great majority suffer no serious symptoms or complications, and the disorder clears up without significant aftereffects." So Choice (A) is right.

Dramatic words, such as *invariably,* are usually (though not invariably) wrong. If you're making a guess (which is always worth doing because the ACT has no penalty for wrong answers), eliminate answers with strong, emphatic words (like *always* and *must*) and look for wimpy words (like *may* and *possibly*).

As for Choices (C) and (D), the passage doesn't discuss either children or diet.

34. **H.** Lines 13–14 state that the site of a pulmonary embolism is often a deep vein of the leg or pelvis. So you know Choice (H) is your answer.

> A question that begins "According to the passage" is usually very straightforward. This type of question is worth an investment of your time. Go back to the passage and find the precise answer.

35. **B.** Although you may have been able to answer this question based on common sense, the theme of the first half of the passage is that thrombosis may turn into an embolism. Choice (A) is out in left field; the passage doesn't say anything about aiding others. Obviously, this is the cheap-trick answer, playing on the word *attendant*.

> You have no information about the degree of risk, although the list of disorders is pretty daunting. So Choice (C) is out. And although women are classified according to childbirth status, the passage never contrasts women and men, so Choice (D) is wrong.

36. **J.** By citing a high percentage of patients who have venous thrombosis after recuperating from hip fractures, the passage implies that the risk of thrombosis worsens.

> This passage uses *exacerbate* in its normal, everyday sense. (The ACT *exacerbates*, or makes worse, your tension headache.) This isn't always the case. A word may have a dozen meanings. Don't be surprised if the ACT uses the least common of those meanings in a passage.

37. **D.** The question directs you to the first sentence of the last paragraph, which gives you a short description of a pulmonary angiography. In that description, you find out that pulmonary angiographies are reliable but that their complexities prevent them from being performed routinely. Choice (D) provides an excellent paraphrase: The properties that prevent some patients from using it repeatedly or routinely are its complexities.

> Choice (B) must be wrong because the paragraph doesn't mention anything about patient allergies. Choice (C) describes the simpler test rather than the pulmonary angiography. You may have had a harder time eliminating Choice (A), but the sentence says that the angiography — not the embolism it detects — is complex.

> Every question in a section counts the same. A basic definition question like this one is easy to answer quickly. If you're short on time (and who isn't on the reading passages?), focus on this type of question.

38. **J.** The best title is often the broadest and most general statement offered. The passage mentions Choice (G) but only in one brief part. The passage never discusses Choices (F) and (H), so cross them out, too. You're left with Choice (J), which is broad and general.

> You can often predict the answer to a main-idea or best-title question. Pretend that your buddy comes up behind you just as you finish reading the passage and asks you what it was about. Your first reaction is the best title: "Oh, I just read this dull passage about what blood clots are and how to recognize them." Bingo! Your prediction leads you right to Choice (J).

39. **C.** This question should have been very easy — if you remembered to expand your search. Often, when a passage sends you to specific lines, the answer isn't there. It's a little above or a little below those lines. Lines 69–71 at the end of the preceding paragraph state that "... other tests may be needed to confirm the diagnosis." The next few paragraphs describe such tests. Choice (C) is the answer you want here.

> Choice (C) is the third correct answer in this passage that uses the word *describe* (see Questions 31 and 38). Many ACT passages, especially science passages, describe a problem or situation. Don't immediately choose *describe* every time you see it, but definitely give *describe* serious consideration. (You can think of *describe* as being "guilty until proven innocent." In other words, assume that *describe* is correct unless you can find something that's clearly better.)

> To *lament* — Choice (A) — is to grieve over. Although you may lament having to take the ACT, few ACT passages themselves lament anything. Choice (B) has the dramatic word *prove*. Few ACT passages definitively prove anything. Also, you can probably eliminate Choice (B) by using common sense — Can *all* of *anything* be diagnosed?

40. **G.** The second-to-last paragraph (the *penultimate* paragraph, if you like to use pretentious language) mentions that pulmonary embolisms are difficult to diagnose on the basis of clinical symptoms alone.

You probably could have chosen Choice (G) based on its wimpy language alone. Dramatic or emphatic answers are rarely correct; hedging or wishy-washy answers are often correct. How can you go wrong saying something like, "should be done cautiously and in conjunction with other tests"? A physician makes a diagnosis cautiously and usually uses more than one test.

Did you fall for the trap answer, Choice (J)? Lines 100–101 mention a complex test that can't be done routinely on all patients — but these lines are talking about pulmonary angiography, not clinical symptoms. If you simply skimmed until you found familiar words, you probably let this cheap trick get the best of you. **Remember:** Just because the passage mentions an answer choice doesn't mean it's the correct answer.

Science Test

Did you remember to slow down and think about the introductory material and examine the tables before you headed to the questions in the Science Test? We know you'll probably want to get right down to business come test day, but be sure to spend at least a minute going over the introductory material you're given. You don't have to understand that material perfectly, but you need to at least identify what the study is about and what the basic results are.

In each of the following sections, we explain how to interpret the tables and figures, as well as the introductory text, that accompany each passage in the Science Test. Then we go into more detailed explanations of the specific questions and their answers.

Passage 1

You've probably watched pole vaulting on television, right? When you're reading through this problem, try to visualize a pole-vaulter running down the runway, planting the pole, zooming skyward, clearing (or crashing into) the bar, and finally falling into the pit. The main point to get out of the intro to this problem is that as the pole unbends, it forces the vaulter up.

From the second paragraph and Table 1, you know that a thick fiberglass pole is harder to bend than a thin fiberglass pole (logically enough) but the carbon fiber pole is harder to bend than a fiberglass pole.

Tables 1 and 2 combine to show that the more force required to bend a pole, the faster the pole bends back. Think of this relationship as a spring. You know that the harder a spring is to stretch, the more forcefully the spring recoils when released.

Okay, you now have the picture in mind and have evaluated the tables. It's time to go on to the questions.

1. **B.** The answer to this question follows from the major relationship noted in the second-to-last paragraph of the analysis of this passage. Remember that the harder a spring is to stretch, the faster it will snap back to its regular position after it's released. Look at the two tables: Pole 3 requires the most force to bend but the least amount of time to snap back; Pole 1 requires the least force to bend but the greatest amount of time to snap back; Pole 2 is intermediate for both force and snap-back time. Choice (B) follows very cleanly from the numerical relationship shown in the two tables. The more force/less time relationship holds for all three poles, so you can't justify Choice (D).

2. **G.** As you see in Table 1, you have to use more force to bend a stiffer pole. In the introductory material before the tables, you find out that Poles 1 and 3 have the same mass (no, you don't have to calculate mass; the passage gives it to you right out, as a gift) and that Pole 2 has the greatest mass. Therefore, Pole 3, the carbon fiber pole, which is one of the least massive poles, is the stiffest. Eliminate Choice (F). On the other hand, when you compare fiberglass to carbon fiber, this smaller-mass-equals-stiffer-pole relationship doesn't hold. Eliminate Choice (H) because with Poles 1 and 2, the more massive pole is stiffer. To choose between Choices (G) and (J), look at Poles 1 and 2, the two fiberglass poles. Because the table indicates that the most massive pole is the stiffest, Choice (G) is the right answer.

3. **A.** This type of question is common in research-summary passages. This question requires you to understand some fundamentals of experimental design. A *controlled variable* (also known as an *independent variable*) is a factor that the experimenter can directly control (duh!). Because ACT questions often ask about controlled variables, you may want to identify those variables as you read through the experimental data upfront. In other words, as you read the problem, say to yourself, "Okay, what's different here?" In Passage 1, the experimenters are fiddling with two factors: the size of the pole and the material it's made of. Those factors are the controlled variables.

   In this study, pole dimensions and material (fiberglass or carbon fiber) are controlled variables. The experimenter can easily change the diameter or length of a pole to a specific value, or he can change the pole's material. Choices (B), (C), and (D) mention factors that result from the experiment, not factors that the experimenters can change as part of the experiment.

4. **G.** Don't despair; this question isn't as tough as the terminology initially suggests. In fact, you can answer this question pretty much by using your common sense. What does *potential* mean? *Potential* is something that can happen but hasn't happened yet. (You have the potential to enjoy these questions . . . but that hasn't happened yet!)

   The pole acts to transfer the energy produced while the vaulter runs into energy that lifts the vaulter upward. When bent, the pole has stored the energy gained from the running, but has not yet moved upward. At this point, the pole has the potential to move with much energy, but it isn't moving yet. Therefore, the pole has a lot of potential energy but no kinetic energy.

5. **D.** The question tells you that the vaulter needs a pole that isn't too massive when it's long. Focus on Choices (B) and (D) because they concern mass. Because low mass is the objective, Choice (D) is correct.

6. **G.** This passage's introduction tells you that beginning vaulters need poles that are relatively easy to bend. That means that Pole 1 is best for beginners.

Passage 2

Always begin a science passage by summarizing to yourself just what the graph (or table, chart, or picture) indicates. This graph shows that the likelihood of death increases as one gets older. Well, duh! This relationship, of course, is what happens in real life. The total number of deaths can never decrease. Fewer people may die in certain years, but when people die, the overall number of deaths goes up until 100 percent of the people are deceased.

Be careful not to interpret the graph as showing that more people die at the age of 100. Because the total number of deaths keeps growing, the number — as well as the percentage — has to be higher at 100 years.

To get an idea of when most people die, look at where the graph makes the steepest climb. This increase appears to be between about 55 and 85 years. The percentage of people who have died grows from about 20 percent to about 80 percent over this time, so more than half of the population dies between the ages of 55 and 85. Not too many people die at 100 because not that many people are left by that time. (They probably took too many ACTs, SATs, and various other agents of neurocellular destruction.)

The graph shows that a typical human being lives to be about 75. (Don't get too depressed. The mere fact that you bought this test-prep book rather than a more serious book shows that you're definitely not typical.) Half of the population dies in 75 years. The remaining half of the population dies after more than 75 years have passed.

7. **B.** Not to worry. This question is a basic test of your graph-reading skills, with a little twist thrown in. First, find 80 years on the horizontal axis. Go straight up from this year (your ACT answer sheet can serve as a straight edge) until you hit the plotted curve. Next, go straight to the left to find the percentage of people who have died. But watch out: If you chose Choice (C), you fell for the trap. The question asks for the percentage *alive* after 80 years. So you must subtract 60 percent from 100 percent to get 40 percent.

Get into the habit of circling precisely what the question is asking for. In this case, circle the word *alive* so that you keep in mind that the percentage alive is what the question wants.

8. **J.** The percentage climbs from 0 percent to only 10 percent or so from 0 to 40 years, so Choices (F) and (G) are out. A good look at the graph shows much bigger increases in later intervals. The graph climbs from about 10 percent to 25 percent (an increase of 15 percent) between 40 and 60 years and from about 25 percent to 70 percent (an increase of 45 percent) between 60 and 80 years. (Quickly looking at the slope of the graph provides the answer for this question.)

9. **A.** With no infant mortality, nobody dies just after 0 years. The graph will stay at 0 for a year or so and then start rising when children start dying from accidents, childhood diseases, and so on.

For Choice (B) to be correct, more people would have to die in the first 20 years. With fewer people dying soon after birth, more people will likely be alive at 20 years, so the graph should be lower. Even if all the people who would have died as infants die before 20, the graph would be the same at 20. Additional people would have to die to make the graph higher.

Choice (C) is out because with more people surviving infancy, more people will have to die at later ages. The graph will be steeper, not less steep, in later years.

Choice (D) is unreasonable because those who survive past 1 year of age are almost certain to die before they reach 100. Most people survive infancy but still don't make it to 100. (Yes, of course, some people do live past 100, but the test doesn't expect you to think of remote possibilities. Curb your argumentative tendencies and go for the logical, common-sense scenario, unless a question specifically says otherwise.) Another reason to eliminate Choice (D) is that it mentions a figure, 110 years, that is far beyond the range shown on the graph. For the graph to get to 110, a significant number of people need to live to 100. Only a small percentage of people die before 1. Keeping these people alive wouldn't swell the number of folks who survive past 100.

10. **H.** You can answer this question by process of elimination. The graph tells you that Choices (F) and (G) are out. A clear majority of people live to 60, which means that the largest number of people have yet to die after 60.

Don't fall for Choice (J). More people die by 95 years than by 75 years, but this fact doesn't mean that more people die between 85 and 95 than between 65 and 75. Only about 10 percent of the people live to 85, so many people aren't left to die between 85 and 95 years. Choice (H) is your only candidate here.

11. **C.** At 15 years — Choice (A) — less than 5 percent have died, so more than 95 percent are still alive. But just because a statement is true doesn't mean it answers the question. Note that the question asks you for the *maximum* number of years. Keep going to find out whether a larger number can be correct. At 35 years — Choice (B) — more than

90 percent are still alive. This larger number eliminates Choice (A). Keep going. At 55 years — Choice (C) — 20 percent have died, so 80 percent are still alive. This number appears in the question, so it's your winner. You can check the last choice just to make sure. At 80 years — Choice (D) — 60 percent have died, so this choice is out.

Did you see the word *maximum* and immediately choose the largest number? Do you really think the ACT is that easy? By all means, check the largest number, but don't automatically assume that it's right.

Passage 3

No, nuclear physics isn't a required course for the ACT. Although this topic may seem incredibly advanced, the reading and interpreting you have to do for this passage are relatively straightforward. You just have to realize that the radioactive substances change in a way that devices can measure and that the rate of change slows down with time. The tables show these relationships: The disintegration rates consistently slow down as time goes on.

Be sure to notice that the time frames used for the two substances differ. Don't assume that Table 1 and Table 2 use the same frame of reference. Treat each table separately.

12. **H.** You can dump Choice (J) immediately. If the substance is down to 125 millicuries after 16 hours, how can it be up to 200 millicuries after 20 hours? Use your common sense to eliminate illogical answers.

Choice (G) penalizes the careless reader who looks at Substance A rather than Substance B.

The most important thing to notice is that the disintegration rate is cut in half every 4 hours. After 20 hours (which is only one 4-hour segment after 16 hours), you can expect that the rate will be half of what it was at 16 hours. Half of 125 is 62.5.

13. **B.** The disintegration rate goes down because the number of radioactive atoms goes down as the substance disintegrates. When fewer atoms are available to disintegrate, the disintegration rate naturally decreases.

So what does all this information mean to you? The number of atoms decreases in the same way that the disintegration rate decreases. At 15 hours, the disintegration rate is only $\frac{25}{200}$ or $\frac{1}{8}$ of what the rate was when the measuring began. The number of atoms must be only $\frac{1}{8}$ of the original 10,000,000. A little simple multiplication finishes the problem: $\frac{1}{8} \times 10,000,000 = 1,250,000$.

14. **F.** Because wimpy or wishy-washy answers usually are better than dramatic or precise answers, eliminate Choices (G) and (J). Think about the choices as follows: If (G) is correct, the test maker also has to accept Choice (F), which really wouldn't be wrong. However, Choice (F) can be correct without Choice (G) being correct. The same thing is true for Choices (H) and (J). If you're going to make a guess, guess Choice (F) or (H), the safer answers.

Just because 1,500 is halfway between 2,000 and 1,000 doesn't mean that the time has to be halfway between the times that are associated with 2,000 and 1,000. Take a look at Table 2. Notice that for every 4-hour interval, the decrease in millicuries is less. For example, the millicuries decrease 1,000 during the first 4 hours but decrease only 500 during the next 4 hours and decrease only 250 during the next 4 hours. You can conclude that more of a decrease occurs during the first 2 hours than during the second 2 hours. At 2 hours, the number of millicuries will be closer to 1,000 than to 2,000. You can conclude that the disintegration rate reached 1,500 a little before 2 hours, making Choice (F) the safe bet.

Although this question is tough, thinking logically about how the test makers construct the test can help you narrow the field. The test makers don't want to have to defend their answers. They're usually going to leave themselves some leeway by choosing less precise answers.

15. **C.** The key is to look for which substance took less time for the disintegration rate (which is directly related to the number of radioactive atoms) to fall to one half of the original value. Substance A went from 200 to 100 in 5 hours, while Substance B went from 2,000 to 1,000 in only 4 hours. Therefore, Substance B has a shorter half-life, which narrows the field to Choices (C) and (D). Choice (D) is full of irrelevant garbage (the fact that the scientists decided to go home after 16 hours doesn't affect the half-life). Choice (C), on the other hand, actually reinforces the definition of half-life.

Choice (A) is misleading because the key isn't the absolute amount of substance present but the amount of substance present relative to the starting amount. Choice (B) is simply wrong. The amount present after 25 hours is half the amount after 20 hours; the amount doesn't completely disappear.

16. **G.** Hey, don't work too hard on this question. All you have to do is look at both tables and find the substance that has the lowest disintegration rate (which means a lower emission rate). You don't have to worry about the rate relative to the starting rate.

Because the disintegration rate is always lower after more time, knock out Choices (F) and (H) right away. Table 1 shows that the rate for Substance A after 20 hours is only 12.5 millicuries, and Table 2 shows 125 millicuries for Substance B after 16 hours.

Passage 4

The key part of this introduction lies in the second paragraph, which tells you that the dispute involves whether the earth is getting too warm because of increases in carbon dioxide. Scientist 1 claims in the second sentence of her paragraph that it is. Scientist 2, on the other hand, professes very directly in the first sentence of his paragraph that it isn't. You have an obvious point of disagreement (as there should be, considering that you're dealing with a conflicting-viewpoints passage.

Both scientists use temperature evidence from the last hundred years to support their claims. Scientist 1 uses some numbers to propose that some significant warming has occurred and that the trend has been most dramatic recently. Scientist 2 mentions the temperature numbers toward the end of the passage and asserts that the recent numbers show that global warming is under control. Although you shouldn't get hung up on details, note that Scientist 1 mentions an increase of $0.6°$ C, while Scientist 2 comes in with an increase of $0.45°$ C over the past hundred years. To reason as a scientist, figure that such discrepancies suggest that the data aren't clear.

Did you notice the correct grammar, "The data aren't clear," in the preceding sentence? In scientific writing, *data* is a plural word, requiring a plural verb. You probably don't think it's fair to make you think of grammar in the middle of the science test . . . but we bet you'll remember this point now!

Scientist 1 cites computer models that indicate future global warming. According to Scientist 1 (don't you love those creative titles?), the increase in temperature will be significant if increases in carbon dioxide stabilize and even more weighty if the carbon dioxide levels continue to increase. Scientist 2 casts doubt on the models. Don't try to follow all of Scientist 2's logic, but note that he says that the models don't account for key factors and that they have already been shown to have exaggerated increases in both carbon dioxide and temperature.

17. **D.** Look at the first two sentences of Scientist 1's argument. She mentions a match between carbon dioxide and temperature variations and then uses the recent large change in carbon dioxide levels as evidence that significant changes in temperature will occur. Scientist 1 goes on to discuss how continued sharp increases in atmospheric carbon dioxide will lead to similar dramatic temperature increases. Scientist 1 implies that the recent carbon dioxide changes have been unprecedented. The data during the past 160,000 years show a correspondence between temperature and carbon dioxide fluctuations, but this correspondence has occurred in the absence of the dramatic changes the earth is now and soon will be experiencing. For Scientist 1 to use the fluctuation correspondence as evidence for what will soon happen, she must assume that the correspondence will continue in light of current and near-future sharp changes. So Choice (D) is right.

    Scientist 2 discusses feedback factors in light of the computer models, which is a good reason to eliminate Choice (A) because the question asks about Scientist 1. You may infer from Scientist 2's discussion that the main difference between the two scientists regarding feedback factors is that Scientist 1 thinks that they'll increase the carbon dioxide-related warming and that Scientist 2 thinks that they'll minimize it.

    Scientist 1 explains that the climate has changed, but she doesn't mention the exact causes of the climate changes. If she doesn't specify that there's a human contribution to the climate changes, you can't say that she assumes that humans can't limit their contribution. Eliminate Choice (B). Scientist 1 contradicts Choice (C) because she mentions that a 0.5° C rise is significant.

18. **H.** Choice (G) is tempting in that only Scientist 2 questions the models currently being used. He claims that a model that appropriately incorporates feedback factors will show that global surface temperatures won't rise as high as models currently predict. The problem with Choice (G) isn't that Scientist 2's viewpoint is inconsistent with the article but that Scientist 1's viewpoint is also consistent. Scientist 1 relies on computer models, so an updated model could very well make Scientist 1's case even stronger. You don't know exactly how those feedback factors will contribute to global warming. Don't take as fact Scientist 2's opinion that the feedback factors will minimize warming. Although either scientist could turn out to be wrong in the face of a new model, both viewpoints are now consistent with the statement in the question. So Choice (H) is the right answer.

19. **A.** As mentioned in the analysis of the passage, the discrepancy in the temperature figures suggests that calculating global temperatures isn't a clear-cut process. Mean global temperature over 100 years entails gathering data from many sites for a long period of time. Some of these sites could have changed. You can also easily assume that scientists around the world don't agree on one accepted way to average all these sites together so they can represent what has happened around the entire world.

    Choice (B) is wrong because a temperature measure is just that, a measure of temperature. The carbon dioxide is important only in that a change in carbon dioxide levels may account for why the temperature levels change. They're not included when numbers for temperature are taken and calculated.

    Choice (C) is wrong because it's relevant only when the change in temperature occurred. Scientist 2 could very well also know about the hot years after 1980. The issue is simply how the present numbers compare to the numbers 100 years ago.

    Choice (D) has to do with the consequences of increasing temperatures, not with the extent to which temperatures have risen.

20. **J.** The breakup of the ice sheet is indicative of global warming. Scientist 1 predicts greater global warming in the next hundred years, so she would expect there to be additional breaking up of Antarctic ice sheets. More breakup should lead to higher water levels and greater vulnerability to flooding.

Choice (F) is something that Scientist 2, who predicts minimal global warming in part because of feedback factors, would predict. Choice (G) is too exact. The passage discusses some numbers regarding the relationship between carbon dioxide and temperature, but it doesn't indicate that the relationship between the two is specifically that when one doubles, the other doubles. Choice (H) may tempt you if you think that ice means cooling, but remember that the ice is melting and melting involves heat. The main problem with Choice (H) is that, even if it were true, you'd have to have some specific science knowledge to say so.

Keep in mind that choosing the correct answer on the ACT never requires you to know specialized scientific information.

21. **A.** Choice (A) is a nice, noncontroversial statement with which both scientists would agree. Scientist 1 stresses that rising carbon dioxide is linked to higher temperature (another factor), while Scientist 2 discusses *feedback factors,* which are factors that respond to carbon dioxide changes and will, in turn, affect the carbon dioxide. Scientist 2, who refers to improved energy technology, clearly disagrees with Choice (B), but so does Scientist 1, who mentions the possibility that carbon dioxide levels will stabilize. Choice (C) is out because Scientist 2 discusses a slowing down in the rate of carbon dioxide level increase. Choice (D) is also out because *directly* is too extreme. Plus, by discussing feedback factors, Scientist 2 certainly doesn't think any direct link exists.

Often, strong or extreme words are incorrect, so view them skeptically.

22. **H.** Scientist 1 asserts that a 0.6° C rise is significant because a 0.5° C change affected crop growth in the past. What if the 0.5° C change were a drop in temperature? Perhaps increased temperatures will do nothing to the crops because the crops will do fine as long as temperatures stay above a certain level.

Eliminate Choice (F) because carbon dioxide has to do with what may cause global warming. It determines what significance increased temperatures will have. In addition, the 150-year figure in this choice doesn't challenge the 100-year figure Scientist 1 presents about temperatures. The time periods still overlap, and the passage discusses a general acceptance that both carbon dioxide and temperature are increasing. The big questions are to what extent the two are related and what the consequences will be.

Choice (G) isn't very important because higher temperatures have clearly occurred toward the end of the 100-year period. Exactly which years had these higher temperatures isn't important. Because relatively few years have passed since 1980, there isn't too much room for variation, anyway. So don't think less of Scientist 1 for omitting the exact years.

Choice (J) is out primarily because this choice has to do with the future, not the past hundred years. Also, Scientist 1 is free to predict a greater increase during the next hundred years because conditions are changing.

23. **B.** Scientist 2 mentions that water vapor and clouds make up 98 percent of the greenhouse effect, so it's reasonable to say that a change in water vapor will affect the greenhouse effect, which, in turn, will affect temperatures. In addition, Scientist 2 discusses how water vapor serves as a feedback factor, which contributes to temperature.

Choice (A) goes too far. Always be on the watch for answers that go beyond what you want, ones that are too extreme or continue past the point required. Scientist 2 mentions improved energy technology, implying that humans can handle some problems brought on by global warming, but you can't say whether Scientist 2 believes that humans can handle anything that comes their way.

Choice (C) picks up on the difference in figures mentioned at the end of the two scientists' passages, but watch out for the word *never.* Scientist 2 believes that the level will be below 1,100 parts per million in 2100, but he could feel that the level eventually will rise to 1,100.

Scientist 2 may believe Choice (D), but you can't say for sure. Scientist 2 believes that the rate of increase will slow and that the world will survive, but Scientist 2 could easily believe that such survival will occur even in the face of continually rising carbon dioxide levels.

Passage 5

Did you look at this experiment and mutter to yourself, "What a blooming mess!"? If so, congratulate yourself: Your humor is becoming almost as sorry as ours. That aside, this passage isn't too bad. This passage doesn't shock the senses by introducing concepts unfamiliar to you. You've seen plants produce flowers at only a certain time of year. You know that the length of daylight is different throughout the year (longer days in summer, shorter days in winter).

After you get a handle on the topic of this passage (the effect of the length of day on plants), you're ready to summarize each experiment. (You may want to write your brief synopsis in the margin.)

- ✔ Experiment 1 shows that interrupting the day has no effect.

- ✔ Experiment 2 shows that interrupting the night changes the plants' responses, indicating that the plants may actually respond to the length of night rather than the length of day. An SD plant is actually a long-night plant, whereas an LD plant is a short-night plant.

- ✔ Experiment 3 may sound complicated, but the gist is that, as with Experiment 1, manipulating the day has no effect on the plants.

- ✔ In Experiment 4, as in Experiment 2, changing a nighttime factor affects the plants.

Taken together, these experiments suggest that the plants are sensitive to changes in the length of night rather than the length of day. Don't economize on time here. Wanting to jump right into the questions is natural, but take a minute or two to think about what you just read. You don't have to be able to quote chapter and verse; you just have to know a little bit of what's going on. If you get confused here, you're likely to miss nearly every question.

24. **J.** Experiments 1 and 2 show that only interruptions that occur during the night affect the flowering response. Eliminate Choices (F) and (H), which mention daytime hours. Choice (J) makes more sense than Choice (G) because, if the total number of hours were critical, a brief interruption would have very little effect. On the other hand, if the plants were somehow measuring the number of continuous nighttime hours, a brief interruption would affect the plant.

25. **C.** One major point of this passage is that SD and LD plants show opposite responses. This difference makes Choices (A) and (D) unlikely. You can make a good guess at this point by choosing between Choices (B) and (C). Remember, the ACT doesn't subtract points for wrong answers, so guessing is always justified. Having a 50-50 choice is a real treat.

When the experimenter presents light in the middle of the 16-hour night, the plants are exposed to only eight hours of uninterrupted night hours. The plant that flowers when nights are short will start flowering. Which plant meets this criterion? The LD plant, which is spinach in this passage, flowers when days are long and nights are short.

You may be saying, "Yes, but what if . . ." Ah, Smart Students' Disease (in which you make things harder than necessary) is back. Don't be too concerned with the exact number of uninterrupted nighttime hours that spinach requires to flower. Although some LD plants may not flower until the number of uninterrupted night hours falls to, say, seven hours, the ACT won't pull this type of trick on you. The ACT doesn't expect you to memorize such obscure facts. What the ACT does test is your understanding that a nighttime interruption effectively shortens the night and, therefore, leads to LD flowering.

The information presented in the first part of the passage reinforces Choice (C). The passage mentions that cocklebur does not flower until day length is less than 15.5 hours. This statement means that nighttime must exceed 8.5 hours ($24 - 15.5 = 8.5$) for cocklebur to flower. When the experimenter flashes light in the middle of the 16-hour night, the night is effectively only 8 hours long, which means that the cocklebur won't flower.

26. **G.** The experimenter can easily choose different plants, keep the lights on or off at a certain time, or change the temperature. Whether the chosen plants flower, on the other hand, has to do with how the plants respond to the conditions presented in the experiment. Flowering depends on what happens to the other variables. Such dependent variables are a step removed from the direct control of the experimenter.

27. **C.** In both sets of experiments, changing the day conditions has no effect on the plants' responses, but changing the night conditions does affect the plants' responses. Choice (D) acknowledges this consistency, but the reason focuses on how the experiments are set up, not on the results. In many biological experiments, experimenters use the same organisms, but doing so doesn't guarantee similar results. (Imagine, for example, that you and your friend both have colds and are both given aspirin. No one can guarantee that both of you would have the same response to the medication just because you're both humans.)

    Choices (A) and (B), besides being flat-out wrong from the start, also provide reasons that focus on the experimental conditions rather than the results. In addition, Choice (A) may not be correct because you have no information regarding the variety of plants used in Experiments 1 and 2. Choice (B) points out a key way that the sets of experiments differ, but the results are similar.

28. **G.** On the horizontal axes, day length increases to the right. The LD plant flowers during long days. This information means that high vertical values are associated with the right side of the graph. Eliminate Choices (H) and (J) because flowering doesn't increase with the increasing day length.

    Choice (G) is better than Choice (F) because with LD plants, no flowering occurs until a critical day length is reached. (The experiments actually show that the LD plant responds when the length of night falls below a certain value, but associating an LD plant's flowering with long days is still okay.) In Choice (F), the graph continually rises, implying that flowering increases as day length increases from 0 hours. Choice (G) correctly shows that flowering doesn't occur when the day length is less than 15 hours.

29. **C.** So many questions are about SD and LD plants that you may have forgotten the third actor in this play, the DN plant. Look at the passage's introduction, which defines a DN plant as one that isn't sensitive to changes in day length. This type of plant should flower in any environment, including near the equator. (So you shouldn't be surprised that some weeds are DN plants.)

    You can eliminate the other choices because the question tells you that around the equator the daylight and nondaylight hours are pretty much equal, which means the plants that require very long or very short days probably won't flower near the equator because the day length stays close to 12 hours and doesn't approach the number of hours necessary for flowering.

Passage 6

Even though you don't need outside knowledge to answer these questions, information you have gained over the years (along with just plain common sense) can be very helpful. The ACT doesn't try to trap or trick you by presenting you with passages that are contrary to actual scientific reality. What you have learned in school or from experience will remain valid and useful for the ACT.

Use what you already know to interpret the first two paragraphs of the passage. What's more spread out — a solid, such as a block of ice, or oxygen gas as it is sprayed from a tank into a room? You know or can visualize that in a gas, particles quickly spread out as much as possible. What happens when you heat ice? The ice melts and turns into liquid water. Further heating leads to boiling, and the water evaporates. These thoughts should help you better understand the second paragraph.

The third paragraph is probably less familiar to you, but the figures should help. You can see from Figure 2, for example, that at 60° C and 0.20 atm, water is a gas, but at 60° C and 0.80 atm, water is a liquid. Try to summarize the information to get the gist or main point. The main point is that pressure affects phases.

The figures reemphasize the association between high temperatures and the gas phase and between low temperatures and the solid phase. When pressure is high, you need a relatively high temperature to turn a liquid into a gas.

30. **G.** This straightforward question simply tests your ability to read a graph. Look at Figure 2, which deals with water. Locate 60° C on the horizontal axis and then go straight up until you're even with 1.00 atm (on the vertical axis). You're in the liquid region.

31. **A.** Look for a point on one of the figures where a solid is next to a gas. Choice (A) looks good. In Figure 1 (bromine), –20° C and 0.05 atm is near the lower-left corner, where a solid and a gas are next to each other. Liquid is out of the way, up and to the right.

    Choice (B) is wrong because at 0° C and 0.80 atm, bromine is near the solid-liquid boundary. Water is also near that boundary at 0° C and 0.80 atm, so Choice (C) is also out. Choice (D) is way off because water is nowhere near a solid at 80° C and 0.50 atm.

32. **G.** The easiest way to answer this question is to use a straightedge (your answer sheet works great) to draw a vertical line from the 30° C mark on each figure. Now, for each figure, mark 0.6 atm and 0.3 atm on the line. On the bromine graph, 0.6 atm is in the liquid region and 0.3 atm is in the gas region when the temperature is 30° C, so Choice (G) is the answer. Don't be careless and pick Choice (F). The pressure is going down, so you're moving from a liquid to a gas, not from a gas to a liquid. The liquid region is generally higher than the gas region. On the water graph, you can see that both of your marks are in the liquid region, eliminating Choices (H) and (J).

33. **D.** Your gut instinct should attract you to Choices (B) and (D) because higher temperatures move particles farther apart. If you're running out of time, go ahead and make a guess. (50/50 odds aren't bad on this test because the ACT has no penalty for wrong answers.) Choice (D) is correct because water at 100° C and 0.60 atm is a gas, while bromine at 50° C and 0.80 atm — Choice (B) — is a liquid. Just to be certain, check Choices (A) and (C). In Choice (A), bromine is a solid. In Choice (C), water is also a solid.

34. **H.** You can probably eliminate Choice (F) by using common sense: Higher altitudes don't necessarily mean your pasta freezes! When an answer seems illogical or even amusing, put it aside for a moment. If none of the other answer choices are correct, you can always come back to it. (For those of you who love Sherlock Holmes, you'll recognize this strategy as a variation on his famous saying, which roughly goes, "When you have eliminated the impossible, whatever remains, however improbable, must be true.")

    Go through the rest of the choices without wasting any time on Choice (F). Choice (G) is out because the water temperature, not the air temperature, is important (because the spaghetti is in the water). A look at Figure 2 confirms the first part of Choice (H): At 1.00 atm, water becomes a gas at about 100° C. At 0.80 atm, water becomes a gas at about 90° C. With the water boiling at a lower temperature, less heat is available to soften the spaghetti. The answer is probably Choice (H), but double-check Choice (J) just to be sure. Figure 2 contradicts Choice (J); think of how you analyzed Choice (H). Besides, in this problem, the water is already boiling, so the length of time required to boil water is irrelevant.

Passage 7

First of all, don't panic if the terminology in this passage isn't familiar to you. You don't have to know what radon is to understand the introduction. Remember that the ACT doesn't presuppose any specific scientific knowledge on your part. Simply note that radon may have something to do with earthquakes and that scientists are going to check out this possibility.

Spend a minute or two looking at the charts. You don't have to understand the charts perfectly, and you certainly don't want to start memorizing the information given. Just realize that Figures 1 through 4 are basically maps. Find the epicenters and note that wells around the epicenters have higher-than-normal amounts of radon emission.

Figure 5 shows a systematic relationship (called a *correlation*) between earthquake magnitude and the *differential,* which is a measure of how much the radon emission exceeds normal. The rightmost point is the only one that bucks the trend. When you see something abnormal, something that doesn't follow the same pattern as the others, pay special attention to it. The chances are good that the test will ask a question about this aberration later. Which earthquake site is represented by the rightmost point? The site had a magnitude of 7.9 and an average differential of 2.5. Scan Figures 1 through 4 and see that the point in question represents China. Note that China has two wells near the epicenter that weren't much above normal. Perhaps these wells were measured inaccurately. Whatever the case, these wells may have something to do with why China is a little off in regard to Figure 5.

35. **B.** Choice (A) doesn't look right. All four sites had radon emissions that were greater than the normal amount found over the earth, making Choice (B) look good.

You should have leaned toward choosing Choice (B) as soon as you saw the wishy-washy, wimpy language in it. A correct answer often has language that isn't extreme or language that hedges a little bit. A conclusion that states that an association is *definitely* present is too strong unless scientists collected a lot more data.

None of the figures shows wells that are 1,000 km (10 cm) away from the epicenter, so you can determine nothing about Choice (C).

The conclusion stated in Choice (D) is also unjustified. For the most part, wells near the epicenters show higher emissions, but the numbers aren't very close to 5 percent and scientists didn't take a measurement right at the epicenter.

36. **H.** The results of the studies indicate some association between earthquakes and radon emissions. Results that go along with the trend found in the studies strengthen the results and any claims derived from the results. You probably crossed out Choice (F) right away. Readings from earthquake sites in another location that aren't much different from average radon emission readings wouldn't provide more evidence for the claim that earthquakes and higher radon emissions are associated. In fact, the information may serve to weaken the claim. Likewise, Choice (G) tends to weaken the claim rather than strengthen it. Similar radon readings from 500 miles away from the earthquake site may indicate that something other than earthquakes is contributing to the high radon readings.

The finding cited in Choice (H) is more helpful. It produces a point that falls in line with the points from the other three sites, so it provides additional support for the claim. Choice (J) doesn't provide enough information. You need to see more earthquakes associated with high radon emissions. Simply having more earthquakes doesn't shed any light on the association between earthquakes and radon emissions.

37. **A.** You have to be careful when dealing with data that show an association (or *correlation,* in more mathematical terms). Just because two things go together doesn't imply that one causes the other. For example, the number of skyscrapers in a city and the number of children who live in that city have a correlation. That is, in general, cities that have more skyscrapers also have more young people. Does this correlation mean that young people are building the skyscrapers? Of course not. A more reasonable explanation is that when a city is large, it has many skyscrapers and youngsters. An underlying cause, namely overall city size, exists. Children don't cause skyscrapers or vice versa.

This study simply measured a correlation. It wasn't designed to investigate any possible mechanism that would convert radon emissions into earthquakes, which knocks out Choices (C) and (D). Choice (B) is out because nothing in the study points to 4 percent as a magic number. (This particular point isn't true, anyway, but even if it were, you wouldn't have to know this information from some specialized outside study. You only have to know the info that the Science Test passages present.)

38. **J.** When scientists obtain a set of experimental results, the responsible factor is often difficult to isolate. For example, if a scientist wanted to study whether a new drug could increase ACT scores, he could give the drug to a group of students and then look at the scores. If the scores were high, the scientist could conclude that the drug had an effect. But what if the group studied included many people who had a history of scoring well on tests similar to the ACT? What if the students did better simply because they believed the drug would help them? By including a control condition, experimenters could rule out these possibilities. Experimenters could find a group that was equal to the drug group on previous test scores and then give these control students a *placebo* (a fake pill) but tell them that this pill is supposed to help raise ACT scores. If the drug group scored higher, experimenters could be more confident that the high scores aren't simply the result of using a high-achieving group or a psychological belief in the drug because the experimenters matched the two groups in terms of these factors. In this case, the chemicals in the drug more likely had something to do with the higher scores. The control condition helped rule out other possible factors.

    In the earthquake studies, scientists measured radon emissions after earthquakes. They obtained high values, but such values could occur even in the absence of an earthquake. Scientists would need to know the radon emission level that normally occurs in the sites studied.

    In a sense, Choices (F) and (H) mention conditions that are included in the studies. The studies compared the wells near the epicenters to worldwide values. Studying more wells from the same areas won't add anything new to the study, and the worldwide averages include virtually earthquake-free areas.

    All Choice (G) would do is add more data to what has already been found. Clearing up the graph in Figure 5 would be particularly helpful, but the condition isn't a control condition.

39. **A.** Approach this question with good old common sense. If you want to predict an earthquake, you have to measure something *before* the earthquake occurs. The problem with the current studies is that scientists measured emissions after the earthquakes. Maybe the earthquakes caused the emissions, making radon pretty useless as a predictor. Choices (B), (C), and (D) wouldn't help unless researchers took measurements before the earthquake.

    You aren't required to have specific science knowledge to answer an ACT question, but the test makers do assume a level of common sense. The ACT doesn't teach or test false science (for example, you won't have an experiment with totally illogical results). This small act of kindness means that you can trust your common sense and general knowledge. The science portion of the ACT has very few traps or tricks in it. The science is pretty straightforward, as are the questions. Don't make these questions harder than they have to be.

40. **H.** Reading through the studies, you don't get a sense of any findings that are *conclusive.* The inclusion of this debatable word in Choice (F) is a big clue that the answer is wrong. Choice (G) is contrary to the findings of Study 2, which show a definite association between earthquake sites and higher radon emission readings. That leaves Choices (H) and (J). The scatter plot in Study 2 graphs the results of Study 1. The graph shows that, generally, as the magnitude of the earthquake increases so does the average differential of the radon emission readings. So Choice (H) is right. You can cross out Choice (J) because the graph shows a positive correlation rather than a negative one. A negative relationship would be if the differential went down as the magnitude increased.

    Be sure you know the definition of positive and negative correlations. You're bound to be asked about them on the test. If two factors have a *positive correlation,* they do the same thing (as one goes up, the other goes up, too). If they have a *negative correlation,* they do opposite things (as one goes up, the other goes down).

Writing Test

See the "Writing Test" section in Chapter 21 for general information on the features that your essay should contain.

The prompt gives you the option of writing for or against funding school expenses with soft drink ads. (It also says you can advocate for another option, but why would you put yourself through the extra work of coming up with something new?) The essay question doesn't have a right answer. You can be for the ads or against them. You just need to pick a position and move on. If your first instinct is that soft drink ads would look better than the peeling paint that currently graces the gym walls, go with it. If the idea of school ads offends you, write on!

Say that you're opposed to the advertising proposal. You may set up your essay this way:

- ✔ **Thesis/Introduction:** Your thesis could be that schools may need a way to meet their budgets, but presenting glaring ads that promote sugary drinks devoid of nutritional value to their susceptible students in a culture that faces skyrocketing statistics of childhood obesity and juvenile diabetes isn't the way to do so.

- ✔ **Body:** Your first body paragraph could then be about the fact that in today's society, kids are bombarded with ads luring them to buy everything from toys to toothpaste. Schools should be a haven from this kind of capitalistic pressure. Students should be especially safeguarded from promotion of things that can harm them.

  The next paragraph could go into detail on the problems associated with drinking soft drinks and could express dismay that kids will think soft drinks are okay because their schools endorse them. Provide specific examples of people you know who are unduly influenced by advertising.

  The last body paragraph could highlight other ways schools could raise money to pay for expenses — maybe by selling to advertisers of healthier products. Schools shouldn't sacrifice the health of students for more activities or better equipment.

- ✔ **Conclusion:** You could conclude with a short summary paragraph that summarizes the main point of each paragraph.

An essay that takes the opposing position could focus on the advantages of pouring corporate money into schools. Corporations can bring in many more dollars than bake sales can. The thesis could point out that the new activities and athletic equipment would give students the ability to engage in physical exercise that would counteract the effects of promoting soft drinks. Without the advertisements, student health would be comprised due to the lack of outlets for physical activity.

Keep in mind that what position you take isn't important. How you support your stance and the quality of your supporting information is very important.

When you're finished reviewing your essay, ask your English teacher to look over your masterpiece for writing errors and to provide general comments about your essay's organization and strength in addressing the given prompt.

Answer Key for Practice Exam 2

English Test

1. C	14. G	27. B	40. G	53. D	66. F
2. G	15. A	28. F	41. B	54. F	67. C
3. C	16. G	29. C	42. H	55. C	68. G
4. J	17. B	30. G	43. A	56. F	69. B
5. B	18. J	31. C	44. G	57. D	70. H
6. G	19. A	32. H	45. C	58. J	71. B
7. C	20. H	33. D	46. G	59. C	72. G
8. F	21. A	34. J	47. A	60. H	73. D
9. D	22. F	35. B	48. F	61. D	74. G
10. H	23. C	36. F	49. A	62. J	75. A
11. D	24. J	37. D	50. G	63. A	
12. G	25. C	38. F	51. B	64. H	
13. C	26. G	39. B	52. G	65. D	

Mathematics Test

1. D	11. D	21. D	31. B	41. D	51. D
2. H	12. K	22. K	32. G	42. H	52. F
3. D	13. A	23. D	33. D	43. B	53. C
4. F	14. J	24. H	34. K	44. H	54. F
5. B	15. E	25. B	35. C	45. B	55. E
6. H	16. J	26. H	36. K	46. H	56. F
7. D	17. E	27. B	37. B	47. A	57. D
8. K	18. H	28. J	38. K	48. H	58. F
9. C	19. E	29. D	39. B	49. A	59. D
10. G	20. J	30. G	40. J	50. J	60. K

Reading Test

1. D	8. F	15. D	22. F	29. B	36. J
2. G	9. A	16. G	23. A	30. G	37. D
3. C	10. J	17. D	24. J	31. B	38. J
4. F	11. D	18. J	25. D	32. H	39. C
5. B	12. G	19. C	26. G	33. A	40. G
6. F	13. C	20. H	27. C	34. H	
7. D	14. J	21. B	28. H	35. B	

Science Test

1. B	8. J	15. C	22. H	29. C	36. H
2. G	9. A	16. G	23. B	30. G	37. A
3. A	10. H	17. D	24. J	31. A	38. J
4. G	11. C	18. H	25. C	32. G	39. A
5. D	12. H	19. A	26. G	33. D	40. H
6. G	13. B	20. J	27. C	34. H	
7. B	14. F	21. A	28. G	35. B	

Chapter 24

Practice Exam 3

· ·

Here comes a chance to practice your ACT test-taking skills. You're probably pretty familiar with the exam format by now, but just in case you've had a momentary bout of amnesia (or you've skipped the first two practice exams in Chapters 20 and 22), we remind you what to expect. The following exam consists of four mandatory tests — a 45-minute English Test, a 60-minute Mathematics Test, a 35-minute Reading Test, and a 35-minute Science Test — and one optional 30-minute Writing Test.

For maximum benefit, take this test under the following normal exam conditions:

- ✔ Sit where you won't be interrupted (even though you'd probably welcome any distractions).

- ✔ Use the answer sheet provided to mark your answers.

- ✔ Set your timer for the time limits indicated at the beginning of each test in this exam.

- ✔ Do not go on to the next test until the time allotted for the test you're taking is up.

- ✔ Check your work only for the test you're taking; don't look at more than one test at a time.

- ✔ Do not take a break in the middle of any test.

- ✔ Give yourself one ten-minute break between the Math Test and the Reading Test.

When you've completed the entire practice exam, turn to Chapter 25, where you find detailed explanations of the answers as well as an abbreviated answer key. Go through the answer explanations to all the questions, not just the ones you missed. We include a bunch of useful information that provides a good review of everything we cover in the other chapters of this book. We've tried to keep your attention by inserting a little corny humor every now and then.

Note: The ACT Writing Test is optional. If you register to take the Writing Test, you'll take it after you've completed the other four tests. For information about the optional Writing Test, see Part VI.

Answer Sheet

Begin with Number 1 for each new test.

English Test

1. Ⓐ Ⓑ Ⓒ Ⓓ
2. Ⓕ Ⓖ Ⓗ Ⓙ
3. Ⓐ Ⓑ Ⓒ Ⓓ
4. Ⓕ Ⓖ Ⓗ Ⓙ
5. Ⓐ Ⓑ Ⓒ Ⓓ
6. Ⓕ Ⓖ Ⓗ Ⓙ
7. Ⓐ Ⓑ Ⓒ Ⓓ
8. Ⓕ Ⓖ Ⓗ Ⓙ
9. Ⓐ Ⓑ Ⓒ Ⓓ
10. Ⓕ Ⓖ Ⓗ Ⓙ
11. Ⓐ Ⓑ Ⓒ Ⓓ
12. Ⓕ Ⓖ Ⓗ Ⓙ
13. Ⓐ Ⓑ Ⓒ Ⓓ
14. Ⓕ Ⓖ Ⓗ Ⓙ
15. Ⓐ Ⓑ Ⓒ Ⓓ
16. Ⓕ Ⓖ Ⓗ Ⓙ
17. Ⓐ Ⓑ Ⓒ Ⓓ
18. Ⓕ Ⓖ Ⓗ Ⓙ
19. Ⓐ Ⓑ Ⓒ Ⓓ
20. Ⓕ Ⓖ Ⓗ Ⓙ
21. Ⓐ Ⓑ Ⓒ Ⓓ
22. Ⓕ Ⓖ Ⓗ Ⓙ
23. Ⓐ Ⓑ Ⓒ Ⓓ
24. Ⓕ Ⓖ Ⓗ Ⓙ
25. Ⓐ Ⓑ Ⓒ Ⓓ
26. Ⓕ Ⓖ Ⓗ Ⓙ
27. Ⓐ Ⓑ Ⓒ Ⓓ
28. Ⓕ Ⓖ Ⓗ Ⓙ
29. Ⓐ Ⓑ Ⓒ Ⓓ
30. Ⓕ Ⓖ Ⓗ Ⓙ
31. Ⓐ Ⓑ Ⓒ Ⓓ
32. Ⓕ Ⓖ Ⓗ Ⓙ
33. Ⓐ Ⓑ Ⓒ Ⓓ
34. Ⓕ Ⓖ Ⓗ Ⓙ
35. Ⓐ Ⓑ Ⓒ Ⓓ
36. Ⓕ Ⓖ Ⓗ Ⓙ
37. Ⓐ Ⓑ Ⓒ Ⓓ
38. Ⓕ Ⓖ Ⓗ Ⓙ
39. Ⓐ Ⓑ Ⓒ Ⓓ
40. Ⓕ Ⓖ Ⓗ Ⓙ
41. Ⓐ Ⓑ Ⓒ Ⓓ
42. Ⓕ Ⓖ Ⓗ Ⓙ
43. Ⓐ Ⓑ Ⓒ Ⓓ
44. Ⓕ Ⓖ Ⓗ Ⓙ
45. Ⓐ Ⓑ Ⓒ Ⓓ
46. Ⓕ Ⓖ Ⓗ Ⓙ
47. Ⓐ Ⓑ Ⓒ Ⓓ
48. Ⓕ Ⓖ Ⓗ Ⓙ
49. Ⓐ Ⓑ Ⓒ Ⓓ
50. Ⓕ Ⓖ Ⓗ Ⓙ

51. Ⓐ Ⓑ Ⓒ Ⓓ
52. Ⓕ Ⓖ Ⓗ Ⓙ
53. Ⓐ Ⓑ Ⓒ Ⓓ
54. Ⓕ Ⓖ Ⓗ Ⓙ
55. Ⓐ Ⓑ Ⓒ Ⓓ
56. Ⓕ Ⓖ Ⓗ Ⓙ
57. Ⓐ Ⓑ Ⓒ Ⓓ
58. Ⓕ Ⓖ Ⓗ Ⓙ
59. Ⓐ Ⓑ Ⓒ Ⓓ
60. Ⓕ Ⓖ Ⓗ Ⓙ
61. Ⓐ Ⓑ Ⓒ Ⓓ
62. Ⓕ Ⓖ Ⓗ Ⓙ
63. Ⓐ Ⓑ Ⓒ Ⓓ
64. Ⓕ Ⓖ Ⓗ Ⓙ
65. Ⓐ Ⓑ Ⓒ Ⓓ
66. Ⓕ Ⓖ Ⓗ Ⓙ
67. Ⓐ Ⓑ Ⓒ Ⓓ
68. Ⓕ Ⓖ Ⓗ Ⓙ
69. Ⓐ Ⓑ Ⓒ Ⓓ
70. Ⓕ Ⓖ Ⓗ Ⓙ
71. Ⓐ Ⓑ Ⓒ Ⓓ
72. Ⓕ Ⓖ Ⓗ Ⓙ
73. Ⓐ Ⓑ Ⓒ Ⓓ
74. Ⓕ Ⓖ Ⓗ Ⓙ
75. Ⓐ Ⓑ Ⓒ Ⓓ

Mathematics Test

1. Ⓐ Ⓑ Ⓒ Ⓓ Ⓔ
2. Ⓕ Ⓖ Ⓗ Ⓙ Ⓚ
3. Ⓐ Ⓑ Ⓒ Ⓓ Ⓔ
4. Ⓕ Ⓖ Ⓗ Ⓙ Ⓚ
5. Ⓐ Ⓑ Ⓒ Ⓓ Ⓔ
6. Ⓕ Ⓖ Ⓗ Ⓙ Ⓚ
7. Ⓐ Ⓑ Ⓒ Ⓓ Ⓔ
8. Ⓕ Ⓖ Ⓗ Ⓙ Ⓚ
9. Ⓐ Ⓑ Ⓒ Ⓓ Ⓔ
10. Ⓕ Ⓖ Ⓗ Ⓙ Ⓚ
11. Ⓐ Ⓑ Ⓒ Ⓓ Ⓔ
12. Ⓕ Ⓖ Ⓗ Ⓙ Ⓚ
13. Ⓐ Ⓑ Ⓒ Ⓓ Ⓔ
14. Ⓕ Ⓖ Ⓗ Ⓙ Ⓚ
15. Ⓐ Ⓑ Ⓒ Ⓓ Ⓔ
16. Ⓕ Ⓖ Ⓗ Ⓙ Ⓚ
17. Ⓐ Ⓑ Ⓒ Ⓓ Ⓔ
18. Ⓕ Ⓖ Ⓗ Ⓙ Ⓚ
19. Ⓐ Ⓑ Ⓒ Ⓓ Ⓔ
20. Ⓕ Ⓖ Ⓗ Ⓙ Ⓚ
21. Ⓐ Ⓑ Ⓒ Ⓓ Ⓔ
22. Ⓕ Ⓖ Ⓗ Ⓙ Ⓚ
23. Ⓐ Ⓑ Ⓒ Ⓓ Ⓔ
24. Ⓕ Ⓖ Ⓗ Ⓙ Ⓚ
25. Ⓐ Ⓑ Ⓒ Ⓓ Ⓔ
26. Ⓕ Ⓖ Ⓗ Ⓙ Ⓚ
27. Ⓐ Ⓑ Ⓒ Ⓓ Ⓔ
28. Ⓕ Ⓖ Ⓗ Ⓙ Ⓚ
29. Ⓐ Ⓑ Ⓒ Ⓓ Ⓔ
30. Ⓕ Ⓖ Ⓗ Ⓙ Ⓚ

31. Ⓐ Ⓑ Ⓒ Ⓓ Ⓔ
32. Ⓕ Ⓖ Ⓗ Ⓙ Ⓚ
33. Ⓐ Ⓑ Ⓒ Ⓓ Ⓔ
34. Ⓕ Ⓖ Ⓗ Ⓙ Ⓚ
35. Ⓐ Ⓑ Ⓒ Ⓓ Ⓔ
36. Ⓕ Ⓖ Ⓗ Ⓙ Ⓚ
37. Ⓐ Ⓑ Ⓒ Ⓓ Ⓔ
38. Ⓕ Ⓖ Ⓗ Ⓙ Ⓚ
39. Ⓐ Ⓑ Ⓒ Ⓓ Ⓔ
40. Ⓕ Ⓖ Ⓗ Ⓙ Ⓚ
41. Ⓐ Ⓑ Ⓒ Ⓓ Ⓔ
42. Ⓕ Ⓖ Ⓗ Ⓙ Ⓚ
43. Ⓐ Ⓑ Ⓒ Ⓓ Ⓔ
44. Ⓕ Ⓖ Ⓗ Ⓙ Ⓚ
45. Ⓐ Ⓑ Ⓒ Ⓓ Ⓔ
46. Ⓕ Ⓖ Ⓗ Ⓙ Ⓚ
47. Ⓐ Ⓑ Ⓒ Ⓓ Ⓔ
48. Ⓕ Ⓖ Ⓗ Ⓙ Ⓚ
49. Ⓐ Ⓑ Ⓒ Ⓓ Ⓔ
50. Ⓕ Ⓖ Ⓗ Ⓙ Ⓚ
51. Ⓐ Ⓑ Ⓒ Ⓓ Ⓔ
52. Ⓕ Ⓖ Ⓗ Ⓙ Ⓚ
53. Ⓐ Ⓑ Ⓒ Ⓓ Ⓔ
54. Ⓕ Ⓖ Ⓗ Ⓙ Ⓚ
55. Ⓐ Ⓑ Ⓒ Ⓓ Ⓔ
56. Ⓕ Ⓖ Ⓗ Ⓙ Ⓚ
57. Ⓐ Ⓑ Ⓒ Ⓓ Ⓔ
58. Ⓕ Ⓖ Ⓗ Ⓙ Ⓚ
59. Ⓐ Ⓑ Ⓒ Ⓓ Ⓔ
60. Ⓕ Ⓖ Ⓗ Ⓙ Ⓚ

Reading Test	Science Test
1. Ⓐ Ⓑ Ⓒ Ⓓ	1. Ⓐ Ⓑ Ⓒ Ⓓ
2. Ⓕ Ⓖ Ⓗ Ⓙ	2. Ⓕ Ⓖ Ⓗ Ⓙ
3. Ⓐ Ⓑ Ⓒ Ⓓ	3. Ⓐ Ⓑ Ⓒ Ⓓ
4. Ⓕ Ⓖ Ⓗ Ⓙ	4. Ⓕ Ⓖ Ⓗ Ⓙ
5. Ⓐ Ⓑ Ⓒ Ⓓ	5. Ⓐ Ⓑ Ⓒ Ⓓ
6. Ⓕ Ⓖ Ⓗ Ⓙ	6. Ⓕ Ⓖ Ⓗ Ⓙ
7. Ⓐ Ⓑ Ⓒ Ⓓ	7. Ⓐ Ⓑ Ⓒ Ⓓ
8. Ⓕ Ⓖ Ⓗ Ⓙ	8. Ⓕ Ⓖ Ⓗ Ⓙ
9. Ⓐ Ⓑ Ⓒ Ⓓ	9. Ⓐ Ⓑ Ⓒ Ⓓ
10. Ⓕ Ⓖ Ⓗ Ⓙ	10. Ⓕ Ⓖ Ⓗ Ⓙ
11. Ⓐ Ⓑ Ⓒ Ⓓ	11. Ⓐ Ⓑ Ⓒ Ⓓ
12. Ⓕ Ⓖ Ⓗ Ⓙ	12. Ⓕ Ⓖ Ⓗ Ⓙ
13. Ⓐ Ⓑ Ⓒ Ⓓ	13. Ⓐ Ⓑ Ⓒ Ⓓ
14. Ⓕ Ⓖ Ⓗ Ⓙ	14. Ⓕ Ⓖ Ⓗ Ⓙ
15. Ⓐ Ⓑ Ⓒ Ⓓ	15. Ⓐ Ⓑ Ⓒ Ⓓ
16. Ⓕ Ⓖ Ⓗ Ⓙ	16. Ⓕ Ⓖ Ⓗ Ⓙ
17. Ⓐ Ⓑ Ⓒ Ⓓ	17. Ⓐ Ⓑ Ⓒ Ⓓ
18. Ⓕ Ⓖ Ⓗ Ⓙ	18. Ⓕ Ⓖ Ⓗ Ⓙ
19. Ⓐ Ⓑ Ⓒ Ⓓ	19. Ⓐ Ⓑ Ⓒ Ⓓ
20. Ⓕ Ⓖ Ⓗ Ⓙ	20. Ⓕ Ⓖ Ⓗ Ⓙ
21. Ⓐ Ⓑ Ⓒ Ⓓ	21. Ⓐ Ⓑ Ⓒ Ⓓ
22. Ⓕ Ⓖ Ⓗ Ⓙ	22. Ⓕ Ⓖ Ⓗ Ⓙ
23. Ⓐ Ⓑ Ⓒ Ⓓ	23. Ⓐ Ⓑ Ⓒ Ⓓ
24. Ⓕ Ⓖ Ⓗ Ⓙ	24. Ⓕ Ⓖ Ⓗ Ⓙ
25. Ⓐ Ⓑ Ⓒ Ⓓ	25. Ⓐ Ⓑ Ⓒ Ⓓ
26. Ⓕ Ⓖ Ⓗ Ⓙ	26. Ⓕ Ⓖ Ⓗ Ⓙ
27. Ⓐ Ⓑ Ⓒ Ⓓ	27. Ⓐ Ⓑ Ⓒ Ⓓ
28. Ⓕ Ⓖ Ⓗ Ⓙ	28. Ⓕ Ⓖ Ⓗ Ⓙ
29. Ⓐ Ⓑ Ⓒ Ⓓ	29. Ⓐ Ⓑ Ⓒ Ⓓ
30. Ⓕ Ⓖ Ⓗ Ⓙ	30. Ⓕ Ⓖ Ⓗ Ⓙ
31. Ⓐ Ⓑ Ⓒ Ⓓ	31. Ⓐ Ⓑ Ⓒ Ⓓ
32. Ⓕ Ⓖ Ⓗ Ⓙ	32. Ⓕ Ⓖ Ⓗ Ⓙ
33. Ⓐ Ⓑ Ⓒ Ⓓ	33. Ⓐ Ⓑ Ⓒ Ⓓ
34. Ⓕ Ⓖ Ⓗ Ⓙ	34. Ⓕ Ⓖ Ⓗ Ⓙ
35. Ⓐ Ⓑ Ⓒ Ⓓ	35. Ⓐ Ⓑ Ⓒ Ⓓ
36. Ⓕ Ⓖ Ⓗ Ⓙ	36. Ⓕ Ⓖ Ⓗ Ⓙ
37. Ⓐ Ⓑ Ⓒ Ⓓ	37. Ⓐ Ⓑ Ⓒ Ⓓ
38. Ⓕ Ⓖ Ⓗ Ⓙ	38. Ⓕ Ⓖ Ⓗ Ⓙ
39. Ⓐ Ⓑ Ⓒ Ⓓ	39. Ⓐ Ⓑ Ⓒ Ⓓ
40. Ⓕ Ⓖ Ⓗ Ⓙ	40. Ⓕ Ⓖ Ⓗ Ⓙ

English Test

> **Time:** 45 minutes for 75 questions
>
> **Directions:** Following are five passages with underlined portions. Alternate ways of stating the underlined portions come after the passages. Choose the best alternative; if the original is the best way of stating the underlined portion, choose NO CHANGE.
>
> The test also has questions that refer to the passages or ask you to reorder the sentences within the passages. These questions are identified by a number in a box. Choose the best answer, and shade in the corresponding oval on your answer sheet.

Passage 1

Hockey Season

The coolness of the ice rink and the hum of the Zamboni means only one thing; it's hockey time! All signs pointing toward a successful season for the Clement Cougars.

Clement's hockey team is not just made up of Clement players. Rounding out the team are players from St. Thomas High School and Our Lady High School, too. Though three schools are represented; the vast majority of the players are from Clement.

Here's a little bit about the players from Clement. Returning to Clement for his senior year, the position of goalie is played by Brendan Sanchez. For the past two years Brendan has been playing hockey in a special league in Washington State. Sanchez's unmatched skills will be an excellent addition to an already great Clement team. Sanchez is surrounded by a great supporting cast that includes such star players as Clement center, Taylor Poldale, St. Thomas senior, Don Silver, Our Lady senior, Nick Woodson, and Clement junior, Justin Frank. Look

for the upperclassmen, to step up and take over the roles vacated by graduated players, Brad Hunt and Steve Wilson. 10

[1] Some of the players, like Sanchez, have been preparing for the rigorous season by joining fall hockey teams. Him and Poldale are currently playing for local AA league teams. [2] It is hoped that this extra practice will give the team the edge to overcome its rival, Apple River High School. [3] Last year, the Clement Cougars won nine games and lost five and played good enough to make the playoffs. [4] The Cougars hope to rebound this season and take home the state championship. 14 [5] Unfortunately, they were dealt a devastating two to one loss in the final seconds at the hands of Coach Jim Quinlan and the Apple River team.

This year will be an exciting one. So grab your jackets, buy your tickets, and come support the Cougars on their way to high school hockey stardom. 15

Go on to next page

1. (A) NO CHANGE
    (B) Zamboni only means
    (C) Zamboni mean only
    (D) Zamboni, means only

2. (F) NO CHANGE
    (G) thing; its hockey
    (H) thing. Its hockey
    (J) thing, it's hockey

3. (A) NO CHANGE
    (B) All signs points toward a successful season
    (C) All signs point toward a successful season
    (D) All signs have pointed toward a successful season

4. (F) NO CHANGE
    (G) are not just made up of
    (H) isn't just made up of
    (J) isn't made up of just

5. (A) NO CHANGE
    (B) are represented, the
    (C) are represented: the
    (D) were represented the

6. Which of the following would be the best way to introduce the paragraph?
    (F) NO CHANGE
    (G) The team has many players.
    (H) Some of the team is the same as last year.
    (J) OMIT the underlined portion.

7. (A) NO CHANGE
    (B) year, the goalie position made up of Brendan Sanchez.
    (C) year, Brendan Sanchez plays goalie.
    (D) year; Brendan Sanchez plays the position of goalie.

8. (F) NO CHANGE
    (G) as: Clement center Taylor Poldale, St. Thomas senior Don Silver, Our Lady senior Nick Woodson, and Clement junior Justin Frank
    (H) as Clement center: Taylor Poldale, St. Thomas senior: Don Silver, Our Lady senior: Nick Woodson, and Clement junior: Justin Frank
    (J) as, Clement center, Taylor Poldale, St. Thomas senior, Don Silver, Our Lady senior, Nick Woodson, and Clement junior, Justin Frank

9. (A) NO CHANGE
    (B) the upperclassmen to step up
    (C) the upperclassmen, to take over
    (D) the upperclassmen to step up and take over

10. At this point in the story, the author is considering including a list of the entire team roster. Would it be appropriate to include that list here?
    (F) Yes, because the primary purpose of the essay is to let the reader know who is on the hockey team.
    (G) Yes, because providing a list of players would make the essay more interesting.
    (H) No, because putting a complete list of players in the middle of the essay would interrupt its flow and interfere with its focus.
    (J) No, because the focus of the essay is how the hockey team performed last year, so knowing this year's roster is irrelevant.

11. (A) NO CHANGE
    (B) Poldale and him
    (C) Him, and Poldale,
    (D) He and Poldale

12. (F) NO CHANGE
    (G) Hopefully, this extra practice
    (H) This extra practice, hopefully,
    (J) Everyone is hopeful that with this extra practice

Go on to next page

13. (A) NO CHANGE
     (B) five games and played sufficiently good enough
     (C) five and played well enough
     (D) five games, and then played sufficiently well enough

14. The most logical position for Sentence 4 is:
     (F) where it is now.
     (G) after Sentence 5.
     (H) after Sentence 2.
     (J) before Sentence 1.

15. This article was written in response to an assignment to provide an article for the high school newspaper that would entice students to attend hockey games. Did the writer fulfill the assignment?
     (A) Yes, because the essay is written in a casual, enthusiastic style that promotes the excitement of following the hockey team's season.
     (B) Yes, because the essay provides detailed information about all of the players so that readers will get to know them better.
     (C) No, because the essay focuses too much on the disappointing season the team experienced the year before.
     (D) No, because the essay is written in a style and uses language that is too formal for a high school newspaper.

Passage 2

Promoting Easy Recycling

It is commonly agreed that recycling being
                                      16
a critical step, in both maintaining a clean and
               17
green environment and sustaining America's

quest for autonomous independence. The sec-
                18
ondary markets for recycled paper, cardboard,
                            19
aluminum, asphalt, copper, plastic, and glass

are at all-time highs and have never been greater.
20

Public education regarding the moral and ethical responsibilities to keep the environment clean has increased. 21 Their is now a large supply
                                        22
and an increasingly strong demand for recycled goods. But we still have problems in one area:
                                          23
the ability to collect and sort recyclables.

[1] Recycle bins have seemingly become depositories for strictly any type of trash, recy-
                        24   25
clable or not from a tattered mattress and last
                                          26
weeks' TV dinner. [2] The recycle bins that newspaper publishers, grocery stores, and big box department stores have traditionally placed in their parking lots have become trash magnets that produce increasingly determined complaints from patrons and neighbors. [3] Part of the reason that the stores are so willing to remove the bins is because of the significant expense involved in having to separate trash from newsprint and other recyclables, including aluminum, cardboard, plastic, and glass. [4] Neighbors frequently ask stores to remove their recycle bins largely because they become displeasing to the eye
                                  27
and unsightly. 28

One solution to the problem has come from entrepreneurs who has begun charging for
                      29
monthly pick-ups of recyclable materials, like paper, aluminum, plastic, and glass, from customers' curbsides. The monthly fee for this service usually pays for the costs incident to

Go on to next page

collection and separation of the materials. Additionally, these businesses sell the materials for a profit on the secondary recyclable market after they separate them. This practice is generally viewed as a "win-win" situation for the businesses and their contented customers, who have to pay only a small fee to contribute toward a cleaner, more energy-independent America. 30

16. (F) NO CHANGE
    (G) could have been
    (H) had been
    (J) is

17. (A) NO CHANGE
    (B) step in both maintaining
    (C) step, in maintaining both
    (D) step, both in maintaining

18. (F) NO CHANGE
    (G) autonomously
    (H) autonomous,
    (J) OMIT the underlined portion.

19. (A) NO CHANGE
    (B) recycled paper; cardboard; aluminum; asphalt; copper; plastic;
    (C) recycled paper: cardboard and aluminum, asphalt, copper, plastic,
    (D) recycled paper and cardboard and aluminum, asphalt, copper, plastic

20. (F) NO CHANGE
    (G) are at all-time highs
    (H) have never been greater and are at all-time highs
    (J) have never been at such an all-time high

21. At this point, the author wants to add this sentence about recycling education:

    While the increase in public education has inspired people to partake in recycling programs, many only do so for a short period of time before reverting to old habits.

    Should the author insert this addition?
    (A) No, because the insertion breaks up an existing cause and effect relationship in the paragraph.
    (B) No, because the sentence brings up a topic that is completely different from information covered in the rest of the paragraph.
    (C) Yes, because the insertion provides information that is necessary to understand the relationship between public education and increased recycling practices.
    (D) Yes, because the sentence adds interesting information about human nature.

22. (F) NO CHANGE
    (G) There is now a large
    (H) There's now a super huge
    (J) Theirs is now a large

23. (A) NO CHANGE
    (B) in one area: the ability to collect and sort recyclables.
    (C) in one area. The ability to collect and sort recyclables.
    (D) in one area which is the ability to collect and sort recyclables.

24. (F) NO CHANGE
    (G) rigorously
    (H) mainly
    (J) virtually

25. (A) NO CHANGE
    (B) trash, recyclable or not,
    (C) trash recyclable or not,
    (D) trash, recyclable, or not,

Go on to next page

26. (F) NO CHANGE
    (G) to last week's TV
    (H) and last weeks TV
    (J) to last weeks' television

27. (A) NO CHANGE
    (B) unsightly and displeasing to the eye
    (C) unsightly
    (D) displeasingly unsightly

28. The most logical and coherent placement for Sentence 4 is:
    (F) where it is now.
    (G) before Sentence 1.
    (H) before Sentence 3.
    (J) at the beginning of the next paragraph.

29. (A) NO CHANGE
    (B) whose begun
    (C) they have begun
    (D) who have begun

30. Given that all of the following sentences are true, which one would most effectively conclude this passage?
    (F) As more people enroll in these recycle programs, the country will become much closer to achieving a greener and more sustainable future.
    (G) More public education would only help further America's sustainability goals.
    (H) If neighbors would stop complaining about recycle bins' being eyesores, the greater public would benefit as a result.
    (J) If more big businesses would step up their game, more small businesses would be likely to follow suit.

Passage 3

The Bill of Rights

The first amendment to the United States Constitution <u>provides that</u> "Congress shall make
31
no law respecting or prohibiting the free exercise thereof; or abridging the freedom of speech, or of the press, or the right of the people peaceably to assemble, and to petition the Government for a redress of grievances." <u>Constituting the Bill of Rights are ten amendments, nine others and this
32
one in the Constitution.</u> The Bill of <u>Rights does protect more than thirty liberties and rights.</u> The
33
Fourteenth Amendment made most of the Bill of Rights applicable to the <u>states, through a process
34
called incorporation.</u>

<u>Originating the Bill of Rights are</u> the English
35
Magna Carta of 1215, the English Bill of Rights of 1689, various other English precedents and acts, and the experience of people in England and America. <u>Once</u> the Bill of Rights was ratified by
36
three-fourths of the fourteen states, virtually all opposition to the U.S. Constitution quickly disappeared.

[1] <u>The effect of the Bill of Rights are deeply
37
embedded</u> in our daily lives. [2] For example, the Bill of Rights <u>by prohibiting</u> most attempts to
38
censor certain types of art or music. [3] It also protects <u>speech, which means</u> you can pretty
39
much say whatever you want about a government official in the editorial section of a

Go on to next page

newspaper or in a blog on the Internet. 40 [4] The Bill of Rights protects our often heated debates on <u>abortion, and school prayer, and the death</u>₄₁ <u>penalty.</u> [5] <u>And the speech you hear</u>₄₂ police officers give on TV shows when they tell someone who has been arrested that he has "the right to remain silent" is also a Bill of Rights issue. 43

[6] This practice is known as reading someone the Miranda rights. [7] The first amendment protection of the rights of extremist groups to peacefully assemble means that any group can stage a protest <u>as long as they are not violent.</u>₄₄ [8] By protecting the civil liberties of even extreme groups, the police and courts seek to preserve the right to freedom of expression for all Americans. 45

31. (A) NO CHANGE
 (B) that provides
 (C) that says
 (D) provides, that,

32. (F) NO CHANGE
 (G) Constituting the Bill of Rights are ten amendments: nine others and this one in the Constitution.
 (H) This amendment and nine others constitute the Bill of Rights, which is comprised of the first ten amendments to our Constitution.
 (J) Constituting the Bill of Rights are ten amendments; nine others and this one in the Constitution.

33. (A) NO CHANGE
 (B) Rights does protect more than thirty liberty's and rights
 (C) Rights protects more than thirty liberties and rights
 (D) Rights, which does protect more than thirty liberties and rights

34. (F) NO CHANGE
 (G) states through a process called incorporation.
 (H) states; through a process called incorporation.
 (J) states: through a process called incorporation.

35. (A) NO CHANGE
 (B) The Bill of Rights originate in
 (C) The Bill of Rights that originate from
 (D) The origins of the Bill of Rights include

36. All of the following would be an acceptable alternative to the underlined portion EXCEPT:
 (F) When
 (G) As soon as
 (H) While
 (J) After

37. (A) NO CHANGE
 (B) The affect of the Bill of Rights are deeply embedded
 (C) The effects of the Bill of Rights is embedded deep
 (D) The effects of the Bill of Rights are deeply embedded

38. (F) NO CHANGE
 (G) prohibits
 (H) prohibit
 (J) that prohibits

39. (A) NO CHANGE
 (B) speech, that means
 (C) speech that means
 (D) speech. Which means

Go on to next page

40. The author is considering deleting Sentence 3. Without this sentence, the paragraph would primarily lack:

    (F) an irrelevant point.

    (G) an example of how the Bill of Rights protects freedom of speech in the daily lives of Americans.

    (H) a thorough explanation of the concept of Freedom of Speech.

    (J) its main idea.

41. (A) NO CHANGE

    (B) abortion, school, prayer, and the death penalty.

    (C) abortion and school prayer, and the death penalty.

    (D) abortion, school prayer, and the death penalty.

42. (F) NO CHANGE

    (G) The speech you hear

    (H) Hearing the speech

    (J) But the speech you hear

43. The author is considering including in Sentence 5 the full text of the Miranda speech rather than the short quote provided. Should the author make this change?

    (A) No, because current television shows do not contain as many instances of police officers reading the Miranda rights as past television programs have.

    (B) No, because the paragraph provides practical examples of more than just one right.

    (C) Yes, because it is difficult to grasp the content of the Miranda rights speech from the short quote provided.

    (D) Yes, because the full text of the speech would provide readers with a better understanding of the pervasiveness of the Bill of Rights in daily life.

44. (F) NO CHANGE

    (G) provided that they are not violent.

    (H) as long as they are nonviolent.

    (J) as long as it is not violent.

45. Suppose the writer had intended to write an essay that thoroughly details the freedoms granted to Americans by the Bill of Rights. Would this essay successfully fulfill the writer's goal?

    (A) Yes, because the author offers real life examples that exemplify how the Bill of Rights apply to daily life.

    (B) Yes, because in explaining its origins, the author implies that the Bill of Rights gives Americans all of the freedoms provided for by various other English precedents and acts.

    (C) No, because the essay fails to include an explanation of the Right to Bear Arms.

    (D) No, because the author describes some freedoms in detail but doesn't deal with all components of the Bill of Rights.

Passage 4

Jackson's Relationship with the Cherokee

[1] Andrew Jackson President signed the
46
Indian Removal Act in 1830, which appropriated
47
$500,000 for the U.S. military to force the
48
Cherokee tribes to march from their homes in
Florida and southern Georgia to Oklahoma. 49

[2] In 1832, the Native Americans, who won a
50
victory supported by most Northern leaders in
the U.S. Supreme Court case of *Worchester v.*
Georgia. The decision held that Native American
nations were independent and not subject to
state regulation. [3] However, after the case deci-
51
sion, President Jackson, provoking, asserted that
52
Chief Justice John Marshall, the longest serving
53
Chief Justice in Supreme Court history, had made
his decision and "now let's see him enforce it."
54

Go on to next page

[4] Although Jackson professed to having what he called the kindest feelings, his actions and subsequent statements <u>belied</u> his words <u>toward the Cherokees</u>.
₅₅   ₅₆

In 1835, Jackson entered into treaty negotiations with the <u>Cherokee, that</u> ended up in the
₅₇
relinquishment of all of their land east of the Mississippi River. <u>Jackson gave the Cherokees
₅₈
until 1838 to leave the area.</u> Some left <u>voluntarily,
₅₉
but</u> most did not. Those who remained were forced by the U.S. military to walk the 1,200 mile "Trail of Tears" from Georgia to lands in Oklahoma, usually with only the clothes they were wearing. The brutal journey in 1838 to 1839 resulted in the deaths of about one-fourth of the Cherokee population from disease, starvation, exposure, and exhaustion. [60]

46.   (F) NO CHANGE
     (G) President Andrew Jackson
     (H) Andrew Jackson, President
     (J) Andrew Jackson, who was president,

47.   (A) NO CHANGE
     (B) that appropriated
     (C) which is appropriating
     (D) that is appropriating

48.   All of the following would be an acceptable alternative to the underlined portion EXCEPT:
     (F) coerce
     (G) command
     (H) help
     (J) compel

49.   The author is considering placing a period after 1830 in Sentence 1 and deleting the rest of the sentence. If the author did this, the paragraph would primarily lose:
     (A) detail about an act that is unrelated to the rest of the information in the passage.
     (B) descriptive detail that provides background information that is key to understanding the struggle set forth in the remainder of the passage.
     (C) irrelevant details that are repeated later in the paragraph.
     (D) information that contradicts the notion later in the passage that Jackson might not have had the best intentions of the Cherokees at heart.

50.   (F) NO CHANGE
     (G) the Native Americans, winners of
     (H) the winning Native Americans
     (J) the Native Americans won

51.   (A) NO CHANGE
     (B) Consequently,
     (C) Additionally,
     (D) Therefore,

52.   (F) NO CHANGE
     (G) Jackson provokingly
     (H) Jackson, provokingly
     (J) Jackson, provoking

53.   At this point, the author is considering eliminating this underlined portion. Should the author make this change?
     (A) Yes, because the information is irrelevant and detracts from the focus of the paragraph.
     (B) Yes, because the information would be more logically placed in the next paragraph.
     (C) No, because the phrase gives the reader background information on John Marshall necessary to an understanding of the significance of the decision.
     (D) No, because the information in the phrase provides an important fact in the history of the United States.

Go on to next page ⟹

54. Which of the following would be an appropriate way to rephrase the underlined portion?

(F) and now he had to live with it.

(G) and now would be singlehandedly responsible for its enforcement.

(H) and that Jackson would play a major role in its enforcement.

(J) but that enforcement would prove nearly impossible.

55. Which of the following would be a suitable substitution for the underlined word?

(A) backed up

(B) contradicted

(C) reiterated

(D) echoed

56. The best placement for the underlined portion would be:

(F) where it is now.

(G) after *the kindest feelings* (but before the comma).

(H) after the word *professed*

(J) after the word *belied*

57. (A) NO CHANGE

(B) Cherokee that

(C) Cherokee that,

(D) Cherokee, that,

58. The author is considering deleting the underlined sentence. If this is done, the passage would primarily lose:

(F) interesting but irrelevant detail about a specific date.

(G) information that is repeated elsewhere in the passage.

(H) a portion of the passage that reveals the true character of Andrew Jackson.

(J) a relevant point that adds to the progression of the timeline explained in the paragraph.

59. (A) NO CHANGE

(B) voluntarily: but

(C) voluntarily, however

(D) voluntarily,

60. Suppose the author's intent was to dispute the argument that Andrew Jackson was an enemy of the Cherokees. Would this passage fulfill the writer's goal?

(F) Yes, because the passage quotes Jackson's affirmation that he only has the "kindest feelings" toward the Cherokees.

(G) Yes, because the passage reveals that Jackson showed animosity toward Chief Justice John Marshall rather than the Cherokees.

(H) No, because the passage talks primarily about Jackson's relationship with Native Americans in general rather than his feelings toward the Cherokees specifically.

(J) No, because the passage focuses on the methods Jackson used to move the Cherokees out of Georgia.

Passage 5

The following paragraphs may or may not be in the most logical order. Each paragraph is numbered in brackets, and Question 74 asks you to choose the most logical placement for Paragraph 2.

Silent Films

[1]

Because it's hard to reveal character without conversation, silent film personalities are essentially one-dimensional. Bad guys are all bad and

61

good guys, all good. Supporting characters are often stereotypes included just to show the theme or add humor.

Go on to next page

[2]

What silent films lack in subtlety; they make
up for in exaggeration.⁶² Without assistance from
dialogue, other means are applied in silent films⁶³
to get their points across. One-dimensional characters, exaggerated movements, ceaseless
action, and expressive musical scores compensate for the lack of words.

[3]

Silent film characters can't tell the audience
what their⁶⁴ thinking, so they must show it.
Therefore, physical actions and gestures are
exaggerated and overacted⁶⁵ far beyond normal
movement. 66 Without the use of words, silent
film stars must talk with their bodies.

[4]

To maintain the attention of its audience, the
silent film is a frenzy of perpetual activity.
Scenes change by the second, and⁶⁷ the transitions between them are choppy. Silent films may
contain car chases, foot chases, jail breaks,
roller skating escapades, and there is lots of⁶⁸
dancing, all occurring in a matter of minutes.
When action cannot clarify the story, placards
expressing dialogue, thoughts, and the passage
of time fill the void.

[5]

Complementing this frenetic motion is an
expressively musical score.⁶⁹ Unlike modern film,
the musical score provides much more than
background accompaniment. 70 The music
plays as large a role in the silent film than does⁷¹
dialogue in the "talkies." Ominous chords signal⁷²
danger, fast-paced jingles heighten chase scenes,
and singing violins encourage romance. In the
absence of words, silent films employ creativity
and ingenuity⁷³ to tell their stories. 74 75

61. (A) NO CHANGE
    (B) Bad guys are all bad; good guys good.
    (C) Bad guys are all bad, good guys are all
        good.
    (D) Bad guys are all bad, which means
        good guys end up being all good.

62. (F) NO CHANGE
    (G) What silent films make up for in sub-
        tlety, they lack in exaggeration.
    (H) Silent films make up for what they lack
        in subtlety and exaggeration.
    (J) What silent films lack in subtlety, they
        make up for in exaggeration.

63. (A) NO CHANGE
    (B) dialogue assistance, other means were
        applied in silent films
    (C) dialogue assistance, silent films applied
        other means
    (D) assistance from dialogue, silent films
        apply other means

Go on to next page

64. (F) NO CHANGE
    (G) there
    (H) they're
    (J) they've been

65. (A) NO CHANGE
    (B) exaggerated
    (C) overacted and exaggerated
    (D) exaggeratedly overacted

66. At this point, the author is considering inserting this sentence:

    For example, a character could demonstrate puzzlement by aggressively scratching his head.

    Should the author make this insertion?

    (F) Yes, because the sentence provides the reader with an image to describe more specifically the point made in the previous sentence.
    (G) Yes, because the sentence gives the reader important insight into human behavior.
    (H) No, because the sentence contradicts information that the author states elsewhere in the passage.
    (J) No, because the sentence conveys a humorous tone that is inappropriate for the passage.

67. (A) NO CHANGE
    (B) and additionally
    (C) because
    (D) furthermore

68. (F) NO CHANGE
    (G) escapades, and many dance numbers
    (H) escapading, and there is lots of dancing
    (J) escapades, dancing from many actors

69. (A) NO CHANGE
    (B) expressively, musically score
    (C) expressive musical score
    (D) musically expressive score

70. At this point, the author wants to add another sentence that compares the role of the musical score in modern films and silent films. Which of the following sentences would best accomplish this goal?

    (F) While the musical score in modern day films is used to enhance viewers' emotional experiences, without music, the silent film audience has no way to identify with the characters other than through visual cues.
    (G) In modern day films, the use of dialogue often offers a clear-cut look into the characters' intents and emotions.
    (H) Silent films, if lacking a musical score, are at a bit of a loss in guiding the audience toward the feelings and emotions the filmmaker and the actors are trying to convey.
    (J) In modern day films, the musical score can help in not only using various chords to signal different emotions, but also through the lyrics in the music chosen for a given scene.

71. (A) NO CHANGE
    (B) the silent film as dialogue,
    (C) the silent film, more than dialogue
    (D) the silent film as dialogue

72. The author is considering deleting the underlined sentence. If the author were to make this deletion, the essay would primarily lose:

    (F) superfluous detail that detracts from the main idea of the paragraph.
    (G) examples of the various musical accompaniments that advance one's understanding of the critical role that musical scores play in modern films.
    (H) an understanding of the most frequent emotions silent filmmakers try to convey through musical scores.
    (J) examples of specific musical accompaniments and how they contribute to advancing the story in silent films.

Go on to next page ⇒

73. (A) NO CHANGE
    (B) and originality
    (C) and also inventiveness
    (D) OMIT the underlined portion.

74. The most logical and coherent position for Paragraph 2 is:
    (F) where it is now.
    (G) before Paragraph 1.
    (H) before Paragraph 4.
    (J) before Paragraph 5.

75. The writer wants to retitle this essay with a more descriptive and appropriate title. Which of the following would best replace the current title?
    (A) Musical Scores Play a Big Role in Silent Films
    (B) The Evolution of Film in the Twentieth Century
    (C) How Silent Films Tell Their Stories
    (D) Why Films Contain Car Chases

Mathematics Test

Time: 60 minutes for 60 questions

Directions: Each question has five answer choices. Choose the best answer for each question and shade the corresponding oval on your answer sheet.

1. Angela has half as much money as Holly, who has three-fourths as much as Dolores. If Angela has $60, how much money does Dolores have?

   (A) $120.00

   (B) $90.00

   (C) $150.00

   (D) $160.00

   (E) $360.00

2. If $y \neq 0$, what is the value of $\dfrac{3}{\left(\dfrac{4}{y}\right)}$?

   (F) $\dfrac{12}{y}$

   (G) $\dfrac{3y}{4}$

   (H) $\dfrac{4}{3y}$

   (J) $\dfrac{y}{12}$

   (K) $\dfrac{3}{4y}$

3. A sailboat has a sail that is 16 ft high. The base of the sail measures 12 feet. What is the measurement in feet from the bottom-left point of the sail's base to the top of the sail?

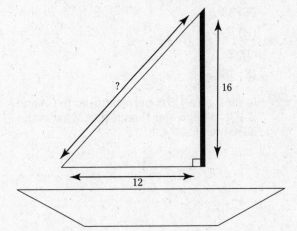

   (A) 18

   (B) 19

   (C) 20

   (D) $\sqrt{2}$

   (E) 28

4. A total of 11 students took an exam, and their average score was 84. If the average score for 6 of the students was 79, what was the average score of the remaining 5 students?

   (F) 88

   (G) 89

   (H) 90

   (J) 91

   (K) 92

Go on to next page ⟩

5. What is the value of x if $x + y = 6$ and $x - y = 4$?

   (A) 1

   (B) 5

   (C) 0

   (D) –1

   (E) –5

6. When adding the fractions $\frac{u}{2}$, $\frac{x}{4}$, $\frac{y}{16}$, and $\frac{z}{24}$, what would you find as the least common denominator?

   (F) 24

   (G) 32

   (H) 48

   (J) 96

   (K) 768

7. In the figure, $\overline{OB}$ is perpendicular to $\overline{OA}$ and $\angle AOC$ is 8° greater than $\angle AOB$. What is the measure of $\angle AOC$?

   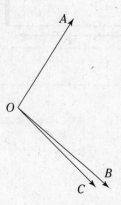

   (A) 82°

   (B) 90°

   (C) 98°

   (D) 172°

   (E) 188°

8. Consider all statements below to be true.

   All Dingbats are blue.

   Homer is a Dingbat.

   Prudence is blue.

   Which of the following statements has to be false?

   (F) Prudence is a Dingbat.

   (G) Homer is blue.

   (H) Prudence could be a Dingbat.

   (J) Prudence is not a Dingbat.

   (K) Homer is not blue.

9. To raise money for a local charity, Bonnie sets up a lemonade stand in her busy neighborhood. Her parents donated the cups, so Bonnie's only costs were her purchase of x pounds of lemons for p dollars per pound and s pounds of sugar at d dollars per pound. Which of the following expresses Bonnie's total cost, in dollars, of producing the lemonade for her sale?

   (A) $(x + s)(p + d)$

   (B) $x + p + s + d$

   (C) $xd + sp$

   (D) $sd + xp$

   (E) $(xp)(sd)$

10. Which of the following expressions is equal to $(x + y)^2$?

    (F) $2x + 2y$

    (G) $x^2 + y^2$

    (H) $x^2 + 2xy + y^2$

    (J) $x^2 - y^2$

    (K) $2xy$

11. If $x^2 = 144$ and $y^2 = 81$, which of the following could be a value for $x + y$?

    (A) –24

    (B) –21

    (C) –18

    (D) 2

    (E) 25

Go on to next page

12. Jan has a necklace on which she strings exactly 3 charms and only 3 charms in no particular order. One of these charms always contains a blue stone, one is always made of silver with no stones, and one is always made of gold with no stones. Jan owns 4 charms with blue stones, 5 charms made of silver with no stones, and 3 charms made of gold with no stones. How many different combinations of 3 charms can Jan string on her necklace?

    (F) 12

    (G) 23

    (H) 60

    (J) 120

    (K) 360

13. Which of these expressions is equal to $9ab(3a^3b^2 + 5ab)$?

    (A) $27a^4b^3 + 45a^2b^2$

    (B) $27a^4b^3 + 5ab$

    (C) $27a^3b^2 + 45ab$

    (D) $9ab(15a^4b^3)$

    (E) $135a^5b^4$

14. Evan has earned $230, $50, and $120 at his last 3 garage sales. He plans to hold one more garage sale next Saturday. If Evan wants to earn an average of exactly $160 on the 4 sales, his earnings for Saturday's garage sale must be:

    (F) $220

    (G) $230

    (H) $240

    (J) $250

    (K) $260

15. If $20^c = 4^3 \times 5^3$, the value of c is:

    (A) 3

    (B) 6

    (C) 9

    (D) 27

    (E) 60

16. At what point does $3x + 7y = 21$ intersect the x-axis?

    (F) $(0, 3)$

    (G) $(3, 0)$

    (H) $(8, 0)$

    (J) $(7, 0)$

    (K) $(0, 7)$

17. If $1 - \dfrac{2}{a} = 3 - \dfrac{4}{a}$, then $1 - \dfrac{2}{a} =$

    (A) -1

    (B) 0

    (C) 1

    (D) $\dfrac{2}{3}$

    (E) $\dfrac{3}{4}$

18. If $a^2 = -1$ and $\left[\left(a^2 \right)^5 \right]^x = 1$, what is the least positive integer value of x?

    (F) 0

    (G) 1

    (H) 2

    (J) 3

    (K) 4

19. If $\square ABCD$ in the figure is reflected across line l, the coordinates of the reflection of point D are:

    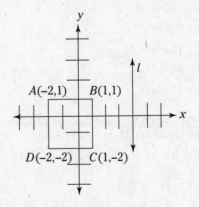

    (A) $(1, -2)$

    (B) $(3, -2)$

    (C) $(4, -2)$

    (D) $(7, -2)$

    (E) $(10, -2)$

Go on to next page

20. The population of Boomtown doubles every 50 years. The number of people in Boomtown this year is 10^3. What will the population of Boomtown be in 3 centuries?

    (F) $3(10^3)$

    (G) $6(10^3)$

    (H) $(10^6)(10^3)$

    (J) $(2^6)(10^3)$

    (K) $(10^3)^6$

21. If $(x-4)$ is a factor of $(x^2 - kx - 28)$, then the value of k is:

    (A) -11

    (B) -7

    (C) -3

    (D) 3

    (E) 7

22. What are all values for z for which $|z-3| < 4$?

    (F) $z < 7$

    (G) $z > 7$

    (H) $0 < z < 6$

    (J) $-1 < z < 7$

    (K) $-6 < z < 0$

23. Which of these expressions is equivalent to $\left(-3x^2 y^5\right)^3$?

    (A) $-27x^5 y^8$

    (B) $-27x^6 y^{15}$

    (C) $-9x^5 y^8$

    (D) $9x^5 y^8$

    (E) $27x^6 y^{15}$

24. What is the slope of the line provided by the equation $32x + 5y + 12 = 0$?

    (F) -32

    (G) $-\dfrac{32}{5}$

    (H) $-\dfrac{5}{32}$

    (J) $\dfrac{32}{5}$

    (K) 12

25. An old lighthouse on a remote part of the coast of Maine can provide a boat that is 4.5 miles away with a flash of light every 20 seconds. The light flashes every time it makes a full rotation. How many degrees does the light rotate in 2 seconds?

    (A) 8

    (B) 9

    (C) 18

    (D) 36

    (E) 81

26. In the figure, $\triangle ACE$ is equilateral and $\overline{FB}$ is parallel to $\overline{DC}$. Point G is the midpoint of $\overline{FB}$. If $\overline{AB}$ measures 4 units and $\overline{BC}$ measures 6 units, what is the measurement in units of the perimeter of the trapezoid formed by points F, B, C, and E?

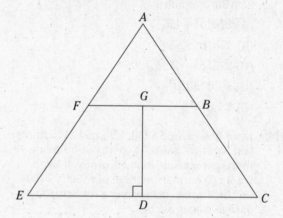

    (F) 18

    (G) 19

    (H) 24

    (J) 26

    (K) 28

27. If $x + 2x + 3x = y$, then $2x - y = ?$

    (A) $-8x$

    (B) $-6x$

    (C) $-4x$

    (D) $-3x$

    (E) $4x$

Go on to next page

28. Which of these is a value of x that satisfies $\log_x 27 = 3$?

    (F) 3

    (G) 9

    (H) 12

    (J) 21

    (K) 27

29. The Swift Express and Douglas Dependable are two trains that travel the same route in opposite directions on parallel tracks. The two trains started at the same time from opposite ends of the 900-mile route. They traveled toward each other at constant rates. The Swift Express completed the 900-mile journey in 3 hours; the Douglas Dependable finished the same trip in 5 hours. How many miles had the Swift Express traveled when it met the Douglas Dependable?

    (A) 300

    (B) 360

    (C) 544.5

    (D) 562.5

    (E) 600

30. In the coordinate plane, point O is the origin, point A has coordinates of $(2, -2)$, point B has coordinates of $(6, 0)$, and point C has coordinates of $(4, -6)$. Any two points can be connected to form a line segment. Which of the following is true about the line segments formed by connecting any two points?

    (F) $\overline{OA} = \overline{AB}$

    (G) $\overline{OC} = \overline{BC}$

    (H) $\overline{AC} = \overline{AB}$

    (J) $\overline{OA} = \overline{OB}$

    (K) $\overline{OB} = \overline{BC}$

31. In the figure, $\triangle MNO$ and $\triangle OPQ$ are similar. The length of $\overline{NM}$ is $\frac{5}{8}$ inch; the length of $\overline{PQ}$ is $\frac{5}{6}$ inch. Which of the following is the value of $\frac{b}{a}$?

    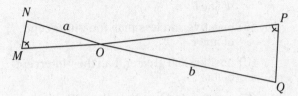

    (A) $\frac{1}{4}$

    (B) $\frac{1}{3}$

    (C) $\frac{3}{4}$

    (D) 1

    (E) $\frac{4}{3}$

32. In 2010, Esteban invested $1,000 in a 10-year certificate of deposit (CD) that pays him interest at an annual percentage rate (APR) of 2.5% compounded annually, which means that the interest he earns each year is added to the principal amount in advance of the next year. The informational brochure that Esteban received provided him with a standard formula he can use to determine the growth of his money: $NV = IV \times (1 + P)^Y$. He read that NV stands for the value of his money at the end of the term of his CD, IV stands for the value of his money at the beginning of the term of his CD, P stands for the percent his money increases, and Y is the number of years in the term of his CD. Rounded to the nearest dollar, what will his accumulated balance be in 2020 when the CD reaches maturity?

    (F) $1,025

    (G) $1,280

    (H) $1,290

    (J) $1,300

    (K) $9,313

Go on to next page

33. Line *l* has a negative slope and a positive *x*-intercept. Line *m* is parallel to line *l* and has a negative *x*-intercept. The *y*-intercept of line *m* must be:

    (A) negative and greater than the *y*-intercept of line *l*.

    (B) negative and less than the *y*-intercept of line *l*.

    (C) positive and greater than the *y*-intercept of line *l*.

    (D) positive and less than the *y*-intercept of line *l*.

    (E) zero.

34. The roots of a quadratic equation have a sum of 3 and a product of 2. Which of the following could be the equation?

    (F) $x^2 + 3x + 2$

    (G) $x^2 - 2x - 3$

    (H) $x^2 + 4x + 3$

    (J) $x^2 + 2x - 3$

    (K) $x^2 - 3x + 2$

35. For the number sequence 2, 6, 10, 14 . . . , which of the following represents the value of the *n*th term?

    (A) $2n$

    (B) $2n^2$

    (C) $n(n-1)$

    (D) $n(n+1)$

    (E) $2(2n-1)$

Use the information that follows to answer Questions 36 through 38.

C and O are the centers of the bases of the right circular cylinder in the figure. The height of the cylinder is 6 inches and $\overline{XY}$ is 4 inches.

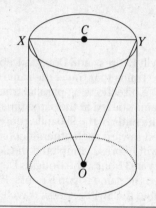

36. Which of these, in inches, is closest to the perimeter of $\triangle XYO$?

    (F) 6.32

    (G) 10.32

    (H) 17

    (J) 16.65

    (K) 20

37. Given that $\triangle XYO$ has no mass, which of these, in cubic inches, is nearest to the volume of the cylinder?

    (A) 38

    (B) 75

    (C) 224

    (D) 301

    (E) 1,000

Go on to next page

38. Which of the following must be true about the angles in the figure?

    (F) $\angle OXY = \angle XYO$

    (G) $\angle XYO < \angle XOY$

    (H) $\angle XOY = \angle OYX$

    (J) $\angle XOY > \angle OXY$

    (K) $\angle OXY < 45°$

39. Which of the following has the least value?

    (A) $\left(100 \times 10^5\right)^{10}$

    (B) 1,000,000,000,000,000

    (C) $1,000^{100}$

    (D) $\left(10 \times 10^{10}\right)^{10}$

    (E) $100^{1,000}$

40. The figure shows a square prism. Which of the given vertices is located in the plane determined by the vertices S, U, and X?

    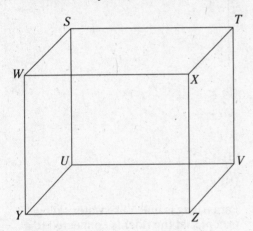

    (F) W

    (G) Z

    (H) Y

    (J) T

    (K) V

41. To create a more refreshing beverage, the snack stand at the beach mixes lemonade with iced tea. The proprietor has found that the best mixture results when the final product is 15 percent lemonade. How many liters of lemonade should the employees mix with 2 liters of iced tea to achieve the best mixture?

    (A) $\dfrac{3}{10}$

    (B) $\dfrac{17}{50}$

    (C) $\dfrac{6}{17}$

    (D) $\dfrac{13}{20}$

    (E) $\dfrac{13}{10}$

42. A line with equation $x = 6$ is graphed on the same xy-coordinate plane as a circle with a center point of (3, 5) and a radius of 4. What are the y-coordinates of the points where the line and the circle intersect?

    (F) 8 and 2

    (G) 7 and –1

    (H) 10 and 0

    (J) 7.65 and 2.35

    (K) 6.87 and –0.87

43. In an attempt to win a pizza baking contest, the employees of Guido's Italian Eatery prepared a crust that was 122 feet in diameter. They cut pepperoni slices from 1-foot pepperoni logs, and they placed the pepperoni slices on the crust so that there were exactly 10 slices per square foot of pizza crust. If they cut exactly 50 slices from each pepperoni log, how many pepperoni logs did they need to fill the pizza?

    (A) 77

    (B) 2,338

    (C) 4,842

    (D) 7,345

    (E) 9,352

Go on to next page

44. All the sides of the right triangle in the figure are measured in the same units of length. What is the value of $\frac{(\sin A)}{(\cos B)}$?

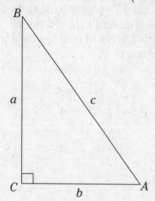

(F) $\frac{a}{c}$

(G) $\frac{c}{a}$

(H) $\frac{a^2}{c^2}$

(J) $\frac{ac}{b^2}$

(K) 1

45. Two positive integers r and s satisfy the relationship $r \dagger s$ only when $q = r^2 + 2$. If s, t, and u satisfy the relations $s \dagger t$ and $t \dagger u$, what is the value of s in terms of u?

(A) $u^2 + 2$

(B) $u^2 + 4$

(C) $u^4 + 4u^2 + 4$

(D) $u^4 + 4u^2 + 6$

(E) $u^4 + 8u^2 + 16$

46. Points D, E, and F lie on a circle. A line drawn from D to F passes through the center of the circle. Which of the following is true about the measurement of the angle formed by points D, E, and F?

(F) $\angle DEF = 90°$

(G) $0° < \angle DEF < 90°$

(H) $90° < \angle DEF < 180°$

(J) $\angle DEF = 180°$

(K) $180° < \angle DEF < 360°$

47. Given that $\begin{pmatrix} a & b \\ c & d \end{pmatrix}$ is that $cd(b^2 - a^2)$.

What is the value of $\begin{pmatrix} 4x & 2y \\ 7y & 3y \end{pmatrix}$ when $x = 4$ and $y = -2$?

(A) $-20,160$

(B) -168

(C) 0

(D) 168

(E) $20,160$

48. In the figure, $z(\sin\theta) = ?$

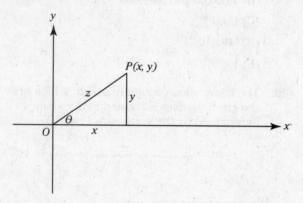

(F) x

(G) y

(H) z

(J) $\frac{y}{z}$

(K) $y + z$

49. Parasailing is much like water-skiing, except that the rider is connected to a parachute rather than water-skis and trails the boat in the air rather than directly behind it. If the rope attached to a parasailer is 50 meters long and the angle created by that rope and the surface of the water is 53°, which of the following is closest to the distance, in meters, from the parasailer to the surface of the water? (Assume that the rope is taut and the water surface is level.)

(A) $(\tan 53°)50$

(B) 50

(C) $(\sin 53°)50$

(D) $(\cos 53°)50$

(E) 53

Go on to next page

50. Which of the following expressions is equivalent to $2x\left(\dfrac{3}{y}+\dfrac{4}{z}\right)$?

    (F) $\dfrac{24x}{yz}$

    (G) $\dfrac{24x}{y+z}$

    (H) $\dfrac{14x}{y+z}$

    (J) $\dfrac{8xy+6xz}{yz}$

    (K) $\dfrac{14x}{yz}$

51. The average salary of the 14 employees of Simon's Crougar Industrial Smoothing, Inc., is \$51,000. When a new employee, George, is hired, the average salary increases to \$51,200. What is George's salary?

    (A) \$51,400

    (B) \$51,700

    (C) \$52,000

    (D) \$53,000

    (E) \$54,000

52. If $\sqrt{5p} = 3.67$, then what is the value of p?

    (F) 0.73

    (G) 1.64

    (H) 2.69

    (J) 8.21

    (K) 18.35

53. Recently, on a day when many Congress members were either ill or attending to matters in their home states, 410 members of the House of Representatives and 90 Senate members voted on a tax increase. A total of 350 members from the two government bodies voted "no" on the tax measure. If the same percentage of members gave a "no" vote in the House of Representatives as gave a "no" vote in the Senate, how many members of the House of Representatives voted "no" on the tax increase?

    (A) 63

    (B) 70

    (C) 206

    (D) 287

    (E) 349

54. The figure shows one cycle of the graph of the function $y = \sin x$ for $0 \le x \le 2\pi$. If the maximum value of the function occurs at point A, what are the coordinates of A?

    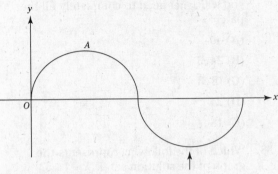

    Note: *Figure not to scale* $y = \sin x$

    (F) $\left(\dfrac{\pi}{4},1\right)$

    (G) $\left(\dfrac{\pi}{4},\pi\right)$

    (H) $\left(\dfrac{\pi}{2},0\right)$

    (J) $\left(\dfrac{\pi}{2},1\right)$

    (K) $\left(\dfrac{\pi}{2},\pi\right)$

55. The solution set for a quadratic equation is 4 and –3. The equation must be which of the following?

    (A) $x^2 - 12$

    (B) $x^2 + x + 12$

    (C) $x^2 + x - 12$

    (D) $x^2 - x + 12$

    (E) $x^2 - x - 12$

56. If a, b, and $c \ne 0$ and if $a^3b^5c^6 = \dfrac{a^2c^6}{3b^{-5}}$, what is the value of a?

    (F) $\dfrac{1}{3}$

    (G) $\dfrac{b^{10}}{3}$

    (H) $3b^{10}$

    (J) $\dfrac{c^{12}}{3}$

    (K) 3

Go on to next page

57. Janet is filling in a patch of lawn with sod. The patch is in the shape of a parallelogram. The length of the patch is 8 feet and its width is 6 feet. One of the interior angles measures 120°. How many square feet of sod will Janet need to completely fill the patch?

(A) 48

(B) $24\sqrt{3}$

(C) $18\sqrt{3}$

(D) 24

(E) 18

58. Which of the following represents the graph of the solution set of $|x| - 1 \leq 3$?

(F)

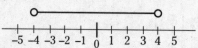

(G)

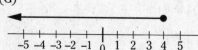

(H)

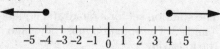

(J)

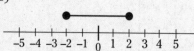

(K)

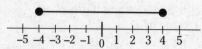

59. The figure shows a cube with a side length of 5 cm. If points W and Z are midpoints of the edges of the cube, what is the area in square centimeters of $\square WXYZ$?

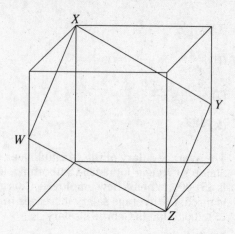

(A) 5.59

(B) 11.18

(C) 22.36

(D) 31.25

(E) 976.56

Go on to next page

60. In the figure, the area of the shaded region bound by the graph of the parabola $y = f(x)$ and the x-axis is 5. What is the area of the region bound by the graph of $y = f(x-3)$ and the x-axis?

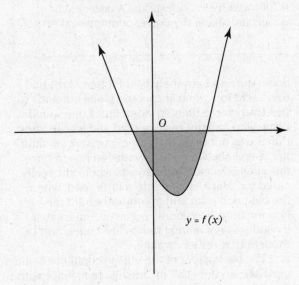

$y = f(x)$

(F) 2

(G) $\dfrac{5}{3}$

(H) 5

(J) 8

(K) 15

Reading Test

> **Time:** 35 minutes for 40 questions
>
> **Directions:** Each of the four passages in this section is followed by ten questions. Answer each question based on what is stated or implied in the passage and shade the corresponding oval on your answer sheet.

Passage 1 — Prose Fiction

This passage is adapted from *A Happy Boy* by Bjørnstjerne Bjørnson, who was a Norwegian poet, novelist, and dramatist.

Line   It was a cloudy evening, not cold; no stars were to be seen; the morrow might bring rain. A drowsy breeze blew over the snow, which was swept clear in patches on the white uplands,

(05) while in other places it had formed deep drifts. Along by the roadside where now snow happened to lie there was a margin of slippery ice; it lay blue-black between the snow and the bare ground, and could be seen glimmering here and

(10) there as far as the eye could reach. On the mountainsides there had been snow-slips; their tracks were black and bare, while on each side of them the snow lay smooth and white, except where the birch-trees clustered together in dark

(15) patches. There was no water to be seen, but half-naked moors and bogs stretched up to river and lowering mountains.

    The farms lay in large clusters in the midst of the level ground; in the dusk of the winter eve-

(20) ning they looked like black masses from which light shot forth over the fields, now from one window, now from another; to judge by the lights there was a great deal going on inside. Young people, grown-up and half-grown up, flocked

(25) together from various quarters. Very few kept to the road; almost all, at any rate, left it when they drew near the farms, and slipped away, one behind the cowhouse, a pair under the storehouse and so forth; while some rushed away

(30) behind the barn and howled like foxes, others answered farther off like cats. One stood behind the wash-house and barked like an old angry dog. The girls came marching along in large bands; they had a few boys, mostly little boys,

(35) with them, who skirmished around them to show off. When one of the gangs of girls came near the house and one or other of the big boys caught sight of them, the girls scattered and fled into the passages or down the garden, and had to be

(40) dragged out and into the rooms one by one.

Some were so extremely bashful that Marit had to be sent for, when she would come out and positively force them in. Sometimes one would come who had not been invited and whose intention it was not to go in, but only to look on, until (45) in the end she would be persuaded just to have one single dance. Those guests whom she really cared for, Marit invited into a little room where the old people sat and grandmother did the honors; they were kindly received and treated. (50) Eyvind was not among the favored ones, and he thought that rather strange.

    The best player of the village could not come until late, so they had meanwhile to manage with the old one, a cottager called Grey Knut. He (55) knew four dances, two spring dances, a halling and an old so-called Napoleon waltz. He struck up, and the dancing began. Eyvind did not dare to join in at first, for there were too many grown-up people; but the half-grown ones soon banded (60) together, pushed each other forward, drank a little strong ale to hearten them, and then Eyvind also joined in. The room grew very hot, the fun and the ale mounted to their heads.

    Marit danced more than anyone else that (65) evening, probably because the party was in her grandparents' house, and so it happened that Eyvind caught her eye, but she always danced with someone else. He wanted to dance with her himself, so he sat out one dance in order to run (70) to her directly when it ended, and this he did; but a tall, swarthy fellow with bushy hair pushed in front of him.

    "Get away, youngster," he cried and gave Eyvind a shove, so that he nearly fell backwards (75) over Marit. Never had such a thing happened to him, never had anyone been other than kind to him, never had he been called "youngster" when wanted to join in anything. He reddened to the roots of his hair, but said nothing, and drew back (80) to where the new musician, just arrived, had taken his seat and was tuning up. Eyvind looked at Marit dancing with the bushy-haired man, she laughed over the man's shoulder so that her white teeth showed, and Eyvind, for the first (85)

Go on to next page

time in his life, was aware of a strange, tingling pain in his breast.

He looked at her again and again, and the more he looked the clearer it seemed to him that (90) Marit was quite grown-up.

1. The passage is most likely part of a:

   (A) fable.

   (B) romance novel.

   (C) coming-of-age tale.

   (D) tragic poem.

2. The character of Marit can best be described as:

   (F) gregarious and influential.

   (G) extremely bashful.

   (H) cold and callous.

   (J) kind and grandmotherly.

3. When the author states in Lines 86–87 that Eyvind experienced a "strange, tingling pain in his breast," he is inferring that Eyvind:

   (A) had drunk too much ale.

   (B) was feeling embarrassed that he had been called "youngster."

   (C) was physically injured by the tall, swarthy fellow's shove.

   (D) was experiencing his first feelings of disappointment.

4. The author suggests that Eyvind is a rather timid individual in all of the following instances EXCEPT:

   (F) when he fails to join in the dancing at first because all of the dancers were older than he.

   (G) when he said nothing in response to the bushy-haired man.

   (H) when he continued to watch Marit dance with the bushy-haired man.

   (J) when he failed to respond to the grandmother's invitation to enter the little room.

5. The author most likely provides the description in the first paragraph to:

   (A) place the events of the house in perspective within the larger realm of the natural world.

   (B) demonstrate how the party attendees braved harsh, cruel conditions in order to reach their destination.

   (C) provide a glimpse into typical Scandinavian life.

   (D) highlight the frigid and potentially dangerous conditions the characters faced every day.

6. The best way to describe Marit's feelings for Eyvind is that she:

   (F) pitied him.

   (G) was secretly in love with him.

   (H) felt repulsed by him.

   (J) was indifferent toward him.

7. The author mentions the little room where the old people sat (Lines 47–50) in order to:

   (A) describe the room where Marit took the timid girls to persuade them to dance just one dance.

   (B) show that Marit cared more for old people than for people her age.

   (C) offer a glimpse of the true nature of the relationship between Marit and Eyvind.

   (D) provide insight into the character of the grandmother.

8. As it is used in Line 34 *bands* most likely refers to:

   (F) gangs of ruffians.

   (G) groupings of young girls.

   (H) members of a parade organized to celebrate a village holiday.

   (J) groups of musicians headed to play at the dance.

Go on to next page

9. It can be reasonably inferred from the passage that Eyvind's attendance at the dance:

   (A) consisted primarily of sitting and watching Marit dance with others.

   (B) resulted in the realization that his life was changing.

   (C) was spent sitting with the grandmother and having conversations with older people.

   (D) ended with his sulking in the corner because the admonishment from the swarthy fellow was the first time he had ever experienced rejection.

10. It is reasonable to conclude that the people who live in Eyvind's village:

    (F) experience cloud cover and cold almost every day because they live very far north.

    (G) engage in activities that involve participation by a variety of age groups.

    (H) are generally fearful of traveling on the designated roads and prefer to move through the countryside by running from farmhouse to farmhouse.

    (J) prefer to dance to music performed by young musicians.

Passage 2 — Social Science

This passage is adapted from *The Rise and Fall of the U.S. Mortgage and Credit Markets: A Comprehensive Analysis of the Market Meltdown* by James R. Barth (Wiley).

Line
The economy is engaged in a massive wave of deleveraging, a scramble to reduce debt and sell assets as well as an attempt to obtain new capital from any willing source, including the
(05) government. Unfortunately, this process has caused a major credit crunch and sent asset prices further downward. Even solid companies with no connection to the real estate and finance sectors have been affected as credit markets
(10) seized up. In the process, a rush to liquidity has created severe difficulties for individuals, small businesses, large corporations, and even state and local governments as they try to obtain short-term funding simply to meet payrolls and
(15) cover ongoing operating expenses.

In many cases, the government has now become the buyer of last, if not first, resort, intervening in the market in ways not seen since the New Deal. To contain the damage, the gov-
(20) ernment invoked some existing but seldom-used powers and created others out of whole cloth. As the financial sector continued to lurch from crisis to crisis in 2008, the government's response has been marked by an improvisational
(25) quality that has failed to restore confidence in the financial system.

The government has attempted to shore up mortgages directly. In July 2008, the Housing and Economic Recovery Act authorized the Federal
(30) Housing Authority to guarantee up to $300 billion in new 30-year fixed-rate mortgages for subprime borrowers. But the guarantees were conditional on lenders voluntarily writing down principal loan balances to 90 percent of current
(35) appraisal value; there are indications that the program has not met with much initial success as of this writing. The Act also provided temporary authority to the Treasury Secretary to purchase any obligations and other securities in any
(40) amounts issued by Fannie Mae and Freddie Mac, the two big government-sponsored enterprises that hold and guarantee most of the nation's mortgages. But by September both institutions had deteriorated sufficiently that they were
(45) placed into conservatorship, or effectively nationalized, to ensure that they would remain solvent. At the same time, the Treasury announced a temporary program to purchase Fannie Mae and Freddie Mac mortgage-backed
(50) securities to help make more mortgage financing available to home buyers.

When all of these government interventions failed to stem the growing crisis, even bolder action was undertaken in October. Congress
(55) passed the Emergency Economic Stabilization Act, granting the Treasury unprecedented powers to use up to $700 billion to stabilize the financial sector. The bailout plan also raised the limit on bank deposits secured by the Federal Deposit
(60) Insurance Corporation (FDIC) from $100,000 to $250,000 per depositor, attempting to reassure depositors that their cash was safe in the banking system. Furthermore, the government announced it was insuring individual investors against losses
(65) in money market mutual funds, instruments that had for decades been regarded as safe havens before one such fund "broke the buck." The SEC also temporarily barred investors from taking any short positions in selected companies, in an effort
(70) to stop the bleeding in the stock market. By late November, the Treasury had injected $179 billion in capital into 30 financial institutions. The FDIC had also extended unlimited insurance coverage to all noninterest-bearing transaction accounts.

Go on to next page ⟶

(75) The Fed, in addition to several other new and historic programs, in the same month took steps to force down home mortgage rates by agreeing to buy up to $600 billion of housing-related securities issued and guaranteed by Fannie Mae,

(80) Freddie Mac, Ginnie Mae, and Federal Home Loan Banks as well as creating a $200 billion program to lend money against securities backed by car loans, student loans, credit card debt, and small-business loans.

(85)   The sheer size of the bailout, with $7.5 trillion or more committed as of late November, provoked a storm of controversy. Many critics have cried foul about the government's lack of transparency; others fume that by rescuing firms

(90) and individuals that took on too much leverage, the government has created thorny new problems of moral hazard (the concept that shielding parties from the full consequences of their risk taking actually encourages them to take even

(95) greater risks in the future). Still others complained that insufficient effort and funds have thus far been devoted to halting the rising tide of home foreclosures. It is ironic to note that the United States has essentially been nationalizing

(100) its financial institutions while China has embarked on privatizing many of its own.

    The government has taken on additional debt in an attempt to shore up the financial system, which only worsens the nation's already stagger-

(105) ing deficit. Future administrations will be grappling with the ramifications of those decisions for years to come. In a very real sense, the bill for this bubble has now been handed to taxpayers.

11. According to the author, all of the following are arguments expressed by critics of the bailout EXCEPT that:

(A) the government has dedicated an inadequate amount of funds to preventing the rapid increase in foreclosures.

(B) the size of the bailout is not enough to promote real change.

(C) the government has provided insufficient disclosure.

(D) the government's practices actually promote financial entities to take on future risk rather than avoid it.

12. As it is used in Line 53, *stem* most likely means to:

(F) originate.

(G) grow slowly.

(H) remove.

(J) stop.

13. One result of the passage of the Emergency Economic Stabilization Act was that:

(A) about $700 billion was used to firm up the financial sector.

(B) a freeze was placed on all foreclosure sales.

(C) the public's confidence in the financial sector was restored.

(D) the government perpetuated an immoral standard.

14. The primary purpose of the first paragraph (Lines 1–15) is to:

(F) reveal the author's anti-government perspective.

(G) summarize how foreclosures played a part in the economic downturn.

(H) present an overview of what the government has chosen to do to combat a growing financial crisis.

(J) describe the pervasiveness of current financial problems and how they have affected individuals and organizations.

15. It is reasonable to infer that the author would agree with which of the following statements about Americans' lack of confidence in the financial sector?

(A) The lack of confidence resulted from a lack of attention to borrowers of government funds.

(B) Americans' confidence was completely restored when the bailout plan raised the limit on bank deposits secured by the Federal Deposit Insurance Corporation from $100,000 to $250,000 per depositor.

(C) The government's seemingly unplanned response to the economic crisis and a series of additional crises continues to erode the public's confidence in its leaders.

(D) The utter size of the financial bailout has created a sense of stability in the United States economy.

Go on to next page

16. One of the steps that the Fed took to stabilize the economy was to:

    (F) limit the power of Fannie Mae, Freddie Mac, and Ginnie Mae.

    (G) temporarily prevent investors from making short sales.

    (H) lower the interest rates that individuals paid for home loans.

    (J) guarantee up to $300 billion in new 30-year fixed-rate mortgages for sub-prime borrowers.

17. Which of the following best summarizes the author's depiction of the Housing and Economic Recovery Act?

    (A) The Act has produced a somewhat positive effect on the economy because it has encouraged lenders to reduce the principal balances of the mortgages of 90 percent of their customers.

    (B) The Act's attempt to stabilize the mortgage market by backing new mortgages of a specific type for particular borrowers has had questionable success because of conditions it places on lenders.

    (C) If it is completely successful, subprime borrowers will be relieved of up to 40 percent of all of their remaining home loan debt.

    (D) The conditions of the Act caused the severe deterioration of the two big government-sponsored enterprises that hold and guarantee most of the nation's mortgages.

18. The author would likely agree with which of the following statements about the state of the U.S. economy at the time of his writing?

    (F) The economy is unlikely to deteriorate further.

    (G) The economy remains in a state of crisis likely to affect taxpayers and future generations for years to come.

    (H) The government has found effective solutions to combat the financial crisis and now just needs to implement these ideas.

    (J) Confidence in the government is growing as corporations and individuals start getting back on their feet.

19. As it is used in Lines 45–46, the phrase "effectively nationalized" is most synonymous with:

    (A) sufficiently deteriorated.

    (B) spread across the country.

    (C) guaranteed unprecedented powers.

    (D) placed under government control.

20. According to the author, all of the following are components of deleveraging the economy EXCEPT:

    (F) offering lower mortgage rates to new homebuyers.

    (G) reducing debt.

    (H) selling assets.

    (J) attempting to gain new capital from any willing source.

Passage 3 — Humanities

This passage is adapted from *A Guide to Early Printed Books and Manuscripts* by Mark Bland (Wiley).

When we look at books as books, we are conscious of more than simply shape, colour, and weight. Imagine, for instance, that on the table is a copy of an early eighteenth-century poem, printed in folio and set in large type with obvious spaces (05) between the lines. If a literary person was asked "What is the most obvious thing about what you are looking at?" their first reply might be something like "It is a poem." To the extent that a poem involves the layout of type on a page in a way that (10) distinguishes it from prose, the answer would have some cunning, but to distinguish the text as 'a poem' is to invite a literary reading of the words as *words*. The most obvious thing about the page (before anything had been 'read') is, in fact, the (15) size of the type and the space between the lines, and that is the step that is often overlooked: large type and extra space meant more paper was used, more paper meant more expense, and someone had to pay the bill — quite possibly not the (20) printer, or publisher. The difference between looking at a page and seeing "a poem," or seeing a relationship between type, paper, and space is the difference between "being literary," and thinking like a bibliographer. The physical aspects of a (25) text are always determined by the economics of book production ('Who paid for this?' is a useful question, if one not always possible to answer), as well as the materials and methods combined to create the document. (30)

Go on to next page ⟶

There is a second point to the example as well, and it has to do with the relationship between form and meaning. To recognize that the text is "a poem" is to recognize something about (35) its form, its conventions, and its readership. In the first instance, the text does not matter. If, to make the point clear, we were to discover that the text was, in fact, a prayer, we would want to know why the conventions of one textual form had been (40) applied to another; and we would want to know who made that decision, why, and whether the text was, in some way, verse. What the text actually said would still be of secondary importance, and would only come into play once we had (45) understood the way in which the formal criteria had been reapplied. Over time, this is how the conventions of textual design evolve: slight adjustments are made to the formal aspects of presentation that cumulatively affect the appearance of the (50) page in quite radical ways. Furthermore, texts get presented in new ways to reflect the changing history of their use: an early edition of Shakespeare was printed according to the conventions of seventeenth-century casual reading; a modern edi-(55) tion is usually designed for the classroom with its accompanying introduction, illustrations, notes, and list of textual variants.

One of the most obvious ways to trace the evolution of a text is to study its typography, or (60) its manuscript equivalent, script. The history of letterforms, and the way in which they are laid out on a page, reflect social conventions as well as individual choice. This is why it is possible, simply by looking at a document, to estimate (65) when it was made to within a period of five or ten years. Bindings similarly reveal periods and tastes, as do the apparently incidental features of format, ornament stocks, and the use of ruled borders. Each of these elements has required a (70) conscious decision by someone at some time, and for this reason it is as necessary to see the text as to read it. Indeed, sometimes it helps not to read the text at all — certainly it helps to read the text only after these other aspects of the (75) book have been taken into consideration.

Bibliography is a historical and analytical discipline concerned with literature in the broadest meaning of that word. Hence, it is an appreciation of literary texts and historical facts that (80) usually shapes a desire to recover more accurately the history of a text through the processes of its making and the ways in which it was read. The point, however, is that in order to understand printed books and manuscripts, the (85) approach to literary documents cannot be limited to 'high' literature.

21. The primary purpose of the passage is best explained as an attempt to:

(A) discredit other authors who define early literary works only by observing their form.

(B) illustrate that the best way to trace the evolution of a text is to examine its typography.

(C) argue that a study of the physical aspects of books is more important to an analysis of early literature than reading its content and observing its form.

(D) show that an analysis of historical literature involves paying attention to more factors than merely what the works actually say.

22. As it is used in Line 12, *cunning* is best defined as:

(F) slyness.

(G) wisdom.

(H) folly.

(J) danger.

23. The author describes all of the following as means of estimating a book's age EXCEPT:

(A) examining its binding.

(B) paying attention to the way it observes social conventions in its ornamentation.

(C) observing whether it is written in the form of a poem, prayer, or other literary type.

(D) looking at the way the letters and words are formed.

Go on to next page

24. The author would argue that the primary difference between the quality of "being literary" and that of "thinking like a bibliographer" is:

    (F) one requires an appreciation for literary texts and historical facts, and the other ignores altogether the texts and their place in history.

    (G) one considers the financial components of book making, and the other does not.

    (H) one looks at the written page and sees a poem, and the other looks at a page and sees the relationship between type, paper, and space.

    (J) one recognizes the relationship between form and meaning, and the other considers only the financial aspects of creating a literary work.

25. Which of the following statements about tracking the development of a text is supported by the passage?

    (A) It is possible to determine the approximate age of a text just by looking at the way its letters are formed.

    (B) Often, the most obvious way to establish a book's age is by examining how its story line reveals social conventions.

    (C) It is possible to estimate the age of a text within a period of five to ten years by observing the kind of paper the bookbinder used.

    (D) The best way to determine the age of a book is by reading the text for content and meaning.

26. *Bibliography,* as it is used in Line 76, most likely refers to:

    (F) a list of books and articles that appears at the end of a publication that references the resources the writer used to develop a thesis on a particular subject.

    (G) a list of publications that the author of this passage used to understand printed books and manuscripts.

    (H) the study of the way texts were created and read in an attempt to comprehend their historical context.

    (J) the ornamental script that early publications used to adorn the text.

27. The author would argue that the style of letterforms in a given document reflects the:

    (A) standard practices of the time when the document was written.

    (B) socioeconomic status of the document's creator.

    (C) exact age of the document.

    (D) document's literary genre.

28. The mention of "'high' literature" in the final paragraph (Line 86) most likely refers to:

    (F) works that can be categorized as having deep meaning.

    (G) works that were costly to produce.

    (H) poems or prayers.

    (J) works that were produced by royalty or high-ranking government leaders.

29. In Lines 54–57, the passage cites that a common component of literature designed for modern classrooms is:

    (A) an accompanying test bank to assess students' learning.

    (B) the use of computerized technology to produce brilliantly colored illustrations.

    (C) a record of variations of the text.

    (D) an extensive biography of the author.

30. Which of the following would the author say best describes the way that the conventions of textual design evolve over time?

    (F) Printers and publishers find more cost-effective strategies of reproduction that result in ever-changing font style and line spacing options.

    (G) Bibliographers' appreciation of literary texts and historical facts produces a system that helps to record more accurately the history of a text's popularity.

    (H) Creators make small alterations to texts' appearances that eventually result in noticeably different page presentations.

    (J) As printers and publishers become more aware of what components are aesthetically pleasing to readers of a given type of text, they develop new ways to format text.

Go on to next page

Passage 4 — Natural Science

Line   When people hear the word "prehistoric,"
they think of animals, especially dinosaurs. But
there were prehistoric plants as well, and they
were just as unusual to modern sensibilities as
(05) the animals of those ancient times. Evidence of
early plant life comes from fossils. Fossils may
have resulted from leaves and stems that fell into
a lake and stuck in the mud at its bottom. The
plants avoided decay because they were buried
(10) quickly in the sediment and were not exposed to
oxygen. As the mud turned into rock the carbon
films and impressions of the plant parts were preserved. Pieces of wood, sometimes whole trees,
became fossilized when water filled all their
(15) pores with silica, which is a hard mineral like
quartz. Eventually the wood turned into stone,
through a process called petrification.

    This fossil record shows scientists how
plants have evolved over time. During the
(20) Jurassic Period the dominant plants were cycads,
gingkoes, conifers and ferns. There is no evidence
of flowering plants until the next period, known as
the Cretaceous Period. One of the oldest known
flowers has been discovered in rocks that are
(25) over 115 million years old.

    Among the most interesting of prehistoric
plants are the cycads, which flourished 65 million to 240 million years ago. Cycads are sometimes called "living fossils" because they reached
(30) their peak around 200 million years ago. Cycads
are a member of the order Cycadales, which contains the most primitive seed-bearing plants.
Cycads are not conifers, but they are related to
conifers because cycads are also cone bearing.

(35)   The plants are extant today, in areas as
widely scattered as South America, Africa,
Australia and Malaysia. Although they primarily
live in the wet tropical or semi-tropical habitats,
some species can not only survive but thrive in
(40) arid regions as well. Scientists long considered
the widespread distribution of the cycad a mystery, as the seeds were too large to be carried by
wind or ocean currents or birds. One popular
theory connects the migration of cycads to the
(45) theory of Continental Drift. Briefly, Continental
Drift hypothesizes that at one point millions of
years ago, there existed just one continent, a
supercontinent named Pangaea. Over the years,
the continents separated, drifting apart and
(50) taking their flora and fauna with them. Thus,
the plants that otherwise would be not as widely
dispersed are found in far-flung areas.

    If these plants provided sustenance to the
gargantuan animals of that time (several times as
large as any animals alive today), the plants   (55)
must have been huge as well. Today's cycads
have trunks that can grow up to 50 feet tall. But
it is the cones that are perhaps the most impressive. There are two different types of cones,
pollen cones (which grow on the male plants)   (60)
and seed cones (which grow on the female
plants), and these can be as long as 36 inches
and weigh up to nearly 100 pounds. One variety
of seed pods produces bright red seeds. These
seeds are ground into flour and used as food-   (65)
stuffs by people in Africa. Some Japanese cooks
mix brown rice with the powdered seeds of some
cycads and ferment the mixture into a miso. In
America, the Seminole Indians of Florida used
the pith of cycads to make bread. Unfortunately,   (70)
some ground cycad seeds have been found to be
carcinogenic (cancer-causing) if not properly
prepared.

    There are also leaves on the cycad plant,
which grow into a sort of crown and thus make   (75)
many people who merely glance at a cycad think
it is a palm tree. The trunks may occasionally
grow underground, leaving an impression that
the leaves are growing directly out of the
ground. In fact, many parts of the cycads are   (80)
underground. Inside the roots of the cycad are
blue-green algae. The conversion of atmospheric
nitrogen into ammonia is one way the cyanobacteria supply the cycad with inorganic nitrogen. It
is fascinating to note that even though the cya-   (85)
nobacteria are in the dark underground, they
have the same membrane structure and pig-
ments of other bacteria that thrive in the sunlight. Why does this strange structure remain?
One theory is that evolution has not yet had suf-   (90)
ficient time to change the portions that at one
point had been essential to the plant's survival.

    Despite its longevity, the cycad, according to
the World Conservation Union's Cycad Specialist
Group, is one of the most threatened groups of   (95)
plants in the world. Of the more than 320 species
in existence, over half are threatened or endangered. Groups like the Cycad Society devote
themselves to funding education and scientific
research efforts to promote cycad conservation   (100)
and ensure this prehistoric plant's survival for
another 200 million years.

Go on to next page

31. The main purpose of the passage is to:

 (A) discuss similarities between prehistoric animals and prehistoric plants.

 (B) refute the theory that cycads were spread via birds.

 (C) contrast and compare prehistoric and current plant life.

 (D) provide an overview of cycads.

32. In Line 35, the word *extant* most nearly means:

 (F) extinct.

 (G) prehistoric.

 (H) narrowly distributed.

 (J) still existing.

33. The passage mentions that scientists have had difficulty coming up with a definitive explanation for:

 (A) why the cycad is found in so many different locations.

 (B) what caused the continents to drift apart.

 (C) why prehistoric plants were so much larger than current plants.

 (D) why the supercontinent separated in the first place.

34. Which of the following is true about the fossil record of early plant life?

 (F) It provides less information about plants than the fossil record of animals provides about animals.

 (G) It provides an explanation of how earlier plant life has developed into modern flora.

 (H) It shows evidence of flowering plants in all known prehistoric periods.

 (J) It was created by decayed plants that had never been exposed to oxygen.

35. The author's purpose in mentioning Pangaea is to:

 (A) provide a possible reason for why the cycad is extinct today.

 (B) prove the cycad was once the largest plant on earth.

 (C) suggest one cause for the cycad's widespread distribution.

 (D) refute the theory that the continents were once connected.

36. The passage suggests that the Jurassic Period:

 (F) contained only non-flowering plants.

 (G) was the period in which cycads, gingkoes, conifers, and ferns became extinct.

 (H) occurred about 115 million years ago.

 (J) existed immediately after the Cretaceous Period.

37. The author includes mention of all of the following EXCEPT:

 (A) a difference between seed cones and pollen cones.

 (B) some medicinal properties of cycad seeds.

 (C) a danger involved in using the seeds of the cycad.

 (D) what kinds of cycad seeds are used in cooking.

38. The author claims that people confuse a cycad with a palm tree because:

 (F) they produce similar types of seeds.

 (G) the cycad grows in the same tropical regions as does the palm tree.

 (H) the cycad's leaves may resemble the fronds of a palm tree.

 (J) both plants are approximately the same size.

Go on to next page

39. According to the passage, one function of cyanobacteria is to:

    (A) allow the cycad to live underground.

    (B) supply the cycad with inorganic nitrogen.

    (C) help the cycad reproduce.

    (D) enable the cycad to live long periods without water.

40. The primary purpose of the last paragraph (Lines 93–102) is most likely to:

    (F) describe a potential reality and mention what steps are being taken to prevent it.

    (G) reveal that most species of cycad plants will become extinct within 200 million years.

    (H) promote the efforts that the World Conservation Union has made in cycad conservation.

    (J) explain what scientific research has revealed about how to best ensure the longevity of cycad species.

STOP DO NOT TURN THE PAGE UNTIL TOLD TO DO SO.
DO NOT RETURN TO A PREVIOUS TEST.

Science Test

Time: 35 minutes for 40 questions

Directions: Following are seven passages and then questions that refer to each passage. Choose the best answer and shade in the corresponding oval on your answer sheet.

Passage 1

Buoyancy is a force that acts in the upward direction on objects which are fully or partially submerged in a fluid. The two laws of buoyancy, which were discovered by Archimedes in the third century B.C., are as follows:

1. For fully submerged objects, the upward buoyant force is equal to the weight of the fluid displaced.

2. For floating objects, the weight of the object is equal to the weight of the fluid displaced.

In general, denser objects are less buoyant, and denser fluids provide more buoyancy to objects submerged in them. A more buoyant object will be able to float and carry more weight before it sinks, while a less buoyant object will sink with less weight applied. The shape of the object also has an effect on buoyancy, particularly for floating objects.

A student performed two studies to investigate how material and fluid type affect buoyancy. In each study, miniature boats were constructed with identical size and dimensions. The masses of the boats were not identical because of the varying material densities. The boats were placed in fluid, and 1 kilogram weights were incrementally placed inside of the boats until the boats no longer floated.

Study 1

In the first study, three different boats with the exact same size and dimensions were constructed from wood, aluminum, and concrete. Each of the boats was placed in pure water, and weights were placed in the center of the boats until the boats sunk. The results are shown in Table 1, indicating the maximum weight that each boat was able to hold before sinking.

Table 1	
Boat Material	**Maximum Weight Supported before Sinking (kg)**
Wood	13
Aluminum	7
Concrete	8

Study 2

In the second study, a single boat made of wood was placed in three different liquids, and weights were placed in the center of the boat until it no longer floated. The three fluids tested were oil, pure water, and sea water. The results are shown in Table 2, indicating the maximum weight the boat was able to hold before sinking in each fluid.

Table 2	
Fluid Used	**Maximum Weight Supported before Sinking (kg)**
Oil	11
Pure water	13
Sea water	14

Go on to next page

1. Which of the following material and fluid combinations was used in both of the two studies?

    (A) concrete and pure water

    (B) wood and oil

    (C) wood and pure water

    (D) aluminum and sea water

2. If a trial had been conducted using an aluminum boat with oil as the fluid, what would have been the maximum weight supported before sinking?

    (F) 7 kg

    (G) greater than 7 kg

    (H) less than 7 kg

    (J) The data from the two studies does not provide enough information to predict the results of that combination.

3. Which of the following conclusions is not supported by the data?

    (A) Pure water provides more buoyancy to floating objects than sea water.

    (B) Oil provides less buoyancy to floating objects than pure water.

    (C) A boat made of concrete is less buoyant than one of the same size made of wood.

    (D) A boat made of wood is more buoyant than one of the same size made of aluminum.

4. Based on the data in Tables 1 and 2, which of the following appears to have the greatest effect on buoyancy?

    (F) boat material

    (G) boat size

    (H) fluid

    (J) The data does not provide enough information to make a conclusion.

5. According to Table 1, which of the following are likely to have similar densities?

    (A) wood and aluminum

    (B) aluminum and concrete

    (C) concrete and wood

    (D) wood and pure water

6. According to Table 2, which of the following fluids is the densest?

    (F) oil

    (G) pure water

    (H) sea water

    (J) gasoline

Go on to next page

Passage 2

Suppose that a 50-kg block is placed on an incline as shown in Figure 1 below. A cable running over a frictionless pulley connects the 50-kg block to another block which is hanging off the edge of the ramp. The coefficient of friction between the block and the ramp, μ_k, is unknown.

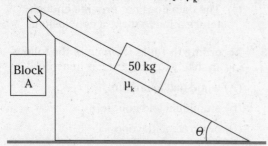

Figure 1: Configuration of blocks.

When the blocks are placed in the configuration shown in Figure 1, the 50-kg block slides up the ramp as Block A moves downward and eventually contacts the ground. Table 1 shows the results of 12 trials where Block A was released from rest in the position shown in the figure. The amount of time it took for Block A to reach the ground was recorded. For each trial, the mass of Block A was varied, as well as the angle θ of the ramp.

Table 1

Mass of Block A (kg)	Angle of Ramp (degrees)	Time for Block A to Reach the Ground (seconds)
40	10	0.62
	20	0.78
	30	1.13
	40	6.38
50	10	0.57
	20	0.66
	30	0.78
	40	1.00
60	10	0.54
	20	0.60
	30	0.68
	40	0.78

7. At which ramp angle did Block A reach the ground fastest?

(A) 10 degrees

(B) 20 degrees

(C) 30 degrees

(D) 40 degrees

8. Suppose an additional trial is performed with the mass of Block A as 70 kg and a ramp angle of 30 degrees. How long will it take for Block A to reach the ground?

(F) 0.74 seconds

(G) 0.62 seconds

(H) 1.15 seconds

(J) 0.68 seconds

9. Table 1 best supports which of the following statements about the time for Block A to reach the ground?

(A) If the ramp angle is increased and the mass of Block A is increased, Block A will reach the ground more slowly.

(B) If the ramp angle is increased and the mass of Block A is decreased, Block A will reach the ground faster.

(C) If the ramp angle is decreased and the mass of Block A is increased, Block A will reach the ground faster.

(D) If the ramp angle is decreased and the mass of Block A is decreased, Block A will reach the ground more slowly.

10. Based on Table 1, which combination of Block A mass and ramp angle would most likely produce equilibrium (no movement) of the blocks?

(F) 50 kg, 24 degrees

(G) 40 kg, 8 degrees

(H) 60 kg, 32 degrees

(J) 40 kg, 41 degrees

Go on to next page

11. Which of the following graphs best repre-
    sents the relationship between ramp angle
    and amount of time for Block A to reach
    the ground?

(A)

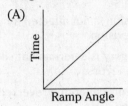

(B)

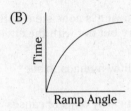

(C)

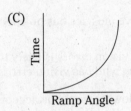

(D)

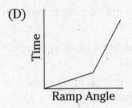

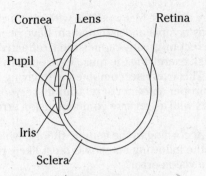

Figure 1: Anatomy of the human eye.

There are multiple viewpoints on the causes
and proper treatment of poor vision, two of
which are explained below.

Genetic Theory

Vision problems in humans are hereditary
and occur regardless of environmental factors.
Vision exams should be conducted on children
beginning at a young age so that issues can be
identified early. The best solutions available to
treat vision errors include eyeglasses, contact
lenses, and eye surgery. These treatments
quickly correct the majority of vision issues and
have been used for centuries in the past, as
shown in artwork and literature. More recently,
contact lenses have been used as a convenient
solution for vision correction, providing an additional treatment option to those with poor
vision. Additionally, laser eye surgery has been
shown to be a long-lasting solution for refractive
vision errors.

Environmental Theory

Poor vision is a result of improper use of the
human eye. When one focuses for too long on
nearby objects, such as books, televisions, or
computers, the eye is weakened, and this leads
to vision errors. When these issues are corrected
through artificial vision correction devices, such
as eyeglasses and contact lenses, the eyes adapt
to this handicap and are allowed to degenerate
further, causing the vision problem to worsen.
Human children who spend a great deal of time
focusing their eyes on nearby objects rather
than playing outside are much more likely to
develop vision defects early on in life. Humans
who make a habit of not focusing on nearby
objects experience much fewer cases of poor
vision.

A more natural and healthier solution to
vision problems is learning to properly exercise
the eyes and to reduce time spent focusing on

Passage 3

Poor vision is a relatively widespread problem among humans. The most common vision
defects include myopia, hyperopia, astigmatism,
and presbyopia. Myopia is commonly called
"nearsightedness" and is characterized by the
ability to see only nearby objects while far-away
objects appear blurry. The opposite of myopia is
hyperopia, commonly called "farsightedness."
This is where the lens of the eye focuses images
behind the retina, making nearby objects difficult to see. Astigmatism is a condition caused
by an irregular cornea or lens where the eye
cannot focus an image properly on the retina,
resulting in blurry vision. Presbyopia occurs
with increased age and results in the inability to
focus on nearby objects, often making reading
difficult. Figure 1 below depicts the basic anatomy of the human eye.

Go on to next page

nearby objects. Many people with vision errors such as myopia and astigmatism have been able to correct or greatly reduce their refractive error through exercising the muscles around their eyes. This exercise, combined with giving the eyes proper amounts of relaxation, serves to prevent as well as reverse common vision errors.

12. According to the genetic theory, which of the following humans is most likely to have a vision error?

    (F) an adult who spends time focusing on nearby objects

    (G) a human who regularly practices eye exercises

    (H) a child whose parents have poor vision

    (J) a child who spends a great deal of time outdoors

13. Which of the following statements about vision errors would be most consistent with both theories?

    (A) Vision errors are caused by a lack of reading.

    (B) Vision errors can be corrected at a young age.

    (C) Vision errors have existed for centuries.

    (D) Vision errors are more common among children than adults.

14. According to those who espouse the environmental theory, which of the following beliefs held by those who follow the genetic theory creates the most significant drawback to correcting vision problems?

    (F) Vision errors are hereditary.

    (G) Humans have experienced vision errors for centuries.

    (H) There are multiple ways to correct vision errors.

    (J) Vision errors should be corrected at a young age with eyeglasses.

15. Those who follow the environmental theory assume that:

    (A) vision problems can develop at any time during life.

    (B) children's vision is not affected by watching television.

    (C) laser eye surgery is a permanent solution to vision errors.

    (D) vision problems cannot be reversed, only prevented.

16. Which of the following is consistent with the genetic theory but not with the environmental theory?

    (F) Eyeglasses allow humans to see correctly.

    (G) Focusing on nearby objects causes vision errors.

    (H) Exercising eye muscles has no effect on vision.

    (J) A child with vision errors is likely to have a sibling who has vision errors.

17. Which of the following would be accepted by advocates of either theory?

    (A) Vision errors may be identified early in life.

    (B) Eye exercises are a healthy alternative to eyeglasses.

    (C) Vision deterioration is less likely in those who wear eyeglasses.

    (D) Children who play outside are less likely to develop vision errors.

18. Evidence suggests that vision errors are more common in some societies in the world and less common in others. Which of the following theories is supported by this evidence?

    (F) the genetic theory

    (G) the environmental theory

    (H) both theories

    (J) neither theory

Go on to next page

Passage 4

Ammonia is added to water to create an ammonia solution. The following reaction shows how ammonia dissociates in water to form ammonium hydroxide:

$$NH_3 + H_2O \Rightarrow NH_4^+ + OH^-$$

As the concentration of ammonia in the water is increased, more of the ammonia dissociates to form ammonium hydroxide, and the pH increases. A higher pH indicates that more OH^- ions are present in the solution. Table 1 shows how the pH of the solution changes as the molarity of the ammonia solution is altered.

Table 1

Molarity (M) of Ammonia Solution	pH
0.000001	7.98
0.00001	8.85
0.0001	9.54
0.001	10.10
0.01	10.62
0.1	11.12
1	11.63
2	11.78
3	11.87
4	11.93
5	11.98
10	12.13

As an ammonia solution is heated, the ammonia becomes less soluble, and ammonia escapes from the water as a vapor. Therefore, the ammonia concentration of the solution decreases. A 1 M ammonia solution at 10°C was slowly heated, and the concentration was measured at various temperatures. Table 2 contains data showing how the molar concentration of ammonia decreased as the solution was heated.

Table 2

Temperature (°C)	Molarity (M) of Ammonia Solution
10	1.00
20	0.82
30	0.66
40	0.52
50	0.40

19. An ammonia solution is desired to have a pH of 10. What molarity of solution is closest to the desired pH?

(A) 10 M

(B) 1 M

(C) 0.0001 M

(D) 0.005 M

20. Which of the following statements about OH^- ions is best supported by Table 1 and the text that precedes it?

(F) A 2 M ammonia solution has more OH^- ions than a 5 M solution.

(G) A 0.001 M ammonia solution has fewer OH^- ions than a 0.0001 M solution.

(H) A 0.0001 M ammonia solution has more OH^- ions than a 10 M solution.

(J) A 1 M ammonia solution has more OH^- ions than a 0.01 M solution.

21. According to Tables 1 and 2, if a 1 M ammonia solution is initially 10°C and is slowly heated by 30°C, what is most likely to be the pH?

(A) 11.63

(B) 11.48

(C) 11.12

(D) 11.87

Go on to next page

22. Which of the following conclusions is best supported by Tables 1 and 2?

    (F) Temperature has no effect on the solubility of ammonia in water.

    (G) The molarity of an ammonia solution has an inverse relationship with pH.

    (H) The concentration of any ammonia solution can be determined by measuring the temperature of the solution.

    (J) The pH of an ammonia solution changes more quickly at lower concentrations of ammonia.

23. Suppose a chemist wishes to decrease the pH of an ammonia solution. Which of the following would help to achieve the desired outcome?

    (A) Heat the ammonia solution.

    (B) Cool the ammonia solution.

    (C) Add more ammonia to the solution.

    (D) Pressurize the ammonia solution.

Passage 5

An electrical circuit is essentially a circular path in which electrons can flow. Typically, a voltage source, such as a battery, will provide the necessary power to keep the electrons flowing through the circuit. The rate of flow of electron charge in the circuit is called electrical current. Electrical current is measured in amperes (A). A student constructed a simple electrical circuit using a battery, resistors, and wire. The potential of a battery is measured in volts (V), and the resistance of resistors is measured in ohms (Ω). Figure 1 represents the electrical circuit configuration.

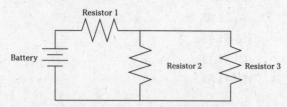

Figure 1: A simple electrical circuit configuration.

The student conducted two studies on the electrical circuit to examine the effect of changing components in the circuit. Each of the studies is described below, followed by the results obtained in the study.

Study 1

In the first study, the battery used to power the circuit was changed, and the voltage across each resistor was measured using a voltmeter by placing the voltmeter in parallel with each resistor. The resistances of Resistors 1, 2, and 3 were 100 Ω, 1,000 Ω, and 5,000 Ω, respectively. Table 1 shows the results.

Table 1			
Voltage Measured across Resistor (Volts)			
Battery Used (V)	**Resistor 1 (100 Ω)**	**Resistor 2 (1,000 Ω)**	**Resistor 3 (5,000 Ω)**
1.5	0.16	1.34	1.34
3.0	0.32	2.68	2.68
4.5	0.48	4.02	4.02
6.0	0.64	5.36	5.36
9.0	0.96	8.04	8.04

Study 2

In the second study, the resistance of Resistor 1 was changed, and the current through each resistor was measured using a digital multimeter. In order to take the measurements, the multimeter was placed in series with each of the resistors. The current measurements taken were very small in magnitude, so they are shown in milliamperes (mA), which are one-thousandth of an ampere. A 9.0 volt battery was used in the circuit. Table 2 shows the results.

Table 2			
Current Measured through Resistor (mA)			
Resistor 1 Resistance (Ω)	**Resistor 1**	**Resistor 2 (1,000 Ω)**	**Resistor 3 (5,000 Ω)**
100	9.64	8.04	1.61
200	8.71	7.26	1.45
300	7.94	6.62	1.32
400	7.30	6.08	1.22
500	6.75	5.63	1.13

Go on to next page ⟹

24. Study 1 suggests that the voltage measured across Resistor 2 is smallest when the battery voltage is:

    (F) 1.5 V.

    (G) 3.0 V.

    (H) 6.0 V.

    (J) 9.0 V.

25. Which of the following best describes the difference between Studies 1 and 2?

    (A) In Study 1, the Resistor 3 resistance was varied; in Study 2, the battery voltage was varied.

    (B) In Study 1, the battery voltage was varied; in Study 2, the Resistor 2 resistance was varied.

    (C) In Study 1, the battery voltage was varied; in Study 2, the Resistor 1 resistance was varied.

    (D) In Study 1, the Resistor 2 resistance was varied; in Study 2, the Resistor 1 resistance was varied.

26. In Study 2, as the Resistor 1 resistance was increased, the current through:

    (F) Resistor 2 increased and the current through Resistor 3 increased.

    (G) Resistor 3 increased and the current through Resistor 1 decreased.

    (H) Resistor 1 decreased and the current through Resistor 2 decreased.

    (J) Resistor 3 decreased and the current through Resistor 2 increased.

27. Which circuit configuration was used in both studies?

    (A) battery voltage of 1.5 V, Resistor 1 resistance of $100 \, \Omega$

    (B) battery voltage of 9.0 V, Resistor 1 resistance of $100 \, \Omega$

    (C) battery voltage of 1.5 V, Resistor 1 resistance of $500 \, \Omega$

    (D) battery voltage of 9.0 V, Resistor 1 resistance of $500 \, \Omega$

28. In Study 1, if a 12.0 V battery had been used, the voltage measured across Resistor 2 would have been closest to:

    (F) 10.71 V.

    (G) 8.04 V.

    (H) 1.29 V.

    (J) 0.96 V.

29. Which of the following conclusions about the electrical circuit is best supported by Studies 1 and 2?

    (A) The voltage across Resistors 1 and 2 is always equal, and the current through Resistor 1 is always greater than the current through Resistor 3.

    (B) The voltage across Resistors 2 and 3 is always equal, and the current through Resistor 2 is always greater than the current through Resistor 1.

    (C) The voltage across Resistors 2 and 3 is always equal, and the current through Resistor 3 is always equal to the current through Resistor 2.

    (D) The voltage across Resistors 2 and 3 is always equal, and the current through Resistor 1 is always equal to the sum of the currents through Resistors 2 and 3.

Passage 6

When astronauts traveled to the Moon during the Apollo Program, they collected samples of the lunar surface and brought them back to the Earth to be studied. If a long-term colony were ever to be constructed on the Moon, there would have to be resources available that could be used for construction materials, fuel, and food. The lunar samples that were brought back to Earth were analyzed and their compositional elements were determined.

Samples from the Moon are categorized depending on where they were collected. Those taken from the dark-colored low-lying areas are considered to be from the lunar lowlands, while those taken from the light-colored elevated areas are considered to be representative of the lunar highlands. Figure 1 is a graph showing the most common elements by weight percent that are typically present in the Earth and how these compare to the elements found in the lunar highlands and lowlands.

Go on to next page

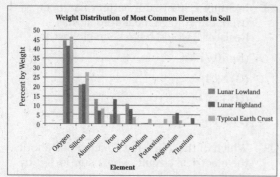

Figure 1: Comparing the elements found in the Earth's surface to those found in the Moon's surface.

Additional elements are found in the Earth's crust as well as on the Moon, but they are present in much smaller weight percentages. Figure 2 compares these less common elements in the lunar highlands and lowlands with typical Earth crust.

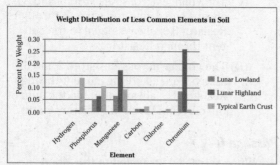

Figure 2: Comparing less common elements in the lunar surface to those in the Earth's crust.

30. Which of the following elements comprises the largest percent by weight in the lunar highlands?

(F) aluminum

(G) iron

(H) calcium

(J) sodium

31. In larger concentrations, chromium can pose a health hazard to humans. According to Figure 2, what location would be the most dangerous for humans to inhabit because of chromium?

(A) lunar lowlands

(B) lunar highlands

(C) Earth landmasses

(D) Earth oceans

32. Which of the following elements are found in higher concentrations in the Earth's crust than in the lunar lowlands?

(F) silicon and aluminum

(G) iron and calcium

(H) sodium and potassium

(J) chlorine and chromium

33. Hydrogen, carbon, and oxygen are important in the production and use of fuel, an essential resource. Which of the following conclusions about the data causes the most concern for prospective lunar inhabitants?

(A) Oxygen is present in soil on the Moon and on the Earth in roughly similar concentrations.

(B) Hydrogen is present in higher concentrations in the lunar lowlands than in the lunar highlands.

(C) Oxygen is present in soil on the Earth in higher concentrations than carbon.

(D) Hydrogen is present in smaller concentrations on the Moon than on the Earth.

34. Which of the following correctly lists elements in the lunar lowlands from lowest to highest concentration?

(F) iron, calcium, aluminum

(G) aluminum, calcium, iron

(H) iron, aluminum, calcium

(J) calcium, iron, aluminum

Go on to next page

Passage 7

A scientist performed two studies to determine the factors affecting the spiciness of jalapeño peppers. Chili peppers like the jalapeño are spicy because of a chemical compound contained within them called capsaicin. To quantify the spiciness, the Scoville heat unit scale is used, which is a measure of the amount of capsaicin in the pepper. Higher capsaicin results in a higher measure of Scoville heat units, which corresponds to a spicier pepper.

The plants used in the studies were grown from a single group of seeds and planted in the same type of soil and given the same amount of light each day. Test groups were designed to vary the watering frequency and soil temperature of the plants to determine the resulting effects on spiciness. There were five plants in each test group, with all plants in a test group being subjected to identical conditions. Multiple peppers from each plant were tested, and the average measured Scoville heat units for all of the peppers from each plant are shown in the tables.

Study 1

In the first study, the watering frequency was varied for each test group. The soil temperature was kept at 25°C for all plants in Study 1. The results of the study are shown in Table 1.

Table 1

Days between Watering	Average Measured Scoville Heat Units of Each Jalapeño Plant in the Test Group					Average of Test Group
1	3,900	3,800	4,300	4,100	4,000	4,020
2	4,400	4,500	4,200	4,300	4,900	4,460
3	5,100	5,100	5,200	4,500	5,100	5,000
4	5,500	5,300	5,700	5,600	5,800	5,580
5	6,300	5,600	6,700	5,200	6,100	5,980

Study 2

In the second study, the temperature of the soil was varied for each test group by placing the pots on heating mats and adjusting the heat to keep the soil at the desired temperature. The plants were watered every three days. The results of the study are shown in Table 2.

Table 2

Temperature of Soil (°C)	Average Measured Scoville Heat Units of Each Jalapeño Plant in the Test Group					Average of Test Group
15	4,700	4,200	4,300	4,100	4,400	4,340
20	4,800	4,600	4,200	4,700	4,800	4,620
25	5,000	5,100	4,900	4,900	5,400	5,060
30	5,100	5,300	4,800	5,300	4,900	5,080

Go on to next page

35. According to Study 1, if a jalapeño plant has a soil temperature of 25°C and produces peppers with an average of 4,500 Scoville heat units, how often is it most likely watered?

    (A) every day
    (B) every two days
    (C) every week
    (D) every two weeks

36. If a jalapeño plant is kept in soil with a temperature of 30°C and is watered every three days, what is the best estimate for the average amount of Scoville heat units contained in its peppers?

    (F) 3,800
    (G) 4,400
    (H) 5,100
    (J) 5,600

37. According to Study 1, as a jalapeño plant is watered more often, the spiciness of its peppers:

    (A) increases.
    (B) decreases.
    (C) stays the same.
    (D) is indeterminate.

38. If a scientist wanted to conduct another study on a factor affecting jalapeño spiciness that was not examined in Studies 1 and 2, she should:

    (F) vary the soil composition.
    (G) vary the soil temperature.
    (H) hold constant the frequency of watering.
    (J) hold constant the light provided to the plants.

39. Based on the studies, which of the following combinations of soil temperature and watering frequency would likely produce the widest variation in spiciness from plant to plant?

    (A) water every 5 days and 25°C soil temperature
    (B) water every 3 days and 25°C soil temperature
    (C) water every 3 days and 30°C soil temperature
    (D) water every 3 days and 20°C soil temperature

40. According to Studies 1 and 2, what conditions are most likely to produce spicy jalapeño peppers?

    (F) lower soil temperature and more frequent watering
    (G) higher soil temperature and more frequent watering
    (H) lower soil temperature and less frequent watering
    (J) higher soil temperature and less frequent watering

STOP DO NOT TURN THE PAGE UNTIL TOLD TO DO SO.
DO NOT RETURN TO A PREVIOUS TEST.

Writing Test

Time: 30 minutes

Directions: Choose a position on the issue presented in the following writing prompt. Present your position in a logical, clear, and well-organized essay that follows the rules of Standard English. Write your essay on a separate sheet of lined paper.

A state politician believes that it is becoming increasingly obvious that the preoccupation with a liberal arts curriculum in higher education is misplaced as the unemployment rate and student loan delinquency rate reach new highs. The politician cites statistics from the U.S. Department of Labor that state that the demand for graduates trained in trades, like plumbers, electricians, mechanics, and other technicians, has never been greater in the last century. Similarly, unemployment rates for vocational grads, who often attend private trade schools rather than state public universities, are also at an all-time low. Based upon these facts, the politician claims it is time for the state legislature to allocate more funding for vocational educational programs instead of for schools that focus on a liberal arts curriculum. A group of professors from the local state college opposes the measure stating that a liberal arts education prepares students for more than just a trade; it provides them with the means to make informed decisions for a lifetime.

Write an essay that takes a position on this issue. Your position can support either one side of the issue or the other, or you may introduce a different point of view on the question. Provide specific examples and reasons to support your opinion.

Chapter 25

Practice Exam 3: Answers and Explanations

• •

Okay. You've completed the practice exam in Chapter 24. We realize that you've had your nose to the grindstone for a long time. You probably need a break. Go ahead. Take a time out. But come right back and read through all the answer explanations we provide in this chapter — yes, even the ones you got right. Along the way, we offer tons of tips and traps — valuable information that you'll be able to use when you face the real ACT on test day.

After you read through the explanations, turn to Chapter 21 to determine what score you would've received if this practice test were real. If you're short on time, skip to the end of this chapter, where we provide an abbreviated answer key.

English Test

1. **C.** At first glance, you may not think the subject of this sentence is plural, but it is: coolness *and* hum. That means you need a plural verb. Believe it or not, *mean* is plural, and the only answer that contains mean is Choice (C).

2. **F.** The words before the punctuation mark create a complete sentence, and the words after the punctuation create a complete sentence. Because no conjunction joins the two clauses, a semicolon does. So the sentence is fine as is. Choice (J) makes the sentence a comma splice.

   Choice (H) may have tempted you because, of course, you can punctuate two independent clauses with a period. Hold on, though. Choice (H) uses *its* (the possessive form) to mean *it's* (the contraction of "it is").

3. **C.** The underlined part isn't a complete sentence. *Pointing* without any assistance from another helping verb doesn't work as a verb. You have to change it to a word that functions as a real verb. The paragraph is in simple present tense, so pick Choice (C) rather than Choice (D). Choice (B) creates a new error by pairing a singular verb with a plural subject.

4. **J.** This question may have been a little tricky because the misplaced modifier is hard to spot at first. But after you see that *just* is in the wrong place, you can fix the sentence in a jiffy. *Just* refers to the kinds of players — they weren't just from Clement. It doesn't refer to "made up," so you can't say that the hockey team was "just made up" (unless perhaps the players had all recently had clown faces painted on).

   Modifiers, words that describe other words, need to be as close to the words they describe as possible.

   The answer that puts *just* in its place is Choice (J). Don't worry that it changes "it is" to *it's*. The tone of the essay is casual, so contractions are okay.

5. **B.** Semicolons separate independent clauses. Whenever you see a semicolon in a sentence, the words that come before it and the words that come after it have to make complete sentences. The words that come before the semicolon in this sentence don't create a complete sentence. They make a dependent clause. You separate a beginning dependent clause from the rest of the sentence with a comma. So Choice (B) is the right answer.

6. **J.** The paragraph is about more than just the players from Clement, so the underlined sentence doesn't provide an accurate idea of what the paragraph is about. Cross out Choice (F) and check out your other options. Eliminate Choice (H) because the paragraph is primarily about Sanchez, who wasn't on the team last year. Plus, Choice (H) awkwardly compares *team* to *year*. Choice (G) is vague and uninformative and would be better introducing a paragraph about the number of players on the team rather than the characteristics of individual members. The best answer is Choice (J). The last sentence of the previous paragraph sets up that the next paragraph is about the players.

7. **C.** This sentence begins with a description of someone who's returning to Clement, but the subject of the sentence is *position*. The position isn't returning. Brendan Sanchez is. Choose the answer that makes Sanchez the subject of the sentence without creating a new error. Choices (C) and (D) correct the error. Choice (D) changes the comma to a semicolon, though. A semicolon doesn't work in this sentence because the information that comes before it isn't a complete sentence. Choice (C) corrects the error and deletes unnecessary words.

Whenever you see a beginning phrase with a comma after it, check the subject of the sentence. The beginning phrase should describe the subject of the sentence. If it doesn't, you have to change it.

8. **F.** This question tests you about comma usage. Commas correctly separate elements in a series from one another and appositives from the nouns they describe. This sentence has both a series and a few appositives. Each player's name needs to be surrounded by commas, just the way it appears in the original sentence. The colon in Choice (G) isn't proper because the words that come before a colon must be a complete sentence. You don't use colons to set apart appositives, so Choice (H) is out. The problem with Choice (J) is that comma with no purpose in between *as* and *Clement*.

9. **D.** You don't have any reason to insert a comma anywhere in the underlined words, so cross out Choices (A) and (C).

Whenever you see a comma in the underlined words, check it carefully to make sure it's used properly and has a definite reason for being there.

Choice (B) gets rid of the comma, but it also cuts out "and take over," which changes the message of the sentence. So (D) is the answer you want here.

10. **H.** The passage is a casual article designed to get readers psyched about the hockey team. Sticking a list of players right in the middle of the article probably wouldn't be appropriate. If a list is necessary, which is debatable, it would work better at the end of the article so that it doesn't interrupt the information in the passage. Because the answer is no, cross out Choices (F) and (G). Then all you have to do is pick the right reason for not including the list. The focus of the essay isn't last year's performance, so the answer has to be Choice (H).

11. **D.** Always check an underlined pronoun to make sure it's used properly. "Him and Poldale" is the subject of the sentence. *Him* is the objective form. You can't use an objective pronoun to fill the position of sentence subject. The only answer that changes *him* to *he* is Choice (D).

12. **F.** As weird as it may sound, "it is hoped" is the proper way to say this expression. *Hopefully* is an adverb and is almost always used incorrectly on the ACT. In Standard English (the way it's written in formal books, not the way most high schoolers speak it), you use *hopefully* only to describe the way you did something. For instance, "I entered the ACT test center hopefully, anticipating an awesome score after many diligent hours of

careful preparation." "Everyone is hopeful" in Choice (J) isn't improper, but the rest of the answer choice doesn't flow with the remainder of the sentence.

Always reread the sentence with your answer inserted to check that it makes sense and to verify that you haven't missed something in your eagerness to make a choice.

13. **C.** *Good* is an adjective. *Well* is an adverb. This sentence uses *good* to describe how the Cougars played. You use adverbs to describe the action of verbs, which means *good* doesn't belong here. The proper construction is "played well." Cross out Choices (A) and (B). Choice (D) is redundant. *Sufficiently* and *enough* mean the same thing. The best answer is Choice (C).

14. **G.** Saying that the Cougars have to rebound before you talk about their previous losses doesn't make a whole lot of sense. Sentence 5 mentions last year's losses, so Sentence 4 needs to come after Sentence 5. Choice (G) is the winner here.

15. **A.** You can eliminate Choice (D) because the tone of the passage isn't formal. The essay mentions last season's losses but doesn't dwell on them, so cross out Choice (C). Choice (A) is a better answer than Choice (B) because the essay doesn't provide details about all the players.

16. **J.** This poor sentence has no verb, which means it's really not a sentence. *Being* can't function as a verb unless it's paired with a helping verb. Choose the answer that gives the sentence a verb. Make sure to use the proper tense. The rest of the paragraph is in present tense. Choice (J) follows that trend. The other two choices suggest that recycling was good in the past.

Use the verbs in the other sentences in the paragraph to figure out what tense the verb should be in the sentence with the underlined words.

17. **B.** The comma in the underlined words has no purpose. Take the poor, aimless punctuation mark out of its misery by removing it from the sentence. The only choice that completes this noble task is Choice (B). Choices (C) and (D) try to move the position of *both* around, but *both* is fine just where it is. Recycling is a step in both maintaining and sustaining.

18. **J.** This sentence provides a classic case of redundancy. *Autonomous* and *independence* mean the same thing, so you don't need both of them. Omit *autonomous* by choosing Choice (J) and move on.

19. **A.** The underlined series is punctuated correctly. A comma comes after every item in the list. Semicolons are overkill in this case, so cross out Choice (B). The colon in Choice (C) suggests that everything that comes after it is an example of recycled paper. And Choice (D) is wrong because you need to replace those extra *ands* at the beginning of the list with commas.

20. **G.** The problem with this sentence is another additional redundant repetition. Yikes! It's contagious. If markets are at all-time highs, they've never been greater. You don't need to say it twice. Choice (G) cures the malady. Choice (J) eliminates *greater* but remains repetitious because "have never been" conveys the same message as *all-time*.

21. **A.** The proposed insertion flows fairly well from the sentence before it, but it doesn't work with the sentence after it. If people tend to discontinue participating in recycle programs, the next statement about increased supply and demand for recycled goods doesn't make sense. So the answer is no. Cross out Choices (C) and (D). Now you just have to decide between Choices (A) and (B). The topic isn't *completely* different from the information in the rest of the paragraph. It's about public education and recycling. Choice (A) is better. Inserting the sentence would break up the information that public education has caused increased supply and demand for recycled goods.

After you determine the short answer to a "no, no, yes, yes" question on the English Test, you've got a 50 percent chance of picking the right answer. These questions are often less time-consuming than they appear.

22. **G.** If you noticed that the underlined words contain the wrong version of *their,* give your-self a strong pat on the back. *Their* is the possessive form of *they,* and a noun always has to follow it. But a noun doesn't come after *their* in this sentence. Choice (G) presents the cor-rect version, and it doesn't change *large* to "super huge," a choice of words that doesn't fit with the relatively formal tone of the rest of the passage.

23. **B.** Check the words that come before and after the semicolon. The words after it aren't a complete sentence, so you know the semicolon isn't right. If a semicolon doesn't work, a period certainly won't either. Cross out Choice (C). Deciding between Choices (B) and (D) may be a little more challenging. *Which* introduces a nonrestrictive (or nonessential) clause, so it needs to be separated from the rest of the sentence by a comma. Cross out Choice (D). The best way to punctuate the sentence out of the four options is with the colon in Choice (B).

24. **J.** In this sentence, *strictly* describes "any type of trash." But the right use of *strictly* is to narrow down something to a specific type rather than the more general *any* type. You need to replace *strictly* with a more accurate word. Cross out Choice (G) because referring to types of trash as rigorous just doesn't make sense. In the context of this sentence, *mainly* means mostly and *virtually* means almost. It makes more sense to say "almost any type of trash" than "mostly any type of trash."

25. **B.** One look at the answer choices tells you exactly what kind of error to focus on. All the choices are the same except for the commas. So your job for this question is to figure out where the commas go. Don't waste time looking for any other error. "Recyclable or not" is a phrase that provides more information about the type of trash. You separate it from the rest of the sentence by surrounding it with commas. The only choice that properly puts commas on either side of the phrase is Choice (B). There's no reason for the comma between "recyclable" and "or" in Choice (D).

Notice that the question doesn't ask you to determine whether the phrase is essential or not. All you have to know is how to punctuate a nonessential phrase.

26. **G.** Examining the answer choices helps you focus on the errors in the underlined words. First, you notice that Choices (G) and (J) change *and* to *to.* The proper construction is "from . . . to," which means that *to* is correct. Mark through Choices (F) and (H) with your No. 2 pencil and take a closer look at the remaining options. Choice (J) changes TV to tele-vision, and Choice (G) changes *weeks'* to *week's. TV* is fine here. The dinners the passage refers to are commonly called "TV dinners" rather than "television dinners." The answer must be Choice (G). It properly changes *weeks'* from the plural possessive to the singular possessive *week's.* There's only one "last week."

27. **C.** *Unsightly* is a more concise way of saying "displeasing to the eye." Including both in the sentence is needlessly repetitious. The answer that corrects the issue is Choice (C).

28. **H.** Sentence 4 provides more detail about the complaints that neighbors make. Therefore, it makes the most sense to put it right after Sentence 2 (and before Sentence 3) because it's the sentence that states that neighbors complain about the "trash magnets" that recy-cle bins have become. Eliminate Choice (G) right away because Sentence 4 would be out of place without knowing the information in Sentence 2. It works better before Sentence 3 because it refers to removing the recycle bins, and Sentence 3 further explains why stores are willing to engage in the removal. Choice (J) would put Sentence 4 in a paragraph about a different topic, the recycling entrepreneurs. Picking Choice (H) provides the best flow of information in the paragraph.

If this question takes you more than half a minute to sift through the answer options, elimi-nate answer choices you know have to be wrong — such as Choices (G) and (J) — and guess from the remaining choices. You don't want to waste precious time on this question when you could use the time to answer easier questions later in the section.

29. **D.** The underlined words have a subject/verb agreement issue. *Who* refers to *entrepreneurs,* which is a plural noun. Therefore, the verb has to be plural — "have begun." Choice (C) creates a run-on sentence, and Choice (B) incorrectly changes *who* to the possessive form *whose.*

30. **F.** Eliminate answers that mention topics that were only covered in other paragraphs. Choice (G) is about public education, which appears only in the first paragraph. Choice (H) talks about neighbor complaints, which appears only in the second paragraph. The last paragraph doesn't distinguish between small and big businesses, so Choice (J) addresses a topic that hasn't been discussed. The best conclusion for the passage is Choice (F) because it refers to the programs discussed in the last paragraph and relates them to the general passage theme of promoting a greener future that's introduced in the first paragraph.

31. **A.** The sentence is fine the way it is. *That* isn't nonessential and shouldn't be separated by commas. Choice (D) is wrong. If you picked Choice (B) or (C), you created an incomplete sentence that leaves you waiting for more information.

Always reread the sentence with your answer choice inserted. This step alerts you to problems with your answer that you may miss otherwise. When you read this sentence with Choice (B) or (C), you immediately notice that something is wrong.

32. **H.** The sentence is unclear and awkward. The reference to "this one" is vague, and it sounds like only "this one" is in the Constitution. Choice (H) changes the reference from "this one" to "this amendment" and clarifies that all ten amendments are in the Constitution.

When a whole sentence is underlined, look for an unclear reference or modifier error. You'll probably have to rewrite the sentence to fix the error.

33. **C.** Cross out Choice (B) because you don't need to change *liberty* to the possessive form; in fact, doing so is wrong. You can also eliminate Choice (D) because it deletes the main verb and makes the sentence incomplete. Between the remaining choices, Choice (C) is more direct and, thus, is the better answer. The emphasis provided by the phrasing in the original sentence is unnecessary.

34. **G.** Knowing how the Fourteenth Amendment made the Bill of Rights applicable is essential to the idea of the sentence. Therefore, you can't separate the underlined portion from the rest of the sentence by any form of punctuation.

35. **D.** The original wording of the sentence is strange. The listed items didn't originate the Bills of Rights. People did. The list includes elements that form the origins of the Bill of Rights. Choice (D) most properly conveys this idea.

36. **H.** Eliminate the answer choice that doesn't show that opposition disappeared soon after the Bill of Rights were ratified. Examine each option by reading it in the sentence. "When the Bill of Rights was ratified," "as soon as the Bill of Rights was ratified," and "after the Bill of Rights was ratified" convey the same general idea as "once the Bill of Rights was ratified." *While* is the same as *during*, which would mean that the opposition decreased at the same time that the Bill of Rights was ratified.

37. **D.** This sentence has a subject/verb agreement problem. The subject *(effect)* is singular and the verb *(are)* is plural. One of them has to change. Cross out Choice (A). *Affect* is almost always used as a verb rather than a noun, so Choice (B) is wrong. Both of the remaining choices change *effect* to the plural, but Choice (C) incorrectly makes the verb singular. Choice (D) corrects the problem without creating a new error.

38. **G.** The phrase "by prohibiting" isn't a verb, so the sentence has no verb and is a fragment. Choice (J) inserts a verb, but *prohibits* goes with *that* rather than "Bill of Rights," which means the sentence is still a fragment. The best answer is Choice (G). It provides a singular verb for the singular subject.

39. **A.** The original sentence correctly uses *which* to introduce a descriptive clause that's not essential to the main point of the sentence, which is that the Bill of Rights protects speech. Choice (D) retains the *which* but creates a sentence fragment. So Choice (A) is the answer here.

Choose *that* to introduce clauses that are essential (or restrictive) and *which* to introduce clauses that aren't essential. Always use a comma to separate clauses that begin with *which* from the rest of the sentence. Don't separate clauses that begin with *that* by inserting a comma.

40. **G.** Approach this question by eliminating answers you know aren't right. The sentence provides an explanation of free speech, but it doesn't go into enough detail to be thorough. Cross out Choice (H). The main idea of the paragraph is that the Bill of Rights affects daily life. Eliminating Sentence 3 wouldn't take away this idea, so Choice (J) can't be right. The sentence introduces the concept of free speech and explains how it affects daily life, so it isn't irrelevant. The answer has to be Choice (G). The sentence gives the specific examples of the editorial section and Internet blogs to show how free speech plays out in daily life.

41. **D.** You need to separate a list of three or more items with commas. The only *and* is the one that comes before the last item. The only answer that follows these rules is Choice (D).

    Choice (B) looks like it corrects the problem, but *school* and *prayer* aren't separate issues, so you shouldn't separate them with a comma. The issue is school prayer. (Americans may debate about education or school issues but not about school itself.)

42. **G.** Eliminate Choice (J) right away. *But* signals a contrasting idea, but this sentence just expands on the ideas in the sentence that come before it. Choice (H) tells you that *hearing* the Miranda speech is a rights issue. The Bill of Rights doesn't particularly give you the right to hear the speech on TV. (Although that would be a great argument to offer your parents when they tell you to turn off the television and get studying for the ACT. "But Mom, watching this cop show is my Constitutional right!")

    The problem with the original sentence is the presence of *and.* You may have been told that you never begin a sentence with *and.* Although that's usually a good practice, it's not a hard and fast rule of Standard English. The issue isn't that the sentence begins with *and.* It's that the *and* is redundant. The sentence later includes *also.* Saying "and the speech is also a *right*" is repetitive. Ditch the *and* and pick Choice (G).

43. **B.** The paragraph provides a series of examples of free speech. Its main idea isn't the Miranda speech, so the full quote would be not only unnecessary but also pretty boring. Eliminate the yes answers, Choices (C) and (D). How many instances of Miranda speeches appear on TV is irrelevant. The best answer is Choice (B). Because the paragraph explores more rights than just Miranda rights, a copy of the full speech would be major overkill.

44. **J.** Pay attention to underlined pronouns. Make sure that they have clear references and that their references agree in number. This sentence says a group can stage a protest as long as the protest is not violent. *They* is plural, but it renames the singular noun *protest.* The proper singular pronoun to refer to *protest* is *it.* The only choice that corrects the problem is Choice (J).

Don't let answer choices that make irrelevant word changes distract you from the real problem in the sentence. In this question, "as long as" and "not violent" aren't improper constructions that require changing.

45. **D.** The essay gives a pretty thorough explanation of the First Amendment, but the author tells you that the Bill of Rights is more than just the First Amendment. Because the essay doesn't go into detail about the freedoms granted by the other amendments, the answer to this question is no. Cross out Choices (A) and (B). Your task is to choose the best answer of the two remaining. Choice (D) is better than Choice (C) because it's more comprehensive. Even if it included an explanation of the Right to Bear Arms, the essay probably wouldn't fulfill the intended goal.

Only one answer can be right. Sometimes you find yourself choosing between two answers that could be right. Pick the one that's "more right" than the other.

46. **G.** When a title follows a person's name, you have to surround it with commas. Choice (F) is wrong. Choice (H) isn't any better. Because the title comes before the name in Choice (G), no commas are necessary. Choice (J) is also technically correct; commas surround the nonessential clause. But Choice (G) is less wordy, so it's a better choice than Choice (J).

47. **A.** Because a comma comes after 1830, the clause that comes after it must be nonessential. You introduce nonessential clauses with *which,* not *that.* The sentence is fine as it is. Choices (C) and (D) use the progressive tense, which makes it sound like the Act is still in the process of appropriating.

48. **H.** Pick the answer that's not like the others. Choices (F), (G), and (J) all imply force without the other's consent. Choice (H) is gentler and more benevolent than the others. It doesn't belong and is, therefore, the correct answer.

49. **B.** The question asks you to determine what the result would be if the author deleted the description of the Indian Removal Act. This description provides relevant information about the event that precipitated the issues between Jackson and Native Americans. You can cross out Choice (C) because the description is definitely relevant. You have to know the ramifications of the Act to understand what the Native Americans fought to win a victory over. Therefore, the information is related to the rest of the passage, and Choice (A) can't be right. Choice (D) is clearly wrong. The information supports rather than contradicts the idea that Jackson didn't care about the interests of the Native Americans. The answer has to be Choice (B).

At first, you may be tempted to hurry through this question or skip it altogether because it seems to require a lot of reading. Give it a chance, though. The incorrect answer choices are pretty easy to eliminate.

50. **J.** The original sentence is a fragment. It doesn't have a main verb. Read each answer choice in the sentence. The only option that gives the sentence a verb is Choice (J).

51. **A.** Pick the appropriate transition word for this sentence. The right answer is the one that shows the relationship between the sentence with the underlined word and the information in the sentence before it. The previous sentence talks about the victory of the Native Americans over Jackson's coercion. The sentence that follows the underlined word is about Jackson's determination to thwart the decision. The two pieces of information contrast each other. Therefore, Choice (A) is the best answer because *however* shows contrast. *Additionally* would work if the sentences had similar ideas, but they don't. Eliminate Choice (C).

The words in Choices (B) and (D) mean the same thing; they both show cause and effect. They can't both be right, so both must be wrong.

52. **G.** The error you need to correct here has to do with the word *provoking*. The word tells you how Jackson asserted, and words that tell how someone performs an action verb need to be adverbs. The adverb form is *provokingly*. Cross out Choices (F) and (J). Choice (H) contains the adverb, but it also sticks in an unjustified comma. The answer that corrects the adverb problem and punctuates the sentence properly is Choice (G).

53. **A.** The passage isn't about Chief Justice Marshall. Although the underlined portion provides you with an interesting tidbit of history, it's not pertinent to the message of the sentence. It actually keeps you from honing in on the main idea of the sentence. Therefore, the best answer is Choice (A).

Even if you aren't sure whether the answer is yes or no, you can eliminate answer choices based on the explanations they give. Information about Chief Justice Marshall definitely doesn't belong in the next paragraph. That paragraph doesn't even mention the Supreme Court. Cross out Choice (B). Knowing that Marshall was the longest-serving Chief Justice doesn't provide a better understanding of the importance of the Court decision presented in the passage, so Choice (C) is out. Eliminating these two choices gives you a 50 percent chance of guessing correctly.

54. **J.** The idea conveyed in the underlined words is that Jackson wouldn't allow the Court decision to be enforced. The answer that best paraphrases that concept is Choice (J). Choice (H) conveys the opposite thought. So does Choice (F), and it's unclear who *he* refers to. Choice (G) doesn't convey that Jackson doesn't want the decision to be enforced.

55. **B.** If you don't know what *belied* means, just reread the sentence with each answer choice inserted. The one that makes sense is the right answer. *Although* at the beginning of the sentence means that the second part of the sentence opposes the idea in the first part. Jackson wasn't kind to the Cherokees. His actions *contradicted* his profession that he had the kindest feelings, so Choice (B) is right. The other choices show similarity between the two ideas in the sentence rather than opposition.

56. **G.** You have kind feelings *toward* someone, but you speak words *to* or *about* someone. Therefore, the underlined portion fits better after feelings. Cross out Choice (F) and pick Choice (G). You don't know who Jackson professed to, and *toward* doesn't work with *professed,* so Choice (H) is out. Likewise, Choice (J) is wrong because you don't belie toward someone.

57. **B.** Here's another question that deals with restrictive and nonrestrictive clauses. *That* introduces restrictive clauses and shouldn't be separated from the rest of the sentence with a comma. Choice (B) takes away the comma.

When you see a comma before *that,* it's almost always wrong.

58. **J.** If you don't know the conditions of the treaty, you don't know why the brutal journey mentioned at the end of the paragraph took place from 1838 to 1839. The information in the sentence isn't irrelevant, and it doesn't appear anywhere else in the passage. You can cross out Choices (F) and (G). Other sentences in the passage are about Jackson's character, but this one isn't. The best answer is Choice (J).

59. **A.** The punctuation in this sentence is correct. The words that come before the comma form a complete thought, and the words that come after it form a complete sentence. The conjunction *but* joins them, which means the comma before *but* is proper. Choice (D) makes the sentence a comma splice because it takes out the conjunction. *However* is a conjunctive adverb, which is a fancy way of saying it needs a semicolon before it and a comma after it. Choice (C) can't be right.

60. **J.** The passage doesn't paint a positive picture of Jackson's relations with the Cherokees, so you can eliminate the yes answers. Then cross out Choice (H) because the passage deals with specific ways that Jackson dealt with the Cherokees. The best answer is Choice (J).

61. **A.** Strangely enough, this sentence is okay the way it's written. Commas can replace missing words in balanced expressions. In this case, the comma takes the place of *are* in the second expression. If you're unsure, you can check the other answers and cross out ones that contain errors. Choice (C) is a comma splice. Choice (D) is wordy and adds a cause-and-effect relationship the original doesn't suggest. Choice (B) deletes a word from the second expression but doesn't replace it with a comma. The best answer is Choice (A).

62. **J.** The problem with this sentence isn't the wording. It's the punctuation. The first clause isn't a complete sentence, so you can't use a semicolon to separate it from the rest of the sentence. Choices (G) and (H) change the meaning of the sentence. Choice (J) properly separates the beginning dependent clause from the rest of the sentence with a comma.

63. **D.** Change the passive voice to active voice and you can also correct the modifier problem. Dialogue isn't assisting "other means"; it's assisting silent films. "Silent films" needs to be the subject of the sentence. Both Choices (C) and (D) make silent films the subject, but Choice (C) is in past tense. The rest of the paragraph is in present tense, so Choice (D) is better.

If the underlined portion of a sentence is in passive voice, pick an answer that changes it to active voice unless that change creates another error. Passive voice isn't necessarily wrong, but active voice is almost always better.

64. **H.** *Their* is the possessive form of *they.* The construction that makes sense in this sentence is *they're,* which is the contraction of "they are." The characters can't tell the audience what they are (or they're) thinking. Choice (H) corrects the error and maintains the simple present verb tense that the rest of the paragraph uses.

65. **B.** *Exaggerated* and *overacted* mean the same thing, so you don't need both of them. Choice (B) takes care of the redundancy.

66. **F.** You may not know right away whether the inserted sentence would be appropriate, but you can apply POE (process of elimination) to help narrow down the choices. Cross out Choice (H). The sentence doesn't contradict anything in the passage. A humorous tone wouldn't be inconsistent with the causal language in the passage. Besides, the sentence isn't particularly humorous. Choice (J) is out. Through POE, you know the answer is yes. Choose the answer that provides the best reason. The sentence provides an example, not a behavioral study. Choice (F) is the best answer.

67. **A.** The sentence seems fine the way it is, but check the other options to be sure. Choice (B) is redundant. Choice (D) doesn't have the right punctuation. (You need a semicolon before *furthermore* and a comma after it.) Choice (C) suggests a cause-and-effect relationship in the sentence that the passage doesn't justify. Keep the status quo with Choice (A).

68. **G.** The underlined series lacks parallel structure. All the elements in a series have to be in the same grammatical form. Everything in the list is a noun except the last item, which is an independent clause. Pick the answer that changes the independent clause to a noun form. Choice (H) keeps the clause, so it's wrong. Choice (J) omits the *and* from the series, so it can't be right. Choice (G) corrects the problem by changing the clause to the noun "dance numbers."

Often, underlined words that are part of a series signal a parallelism issue. When you see a series, check the punctuation and make sure all the elements are in the same grammatical form.

69. **C.** This sentence uses the adverb *expressively* to describe the noun "music score." Adverbs describe actions verbs, not nouns. Choice (C) changes the adverb to an adjective. Choice (B) makes the situation worse by changing musical to musically and inserting an unjustified comma. Choice (D) changes the meaning of the sentence.

70. **F.** Eliminate answers that aren't about the effects of the musical score. Choice (G) talks about dialogue and doesn't mention music. Cross out answers that don't compare the modern film experience to the silent film experience. Choice (H) talks only about silent films. Choice (J) discusses only modern films. The only answer that deals with music and compares the two kinds of films is Choice (F).

When you remember to use POE (process of elimination, that is), this question suddenly gets much easier.

71. **D.** This sentence has a bad case of comparisonitis. The words it uses to compare music to dialogue are simply wrong. To cure the problem, realize that the proper construction is "as large as" rather than "as large than." Choice (C) doesn't add the *as*. So cross it out. Choices (B) and (D) include *as,* but Choice (B) slips in an incorrect comma after dialogue. The best answer is Choice (D).

If you picked Choice (B), you probably read it too quickly and failed to see the comma. If you reread the sentence with Choice (B) inserted, you can see right away that it has a problem comma. Always reread the sentence with your answer inserted before you move to the next question.

72. **J.** The underlined sentence has a bunch of examples of how music conveys information in silent films. The right answer probably has the word *examples* in it. That knowledge leads you to Choices (G) and (J). Choice (G) is about modern films, so eliminate it. The answer is probably Choice (J), but check the others just to be sure. The examples aren't *superfluous* (or unnecessary fluff), so cross out Choice (F). They help you understand the concept in the previous sentence. The examples aren't of emotions, so Choice (H) isn't accurate. Choice (J) is the answer.

73. **D.** *Creativity* and *ingenuity* mean the same thing. To correct the redundancy, pick Choice (D). *Originality* and *inventiveness* are other synonyms of creativity, so Choices (B) and (C) don't fix the problem.

74. **G.** You knew this one was coming. The test warned you about it from the beginning of the passage. As you read through the passage, you may have been looking for paragraphs that seemed out of place. The question tells you that the paragraph to consider is Paragraph 2. As you read through the paragraph, you may notice that it summarizes the points that the other paragraphs make. This summarizing feature may indicate that it's an introduction or conclusion paragraph. The choices don't give you the option of ending with Paragraph 2, so it probably belongs at the beginning, before Paragraph 1.

The paragraph doesn't belong before Paragraph 5 because the first sentence of Paragraph 5 refers to the "frenetic motion" in Paragraph 4. If you put Paragraph 2 between them, that reference wouldn't make sense. Nothing in Paragraphs 3 and 4 tells you that Paragraph 2 should go between them, either. Therefore, the best answer is Choice (G).

This question comes at the end of the section when you're probably running out of time. If you're pretty sure the answer is Choice (G), save time by marking it on your answer sheet and moving on to the next question. If you have time at the end of the section, go back to this question to check the other answer options.

75. **C.** Pick an answer that summarizes a majority of the passage and isn't too general or too specific. The passage talks about musical scores in only one paragraph, so Choice (A) is wrong. Choice (B) is about film in general rather than silent films. Cross it out. Choice (D) is both too general (it's about all films) and too specific (just car chases). The best answer is Choice (C).

Mathematics Test

1. **D.** Keep in mind that the question asks for the amount Dolores has. But to figure out Dolores's amount, you have to know what Holly has. That Angela has half as much money as Holly is the same as saying that Holly has twice as much as Angela. Make an equation. Let A = Angela and H = Holly. That gives you $2A = H$; $2(\$60) = H$; $\$120 = H$. Holly has $120.

   Next, if Holly has $\frac{3}{4}$ as much as Dolores, then Dolores has $\frac{4}{3}$ as much as Holly (let D = Dolores): $D = \frac{4}{3}H$; $D = \frac{4}{3}(\$120)$; $D = \$160$. Dolores has $160.

   If you picked Choice (A), you mixed up Holly and Dolores. Choice (B) is what you get if you multiplied $120 by $\frac{3}{4}$ rather than $\frac{4}{3}$. If you chose Choice (C), you correctly doubled $60 to get $120, but then you mistakenly figured that if Holly's $120 was $\frac{4}{3}$ of Dolores's amount, you just had to add $\frac{3}{4}$ of $120 to it. Finally, Choice (E) is just wishful thinking on Dolores's part.

2. **G.** You remember how to divide by a fraction, right? You just multiply by the reciprocal. In this case, change the first division bar to a multiplication symbol and then flip the fraction underneath from $\frac{4}{y}$ to $\frac{y}{4}$. Then multiply. You get $\frac{3y}{4}$.

   Don't let the $y \neq 0$ throw you. Just ignore it. It's just there to let you know that the answer isn't an undefined number.

   If you picked Choice (F), you spaced the reciprocal rule and multiplied by $\frac{4}{y}$. Choice (H) flips the numerator rather than the denominator. Choice (J) results from flipping $\frac{4}{y}$ and leaving the 3 on the bottom rather than on the top. Finally, Choice (K) is wrong because it uses the wrong division bar for the problem. The parentheses clearly indicate that you're not supposed to divide $\frac{3}{4}$ by y.

3. **C.** The problem tells you that the height of the sail is perpendicular to its base, which means the sail forms a right triangle. The question asks you to find the measurement of the hypotenuse of that triangle. Before you call on Pythagoras and his theorem, check the ratio of the triangle. It's $12:16:x$. Notice that 12 is 4 times 3 and 16 is 4 times 4. Looks like a 3:4:5 right triangle to us! Multiply 5 by 4 to complete the proportion. The answer has to be 20, which is Choice (C). If you chose any other answer, you were just guessing.

   If you forget the common ratios of right triangles, you can rely on the Pythagorean theorem to find the measurement. The theorem states that the hypotenuse squared is equal to the sum of the squares of the other sides: $c^2 = a^2 + b^2$. Plug in the two side lengths and solve for c:

   $$c^2 = 12^2 + 16^2$$
   $$c^2 = 144 + 256$$
   $$c^2 = 400$$
   $$c = 20$$

4. **H.** You need to find the average score of several members of a larger group. Use the average formula.

By definition, an *average* equals the sum of all the scores divided by the number of scores:

$$\text{Average} = \frac{\text{Sum of scores}}{\text{Number of scores}}$$

For a detailed discussion of averages and means, check out Chapter 7. Set up the equation and plug in what you know. On the left of the equation is the average of the scores, which the problem tells you is 84. On the right is the sum of all 11 scores divided by the total number of scores, which is 11. Put 11 as your denominator.

Figuring what goes in the numerator is a little trickier. You don't know each individual score, but you do know a little about their averages. The problem tells you that the average of the first 6 scores is 79. If you apply the average formula to this information, you know that their sum is 474:

$$79 = \frac{\text{Sum}}{6}; \ 79 \times 6 = \text{Sum}; \ 474 = \text{Sum}$$

Similarly, the sum of the last 5 scores can be represented by $5x$ (meaning 5 times x), with x representing the average score of the 5 remaining students. The equation looks like this:

$$84 = \frac{474 + 5x}{11}$$

Solve for x to get your answer: $972 = 474 + 5x$; $450 = 5x$; $90 = x$.

The answer is Choice (H). If you picked any of the other options, you either guessed or made a math error. Be careful with your calculations.

5. **B.** You can solve simultaneous equations two ways. The faster way is by elimination; just stack them and add. The $+y$ and $-y$ cancel out and you're left with $2x = 10$. You can quickly see that $x = 5$.

The other way is to solve the first equation for y "in terms of x" (which is a fancy way of saying solve for y with x still in the equation) and then substitute what you get for y into the second equation. When you solve for y in the first equation, you get $y = 6 - x$. Substitute $6 - x$ for y in the second equation: $x - (6 - x) = 4$; $x - 6 + x = 4$. Combine like terms: $2x - 6 = 4$. Solve for x: $2x = 10$. What a coincidence! $x = 5$.

6. **H.** The *least common denominator* is the smallest number that all denominators go into.

The fastest way to solve this problem is by examining the answer options. Because you're looking for the smallest number, start with the smallest answer. Choice (F) is smallest, but 16 isn't a factor of 24. The next value is 32. 16 goes into 32, but 24 doesn't. Choice (G) is out. Try Choice (H): 2, 4, and 24 are definitely factors of 48. And 16 goes into 48 an even 3 times. You have your winner!

You don't have to test the other two options, because they're larger than 48 and you're looking for the lowest value.

7. **C.** If ray *OB* and ray *OA* are perpendicular, they form a right angle measuring 90 degrees. If angle *AOC* is 8 degrees greater than angle *AOB*, then it must measure 98 degrees.

Choice (A) is incorrect because it subtracts 8 degrees from 90 degrees instead of adding it. Choice (B) doesn't work because it's the measure of right angle *AOB*. If you picked either Choice (D) or (E), you mistakenly thought perpendicular lines formed an angle that measures 180 degrees (the measure of a straight angle or a straight line).

8. **K.** This question may not seem like a math question at all. But don't panic! The ACT may throw a few logic questions into the Math Test.

Sometimes drawing diagrams can help you keep things straight in logic problems. A simple Venn diagram is good for problems that group information as this one does.

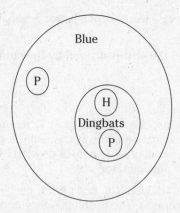

The first statement says that all Dingbats are blue. That tells you that a smaller circle, Dingbats, fits into a larger circle, blue. Homer (H) is an even smaller category. He fits into the Dingbats circle. That tells you that Homer must be blue. Prudence (P) isn't so cut and dry. She's blue alright, but that means she can fit anywhere in the big blue circle. She can be a Dingbat like Homer, but she doesn't have to be.

Now before you rush right into the answer choices with your newfound knowledge, check the question. It asks you for what must be *false*. Use your diagram to eliminate options that must be or could be true. Prudence could be a Dingbat or not. Cross out Choices (F), (H), and (J). Homer is indeed always blue. (Poor guy!) So Choice (G) is wrong. The right answer has to be Choice (K).

9. **D.** The problem tells you that Bonnie's only costs were the lemons and sugar she had to buy to make the lemonade. The correct formula is the one that shows how much she paid for the lemons and sugar.

TIP

If the proper formula isn't immediately obvious to you, you could spend a whole bunch of time trying to figure it out. Or you could save some time and substitute numbers for the variables in the problem to see which answer works out. We vote for saving time!

When you're substituting numbers for variables, pick easy numbers to work with. Say that she bought 10 pounds of lemons for $2 a pound and 5 pounds of sugar for $3 a pound. That means that $x = 10$, $p = 2$, $s = 5$, and $d = 3$. Write this information in your test booklet. Bonnie spent $20 on lemons (10 times $2) and $15 on sugar (5 times $3) for a total cost of $35. Plug your made-up numbers into the answer choices to see which one equals 35.

Choice (A) works out to 75: $(10 + 5)(2 + 3) = (15)(5) = 75$. Cross it out and check Choice (B): $10 + 2 + 5 + 3 = 20$. That can't be right. For Choice (C), multiply 10 and 3 to get 30 and 5 and 2 to get 10. Then add them together to get $30 + 10$ or 40. Keep looking. Choice (D) has you multiply 5 and 3 to get 15 (which is what Bonnie spent on sugar) and 10 and 2 to get 20 (which was her cost for lemons) and add the sums: $15 + 20 = 35$. That works! If you have time, check Choice (E): $xp = 10$ and $sd = 15$. If you multiply them, you end up with 150.

10. **H.** First, recognize that $(x + y)^2$ is the same as $(x + y)(x + y)$. As you may remember from algebra class (or Chapter 9), the product of two identical added terms is always the square of the first term (x) plus the square of the last term (y) plus 2 times the product of both terms (xy). In this case, that works out to be Choice (H): $x^2 + 2xy + y^2$. If you forgot the rule, you could use the FOIL method to multiply the expressions. The product of the First terms is x^2, the product of the Outer terms is y^2, and the products of the Inner terms are xy and xy. Put them all together and you get $x^2 + xy + xy + y^2$, or $x^2 + 2xy + y^2$.

You know you can eliminate Choice (J) because the product of positive values can't result in an expression that contains a negative.

11. **B.** This one isn't too hard. You should've immediately noticed that 144 and 81 are perfect squares. You remember from those dreaded memorized multiplication tables that 12 times 12 is 144 and 9 times 9 is 81. You can easily see that $x = 12$ and $y = 9$. All you have to do is add them together, right? $12 + 9 = 21$. But wait! 21 doesn't appear in the answer choices.

Because the product of two negative values is positive, x could be 12 or –12 and y could be either 9 or –9. Therefore, $x + y$ could be 21, –21, 3, or –3. The only one of these answers that appears is –21, Choice (B).

12. **H.** You could write out all the possibilities, but you don't have all day! The order of the charms doesn't matter. All you have to do is multiply together the number of charms in each category: $4 \times 5 \times 3 = 60$. That means there are 60 possible 3-charm combinations for Jan's necklace. If you picked Choice (F), you added the number of charms instead of multiplying them.

13. **A.** All this question takes is a little distributing. Multiply $9ab$ by the first term: $9ab \times 3a^3b^2 = 27a^4b^3$. Eliminate Choices (C), (D), and (E) because they have a different first term. You can take the time to multiply $9ab$ by the second term, but you already know the answer has to be Choice (A) because the second term can't still be $5ab$ after you multiply it by $9ab$.

REMEMBER

If you picked Choice (D) or (E), you forgot that you can't add terms that aren't exactly alike.

14. **H.** You know the formula for finding an average. You just have to arrange it to fit the question. You know the average amount per sale ($160), the number of sales Evan has (4), and the amount he's made at the first 3 sales ($230, $50, and $120). You just don't know the amount of Saturday's sale because it hasn't happened yet. Let x equal the amount he has to make at the fourth sale. Now you can set up the equation and solve for x:

$$\text{Average} = \frac{\text{Sum of amounts}}{\text{Number of sales}}$$

$$160 = \frac{230 + 50 + 120 + x}{4}$$

$$640 = 230 + 50 + 120 + x$$

$$640 = 400 + x$$

$$240 = x$$

Evan needs to make $240 on Saturday's sale, which is Choice (H). If you picked anything other than Choice (H), you either guessed or miscalculated.

15. **A.** You could solve this problem by figuring out the value of the right side of the equation and then playing with your calculator until you find out what power of 20 that equals. How tedious!

The faster way to solve this problem is to notice that $20^c = (4 \times 5)^c$, which is the same as $20^c = 4^c \times 5^c$. All the exponents must be the same, and c must be 3. (Review the rules for multiplying bases and exponents in Chapter 7.)

16. **J.** The y-coordinate of a point where a line intersects the x-axis is 0, and the y-coordinate is always listed last. Eliminate the choices that list 0 first: Choices (F) and (K). Because you know that $y = 0$, all you have to do now is substitute 0 for y in the equation: $3x + 7(0) = 21$. This simplifies to $3x = 21$. Divide both sides by 3, and you get $x = 7$. The point's coordinates are $(7, 0)$.

Another (but more time-consuming) way to approach this question would be to put the equation in the slope-intercept form by getting y by itself on the left side of the equation:

$$3x + 7y = 21;\ 7y = -3x + 21;\ y = -\frac{3}{7}x + 3$$

This equation tells you that the line intercepts the y-axis at $(0, 3)$ and the line has a slope of $-\frac{3}{7}$. Now you can graph the line on the coordinate plane. Begin at $(0, 3)$ and draw a line with a negative slope. That means to find the next point on the line, you count 3 points down and 7 points to the right (because lines with negative slope fall from left to right). What do you know? This point lies on the x-axis at point $(7, 0)$.

17. **A.** Just solve the first equation for a: $1 - \frac{2}{a} = 3 - \frac{4}{a}$; $1 + \frac{2}{a} = 3$; $\frac{2}{a} = 2$; $2 = 2a$; $1 = a$.

Wait, you're not done yet! You know that $a = 1$, but that's not what the question asks. You need to come up with the value of $1 - \frac{2}{a}$. Substitute 1 for a and you get $1 - \frac{2}{1} = 1 - 2 = -1$.

18. **H.** This one is easier than it looks. Start out by substituting –1 for a^2 in the second equation: $\left[(-1)^5 \right]^x = 1$. Simplify: $(-1)^5 = -1$, which means the equation is now $(-1)^x = 1$.

To make –1 a positive number, its exponent has to be even. The value of x has to be an even number; the least positive integer that is also an even number is 2.

Choice (A) may have tempted you. By definition any number raised to the zero power = 1, but don't be fooled! 0 can't be right because 0 is neither negative nor positive and the question asks for a positive integer.

19. **E.** For this problem, you need to know what it means to reflect a figure.

When you reflect a shape, it flips over at one of its ends to form a kind of mirror image. The problem tells you that the shape is reflected across line l. That means the shape flips and flies across line l until its left side is the same distance from line l as its right side was before. Line l forms a center line between the edge of the original shape and the edge of the reflected shape. The following figure can help you picture the reflection.

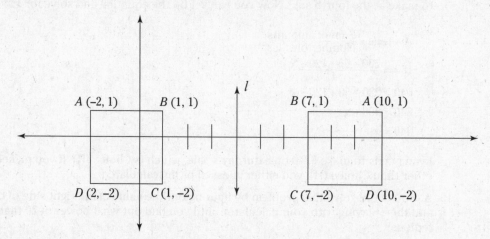

As you can see from the answer choices, the y-coordinates stay exactly the same. You're only concerned with the x-coordinate of point D. In its new position, point D holds the spot 10 spaces away from the y-axis. Its new coordinates are (10, –2), Choice (E).

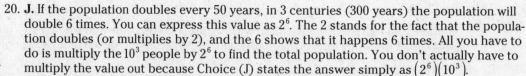

Don't let the y-axis confuse you; line l is the critical center line in this problem. And don't worry if you weren't particularly fond of this question. Problems about reflected shapes crop up only every once in a while on the ACT.

20. **J.** If the population doubles every 50 years, in 3 centuries (300 years) the population will double 6 times. You can express this value as 2^6. The 2 stands for the fact that the population doubles (or multiplies by 2), and the 6 shows that it happens 6 times. All you have to do is multiply the 10^3 people by 2^6 to find the total population. You don't actually have to multiply the value out because Choice (J) states the answer simply as $\left(2^6 \right) \left(10^3 \right)$.

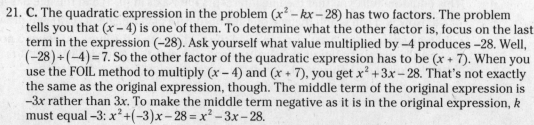

Before you spend a lot of time performing calculations, check the answer choices to see what form they're in. Sometimes you don't have to figure things out completely.

21. **C.** The quadratic expression in the problem $(x^2 - kx - 28)$ has two factors. The problem tells you that $(x - 4)$ is one of them. To determine what the other factor is, focus on the last term in the expression (–28). Ask yourself what value multiplied by –4 produces –28. Well, $(-28) \div (-4) = 7$. So the other factor of the quadratic expression has to be $(x + 7)$. When you use the FOIL method to multiply $(x - 4)$ and $(x + 7)$, you get $x^2 + 3x - 28$. That's not exactly the same as the original expression, though. The middle term of the original expression is $-3x$ rather than $3x$. To make the middle term negative as it is in the original expression, k must equal –3: $x^2 + (-3)x - 28 = x^2 - 3x - 28$.

Be careful when you choose a value for k. In the problem, the quadratic expression specifically shows that k is negative. So, k must be –3.

22. **J.** When you solve the inequality for z, you discover that $z < 7$, which means you can cross out Choices (G), (H), and (K). Don't stop there and pick Choice (F), though. Because the value has to be positive (because it's an absolute value), there's a lower limit to the values that can equal z. Eliminate Choice (F) and mark Choice (J) as your answer.

The *absolute value* of a number is always positive. It simply refers to how far the number is from 0. No matter what, the expression $z - 3$ is positive. As long as you realize that the possible values for z have a lower limit, you don't have to figure out what that lower limit is to solve the problem. To verify your answer, though, substitute –1 for z: $|-1-3| < 4$. The absolute value of –4 is 4, which equals 4. Therefore, –1 doesn't satisfy the conditions and z must be greater than –1. The possible values for z are 0, 1, 2, 3, 4, 5, and 6.

23. **B.** You can write $\left(-3x^2y^5\right)^3$ as $(-3)^3\left(x^2\right)^3\left(y^5\right)^3$. As long as you remember that you multiply the exponents, you're smooth sailing on this problem. $-3^3 = -27$, which means you can cross out Choices (C), (D), and (E) because none has a coefficient of –27. The difference between Choice (A) and Choice (B) is that Choice (A) adds the exponents instead of multiplies them. Choice (A) has to be wrong. So Choice (B) has to be right.

24. **G.** Aren't you glad you know the slope intercept form for the equation of a line? (If you need a refresher, check out Chapter 8.) Just isolate y on the left side of the equation by subtracting 12 and $32x$ from both sides and then dividing by 5: $32x + 5y + 12 = 0$; $5y = -32x - 12$; $y = -\dfrac{32}{5}x - \dfrac{12}{5}$. The resulting coefficient of x $(-\dfrac{32}{5})$ is the slope! What could be easier? Just make sure you keep your negative and positive signs straight and you'll breeze right through these types of questions.

25. **D.** This question may have you daydreaming of quaint New England lighthouses and ocean landscapes. Snap out of it! Sit forward in your uncomfortable chair, take up your No. 2 pencil, and realize that this is just a standard circle problem.

As it rotates, the light in the lighthouse moves full circle, or 360 degrees. Because the light takes 20 seconds to complete one full rotation, the lighthouse rotates 18 degrees per second: $\dfrac{360}{20} = 18$.

Hold it! Don't stop there and pick Choice (C). The question asks for the number of degrees the light rotates in 2 seconds, not 1. Multiply 18 by 2 seconds and you get 36 degrees.

If you marked Choice (E), you tried to work the 4.5 miles into the problem and multiplied 18 by 4.5. The number of miles that the lighthouse projects its light has no bearing on its rotation speed. The ACT question creators just put that information in there to test your ability to weed out unnecessary information. Impress them with your gardening skills (weed out — get it?) and focus only on the information that's relevant to answering the question.

26. **J.** To determine the perimeter of trapezoid *FBCE*, you have to figure out the lengths of segments *FB*, *BC*, *EC*, and *FE* so you can add them together. The problem gives you the length of two of the sides. *BC* = 6 units and the left and right sides of the trapezoid are equal because the triangle is equilateral, which means that *FE* = 6 units, too. Find the measurements of *FB* and *EC* and you're done!

Apply what you know about triangles. If triangle *ACE* is equilateral, all angles measure 60 degrees and the side lengths are equal. *EC* has to be 10 units. *AB* added to *BC* forms one side of triangle *ACE* (side *AC*). *AB* = 4 units and *BC* = 6 units. That means that *AC* is 10 units (4 + 6 = 10), and *AC* = *EC*. So far the perimeter is 6 + 6 + 10, or 22, units. You can eliminate Choices F and G.

Your remaining task is to find the length of *FB*. Accomplish this task by recognizing that triangle *ABF* is also equilateral. You know that *FB* and *EC* are parallel. You should note that lines *AE* and *AC* are transversals that cut through these parallel lines. That means that the corresponding angles these lines form are equal. Angles *AEC*, *AFB*, *ACE*, and *ABF* all equal 60 degrees, which means that triangle *ABF* is also equilateral and has equal side lengths. Because *AB* = 4, *FB* = 4. Add 4 to 22 to get 26, and you know that Choice (J) is the perimeter of the trapezoid.

Note that the fact that point *G* is the midpoint of *FB* is irrelevant to the problem. We hope you didn't spend too much time trying to use that useless information to solve the problem.

27. **C.** Because you're supposed to solve for $2x - y$ and the equation contains the terms $2x$ and y, all you have to do is get $2x - y$ on one side of the equation and the rest of the terms on the other side. To accomplish this task, just subtract x and $3x$ from the left side of the equation and subtract y from the right: $x + 2x + 3x = y$; $2x - y = -x - 3x$; $2x - y = -4x$.

You can solve many ACT math problems in more than one way. You could also solve this problem by solving the first equation for *y* and substituting that value for *y* in the second equation: $x + 2x + 3x = 6x$, so $6x = y$. When you substitute $6x$ for *y* in the second equation, you get $2x - 6x$, which equals $-4x$.

28. **F.** Questions that involve logarithms are scarce on the ACT, which probably suits you just fine, but they're also pretty simple. Even if you've never studied logarithms in your life, you can handle these questions. All you have to know is that $\log_x 27 = 3$ means that it takes 3 *x* times to get 27. Therefore, $x = 3$. You multiply 3 three times to get 27. That's all there is to it!

29. **D.** This word problem is a distance problem. The formula for finding distance (*d*) is rate (*r*) × time (*t*).

To find out how many miles the Swift Express travels before it meets up with the Douglas Dependable, first determine the rate of each train by applying the distance formula and plugging in numbers you know. If distance = rate × time, then rate = $\frac{distance}{time}$. Swift Express's rate is $\frac{900}{3}$, or 300 miles/hour. The Douglas Dependable travels at a rate of $\frac{900}{5}$, or 180 miles/hour.

To continue with the solution, ask yourself which of the three elements of the formula (rate, time, or distance) both trains have in common when they meet in the middle. It's not rate, because you know from your calculations that the rates are different. It's not distance, because the faster train must travel more miles than the slower train. It must be time. Don't let the 3 hour and 5 hour designations fool you. These tell you the total time each train took to travel the entire distance. But you're looking for the time it takes them to meet in the middle. Both trains travel the same amount of time before they meet.

Modify the distance formula to solve for time. Then set up an equation that makes the two trains' times equal to each other. You can let 1 stand for the Swift Express and 2 stand for the Douglas Dependable:

$$t = \frac{d}{r}$$

$$\frac{d_1}{r_1} = \frac{d_2}{r_2}$$

Plug the values you know into the equation with *x* standing for the distance the Swift Express has traveled when the two trains meet. If Swift Express has traveled *x* miles when they meet, Douglas Dependable will have traveled $900 - x$ miles, or the difference between the total 900 miles and the *x* miles that Swift Express has traveled. Here's what your equation looks like:

$$\frac{x}{300} = \frac{900 - x}{180}$$

Cross-multiply to solve for *x*:

$$180x = 300(900 - x)$$
$$180x = 270,000 - 300x$$
$$480x = 270,000$$
$$x = 562.50$$

The answer is Choice (D).

30. **H.** When you look at the answer choices, you realize that you need to find out which line segments are equal. Approach this problem by using the distance formula to figure out the length of each line segment:

$$d = \sqrt{(y_2 - y_1)^2 (x_2 - x_1)^2}$$

If you have a hard time envisioning this question without a picture of the points on the coordinate plane, sketch out a quick graph, like this one:

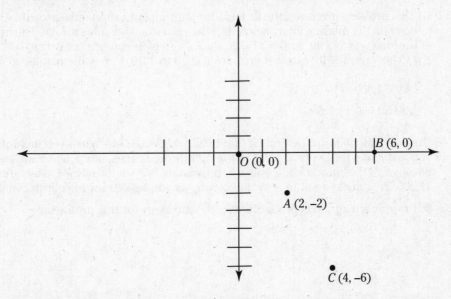

When you look at the graph, you may think that lines *AB* and *AC* have similar lengths. Don't rely on your eye to answer this question, but start your calculations with these points. Find the length (distance) of line *AC*:

$$d_{AC} = \sqrt{\left[-6 - (-2)\right]^2 + (4 - 2)^2}$$
$$d_{AC} = \sqrt{(-4)^2 + 2^2}$$
$$d_{AC} = \sqrt{16 + 4}$$
$$d_{AC} = \sqrt{20}$$

Follow the same process for line *AB*:

$$d_{AB} = \sqrt{\left[0 - (-2)\right]^2 + (6 - 2)^2}$$
$$d_{AB} = \sqrt{2^2 + 4^2}$$
$$d_{AB} = \sqrt{4 + 16}$$
$$d_{AB} = \sqrt{20}$$

Lines *AB* and *AC* are the same length. Choice (H) is the correct answer. If you calculate the length of the other lines, you'll find that *OA* is $\sqrt{8}$, *OC* is $\sqrt{52}$, *BC* is $\sqrt{40}$, and *OB* is 6.

31. **E.** When two triangles are similar, one is an enlargement of the other with the same angles and respective sides in the same proportion to one another. You can set up a proportion to solve this problem.

You know that lines *NM* and *PQ* are similar sides of the two triangles because they're across from equal angles. Likewise, *a* and *b* are similar sides because they're across from equal angles. So the ratio of *b* to *a* is the same as the ratio of line *PQ* to line *NM*, or $\frac{5}{6} : \frac{5}{8}$.

A ratio is like a division problem: $\frac{5}{6} : \frac{5}{8} = \frac{\frac{5}{6}}{\frac{5}{8}}$. Solve the problem to find the ratio of the two

triangles: $\frac{\frac{5}{6}}{\frac{5}{8}} = \frac{5}{6} \times \frac{8}{5} = \frac{40}{30} = \frac{4}{3}$. Because the ratio of the two triangles is $\frac{4}{3}$, the value of $\frac{b}{a}$ is

also $\frac{4}{3}$. So Choice (E) is right.

If you picked Choice (B), you found the ratio of the small triangle to the large triangle rather than the other way around. Order matters with ratios, so work carefully.

32. **G.** This problem gives you the formula for figuring out exponential growth. All you have to do is fill the missing information into the equation and solve for *NV*. The initial value of the loan was $1,000, so IV = $1,000. P = 2.5% (which you can convert to 0.025) and Y = 10 because the investment grew from 2000 to 2010. Here's the resulting equation:

$$NV = 1,000 \times (1 + 0.025)^{10}$$
$$NV = 1,000 \times 1.025^{10}$$

Use your calculator to determine that $1.025^{10} = 1.280084544$. When you multiply by 1,000, you just move the decimal point to the right three spaces, but you already know that because all the answer choices are in thousands. NV = 1,280.084544, which rounds to $1,280. This question is an easy one as long as you keep track of your decimal points.

33. **B.** Drawing a diagram is probably your best strategy for this problem.

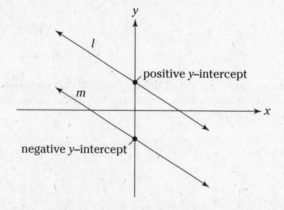

Line *l* has a negative slope and a positive *x*-intercept (meaning it's to the right of the *y*-axis). Its *y*-intercept is positive as well (meaning it's above the *x*-axis). If line *m* is parallel to line *l* and line *l* has a negative slope, line *m* also has a negative slope. A line with a negative slope falls from left to right. So if a line with a negative slope has a negative *x*-intercept, that line has to also have a negative *y*-intercept. Eliminate Choices (C), (D), and (E) because they say that the *y*-intercept of line *m* is positive or zero. If the *y*-intercept of line *m* is negative and the *y*-intercept of line *l* is positive, the *y*-intercept of line *m* has to be less than the *y*-intercept of line *l*, so Choice (B) must be the correct answer.

34. **K.** The values that add up to 3 and multiply to 2 are 2 and 1. Be careful, though, these values are the roots of the equation, not the factors. The factors that result in roots of 2 and 1 are $(x - 2)(x - 1)$. Now all you have to do is FOIL. (No, we didn't say FOLD. Hang in there. You still have 26 questions to go. Check out Chapter 9 if you don't remember how to FOIL.)

The quickest way to move through the problem is to exert a little POE (that's short for process of elimination). All choices have the same first term, so you don't have to figure that out. The last term should be +2 ($-2 \times -1 = 2$). Feel free to cross out Choices (G), (H), and (J). The outer terms equal $-1x$, and the inner terms result in $-2x$. The answer has to be Choice (K) because it has a negative middle term.

You can also approach this problem by simply factoring each answer choice to see which one has roots of 2 and 3. The process goes more quickly when you recognize that factoring Choices (F) and (H), which have all positive terms, will give you only negative roots. In that case, the last term will be positive, but the middle term will be negative. That way you'd only have to try Choices (G), (J), and (K). The roots of Choice (G) are 3 and –1. Choice (J)'s roots are –3 and 1.

35. **E.** Just using a quick number substitution for each possible answer is the fastest way to solve this problem. You can eliminate answers that fail to give you 2, 6, and 10 when you substitute 1, 2, and 3 for n. For instance, you can cross out Choice (A) because, although $2(1) = 2$, $2(2)$ isn't 6 and $2(3)$ isn't 10. Choices (B), (C), and (D) don't work for all three of the first terms in the sequence. Choice (E) is the ticket: $2[2(1) – 1] = 2(1) = 2$; $2[2(2) – 1] = 2(3) = 6$; and $2[2(3) – 1] = 10$.

36. **J.** To find the perimeter of the triangle, you have to know its side lengths. You know the length of one side. Line XY measures 4 inches. The other two sides are equal. When you find the value of one, you'll know the value of the other.

Your job is much easier after you notice that the side you need to know is also the hypotenuse of a right triangle that's formed when you draw a line through point O that joins the sides of the cylinder as shown in the following figure.

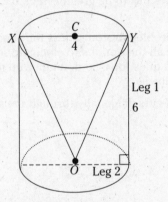

Leg 1 of the triangle is 6 inches. Leg 2 is 2 inches because it's the radius of a circle with a diameter that measure 4 inches and the radius is half the diameter.

The side lengths aren't in one of those handy Pythagorean triples we talk about in Chapter 8, so you have to apply the Pythagorean theorem:
$c^2 = a^2 + b^2$; $c^2 = 6^2 + 2^2$; $c^2 = 36 + 4$; $c^2 = 40$; $c = \sqrt{40}$.

The square root of 40 is a little more than 6, but don't pick Choice (F). You're not done yet. You have to add up the sides of the original triangle to find its perimeter. The sum is $\sqrt{40} + \sqrt{40} + 4$, which is a little more than $6 + 6 + 4$, or 16. The closest answer is Choice (J).

37. **B.** The language of the question tells you that you're supposed to find the volume of the cylinder and ignore the triangle inside. The formula for the volume of a cylinder is $V = \pi r^2 h$. If you've memorized the formula, the rest of the question is simple. The height is 6 inches and the radius is 2 inches. Substitute the values in the formula and solve for V: $V = \pi (2)^2 6$; $V = \pi 24$.

The answers don't contain the π sign, so use your power of estimation. π is about 3.14, which is just a little over 3, and 24 times a little over 3 is a little more than 72. The answer choice that's closest to a little more than 72 is 75, Choice (B).

38. **F.** Because O is the center of the base, the lines that connect it to opposite sides of the top have to be equal. (You figured that out in Question 36.) If the sides are equal, the angles opposite them are also equal. The answer has to be Choice (F).

If that seemed too easy, you may want to check the other options. You know that Choices (G), (H), and (J) are untrue. Line *XY* is shorter than the other two sides of the triangle, so its angle also must be smaller than the other angles.

Note: Because you know that Choice (F) is true, don't spend too much time considering Choice (K). You know from working out Question 36 that the angle next to angle *OXY* in one of the right triangles you drew is the smallest of the three angles in the right triangle. One of the other angles is 90 degrees. That means the other two angles have to add up to 90 degrees. If the two angles were equal, they'd both measure 45 degrees. They're not equal, so the smaller angle has to be less than 45 degrees. That small angle and angle *OXY* form a 90-degree angle. If the small angle is less than 45 degrees, angle *OXY* must be more than 45 degrees.

39. **B.** This problem focuses on the rules of bases and exponents. The easiest way to solve this problem is to reduce each expression to a single power of 10 (10^x). Then you can compare the quantities in a similar format. Choice (E) is already in that format. The next easiest answer to evaluate is Choice (B). Count the zeros to find the exponent. 1,000,000,000,000,000 is also 10^{15}, which is less than 10^{100}. Cross out Choice (E).

Eliminate Choice (C), too: $1,000^{100}$ has to be greater than 10^{15}. Don't work out Choice (A). As soon as you notice that you have to multiply 10^5 ten times, you know it can't be less than 10^{15}. The same goes for Choice (D): 10^{10} ten times has to be greater than 10^{15}. Choice (B) has the least value.

When you compare the answer choices, this problem becomes less time-consuming than it originally seemed. You don't have to calculate all the options to eliminate some wrong answers, which is the case for many ACT math questions. So don't give up on a question before you look for shortcuts in the answer choices.

40. **G.** The plane that contains vertices *S*, *U*, and *X* cuts diagonally through the square prism from back-left to front-right.

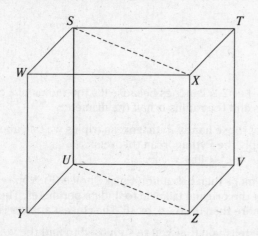

As shown in the figure, that plane also contains vertex *Z* in the lower-right corner. None of the other vertices falls in this plane. So Choice (G) is the winner.

41. **C.** Lemonade has to end up being 15 percent of the total beverage, so the best way to solve the problem is to set up a proportion with lemonade on the top and total liquid on the bottom.

On the left side, put $\frac{15}{100}$ to represent that lemonade will be 15 percent of the total or 15 parts per 100. On the right side of the proportion, make the numerator the total amount of lemonade that ends up in the beverage; call that *x* because it's what the problem asks you to figure out. The denominator is the total amount of combined liquid. You can represent that with $2 + x$, which is the two liters of iced tea plus *x* amount of lemonade. The proportion is $\frac{15}{100} = \frac{x}{2 + x}$.

Cross-multiply and solve: $15(2 + x) = 100x$; $30 + 15x = 100x$; $30 = 85x$; $x = \frac{30}{85} = \frac{6}{17}$.

If you picked Choice (A), you incorrectly multiplied the 2 liters of iced tea by 15 percent. Doing so doesn't account for the additional liquid required to create the combination.

42. **J.** Drawing a graph may help you visualize the problem, but you can't solve it visually and graphing eats up precious time. So working out the necessary calculations is a better way to go. This problem involves two equations and substitution.

The first equation you know is the equation of the line: $x = 6$. The second equation is the equation of the circle. The general equation for a circle is $(x-h)^2 + (y-k)^2 = r^2$, where h and k are the x- and y-coordinates of the center of the circle and r is its radius. Thus, the equation for this specific circle is $(x-3)^2 + (y-5)^2 = 4^2$.

The first equation tells you that $x = 6$, so substitute 6 for x in the equation and solve for y: $(6-3)^2 + (y-5)^2 = 4^2$; $9 + (y-5)^2 = 16$; $(y-5)^2 = 7$; $y-5 = \pm\sqrt{7}$; $y = 5 \pm \sqrt{7}$.

Use the square root key on your calculator to find that the y-coordinates are 7.65 and 2.35, or Choice (J).

If you picked Choice (F), you probably sketched out a rough graph and tried to eyeball the right answer.

Reading through this question may have inspired you to guess and run, which may not be a bad idea if you're pressed for time by this point in the exam and haven't memorized the equation of a circle. Bubble in something for this time-consumer and move on to the next problem. Be sure to mark it so that you'll know to come back to it if you have time at the end of the section.

43. **B.** Use the formula for the area of a circle $\left(A = \pi r^2\right)$ to find the pizza's area. Divide the diameter of 122 feet by 2 to get the correct radius of 61 feet: $A = \pi(61)^2$; $A = \pi(3{,}721)$; $A = 11{,}689.87$ square feet.

You need 10 pepperoni slices per square foot, so multiply that number by 10 to get 116,898.70 total slices of pepperoni on the pizza. Then divide that large number by 50 to figure out how many pepperoni sticks the pizza makers need. The answer is 2,337.97 sticks. Don't forget to round up to 2,338 so you don't run out of pepperoni! If you picked Choice (A), you used the formula for circumference instead of area.

If this problem doesn't give you real incentive to do well on the ACT so you can go to college and get a good education so you don't have to cut up 2,338 pepperoni sticks at a pizza restaurant for a living, we don't know what will!

44. **K.** You just need to know a few basic trig rules to answer this question. Don't worry. No prior trigonometry class required. Merely memorize SOH CAH TOA. (Review Chapter 9 if you can't remember what this acronym means.) All you have to do is divide $\sin A$ by $\cos B$. To determine $\sin A$, find angle A on the figure. The opposite side of angle A is a, and the hypotenuse of the triangle (the side opposite the 90-degree angle) is c. Therefore, $\sin A = \dfrac{a}{c}$. To find $\cos B$, work with angle B on the figure. The side adjacent (or next) to it is a. The hypotenuse is still c. That means $\cos B = \dfrac{a}{c}$. What do you know? The value of $\sin A$ is the same as the value of $\cos B$. Any number divided by itself is 1. The answer is Choice (K). That wasn't so bad!

45. **D.** Making sense of this problem requires a little language interpretation.

Two positive integers r and s satisfy the relationship $r \dagger s$ only when $r = s^2 + 2$. The funny symbol between r and s means that whenever you have two values with the symbol between them you create the given equation with those values inserted.

So this problem results in two equations: $s \dagger t$ gives you $s = t^2 + 2$, and $t \dagger u$ means $t = u^2 + 2$. Because you're solving for s in terms of u, you have to make the t's disappear. The second equation solves for t in terms of u. Substitute $u^2 + 2$ for t in the first equation: $s = \left(u^2 + 2\right)^2 + 2$. Use FOIL to square the first expression: $\left(u^2 + 2\right)\left(u^2 + 2\right) = u^2 + 4u^2 + 4$. Add 2 and combine: $s = u^4 + 4u^2 + 6$. After you get past the language barrier, this problem practically solves itself.

46. **F.** This problem describes an inscribed angle in a semicircle. Here's what it looks like:

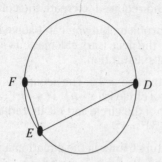

Thales's theorem states that an inscribed angle in a semicircle is a right (90-degree) angle. That's all the information you need to pick Choice (F) and eliminate the others.

47. **A.** If you know how to substitute, you can solve this problem. The *determinant* tells you how to determine which values constitute a, b, c, and d. The equation shows you where to put the values when you know what they are. This is all just a fancy way of saying that $a = 4x$, $b = 2y$, $c = 7y$, and $d = 3y$. Insert these values into the equation: $(7y \times 3y)\left[(2y)^2 - (4x)^2\right]$. Finish up by substituting 4 for x and –2 for y and solving the equation:

$$(7(-2) \times 3(-2))\left[(2(-2))^2 - (4(4))^2\right] = (-14 \times -6)(-4^2 - 16^2) = 84(16 - 256) = -20{,}160$$

48. **G.** Find the value of $\sin\theta$, multiply it by z, and you're done. Remember that SOH tells you $\sin\theta = \dfrac{\text{opposite}}{\text{hypotenuse}}$. The opposite side is y. The hypotenuse is z. The final answer is $z\sin\theta = z \times \dfrac{y}{z} = y$, Choice (G). If you picked Choice (F), you were thinking cosine, not sine.

49. **C.** It's arts and crafts time. Sketch the little boat. Add the water. Draw the rope. Draw a person in the air. Behold! Your masterpiece reveals a right triangle. Its vertices are the boat, the parasailer, and the point in the water directly beneath the parasailer:

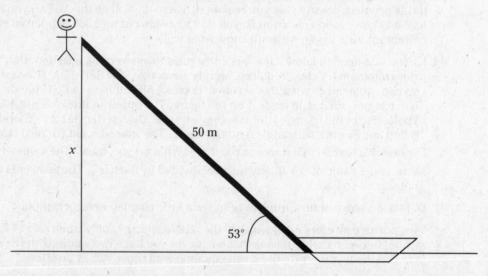

TIP You know that Choice (B) isn't right even before you do any calculating. After all, the hypotenuse of a right triangle is always longer than either of the other two sides.

As the problem explains, the angle that the rope makes with the surface of the water is 53 degrees. You know the length of the hypotenuse (50 meters), and you want to know the length of the side that's opposite of the 53-degree angle (x). Sounds like you need to apply sine: SOH or $\sin 53° = \dfrac{\text{opposite}}{\text{hypotenuse}}$. Delete Choices (A) and (D) because they use tangent and cosine. Plug in the values and solve for x: $\sin 53° = \dfrac{x}{50}$; $x = (\sin 53°)50$.

50. **J.** To evaluate the expression, engage in a little distribution. Multiply $2x$ by both terms inside the parentheses: $2x\left(\dfrac{3}{y}\right) = \dfrac{6x}{y}$; $2x\left(\dfrac{4}{z}\right) = \dfrac{8x}{z}$. The new expression is $\dfrac{6x}{y} + \dfrac{8x}{z}$. Unfortunately, that's not an answer option, so you must press on.

Fractions have to have the same denominator before you can add them. To find the lowest common denominator of two variables, just multiply them. The product of y and z is yz.

Convert each fraction so its denominator is yz. Multiply the top and bottom of the first term by z. That gives you $\dfrac{6xz}{yz}$. Multiply the top and bottom of the second fraction by y and you get $\dfrac{8xy}{yz}$. When you add the two fractions together, you get $\dfrac{8xy + 6xz}{yz}$, or Choice (J). If you picked Choice (F), you multiplied the fractions instead of adding them.

51. **E.** The formula for finding average is simple. It's just the sum of all the salaries divided by the number of salaries. The trick for this question is to figure out where to put what you know in the equation. The question gives you the average of all the salaries: $51,200. Insert that value for *average* in the equation. The total number of salaries is 15. That's the number you divide by. The tricky part is determining how to represent the sum of all salaries. You know that the first 14 salaries average $51,000. Apply the average formula again: $51,000 times 14 must be the sum of the other 14 salaries. Let x stand for George's salary and add that to the sum of the other salaries. Your equation looks like this: $51,200 = \dfrac{(14 \times 51,000) + x}{15}$.

Solve for x and you're through: $768,000 = 714,000 + x$; $54,000 = x$. George's salary is above average. If you chose Choice (A), you probably made the mistake of adding George's salary (x) to just one $51,000 salary rather than 14 of them.

52. **H.** Don't let the square root sign throw you. Solve this equation in the same way you would any other equation. For this problem, you have to "break out" the variable p from the square root "jail" it's trapped in.

Get the variable by itself on one side of the equation by performing the opposite function to both sides of the equation. The opposite of taking the square root of something is to square it. Square everything on both sides of the equation. You end up with $\sqrt{5p} \times \sqrt{5p} = 3.67 \times 3.67$, or $5p = 13.4689$. When you divide both sides by 5, you get 2.69, Choice (H).

53. **D.** This word problem has you working with percentages. Make sure you're clear about what you're supposed to figure out and what you know. The answer you're looking for is the number of Representatives who voted no. You know that the percentage of no votes is the same in both groups, but you don't know what that percentage is. You can set up an equation to figure out the percentage of no votes. Make x the percentage of members that voted no in each group: $(410)x + (90)x = 350$. This means that a certain percentage of 410 Representatives and the same percentage of Senators adds up to a total of 350 members who voted no. Solve for x: $500x = 350$; $x = 0.7$, which is 70%.

Don't get all excited and select Choice (B). The question doesn't ask you for the percentage of no votes. It wants you to figure out the number of no votes in the House of Representatives.

Multiply 410 by 70% (or 0.7) to get 287 naysayers. If you picked Choice (A), you figured out the number of Senators who voted no.

54. **J.** The information you need to help you find the answer is hidden in the problem. It helps to know that $\sin \pi = 0$ (or use your calculator to figure it out). Read through the problem and add information to the figure it provides.

Following the x-axis from left to right; you have three x-intercepts (where the graph of the function crosses the x-axis and $y = 0$). The first x-intercept is the origin $(0, 0)$. According to the function, the last x-intercept has coordinates of $(2\pi, 0)$. When you know that $\sin \pi = 0$, you can deduce that the middle x-intercept has coordinates of $(\pi, 0)$. Point A then must have x-coordinates between 0 and π and a y-coordinate greater than 0. The range of values for sine lies between -1 and 1 $(-1 \le \sin x \le 1)$. Because point A represents the maximum y-value of $\sin x$, the y-coordinate is 1.

The figure states that it's not drawn to scale, so you can't assume by looking at it that point A is $\left(\frac{\pi}{2}, 1\right)$ even though the x-coordinate appears to be halfway between 0 and π.

To confirm your answer, use your calculator to determine the sine of $\frac{\pi}{2}$. Sure enough, it equals 1.

If you guessed Choice (A) or (B), you incorrectly approached the graph as though it represented $0 \leq x \leq \pi$. Choice (C) can't be right because clearly y doesn't equal 0. You can eliminate Choice (E) right off the bat because $\sin x$ can't equal π because π is approximately 3.14 and the sine of a number can't be greater than 1. If this explanation seems like Greek to you, don't worry. You don't need to learn a new language. These types of questions appear rarely on the ACT. Spend your time and effort on questions you understand instead.

55. **E.** If 4 and –3 are the solution set of a quadratic equation, the factors must be $(x-4)(x+3)$. Use FOIL to multiply the expressions. You end up with $x^2 - x - 12$, Choice (E).

56. **F.** This question is about multiplying and dividing bases with exponents.

Keep these rules in mind as you solve this problem:

- You can multiply and divide exponents only when the bases are the same.

- When you see a base raised to a negative exponent, it equals the reciprocal of the base raised to the positive version of the exponent.

To get a by itself, divide both sides of the equation by c^6. That gives you $a^3 b^5 = \frac{a^2}{3b^{-5}}$.

Convert b^{-5} into $\frac{1}{b^5}$. To divide by a fraction, multiply by the reciprocal: $\frac{a^2}{3} \times \frac{b^5}{1} = \frac{a^2 b^5}{3}$. This gives you $a^3 b^5 = \frac{a^2 b^5}{3}$. Divide both sides by b^5 to eliminate that term. To isolate a, divide both sides by a^2. This gives you $a = \frac{1}{3}$.

57. **B.** The number of square feet of sod is the area of the parallelogram. The area of a parallelogram is bh. The base of the garden is the length of one of its sides (let's say the longer one measures 8 feet.) Because the garden is shaped like a parallelogram, you can't assume that the measure of its width is the 6-feet measure on the other side. To find the width measure, draw a parallelogram that slants to the right and create a right triangle by drawing a line from its top left corner that's perpendicular to the base.

The angle your new line extends from measures 120 degrees. Opposite angles in a parallelogram have the same measurements, and all four angles add up to 360 degrees. That means the two smaller angles of the garden measure 60 degrees and the other large angle measures 120 degrees.

The right triangle you've created is a 30:60:90 right triangle. The side ratio of a 30:60:90 triangle is $s : s\sqrt{3} : 2s$.

The smaller side (the one opposite the 30-degree angle) is equal to half the hypotenuse, and the longer side (the one opposite the 60-degree angle) is equal to the smaller side multiplied by $\sqrt{3}$. The smaller side is half of 6, which is 3, and the longer side, the height of the parallelogram, is $3\sqrt{3}$. Multiply that value by the base of 8. The number of square feet of sod that Janet needs is $24\sqrt{3}$.

58. **K.** The absolute value of x is the number of spaces x is from 0 on the number line. When you solve the inequality by adding 1 to both sides, you learn that $|x| \leq 4$. That means that x includes –4 and 4 and all numbers between them on the number line. Eliminate Choices (G) and (H) because they show that values for x are unlimited in at least one direction. Choice (J) results from subtracting 1 from both sides of the inequality instead of adding it. If you picked Choice (F), you forgot that x includes –4 and 4. The best answer is Choice (K). The solid points at –4 and 4 indicate that the two values are included in the solution set.

59. **D.** To find the area of $WXYZ$, you have to know the length of its sides. As it turns out, all four sides are the hypotenuses of equal right triangles. Each triangle has one leg that

measures 5 cm (the length of one edge of the cube) and a second leg that measures 2.5 cm (half the length of one side of the cube). Apply your trusty friend the Pythagorean theorem to find the length of the hypotenuse (which is the length of each side of *WXYZ*): $c^2 = a^2 + b^2 = (5)^2 + (2.5)^2 = 25 + 6.25 = 31.25$.

Note: You could figure out the square root of 31.25 to discover the length of the hypotenuse, but then you'd just have to square it again to get the area of *WXYZ*. Because the sides of *WXYZ* are equal, it's a square. The area of a square is the square of one of its side lengths. The side length of *WXYZ* is the square root of 31.25, and, therefore, 31.25 is the area of the square.

If you chose Choice (A), you didn't finish the problem, and Choice (E) incorrectly squares 31.25 a second time.

60. **H.** Replacing *f(x)* with *f(x – 3)* does nothing more than shift the parabola over 3 units to the right. That move has no effect on the area. The area remains 5, or Choice (H).

The last three questions in this section were probably easier for you than some of the questions that come before them. Don't spend too much time on really difficult questions that may prevent you from getting to easier questions later in the test. If it takes you more than a minute to answer a question, mark your best guess and move along.

Reading Test

1. **C.** The passage is clearly not a poem, so cross out Choice (D). A *fable* tells a story with a moral lesson and often uses humanized animals as its main characters. That definition is too specific to apply to this passage. So you can narrow down your options to Choices (B) and (C). You may have noticed a hint of romance in the story, but it's mostly about an instance when the young protagonist, Eyvind, has experiences, such as watching Marit outgrow him and experiencing embarrassment at being called a *youngster,* that mark his development from a child to a young man. Choice (C) is the best answer.

2. **F.** Marit is the one who coaxes the bashful children into the party. She dances more than anyone else. You can hardly describe her as bashful. Cross out Choice (G). You probably wouldn't use the adjective *grandmotherly* to describe a tireless dancer, either. Choice (J) is out. Marit doesn't pay much attention to Eyvind, but that doesn't categorize her as callous. The best answer is Choice (F). *Gregarious* means social and outgoing.

3. **D.** The tingling sensation occurs in the last line of the paragraph that describes the scene in which the tall fellow pushes Eyvind away. The tingling doesn't occur right after the fellow calls him a youngster, though. It happens after he sees Marit laughing and dancing. The line says that this is the first time Eyvind has experienced this feeling, and it implies that he's disappointed that Marit has outgrown him. The best answer is Choice (D). The passage doesn't say that Eyvind drank ale. Nor does the paragraph give any indication that Eyvind experienced physical injury from the push.

4. **J.** Cross out the answers that express a legitimate time when Eyvind was timid. Start with Choice (F) because Lines 58–59 say that he didn't dare join in the dancing at first. He didn't stand up for himself when the bushy-haired man pushed him, so you can cross out Choice (G), too. The passage says that Eyvind moved back away from the dance floor when he watched Marit dance, which suggests timidity. Choice (H) is out. The passage says that Eyvind didn't get an invitation to enter the little room, so he definitely didn't fail to respond to it. Choice (J) describes the one time when Eyvind wasn't timid because it didn't happen.

5. **A.** The description doesn't portray particularly harsh or dangerous conditions, which means that Choices (B) and (D) aren't right. The first paragraph doesn't mention anything about Scandinavian life. The answer has to be Choice (A). The introductory paragraph sets the natural backdrop for the main events of the story.

Using the power of POE (process of elimination) can really help you out on the Reading Test. When you first look at the answer choices, you may feel a bit overwhelmed. They may all look right or all look wrong, or they may seem like they're about a completely different subject than the passage you read! Cross out answers that are obviously wrong. Soon, you'll be able to focus on the best option.

6. **J.** Marit doesn't pay much attention to Eyvind. The answer that best describes this fact is Choice (J). Nothing in the passage implies that she loves Eyvind, and her feelings toward him aren't strong enough to be repulsion or pity.

Unless something in the passage specifically suggests a strong answer choice, the right answer is probably fairly neutral.

7. **C.** The author describes the little room to point out that Eyvind didn't get invited to Marit's family's inner circle. You don't have to make any inferences to cross out Choice (A). No one danced in the little room. The grandmother isn't a major figure in the passage, so the purpose of the scene probably isn't to learn more about her. Eliminate Choice (D). Old people were in the room but not necessarily because Marit invited them. Choice (B) isn't right. The best answer is Choice (C). The passage says that Marit invited guests she really cared for to the room. She didn't invite Eyvind. So she must not really care for Eyvind, something that Eyvind finds strange. From this little scene, you realize that Eyvind makes more of his relationship with Marit than she does.

8. **G.** *Bands* refers to the groups of girls that walked together to the party. The passage also refers to them as *gangs,* but it doesn't give a negative impression of them. They aren't ruffians. Keep Choice (G) in mind and cross out Choice (F). The passage says they marched along, but that doesn't mean they were in a parade. Choice (H) is wrong. If you picked Choice (J), you probably tried to answer the question without looking at the passage. A *band* is often a group of musicians, but that's not the case in this passage.

Don't answer reading questions based on your outside knowledge. Use the passage to answer every question.

9. **B.** POE to the rescue! Cross out choices that make you think beyond the scope of the passage or that are just plain wrong. Choice (C) is one of the just plain wrong ones. Eyvind wasn't invited to the grandmother's room, so he couldn't have spent all his time there. The passage says that Eyvind danced, so he didn't just sit and watch Marit. Cross out Choice (A). The passage doesn't specifically state that Eyvind was in the corner or that he sulked. He seemed to be in a state of shock rather than depression. Cross out Choice (D). The fact that he was experiencing new feelings and noticing changes in Marit implies that he realized his life was changing. Choice (B) is best.

10. **G.** You can't make assumptions about everyday weather in the village from the description of one evening. Choice (F) makes you infer way beyond the information in the passage. Likewise, just because groups of children make their way to the party by running from farmhouse to farmhouse doesn't mean that all villagers travel that way. Lines 53–55 suggest that the villagers prefer dancing to the new musician rather than the old one, but that's because he's a better player and knows more songs. The passage doesn't say that he's necessarily older. Cross out Choices (H) and (J) and consider Choice (G). Because the passage tells you that people of different ages attended the dance, you can reasonably assume that the villagers participate in activities with different age groups, even if those activities include just this one dance.

11. **B.** This passage contains a lot of information that you may have a hard time keeping straight. As you read each paragraph, summarize its topic in your head and write one or two words in the margin next to the paragraph that help you remember the information it covers. To answer this particular question, head for the paragraph you marked as being about criticism of the bailouts.

The passage first mentions *bailout* in the fourth paragraph. The next paragraph, though, is the one that lists the complaints against it. Refer to this paragraph as you read through the answer choices. Remember to cross out the choices that are arguments against the bailout. The remaining answer is the right one.

Lines 95–98 list the complaint that not enough funds have been devoted to halting foreclosures, which sounds a lot like Choice (A). Cross out that answer. According to Lines 85–87, the size of the bailout is a problem but not because it's too small. On the contrary, it's too large. Choice (B) is probably the answer, but check the others to be sure. Choice (C) paraphrases Lines 87–89, which mention the lack of transparency, so it's not right. Choice (D) appears in Lines 92–95 as well. Cross out Choice (D) and stick with Choice (B).

The answer choices often paraphrase the wording in the passage, so you may have to do a little translation to evaluate the options.

12. **J.** To answer vocabulary-in-context questions, replace the original word with each answer choice to see which one makes sense. The original sentence says that the interventions failed to *stem* the growing crisis. The interventions didn't fail to *originate* the growing crisis, so Choice (F) doesn't fit. Choice (G) sounds way too awkward. You're down to Choices (H) and (J). You may be able to say that the interventions failed to *remove* the growing crisis, but the better answer is Choice (J). It sounds better to say that interventions failed to *stop* the growth rather than *remove* it.

Don't choose an answer to a vocabulary-in-context question based on what you think the word's definition is. The ACT often tests you on words that have several alternative definitions.

13. **A.** The Act appears in the fourth paragraph. Compare each answer choice to the information in the paragraph to see which one is a result of the Act's passage. Choice (A) paraphrases Lines 57–58, which say that the Act used $700 to stabilize the financial sector. *Stabilize* means to firm up. Choice (A) is the answer.

14. **J.** The first paragraph isn't about foreclosures. Cross out Choice (G). The passage doesn't talk about the role of government until the next paragraph, so Choices (F) and (H) are out, too. The best answer is Choice (J). The paragraph starts with a description of the problems and follows with the various ways different entities have been affected.

15. **C.** Look in the second paragraph where it says that the government's *improvisational* (or unplanned) response to the crisis has contributed to the public's failing confidence in its ability to restore the financial system. Choice (C) provides a nice paraphrase of this idea. Choice (D) contradicts information in Lines 85–87. Choice (B) contains one of those debatable words — *completely* — that raises a red flag. Nothing in the passage suggests that anyone's confidence has been completely restored. Because Choice (C) answers the question, don't waste time trying to find Choice (A). The passage doesn't associate lack of confidence with lack of attention to borrowers.

16. **H.** Focus on the fourth paragraph, where the passage mentions the Fed. Lines 75–79 say that the Fed took steps to force down home mortgage rates. That fact corresponds with Choice (H); mortgage rates are interest rates. None of the other choices work. You can't assume that buying housing-related securities was an attempt to limit the power of Fannie Mae, Freddie Mac, and Ginnie Mae. The passage doesn't mention short sales. And the new fixed-rate mortgages were part of the Housing and Economic Recovery Act discussed in the prior paragraph, not the Stabilization Act.

If you need more than a minute to work through this problem, move on. Eliminate obviously incorrect choices and guess. Don't let a time-consuming question early in the Reading Test prevent you from getting to other questions later on.

17. **B.** From the third paragraph, you know that the purpose of the Act was to shore up mortgages and that it wasn't too successful. Choice (B) paraphrases the idea, so it's your answer. Choice (A) contradicts the author's assertion that the Act wasn't very successful. The passage doesn't contain enough information to be specific about the percentage of debt that subprime borrowers would be relieved of, so Choice (C) can't be right. The paragraph says that Fannie Mae and Freddie Mac had deteriorated, but it doesn't suggest that the Act caused their deterioration. Eliminate Choice (D).

18. **G.** The author summarizes his conclusion in the last paragraph. He predicts that government intervention in the crisis will pose problems for many years. Choices (F), (H), and (J) contradict this opinion. Choice (G) provides a good paraphrase of the last paragraph.

19. **D.** "Effectively nationalized" means that Freddie Mac and Fannie Mae were put into a conservatorship to prevent future deterioration. It doesn't mean that they were deteriorated. Cut Choice (A). Saying that the enterprises were spread across the country doesn't make sense, so cut Choice (B), too. The best answer is Choice (D). The enterprises were placed in a conservatorship, which means that they were controlled by another entity. *Nationalized* suggests that this entity was the government. Nothing in the sentence suggests Choice (C).

20. **F.** This question was a pretty easy one. *Deleveraging* appears in the first sentence, so you don't have to look deep in the passage to find it. The first passage says that it means to reduce debt, sell assets, and obtain capital from any source. So you can cross out Choices (G), (H), and (J) with confidence. The only answer left is Choice (F). Home mortgage rates aren't part of the definition.

21. **D.** You can begin eliminating answer choices just by reading the first word in each option. The passage is more informative than argumentative, so you can make a pretty good bet that its purpose isn't to discredit or argue. You may not want to cross out Choices (A) and (C) based on this observation alone, but you should definitely examine the other two choices more closely. Choice (B) is too specific for a main-idea question. The passage discusses more elements than just typography. Choice (D) sounds right. It's general enough to encompass the whole passage and is a good summary of the last paragraph, which says that *bibliography* requires attention to many aspects of the text.

If you're pressed for time, mark Choice (D) on your answer sheet and press on. If you're on track time-wise, take a couple of seconds to consider Choices (A) and (C). The passage doesn't talk about authors, so Choice (A) can't be right. When you read through Choice (C), you see that it's wrong, too. The passage doesn't get into what elements of study are most important. It just says that analyzing many aspects is important. Now you can be confident that Choice (D) is the best answer.

22. **G.** Don't try to answer this question based on your own definition of *cunning*. Substitute each choice for *cunning* in the passage and pick the one that makes the most sense. The sentence before the reference presents what would be a logical answer to a question. Then the author says that this answer would have some *cunning* (or correctness) given certain circumstances. Choices (F), (H), and (J) don't convey the same meaning. The answer that's most similar to *correctness* is Choice (G): The answer would have some wisdom given certain circumstances.

If you tried to answer this question based on what you know *cunning* means, you may have picked Choice (A). One of the definitions of *cunning* is slyness, but that meaning doesn't fit in this context. Always analyze the answers to vocabulary-in-context questions by putting them in the passage.

23. **C.** This question is pretty easy after you figure out which part of the passage gives you the answer. If you skim the questions before you read the passage, you know that you'll encounter a question about estimating a book's age. When you get to the third paragraph and read about estimating the age of a book within five to ten years, you know to mark that particular sentence.

Don't actually try to answer the question while you read the passage. Just mark the information in the passage so you know where to return later when you're in question-answering mode.

Lines 61–63 say that the way letters are laid out on a page reflects social conventions. The next sentence says that this is why you can estimate a document's age by looking at it. The answer that paraphrases this information is Choice (D), so you can cross it out. Binding and ornamentation appear in Lines 66–69 as additional ways that documents reveal their age. Cross out Choices (A) and (B). Choice (C) must be the answer, which makes sense. The author talks about literary types in another paragraph, and all periods produce different types of literature.

24. **H.** The quotes in the question appear in Lines 24–25 in the first paragraph. From this sentence, you know that "being literary" means looking at a page and seeing a poem. Someone who thinks "like a bibliographer" sees the physical aspects of the document, such as type (meaning the style of the letters), paper, and space on the page. Choice (H) is almost a word-for-word copy of the passage.

If you picked Choice (G) or (J), you read too much into the passage. The passage says that physical aspects are determined by economics, but that fact doesn't mean that the bibliographer is especially concerned with the financial aspects of creating a document. The bibliographer's primary focus is on the physical aspects themselves. The debatable word *altogether* in Choice (F) should have raised a red flag.

25. **A.** If you answered Question 23 correctly, you probably got this one, too. The third paragraph states that looking at a document's physical aspects reveals its age. Choices (B) and (D) concern style and story rather than physical elements. Cross out both of them. The paragraph specifically mentions letterforms, bindings, format, ornament stocks, and ruled borders as revealing age but not paper type. Choice (A) is a better answer than Choice (C).

26. **H.** The last paragraph defines *bibliography*. Pick the answer that best summarizes the last paragraph. Its gist is that bibliography is the broad study of texts, including the history of how the text was made and how it was read. Choice (J) focuses on one specific element of the way a text was made. Cross it out. Choice (H) is the best summary.

If you picked Choice (F) or (G), you relied on the definition of bibliography that you're familiar with — the list of resources your teachers make you include at the end of your research papers. The result of that tedious task isn't what the author of this passage is talking about.

27. **A.** A discussion of letterforms appears in the third paragraph. The author says they reflect the social conventions of the time they were created. "Social conventions" and "standard practices" have pretty much the same meaning. Pick Choice (A). Beware of Choice (C): It contains the debatable word *exact*. The passage says you can estimate a document's age from its letterforms. Estimating isn't the same as knowing its exact age. The passage never says that the way letters are formed in a work reveals whether it's a poem, prayer, or other type of literature, so Choice (D) is wrong. If you picked Choice (B), you probably read in the first paragraph that the physical aspects of a document are always determined by the economics of book production. That's not enough information to say that the style of letterforms reveals the creator's specific socioeconomic status.

Don't choose an answer that makes you read too much into what the passage actually says. For this question, you have to take too big of a stretch to say that the economics of book production is related to the socioeconomic status of an individual.

28. **F.** The best way to answer this question is to begin with POE. The passage isn't clear about exactly what high literature is, so you have to figure out what it is not. Choice (J) can't be right because the passage doesn't say anything about works produced by royalty. The passage talks about poems and prayers specifically, but it doesn't suggest that these two genres form a separate kind of literature. So cross out Choice (H). Choice (G) is probably wrong, too. The point of the last paragraph is that analyzing literature should include the way it was made as well as whatever is traditionally done with "high" literature. The passage associates costs of production with the physical aspects of a document (the way it's made), so the cost of production doesn't distinguish "high" literature. The only answer choice left standing is Choice (F). The author advocates examining the physical aspects of a work as well as its literary value. The first sentence of paragraph two refers to the relationship between form and meaning, suggesting that those who are literary focus more on meaning than form. *Bibliography,* then, takes into consideration form and meaning and isn't limited to analyzing just meaning in the way that those that study only "high" literature are.

This question requires you to engage in a lengthy thought process. Don't waste too much time trying to answer it. Eliminate answers that are obviously wrong, guess, and go on to questions that are easier to answer.

29. **C.** The passage lists the common components as the introduction, illustrations, notes, and list of textual variants. Eliminate answers that don't relate to these components. The passage doesn't mention test banks, so cross out Choice (A). Choice (B) refers to illustrations, but the passage doesn't get specific enough for you to say that the illustrations are computerized. So Choice (B) is wrong. An author's biography could be part of an introduction, but the passage doesn't say so. Choice (D) is out. Textual variants refer to different variations of the text. The best answer is Choice (C).

30. **H.** Lines 46–50 in the second paragraph tell you how the conventions of textual design evolve. The answer that paraphrases this sentence is Choice (H). The passage doesn't discuss what makes a text more aesthetically pleasing or popular, so Choices (G) and (J) aren't right. Choice (F) doesn't work because although the passage mentions that costs affect style, it doesn't say anything about how costs concern the way texts evolve.

31. **D.** A *main purpose* or *main idea* is by definition broad and general. So an answer with the word *overview* is often correct because it encompasses nearly everything. Hence, Choice (D) is your winner here. Choice (A) is wrong because the passage barely mentions prehistoric animals. In Choice (B), *refute,* which means to disprove, is rarely a correct answer. (Passages discuss or describe; they don't often refute or criticize. Chapter 13 covers this concept in more detail.)

The fact that Choice (B) may be a true statement is irrelevant (the cycad seeds were too large to be spread by birds). The mere fact that an answer is true doesn't mean it's the correct answer to the question.

Choice (C) is overly broad. The passage includes little discussion of current plant life, and what's there is limited to cycads, not to plants in general.

32. **J.** The line implies that the plants, although prehistoric, still exist today and goes on to tell you where they may be found. Choice (F) is exactly backward; the plants are *not* extinct. Choice (G) is illogical in the context of the passage. Choice (H) contradicts the rest of the sentence, which tells you how widespread the plants are.

33. **A.** This question is about pure detail. Lines 40–43 state that scientists considered the widespread distribution of the cycad a mystery.

34. **G.** The answer to this specific-information question comes right out of the passage. The first sentence of the second paragraph says that this fossil record (referring to the early plant life fossils discussed in the first paragraph) shows how plants have evolved over time. Choice (G) is a nice paraphrase of this statement. The passage doesn't compare plant fossils to animal fossils, so Choice (F) is out. The word *all* in Choice (H) indicates that it's probably not right. The first paragraph says that the fossils develop from plants that haven't decayed, so cross out Choice (J).

35. **C.** A passage often suggests; it rarely refutes (to *refute* is to disprove). Pangaea, which appears in paragraph four, was the one large supercontinent that later broke into smaller continents, taking the cycad seeds and plants with them. The author mentions this idea as a possible way to explain the seeds' widespread distribution. Choice (A) is wrong because the cycad is not extinct today; it's *extant* (still in existence). Choice (B) is going too far. Although the passage says that the plants in prehistoric times were huge, it doesn't mention or imply that the cycad was the largest plant.

36. **F.** You know that Choice (G) can't be right. Cycads still exist, so they didn't become extinct in the Jurassic Period. The second paragraph says that the Cretaceous Period came after the Jurassic Period, so cross out Choice (J). If you picked Choice (H), you focused on the age of rocks that contain fossils of flowers rather than the age of the Jurassic Period. The best answer is Choice (F). If no evidence of flowers exists until the period after the Jurassic Period, the Jurassic Period probably didn't have any flowering plants.

37. **B.** Paragraph five tells you that the seed cones are female and the pollen cones are male. The paragraph also warns of the cancer-causing properties of the seeds, but it never mentions any medicinal properties.

A question like this one requires an investment of time. Unless you're a reader who retains everything after one quick reading, you're probably wise to go back and double-check your memory. Look for the precise answer; don't depend on remembering everything.

38. **H.** Paragraph six states that the leaves of the cycad plant grow into a crown that makes people think the plant is a palm tree.

39. **B.** A question that begins "according to the passage" is often a gift to you. It's usually a simple detail-related question that requires little thought. All you have to do is go back and find the answer in the passage, usually stated very clearly and directly. Here, paragraph five says that "the conversion of atmospheric nitrogen into ammonia is one way the cyanobacteria supply the cycad with inorganic nitrogen."

40. **F.** The last paragraph focuses on the possible extinction of cycads and the steps groups are taking to prevent it. Hey, that's exactly what Choice (F) says! The passage doesn't include enough specific information to verify Choice (G) or (J). The article is more informative than persuasive, so Choice (H) isn't the primary purpose of the paragraph.

Science Test

In each of the following sections, we explain how to interpret the tables and figures, as well as the introduction material, that accompany each passage in the Science Test. After all, it's important that you read all the introductory material before you try to answer any of the questions. Then we go into more detailed explanations of the specific questions and their answers.

Passage 1

Be sure to read over the given information for this research-summary passage and understand what data the tables provide before you tackle the questions. In the first study, the student changes the boat material and holds the fluid type constant as pure water. In the second study, the student changes the fluid type and holds the boat material constant as wood. The passage tells you that denser objects are less buoyant and denser fluids provide more buoyancy. It also indicates that more buoyant objects can support more weight before they sink. You can use this information to interpret the tables and determine the relative densities of the boat materials and fluids. Wood supports the most weight, so it's the least dense material. Sea water allows the wood to support the most weight, so sea water must be the densest fluid.

1. **C.** Study 1 used pure water for all three trials. Study 2 used wood for all three trials. This info immediately leads you to the correct answer: wood and pure water. Only Study 1 used Choice (A), concrete and pure water, while only Study 2 used Choice (B), wood and oil. Neither study used Choice (D), aluminum and sea water.

2. **H.** For this question, you have to understand what both tables are telling you and then combine the information. Aluminum is the densest of the three materials and, therefore, has the least buoyancy, as shown in Table 1. By looking in Table 2, you can see that oil is the least dense of the fluids and thus provides the least buoyancy. The combination of the least buoyant material and the least buoyant fluid would mean that the maximum weight supported would be less than any of the other combinations given and, therefore, less than 7 kg.

Be sure to look at all the information provided, and don't assume that you'll be able to answer each question using only a single table.

3. **A.** You're looking for the answer that the passage *doesn't* support. Pay careful attention to what the statements say. If you confuse more buoyant and less buoyant, you'll quickly reach the wrong conclusion. Even if you pick Choice (A) right away as the correct answer, check the others to make sure you haven't missed something important.

   Choices (A) and (B) refer to Table 2. Choices (C) and (D) refer to Table 1. From the tables, you can see that sea water provided the most buoyancy because it supported the maximum weight before the wood boat sank. Oil provided the least buoyancy. From Table 1, you can conclude that wood was the most buoyant boat material. Aluminum was the least. Choices (C) and (D) are true because wood was the most buoyant.

4. **F.** This question involves looking at the weights supported and evaluating the effect of varying boat material and fluid type. Table 1 tells you that the wooden boat was significantly more buoyant than the other materials. It supported a weight of nearly twice that of the aluminum boat. Table 2 shows you that the range of weight supported by the different fluids was small, varying only from 11 to 14. This small range indicates that fluid type had a smaller effect on buoyancy than material type.

   Cross out Choice (G) right away. The question clearly states that you should base your answer on the data in Tables 1 and 2. Boat size isn't a part of the studies, so you can't conclude anything about it.

5. **B.** The text that comes before the tables tells you how density relates to buoyancy and how buoyancy relates to the weight applied to the object before it sinks. After you figure out that substances with similar densities have similar buoyancies, you can look in the tables to find which boat materials had a similar amount of weight applied to them before the boat sank. In Table 1, aluminum and concrete were very similar, whereas wood was much different. Go ahead and eliminate Choices (A) and (C) because you know that the density of wood isn't similar to aluminum or concrete. Pick Choice (B).

   Choice (D) is a trick. You can't tell from the data whether wood and pure water have similar densities. Don't let this bother you, though, because the question asks you to answer according to Table 1, which gives information only about boat materials.

6. **H.** To answer this question correctly, make sure you understand that denser fluids provide more buoyancy to objects submerged in them and that a more buoyant object can float and carry more weight before it sinks. Armed with this knowledge, you can go to Table 2 and see that sea water provided the most buoyancy to the boat because it supported the maximum weight. Therefore, sea water is the densest. Choice (J) is obviously wrong because the studies don't address gasoline at all.

Passage 2

For this data-representation passage, your first step is to look at Figure 1 and understand how the 50-kg block will move up the ramp and how Block A will lower until it reaches the ground. All the data provided in Table 1 is based on how long it takes for this simple action to take place. When you understand exactly what's being timed, the questions become fairly straightforward. You just have to look at Table 1 to find the right answers.

Table 1 consists of time data that shows how the time changed when the mass of Block A and the ramp angle were varied. For each of the three Block A masses, you see four ramp angles. The table shows you two clear trends. The first trend is a positive correlation between ramp angle and the time it took Block A to reach the ground. As the angle of the ramp increased, the time for Block A to reach the ground also increased. This trend is true for all three Block A masses used. The other trend is a negative correlation between mass and time. As the mass of Block A increased, the time it took for the block to reach the ground decreased.

7. **A.** You can look at any of the three masses for Block A to answer this question. For each mass, the ramp angle of 10 degrees produced the smallest time for Block A to reach the ground. So Choice (A) is your answer.

   You can also think about this question logically to check your answer. Based on Figure 1, you see that as the ramp angle was reduced, the 50-kg weight hung by the cord less and less and was supported by the ramp more and more. Therefore, as the ramp angle decreased, the friction between the ramp and the 50-kg block became more significant and the weight of the 50-kg block became less significant in slowing the fall of Block A. The friction force was smaller in magnitude than the weight of the 50-kg block, which means that as the ramp angle decreases, Block A reaches the ground in a smaller amount of time.

8. **G.** For this question, pay attention to the trends shown in Table 1. One of the trends is that as the mass of Block A increased, the time for Block A to reach the ground decreased. This trend makes sense logically because a heavier block would more easily overcome the frictional and gravitational forces exerted on the cable by the 50-kg block. Look at Table 1 at a ramp angle of 30 degrees and a Block A mass of 60 kg. You see that Block A took 0.68 seconds to reach the ground. So if the mass of Block A were increased to 70 kg, you know that the time for Block A to reach the ground would have to decrease. Therefore, the answer has to be something less than 0.68 seconds. The only choice that's less than 0.68 seconds is Choice (G).

9. **C.** Consider the trends in Table 1 to help you with this question. A lower ramp angle made Block A reach the ground faster. So did a higher mass of Block A. Armed with this knowledge, you can quickly pick Choice (C). Rule out Choice (B) because none of the data supports it.

   Choices (A) and (D) may trick you if you look only at specific instances in the table. When the ramp angle was increased from 20 to 30 degrees and the mass of Block A was increased from 50 to 60 kg, Block A did reach the ground more slowly. But when the ramp angle was increased from 30 to 40 degrees and the mass of Block A was increased from 40 to 50 kg, Block A reached the ground faster. Choice (A) isn't consistently true for every case. The question asks for the answer that's best supported. Choices (A) and (D) have to be incorrect because they're not always true; the data always supports Choice (C).

10. **J.** For this question, think about what the amount of time it takes for Block A to reach the ground means. A small amount of time means that the block slid quickly and wasn't at all in equilibrium. A large amount of time means that the block was moving slowly and wasn't far from being in equilibrium. In other words, as the amount of time to reach the ground increased, the system came closer to equilibrium. If the system were perfectly at equilibrium, then the time for Block A to reach the ground would be infinitely large. From Table 1, you can see that the largest time occurred with a ramp angle of 40 degrees and a Block A mass of 40 kg. Based on the trends in the table, you know that as the ramp angle was increased, the time for Block A to reach the ground also increased. Therefore, with a mass of 40 kg and a ramp angle larger than 40 degrees, you'd expect the system to be close to equilibrium. Hence, Choice (J) is the winner here.

    Using the same logic, you can eliminate the other choices. From the table, you'd expect Choice (A) to yield a time somewhere between 0.66 seconds and 0.78 seconds, which wouldn't indicate equilibrium. Similarly, you'd expect Choice (D) to yield a time between known data points in the table. For Choice (G), you'd expect a time faster than 0.62 seconds based on the trends, meaning that Choice (J) is the only possible answer.

11. **C.** This question asks you to apply your knowledge of the trends shown in the table to a graphical representation. All the choices indicate that as the ramp angle increases, time also increases, so you have to look more closely at the numbers shown in the table to determine the correct answer. Increasing the ramp angle from 10 to 20 degrees increased the time a small amount. You can look at any of the masses used to verify this trend. Increasing the ramp angle from 20 to 30 degrees increased the time by a larger amount,

and increasing it from 30 to 40 degrees increased the time by an even larger amount. After you see this trend, you can determine that the time for Block A to reach the ground grows exponentially with ramp angle. In other words, the graph's curve gets steeper as it moves up to the right, just as the one shown in Choice (C) does. For Choice (A) to be right, the relationship between ramp angle and time would have to be steady. The line in Choice (B) becomes less steep as it moves to the right. Choice (D) may be tempting, but it would work only if the data increased linearly between three data points.

Passage 3

Don't get too hung up on the information given in the beginning of this conflicting-viewpoint passage. It's there only to provide background for the two theories and isn't needed to answer the specific questions. The best strategy for these questions is to skim through both theories to get a general idea of what they're talking about and where they stand on the issue. Then go to the questions and answer them by referring back to the theories for the specifics.

The key point of the genetic theory is that parents pass vision errors down to children and that the best way to correct those errors is by using artificial devices. The main idea of the environmental theory is that how the eyes are used causes vision errors and that altering eye use has an effect on vision.

12. **H.** The genetic theory supports the idea that vision problems are hereditary and can't be changed by using eyes in a certain way. Choices (F), (G), and (J) all talk about a specific use of one's vision, which isn't part of the genetic theory. Choice (H) is the only possible answer here.

Generalizing the gist of the answer choices makes associating them with one theory or the other much easier to do. According to the genetic theory, the only way vision errors occur is if they're passed on from parents to their children. Any answer that says you can correct error through eye use can't be part of the genetic theory.

13. **B.** Both theories discuss correcting vision at a young age, but the method of correction differs. You can eliminate all the choices besides Choice (B) by noticing that they're either referenced by only one or none of the theories. Neither theory supports Choice (A) (though the environmental theory would say that a lot of reading affects vision). Only the genetic theory discusses Choice (C), and neither theory discusses Choice (D).

14. **J.** To answer this question, you need to identify the belief that the environmental theory discusses negatively and that the genetic theory supports. The environmental theory doesn't specifically address any negative effects of thinking that vision problems are hereditary. People who assume that vision errors are hereditary can still correct their vision by using the methods of the environmental theory. So cross out Choice (F). Choice (G) is wrong for the same reason. Thinking that vision problems have been around for awhile doesn't create more vision problems. Both theories suggest that you can correct vision errors through multiple ways, so Choice (H) isn't right, either. Environmental theorists talk about the negative effects of wearing glasses at an early age, which is a practice endorsed by the genetic theory folks. The environmental theorists say that the practice of wearing glasses promotes more vision problems. Choice (J) is the correct answer.

15. **A.** For this question, just look closely at the environmental theory to see which choice it supports. Choice (A) is correct because the environmental theory says that vision errors result from focusing too long on nearby objects, which is something that could happen at any time in life. Choice (B) is incorrect because the environmental theory makes the exact opposite claim, stating that watching television affects vision. Choice (C) is incorrect because the environmental theory doesn't support laser eye surgery. The theory also supports the idea that vision problems can be both prevented and reversed, which makes Choice (D) incorrect.

16. **H.** Skim through the choices to see which ones are inconsistent with the environmental theory. From the remaining answers, choose the one that's consistent with the genetic theory.

    Cross out Choice (F) because the environmental theory never claims that eyeglasses don't allow humans to see well. It just argues that glasses aren't a strong solution to underlying vision errors. The environmental theory states that focusing on nearby objects creates vision problems, so eliminate Choice (G). This leaves you with Choices (H) and (J) as possibilities. Choice (J) is consistent with both theories because siblings have similar genetic makeups and are brought up in similar environments. The correct answer has to be Choice (H). Exercising eye muscles promotes vision according to the environmental theory but isn't helpful according to those who hold to the genetic theory.

17. **A.** Look at the choices to find one that both theories support. Choice (A) works because both theories say that vision errors can be identified in children. The genetic theory doesn't support Choices (B) and (D), and Choice (C) doesn't go along with the environmental theory's premise that glasses make vision problems worse.

18. **H.** Think about what traits people who come from the same societies may have in common. In many cases, people in the same society have shared genetics because their families and ethnicities have lived near each other for generations. They may also share similar environmental factors, such as hobbies and lifestyles, because of societal customs. Therefore, societies that are more prone to vision errors could be that way because of genetic factors or environmental factors. So evidence that vision errors are more common in certain societies and less common in others supports both the genetic theory and the environmental theory.

Passage 4

The equation shows the reversible chemical reaction where ammonia (NH_3) in water (H_2O) dissociates into ammonium (NH_4^+) and hydroxide (OH^-). As the passage states, a higher ammonia concentration causes more ammonia to dissociate and, therefore, increases the amount of ammonium and hydroxide in the solution. A higher pH indicates that a solution has more hydroxide ions. Table 1 shows how the molarity of an ammonia solution affects pH. As the molarity increases, the pH also increases. The increments of molarity are very small at the top of the table and become increasingly larger as you go down the table. The pH increases in the opposite manner. Near the top of the table where molarity increases by very small increments, you can see that the pH increases a great deal. Near the bottom of the table, the pH increases very slowly.

Table 2 shows data from a 1 M ammonia solution at 10 degrees C that was slowly heated. The concentration was measured at various temperatures. As the temperature increased, the molarity of the solution decreased. As the text that comes before Table 2 states, ammonia becomes less soluble in water with increasing temperature, so ammonia leaves the water in the form of vapor.

19. **C.** Look at Table 1 to find the data point that's closest to a pH of 10. From the table, you can see that a solution with a pH of 10 would have a molarity between 0.0001 and 0.001. Only one of these molarities is a choice, which means the answer must be 0.0001 M. Verify your answer by looking at the other choices and checking their pHs. Choice (A), 10 M, would have a pH of 12.13, and Choice (B), 1 M, would have a pH of 11.63. These are easy to eliminate quickly because they're shown as data points in the table. Choice (D), 0.005 M, would have a pH between 10.10 and 10.62, which is closer to the desired pH of 10, but it isn't as close as Choice (C).

    Don't let Choice (A) trick you; a pH of 10 is different from a 10 M solution. You must look closely at the information and tables provided to answer the questions correctly.

20. **J.** You need to use two pieces of information to answer this question. First, you need to know that more OH^- ions correspond to a higher pH. Second, you need to realize from looking at Table 1 that a higher molarity corresponds to a higher pH and, therefore, more OH^- ions. Choice (F) is incorrect because a 2 M solution is lower in molarity than a 5 M solution and so has a lower pH and fewer OH^- ions. The same logic applies to Choices (G) and (H), so you can dismiss them, too. Choice (J) is the right answer because a 1 M solution is higher in concentration than a 0.01 M solution and, thus, has a higher pH and more OH^- ions.

21. **B.** For this question, you start with a 1 M ammonia solution initially at 10 degrees C and heat the solution. Table 2 describes this exact scenario. If the solution were heated by 30 degrees C, the final temperature would be 40 degrees C. According to Table 2, this temperature would result in a 0.52 M ammonia solution. At this point, you can go to Table 1 to see what pH would be most likely for a 0.52 M solution. The molarity for a 0.52 M solution is between 0.1 M and 1 M, which means the pH would be between 11.12 and 11.63. So the correct answer has to be Choice (B), 11.48.

Make sure you read the whole question before trying to jump to the answer. If you read too quickly, you might mistakenly think that you're looking for the pH of a 1 M ammonia solution and arrive at the incorrect answer of Choice (A).

22. **J.** You need a good understanding of both tables to answer this question, because each of the conclusions relates to different aspects of the passage. Choice (A) is incorrect because the text preceding Table 2 states that temperature affects the solubility of ammonia in water. Choice (B) is incorrect because pH increased with increased molarity of ammonia solution. This is a direct (positive) relationship, not an inverse (negative) one. Choice (H) is incorrect because ammonia solutions of a constant temperature may have varying concentrations, as you can see in Table 1, where concentration varied with a constant temperature. Table 2 shows that heating the solution decreased the molarity but not that temperature always indicated a specific molarity. Choice (J) is the correct answer. As shown in Table 1, the pH of the ammonia solution increased rapidly when the concentration was lower. As the concentration increased, the pH changed much more slowly.

23. **A.** To answer this question, you have to use information from both tables. Table 1 shows you that a lower concentration of ammonia in the solution had a lower pH, and Table 2 shows you how heating the solution lowered the concentration. So pick Choice (A). Choice (B) is incorrect because the passage never provides information on what happens to the concentration of an ammonia solution when it's cooled. Choice (C) can't be right because adding more ammonia solution would increase the pH, as shown in Table 1. Pressurizing the ammonia solution would increase the solubility of the ammonia in water, which eliminates Choice (D).

Passage 5

You don't have to know anything about how electrical circuits work or exactly what the wording in Figure 1 means to answer the questions in this research-summary passage. Just read the text carefully and make sure you know what the tables show.

The two studies involve simply replacing components in the circuit described and then measuring current and voltage for each of the three resistors. Study 1 uses five different batteries with varying voltages. Table 1 shows the resulting voltage across each resistor. Study 2 replaces Resistor 1 with five different resistors with varying resistance. Table 2 shows the current through each resistor. The main trend in Study 1 is that with increasing battery voltage, the voltage across each resistor also increased. The trend in Table 2 is that with increasing Resistor 1 resistance, the current through each resistor decreased. If you keep these two major trends in mind, you'll be able to answer the questions quickly and easily.

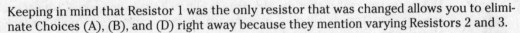

24. **F.** This question asks you to look at Table 1, which portrays the data for Study 1, and find when the voltage across Resistor 2 was smallest. The column labeled "Resistor 2 (1,000 Ω)" shows you that the smallest voltage measured was 1.34 V and that this voltage occurred when the battery used was 1.5 V. Choice (F) is the correct answer. You can also figure this one out simply by knowing the trends from Study 1. The voltage across each resistor increased when the battery voltage increased. Therefore, you know that the smallest voltage across any of the resistors occurred with the smallest battery voltage, which was 1.5 V.

25. **C.** You have to look at the text for each study to find the answer to this question. The first study varied the battery voltage and measured the voltage across each resistor. The second study varied the Resistor 1 resistance and measured the current through each resistor. This information corresponds with Choice (C).

    Keeping in mind that Resistor 1 was the only resistor that was changed allows you to eliminate Choices (A), (B), and (D) right away because they mention varying Resistors 2 and 3.

26. **H.** This question is about Study 2, so look at Table 2. As you can see, the current through each of the three resistors decreased as the Resistor 1 resistance increased. This trend tells you to jump straight to Choice (H) because it's the only one that says that both currents decreased. Even if you didn't recognize this overall trend, you can look at Table 2 and find the decreasing trend for each individual resistor. Choices (F), (G), and (J) are incorrect because they say that the current through one of the resistors increased as Resistor 1 resistance increased.

27. **B.** The two main components of the circuit examined in these studies were the battery used and the resistance of Resistor 1. For both studies, one of these components was varied while the other was held constant. In Study 1, battery voltage was varied, while Resistor 1 resistance was held constant at 100 Ω. In Study 2, Resistor 1 resistance was varied and battery voltage was held constant at 9.0 V. Therefore, the configuration used in both studies was a battery voltage of 9.0 V and a Resistor 1 resistance of 100 Ω. You can tell that Choices (A) and (C) are incorrect because Study 2 didn't use a battery voltage of 1.5 V. Similarly, Choices (C) and (D) are incorrect because Study 1 didn't use a Resistor 1 resistance of 500 Ω.

28. **F.** To answer this question, you have to extrapolate the data given in Table 1. The table tells you that the voltage measured across Resistor 2 increased as the battery voltage increased. The question asks you to extrapolate out to a battery voltage of 12.0 V, which would mean that the voltages across each of the resistors would increase. With a 9.0 V battery, the voltage across Resistor 2 was 8.04 V, so you know the answer you're looking for has to be greater than 8.04 V. Choice (F) is the only one greater than 8.04 V, so it's the correct answer.

    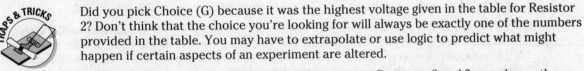

    Did you pick Choice (G) because it was the highest voltage given in the table for Resistor 2? Don't think that the choice you're looking for will always be exactly one of the numbers provided in the table. You may have to extrapolate or use logic to predict what might happen if certain aspects of an experiment are altered.

29. **D.** From Table 1, you can see that the voltage across Resistors 2 and 3 was always the same; that's because they were arranged in parallel in the circuit. Armed with this info, you can eliminate Choice (A). When you look at Table 2, you may notice that the current through Resistor 1 was always equal to the sum of the currents through Resistors 2 and 3. This trend leads you to the correct answer of Choice (D). Even if you didn't notice this trend, though, you can go ahead and determine that the other choices are incorrect. The current through Resistor 2 was never greater than the current through Resistor 1, so Choice (B) is wrong. The current through Resistors 2 and 3 was never equal, so Choice (C) is also incorrect.

Passage 6

The graphs here illustrate the variations in concentration of elements in soil on the Earth and on the Moon. For each element, the percent by weight is shown for the lunar lowlands, the lunar highlands, and in typical Earth crust. The first graph, Figure 1, shows the most common elements, with oxygen making up nearly half of the soil. If you look at the concentrations in typical Earth crust, you see that the chart goes from left to right showing the most to least common elements in soil on the Earth. The second graph, Figure 2, shows only the less common elements, which are in very small concentrations. If the two graphs were shown on the same scale, you wouldn't be able to distinguish any difference between the concentrations of the less common elements because they'd all appear to be close to 0.

Make sure you realize that the elements in Figure 2 are in very small concentrations when compared to those in Figure 1 even though the bars appear to be quite large. Always pay attention to the axis labels when looking at graphs.

30. **G.** Look for the largest percent by weight but focus only on the elements listed in the answer choices. Figure 1 provides what you need to get the right answer. The largest concentrations overall are oxygen and silicon, but neither of those are choices, so you have to keep going to the right to find the next highest element.

Did you put down aluminum because it comprises the largest concentration in the typical Earth crust of the four choices given? The question asks specifically about the lunar highlands, so Choice (F) is incorrect. In the lunar highlands, the element with the next highest percent by weight is iron, so Choice (G) is the correct answer. Choices (H) and (J) are incorrect because calcium and sodium are present in smaller concentrations than iron.

31. **B.** You need to look at Table 2 to answer this question. The question states that chromium is dangerous in larger concentrations, so locate the place with the highest percent by weight of chromium. That place is the lunar highlands, Choice (B). Choice (A) is incorrect because the lunar lowlands have lower concentrations than the lunar highlands (although the percent by weight in the lowlands is also potentially hazardous). Choices (C) and (D) are wrong because the graph shows that the concentrations of chromium on the Earth are the smallest.

32. **H.** To answer this question, you just need to find which elements are present in higher concentrations in the Earth's crust than in the lunar lowlands. The elements that fit this description are oxygen, silicon, sodium, potassium, hydrogen, phosphorus, manganese, carbon, and chlorine. This information leads you to Choice (H) because both sodium and potassium are present in higher concentrations on the Earth than in the lunar lowlands. Choice (F) is wrong because aluminum is present in higher concentrations in the lunar lowlands than in the Earth's crust. The same applies to Choices (G) and (J).

33. **D.** The question says that hydrogen, oxygen, and carbon are all important for fuel, which lets you know that they're desirable on the Moon. So, ideally, they'd be in at least as high of a concentration on the Moon as they are in the Earth's crust. Choice (A) isn't an issue because it says that the oxygen levels in the soil are satisfactory. Choice (B) might cause enough concern to prevent an outpost construction in the lunar highlands, but if you look at the graph, you see a more pertinent issue with hydrogen. Choice (D) causes a lot of concern because hydrogen is necessary for fuel, yet it's present in much smaller concentrations on the Moon than on the Earth. Choice (D) is the correct answer. Choice (C) talks only about the Earth, so it isn't particularly relevant to prospective lunar inhabitants.

34. **F.** This question requires you to look at three elements and list them in order from lowest to highest concentration according to their presence in the lunar lowlands. You can answer this one pretty quickly just by looking at Figure 1. Of calcium, iron, and aluminum, iron has the lowest percent by weight. Calcium comes next, and aluminum has the highest percent by weight. Choice (F) is the correct answer.

Passage 7

The main concepts you need to pull out of this passage have to do with spiciness, capsaicin content, and the Scoville heat unit. Higher capsaicin corresponds to more spiciness, which corresponds to a larger number of Scoville heat units in the tables. You need to have this relationship down in order to answer most of the questions.

After you have an idea of what the two tables show, focus on the nature of the two studies that were conducted. In the first study, the only thing that the scientist varied was how often the plants were watered. As you can see in Table 1, more frequent watering (fewer days between applications) resulted in a lower average spiciness. In the second study, the only thing that the scientist varied was the soil temperature. The scientist held all the other parameters constant. Table 2 shows that as soil temperature increased, the average spiciness also increased.

35. **B.** To answer this question, go to Table 1 to find out which watering frequency would result in an average of 4,500 Scoville heat units. The test group that had the closest to this number of heat units was the group with two days between watering. It had an average of 4,460 Scoville heat units. Choice (B) is the best answer.

Make sure you pay attention to the units. If you just saw the number 2 and didn't look to see that it was being measured in days, you might have mistakenly put down Choice (D), every two weeks, which is an incorrect answer.

36. **H.** To answer this question, focus on Table 2, which shows the results of Study 2, which consisted of watering the plants every three days. When you look at the data for 30 degrees C, you see that the average number of Scoville heat units for the test group was 5,080. This is very close to Choice (H), which is the correct answer. None of the other choices are very close to 5,080. Choice (F) is so low that it doesn't seem at all likely to occur in Study 2, in which the plants received water every three days.

37. **B.** For this question, focus on the trends that the data present. Table 1 shows that when the scientist watered the plants every five days, the average number of Scoville heat units was 5,980. However, when the scientists watered the plants more often, such as every day, the average number of Scoville heat units was only 4,020. These results indicate that the increase in watering frequency resulted in less spicy peppers. Therefore, when a jalapeño plant is watered more often, the spiciness of its peppers decreases. Choice (B) is the correct answer.

Observe trends in the data whenever you can. Even though the measured Scoville heat units varied quite a bit from plant to plant, the overall average of the test group showed a clear trend.

38. **F.** The correct answer to this question conveys the element that wasn't tested in either of the studies. Choice (F) is the correct answer because neither study varied the soil composition. Choice (G) is incorrect because the point of Study 2 was to vary the soil temperature and observe the effects. Choice (H) is incorrect because the frequency of water was held constant in Study 2, and holding a variable constant doesn't generate more data. Eliminate Choice (J) because the light provided to the plants was held constant in both studies.

39. **A.** You have to look up each of the answer choices individually in the tables to answer this question. Choice (A) appears in Table 1 and shows the Scoville heat units ranging from 5,200 to 6,700, which is a range of 1,500. Choice (B) appears in both Table 1 and Table 2; it shows a range of 700 in Table 1 and 600 in Table 2. Choice (C) is present in Table 2 and shows a range of 500 Scoville heat units. Choice (D) appears in Table 2 and shows a range of 600. Choice (A) has the largest range by a long shot, which makes it the correct answer.

This question takes longer to answer than some others because you have to look through both tables and examine each answer choice. Spotting the wide variation recorded in Table 1 with five days between watering may be fairly easy to do. But if you're running out of time at the end of the section, mark a guess for time-consuming questions like this one and move on to the remaining questions. If you have time, you can go back and spend more time working out the answer.

40. **J.** The key to answering this one correctly is recognizing the trends shown in Tables 1 and 2. Table 1 shows that the spiciest peppers were produced with the least frequent watering (every 5 days), and Table 2 shows that the spiciest peppers were produced with the highest soil temperature (30 degrees Celsius). The combination of these factors should result in the spiciest jalapeño peppers, assuming that the plants survive the hot and dry conditions.

Writing Test

See the "Writing Test" section in Chapter 21 for general information on the features that your essay should contain.

The prompt gives you the option of writing for or against funding vocational training programs more than liberal arts curricula in higher education. (It also says you can advocate for another point of view, but why waste time trying to come up with something new?) The prompt doesn't have a right or wrong answer. You can be for the funding or against it. You just need to pick a position and move on. If your first instinct is that vocational training should be funded more than liberal arts, go for it. If you're a liberal arts advocate, however, make your voice heard!

For example, if you're all for funding vocational training, you may have set up your essay this way:

- ✔ **Thesis/Introduction:** Your thesis is that vocational programs provide more opportunities for students to obtain jobs and contribute to the economy when they graduate; therefore, the state benefits more from funding them than it does from funding liberal arts programs.

- ✔ **Body:** The first body paragraph provides evidence that vocational programs provide a better job guarantee than liberal arts programs. You explain that vocational programs lead to specific careers and can be tailored to careers that are in high demand. Provide examples of people you know who got good-paying jobs right after graduating from a vocational program or people you know who graduated from liberal arts colleges and are still living with their parents.

  The next paragraph covers how vocational programs contribute to the economy and, therefore, benefit the public good. Be as specific as possible.

  In another paragraph, address the point raised by the opposing view. Explain why the fact that a liberal arts curriculum prepares students for decision making isn't enough.

- ✔ **Conclusion:** Conclude with a short summary paragraph that summarizes the main point of each paragraph.

An essay that takes the opposing position could focus on the drawbacks of training for just one career. It could explain that liberal arts graduates are more prepared for today's quickly changing technological society because they've been trained to make decisions for all types of circumstances rather than those that apply to just one field. Make the point that a population that can adjust to changes will be better for society in the long run as the careers that vocational programs train for become obsolete.

The position you take isn't important, but the way that you support your stance and the quality of your supporting information are very important.

When you're finished reviewing your essay, ask your English teacher to look over your masterpiece for writing errors and to provide general comments about your essay's organization and strength in addressing the given prompt.

Answer Key for Practice Exam 3

English Test

1. C	14. G	27. C	40. G	53. A	66. F
2. F	15. A	28. H	41. D	54. J	67. A
3. C	16. J	29. D	42. G	55. B	68. G
4. J	17. B	30. F	43. B	56. G	69. C
5. B	18. J	31. A	44. J	57. B	70. F
6. J	19. A	32. H	45. D	58. J	71. D
7. C	20. G	33. C	46. G	59. A	72. J
8. F	21. A	34. G	47. A	60. J	73. D
9. D	22. G	35. D	48. H	61. A	74. G
10. H	23. B	36. H	49. B	62. J	75. C
11. D	24. J	37. D	50. J	63. D	
12. F	25. B	38. G	51. A	64. H	
13. C	26. G	39. A	52. G	65. B	

Mathematics Test

1. D	11. B	21. C	31. E	41. C	51. E
2. G	12. H	22. J	32. G	42. J	52. H
3. C	13. A	23. B	33. B	43. B	53. D
4. H	14. H	24. G	34. K	44. K	54. J
5. B	15. A	25. D	35. E	45. D	55. E
6. H	16. J	26. J	36. J	46. F	56. F
7. C	17. A	27. C	37. B	47. A	57. B
8. K	18. H	28. F	38. F	48. G	58. K
9. D	19. E	29. D	39. B	49. C	59. D
10. H	20. J	30. H	40. G	50. J	60. H

Reading Test

1. C	8. G	15. C	22. G	29. C	36. F
2. F	9. B	16. H	23. C	30. H	37. B
3. D	10. G	17. B	24. H	31. D	38. H
4. J	11. B	18. G	25. A	32. J	39. B
5. A	12. J	19. D	26. H	33. A	40. F
6. J	13. A	20. F	27. A	34. G	
7. C	14. J	21. D	28. F	35. C	

Science Test

1. C	8. G	15. A	22. J	29. D	36. H
2. H	9. C	16. H	23. A	30. G	37. B
3. A	10. J	17. A	24. F	31. B	38. F
4. F	11. C	18. H	25. C	32. H	39. A
5. B	12. H	19. C	26. H	33. D	40. J
6. H	13. B	20. J	27. B	34. F	
7. A	14. J	21. B	28. F	35. B	

Part VIII
The Part of Tens

The 5th Wave   By Rich Tennant

"My weight? Can we list it algebraically as a variable of x?"

In this part . . .

Party time! Sure, you can actually learn a few new things in these chapters, but you can also have a lot of fun with the ten hottest rumors about the ACT that absolutely aren't true. And we offer you a chance to get your parents involved with ten ways they can help you succeed on the ACT.

Chapter 26

Ten Wrong Rumors about the ACT

In This Chapter
▶ Recognizing that not everything you hear is true
▶ Finding out what's true and what isn't

They're whispered in the bathrooms and written in notes passed in the classroom. What are they? They're the vile and vicious rumors about the ACT — rumors that seem to grow with each telling. One of our jobs as test-preparation instructors is to reassure students and their parents that the latest rumors they've heard about the ACT are completely false. Here, we address ten of the rumors you may have heard. Quick hint: They're all wrong!

You Can't Study for the ACT

If you really believed this rumor, you wouldn't have bought this book (and we're really glad you did!). Of course you can study for the ACT!

The ACT tests grammar; you can certainly refresh your memory of the grammar rules. The ACT tests algebra, geometry, and arithmetic; you can definitely study formulas and rules in those areas. In addition, a little preparation can make you very comfortable with the format and timing of the test, which reduces your test-taking anxiety and ultimately improves your score. This book, in particular, discusses tricks and traps that the test takers build into the exam; by knowing what they are ahead of time, you can avoid falling into them on test day.

Different States Have Different ACTs

This rumor is based on the fact that the score sheet compares your performance to that of other students who have taken the ACT in your state. When you receive your ACT score, you find out your percentile rank nationally and within your state. However, all students in all states take the exact same ACT on any one test date. (Of course, the ACT changes from one date to the next; otherwise, you could keep retaking the same test. You'd be surprised how many students don't realize this little nuance and merrily say to us, "Oh, I remember the questions from last time, so I'll do great next time.")

The ACT Has a Passing Score

The ACT has no such thing as a passing or failing score. By looking at the college websites of the schools you're interested in attending, you can get a pretty good idea of the score you need to get based on your GPA. If you have a high GPA, your ACT score can be lower than if you have a low GPA. In fact, you may be pleasantly surprised how low your ACT score can be. Scoring on the ACT isn't like scoring on high school exams, for which a 65th percentile is failing. If your score is in the 65th percentile on the ACT, you've actually done above average, better than 65 percent of the others who've taken the test.

The ACT Tests IQ

The ACT is a college entrance exam. It tests your potential for doing well in college. If you're the type who normally studies hard for an exam, you'll probably study hard for the ACT and do well on it and then study hard for college exams and do well on them, too. The key is in the preparation. You have the same opportunity to do well on the ACT regardless of whether you're a SuperBrain or as cerebrally challenged as the rest of us. With this book, you find out how to improve your ACT scores with all sorts of tricks, tips, and techniques — something that's much harder to do on IQ exams.

You Can't Use a Calculator on the ACT

Back when your parents took the ACT, you couldn't bring a calculator. Nowadays, though, using a calculator is perfectly acceptable, and recommended, for the Mathematics Test. You can't use it on any other section, however. Just make sure your calculator meets the specifications listed on the official ACT website (www.actstudent.org). The ACT's requirements for calculators are a little more stringent than the SAT's.

You Should Never Guess on the ACT

Wrong, wrong, wrong. You should always guess on the ACT. This exam has no penalty for guessing. Never leave an answer blank. Fill in something, anything, on the chance that you may get lucky and get the question correct.

If you're also taking the SAT, notice that the two exams are different in this respect. The SAT penalizes you a fraction of a point for each wrong answer (except on the grid-in math portion), so random guessing on that test isn't a good idea. Random guessing on the ACT, however, can only help you.

The ACT Is Easier Than the SAT

Maybe. Maybe not. The exams test similar subjects. Both have grammar, reading, and math questions. The ACT reading passages — both in the Reading Test and in the Science Test — tend to be slightly longer than some of the reading passages on the SAT, but their length doesn't necessarily mean they're more difficult. The math questions on the ACT are all straightforward multiple-choice with none of the tricky grid-in questions featured on the SAT. However, the ACT does feature a few trigonometry questions (only about four; don't sweat 'em) that aren't on the SAT.

The SAT and ACT present questions in slightly different ways, so we suggest that you take both tests to see which one you feel more comfortable with.

The ACT Is the Same as the Achievement Test

Many people, especially parents, confuse ACT with ACH. The SAT Subject Tests used to be called the *Achievement Test,* or the ACH. Neither has anything to do with the ACT, which stands for *American College Testing.* SAT Subject Tests consist of single-subject tests that require you to actually know things like Chinese verbs or botany rules. The ACT doesn't test single subjects, but it does test general knowledge and reasoning skills.

You Have to Write an Essay

Wrong. You don't have to write an essay during the ACT. It's optional. However, a growing number of colleges want to see an essay score from either the ACT or SAT, and some require that you complete the ACT essay. Taking this portion of the test is a good idea even though you really don't want to.

You Shouldn't Take Both the SAT and the ACT

Wrong, wrong, wrong. Many students take both exams. Usually, the ACT is offered a week or two after the SAT. You may get burned out taking two exams this close together or have trouble studying for both of them, but you certainly may take both tests. Almost all colleges accept either your SAT or ACT score. When we counsel students, we suggest that they take both exams. You may do better on one than you do on the other, and you won't know which one you're better at until you take them both.

Chapter 27

Attention, Parents! Ten Ways You Can Help Your Student Succeed on the ACT

In This Chapter
▶ Discovering constructive ways to help your son or daughter prepare for the ACT
▶ Pointing out your role the day of the test

As a parent, you may wonder what you can do to help your student study for the ACT. Well, wonder no longer! This chapter has ten specific steps for helping your child do his best.

Give Him Awesome Test-Prep Materials

If you bought this book for your child, you did him a huge favor. Reading this book and taking the full-length practice tests in Chapters 20, 22, and 24 give your child an edge over other juniors and seniors who haven't prepared. Nicely done!

Encourage Her to Study

Possessing this book is one thing; actually using it is another. Help your child work out a study schedule and give her incentives to stick to it, such as picking out the family's dinner menu for one week or allotting her a larger share of the family's phone minutes.

Supply Him with a Good Study Environment

Make sure your student has a quiet study area where he can concentrate without being disturbed by siblings, pets, friends, TV, the computer, or his cellphone. Quality study time is time spent without distractions.

Take Practice Tests with Her

You'll be better able to discuss the questions and answers with your child if you take the practice tests, too. Pretend you're a test proctor and be the official timer for your student when she takes the full-length practice tests. After she's done, read through the answer explanation chapters (Chapters 21, 23, and 25) with your kid and help her discover which question types she may need to improve on. Then look up those particular topics in earlier chapters for a refresher on the rules that govern them.

Model Good Grammar for Him

Help your child recognize mistakes in English usage questions by speaking properly with him and *gently* correcting his grammar mistakes in your conversations. Before you know it, he'll be correcting you!

Help Her Memorize Math Formulas

The online Cheat Sheet for this book has a list of formulas your student needs to memorize for the test; check it out at www.dummies.com/cheatsheet/act. Quiz her to make sure she remembers them.

Encourage Him to Read

One of the best ways to improve reading scores is to actually read. Go figure! Incorporate reading into your family's schedule and set up times to read short passages together and discuss their meanings.

Explore Colleges with Her

Your child's ACT score becomes more important to her when she realizes what's at stake. Taking her to college fairs and campus visits can foster her enthusiasm for college and make taking the ACT more relevant.

Get Him to the Test Site on Time

If the test site is unfamiliar to you, take a test drive before the exam date to make sure you don't get lost or encounter unexpected roadwork on the morning of the test. That day, make sure your kid's alarm is set properly so he rises with plenty of time to get dressed, eat a healthy breakfast, and confirm he has the items he needs to take with him to the exam.

Help Her Keep a Proper Perspective

Remind your student that, although the ACT is important, it isn't more important than her schoolwork or being good to her family. Her exam score isn't a reflection of her worth (or your parenting skills). It's just one of many tools colleges use to assess students' skills and determine whether they're a proper fit for their freshman classes.

Index

• *Symbols* •

' (apostrophe), 35–36
: (colon), 35
, (comma), 33–35
- (dash), 35
≥ (greater than or equal to), 104
≤ (less than or equal to), 104
≠ (not equal to), 104
( ) (parentheses), order of operations, 67
. (period), 33
? (question mark), 33
; (semicolon), 35
θ (theta symbol), 113

• *A* •

abbreviations, punctuating, 33, 34
absolute value, 58
ACH versus ACT, 483
ACT. *See also specific practice exams*
  versus ACH, 483
  breakdown by section, 11
  breaks, 11
  learning disabilities, 13
  military duty, 13
  number of questions, 11
  physical disabilities, 13
  religious obligations, 13
  repeating, 15–16, 22
  versus SAT, 482–483
  subjects tested, 14–15
  Test Administration telephone number, 11
  test center, 11–13
  time limit, 11
  timing yourself, 13
  Web site, 12
ACT Math For Dummies, 3
ACT scores. *See* scoring
action verbs, 30, 201
acute angles, 72
addition
  algebraic expressions, 99
  definition, 59
  fractions, 62–63
  order of operations, 67
  radicals, 108
  in word problems, 117–118
additional-result questions, Science Test, 167
adjacent side, trigonometry, 112

adjectives, 31
admission ticket, 11
admission to college. *See* college admission;
    college admission factors
adverb phrases, 31
adverbs, 31
affect/effect, 40
algebra. *See also* geometry; math operations;
    Mathematics Test; trigonometry
  binomials
    definition, 100
    dividing, 100
    FOIL (First, Outer, Inner, Last) method,
      100–101
    multiplying, 100–101
  coefficients, 97
  constants, 97
  factoring, 101–103
  functions
    on coordinate plane, 110–111
    piecewise, 111
    as symbols, 110
    types of, 110
  like terms, 98
  origin of, 98
  polynomials, multiplying, 100
  quadratic equations, factoring, 101–103
  questions on Mathematics Test, 130
  solving for *x,* 98–99
  substitution, 104
  symbols
    functions as, 110
    of inequality, 104
    substituting for, 106–107
    for variables, 106–107
  terms, 97
  variables, 97–98
Algebra I For Dummies, 3
Algebra II For Dummies, 3
algebraic expressions
  adding/subtracting, 99
  definition, 97
  multiplying/dividing, 100
although, subordinating conjunction, 32
among/between, 40
amount/number, 40
analyzing underlined words on English Test,
    44–45
anchor schools, 24
and, coordinating conjunction, 32

angles. *See also* triangles
  acute, 72
  complementary, 73
  corresponding, 74
  obtuse, 73
  reflex, 73
  right, 72
  straight, 73
  supplementary, 73
  types of, 72–74
  vertical, 74
answer key. *See also specific tests*
  Practice Exam 1, 296–297
  Practice Exam 2, 385–386
  Practice Exam 3, 477–478
answer sheet. *See also specific tests*
  incorrect markings on, 19
  Practice Exam 1, 211–212
  Practice Exam 2, 301–302
  Practice Exam 3, 389–390
answers and explanations
  Practice Exam 1
    English Test, 257–265
    Mathematics Test, 265–276
    Reading Test, 276–282
    Science Test, 282–293
    Writing Test, 293–294
  Practice Exam 2
    English Test, 345–354
    Mathematics Test, 354–365
    Reading Test, 365–372
    Science Test, 372–383
    Writing Test, 384
  Practice Exam 3
    English Test, 437–446
    Mathematics Test, 446–461
    Reading Test, 461–467
    Science Test, 467–476
    Writing Test, 476
apostrophe ('), 35–36
appositives, punctuating, 34
arcs, circles, 88
area. *See also* TSA (total surface area)
  circle, 87
  parallelogram, 81–82
  quadrilateral, 81–82
  rectangle, 81
  rhombus, 81
  shaded area, 138–139
  square, 81
  trapezoid, 82
  triangle, 78
arithmetic. *See* Mathematics Test; *specific topics*
as . . . as, 40
aside, punctuating, 34

as/like, 41
attitude questions, Reading Test, 149–150
average
  formula, 67–68
  median, 68
  mode, 68
  weighted, 68
axis of symmetry, 94–95

• B •

base, numeric, 66
because, subordinating conjunction, 32
best/better, 40
binomials
  definition, 100
  dividing, 100
  FOIL (First, Outer, Inner, Last) method, 100–101
  multiplying, 100–101
"blah blah blah," in Bulgarian, 123
books
  ACT Math For Dummies, 3
  Algebra I For Dummies, 3
  Algebra II For Dummies, 3
  English Grammar For Dummies, 3
  English Grammar Workbook For Dummies, 3
  SAT Math For Dummies, 3
  use during the test, 13
breaks during test, 11
Bulgarian for "thank you," 123
but, coordinating conjunction, 32
but also/not only, correlative conjunction
  common errors, 42
  description, 32

• C •

calculator, use during test, 12, 482
calculus questions, Mathematics Test, 130
canceling out fractions, 62
careless mistakes. *See* mistakes, taking the test
Cartesian coordinate plane. *See* coordinate plane
Casner, Gael M., 24
cellphones, use during test, 12
central angles, circles, 87
charity, influence on college admission, 23
chart. *See* coordinate plane
charting math word problems, 121–122
cheating, 19
checking your work, 20
chord, circle, 87
circle
  arc, 88
  area, 87
  central angle, 87

chord, 87
    degrees in, 88
    diameter, 86
    equation of, 95–96
    inscribed angle, 87–88
    midpoint, 86
    radius, 86
    sample questions, 89–91
    sector, 88
clause(s)
    definition, 33
    dependent, 33
    independent, 33
    joining, 32
    nonrestrictive, punctuating, 34
    separating with punctuation, 34
clothing, for test, 12
coefficient, algebraic, 97
college admission
    anchor schools, 24
    final decision, 25
    high school life versus college, 25
    interview strategies, 23–24
    mistakes in planning for, 24–25
    picking a school, 24, 486
    reach schools, 24
    taking ACT for, 22
college admission factors
    ACT scores, 22
    charity, 23
    high school classes, 22
    repeating the ACT, 22
    sports, 23
    what colleges look for, 21
colon (:), 35
comma (,), 33–35
common denominator, finding, 62–63
common mistakes. *See* mistakes, taking the test
comparative form, 40
complementary angles, 73
complement, 32
complex sentence, punctuating, 34
composite numbers, 58, 107
composite score, 14
compound inequalities, 105
compound subjects, subject/verb agreement, 38
computers, use during test, 12
conclusion/result questions, Science Test, 167
conclusion in essay, 200
conflicting-viewpoints passages, Science Test, 167–170
conjunctions. *See also specific conjunctions*
    coordinating, 32
    correlative, 32
    definition, 31–32
    subordinating, 32

constant, algebraic, 97
contraction, punctuating, 34
controlled variables, 163
converting fractions to/from decimals, 61
coordinate geometry. *See* coordinate plane
coordinate plane
    axis of symmetry, 94–95
    definition, 91
    distance formula, 93
    equation of a circle, 95–96
    equation of a line, 93–94
    evaluating functions, 110–111
    example of, 92
    formulas for, 92–94
    graphing linear inequalities, 94–95
    graphing quadratic equations, 94
    horizontal axis, 91
    midpoint formula, 92
    ordered pair, 91
    origin, 91
    parabolas, 94–95
    point-slope formula, 94
    quadrant, 91
    questions on test, 130
    rise over run, 93
    sample questions, 95–96
    slope formula, 93
    vertex, 94–95
    vertical axis, 91
    x-axis, 91
    y-axis, 91
coordinating conjunctions, 32
correlation, negative/positive, 164
correlative conjunctions, 32
corresponding angles, 74
cosecant (csc), 113
cosine (cos), 112
cotangent (cot), 113
cube
    total surface area of, 85
    volume of, 84
cube roots, 107
cylinder
    total surface area of, 85–86
    volume of, 85

● **D** ●

dash (-), 35
data-analysis questions, Science Test, 164–165
data-representation questions, Science Test, 162–165
dates, punctuating, 34
Davis, Kimberly (college admissions expert), 22
degrees, in a circle, 88
denominator, 61

dependent clause, 33
dependent variable, 163
detail questions, Reading Test, 149
diagrams, Science Test, 164–165
diameter, circle, 86
difference, subtraction, 59
different from, 40
direct object, 32
directions to test center, 12
distance formula, 93
distance versus quantity, 40
distinctions, punctuating, 34
distributive property, 59
dividend, 59
division
  algebraic expressions, 100
  binomials, 100
  definition, 59
  dividends, 59
  divisor, 59
  fractions, 62
  order of operations, 67
  quotient, 59
  radicals, 108–109
  in word problems, 117–118
divisor, 59
double-checking your work, 20

• E •

editing essays, 200–201
effect/affect, 40
either/or, correlative conjunction
  description, 32
  rules for, 40
electronic devices, use during test, 13
engaging the reader, in essay, 196
English Grammar For Dummies, 3
English Grammar Workbook For Dummies, 3
English Test. *See also* grammar; Writing Test
  format, 44–46
  ignoring the big picture, 47
  NO CHANGE option, 47
  OMIT option, 47
  "other word" option, 47
  overview, 14
  passages, 44
  Practice Exam 1
    answer key, 296
    answer sheet, 211
    answers and explanations, 257–265
    questions, 213–222
    timing, 209
  Practice Exam 2
    answer key, 385
    answer sheet, 301
    answers and explanations, 345–354

  questions, 303–313
  timing, 299
  Practice Exam 3
    answer key, 477
    answer sheet, 389
    answers and explanations, 437–446
    questions, 391–402
    timing, 387
  practice questions, 49–54
  question types
    analyzing underlined words, 44–45
    categories of, 43
    organization, 46
    sentence structure, 46
    style, 47
    writing, 45–46
  rhetorical skills questions, 43
  traps, 47
  usage and mechanics questions, 43
  wasting time, 47
equation of a circle, 95–96
equation of a line, 93–94
equilateral triangle, 75
er/est, 40
essays. *See* Writing Test, essays
Example icon, explained, 5
examples. *See also* practice questions; *specific test sections*
  in essays, 197
  of essays, 198–199
exams. *See* ACT; *specific practice exams*
exception questions, Reading Test, 150
experiment-design questions, Science Test, 166–167
exponents, 66–67, 109
extrapolation, 165
eyeglasses, for test, 12

• F •

factoring, algebraic, 101–103
factors (prime numbers), 58
failing/passing the ACT, 481–482
farther/further, 40
fewer/less, 41
FOIL (First, Outer, Inner, Last) method, 100–101
for, coordinating conjunction, 32
Fothergill, Todd (college admissions expert), 22
four-sided figures. *See* quadrilaterals
fractions
  adding, 62–63
  canceling out, 62
  common denominator, finding, 62–63
  converting, 61
  decimal conversion, 61
  denominator, 61
  dividing, 62
  greatest common factor, 61

improper, 63
least common denominator, 62–63
mixed numbers, 63
multiplying, 62
numerators, 61
reciprocals, 62
simplifying, 61
subtracting, 62–63
functions, algebraic
  on coordinate plane, 110–111
  piecewise, 111
  as symbols, 110
  types of, 110
further/farther, 40
future tense, 30

• G •

geometry. *See also* algebra; math operations;
    Mathematics Test; *specific shapes;*
    trigonometry
angles
  acute, 72
  complementary, 73
  corresponding, 74
  obtuse, 73
  reflex, 73
  right, 72
  straight, 73
  supplementary, 73
  types of, 72–74
  vertical, 74
circle
  arc, 88
  area, 87
  central angle, 87
  chord, 87
  degrees in, 88
  diameter, 86
  inscribed angle, 87–88
  midpoint, 86
  radius, 86
  sample questions, 89–91
  sectors, 88
coordinate plane
  axis of symmetry, 94–95
  definition, 91
  distance formula, 93
  equation of a circle, 95–96
  equation of a line, 93–94
  examples, 92
  formulas for, 92–94
  graphing linear inequalities, 94–95
  graphing quadratic equations, 94
  horizontal axis, 91
  midpoint formula, 92
  ordered pair, 91

origin, 91
parabola, 94–95
point-slope formula, 94
quadrant, 91
rise over run, 93
sample questions, 95–96
slope formula, 93
vertex, 94–95
vertical axis, 91
x-axis, 91
y-axis, 91
line segments, 71
line(s)
  definition, 71
  horizontal, 71
  intersection of, 71
  midpoint, 71
  at 90-degree angles, 72
  parallel, 72
  perpendicular, 72
  vertical, 71
polygon. *See also* quadrilateral; triangle
  average angle measure, 83–84
  definition, 83
  exterior angle measure, 83
  interior angle measure, 83
  perimeter, 83
  regular, 83
  sum of exterior angles, 83
  sum of interior angles, 83
  total surface area of, 85–86
  volume of, 84–85
quadrilateral. *See also* polygon
  leftover problems, 82–83
  parallelogram, 81–82
  rectangle, 81
  rhombus, 81
  shaded-area problems, 82–83
  square, 79, 81
  trapezoid, 82
questions on the Mathematics Test, 130
triangle. *See also* polygon
  angles, measuring, 75–76
  area, 78
  common ratios, 79–80
  equilateral, 75
  exterior angles, measuring, 76
  isosceles, 75
  largest angle, 75–76
  perimeter, 78
  Pythagorean theorem, 78
  Pythagorean triples, 79–80
  scalene, 75
  sides, measuring, 75–76
  similar, 76–77
  sum of interior angles, 76
  types of, 75–77

ghost words, 200
good/well, 40
grammar. *See also* English Test; Writing Test
  commonly tested errors
    hardly, 42
    hopefully, 42
    idiomatic constructions, 39–42
    if/would, 42
    misplaced modifiers, 39–42
    parallelism, 39
    pronouns, 36–37
    redundancy, 39
    in regard to/in regards to, 42
    sentence fragments, 38
    subject/verb agreement, 37–38
    verb tense, 38–39
    wordiness, 39
  English Grammar For Dummies, 3
  English Grammar Workbook For Dummies, 3
  parts of speech, 30–32. *See also specific parts*
  punctuation, 33–36. *See also specific punctuation*
  sentence parts, 32–33. *See also specific parts*
graphing. *See also* coordinate plane
  linear inequalities, 94–95
  quadratic equations, 94
graphs, Science Test, 164–165. *See also*
    coordinate plane
greater than or equal to (≥), 104
greatest common factor, 61
grid. *See* answer sheet
grid-in questions, Mathematics Test, 130
guessing, 13–14, 482

• *H* •

hamburger writing, 198–200
handwriting legibility, 201
hard problems, getting stuck on, 20
hardly, 42
he, subjective pronoun, 31
heartbeat problems, 64
her
  objective pronoun, 31
  possessive pronoun, 31
hers, possessive pronoun, 31
herself, reflexive pronoun, 31
high school
  classes, influence on college admission, 22
  versus college life, 25
him, objective pronoun, 31
himself, reflexive pronoun, 31
his, possessive pronoun, 31
hooking the reader, in essay, 196
hopefully, 42
horizontal axis, 91

horizontal lines, 71
humanities, Reading Test
  practice questions, 156–157
  topic, 145
hypotenuse, trigonometry, 112. *See also* triangle

• *I* •

I, subjective pronoun, 31
icons used in this book, 5
idiomatic constructions, 39–41
if, subordinating conjunction, 32
if/whether, 40
if/would, 42
I/me, 37
imply/infer, 40
improper fractions, 63
in regard to/in regards to, 42
indefinite pronouns, 31, 38
independent clause, 33–34
independent variable, 163
indirect object, 32
inequalities
  compound, 105
  multiplying by a negative number, 105
  range of numbers, 105
  solving for *x,* 105
  symbols for, 104
inference questions, Reading Test, 149–150
infer/imply, 40
initials, punctuating, 33
inscribed angle, 87–88
integers, 57
interest problems
  definition, 122
  percent growth, 123
  simple interest, 122
interpolation, 165
intersections, lines, 71
interviews, strategies for, 23–24
introduction, in essays, 198
IQ testing, 482
irrational numbers, 57
isosceles triangle, 75
it
  objective pronoun, 31
  subjective pronoun, 31
its, possessive pronoun, 31
itself, reflexive pronoun, 31

• *J* •

Johnson, Todd (college admissions expert), 23
judgments, in essays, 194

• L •

Lawrence, Carolyn Z. (college admissions expert), 25
lay/lie, 41
learning disabilities, 13
least common denominator, 62–63
least/less, 41
leftover problems, solving with quadrilaterals, 82–83
less than or equal to (≤), 104
less/fewer, 41
less/least, 41
lie/lay, 41
like terms in algebra, 98
like/as, 41
line segments, 71
linear inequalities, graphing, 94–95
lines
 definition, 71
 equation of, 93–94
 horizontal, 71
 intersection of, 71
 midpoint, 71
 at 90-degree angles, 72
 parallel, 72
 perpendicular, 72
 vertical, 71
linking verbs, 30
Linzer, Helane (college admissions expert), 22
logarithms, 109
Long, James E. (college admissions expert), 23
losing concentration, 18–19

• M •

main-idea questions, Reading Test, 148–149
many/much, 41
map to test center, 12
math help
 ACT Math For Dummies, 3
 Algebra I For Dummies, 3
 Algebra II For Dummies, 3
 counterparts for common words, 117–118
 memorizing formulas, 486
 from parents, 485–486
 SAT Math For Dummies, 3
math operations. *See also* Mathematics Test; numbers; *specific operations*
 addition, 59
 average
  formula for, 67–68
  median, 68
  mode, 68
  weighted, 68

difference, 59
distributive property, 59
dividend, 59
division, 59
divisor, 59
exponents, 66–67, 109
fractions
 adding, 62–63
 canceling out, 62
 common denominator, finding, 62–63
 converting to decimals, 61
 denominator, 61
 dividing, 62
 greatest common factor, 61
 improper, 63
 least common denominator, 62–63
 mixed numbers, 63
 multiplying, 62
 numerator, 61
 reciprocal, 62
 simplifying, 61
 subtracting, 62–63
inequalities
 compound, 105
 multiplying by a negative number, 105
 range of numbers, 105
 solving for *x,* 105
 symbols for, 104
logarithms, 109
multiplication, 59
number bases, 66
numerical coefficients, 66
odd/even numbers, 60
order of, 67
percentages, 63–64
percent/decimal conversions, 61
positive/negative numbers, 60–61
PPMDAS, order of operations mnemonic, 67
product, 59
proportions, 65–66
quotient, 59
radicals
 adding/subtracting, 108
 multiplying/dividing, 108–109
 order of operations, 109
range, 68
ratios, 64–65
roots, 107
subtraction, 59
sum, 59
math word problems
 charting, 121–122
 interest problems
  definition, 122
  percent growth, 123
  simple interest, 122

math word problems *(continued)*
math counterparts for common words, 117–118
mixture problems, 121–122
percent increase/decrease, 124–126
probability, 126–127
rate problems, 120–121
work problems
definition, 118
total production, 119
total time, 119–120
Mathematics Test. *See also specific topics*
arithmetic questions, 129–130
do's and don'ts, 133–134
format, 129–130
number of questions, 129
overview, 15
Practice Exam 1
answer key, 296
answer sheet, 211
answers and explanations, 265–276
questions, 223–231
timing, 209
Practice Exam 2
answer key, 385
answer sheet, 301
answers and explanations, 354–365
questions, 314–322
timing, 299
Practice Exam 3
answer key, 477
answer sheet, 389
answers and explanations, 446–461
questions, 403–413
timing, 387
practice questions, 135–141
strategy for, 131–133
timing, 132–133
traps, 131
types of questions
algebra, 130
arithmetic, 129–130
calculus, 130
coordinate geometry, 130
grid-in, 130
multiple-choice, 131–132
plane geometry, 130
pre-algebra, 129–130
quantitative comparisons, 130
trigonometry, 130
McKenzie, Erin (college admissions expert), 24
me, objective pronoun, 31
median, 68
me/I, 37
memorizing math formulas, 486

midpoint
circles, 86
formula, coordinate plane, 92
lines, 71
military duty, 13
mine, possessive pronoun, 31
misconceptions about the ACT, 481–483
misplaced modifiers, 39–42
mistakes, planning for college admission, 24–25
mistakes, taking the test
cheating, 19
failing to double-check your work, 20
losing concentration, 18–19
making incorrect grid markings, 19
overemphasizing hard problems, 20
panicking about time, 19
rubbernecking, 19
worrying about previous sections, 20
mixed numbers, 63
mixture problems, 121–122
mode, 68
modifiers, misplaced, 41–42
more/most, 41
much/many, 41
multiple-choice questions, Mathematics Test, 131–132
multiplication
algebraic expressions, 100
binomials, 100–101
definition, 59
fractions, 62
inequalities by a negative number, 105
order of operations, 67
polynomials, 100
radicals, 108–109
in word problems, 117–118
my, possessive pronoun, 31
myself, reflexive pronoun, 31

natural numbers, 57
natural science, Reading Test
practice questions, 157–158
topic, 146
negative correlation, 164
negative integers, 57
negative/positive numbers, mathematical operations, 60–61
neither/nor, correlative conjunction
description, 32
rules for, 40
NO CHANGE option, 47
nonessential information, punctuating, 34
nonrestrictive clause, punctuating, 34

nor, coordinating conjunction, 32
Norman, Bari (college admissions
    expert), 21
not equal to (≠), 104
not only/but also, correlative conjunction
  common errors, 42
  description, 32
note paper, for test, 13
notes, use during test, 13
nouns. *See also* pronouns; subject/verb
    agreement
  connecting descriptions to, 31
  definition, 31
  renaming, 31
  as subjects, 32
number bases, 66
number lines, 58
numbers. *See also* Mathematics Test;
    specific topics
  absolute value, 58
  composite, 58
  factors, 58
  integers, 57
  irrational, 57
  natural, 57
  prime, 58
  prime factorization, 58
  rational, 57
  real, 57
  types of, 57–58
numerator, 61
numerical coefficients, 66

• *O* •

objective pronouns, 31, 37
obtuse angles, 73
odd/even numbers, 60
OMIT option, 47
omitted words, punctuating, 34
opposite side, trigonometry, 112
or, coordinating conjunction, 32
order of operations, 67, 109
ordered pair, 91
or/either, correlative conjunction
  description, 32
  rules for, 40
organization questions, English Test, 46
origin, coordinate plane, 91
"other word" option, 47
our, possessive pronoun, 31
ours, possessive pronoun, 31
ourselves, reflexive pronoun, 31

• *P* •

panicking about time, 19
parabola, 94–95
paragraphs in essays, examples of, 198–199
parallel lines, 72
parallelism, common errors, 39
parallelogram, 81–82
parentheses (( )), order of operations, 67
parents, tips for, 485–486
parts of speech, 30–32. *See also specific parts*
passages
  English Test, 44
  Reading Test, 145–146
  Science Test, 161–162, 162–165, 165–167,
    167–170
passing/failing the ACT, 481–482
past tense, 30
past-perfect tense, 30
pencils, for the test, 11
percent growth, 123
percent increase/decrease, 124–126
percentages
  decimal conversions, 61
  description, 63–64
  of increase/decrease, 124–126
  in word problems, 117–118
percentile score, 14
perimeter
  polygons, 83
  triangles, 78
period (.), 33
perpendicular lines, 72
personal pronouns, 31
photo ID, for test, 12
phrases
  definition, 33
  joining, 32
physical disabilities, 13
picking a school. *See* college admission
piecewise functions, 111
place names, punctuating, 34
plane geometry questions, Mathematics Test, 130
point-slope formula, 94
polygon. *See also* quadrilateral; triangle
  average angle measure, 83–84
  definition, 83
  exterior angle measure, 83
  interior angle measure, 83
  perimeter, 83
  regular, 83
  sum of exterior angles, 83
  sum of interior angles, 83
  total surface area, 85–86
  volume, 84–85

polynomials, multiplying, 100
positive correlation, 164
positive integers, 57
positive thinking, 18
positive/negative numbers, mathematical
    operations, 60–61
possessive pronouns, 31
possessives, punctuating, 34–35
powers. *See* exponents
PPMDAS, order of operations mnemonic, 67
Practice Exam 1
  answer key, 296–297
  answer sheet, 211–212
  English Test
    answers and explanations, 257–265
    practice questions, 213–222
  exam conditions, 209
  Mathematics Test
    answers and explanations, 265–276
    practice questions, 223–231
  Reading Test
    answers and explanations, 276–282
    practice questions, 232–240
  Science Test
    answers and explanations, 282–293
    practice questions, 241–255
  scoring, 294–295
  timing, 209
  Writing Test
    answers and explanations, 293–294
    practice questions, 256
Practice Exam 2
  answer key, 385–386
  answer sheet, 301–302
  English Test
    answers and explanations, 345–354
    questions, 303–313
  exam conditions, 299
  Mathematics Test
    answers and explanations, 354–365
    questions, 314–322
  Reading Test
    answers and explanations, 365–372
    questions, 323–331
  Science Test
    answers and explanations, 372–383
    questions, 332–342
  timing, 299
  Writing Test
    answers and explanations, 384
    questions, 343
Practice Exam 3
  answer key, 477–478
  answer sheet, 389–390
  English Test
    answers and explanations, 437–446
    questions, 391–402

    exam conditions, 387
  Mathematics Test
    answers and explanations, 446–461
    questions, 403–413
  Reading Test
    answers and explanations, 461–467
    questions, 414–423
  Science Test
    answers and explanations, 467–476
    questions, 424–434
  timing, 387
  Writing Test
    answers and explanations, 476
    questions, 435
practice exams, parental help with, 485–486
practice questions
  English Test
    examples, 49–54
    Practice Exam 1, 213–222
    Practice Exam 2, 303–313
    Practice Exam 3, 391–402
  Mathematics Test
    examples, 135–141
    Practice Exam 1, 223–231
    Practice Exam 2, 314–322
    Practice Exam 3, 403–413
  Reading Test
    humanities, 156–157
    natural science, 157–158
    Practice Exam 1, 232–240
    Practice Exam 2, 323–331
    Practice Exam 3, 414–423
    prose fiction, 153–154
    social science, 155–156
  Science Test
    examples, 171–179
    Practice Exam 1, 241–255
    Practice Exam 2, 332–342
    Practice Exam 3, 424–434
  Writing Test
    essay examples, 203–205
    Practice Exam 1, 256
    Practice Exam 2, 343
    Practice Exam 3, 435
pre-algebra questions, 129–130
predicate adjective, 32
predicate noun, 32
predicate pronoun, 32
predicate
  complement, 32
  definition, 32
  direct object, 32
  indirect object, 32
prepositions, 31–32
present tense, 30
present-perfect tense, 30
prime factorization, 58

prime numbers, 58, 107
probability problems, 126–127
product, multiplication, 59
pronouns. *See also* nouns; *specific pronouns*
　common errors, 36–37
　connecting descriptions to nouns, 31
　definition, 31
　faulty references, 36
　improper forms, 36
　indefinite, 31
　objective, 31
　as objects in sentences, 31
　personal, 31
　possessive, 31
　reflexive, 31
　relative, 31
　renaming general nouns, 31
　renaming specific nouns, 31
　rules for using, 37
　subjective, 31
　as subjects in sentences, 31
　unclear references, 36
proofreading essays, 200–201
proportions, 64–66
prose fiction, Reading Test
　practice questions, 153–154
　topic, 145
punctuation, forms of
　' (apostrophe), 35–36
　: (colon), 35
　, (comma), 33–35
　- (dash), 35
　. (period), 33
　? (question mark), 33
　; (semicolon), 35
punctuation, uses for
　abbreviations, 33, 34
　appositives, 34
　asides, 34
　clarifying complex sentences, 34
　contractions, 34
　dates, 34
　direct questions, 33
　distinctions, 34
　ending sentences, 33
　essays, 201
　initials, 33
　joining clauses, 34
　with nonrestrictive clauses, 34
　omitted words, 34
　place names, 34
　possessives, 34–35
　separating independent clauses, 34
　series of expressions, 33
　setting off nonessential information, 34
　titles, 34
Pythagorean theorem, 78
Pythagorean triples, 79–80

• Q •

quadrant, coordinate plane, 91
quadratic equation
　factoring, 101–103
　graphing, 94
quadrilateral. *See also* polygon
　area, 81–82
　leftover problems, 82–83
　parallelogram, 81–82
　rectangle, 81
　rhombus, 81
　shaded-area problems, 82–83
　square, 79, 81
　trapezoid, 82
quantitative comparison questions, 130
question mark (?), 33
questions, practice. *See* practice questions
questions, punctuating, 33
quotient, 59

• R •

radicals
　adding/subtracting, 108
　multiplying/dividing, 108–109
　order of operations, 109
radius, circle, 86
range of numbers
　definition, 68
　in inequalities, 105
rate problems, 120–121
rational numbers, 57
ratios, 64–66
reach schools, 24
Reading Test
　number of questions, 145
　overview, 15, 145–146
　Practice Exam 1
　　answer key, 297
　　answer sheet, 212
　　answers and explanations, 276–282
　　questions, 232–240
　　timing, 209
　Practice Exam 2
　　answer key, 386
　　answer sheet, 302
　　answers and explanations, 365–372
　　questions, 323–331
　　timing, 299
　Practice Exam 3
　　answer key, 478
　　answer sheet, 390
　　answers and explanations, 461–467
　　questions, 414–423
　　timing, 387

Reading Test *(continued)*
  practice questions
    humanities, 156–157
    natural science, 157–158
    prose fiction, 153–154
    social science studies, 155–156
  scoring, 146
  strategies, 146–148
  timing, 146
  tips and traps, 150–151
  topics, 145–146
  types of questions
    attitude, 149–150
    detail, 149
    exception, 150
    inference, 149–150
    main-idea, 148–149
    tone, 149–150
    vocabulary-in-context, 150
real numbers, 57
reciprocals, fractions, 62
rectangle, 81
rectangular solid
  total surface area, 85
  volume, 84
redundancy, common error, 39
Reed, Colleen (college admissions expert), 24
reflex angles, 73
reflexive pronouns, 31, 37
regular polygon, 83
relative pronouns, 31
religious obligations, 13
Remember icon, explained, 5
repeating the test
  influence on college admission, 22
  pros and cons, 15–16
repetition, in essays, 201
research summaries, Science Test, 165–167
result/conclusion questions, Science Test, 167
reviewing your work, 20. *See also* mistakes,
    taking the test
rhetorical skills questions, 43
rhombus, 81
right angles, 72
rise over run, 93
roots, 107
rubbernecking, 19
rumors about the ACT, 481–483
Ryan, Mark (author), 3

• S •

S.A.M.A.N. (Say, man...) rule, 38
sample questions. *See* practice questions
SAT Math For Dummies, 3
SAT versus ACT, 482–483

scalene triangle, 75
Schaefer, Diane (college admissions expert), 25
Science Test
  conflicting-viewpoints passages, 167–170
  controlled variables, 163
  dependent variables, 163
  diagrams, 164–165
  extrapolation, 165
  format, 161–162
  graphs, 164–165
  independent variables, 163
  interpolation, 165
  negative correlation, 164
  number of questions, 161
  overview, 15
  positive correlation, 164
  Practice Exam 1
    answer key, 297
    answer sheet, 212
    answers and explanations, 282–293
    questions, 241–255
    timing, 209
  Practice Exam 2
    answer key, 386
    answer sheet, 302
    answers and explanations, 372–383
    questions, 332–342
    timing, 299
  Practice Exam 3
    answer key, 478
    answer sheet, 390
    answers and explanations, 467–476
    questions, 424–434
    timing, 387
  practice questions, 171–179
  research-summary passages, 165–167
  strategies
    conflicting-viewpoints passages, 168–169
    data-analysis questions, 164–165
    data-representation questions, 162–164
    research-summary passages, 165–167
  tables, 164–165
  types of questions, 162–167
scoring
  composite score, 14
  description, 13, 14
  guessing, 13–14
  influence on college admission, 22
  passing/failing, 481–482
  percentile score, 14
  on practice exams, 294–295
  on Reading Test, 146
  sample report, 14
  state-to-state differences, 481
  subscores, 14
scratch paper, use during test, 13

secant (sec), 113

sector, circle, 88

semicolon (;), 35

sentence fragment, 38

sentence structure. *See also* conjunctions

  clauses, 33

  complements, 32

  direct objects, 32

  ending punctuation, 33

  fragment, 38

  indirect objects, 32

  joining parts of speech, 31–32

  misplaced modifiers, 41–42

  phrases, 33

  predicate, 32

  prepositions, 31–32

  questions about, 46

  subject, 32

series of expressions, punctuating, 33

shaded-area problems, solving with
    quadrilaterals, 82–83

she, subjective pronoun, 31

similar triangles, 76–77

simple interest, 122

simplifying fractions, 61

sine (sin), 112

slope formula, 93

snacks, during test, 12

so, coordinating conjunction, 32

social science studies, Reading Test

  practice questions, 155–156

  topic, 145

SOH CAH TOA ratios, 111–115

solving for *x*, 98–99, 105

special circumstances, 13

spell check, essays, 200

sports, influence on college admission, 23

square roots, 107

squares, 79, 81

state-to-state ACT differences, 481

Sterling, Mary Jane (author), 3

straight angles, 73

stress management, 17–18

stretching exercises, 17

studying for the ACT

  memorizing math formulas, 486

  practicality of, 481

  proper environment, 485

  taking practice tests, 485–486

  test-prep materials, 485

  time required, 7

  tips for parents, 485–486

style questions, 47

subjective pronouns, 31, 37

subjects (of sentences), 32

subjects (of test), 14–15. *See also specific subjects*

subject/verb agreement

  common errors, 37–38

  compound subjects, 38

  indefinite pronouns, 38

  plural versus singular subjects, 38

  S.A.M.A.N. (Say, man...) rule, 38

  in test questions, 45

subordinating conjunctions, 32

subscores, 14

substitution, algebraic, 104, 106

subtraction

  algebraic expressions, 99

  definition, 59

  fractions, 62–63

  order of operations, 67

  radicals, 108

  in word problems, 117–118

sum, addition, 59

sum of exterior angles, 83

sum of interior angles

  polygons, 83

  triangles, 76

superlative form, 40

supplementary angles, 73

symbols, algebraic. *See also specific symbols*

  functions as, 110

  of inequality, 104

  substituting for, 106–107

  for variables, 105–107

• T •

tables, Science Test, 164–165

tangent (tan), 112

terms, in algebraic expression, 97

Test Administration, telephone number, 11

test center. *See also* ACT

  directions to, 12

  punctual arrival, 12

  things to take with you, 11–13

test-prep materials, 485

tests. *See specific practice exams*

"thank you," in Bulgarian, 123

that, relative pronoun, 31, 37

their, possessive pronoun, 31

theirs, possessive pronoun, 31

them, objective pronoun, 31

themselves, reflexive pronoun, 31

theta symbol (θ), 113

they, subjective pronoun, 31

three-sided figure. *See* triangle

ticket to the test, 11

time limit, 11

timing. *See also specific tests*
  arrival at the test site, 486
  calculating in work problems, 119–120
  panicking about, 19
  Practice Exam 1, 209
  Practice Exam 2, 299
  Practice Exam 3, 387
  Reading Test topic, 146
  studying, 7
timing yourself, 12
Tip icon, explained, 5
titles, punctuating, 34
to be verbs, 30
tone questions, Reading Test, 149–150
total production, 119
total surface area (TSA). *See* TSA (total surface area)
transitions, in essays, 199
trapezoid, 82
Traps & Tricks icon, explained, 5
triangle. *See also* angles; polygon; trigonometry
  angles, measuring, 75–76
  area, 78
  common ratios, 79–80
  equilateral, 75
  exterior angles, measuring, 76
  isosceles, 75
  largest angle, 75–76
  perimeter, 78
  Pythagorean theorem, 78
  Pythagorean triples, 79–80
  scalene, 75
  sides, measuring, 75–76
  similar, 76–77
  sum of interior angles, 76
  types of, 75–77
trigonometry. *See also* algebra; geometry; math operations; Mathematics Test; triangle
  adjacent side, 112
  cosecant (csc), 113
  cosine (cos), 112
  cotangent (cot), 113
  definition, 111
  hypotenuse, 112
  opposite side, 112
  questions on the Mathematics Test, 130
  sample questions, 113–115
  secant (sec), 113
  sine (sin), 112
  SOH CAH TOA ratios, 111–115
  tangent (tan), 112
  test scope, 115
  θ (theta symbol), 113
TSA (total surface area). *See also* area
  cube, 85
  cylinder, 85–86
  rectangular solid, 85

• U •

underlined words, English Test questions, 44–45
units of measure
  length, 70
  quantities, 70
  time, 70
us, objective pronoun, 31
usage and mechanics, English Test questions, 43

• V •

variable
  algebraic, 97–98
  in word problems, 117–118
verb tense
  common errors, 38–39
  future, 30
  past, 30
  past perfect, 30
  present, 30
  present perfect, 30
verbs, 30. *See also* predicates; subject/verb agreement
vertex, coordinate plane, 94–95
vertical angles, 74
vertical axis, 91
vertical lines, 71
visualization, 18
vocabulary-in-context questions, Reading Test, 150
volume
  cube, 84
  cylinder, 85
  rectangular solid, 84

• W •

wasting time, English Test, 47
watch, for test, 12
we, subjective pronoun, 31
weighted average, 68
well/good, 40
when, subordinating conjunction, 32
whether/if, 40
which, relative pronoun
  description, 31
  rules for using, 37
while, subordinating conjunction, 32
who, relative pronoun
  description, 31
  rules for using, 37
whom, relative pronoun, 31
whose, relative pronoun, 31
Woods, Geraldine (author), 3

word problems
  charting, 121–122
  interest problems, 122–123
  math counterparts for common words, 117–118
  mixture problems, 121–122
  percent increase/decrease, 124–126
  probability, 126–127
  rate problems, 120–121
  work problems, 118–120
wordiness, common error, 39
work problems
  definition, 118
  total production, 119
  total time, 119–120
worse/worst, 40
would/if, 42
writing questions, English Test, 45–46
Writing Test. *See also* English Test; grammar
  essays
    action verbs, 201
    conclusion, 200
    editing, 200–201
    examples in, 197
    examples of, 186–191, 198–199
    first paragraph, 196
    ghost words, 200
    hamburger writing, 198–200
    handwriting legibility, 201
    hooking the reader, 196
    incorporating the question, 194–195
    introduction, 198
    making a judgment, 194
    practice questions, 203–205
    proofreading, 200–201
    punctuation, 201
    repetition, 201
    spell check, 200
    strategic checklist, 193

    taking a position, 195
    transitions, 199
  overview, 15
  Practice Exam 1
    answers and explanations, 293–294
    questions, 256
    timing, 209
  Practice Exam 2
    answers and explanations, 384
    questions, 343
    timing, 299
  Practice Exam 3
    answers and explanations, 476
    questions, 435
    timing, 387
  scoring, 186
  strategies, 183–186

x-axis, 91

y-axis, 91
yet, coordinating conjunction, 32
you
  objective pronoun, 31
  subjective pronoun, 31
your, possessive pronoun, 31
yours, possessive pronoun, 31
yourself, reflexive pronoun, 31
yourselves, reflexive pronoun, 31

• Z •

Zegarelli, Mark (author), 3

Workspace

Workspace

Workspace

Workspace

Workspace

ple & Macs

ad For Dummies
78-0-470-58027-1

hone For Dummies,
h Edition
78-0-470-87870-5

acBook For Dummies, 3rd
dition
78-0-470-76918-8

ac OS X Snow Leopard For
ummies
78-0-470-43543-4

usiness

ookkeeping For Dummies
78-0-7645-9848-7

b Interviews
or Dummies,
d Edition
78-0-470-17748-8

esumes For Dummies,
h Edition
78-0-470-08037-5

arting an
nline Business
or Dummies,
h Edition
78-0-470-60210-2

ock Investing
or Dummies,
d Edition
78-0-470-40114-9

uccessful
me Management
or Dummies
78-0-470-29034-7

Computer Hardware

BlackBerry
For Dummies,
4th Edition
978-0-470-60700-8

Computers For Seniors
For Dummies,
2nd Edition
978-0-470-53483-0

PCs For Dummies,
Windows 7
Edition
978-0-470-46542-4

Laptops For Dummies,
4th Edition
978-0-470-57829-2

Cooking & Entertaining

Cooking Basics
For Dummies,
3rd Edition
978-0-7645-7206-7

Wine For Dummies,
4th Edition
978-0-470-04579-4

Diet & Nutrition

Dieting For Dummies,
2nd Edition
978-0-7645-4149-0

Nutrition For Dummies,
4th Edition
978-0-471-79868-2

Weight Training
For Dummies,
3rd Edition
978-0-471-76845-6

Digital Photography

Digital SLR Cameras &
Photography For Dummies,
3rd Edition
978-0-470-46606-3

Photoshop Elements 8
For Dummies
978-0-470-52967-6

Gardening

Gardening Basics
For Dummies
978-0-470-03749-2

Organic Gardening
For Dummies,
2nd Edition
978-0-470-43067-5

Green/Sustainable

Raising Chickens
For Dummies
978-0-470-46544-8

Green Cleaning
For Dummies
978-0-470-39106-8

Health

Diabetes For Dummies,
3rd Edition
978-0-470-27086-8

Food Allergies
For Dummies
978-0-470-09584-3

Living Gluten-Free
For Dummies,
2nd Edition
978-0-470-58589-4

Hobbies/General

Chess For Dummies,
2nd Edition
978-0-7645-8404-6

Drawing
Cartoons & Comics
For Dummies
978-0-470-42683-8

Knitting For Dummies,
2nd Edition
978-0-470-28747-7

Organizing
For Dummies
978-0-7645-5300-4

Su Doku For Dummies
978-0-470-01892-7

Home Improvement

Home Maintenance
For Dummies,
2nd Edition
978-0-470-43063-7

Home Theater
For Dummies,
3rd Edition
978-0-470-41189-6

Living the
Country Lifestyle
All-in-One
For Dummies
978-0-470-43061-3

Solar Power Your Home
For Dummies,
2nd Edition
978-0-470-59678-4

vailable wherever books are sold. For more information or to order direct: U.S. customers visit www.dummies.com or call 1-877-762-2974.
.K. customers visit www.wileyeurope.com or call (0) 1243 843291. Canadian customers visit www.wiley.ca or call 1-800-567-4797.

Internet

Blogging For Dummies,
3rd Edition
978-0-470-61996-4

eBay For Dummies,
6th Edition
978-0-470-49741-8

Facebook For Dummies,
3rd Edition
978-0-470-87804-0

Web Marketing
For Dummies,
2nd Edition
978-0-470-37181-7

WordPress
For Dummies,
3rd Edition
978-0-470-59274-8

Language & Foreign Language

French For Dummies
978-0-7645-5193-2

Italian Phrases
For Dummies
978-0-7645-7203-6

Spanish For Dummies,
2nd Edition
978-0-470-87855-2

Spanish
For Dummies,
Audio Set
978-0-470-09585-0

Math & Science

Algebra I
For Dummies,
2nd Edition
978-0-470-55964-2

Biology For Dummies,
2nd Edition
978-0-470-59875-7

Calculus For Dummies
978-0-7645-2498-1

Chemistry For Dummies
978-0-7645-5430-8

Microsoft Office

Excel 2010 For Dummies
978-0-470-48953-6

Office 2010 All-in-One
For Dummies
978-0-470-49748-7

Office 2010 For Dummies,
Book + DVD Bundle
978-0-470-62698-6

Word 2010 For Dummies
978-0-470-48772-3

Music

Guitar For Dummies,
2nd Edition
978-0-7645-9904-0

iPod & iTunes For
Dummies, 8th Edition
978-0-470-87871-2

Piano Exercises
For Dummies
978-0-470-38765-8

Parenting & Education

Parenting For Dummies,
2nd Edition
978-0-7645-5418-6

Type 1 Diabetes
For Dummies
978-0-470-17811-9

Pets

Cats For Dummies,
2nd Edition
978-0-7645-5275-5

Dog Training For Dummies,
3rd Edition
978-0-470-60029-0

Puppies For Dummies,
2nd Edition
978-0-470-03717-1

Religion & Inspiration

The Bible For Dummies
978-0-7645-5296-0

Catholicism For Dummies
978-0-7645-5391-2

Women in the Bible
For Dummies
978-0-7645-8475-6

Self-Help & Relationship

Anger Management
For Dummies
978-0-470-03715-7

Overcoming Anxiety
For Dummies,
2nd Edition
978-0-470-57441-6

Sports

Baseball
For Dummies,
3rd Edition
978-0-7645-7537-2

Basketball
For Dummies,
2nd Edition
978-0-7645-5248-9

Golf For Dummies,
3rd Edition
978-0-471-76871-5

Web Development

Web Design
All-in-One
For Dummies
978-0-470-41796-6

Web Sites
Do-It-Yourself
For Dummies,
2nd Edition
978-0-470-56520-9

Windows 7

Windows 7
For Dummies
978-0-470-49743-2

Windows 7
For Dummies,
Book + DVD Bundle
978-0-470-52398-8

Windows 7 All-in-One
For Dummies
978-0-470-48763-1

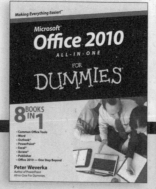

Available wherever books are sold. For more information or to order direct: U.S. customers visit www.dummies.com or call 1-877-762-297
U.K. customers visit www.wileyeurope.com or call (0) 1243 843291. Canadian customers visit www.wiley.ca or call 1-800-567-4797.

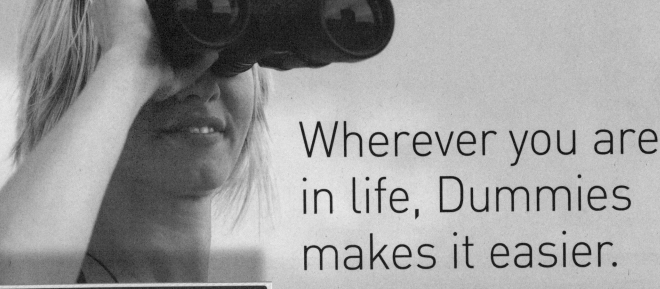

DUMMIES.COM®

Wherever you are in life, Dummies makes it easier.

From fashion to Facebook®,
wine to Windows®, and everything in between,
Dummies makes it easier.

Visit us at Dummies.com

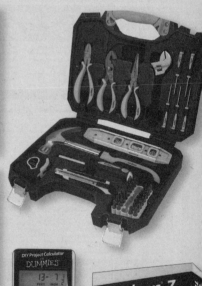